CONTENTS

INTRODUCTION

Whether you are a longtime Lionel enthusiast or a newcomer to the toy train hobby, this guide contains the information you need to identify and evaluate thousands of items made by Lionel since 1901. Most of all, you'll have at your fingertips the most up-to-date prices for locomotives, freight cars, passenger cars, stations, tunnels, signals, track sections, transformers, and other items.

What is listed

Almost every Lionel O gauge toy train produced over the years is listed in the pages that follow.

This edition of the *Lionel Pocket Price Guide* contains information about new additions to the product line as described in Lionel catalogs, press releases, and other sources. Any additions that Lionel makes to its line after this book is printed will be reported in the next edition.

In addition, the *Lionel Pocket Price Guide* provides information about items associated with Lionel yet not mentioned in its catalogs. These uncataloged or promotional items include unique models and specially decorated locomotives and cars that Lionel produces for national and regional toy train collecting and operating groups, museums, local railroad clubs, and other customers.

When to consult this guide

Many readers of the *Lionel Pocket Price Guide* use it after the fact. They already have some trains and accessories and now want to identify and evaluate those items. Maybe someone lucked upon a bridge at a garage sale and wants to know whether it's a 300 Hellgate or a 314 deck girder type. Somebody else needs to provide his or her insurance agent with a complete list of O gauge locomotives that includes their conditions and current values. This guide contains the information needed to identify that bridge as well as determining present values for that engine roster.

In addition, the *Lionel Pocket Price Guide* can help you think about what to acquire in the future. That's really when the fun begins! You just have to spend some time considering how you want to approach the hobby. Collect, operate, or both? Prewar, postwar, or modern? Particular types of locomotives or cars? Favorite railroads? Promotional items?

Once you have a general idea of how to enjoy this hobby, you can make informed decisions about which trains you want.

2015 EDITION

Greenberg's
GUIDES®

LIONEL® TRAINS

POCKET PRICE GUIDE

Edited by Roger Carp

KALMBACH BOOKS

Kalmbach Books
21027 Crossroads Circle
Waukesha, Wisconsin 53186
www.Kalmbach.com/Books

Published in 2014
Thirty-fifth Edition

Manufactured in the United States of America

ISBN: 978-1-62700-126-7
EISBN: 978-1-62700-132-8

Front cover photo: 2351 Milwaukee Road EP-5 Electric
Locomotive, model courtesy Manny Piazza

Back cover photo: Lionel Corporation Tinplate 11-6020
UP City of Denver Passenger Train Set, courtesy
MTH Electric Trains

We constantly strive to improve Greenberg's Pocket Price Guides. I
you find missing items or detect misinformation, please contact us
Send your comments, new information, or corrections via e-mail
to books@kalmbach.com or by mail to Lionel Pocket Price Guide
Editor at the address above.

UNDERSTANDING VALUES

The values presented here are an averaged reflection of prices for items bought and sold across the country during the year prior to the publication of this edition. These values are offered as guidelines and should be viewed as starting points that buyers and sellers can use to begin informed and reasonable negotiations.

In a listing for a steam locomotive, the value includes a tender, even if the tender is not listed in the description. The value of steam locomotives, particularly prewar items, may be affected significantly by the type of tender included.

Values for individual items may differ from what is listed in this price guide due to a few key factors. Where collectible trains are scarce and demand outruns supply, actual values may exceed what is shown. Values may also rise where certain items are especially popular, often because of their road names. And as with all collectibles, national and local economic conditions will impact values, which tend to drop when times are tough and demand falls.

Original packaging

Items in Like New or better condition require their original packaging to maintain their high level of value. The values given for items in Good and Excellent condition are not based on the expectation that a box and other associated items are present.

Items that do have their original packaging, especially if it is complete and undamaged, command a premium among collectors of prewar and postwar trains. No hard-and-fast rules can be stated as to how much higher their value is over the same items in Excellent condition. Generally speaking, though, boxed items in Like New condition are valued about 50 percent above the same item without a box.

Using the values

The values listed are what a consumer would pay—more or less—to get a particular item in a specific condition. One collector selling that item to another would probably ask the stated value and expect to get something close to it.

However, someone selling that same item to a person or business that intends to resell it (a train dealer) is unlikely to receive the stated value. Experience shows that sellers get about half the amount. Dealers offer less so they can earn a profit when reselling an item.

When buying or selling a toy train, you should learn more about it. Start by consulting this price guide and then look for more about it in a reference guide or website on toy trains. You can also ask more experienced hobbyists for their opinion about the item's condition and value.

FINDING A PRODUCT

The *Lionel Pocket Price Guide* has been divided into seven major sections.

Section 1: Prewar 1901–1942

Section 1 of the *Lionel Pocket Price Guide* is devoted to the prewar period. The entries cover just about every train, accessory, and transformer associated with Lionel's line during its first 42 years.

The only outfits (sets) listed are those of articulated streamlined trains that consist of a powered unit and attached unpowered cars.

In an item's listing, the basic description specifies its gauge (the distance between the inside of the outermost rails). During this time, Lionel catalogued models in four sizes. It is noted in parentheses whether an item is 2⅞-inch, Standard (2⅛ inches), O (1¼ inches), or OO (¾ inches). O gauge models intended to run on tighter 27-inch-diameter track belong to Lionel's O27 gauge line and are identified as such.

Transformers, rheostats, and many accessories were not limited to a single gauge, so their descriptions do not specify a gauge.

Section 2: Postwar 1945–1969

Section 2 concentrates on the postwar period. Nearly every train and accessory (except outfits) that Lionel cataloged between 1945 and 1969 has its own listing. By this time, Lionel no longer made trains in 2⅞-inch, Standard, or OO gauge. Instead, it offered trains that ran on track that had a diameter of either 31 inches (O gauge) or 27 inches (O27 gauge). However, the entries in this section do not distinguish between O and O27 since only a handful of locomotives and cars could operate solely on the wider curves.

Section 3: Modern Era 1970–2015

Section 3 shows the trains, accessories, transformers, and other items that Lionel has cataloged since 1970. The modern era encompasses the products of three companies: Model Products Corp. (MPC, a division of General Mills), 1970–85; Lionel Trains Inc. (LTI), 1986–95; and Lionel LLC (LLC), 1996–2015.

These incarnations of Lionel are responsible for an enormous inventory of trains, rolling stock, transformers, and accessories. Cataloged and uncataloged O gauge items (ranging from the near-scale Standard O to the toy-like O27) can be found within the pages of this section.

All items in Section 3 are arranged according to their Lionel catalog number (omitting the numeral 6 used as a prefix). The descriptions of products made during the modern era may include information that relates to where in the product line a particular item belongs. Models derived from MPC designs have been described as *traditional*. Rolling stock whose dimensions and features approach scale realism may be designated as Standard O (abbreviated as std O). Locomotives equipped with TrainMaster Command Control or its successor, Legacy, are identified with the abbreviation CC.

Section 4: Lionel Corporation Tinplate

Section 4 features 700 products developed jointly by Lionel and MTH Electric Trains since 2009. These Lionel Corporation trains and accessories are reproductions of Lionel (and some American Flyer) tinplate items from the prewar era. You'll find trains here that operate as tinplate trains did prior to 1942 as well as others that have been updated with modern features and technology, such as Proto-Sound. The retail prices are listed for these products.

Section 5: Club Cars and Special Production

Section 5 gathers the various items, principally locomotives and rolling stock, that Lionel has made or sponsored for different hobby organizations, museums, and businesses since the 1970s. These uncataloged club cars and special production items are arranged according to the groups that offered them for sale. Those groups are listed alphabetically; regional divisions of national organizations follow the parent organization's listing. Within each subordinate section, items are listed in a numerical (not chronological) order, with a basic description similar to that used for cataloged entries.

Section 6: Boxes

Over the past 20 years, original boxes and other forms of packaging have assumed significance for some collectors. These hobbyists insist that the trains they buy come in the boxes and have the paperwork and ancillary pieces (inserts, instruction sheets, and envelopes) that the manufacturer packed with them before offering them for sale.

Cardboard boxes, inserts, and assorted sheets of paper are more fragile than die-cast metal or plastic trains. They were also deemed to be less important to the children playing with toy trains long ago and so were not treated with the same care. Instruction sheets were lost, and boxes were discarded. As a result, fewer boxes and instruction sheets have survived than have the trains and accessories that went with them. In some cases, the box that a particular locomotive, car, or even set came in is now valued more than the item itself.

Boxes are evaluated according to standards and conditions established by the Train Collectors Association, similar to those developed for toy trains and accessories:

P-10   **Mint:** Brand new, complete, all original as manufactured, and unused. Flaps appear to never have been opened, and edges are crisp. No tears, fading, or wear marks. Contains original contents and all applicable sealing tape, wrap, and staples.

P-9   **Store New:** Complete, all original, and unused. Box may have merchant additions such as store stamps and price tags. Must have appropriate inner liners.

P-8   **Like New:** Complete and all original. There is evidence of light use and aging. Box may have notations (discrete) added since leaving the manufacturer.

P-7   **Excellent:** Complete and all original. Box shows moderate signs of being opened and closed including edge and corner wear. All flaps must be intact.

P-6   **Very Good:** Complete and all original. Box shows signs of usage such as minor abrasions, small tears, color changes, and minor soiling. Inner liners may be missing, and inner flaps may require strengthening. The box can still safely store its original contents.

P-5   **Good:** Box shows substantial wear, and edges may be damaged. Box may have extensive color fading but no evident water damage or cardboard deterioration. Exterior flaps are present, but their connection to the box may require repair. Inner liners may be missing. With care, the box can still store contents. (Any box that has been repaired cannot be graded above P-5.)

P-4   **Fair:** Box shows heavy damage and may have been repaired. Inner flaps may be missing. Box cannot store its original contents. Water damage may be present.

Values for postwar boxes in this section are shown for Good (P-5) and Excellent (P-7) conditions.

Lionel used these box types during the postwar years:

Art Deco: Original postwar box with bold orange and blue design and lettering. It was used in 1946 and 1947.

Classic: More understated design than Art Deco. It was the main component box from 1948 through 1958. Boxes can be divided into Early (1948–49), Middle (1949–55), and Late (1956–58) Classic designs, which are marked by minor lettering changes.

Orange Perforated: This was a significant change from the Classic design. The solid orange box features white lettering and a tear-out perforated front panel. It was used in 1959 and 1960.

Orange Picture: Instead of a perforated panel, this version of the Orange Perforated box features an illustration of a steam locomotive and an F3 diesel on the front. It was used from 1961 to 1964.

Hillside Orange Picture: Similar to an Orange Picture box, it is labeled with Hillside, N.J., where Lionel's plant was located. It was used in 1965.

Cellophane: Used in 1966, this box features a clear cellophane window on the front.

Hagerstown Checkerboard: It has a Lionel checkerboard pattern and Hagerstown, Maryland, printed on end flap bottoms. The box was used in 1968.

Hillside Checkerboard: This 1969 box is the same as the Hagerstown Checkerboard box, but with Hillside, New Jersey, printed on it.

Lionel also used brown corrugated and plain white boxes.

Section 7: Sets

This section lists boxed train sets catalogued by Lionel during the postwar years, 1945–1969. When collecting sets, it is important that the sets, or outfits, contain all the items, including ancillary ones, that Lionel packed with them. These items include the locomotive (and tender if a steam engine) rolling stock, any accessories, track, transformer, instructions and other paper pieces, component boxes, and the set box.

The listings include the set's catalog number, a short description, and product numbers for the locomotives, rolling stock, and any major accessories. Sets came with O27 gauge, O gauge, or Super O track. O27 and Super O track are listed in the set's description. If no track is listed, the set came with O gauge.

Set values are listed for Excellent (C-7) condition. The presence and condition of original component boxes, set boxes, inserts and other packaging materials can have a significant effect on a set's value. The values reflect the inclusion of these materials. Values of individual set and component boxes can be found in Section 6.

Due to space constraints, not every item found in a set is listed in the description. You can find more complete information on a set's contents on various websites and in *Greenberg's Guide to Lionel Trains 1945–1969 Volume III: Catalogued Sets* by Paul Ambrose. (Although the book is out of print, it is available from booksellers on the Internet.)

USING THE GUIDE

Number	Description	Condition ——Good	Exc	Cond/$
2561	Vista Valley Observation Car, *59–61**	115	282	___
X6454	NYC Boxcar, *48*			
	(A) Brown body	19	52	___
	(B) Orange body	65	133	___
	(C) Tan body	22	56	___
6475	Libby's Crushed Pineapple Vat Car, *63 u*	33	83	___

Identifying a catalog number

A Lionel catalog number is usually stamped, printed, or painted on an item. However, some products do not contain a catalog number. In these cases, you can match the product with its catalog number using a comprehensive reference book or website, including Lionel.com, which contains past and current catalogs.

Two-, three-, and four-digit numbers predominated during the prewar (1901–42) and postwar (1945–69) periods. Four- and five-digit numbers have been most common during the modern era (1970–2015).

On the models, catalog numbers often double as road numbers, although sometimes separate road numbers were added.

Locating an item

Sections are arranged in numerical order of catalog numbers. Items having one or more zeroes as placeholders are listed before those without placeholders. For example, a 004 4-6-4 Locomotive is listed before a 4 Electric Locomotive.

In the prewar and postwar sections, some items such as transformers and track pieces, are identified by a letter. These products follow the numbered items.

Reading an entry

Every entry begins with the product's catalog number assigned by Lionel. (Club and special production cars may have numbers that were assigned by the group.)

A basic description of the model follows. It gives the type of product, lists the name of any railroad identified with it, and includes identifying characteristics, such as color or lettering. If the item has a road number that differs from its catalog number, that number is shown in quotation marks. (Most of these are seen in Section 3). Abbreviations used in the descriptions, including those of railroad names, are listed at the back of the price guide.

Next, you'll find the year or years during which that item was part of Lionel's cataloged product line. The years are shown in italics. If a year is followed by a *u*, this item is considered to be uncataloged. It was not part of the cataloged line but a promotional item that Lionel made or sponsored for an outside business or group.

Entries that show an asterisk (*) after the year have had one or more reissues of the item made.

Many entries feature variations, each indicated by a separate letter (A, B, and so forth). Variations amount to slight yet noteworthy differences in appearance that distinguish models that otherwise seem identical. These differences can relate to color, lettering, and details that were added or deleted. For items having many variations, an entry may not include every variation.

An entry concludes with an indication of the value of the item for several common conditions.

Condition

Lionel enthusiasts should be familiar with the condition and grading standards established by the Train Collectors Association, which are used as the basis for evaluating the condition of toy trains and accessories:

C-10 Mint: Brand new—all original, unused, and unblemished.

C-9 Factory New: Same condition as Mint but with evidence of factory rubs or slight signs of handling, shipping, and being test run at the factory.

C-8 Like New: Complete and all original with no rust or no missing parts; may show effects of being displayed or signs of age and may have been run.

C-7 Excellent: All original and may have minute scratches and paint nicks; no rust, no missing parts, and no distortion of component parts.

C-6 Very Good: Has minor scratches, paint nicks, or minor spots of surface rust; is free of dents and may have minor parts replaced.

C-5 Good: Shows evidence of heavy use and signs of play wear—small dents, scratches, minor paint loss, and minor surface rust.

C-4 Fair: Shows evidence of heavy use—scratches and dents, moderate paint loss, missing parts, and surface rust.

C-3 Poor: Requires major body repair and is a candidate for restoration; major rust, missing parts, and heavily scratched.

C-2 Restoration: Needs to be restored.

C-1 Junk: Parts value only.

Values are listed for prewar and postwar trains in Good (C-5) and Excellent (C-7) conditions. For modern-era trains, including special production and club cars, the values for Excellent (C-7) and Mint (C-10) are shown.

You may also see NRS listed as a value. NRS (No Reported Sales) refers to an item with limited pricing data since only a handful of these scarce items may have been reported.

Determining a model's condition

Look over a model carefully to see whether it has suffered serious damage, including warping and breaking. Then note whether any parts are missing. Feel for dents in metal and cracks in plastic. Check for areas marred by rust, mildew, or chipped paint.

The TCA condition standards will assist you in evaluating your model, such as deciding whether a prewar or postwar model falls below Good or above Excellent.

The assessment of a toy train's value is based on the expectations that it has not been modified and that all parts are present and original to it. Repainting or relettering a model seriously undermines a train's value, regardless of how beat-up and scratched it may have been before undergoing modification. Any model that has been altered should be labeled as a restoration; potential buyers deserve to be informed about how it has been modified, so they do not mistake it for an original.

A model that is missing some parts should be sold *as is* or have those parts replaced by identical originals. A tank car cataloged in 1935 that needs a brake wheel must have a part from 1935 put on it to be considered a true original. Adding a brake wheel from 1936 undermines the car's legitimacy as much as adding one from 2014 does.

The same rule applies to the ancillary items that came with various models. The value of a flatcar may depend largely on the miniature airplane or rocket packed with it; therefore, having a load that is a genuine original is essential to maintaining the value of that flatcar. Similarly, freight loaders must have whatever cargo came with them (coal, logs, trailers, and so forth). Reproductions should be identified as such.

		Good	Exc	
001	4-6-4 Locomotive (OO), *38–42*	195	395	____
1	Bild-A-Motor (O), *28–31*	60	140	____
1	Trolley (std), *06–14*			
	(A) Cream body, orange band and roof	1900	4750	____
	(B) White body, blue band and roof	1750	4750	____
	(C) Cream body, blue band and roof	1300	3150	____
	(D) Cream body, blue band and roof, Curtis Bay	2150	5550	____
	(E) Blue, cream band, blue roof	1450	3150	____
1/111	Trolley Trailer (std), *06–14*	1000	2700	____
002	4-6-4 Locomotive (OO), *39–42*	160	315	____
2	Bild-A-Motor (std), *28–31*	100	180	____
2	Trolley (std), *06–16**			
	(A) Yellow, red band	1200	2250	____
	(B) Red, yellow band	1200	2250	____
2/200	Trolley Trailer (std), *06–16*	1000	1800	____
003	4-6-4 Locomotive (OO), *39–42*			
	(A) 003W whistling Tender	190	395	____
	(B) 003T nonwhistling Tender	175	355	____
3	Trolley (std), *06–13*			
	(A) Cream, orange band	1400	3100	____
	(B) Cream, dark olive green band	1400	3100	____
	(C) Orange, dark olive green band	1400	3100	____
	(D) Dark green, cream windows	1400	3100	____
	(E) Green, cream windows, Bay Shore	1650	3700	____
3/300	Trolley Trailer (std), *06–13*	1500	3500	____
004	4-6-4 Locomotive (OO), *39–42*			
	(A) 004W whistling Tender	210	350	____
	(B) 004T nonwhistling Tender	190	310	____
4	Electric Locomotive 0-4-0 (O), *28–32**			
	(A) Orange, black frame	550	875	____
	(B) Gray, apple green stripe	580	1050	____
4	Trolley (std), *06–12*			
	(A) Cream, dark olive green band	3000	4950	____
	(B) Green or olive green, cream roof	3000	4950	____
4U	No. 4 Kit Form (O), *28–29*	1150	1600	____
5	0-4-0 Locomotive, no tender, early (std), *06–07*			
	(A) NYC & HRR	1000	1450	____
	(B) Pennsylvania	1400	2300	____
	(C) NYC & HRRR (3 Rs)	1250	2050	____
	(D) B&O RR	1500	2400	____
5	0-4-0 Locomotive, tender, early Special (std), *06–09*	980	1300	____

			Good	Exc
___	5	0-4-0 Locomotive, no tender, later (std), *10–11*	750	1150
___	5	0-4-0 Locomotive, tender, later Special (std), *10–11*	920	1200
___	5/51	0-4-0 Locomotive, tender, latest (std), *12–23*	800	1100
___	6	4-4-0 Locomotive (std), *06–23*	860	1250
___	6	0-4-0 Locomotive Special (std), *08–09*	2050	2950
___	7	Steam 4-4-0 Locomotive (std), *10–23**	1850	2300
	8	Electric Locomotive 0-4-0 (std), *25–32*		
___		(A) Maroon or Mojave, brass windows and trim	130	250
___		(B) Olive green, brass windows	155	205
___		(C) Red, brass or cream windows	195	250
___		(D) Peacock, orange windows	520	750
	8	Trolley (std), *08–14**		
___		(A) Cream, orange band and roof	3000	5400
___		(B) Dark green, cream windows	3000	5400
	8E	Electric Locomotive 0-4-0 (std), *26–32*		
___		(A) Mojave, brass windows and trim	175	250
___		(B) Red, brass or cream windows	150	225
___		(C) Peacock, orange windows	370	590
___		(D) Pea green, cream stripe	465	670
___	9	Electric Locomotive 0-4-0 (std), *29**	1200	2150
___	9	Motor Car (std), *09–12*		NRS
___	9	Trolley (std), *09*	3000	5400
	9E	Electric Locomotive (std), *28–35**		
___		(A) 0-4-0, orange	700	1250
___		(B) 2-4-2, two-tone green	880	1600
___		(C) 2-4-2, gunmetal gray	860	1100
___	9U	Electric Locomotive 0-4-0 Kit (std), *28–29*	1050	1750
	10	Electric Locomotive 0-4-0 (std), *25–29**		
___		(A) Mojave, brass trim	150	215
___		(B) Gray, brass trim	125	205
___		(C) Peacock, brass inserts	145	205
___		(D) Red, cream stripe	580	880
	10	Interurban (std), *10–16*		
___		(A) Maroon	3000	5750
___		(B) Dark olive green	1200	2150
	10E	Electric Locomotive 0-4-0 (std), *26–30*		
___		(A) Olive green, black frame		NRS
___		(B) Peacock, dark green or black frame	245	400
___		(C) State brown, dark green frame	435	630
___		(D) Gray, black frame	165	220
___		(E) Red, cream stripe	620	890
___	011	Switches, pair (O), *33–37*	17	35
___	11	Flatcar, early (std), *06–08*	150	360
___	11	Flatcar, later (std), *09–15*	50	90

		Good	Exc
11	Flatcar, latest (std), *16–18*	50	90 ____
11	Flatcar, Lionel Corp. (std), *18–26*	50	80 ____
012	Switches, pair (O), *27–33*	21	42 ____
12	Gondola, early (std), *06–08*	150	360 ____
12	Gondola, later (std), *09–15*	50	100 ____
12	Gondola, latest (std), *16–18*	45	70 ____
12	Gondola, Lionel Corp. (std), *18–26*	50	70 ____
013	012 Switches and 439 panel board, *27–33*	120	190 ____
13	Cattle Car, early (std), *06–08*	300	450 ____
13	Cattle Car, later (std), *09–15*	150	225 ____
13	Cattle Car, latest (std), *16–18*	65	115 ____
13	Cattle Car, Lionel Corp. (std), *18–26*	65	115 ____
0014	Boxcar (OO), *38–42*		
	(A) Yellow, Lionel Lines	80	155 ____
	(B) Tuscan, Pennsylvania	50	75 ____
14	Boxcar, early (std), *06–08*	195	435 ____
14	Boxcar, later (std), *09–15*	80	105 ____
14	Boxcar, latest (std), *16–18*	80	105 ____
14	Boxcar, Lionel Corp. (std), *18–26*	80	105 ____
0015	Tank Car (OO), *38–42*		
	(A) Silver, Sun Oil	40	90 ____
	(B) Black, Shell	40	75 ____
15	Oil Car, early (std), *06–08*	200	360 ____
15	Oil Car, later (std), *09–15*	75	115 ____
15	Oil Car, latest (std), *16–18*	75	115 ____
15	Oil Car, Lionel Corp. (std), *18–26*	75	115 ____
0016	Hopper Car (OO), *38–42*		
	(A) Gray	75	145 ____
	(B) Black	75	115 ____
16	Ballast Dump Car, early (std), *06–11*	400	700 ____
16	Ballast Dump Car, later (std), *09–15*	95	175 ____
16	Ballast Dump Car, latest (std), *16–18*	95	175 ____
16	Ballast Dump Car, Lionel Corp. (std), *18–26*	95	175 ____
0017	Caboose (OO), *38–42*	50	90 ____
17	Caboose, early (std), *06–08*	220	440 ____
17	Caboose, later (std), *09–15*	70	135 ____
17	Caboose, latest (std), *16–18*	75	135 ____
17	Caboose, Lionel Corp. (std), *18–26*	50	90 ____
18	Pullman Car (std), *08*		
	(A) Dark olive green, nonremovable roof	700	2150 ____
	(B) Dark olive green, removable roof	105	215 ____
	(C) Yellow-orange, removable roof	315	870 ____
	(D) Orange, removable roof	90	205 ____
	(E) Mojave, removable roof	305	890 ____
18	Pullman Car (std), *11–13*	600	900 ____

			Good	Exc
___	18	Pullman Car (std), *13–15*	150	270
___	18	Pullman Car (std), *15–18*	150	270
___	18	Pullman Car (std), *18–22*	90	155
___	18	Pullman Car (std), *23–26*	270	530
	19	Combine Car (std), *08*		
___		(A) Dark olive green, nonremovable roof	1100	2600
___		(B) Dark olive green, removable roof	90	145
___		(C) Yellow-orange, removable roof	260	430
___		(D) Orange, removable roof	115	205
___		(E) Mojave, removable roof	305	890
___	19	Combine Car (std), *11–13*	600	900
___	19	Combine Car (std), *13–15*	200	270
___	19	Combine Car (std), *15–18*	200	270
___	19	Combine Car (std), *18–22*	90	155
___	19	Combine Car (std), *23–26*	265	520
___	020	90-degree Crossover (O), *15–42*	2	5
___	020X	45-degree Crossover (O), *17–42*	2	9
___	20	90-degree Crossover (std), *09–32*	4	10
___	20	Direct Current Reducer, *06*		195
___	20X	45-degree Crossover (std), *28–32*	5	10
___	021	Switches, pair (O), *15–37*	20	48
___	21	90-degree Crossover (std), *06*	10	18
___	21	Switches, pair (std), *15–25*	40	70
___	022	Remote Control Switches, pair (O), *38–42*	38	70
___	22	Manual Switches, pair (std), *06–25*	47	75
___	023	Bumper (O), *15–33*	15	37
___	23	Bumper (std), *06–23*	17	39
___	0024	Pennsylvania Boxcar (OO), *39–42*	45	75
___	24	Railway Station (std), *06*		NRS
___	025	Bumper (O), *28–42*	22	33
	0025	Tank Car (OO), *39–42*		
___		(A) Black, Shell	40	90
___		(B) Silver, Sunoco	40	80
___	25	Open Station (std), *06*		NRS
___	25	Bumper (std), *27–42*	30	47
___	26	Passenger Bridge (std), *06*		40
___	0027	Caboose (OO), *39–42*	40	70
___	27	Lighting Set, *11–23*	15	41
___	27	Station (std), *09–12*		NRS
___	28	Double Station with dome, *09–12*		NRS

		Good	Exc	
29	Day Coach (std), *07–22*			
	(A) Dark olive green, 9 windows	1500	3000	____
	(B) Maroon, 10 windows	1200	1500	____
	(C) Dark green, 10 windows	3000	4500	____
	(D) Dark olive green, 10 windows	680	1000	____
	(E) Dark green, 10 windows	500	900	____
0031	2-rail 13" Curve Track (OO), *39–42*	5	10	____
31	Combine Car (std), *21–25*			
	(A) Maroon	70	90	____
	(B) Orange	125	195	____
	(C) Dark olive green	70	90	____
	(D) Brown	75	95	____
0032	2-rail 12" Straight Track (OO), *39–42*	10	15	____
32	Mail Car (std), *21–25*			
	(A) Maroon	85	125	____
	(B) Orange	120	185	____
	(C) Dark olive green	65	85	____
	(D) Brown	70	90	____
32	Miniature Figures, *09–18*	93	253	____
33	Electric Locomotive 0-6-0, early (std), *13*			
	(A) Dark olive green, NYC in oval	90	175	____
	(B) Black, NYC	440	950	____
	(C) Dark olive green, NYC	440	950	____
	(D) Pennsylvania RR	580	1250	____
33	Electric Locomotive 0-4-0, later (std), *13–24*			
	(A) Dark olive green or black, NYC	105	170	____
	(B) Black, lettered C&O	395	720	____
	(C) Maroon, red, or peacock	340	620	____
0034	2-rail 13" Curve Track, electrical connectors (OO), *39–42*	10	15	____
34	Electric Locomotive 0-6-0, early (std), *12*	520	860	____
34	Electric Locomotive 0-4-0 (std), *13*	200	385	____
35	Pullman Car (std), *12–13*			
	(A) Dark blue	470	900	____
	(B) Dark olive green	170	235	____
35	Pullman Car (std), *14–16*			
	(A) Dark olive green, maroon windows	50	70	____
	(B) Maroon, green windows	85	105	____
	(C) Orange, maroon windows	135	195	____
35	Pullman Car (std), *15–18*	50	70	____

			Good	Exc
	35	Pullman Car (std), *18–23*		
____		(A) Dark olive green, maroon windows	36	50
____		(B) Maroon, green windows	30	45
____		(C) Orange, maroon windows	120	210
____		(D) Brown, green windows	36	50
____	35	Boulevard Street Lamp, 6⅛" high, *40–42*	25	50
____	35	Pullman Car (std), *24*	40	55
____	35	Pullman Car (std), *25–26*	40	55
	36	Observation Car (std), *12–13*		
____		(A) Dark blue	315	810
____		(B) Dark olive green	145	205
	36	Observation Car (std), *14–16*		
____		(A) Dark olive green, maroon windows	70	95
____		(B) Maroon, green windows	50	70
____		(C) Orange, maroon windows	180	290
____		(D) Brown, green windows	60	75
____	36	Observation Car (std), *15–18*	60	80
	36	Observation Car (std), *18–23*		
____		(A) Dark olive green, maroon windows	40	55
____		(B) Maroon, green windows	40	55
____		(C) Orange, maroon windows	130	215
____		(D) Brown, green windows	40	55
____	36	Observation Car (std), *24*	40	55
____	36	Observation Car (std), *25–26*	40	55
	38	Electric Locomotive 0-4-0 (std), *13–24*		
____		(A) Black	100	135
____		(B) Red	475	680
____		(C) Mojave or pea green	405	540
____		(D) Dark green	270	360
____		(E) Brown	270	315
____		(F) Red, cream trim	405	540
____		(G) Maroon	170	270
____		(H) Gray	110	125
____	41	Accessory Contactor, *37–42*	3	7
____	042	Switches, pair (O), *38–42*	17	39
____	42	Electric Locomotive 0-4-4-0, square hood, early (std), *12**	760	1650
	42	Electric Locomotive 0-4-4-0 , round hood, later (std), *13–23*		
____		(A) Black or gray	300	510
____		(B) Maroon	1250	2050
____		(C) Dark gray	375	600
____		(D) Dark green or Mojave	500	800
____		(E) Peacock	1100	1800
____		(F) Olive or dark olive green	750	1200

		Good	Exc	
043/43	Bild-A-Motor Gear Set, *29*		85	___
0044	Boxcar (OO), *39–42*	41	80	___
0044K	Boxcar Kit (OO), *39–42*	75	120	___
0045	Tank Car (OO), *39–42*			
	(A) Black, Shell	40	95	___
	(B) Silver, Sunoco	40	80	___
0045K	Tank Car Kit (OO), *39–42*	75	120	___
45N	Automatic Gateman (std O), *37–42*	40	89	___
0046	Hopper Car (OO), *39–42*	50	90	___
0046K	Hopper Car Kit (OO), *39–42*			
	(A) Southern Pacific	75	135	___
	(B) Reading		NRS	___
46	Crossing Gate, *39–42*	75	120	___
0047	Caboose (OO), *39–42*	31	60	___
0047K	Caboose Kit (OO), *39–42*	75	135	___
47	Crossing Gate, *39–42*	70	140	___
48W	Whistle Station, *37–42*	22	65	___
50	Electric Locomotive 0-4-0 (std), *24*			
	(A) Dark green or dark gray	145	250	___
	(B) Maroon	315	600	___
	(C) Mojave	175	345	___
50	Cardboard Train, Cars, Accessory (O), *43**	200	360	___
0051	7" Curve Track (OO), *39–42*	5	15	
51	0-4-0 Locomotive, late, 8-wheel (std), *12–23*	800	1150	___
0052	7" Straight Track (OO), *39–42*	10	15	___
52	Lamp Post, *33–41*	44	95	___
53	Electric Locomotive 0-4-4-0, early (std), *12–14*	1200	2450	___
53	Electric Locomotive 0-4-0, later (std), *15–19*			
	(A) Maroon	550	950	___
	(B) Mojave	670	1350	___
	(C) Dark olive green	560	1150	___
53	Electric Locomotive 0-4-0, latest (std), *20–21*	200	450	___
53	Electric Locomotive 0-6-6-0, early (std), *11*		NRS	___
53	Lamp Post, *31–42*	33	49	___
0054	7" Curve Track, electrical connectors (OO), *39–42*	10	15	___
54	Electric Locomotive 0-4-4-0, early (std), *12**	2500	4050	___
54	Electric Locomotive 0-4-4-0, late (std), *13–23*	1800	2700	___
54	Lamp Post, *29–35*	55	129	___

			Good	Exc
	56	Lamp Post, removable lens and cap, *24–42*		
____		(A) Mojave	85	187
____		(B) Dark gray	50	90
____		(C) 45N green	30	45
____		(D) Pea green	30	48
____		(E) Aluminum	30	45
____		(F) Copper	60	115
____		(G) Dark green	30	45
	57	Lamp Post with street names, *22–42*		
____		(A) Orange post, Main St. & Broadway	35	50
____		(B) Orange post, Fifth Ave. & 42nd St.	40	100
____		(C) Orange post, Broadway & 21st St.	50	90
____		(D) Orange post, Broadway, 42nd St., Fifth Ave. & 21st St.	60	120
____		(E) Yellow post, Main St. & Broadway	45	80
	58	Lamp Post, 7⅜" high, *22–42*		
____		(A) Cream	33	57
____		(B) Peacock	33	60
____		(C) Silver	33	60
____		(D) Maroon	30	87
____		(E) Dark green	30	60
____		(F) Orange	30	60
____	59	Lamp Post, 8¾" high, *20–36*	40	85
____	060	Telegraph Post (O), *29–42*	13	23
____	60	Telegraph Post (std), *20–28*	13	23
____	60	Electric Locomotive 0-4-0, FAO Schwartz (std), *15 u*		NRS
____	0061	7" Curve Track, tubular (OO), *38*	3	8
____	61	Lamp Post, one globe, *14–36*	40	65
____	61	Electric Locomotive 0-4-4-0, FAO Schwartz (std), *15 u*		NRS
____	0062	7" Straight Track, tubular (OO), *38*	5	10
____	62	Semaphore, *20–32*	28	50
____	62	Electric Locomotive 0-4-0, FAO Schwartz (std), *24–32 u*		NRS
____	0063	Half Curve Track, tubular (OO), *38–42*	8	15
____	63	Semaphore, single arm, *15–21*	25	50
____	63	Lamp Post, two globes, *33–42*	135	265
____	0064	7" Curve Track, tubular, electrical connectors (OO), *38*	8	15
____	64	Lamp Post, *40–42*	37	70
____	64	Semaphore, double arm, *15–21*	30	60
____	0065	Half Straight Track, tubular (OO), *38–42*	10	15
____	65	Semaphore, one-arm, *15–26*	30	60
____	65	Whistle Controller, *35*	5	7
____	0066	5⅝" Straight Track (OO), *38–42*	10	15

		Good	Exc	
66	Semaphore, two-arm, *15–26*	35	70	____
66	Whistle Controller, *36–39*	9	10	____
67	Lamp Post, *15–32*	85	145	____
67	Whistle Controller, *36–39*	4	8	____
068	Warning Signal (0), *25–42*	11	23	____
69N	Electric Warning Signal (std 0), *36–42*	33	72	____
0070	90-degree Crossing, *38–42*	5	10	____
70	Outfit: 62 (2), 59 (1), 68 (1), *21–32*	60	130	____
071	060 Telegraph Poles, 6 pieces (std), *24–42*	70	160	____
71	60 Telegraph Post Set, 6 pieces, *21–31*	70	160	____
0072	Remote Control Switches, pair (00), *38–42*	175	288	____
0072L	Remote Control Switch, left hand (00), *38–42*	50	95	____
0072R	Remote Control Switch, right hand (00)	50	95	____
0074	Boxcar (00), *39–42*	36	70	____
0075	Tank Car (00), *39–42*	48	90	____
076	Block Signal (0), *23–28*	25	78	____
76	Warning Bell and Shack, *39–42*	65	179	____
0077	Caboose (00), *39–42*	34	60	____
77/077	Automatic Crossing Gate, *23–35*	28	49	____
78/078	Train Signal, *24–32*	40	100	____
79	Flashing Signal, *28–42*	120	148	____
80/080	Semaphore, *26–35*	50	120	____
81	Controlling Rheostat, *27–33*	2	6	____
82/082	Semaphore, *27–35*	50	120	____
83	Flashing Traffic Signal, *27–42*	65	195	____
084	Semaphore, *28–32*	60	100	____
84	Semaphore, *27–32*	55	85	____
85	Telegraph Pole (std), *29–42*	15	27	____
86	Telegraph Poles, 6 pieces, *29–42*	60	120	____
87	Flashing Crossing Signal, *27–42*	85	300	____
88	Rheostat, *15–27*	3	9	____
88	Direction Controller, *33–42*	4	8	____
89	Flagpole, *23–34*	44	75	____
90	Flagpole, *27–42*	39	95	____
91	Circuit Breaker, *30–42*	34	48	____
092	Signal Tower, *23–27*	83	190	____
92	Floodlight Tower, *31–42**	150	290	____
93	Water Tower, *31–42*	60	107	____
94	High Tension Tower, *32–42**	150	290	____
95	Controlling Rheostat, *34–42*	2	6	____
96	Coal Elevator, manual, *38–40*	165	220	____
097	Telegraph Set (0)	50	75	____
97	Coal Elevator, *38–42*	125	200	____
98	Coal Bunker, *38–40*	160	318	____
99N	Train Control Block Signal, *36–42*	44	155	____

			Good	Exc
____	100	Wooden Gondola (2⅞"), 01		NRS
____	100	Bridge Approaches, 2 ramps (std), 20–31	20	36
____	100	Electric Locomotive (2⅞"), 03–05*	2900	5200
	100	Trolley (std), 10–16		
____		(A) Blue, white windows	1300	2700
____		(B) Blue, cream windows	1850	3600
____		(C) Red, cream windows	1300	2700
____	101	Bridge, span (104) and 2 approaches (100), 20–31	65	120
____	101	Summer Trolley (std), 10–13	1300	2700
____	102	Bridge, 2 spans (104) and 2 approaches (100), 20–31	70	175
____	103	Bridge (std), 13–16	50	70
____	103	Bridge, 3 spans (104) and 2 approaches (100), 20–31	60	145
____	104	Bridge Center Span (std), 20–31	20	45
____	104	Tunnel, papier mache (std), 09–14	50	135
____	105	Bridge (std), 11–14	40	70
____	105	Bridge Approaches, 2 ramps (0), 20–31	50	70
____	106	Bridge, span (110) and 2 approaches (105), 20–31	30	65
____	106	Rheostat, 11–14	3	9
____	107	DC Reducer, 110V, 23–32		NRS
____	108	Bridge, 2 spans (110) and 2 approaches (105), 20–31	50	90
____	109	Bridge, 3 spans, (110) and 2 approaches (105), 20–32	50	115
____	109	Tunnel, papier mache (std), 13–14	30	70
____	110	Bridge Center Span (0), 20–31	12	23
____	111	Box of 50 Bulbs, 20–31	55	105
____	112	Gondola, early (std), 10–12	225	400
____	112	Gondola, later (std), 12–16	40	65
____	112	Gondola, latest (std), 16–18	40	65
____	112	Gondola, Lionel Corp. (std), 18–26	40	65
____	112	Station, 31–35	145	270
____	113	Cattle Car, later (std), 12–16	50	70
____	113	Cattle Car, latest (std), 16–18	50	70
____	113	Cattle Car, Lionel Corp. (std), 18–26	40	55
____	113	Station with light fixtures, 31–34	150	310
____	114	Boxcar, later (std), 12–16	50	90
____	114	Boxcar, latest (std), 16–18	40	70
____	114	Boxcar, Lionel Corp. (std), 18–26	40	70
____	114	Station with light fixtures, 31–34	530	1200
____	115	Station with train control, 35–42*	185	368
____	116	Ballast Car, early and later (std), 10–16	85	115
____	116	Ballast Car, latest (std), 16–18	65	105

		Good	Exc	
116	Ballast Car, Lionel Corp. (std), *18–26*	55	95	___
116	Station with train control, *35–42**	640	923	___
117	Caboose, early (std), *12*	60	70	___
117	Caboose, later (std), *12–16*	50	70	___
117	Caboose, latest (std), *16–18*	50	70	___
117	Caboose, Lionel Corp. (std), *18–26*	38	60	___
117	Station, *36–42*	90	235	___
118	Tunnel, metal, 8" long (O), *20–32*	20	55	___
118L	Tunnel, metal, lighted, 8" long, *27*	20	55	___
119	Tunnel, metal, 12" long, *20–42*	22	60	___
119L	Tunnel, metal, lighted, 12" long, *27–33*	20	55	___
120	Tunnel, metal, 17" long, *22–27*	27	75	___
120L	Tunnel, metal, lighted, 17" long, *27–42*	75	140	___
121	Station, lighted (std), *09–16*			
	(A) 14" x 10" x 9"		NRS	___
	(B) 13" x 9" x 13"	150	300	___
121	Station (std), *20–26*	75	165	___
121X	Station (std), *17–19*	110	255	___
122	Station (std), *20–30*	80	190	___
123	Station (std), *20–23*	75	205	___
123	Tunnel, paperboard base, 18½" long (O), *33–42*	105	235	___
124	Lionel City Station, *20–36**			
	(A) Tan or gray base, pea green roof	90	200	___
	(B) Pea green base, red roof	200	360	___
125	Lionelville Station, *23–25*	80	185	___
125	Track Template, *38*	1	5	___
126	Lionelville Station, *23–36*	95	205	___
127	Lionel Town Station, *23–36*	83	160	___
128	115 Station and 129 Terrace, *35–42**	900	1900	___
128	124 Station and 129 Terrace, *31–34**	900	1900	___
129	Terrace, *28–42**	600	1100	___
130	Tunnel, 26" long (O), *20–36*	100	450	___
130L	Tunnel, lighted, 26" long, *27–33*	150	450	___
131	Corner Display, *24–28*	125	295	___
132	Corner Grass Plot, *24–28*	125	295	___
133	Heart-shaped Plot, *24–28*	125	295	___
134	Lionel City Station with stop, *37–42*	230	445	___
134	Oval-shaped Plot, *24–28*	125	300	___
135	Circular Plot, *24–28*	125	295	___
136	Large Elevation, *24–28*		NRS	___
136	Lionelville Station with stop, *37–42*	85	180	___
137	Station with stop, *37–42*	85	135	___
140L	Tunnel, lighted, 37" long, *27–32*	460	1050	___
150	Electric Locomotive 0-4-0, early (O), *17*	90	160	___

			Good	Exc
	150	Electric Locomotive 0-4-0, late (O), *18–25*		
___		(A) Brown, brown or olive windows	95	150
___		(B) Maroon, dark olive windows	90	135
	152	Electric Locomotive 0-4-0 (O), *17–27*		
___		(A) Dark green	90	135
___		(B) Gray	115	160
___		(C) Mojave	340	680
___		(D) Peacock	340	680
___	**152**	Crossing Gate, *40–42*	18	42
___	**153**	Block Signal, *40–42*	23	45
	153	Electric Locomotive 0-4-0 (O), *24–25*		
___		(A) Dark green	100	160
___		(B) Gray	100	160
___		(C) Mojave	100	160
___	**154**	Electric Locomotive 0-4-0 (O), *17–23*	100	180
	154	Highway Signal, *40–42*		
___		(A) Black base	21	49
___		(B) Orange base	59	265
	155	Freight Shed, *30–42**		
___		(A) Cream base, terra cotta floor	180	320
___		(B) Ivory base, red floor	240	400
___	**156**	Electric Locomotive 0-4-0 (O), *17–23*	400	720
___	**156**	Station Platform, *39–42*	85	133
	156	Electric Locomotive 4-4-4 (O), *17–23*		
___		(A) Dark green	475	810
___		(B) Maroon	540	890
___		(C) Olive green	600	1050
___		(D) Gray	670	1200
	156X	Electric Locomotive 0-4-0 (O), *23–24*		
___		(A) Maroon	380	495
___		(B) Olive green	440	550
___		(C) Gray	530	710
___		(D) Brown	470	600
___	**157**	Hand Truck, *30–32*	25	41
	158	Electric Locomotive 0-4-0 (O), *19–23*		
___		(A) Gray or red windows	75	205
___		(B) Black	95	250
___	**158**	Station Set: 136 Station and 2 platforms (156), *40–42*	120	280
___	**159**	Block Actuator, *40*	10	27
___	**161**	Baggage Truck, *30–32**	42	80
___	**162**	Dump Truck, *30–32**	42	80
___	**163**	Freight Accessory Set: 2 hand trucks (157), baggage truck (161), and dump truck (162), *30–42**	220	360
___	**164**	Log Loader, *40–42*	160	225

		Good	Exc	
165	Magnetic Crane, *40–42*	175	285	____
165-22	Scrap Steel with bag, *40–42*	50	125	____
165-83	Scrap Steel with bag, *40–42*		128	____
166	Whistle Controller, *40–42*	3	7	____
167	Whistle Controller, *40–42*	6	23	____
167X	Whistle Controller (OO), *40–42*	5	14	____
168	Magic Electrol Controller, *40–42*		77	____
169	Controller, *40–42*	3	8	____
170	DC Reducer, 220V, *14–38*	3	8	____
171	DC to AC Inverter, 110V, *36–42*	3	15	____
172	DC to AC Inverter, 229V, *39–42*	3	7	____
180	Pullman Car (std), *11–13*			
	(A) Maroon body and roof	145	205	____
	(B) Brown body and roof	145	255	____
180	Pullman Car (std), *13–15*	80	160	____
180	Pullman Car (std), *15–18*	80	160	____
180	Pullman Car (std), *18–22*	80	135	____
181	Combine Car (std), *11–13*			
	(A) Maroon, dark olive doors	145	205	____
	(B) Brown, dark olive doors	145	205	____
	(C) Yellow-orange, orange doors	350	495	____
181	Combine Car (std), *13–15*	80	160	____
181	Combine Car (std), *15–18*	80	160	____
181	Combine Car (std), *18–22*	80	135	____
182	Observation Car (std), *11–13*			
	(A) Maroon, dark olive doors	145	205	____
	(B) Brown, dark olive doors	145	205	____
	(C) Yellow-orange, orange doors	350	495	____
182	Observation Car (std), *13–15*	80	160	____
182	Observation Car (std), *15–18*	80	160	____
182	Observation Car (std), *18–22*	80	135	____
184	Bungalow, illuminated, *23–32**	65	110	____
185	Bungalow, *23–24*	50	115	____
186	184 Bungalows, set of 5, *23–32*	195	610	____
186	Log Loader Outfit, *40–41*	130	340	____
187	185 Bungalows, set of 5, *23–24*	170	590	____
188	Elevator and Car Set, *38–41*	115	370	____
189	Villa, illuminated, *23–32**	133	225	____
190	Observation Car (std), *08*			
	(A) Dark olive green, nonremovable roof	1150	2600	____
	(B) Dark olive green, removable roof	115	205	____
	(C) Yellow-orange, removable roof	320	620	____
	(D) Orange, removable roof	115	205	____
	(E) Mojave, removable roof	345	870	____

			Good	Exc
____	190	Observation Car (std), *11–13*	600	900
____	190	Observation Car (std), *13–15*	200	295
____	190	Observation Car (std), *15–18*	200	295
____	190	Observation Car (std), *18–22*	80	135
____	190	Observation Car (std), *23–26*	230	475
____	191	Villa, illuminated, *23–32**	123	325
____	192	Illuminated Villa Set: 189, 191, 184 (2), *27–32*		800
____	193	Automatic Accessory Set (O), *27–29*	150	325
____	194	Automatic Accessory Set (std), *27–29*	100	325
____	195	Terrace, *27–30*	350	740
____	196	Accessory Set, *27*	200	335
____	200	Electric Express (2⅞"), *03–05**	4000	6300
____	200	Trailer, matches No. 2 Trolley (std), *11–16*		2400
____	200	Turntable (std), *28–33**	85	190
	201	0-6-0 Locomotive (O), *40–42*		
____		(A) 2201B Tender, bell	375	760
____		(B) 2201T Tender, no bell	345	690
	202	Summer Trolley (std), *10–13*		
____		(A) Electric Rapid Transit	1300	2700
____		(B) Preston St.	3250	4500
____	203	Armored 0-4-0 (O), *17–21*	1100	1800
	203	0-6-0 Locomotive (O), *40–42*		
____		(A) 2203B Tender, bell	400	495
____		(B) 2203T Tender, no bell	365	550
	204	2-4-2 Locomotive (O), *40–42 u*		
____		(A) Black	55	105
____		(B) Gunmetal gray	80	165
____	205	Merchandise Containers, 3 pieces, *30–38**	130	320
____	206	Sack of Coal, *38–42*	5	18
____	208	Tool Set: 6 assorted tools, *34–42**	65	150
	0209	Barrels, wooden, 6 pieces (O), *34–42*		
____		(A) Solid barrels	8	26
____		(B) 2-piece barrels	83	169
____	209	Barrels, wooden, 4 pieces (std), *34–42*	10	22
____	210	Switches, pair (std), *26, 34–42*	42	75
____	211	Flatcar (std), *26–40**	125	225
	212	Gondola (std), *26–40**		
____		(A) Gray or light green	100	205
____		(B) Maroon	75	135
	213	Cattle Car (std), *26–40**		
____		(A) Mojave, maroon roof	160	365
____		(B) Terra-cotta, pea green roof	130	285
____		(C) Cream, maroon roof	300	650

		Good	Exc	
214	Boxcar (std), *26–40**			
	(A) Terra-cotta, dark green roof	195	387	____
	(B) Cream body, orange roof	150	270	____
	(C) Yellow, brown roof	300	495	____
214R	Refrigerator Car (std), *29–40**			
	(A) Ivory or white, peacock roof	325	495	____
	(B) White, light blue roof	435	790	____
215	Tank Car (std), *26–40**			
	(A) Pea green	150	215	____
	(B) Ivory	220	360	____
	(C) Aluminum	315	720	____
216	Hopper Car (std), *26–38**			
	(A) Dark green, brass plates	195	335	____
	(B) Dark green, nickel plates	445	1100	____
217	Caboose (std), *26–40**			
	(A) Orange, maroon roof	250	510	____
	(B) Red, peacock roof	120	235	____
	(C) Red body and roof, ivory doors	150	320	____
217	Lighting Set, *14–23*		NRS	____
218	Dump Car (std), *26–38**	220	365	____
219	Crane Car (std), *26–40**			
	(A) Peacock, red boom	135	255	____
	(B) Yellow, light green or red boom	270	440	____
	(C) Ivory, light green boom	270	480	____
220	Floodlight Car (std), *31–40**			
	(A) Terra-cotta base	225	385	____
	(B) Green base	340	485	____
220	Switches, pair (std), *26**	25	90	____
222	Switches, pair (std), *26–32*	40	100	____
223	Switches, pair (std), *32–42*	33	120	____
224/224E	2-6-2 Locomotive (O), *38–42*			
	(A) Black, die-cast 2224 Tender	155	253	____
	(B) Black, plastic 2224 Tender	110	195	____
	(C) Gunmetal, die-cast 2224 Tender	385	950	____
	(D) Gunmetal, sheet-metal 2689 Tender	120	210	____
225	222 Switches and 439 Panel, *29–32*	115	260	____
225/225E	2-6-2 Locomotive (O), *38–42*			
	(A) Black, 2235 or 2245 Tender	210	370	____
	(B) Black, 2235 plastic Tender	185	320	____
	(C) Gunmetal, 2225 or 2265 Tender	210	360	____
	(D) Gunmetal, 2235 die-cast Tender	285	730	____
226/226E	2-6-4 Locomotive (O), *38–41*	275	632	____
227	0-6-0 Locomotive (O), *39–42*			
	(A) 2227B Tender, bell	600	1250	____
	(B) 2227T Tender, no bell	600	1150	____

		Good	Exc
228	0-6-0 Locomotive (O), *39–42*		
___	(A) 2228B Tender, bell	600	1250
___	(B) 2228T Tender, no bell	600	1150
229	2-4-2 Locomotive (O), *39–42*		
___	(A) Black or gunmetal, 2689W Tender	155	263
___	(B) Black or gunmetal, 2689T Tender	120	200
___	(C) Black, 2666W whistle Tender	155	280
___	(D) Black, 2666T nonwhistling Tender	120	200
___ **230**	0-6-0 Locomotive (O), *39–42*	1100	2050
___ **231**	0-6-0 Locomotive (O), *39*	1000	1800
___ **232**	0-6-0 Locomotive (O), *40–42*	1000	1800
___ **233**	0-6-0 Locomotive (O), *40–42*	1000	1800
___ **238**	4-4-2 Locomotive (O), *39–40 u*	430	710
238E	4-4-2 Locomotive (O), *36–38*		
___	(A) 265W or 2225W whistle Tender	280	343
___	(B) 265 or 2225T nonwhistling Tender	275	360
___ **248**	Electric Locomotive 0-4-0 (O), *27–32*	150	240
249/249E	2-4-2 Locomotive (O), *36–39*		
___	(A) Gunmetal, 265T or 265W Tender	100	269
___	(B) Black, 265W Tender	110	210
___ **250**	Electric Locomotive 0-4-0, early (O), *26*	125	220
250	Electric Locomotive 0-4-0, late (O), *34*		
___	(A) Yellow-orange body, terra-cotta frame	145	245
___	(B) Terra-cotta body, maroon frame	160	270
___ **250E**	4-4-2 Hiawatha Locomotive (O), *35–42**	400	1100
251	Electric Locomotive 0-4-0 (O), *25–32*		
___	(A) Gray body, red windows	190	340
___	(B) Red body, ivory stripe	215	410
___	(C) Red body, no ivory stripe	200	380
251E	Electric Locomotive 0-4-0 (O), *27–32*		
___	(A) Red body, ivory stripe	225	425
___	(B) Red body, no ivory stripe	215	395
___	(C) Gray, red trim	195	350
252	Electric Locomotive 0-4-0 (O), *26–32*		
___	(A) Peacock or olive green	95	170
___	(B) Terra-cotta or yellow-orange	125	214
252E	Electric Locomotive 0-4-0 (O), *33–35*		
___	(A) Terra-cotta	145	250
___	(B) Yellow-orange	125	205

		Good	Exc	
253	Electric Locomotive 0-4-0 (O), *24–32*			
	(A) Maroon	180	430	____
	(B) Dark green	105	249	____
	(C) Mojave	105	235	____
	(D) Terra-cotta	180	430	____
	(E) Peacock	95	195	____
	(F) Red	210	475	____
253E	Electric Locomotive 0-4-0 (O), *31–36*			
	(A) Green	150	205	____
	(B) Terra-cotta	190	305	____
254	Electric Locomotive 0-4-0 (O), *24–32*	240	340	____
254E	Electric Locomotive 0-4-0 (O), *27–34*	190	263	____
255E	2-4-2 Locomotive (O), *35–36*	485	1000	____
256	Electric Locomotive 0-4-4-0 (O), *24–30**			
	(A) Rubber-stamped lettering	470	1250	____
	(B) No outline around Lionel	425	770	____
	(C) Lionel Lines and No. 256 on brass	450	1050	____
257	2-4-0 Locomotive (O), *30–35 u*			
	(A) Black tender	145	300	____
	(B) Black crackle-finish tender	240	435	____
258	2-4-0 Locomotive, early (O), *30–35 u*			
	(A) 4-wheel 257 Tender	85	170	____
	(B) 8-wheel 258 Tender	100	195	____
258	2-4-2 Locomotive, late (O), *41 u*			
	(A) Black	60	90	____
	(B) Gunmetal	85	135	____
259	2-4-2 Locomotive (O), *32*	70	135	____
259E	2-4-2 Locomotive (O), *33–42*	80	155	____
260E	2-4-2 Locomotive (O), *30–35**			
	(A) Black body, green or black frame	385	548	____
	(B) Dark gunmetal body and frame	440	640	____
261	2-4-2 Locomotive (O), *31*	125	210	____
261E	2-4-2 Locomotive (O), *35*	190	285	____
262	2-4-2 Locomotive (O), *31–32*	215	311	____
262E	2-4-2 Locomotive (O), *33–36*			
	(A) Gloss black, copper and brass trim	100	210	____
	(B) Satin black, nickel trim	125	258	____
263E	2-4-2 Locomotive (O), *36–39**			
	(A) Gunmetal gray	315	610	____
	(B) 2-tone blue, from Blue Comet	415	950	____
264E	2-4-2 Locomotive (O), *35–36*			
	(A) Red, Red Comet	138	295	____
	(B) Black	220	380	____

			Good	Exc
	265E	2-4-2 Locomotive (O), *35–40*		
___		(A) Black or gunmetal	170	330
___		(B) Light blue, Blue Streak	460	800
___	**267E/W**	Set: 616, 617 (2), 6*18, 35–41*		560
___	**270**	Bridge, 10" long (O), *31–42*	18	50
___	**270**	Lighting Set, *15–23*		NRS
___	**271**	270 Bridges, set of 2, *31–33, 35–40*	65	150
___	**271**	Lighting Set, *15–23*		NRS
___	**272**	270 Bridges, set of 3, *31–33, 35–40*	60	165
___	**280**	Bridge, 14" long (std), *31–42*	50	115
___	**281**	280 Bridges, set of 2, *31–33, 35–40*	90	205
___	**282**	280 Bridges, set of 3, *31–33, 35–40*	105	265
___	**289E**	2-4-2 Locomotive (O), *37 u*	120	305
___	**300**	Electric Trolley Car (2⅞"), *01–05*	2000	3600
	300	Hellgate Bridge (std), *28–42**		
___		(A) Cream towers, green truss	800	1350
___		(B) Ivory towers, aluminum truss	763	1600
___	**303**	Summer Trolley, *10–13*	1500	3150
___	**308**	Signs, set of 5 (O), *40–42*	26	70
___	**309**	Electric Trolley Trailer (2⅞"), *01–05*	2500	4050
	309	Pullman Car (std), *26–39*		
___		(A) Maroon body and roof, Mojave windows	100	160
___		(B) Mojave body and roof, maroon windows	100	160
___		(C) Light brown body, dark brown roof	120	190
___		(D) Medium blue body, dark blue roof	170	280
___		(E) Apple green body, dark green roof	170	280
___		(F) Pale blue body, silver roof	100	185
___		(G) Maroon body, terra-cotta roof	130	195
___	**310**	Rails and Ties, complete section (2⅞"), *01–02*	5	14
	310	Baggage Car (std), *26–39*		
___		(A) Maroon body and roof, Mojave windows	100	160
___		(B) Mojave body and roof, maroon windows	85	160
___		(C) Light brown body, dark brown roof	115	185
___		(D) Medium blue body, dark blue roof	170	280
___		(E) Apple green body, dark green roof	170	280
___		(F) Pale blue body, silver roof	100	175
	312	Observation Car (std), *24–39*		
___		(A) Maroon body and roof, Mojave windows	100	160
___		(B) Mojave body and roof, maroon windows	83	160
___		(C) Light brown body, dark brown roof	120	185
___		(D) Medium blue body, dark blue roof	170	280
___		(E) Apple green body, dark green roof	170	280
___		(F) Pale blue body, silver roof	100	175
___		(G) Maroon body, terra-cotta roof	130	195

		Good	Exc
313	Bascule Bridge (O), *40–42*		
	(A) Silver bridge	235	500 ___
	(B) Gray bridge	250	590 ___
314	Girder Bridge (O), *40–42*	17	40 ___
315	Trestle Bridge (O), *40–42*	28	80 ___
316	Trestle Bridge (O), *40–42*	21	48 ___
318	Electric Locomotive 0-4-0 (std), *24–32*		
	(A) Gray, dark gray, or Mojave	150	250 ___
	(B) Pea green	150	250 ___
	(C) State brown	250	395 ___
318E	Electric Locomotive 0-4-0, *26–35*		
	(A) Gray, Mojave, or pea green	150	250 ___
	(B) State brown	275	440 ___
	(C) Black	550	1275 ___
319	Pullman Car (std), *24–27*	105	175 ___
320	Baggage Car (std), *25–27*	100	175 ___
320	Switch and Signal (2⅞"), *02–05*		NRS ___
322	Observation Car (std), *24–27, 29–30 u*	100	175 ___
330	90-degree Crossing (2⅞"), *02–05*		NRS ___
332	Baggage Car (std), *26–33*		
	(A) Red body and roof, cream doors	80	120 ___
	(B) Peacock body and roof, orange doors	75	115 ___
	(C) Gray body and roof, maroon doors	75	115 ___
	(D) Olive green body and roof, red doors	90	145 ___
	(E) State brown body, dark brown roof	190	430 ___
337	Pullman Car (std), *25–32*		
	(A) Red body and roof, cream doors	95	190 ___
	(B) Mojave body and roof, maroon doors	95	190 ___
	(C) Olive green body and roof, red doors	105	225 ___
	(D) Olive green body and roof, maroon doors	95	190 ___
	(E) Pea green body and roof, cream doors	210	500 ___
338	Observation Car (std), *25–32*		
	(A) Red body and roof, cream doors	95	190 ___
	(B) Mojave body and roof, maroon doors	95	190 ___
	(C) Olive green body and roof, red doors	105	225 ___
	(D) Olive green body and roof, maroon doors	95	190 ___
339	Pullman Car (std), *25–33*		
	(A) Peacock body and roof, orange doors	55	88 ___
	(B) Gray body and roof, maroon doors	55	100 ___
	(C) State brown body, dark brown roof	135	380 ___
	(D) Peacock body, dark green roof	75	130 ___
	(E) Mojave body, maroon roof and doors	145	230 ___
340	Suspension Bridge (2⅞"), *02–05**		NRS ___

			Good	Exc
	341	Observation Car (std), *25–33*		
___		(A) Peacock body and roof, orange doors	50	70
___		(B) Gray body and roof, maroon doors	50	70
___		(C) State brown body, dark brown roof	125	157
___		(D) Peacock body, dark green roof	65	95
___		(E) Mojave body, maroon roof and doors	135	165
___	**350**	Track Bumper (2⅞"), *02–05*		550
___	**380**	Elevated Pillars (2⅞"), *04–05**	30	70
___	**380**	Electric Locomotive 0-4-0 (std), *23–27*	310	440
	380E	Electric Locomotive 0-4-0 (std), *26–29*		
___		(A) Mojave	445	630
___		(B) Maroon	295	400
___		(C) Dark green	370	460
___	**381**	Electric Locomotive 4-4-4 (std), *28–29**	1600	2100
	381E	Electric Locomotive 4-4-4 (std), *28–36**		
___		(A) State green, apple green subframe	1500	2500
___		(B) State green, red subframe	1900	3250
___	**381U**	Electric Locomotive 4-4-4 Kit (std), *28–29*	1600	4100
___	**384**	2-4-0 Locomotive (std), *30–32**	415	730
___	**384E**	2-4-0 Locomotive (std), *30–32**	425	650
___	**385E**	2-4-2 Locomotive (std), *33–39**	370	670
___	**390**	2-4-2 Locomotive (std), *29**	460	820
	390E	2-4-2 Locomotive (std), *29–31**		
___		(A) Black, with or without orange stripe	460	690
___		(B) 2-tone blue, cream-orange stripe	650	1050
___		(C) 2-tone green, orange or green stripe	990	2050
	392E	4-4-2 Locomotive (std), *32–39**		
___		(A) Black, 384 Tender	750	1250
___		(B) Black, large 12-wheel tender	1050	1850
___		(C) Gunmetal gray	1000	1800
___	**400**	Express Trail Car (2⅞"), *03–05**	3500	5850
	400E	4-4-4 Locomotive (std), *31–39**		
___		(A) Black	1400	2150
___		(B) Blue	1550	2350
___		(C) Gunmetal or light blue	1650	2800
___		(D) Black crackle finish	1600	3500
___	**402**	Electric Locomotive 0-4-4-0 (std), *23–27*	365	570
___	**402E**	Electric Locomotive 0-4-4-0 (std), *26–29*	345	550
___	**404**	Summer Trolley (std), *10*		NRS
	408E	Electric Locomotive 0-4-4-0 (std), *27–36**		
___		(A) Apple green or Mojave, red pilots	770	980
___		(B) State brown, brown pilots	2000	3000
___		(C) State green, red pilots	2000	3800

		Good	Exc	
412	California Pullman Car (std), *29–35**			
	(A) Light green body, dark green roof	590	1750	____
	(B) Light brown body, dark brown roof	620	2100	____
413	Colorado Pullman Car (std), *29–35**			
	(A) Light green body, dark green roof	590	1750	____
	(B) Light brown body, dark brown roof	620	2100	____
414	Illinois Pullman Car (std), *29–35**			
	(A) Light green body, dark green roof	590	1750	____
	(B) Light brown body, dark brown roof	620	2050	____
416	New York Observation Car (std), *29–35**			
	(A) Light green body, dark green roof	590	1750	____
	(B) Light brown body, dark brown roof	620	2100	____
418	Pullman Car (std), *23–32**	225	320	____
419	Combination (std), *23–32**	205	280	____
420	Faye Pullman Car (std), *30–40**			
	(A) Brass trim	485	900	____
	(B) Nickel trim	500	1200	____
421	Westphal Pullman Car (std), *30–40**			
	(A) Brass trim	500	900	____
	(B) Nickel trim	500	1200	____
422	Tempel Observation Car (std), *30–40**			
	(A) Brass trim	485	900	____
	(B) Nickel trim	500	1200	____
424	Liberty Bell Pullman Car (std), *31–40**			
	(A) Brass trim	350	530	____
	(B) Nickel trim	385	650	____
425	Stephen Girard Pullman Car (std), *31–40**			
	(A) Brass trim	350	530	____
	(B) Nickel trim	385	650	____
426	Coral Isle Observation Car (std), *31–40**			
	(A) Brass trim	350	530	____
	(B) Nickel trim	385	650	____
428	Pullman Car (std), *26–30**			
	(A) Dark green body and roof	250	385	____
	(B) Orange body and roof, apple green windows	390	890	____
429	Combine Car (std), *26–30**			
	(A) Dark green body and roof	250	385	____
	(B) Orange body and roof, apple green windows	390	890	____
430	Observation Car (std), *26–30**			
	(A) Dark green body and roof	250	385	____
	(B) Orange body and roof, apple green windows	390	890	____

		Good	Exc
431	Diner (std), *27–32**		
____	(A) Mojave body, screw-mounted roof	350	540
____	(B) Mojave body, hinged roof	465	720
____	(C) Dark green body, orange windows	410	720
____	(D) Orange body, apple green windows	410	720
____	(E) Apple green body, red windows	410	720
____ **435**	Power Station, *26–38**	215	400
436	Power Station, *26–37**		
____	(A) Power Station plate	135	265
____	(B) Edison Service plate	270	610
____ **437**	Switch Signal Tower, *26–37**	190	430
438	Signal Tower, *27–39**		
____	(A) Mojave base, orange house	215	321
____	(B) Black base, white house	325	640
____ **439**	Panel Board, *28–42**	80	145
____ **440/0440**	Signal Bridge, *32–35**	180	473
____ **440C**	Panel Board, *32–42*	90	145
____ **441**	Weighing Station (std), *32–36*	495	1325
____ **442**	Landscaped Diner, *38–42*	198	258
____ **444**	Roundhouse (std), *32–35**	1350	2850
____ **444-18**	Roundhouse Clip, *33*		NRS
450	Electric Locomotive 0-4-0, Macy's (O), *30 u*		
____	(A) Red, black frame	295	700
____	(B) Apple green, dark green frame	415	880
____ **450**	Set: 450, matching 605, 606 (2), *30 u*	750	1800
____ **490**	Observation Car (std), *23–32**	190	255
____ **500**	Electric Derrick Car (2⅞"), *03–04**	5000	6750
511	Flatcar (std), *27–40*		
____	(A) Dark green	65	115
____	(B) Medium green	75	165
512	Gondola (std), *27–39*		
____	(A) Peacock	38	58
____	(B) Light green	50	95
513	Cattle Car (std), *27–38*		
____	(A) Olive green, orange roof	70	165
____	(B) Orange, pea green roof	60	110
____	(C) Cream, maroon roof	90	250
514	Boxcar (std), *29–40*		
____	(A) Cream, orange roof	90	155
____	(B) Yellow, brown roof	115	285
514	Refrigerator Car, ivory or white, peacock roof, (std), *27–28*	240	400
514R	Refrigerator Car (std), *29–40*		
____	(A) Ivory, peacock roof	140	190
____	(B) White, light blue roof	420	580

		Good	Exc	
515	Tank Car (std), *27–40*			
	(A) Terra-cotta	90	145	____
	(B) Ivory	105	185	____
	(C) Aluminum	90	175	____
	(D) Orange, red Shell decal	340	750	____
516	Hopper Car (std), *28–40*			
	(A) Red	170	240	____
	(B) Red, rubber-stamped data	200	300	____
	(C) Light red, nickel trim	200	325	____
517	Caboose (std), *27–40*			
	(A) Pea green body, red roof	50	100	____
	(B) Red body and roof	105	155	____
	(C) Red body, black roof, orange windows	355	640	____
520	Floodlight Car (std), *31–40*			
	(A) Terra-cotta base	110	210	____
	(B) Green base	110	240	____
529	Pullman Car (O), *26–32*			
	(A) Olive green body and roof	25	45	____
	(B) Terra-cotta body and roof	25	60	____
530	Observation Car (O), *26–32*			
	(A) Olive green body and roof	25	45	____
	(B) Terra-cotta body and roof	25	63	____
550	Miniature Figures, boxed (std), *32–36**	175	431	____
551	Engineer (std), *32*	25	45	____
552	Conductor (std), *32*	21	42	____
553	Porter with stool (std), *32*	25	50	____
554	Male Passenger (std), *32*	25	45	____
555	Female Passenger (std), *32*	25	45	____
556	Red Cap with suitcase (std), *32*	25	65	____
600	Derrick Trailer (2⅞"), *03–04**	5000	8550	____
600	Pullman Car, early (O), *15–23*			
	(A) Dark green	65	170	____
	(B) Maroon or brown	48	85	____
600	Pullman Car, late (O), *33–42*			
	(A) Light red or gray, red roof	50	90	____
	(B) Light blue, aluminum roof	70	120	____
601	Observation Car, late (O), *33–42*			
	(A) Light red body and roof	50	90	____
	(B) Light gray, red roof	50	90	____
	(C) Light blue body, aluminum roof	70	120	____
601	Pullman Car, early (O), *15–23*	50	70	____
602	Lionel Lines Baggage Car, late (O), *33–42*			
	(A) Light red or gray, red roof	60	110	____
	(B) Light blue, aluminum roof	90	150	____

			Good	Exc
___	602	NYC Baggage Car (0), *15–23*	30	45
___	602	Observation Car (0), *22 u*	30	36
___	603	Pullman Car, early (0), *22 u*	40	70
___	603	Pullman Car, later (0), *20–25*	20	45
	603	Pullman Car, latest (0), *31–36*		
___		(A) Light red body and roof	45	85
___		(B) Red body, black roof	35	60
___		(C) Stephen Girard green body, dark green roof	35	60
___		(D) Maroon body and roof, Macy Special	60	125
___	604	Observation Car, later (0), *20–25*	35	60
	604	Observation Car, latest (0), *31–36*		
___		(A) Light red body and roof	44	85
___		(B) Red body, black roof	35	60
___		(C) Yellow-orange body, terra-cotta roof	35	60
___		(D) Stephen Girard green body, dark green roof	35	60
___		(E) Maroon body and roof	70	150
	605	Pullman Car (0), *25–32*		
___		(A) Gray, Lionel Lines	85	170
___		(B) Gray, Illinois Central	85	170
___		(C) Red, Lionel Lines	170	255
___		(D) Red, Illinois Central	255	340
___		(E) Orange, Lionel Lines	170	255
___		(F) Orange, Illinois Central	300	430
___		(G) Olive green, Lionel Lines	255	340
	606	Observation Car (0), *25–32*		
___		(A) Gray, Lionel Lines	130	215
___		(B) Gray, Illinois Central	90	170
___		(C) Red, Lionel Lines	170	255
___		(D) Red, Illinois Central	255	340
___		(E) Orange, Lionel Lines	170	255
___		(F) Orange, Illinois Central	170	255
___		(G) Olive green, Lionel Lines	255	340
	607	Pullman Car (0), *26–27*		
___		(A) Peacock, Lionel Lines	50	70
___		(B) Peacock, Illinois Central	75	115
___		(C) 2-tone green, Lionel Lines	50	75
___		(D) Red, Lionel Lines	75	110
	608	Observation Car (0), *26–37*		
___		(A) Peacock, Lionel Lines	50	70
___		(B) Peacock, Illinois Central	75	115
___		(C) 2-tone green, Lionel Lines	50	75
___		(D) Red, Lionel Lines	75	110
___	609	Pullman Car (0), *37*	60	85

		Good	Exc	
610	Pullman Car, early (O), *15–25*			
	(A) Dark green body and roof	50	65	____
	(B) Maroon body and roof	60	95	____
	(C) Mojave body and roof	60	95	____
610	Pullman Car, late (O), *26–30*			
	(A) Olive green body and roof	65	80	____
	(B) Mojave body and roof	55	80	____
	(C) Terra-cotta body, maroon roof	100	155	____
	(D) Pea green body and roof	70	115	____
	(E) Light blue body, aluminum roof	130	260	____
	(F) Light red body, aluminum-painted roof	100	155	____
611	Observation Car (O), *37*	55	90	____
612	Observation Car, early (O), *15–25*			
	(A) Dark green body and roof	50	60	____
	(B) Maroon body and roof	70	90	____
	(C) Mojave body and roof	70	90	____
612	Observation Car, late (O), *26–30*			
	(A) Olive green body and roof	55	80	____
	(B) Mojave body and roof	55	80	____
	(C) Terra-cotta body, maroon roof	100	155	____
	(D) Pea green body and roof	70	115	____
	(E) Light blue body, aluminum roof	130	260	____
	(F) Light red body, aluminum-painted roof	100	155	____
613	Pullman Car (O), *31–40**			
	(A) Terra-cotta body, maroon/terra-cotta roof	85	195	____
	(B) Light red body, light red/aluminum roof	175	350	____
	(C) Blue, two-tone blue roof	115	225	____
614	Observation Car (O), *31–40**			
	(A) Terra-cotta body, maroon/terra-cotta roof	100	190	____
	(B) Light red body, light red/aluminum roof	175	350	____
	(C) Blue, two-tone blue roof	115	225	____
615	Baggage Car (O), *33–40**	150	260	____
616E/W	Diesel only (O), *35–41*	90	215	____
616E/W	Set: 616, 617 (2), 618	218	570	____
617	Coach (O), *35–41*			
	(A) Blue and white	55	85	____
	(B) Chrome, gunmetal skirts	55	85	____
	(C) Chrome, chrome skirts	55	85	____
	(D) Silver-painted	55	85	____
618	Observation Car (O), *35–41*			
	(A) Blue and white	55	85	____
	(B) Chrome, gunmetal skirts	55	85	____
	(C) Chrome, chrome skirts	55	85	____
	(D) Silver-painted	55	85	____

		Good	Exc
619	Combine Car (0), *36–38*		
____	(A) Blue, white windows band	100	205
____	(B) Chrome, chrome skirts	100	205
____ **620**	Floodlight Car (0), *37–42*	50	85
629	Pullman Car (0), *24–32*		
____	(A) Dark green body and roof	30	40
____	(B) Orange body and roof	30	40
____	(C) Red body and roof	20	32
____	(D) Light red body and roof	40	55
630	Observation Car, *24–32*		
____	(A) Dark green body and roof	30	40
____	(B) Orange body and roof	30	40
____	(C) Red body and roof	20	32
____	(D) Light red body and roof	40	55
____ **636W**	Diesel only (0), *36–39*	90	175
____ **636W**	Set: 636W, 637 (2), 6*38, 36–39*	375	640
____ **637**	Coach (0), *36–39*	70	105
____ **638**	Observation Car (0), *36–39*	70	105
____ **651**	Flatcar (0), *35–40*	28	55
____ **652**	Gondola (0), *35–40*	28	55
____ **653**	Hopper Car (0), *34–40*	35	65
654	Tank Car (0), *34–42*		
____	(A) Orange or aluminum	38	60
____	(B) Gray	42	75
655	Boxcar (0), *34–42*		
____	(A) Cream, maroon roof	35	60
____	(B) Cream, tuscan roof	47	75
656	Cattle Car (0), *35–40*		
____	(A) Light gray, vermilion roof	40	100
____	(B) Burnt orange, tuscan roof	70	125
657	Caboose (0), *34–42*		
____	(A) Red body and roof	20	34
____	(B) Red body, tuscan roof	25	42
____ **659**	Dump Car (0), *35–42*	40	75
____ **700**	Electric Locomotive 0-4-0 (0), *15–16*	360	690
____ **700E**	4-6-4 NYC Hudson "5344," scale (0), *37–42**	1400	2950
____ **700K**	4-6-4 Locomotive, unbuilt gray primer (0), *38–42*	4400	5950
____ **701**	0-6-0 PRR Locomotive "8976," *41*		2097
____ **701**	Electric Locomotive 0-4-0 (0), *15–16*	390	660
____ **702**	Baggage Car (0), *17–21*	115	305
____ **703**	Electric Locomotive 4-4-4 (0), *15–16*	1400	2350
____ **706**	Electric Locomotive 0-4-0 (0), *15–16*	375	630
____ **708**	0-6-0 PRR Locomotive "8976" (0), *39–42**	1450	2850

		Good	Exc	
710	Pullman Car (O), *24–34*			
	(A) Red, Lionel Lines	200	300	____
	(B) Orange, Lionel Lines	150	225	____
	(C) Orange, New York Central	175	225	____
	(D) Orange, Illinois Central	300	450	____
	(E) 2-tone blue, Lionel Lines	300	415	____
	(F) Orange, New York Central	200	260	____
711	Remote Control Switches, pair (072), *35–42*	80	150	____
712	Observation Car (O), *24–34*			
	(A) Red, Lionel Lines	185	355	____
	(B) Orange, Lionel Lines	140	265	____
	(C) Orange, New York Central	168	310	____
	(D) Orange, Illinois Central	280	530	____
	(E) 2-tone blue, Lionel Lines	280	485	____
714	Boxcar (O), *40–42**	350	610	____
714K	Boxcar, unbuilt (O), *40–42*		480	____
715	Tank Car (O), *40–42**			
	(A) SEPS 8124 decal	340	610	____
	(B) SUNX 715 decal	435	880	____
715K	Tank Car, unbuilt (O), *40–42*		530	____
716	Hopper Car (O), *40–42**	310	392	____
716K	Hopper Car, unbuilt (O), *40–42*		730	____
717	Caboose (O), *40–42**	340	510	____
717K	Caboose, unbuilt (O), *40–42*		590	____
720	90-degree Crossing (072), *35–42*	21	40	____
721	Manual Switches, pair (072), *35–42*	50	105	____
730	90-degree Crossing (072), *35–42*	20	36	____
731	Remote Control Switches, pair, T-rail (072), *35–42*	80	135	____
751E/W	Set: 752, 753 (2), 754 (O), *34–41**	640	1050	____
752E	Diesel only (O), *34–41**			
	(A) Yellow and brown	168	355	
	(B) Aluminum	145	340	____
753	Coach (O), *36–41*			
	(A) Yellow and brown	83	185	____
	(B) Aluminum	75	180	____
754	Observation Car (O), *36–41*			
	(A) Yellow and brown	80	185	____
	(B) Aluminum	75	180	____
760	Curved Track, 16 pieces, (072), *35–42*	37	80	____
761	Curved Track (072), *34–42*	1	2	____
762	Straight Track (072), *34–42*	1	2	____
762S	Insulated Straight Track (072), *34–42*	2	5	____

			Good	Exc
	763E	4-6-4 Locomotive (O), *37–42*		
___		(A) Gunmetal, 263 or 2263W Tender	1000	2650
___		(B) Gunmetal, 2226X or 2226WX Tender	1150	2950
___		(C) Black, 2226WX Tender	965	2650
___	**771**	Curved Track, T-rail (O72), *35–42*	3	10
___	**772**	Straight Track, T-rail (O72), *35–42*	4	12
___	**773**	Fishplate Set, 50 plates (O72), *36–42*	25	32
___	**782**	Hiawatha Combine Car (O), *35–41**	230	380
___	**783**	Hiawatha Coach (O), *35–41**	140	290
___	**784**	Hiawatha Observation Car (O), *35–41**	205	445
___	**792**	Rail Chief Combine Car (O), *37–41**	215	580
___	**793**	Rail Chief Coach (O), *37–41**	290	800
___	**794**	Rail Chief Observation Car (O), *37–41**	250	800
___	**800**	Boxcar (2 7/8"), *04–05**	2500	4050
	800	Boxcar (O), *15–26*		
___		(A) Light orange body, brown-maroon roof	45	70
___		(B) Orange body and roof, PRR	30	43
___	**801**	Caboose (O), *15–26*	36	46
___	**802**	Stock Car (O), *15–26*	43	60
___	**803**	Hopper Car, early (O), *23–28*	28	55
___	**803**	Hopper Car, late (O), *29–34*	39	55
___	**804**	Tank Car (O), *23–28*	22	45
	805	Boxcar (O), *27–34*		
___		(A) Pea green, terra-cotta roof	35	55
___		(B) Pea green, maroon roof	44	115
___		(C) Orange, maroon roof	44	95
	806	Stock Car (O), *27–34*		
___		(A) Pea green, terra-cotta roof	42	75
___		(B) Orange, various color roofs	35	50
	807	Caboose (O), *27–40*		
___		(A) Peacock body, dark green roof	20	35
___		(B) Red body, peacock roof	20	38
___		(C) Light red body and roof	23	40
	809	Dump Car (O), *31–41*		
___		(A) Orange bin	40	70
___		(B) Green bin	40	85
	810	Crane Car (O), *30–42*		
___		(A) Terra-cotta cab, maroon roof	170	270
___		(B) Cream cab, vermilion roof	130	205
	811	Flatcar (O), *26–40*		
___		(A) Maroon	40	70
___		(B) Aluminum	47	100
___	**812**	Gondola (O), *26–42*	44	83
___	**812T**	Tool Set: pick, shovel, spade, *30–41*	40	95

		Good	Exc
813	Stock Car (O), *26–42*		
	(A) Orange body, pea green roof	65	145 ____
	(B) Orange body, maroon roof	55	135 ____
	(C) Cream body, maroon roof	100	225 ____
	(D) Tuscan body and roof		1600 ____
814	Boxcar (O), *26–42*		
	(A) Cream, orange roof	46	105 ____
	(B) Cream, maroon roof	115	140 ____
	(C) Yellow, brown roof	110	120 ____
814R	Refrigerator Car (O), *29–42*		
	(A) Ivory, peacock roof	100	198 ____
	(B) White, light blue roof	120	265 ____
	(C) Flat white, brown roof	600	900 ____
815	Tank Car (O), *26–42*		
	(A) Pea green, maroon frame	250	510 ____
	(B) Pea green, black frame	70	155 ____
	(C) Aluminum, black frame	50	115 ____
	(D) Orange-yellow, black frame	150	255 ____
816	Hopper Car (O), *27–42*		
	(A) Olive green	85	155 ____
	(B) Red body	65	115 ____
	(C) Black body	370	680 ____
817	Caboose (O), *26–42*		
	(A) Peacock body, dark green roof	45	70 ____
	(B) Red body, peacock roof	45	80 ____
	(C) Light red body and roof	45	80 ____
820	Boxcar (O), *15–26*		
	(A) Orange, Illinois Central	38	80 ____
	(B) Orange, Union Pacific	48	105 ____
820	Floodlight Car (O), *31–42*		
	(A) Terra-cotta	100	180 ____
	(B) Green	100	175 ____
	(C) Light green	105	180 ____
821	Stock Car (O), *15–16, 25–26*	45	85 ____
822	Caboose (O), *15–26*	35	65 ____
831	Flatcar (O), *27–34*	24	43 ____
840	Industrial Power Station, *28–40**	1200	3050 ____
900	Ammunition Car (O), *17–21*	120	340 ____
900	Box Trail Car (2⅞"), *04–05**	2000	3600 ____
901	Gondola (O), *19–27*	25	49 ____
902	Gondola (O), *27–34*	29	45 ____
910	Grove of Trees, *32–42*	70	155 ____
911	Country Estate, *32–42*	195	410 ____
912	Suburban Home	300	620 ____
913	Landscaped Bungalow, *40–42*	140	285 ____

		Good	Exc
____ 914	Park Landscape, *32–35*	90	205
____ 915	Tunnel, 65" or 60" long, *32–33, 35*	160	435
____ 916	Tunnel, 29" long, *35*	95	180
____ 917	Scenic Hillside, 34" x 15", *32–36*	90	205
____ 918	Scenic Hillside, 30" x 10", *32–36*	90	205
____ 919	Park Grass, cloth bag, *32–42*	8	17
____ 920	Village, *32–33*	600	1600
____ 921	Scenic Park, 3 pieces, *32–33*	980	2600
____ 921C	Park Center, *32–33*	400	1050
____ 922	Terrace, *32–36*	90	175
____ 923	Tunnel, 40" long, *33–42*	90	225
____ 924	Tunnel, 30" long (072), *35–42*	50	135
____ 925	Lubricant, *35–42*	24	116
____ 927	Flag Plot, *37–42*	70	135
____ 1000	Passenger Car (2⅞"), *05**	4500	6750
____ 1000	Trolley Trailer (std), *10–16*	1400	2250
____ 1010	Electric Locomotive 0-4-0, Winner Lines (O), *31–32*	90	160
____ 1010	Interurban Trailer (std), *10–16*	1000	1800
____ 1011	Pullman Car, Winner Lines (O), *31–32*	55	75
____ 1012	Station, *32*	50	70
____ 1015	0-4-0 Locomotive (O), *31–32*	100	205
____ 1017	Winner Station, *33*	25	70
____ 1019	Observation Car (O), *31–32*	50	70
____ 1020	Baggage Car (O), *31–32*	65	110
____ 1021	90-degree Crossover (027), *32–42*	1	4
____ 1022	Tunnel, 18" long (O), *35–42*	15	32
____ 1023	Tunnel, 19" long, *34–42*	20	41
____ 1024	Switches, pair (027), *37–42*	4	15
____ 1025	Bumper (027), *40–42*	14	25
____ 1027	Transformer Station, *34*	50	115
____ 1028	Transformer, 40 watts, *39*	3	11
____ 1029	Transformer, 25 watts, *36*	6	18
____ 1030	Electric Locomotive 0-4-0 (O), *32*	75	135
____ 1030	Transformer, 40 watts, *35–38*	6	23
____ 1035	0-4-0 Locomotive (O), *32*	75	115
____ 1037	Transformer, 40 watts, *40–42*	7	23
____ 1038	Transformer, 30 watts, *40*	2	4
____ 1039	Transformer, 35 watts, *37–40*	7	18
____ 1040	Transformer, 60 watts, *37–39*	12	27
____ 1041	Transformer, 60 watts, *39–42*	13	30
____ 1045	Watchman, *38–42*	30	65
____ 1050	Passenger Car Trailer (2⅞"), *05**	5000	7200
____ 1100	Summer Trolley Trailer (std), *10–13*		NRS

PREWAR 1901-1942

		Good	Exc	
1100	Mickey Mouse Handcar, *35–37**			
	(A) Red base	405	640	___
	(B) Apple green base, orange shoes	500	880	___
	(C) Orange base	600	1225	___
1103	Peter Rabbit Handcar (O), *35–37**	330	820	___
1105	Santa Claus Handcar (O), *35–35**			
	(A) Red base	660	1050	___
	(B) Green base	720	1200	___
1107	Transformer Station, *33*	25	70	___
1107	Donald Duck Handcar (O), *36–37**			
	(A) White dog house, red roof	475	1200	___
	(B) White dog house, green roof	450	1100	___
	(C) Orange dog house, green roof	640	1850	___
1121	Switches, pair (O27), *37–42*	15	34	___
1506L	0-4-0 Locomotive (O), *33–34*	95	125	___
1506M	0-4-0 Locomotive (O), *35*	250	430	___
1508	0-4-0 Commodore Vanderbilt with 1509 Mickey Mouse stoker Tender, *35*	420	690	___
1511	0-4-0 Locomotive (O), *36–37*	110	160	___
1512	Gondola (O), *31–33, 36–37*	29	47	___
1514	Boxcar (O), *31–37*	23	41	___
1515	Tank Car (O), *33–37*	25	41	___
1517	Caboose (O), *31–37*	25	41	___
1518	Mickey Mouse Circus Dining Car (O), *35*	120	260	___
1519	Mickey Mouse Band Car (O), *35*	120	260	___
1520	Mickey Mouse Circus Car (O), *35*	120	260	___
1536	Mickey Mouse Circus Set: 1508, 1509, 1518, 1519, 1520, *35*	770	1350	___
1550	Switches, for windup trains, pair, *33–37*	2	5	___
1555	90-degree Crossover, for windup trains, *33–37*	1	2	___
1560	Station, *33–37*	15	34	___
1569	Accessory Set, 8 pieces, *33–37*	35	70	___
1588	0-4-0 Locomotive (O), *36–37*	150	250	___
1630	Pullman Car (O), *38–42*			
	(A) Aluminum windows	35	70	___
	(B) Light gray windows	47	80	___
1631	Observation Car (O), *38–42*			
	(A) Aluminum windows	35	70	___
	(B) Light gray windows	47	80	___
1651E	Electric Locomotive 0-4-0 (O), *33*	130	240	___
1661E	2-4-0 Locomotive (O), *33*	75	160	___
1662	0-4-0 Locomotive (O27), *40–42*	275	420	___
1663	0-4-0 Locomotive (O27), *40–42*	200	385	___

			Good	Exc
1664/E	2-4-2 Locomotive (027), *38–42*			
____	(A) Gunmetal		60	100
____	(B) Black		60	95
1666/E	2-6-2 Locomotive (027), *38–42*			
____	(A) Gunmetal		115	170
____	(B) Black		95	145
1668/E	2-6-2 Locomotive (027), *37–41*			
____	(A) Gunmetal		75	115
____	(B) Black		75	130
1673	Coach (0), *36–37*			
____	(A) Aluminum windows		35	75
____	(B) Light gray windows		47	90
____ **1674**	Pullman Car (0), *36–37*		35	75
____ **1675**	Observation Car (0), *36–37*		30	70
1677	Gondola (0), *33–35, 39–42*			
____	(A) Light blue, Ives		40	60
____	(B) Blue or red, Lionel		21	37
1679	Boxcar (0), *33–42*			
____	(A) Cream, Ives		23	38
____	(B) Cream, Lionel		23	38
____	(C) Cream or yellow, Baby Ruth		19	38
1680	Tank Car (0), *33–42*			
____	(A) Aluminum, Ives Tank Lines		80	95
____	(B) Aluminum, no Ives lettering		19	34
____	(C) Orange, Shell Oil		15	29
1681	2-4-0 Locomotive (0), *34–35*			
____	(A) Black, red frame		55	120
____	(B) Red, red frame		110	145
1681E	2-4-0 Locomotive (0), *34–35*			
____	(A) Black, red frame		65	130
____	(B) Red, red frame		130	165
1682	Caboose (0), *33–42*			
____	(A) Vermilion, Ives		34	70
____	(B) Red or tuscan, Lionel		17	40
1684	2-4-2 Locomotive (027), *41–42*			
____	(A) Black		45	70
____	(B) Gunmetal		45	70
1685	Coach (0), *33–37 u*			
____	(A) Gray, maroon roof		240	495
____	(B) Red, maroon roof		170	335
____	(C) Blue, silver roof		170	315
1686	Baggage Car (0), *33–37 u*			
____	(A) Gray, maroon roof		240	495
____	(B) Red, maroon roof		170	335
____	(C) Blue, silver roof		170	315

		Good	Exc	
1687	Observation Car (O), *33–37 u*			
	(A) Gray, maroon roof	170	315	___
	(B) Red, maroon roof	180	315	___
	(C) Blue, silver roof	170	315	___
1688/E	2-4-2 Locomotive (027), *36–46*	50	95	___
1689E	2-4-2 Locomotive (027), *36–37*			
	(A) Gunmetal	75	115	___
	(B) Black	60	100	___
1690	Pullman Car (O), *33–40*	35	60	___
1691	Observation Car (O), *33–40*	35	60	___
1692	Pullman Car (027), *39 u*	45	70	___
1693	Observation Car (027), *39 u*	45	70	___
1700E	Diesel, power unit only (027), *35–37*	45	70	___
1700E	Set: 1700, 1701 (2), 17*02, 35–37 u*			
	(A) Aluminum and light red	140	250	___
	(B) Chrome and light red	140	250	___
	(C) Orange and gray	155	285	___
1701	Coach (027), *35–37*			
	(A) Chrome sides and roof	20	46	___
	(B) Silver sides and roof	30	55	___
	(C) Orange and gray	75	150	___
1702	Observation Car (027), *35–37*			
	(A) Chrome sides and roof	20	46	___
	(B) Silver sides and roof	30	55	___
	(C) Orange and gray	75	150	___
1703	Observation Car, hooked coupler, *35–37 u*	49	110	___
1717	Gondola (O), *33–40 u*	30	48	___
1717X	Gondola (O), *40 u*	27	48	___
1719	Boxcar (O), *33–40 u*	30	50	___
1719X	Boxcar (O), *41–42 u*	30	50	___
1722	Caboose (O), *33–42 u*	25	50	___
1722X	Caboose (O), *39–40 u*	26	41	___
1766	Pullman Car (std), *34–40**			
	(A) Terra-cotta, maroon roof, brass trim	300	650	___
	(B) Red, maroon roof, nickel trim	300	540	___
1767	Baggage Car (std), *34–40**			
	(A) Terra-cotta, maroon roof, brass trim	295	850	___
	(B) Red, maroon roof, nickel trim	295	700	___
1768	Observation Car (std), *34–40**			
	(A) Terra-cotta, maroon roof, brass trim	300	650	___
	(B) Red, maroon roof, nickel trim	300	540	___
1811	Pullman Car (O), *33–37*	32	70	___
1812	Observation Car (O), *33–37*	30	65	___
1813	Baggage Car (O), *33–37*	60	135	___
1816/W	Diesel (O), *35–37*	100	240	___

			Good	Exc
___	**1817**	Coach (O), *35–37*	22	50
___	**1818**	Observation Car (O), *35–37*	22	50
___	**1835E**	2-4-2 Locomotive (std), *34–39*	470	730
___	**1910**	Electric Locomotive 0-6-0, early (std), *10–11*	920	1550
___	**1910**	Electric Locomotive 0-6-0, late (std), *12*	550	1350
___	**1910**	Pullman Car (std), *09–10 u*	860	1800
___	**1911**	Electric Locomotive 0-4-0, early (std), *10–12*	860	1700
___	**1911**	Electric Locomotive 0-4-0, late (std), *13*	700	1100
___	**1911**	Electric Locomotive 0-4-4-0 Special (std), *11–12*	860	2500
	1912	Electric Locomotive 0-4-4-0 (std), *10–12**		
___		(A) New York, New Haven & Hartford	1550	3200
___		(B) New York Central Lines	1300	2700
___	**1912**	Electric Locomotive 0-4-4-0 Special (std), *11**	2500	4500
___	**2200**	Summer Trolley Trailer (std), *10–13*	1100	2250
___	**2600**	Pullman Car (O), *38–42*	80	155
___	**2601**	Observation Car (O), *38–42*	60	115
___	**2602**	Baggage Car (O), *38–42*	90	185
	2613	Pullman Car (O), *38–42**		
___		(A) Blue, 2-tone blue roof	100	270
___		(B) State green, 2-tone green roof	200	440
	2614	Observation Car (O), *38–42**		
___		(A) Blue, 2-tone blue roof	100	270
___		(B) State green, 2-tone green roof	200	440
	2615	Baggage Car (O), *38–42**		
___		(A) Blue, 2-tone blue roof	115	270
___		(B) State green, 2-tone green roof	200	420
___	**2620**	Floodlight Car (O), *38–42*	65	100
	2623	Pullman Car (O), *41–42*		
___		(A) Irvington	175	335
___		(B) Manhattan	165	310
___	**2624**	Pullman Car (O), *41–42*	750	1700
___	**2630**	Pullman Car (O), *38–42*	30	70
___	**2631**	Observation Car (O), *38–42*	30	70
	2640	Pullman Car, illuminated (O), *38–42*		
___		(A) Light blue, aluminum roof	30	70
___		(B) State green, dark green roof	28	70
	2641	Observation Car, illuminated (O), *38–42*		
___		(A) Light blue, aluminum roof	30	70
___		(B) State green, dark green roof	28	70
___	**2642**	Pullman Car (O), *41–42*	32	70
___	**2643**	Observation Car (O), *41–42*	30	65
___	**2651**	Flatcar (O), *38–42*	30	50
___	**2652**	Gondola (O), *38–41*	26	55

		Good	Exc
2653	Hopper Car (O), *38–42*		
	(A) Stephen Girard green	38	70 ____
	(B) Black	60	132 ____
2654	Tank Car (O), *38–42*		
	(A) Aluminum, Sunoco	35	60 ____
	(B) Orange, Shell	35	60 ____
	(C) Light gray, Sunoco	41	70 ____
2655	Boxcar (O), *38–42*		
	(A) Cream, maroon roof	35	65 ____
	(B) Cream, tuscan roof	38	75 ____
2656	Stock Car (O), *38–41*		
	(A) Light gray, red roof	45	75 ____
	(B) Burnt orange, tuscan roof	75	115 ____
2657	Caboose (O), *40–41*	31	45 ____
2657X	Caboose (O), *40–41*	25	41 ____
2659	Dump Car (O), *38–41*	40	70 ____
2660	Crane Car (O), *38–42*	85	115 ____
2672	Caboose (027), *41–42*	22	35 ____
2677	Gondola (027), *39–41*	26	37 ____
2679	Boxcar (027), *38–42*	26	29 ____
2680	Tank Car (027), *38–42*		
	(A) Aluminum, Sunoco	15	41 ____
	(B) Orange, Shell	15	41 ____
2682	Caboose (027), *38–42*	18	32 ____
2682X	Caboose (027), *38–42*	22	35 ____
2717	Gondola (O), *38–42 u*	21	41 ____
2719	Boxcar (O), *38–42 u*	29	50 ____
2722	Caboose (O), *38–42 u*	25	50 ____
2755	Tank Car (O), *41–42*	73	128 ____
2757	Caboose (O), *41–42*	26	44 ____
2757X	Caboose (O), *41–42*	25	36 ____
2758	Automobile Boxcar (O), *41–42*	38	60 ____
2810	Crane Car (O), *38–42*	145	205 ____
2811	Flatcar (O), *38–42*	65	95 ____
2812	Gondola (O), *38–42*		
	(A) Green	42	83 ____
	(B) Dark orange	44	95 ____
2813	Stock Car (O), *38–42*	120	223 ____
2814	Boxcar (O), *38–42*		
	(A) Cream, maroon roof	85	198 ____
	(B) Orange, brown roof, rubber-stamped lettering	200	700 ____
2814R	Refrigerator Car (O), *38–42*		
	(A) White, light blue roof, nickel plates	150	258 ____
	(B) White, brown roof, no plates	375	660 ____

			Good	Exc
2815		Tank Car (O), *38–42*		
____		(A) Aluminum	85	165
____		(B) Orange	135	250
2816		Hopper Car (O), *35–42*		
____		(A) Red	100	190
____		(B) Black	110	220
2817		Caboose (O), *36–42*		
____		(A) Light red body and roof	90	145
____		(B) Flat red body, tuscan roof	140	225
2820		Floodlight Car (O), *38–42*		
____		(A) Stamped nickel searchlights	110	205
____		(B) Gray die-cast searchlights	120	260
____	**2954**	Boxcar (O), *40–42**	145	349
	2955	Sunoco Tank Car (O), *40–42**		
____		(A) Shell decal	225	498
____		(B) Sunoco decal	340	690
____	**2956**	Hopper Car (O), *40–42**	160	400
____	**2957**	Caboose (O), *40–42**	70	313
____	**3300**	Summer Trolley Trailer (std), *10–13*	1400	2250
____	**3651**	Operating Lumber Car (O), *39–42*	24	55
____	**3652**	Operating Gondola (O), *39–42*	36	85
____	**3659**	Operating Dump Car (O), *39–42*	26	32
____	**3811**	Operating Lumber Car (O), *39–42*	33	77
____	**3814**	Operating Merchandise Car (O), *39–42*	125	245
____	**3859**	Operating Dump Car (O), *38–42*	44	100

Other Transformers and Motors

			Good	Exc
____	A	Miniature Motor, *04*	50	95
____	A	Transformer, 40, 60 watts, *21–37*	8	25
____	B	New Departure Motor, *06–16*	75	135
____	B	Transformer, 50, 75 watts, *16–38*	6	24
____	C	New Departure Motor, *06–16*	100	180
____	D	New Departure Motor, *06–14*	100	180
____	E	New Departure Motor, *06–14*	100	180
____	F	New Departure Motor, *06–14*	100	180
____	G	Fan Motor, battery-operated, *06–14*	100	180
____	K	Transformer, 150, 200 watts, *13–38*	19	95
____	L	Transformer, 50, 75 watts, *13–16, 33–38*	8	24
____	M	Peerless Motor, battery-operated, *15–20*	30	80
____	N	Transformer, 50 watts, *41–42*	7	23
____	Q	Transformer, 50 watts, *14–15*	13	32
____	Q	Transformer, 75 watts, *38–42*	15	40
____	R	Peerless Motor, battery-operated, reversing, *15–20*	30	75
____	R	Transformer, 100 watts, *38–42*	27	60

		Good	Exc	
S	Transformer, 50 watts, *14–17*	18	37	____
T	Transformer, 75, 100, 150 watts, *14–28*	10	28	____
U	Transformer, Aladdin, *32–33*	6	16	____
V	Transformer, 150 watts, *39–42*	55	95	____
W	Transformer, 75 watts, *32–33*	7	37	____
Y	Peerless Motor, battery-operated, 3-speed, *15–20*	40	80	____
Z	Transformer, 250 watts, *39–42*	118	170	____

Track, Lockons, and Contactors

	Good	Exc	
O Straight		1	____
O Curve		1	____
072 Straight	1	2	____
072 Curve	1	2	____
027 Straight		1	____
027 Curve		1	____
Standard Straight	1	3	____
Standard Curve	1	2	____
Standard Insulated Straight, *33–42*	2	4	____
Standard Insulated Curve, *33–42*	1	2	____
O Gauge Lockon		1	____
Standard Gauge Lockon		1	____
UTC Lockon		1	____
145C Contactor	3	10	____
153C Contactor	3	7	____
Track Clips, dozen (O), *37*	4	12	____

		Good	Exc
011-11	Fiber Pins, dozen (O), *46–50*		3
011-43	Insulating Pins, dozen (O), *61*	1	2
020	90-degree Crossover (O), *45–61*	4	8
020X	45-degree Crossover (O), *46–59*	6	11
022	Remote Control Switches, pair (O), *45–69*	24	47
022-500	Adapter Set (O), *57–61*	1	6
022A	Remote Control Switches, pair (O), *47*	29	120
25	Bumper (O), *46–47*	6	20
26	Bumper, *48–50*		
	(A) Red, *49–50*	7	12
	(B) Gray, *48*	18	53
027C-1	Track Clips, box of 12 (O27), *47, 49*	4	14
027C-1	Track Clips, box of 50 (O27)	35	105
30	Water Tower, *47–50*	38	96
31	Curved Track (Super O), *57–66*	1	2
31-7	Power Blade Connection, dozen (Super O), *57–60*		7
31-15	Ground Rail Pin, dozen (Super O), *57–66*		5
31-45	Power Blade Connection, dozen (Super O), *61–66*		6
32	Straight Track (Super O), *57–66*	1	4
32-10	Insulating Pin, dozen (Super O), *57–60*		5
32-20	Power Blade Insulator, dozen (Super O), *57–60*		3
32-25	Insulating Pin (Super O), *57–61*		1
32-30	Ground Pin (Super O), *57–61*		1
32-31	Power Pin (Super O), *57–61*		1
32-32	Insulating Pin (Super O), *57–61*		1
32-33	Ground Pin (Super O), *57–61*		1
32-34	Power Pin (Super O), *57–61*		1
32-35	Insulating Pin, dozen (Super O to O27), *57–61*		3
32-45	Power Blade Insulators, dozen (Super O), *61–66*	3	8
32-55	Insulating Pins, dozen (Super O), *61–66*	3	8
33	Half Curved Track (Super O), *57–66*	1	3
34	Half Straight Track (Super O), *57–66*	1	3
35	Boulevard Lamp, *45–49*	12	38
36	Operating Car Remote Control Set (Super O), *57–66*	11	22
37	Uncoupling Track Set (Super O), *57–66*	8	16
38	Accessory Adapter Tracks, pair (Super O), *57–61*	6	13
38	Operating Water Tower, *46–47*	118	308
39	Operating Set (Super O), *57*	4	8

		Good	Exc	
39-5	Operating Set (Super O), *57–58*	4	8	___
39-6	Operating Set (Super O), *57–58*	4	25	___
39-10	Operating Set (Super O), *58*	4	8	___
39-15	Operating Set with blade (Super O), *57–58*	4	8	___
39-20	Operating Set (Super O), *57–58*	4	8	___
39-25	Operating Set (Super O), *61–66*	4	29	___
39-35	Operating Set (Super O), *59*	4	30	___
40	Hookup Wire, *50–51, 53–63*			
	(A) Single reel, orange or gray, with tape	6	42	___
	(B) 8 sealed reels in dealer box	125	500	___
40-25	Conductor Wire with envelope, *56–59*	11	54	___
40-50	Cable Reel with envelope, *60–61*	10	53	___
41	Contactor (Super O)	1	2	___
41	U.S. Army Switcher, *55–57*			
	(A) Unpainted black body	58	102	___
	(B) Black-painted body	250	650	___
042/42	Manual Switches, pair (O), *46–59*	15	31	___
42	Picatinny Arsenal Switcher, *57*	104	295	___
43	Power Track (Super O), *59–66*	4	13	___
44	U.S. Army Mobile Launcher, *59–62*	71	192	___
44-80	Missiles, *59–60*	11	26	___
45	U.S. Marines Mobile Launcher, *60–62*	109	265	___
45	Automatic Gateman, *46–49*	17	45	___
45N	Automatic Gateman, *45*	22	50	___
48	Insulated Straight Track (Super O), *57–66*	4	10	___
49	Insulated Curved Track (Super O), *57–66*	4	10	___
50	Section Gang Car, *54–64*			
	(A) Gray bumpers, rotating blue man and fixed olive men, center horn, *54*	250	692	___
	(B) Blue bumpers, rotating olive man and fixed blue men, center horn	29	69	___
	(C) Blue bumpers, rotating olive man and fixed blue men, off-center horn	28	53	___
51	Navy Yard Switcher, *56–57*	70	171	___
52	Fire Car, *58–61*	80	191	___
53	Rio Grande Snowplow, *57–60*			
	(A) Backwards "a" in Rio Grande	66	216	___
	(B) Correctly printed "a"	169	571	___
54	Ballast Tamper, *58–61, 66, 68–69*	78	165	___
55	PRR Tie-Jector Car, *57–61*	43	114	___
	(A) Ventilation slot behind motorman	50	200	___
	(B) No slot behind motorman	35	105	___
55-150	Ties, 24 pieces, *57–60*	9	35	___
56	Lamp Post, *46–49*	23	49	___
56	M&StL Mine Transport, *58*	167	353	___
57	AEC Switcher, *59–60*	192	553	___
58	GN Snowplow, *59–61*	164	422	___

		Good	Exc
____ 58	Lamp Post, *46–50*	20	48
____ 59	Minuteman Switcher, *62–63*	196	487
60	Lionelville Rapid Transit Trolley, *55–58*		
____	(A) Metal motorman silhouettes	90	290
____	(B) No motorman silhouettes	38	105
____ 61	Ground Lockon (Super O), *57–66*	1	6
61-25	Super O Ground clips, dozen, with dealer envelope		
____		5	20
____ 62	Power Lockon (Super O), *57–66*	1	4
____ 64	Street Lamp, *45–49*	21	42
65	Handcar, *62–66*		
____	(A) Light yellow	113	272
____	(B) Dark yellow	100	258
____ 68	Executive Inspection Car, *58–61*	89	189
____ 69	Maintenance Car, *60–62*	85	228
____ 70	Yard Light, *49–50*	15	36
____ 71	Lamp Post, *49–59*	8	16
____ 75	Goose Neck Lamps, set of 2, *61–63*	12	21
76	Boulevard Street Lamps, set of 3, *59–66, 68–69*		
____		16	35
____ 88	Controller, *46–60*	5	16
____ 89	Flagpole, *56–58*	10	49
90	Controller, *55–66*		
____	(A) Metal clip	7	15
____	(B) No metal clip	6	10
____ 91	Circuit Breaker, *57–60*	11	27
____ 92	Circuit Breaker, *59–66, 68–69*	6	13
____ 93	Water Tower, *46–49*	20	51
____ 96C	Controller, *45–54*	3	10
____ 97	Coal Elevator, *46–50*	67	166
____ 108	Trestle Set, 12 black piers	14	31
____ 109	Partial Trestle Set, *61*	5	17
____ 110	Graduated Trestle Set, 22 or 24 piers, *55–69*	10	21
____ 110-75	Graduated Trestle Set with 110-78 envelope	10	48
____ 111	Elevated Trestle Set, 10 A piers, *56–69*	7	13
____ 111-100	Elevated Trestle Piers, set of 2, *60–63*	13	43
112	Remote Control Switches, pair (Super O), *57–66*		
____		58	91
____ 114	Newsstand with horn, *57–59*	39	86
____ 115	Passenger Station, *46–49*	139	317
____ 118	Newsstand with whistle, *57–58*	41	95
____ 119	Landscaped Tunnel, *57–58*		NRS
____ 120	90-degree Crossing (Super O), *57–66*	7	15
____ 121	Landscaped Tunnel, *59–66*		NRS
____ 122	Lamp Assortment, *48–52*	28	192
____ 123	Lamp Assortment, *55–59*	68	185
____ 123-60	Lamp Assortment, *60–63*	23	163

		Good	Exc	
125	Whistle Shack, *50–55*			
	(A) Gray base	12	38	___
	(B) Green base	18	50	___
128	Animated Newsstand, *57–60*	70	120	___
130	60-degree Crossing (Super O), *57–66*	7	11	___
131	Curved Tunnel, *59–66*		NRS	___
132	Passenger Station, *49–55*	48	79	___
133	Passenger Station, *57, 61–62, 66*	32	65	___
138	Water Tower, *53–57*	34	74	___
140	Automatic Banjo Signal, *54–66*	13	31	___
142	Manual Switches, pair (Super O), *57–66*	32	49	___
145	Automatic Gateman, *50–66*			
	(A) Red roof	12	35	___
	(B) Maroon roof	14	40	___
145C	Contactor, *50–60*	3	12	___
147	Whistle Controller, *61–66*	2	7	___
148	Dwarf Trackside Signal, *57–60*	23	61	___
148-100	Controller (SPDT switch), *57–60*	7	18	___
150	Telegraph Pole Set, *47–50*	29	55	___
151	Automatic Semaphore, *47–69*			
	(A) Green base, yellow blade, *47*	19	76	___
	(B) Black base, yellow blade, *47*	17	27	___
	(C) Black base, red blade, *47*	140	411	___
	(D) Green base, yellow blade with raised lenses	31	134	___
152	Automatic Crossing Gate, *45–49*	12	23	___
153	Automatic Block Control Signal, *45–59*	17	23	___
153C	Contactor	3	11	___
154	Automatic Highway Signal, *45–69*	16	25	___
154C	Contactor	5	15	___
155	Blinking Light Signal with bell, *55–57*	24	46	___
156	Station Platform, *46–49*	40	90	___
156-5	Station Platform Fence with envelope	33	75	___
157	Station Platform, *52–59*			
	(A) Maroon base	18	35	___
	(B) Red base	22	80	___
157-23	Station Platform Fence with envelope	12	64	___
160	Unloading Bin, *52–57*			
	(A) Black plastic	2	6	___
	(B) Black metal	25	62	___
	(C) Multicolor Bakelite	7	23	___
161	Mail Pickup Set, *61–63*	20	63	___
163	Single Target Block Signal, *61–69*	16	30	___
164	Log Loader, *46–50*	80	182	___
164	Log Set, 5 pieces, *52–58*		85	___
167	Whistle Controller, *45–46*	3	10	___
175	Rocket Launcher, *58–60*	60	183	___

			Good	Exc
____	**175-50**	Extra Rocket, *59–60*	10	26
____	**182**	Magnetic Crane, *46–49*	129	245
____	**182-22**	Steel Scrap with bag, *46–49*	37	107
____	**192**	Operating Control Tower, *59–60*	120	248
	193	Industrial Water Tower, *53–55*		
____		(A) Red	58	85
____		(B) Black, *53*	95	183
	195	Floodlight Tower, *57–69*		
____		(A) Medium tan base, rubber-stamped lettering	27	68
____		(B) All other variations	27	59
____	**195-75**	Floodlight Extension, 8-bulb (with box), *58–60*	17	72
____	**196**	Smoke Pellets, *46–47*	27	115
	197	Rotating Radar Antenna, *57–59*		
____		(A) Orange platform	55	135
____		(B) Gray platform	40	83
____	**197-75**	Separate Sale Radar Head	50	219
____	**199**	Microwave Relay Tower, *58–59*	33	75
____	**202**	UP Alco Diesel A Unit, *57*	36	80
____	**204**	Santa Fe Alco Diesel AA Units, *57*	79	240
	205	Missouri Pacific Alco Diesel AA Units, *57–58*		
____		(A) Pilot without support	44	137
____		(B) Pilot with painted metal support	70	185
____	**206**	Artificial Coal, large bag, *46–68*	10	20
____	**207**	Artificial Coal, small bag, *46–48*	6	12
____	**208**	Santa Fe Alco Diesel AA Units, *58–59*	72	221
____	**209**	New Haven Alco Diesel AA Units, *58*	234	711
____	**209**	Wooden Barrels, set of 6, *46–50*	10	19
____	**210**	Texas Special Alco Diesel AA Units, *58*	50	149
____	**211**	Texas Special Alco Diesel AA Units, *62–66*	60	150
____	**212**	Santa Fe Alco Diesel AA Units, *64–66*	80	175
____	**212**	USMC Alco Diesel A Unit, *58–59*	80	175
____	**212T**	USMC Diesel Dummy A Unit, *58 u*	372	920
____	**213**	M&StL Alco Diesel AA Units, *64*	75	255
____	**214**	Plate Girder Bridge, *53–69*	6	22
	215	Santa Fe Alco Diesel Units, *65 u*		
____		(A) AB Units	61	132
____		(B) AA Units	75	150
____	**216**	Burlington Alco Diesel A Unit, *58*	105	362
____	**216**	M&StL Alco Diesel AA Units, *64 u*	70	193
____	**217**	B&M Alco Diesel AB Units, *59*	89	225

		Good	Exc	
218	Santa Fe Alco Diesel Units, *59–63*			
	(A) AA Units	70	165	___
	(B) AB Units	63	153	___
	(C) AA Units, solid nose decal	78	275	___
219	Missouri Pacific Alco Diesel AA Units, *59 u*	73	177	___
220	Santa Fe Alco Diesel Units, *60–61*			
	(A) A Unit	41	118	___
	(B) AA Units	70	205	___
221	2-6-4 Locomotive, 221W Tender, *46–47*			
	(A) Gray body, black drivers	56	152	___
	(B) Black body, nickel-rimmed black drivers, *47*	71	174	___
	(C) Gray body, cast-aluminum drivers, *46*	112	254	___
221	Rio Grande Alco Diesel A Unit, *63–64*	32	68	___
221	Santa Fe Alco Diesel A Unit, *63–64 u*	180	675	___
221	U.S. Marine Corps Alco Diesel A Unit, *63–64 u*	154	550	___
221T	Tender, gray		35	___
221W	Whistle Tender		45	___
222	Rio Grande Alco Diesel A Unit, *62*	25	60	___
223	Santa Fe Alco Diesel AB Units, *63*	86	240	___
224	2-6-2 Locomotive, 2466W or 2466WX Tender, *45–46*			
	(A) Blackened handrails, *45*	125	245	___
	(B) Silver handrails	85	165	___
224	U.S. Navy Alco Diesel AB Units, *60*	121	262	___
225	C&O Alco Diesel A Unit, *60*	55	99	___
226	B&M Alco Diesel AB Units, *60 u*	73	181	___
227	CN Alco Diesel A Unit, *60 u*	85	155	___
228	CN Alco Diesel A Unit, *61 u*	80	145	___
229	M&StL Alco Diesel Units, *61–62*			
	(A) A Unit, *61*	65	118	___
	(B) AB Units, *62*	95	213	___
230	C&O Alco Diesel A Unit, *61*	65	128	___
231	Rock Island Alco Diesel A Unit, *61–63*			
	(A) With red stripe	65	139	___
	(B) Without red stripe	120	315	___
232	New Haven Alco Diesel A Unit, *62*	67	149	___
233	2-4-2 Scout Locomotive, 233W Tender, *61–62*	39	75	___
233W	Whistle Tender		48	___
234W	Whistle Tender	28	54	___
235	2-4-2 Scout Locomotive, 1130T or 1060T Tender, *60 u*	77	218	___
236	2-4-2 Scout Locomotive, *61–62*			
	(A) 1050T slope-back Tender	20	46	___
	(B) 1130T Tender	20	46	___

		Good	Exc
237	2-4-2 Scout Locomotive, *63–66*		
___	(A) 1060T Tender	25	55
___	(B) 234W Tender	40	85
238	2-4-2 Scout Locomotive, stripe on running board, 234W Tender, *63–64*	75	199
239	2-4-2 Scout Locomotive, 234W Tender, *65–66*	55	90
___ **240**	2-4-2 Scout Locomotive, 242T Tender, *64 u*	115	281
241	2-4-2 Scout Locomotive, *65 u*		
___	(A) Narrow stripe, 234W Tender	35	131
___	(B) Wide stripe, 1130T Tender	28	95
242	2-4-2 Scout Locomotive, 1060T or 1062T Tender, *62–66*	21	42
___ **243**	2-4-2 Scout Locomotive, 243W Tender, *60*	41	110
___ **243W**	Whistle Tender	19	39
244	2-4-2 Scout Locomotive, 244T or 1130T Tender, *60–61*	25	42
___ **244T**	Tender		19
___ **245**	2-4-2 Scout Locomotive, 1130T Tender, *59 u*	30	76
246	2-4-2 Scout Locomotive, 244T or 1130T Tender, *59–61*	18	24
___ **247**	2-4-2 Scout Locomotive, 247T Tender, *59*	26	56
___ **248**	2-4-2 Scout Locomotive, 1130T Tender, *58*	32	96
___ **249**	2-4-2 Scout Locomotive, 250T Tender, *58*	24	58
___ **250**	2-4-2 Scout Locomotive, 250T Tender, *57*	24	58
___ **250T**	Tender		29
251	2-4-2 Scout Locomotive, *66 u*		
___	(A) 1062T slope-back Tender	118	278
___	(B) 250T-type Tender	117	277
___ **252**	Crossing Gate, *50–62*	13	25
___ **253**	Block Control Signal, *56–59*	14	28
256	Illuminated Freight Station, *50–53*		
___	(A) Standard	23	43
___	(B) Light green roof	69	164
257	Freight Station with diesel horn, *56–57*		
___	(A) Maroon base	30	100
___	(B) Brown base	38	120
___	(C) Maroon or brown base, light green roof	70	208
260	Bumper, *51–69*		
___	(A) Die-cast	6	13
___	(B) Black plastic	17	34
___ **262**	Highway Crossing Gate, *62–69*	21	52
___ **264**	Operating Forklift Platform, *57–60*	134	249
___ **270**	Metal Bridge (O), *46*	13	47
___ **282**	Gantry Crane, *54–57*	101	169
___ **282R**	Gantry Crane, *56–57*	87	165
___ **299**	Code Transmitter Beacon Set, *61–63*	56	107
___ **308**	Railroad Sign Set, die-cast, *45–49*	25	41

		Good	Exc	
309	Yard Sign Set, plastic, *50–59*	12	27	___
310	Billboard Set, *50–68*	14	21	___
313	Bascule Bridge, *46–49*	126	397	___
313-82	Fiber Pins, dozen, *46–60*	1	2	___
313-121	Fiber Pins, dozen, *61*	1	2	___
314	Scale Model Girder Bridge, *45–50*	12	35	___
315	Trestle Bridge, *46–48*	40	105	___
316	Trestle Bridge, *49*	15	37	___
317	Trestle Bridge, *50–56*	18	32	___
321	Trestle Bridge, *58–64*	13	36	___
321-100	Trestle Bridge	18	63	___
332	Arch-Under Trestle Bridge, *59–66*	20	40	___
334	Operating Dispatching Board, *57–60*	78	226	___
342	Culvert Loader, *56–58*	125	333	___
345	Culvert Unloader, *57–59*	148	350	___
346	Culvert Unloader, manual, *65 u*	60	155	___
347	Cannon Firing Range Set, *64 u*	183	590	___
348	Culvert Unloader, manual, *66–69*	80	173	___
350	Engine Transfer Table, *57–60*	138	300	___
350-50	Transfer Table Extension, *57–60*	93	199	___
352	Ice Depot with 6352 Ice Car, *55–57*	84	150	___
353	Trackside Control Signal, *60–61*	14	33	___
356	Operating Freight Station, *52–57*			
	(A) Dark green roof, *52–57*	43	95	___
	(B) Light green roof, *57*	67	214	___
362	Barrel Loader, *52–57*			
	(A) Gold lettering	32	82	___
	(B) Red lettering	122	408	___
362-78	Wooden Barrels, 6 pieces, *52–57*			
	(A) Brown	7	21	___
	(B) Red	98	267	___
364	Conveyor Lumber Loader, *48–57*	37	90	___
364C	On/Off Switch, *48–64*	4	14	___
385	Dispatching Station, *58–59*	75	158	___
375	Turntable, *62–64*	91	202	___
390C	Switch, double-pole, double-throw, *60–64*	6	16	___
394	Rotary Beacon, *49–53*			
	(A) Steel tower, red platform	18	45	___
	(B) Steel tower, green platform	33	95	___
	(C) Aluminum tower, platform, and base	17	40	___
	(D) Aluminum tower, red steel base	28	73	___
	(E) Steel tower, red platform, stick-on nameplate	20	80	___

		Good	Exc
395	Floodlight Tower, *49–56*		
____	(A) Light green, silver, or unpainted aluminum	24	53
____	(B) Red	28	140
____	(C) Dark green	111	392
____	(C) Yellow	51	150
397	Operating Coal Loader, *48–57*		
____	(A) Yellow generator, *48*	167	390
____	(B) Blue generator, *49–57*	47	98
____ **400**	B&O Passenger Rail Diesel Car, *56–58*	97	198
____ **404**	B&O Baggage-Mail Rail Diesel Car, *57–58*	165	348
____ **410**	Billboard Blinker, *56–58*	28	51
____ **413**	Countdown Control Panel, *62*	30	66
____ **415**	Diesel Fueling Station, *55–57*	60	139
____ **419**	Heliport Control Tower, *62*	165	388
443	Missile Launching Platform with ammo		
____	dump, *60–62*	21	53
____ **445**	Switch Tower, lighted, *52–57*	25	56
____ **448**	Missile Firing Range Set, *61–63*	55	138
____ **450**	Operating Signal Bridge, *52–58*	26	49
____ **450L**	Signal Light Head, *52–58*	16	32
____ **452**	Overhead Gantry Signal, *61–63*	65	125
455	Operating Oil Derrick, *50–54*		
____	(A) Dark green tower, green top	53	146
____	(B) Dark green tower, red top	60	175
____	(C) Apple green tower, red top	95	375
____ **456**	Coal Ramp with 3456 Hopper, *50–55*	80	211
460	Piggyback Transportation Set, *55–57*		
____	(A) Metal stick-on signs on lift truck	65	135
____	(B) Rubber-stamped lettering on lift truck	75	170
____ **460P**	Piggyback Platform, *55–57*	22	65
____ **461**	Platform with truck and trailer, *66*	78	175
____ **462**	Derrick Platform Set, *61–62*	126	309
____ **464**	Lumber Mill, *56–60*	65	155
____ **465**	Sound Dispatching Station, *56–57*	64	110
470	Missile Launching Platform with target car, *59–62*		
____		65	113
479-1	Truck for 6362 Truck Car with envelope, *55–56*		
____		24	100
____ **480-25**	Conversion Magnetic Coupler, *50–60*	1	5
____ **480-32**	Conversion Magnetic Coupler, *61–69*	1	5
494	Rotary Beacon, *54–66*		
____	(A) Painted steel	26	45
____	(B) Unpainted aluminum	25	63
____ **497**	Coaling Station, *53–58*	73	169

		Good	Exc	
520	LL Boxcab Electric Locomotive, *56–57*			
	(A) Black pantograph	30	85	____
	(B) Copper-colored pantograph	40	116	____
600	MKT NW2 Switcher, *55*			
	(A) Black frame, black end rails	75	122	____
	(B) Gray frame, yellow or black end rails	128	255	____
601	Seaboard NW2 Switcher, *56*			
	(A) Red stripes with square ends	82	172	____
	(B) Red stripes with round ends	103	163	____
602	Seaboard NW2 Switcher, *57–58*	105	173	____
610	Erie NW2 Switcher, *55*			
	(A) Black frame	80	135	____
	(B) Yellow frame	168	463	____
	(C) Replacement body with nameplates	105	244	____
611	Jersey Central NW2 Switcher, *57–58*	90	155	____
613	UP NW2 Switcher, *58*	130	241	____
614	Alaska NW2 Switcher, *59–60*			
	(A) Plastic bell, no brake	115	175	____
	(B) No bell, yellow brake	118	234	____
	(C) "Built by Lionel" outlined in yellow near nose	192	338	____
616	Santa Fe NW2 Switcher, *61–62*			
	(A) Open E-unit slot and bell/horn slots	105	190	____
	(B) Plugged E-unit slot and open bell/horn slots	119	227	____
	(C) Plugged E-unit slot and bell/horn slots	110	371	____
617	Santa Fe NW2 Switcher, *63*	123	321	____
621	Jersey Central NW2 Switcher, *56–57*	75	163	____
622	Santa Fe NW2 Switcher, *49–50*			
	(A) Large GM decal on cab	175	302	____
	(B) Small GM decal on side	116	243	____
623	Santa Fe NW2 Switcher, *52–54*	101	167	____
624	C&O NW2 Switcher, *52–54*	93	190	____
625	LV GE 44-ton Switcher, *57–58*	67	117	____
626	B&O GE 44-ton Switcher, *56–57, 59*	122	308	____
627	LV GE 44-ton Switcher, *56–57*	55	101	____
628	NP GE 44-ton Switcher, *56–57*	76	127	____
629	Burlington GE 44-ton Switcher, *56*	120	342	____
633	Santa Fe NW2 Switcher, *62*	92	157	____
634	Santa Fe NW2 Switcher, *63, 65–66*			
	(A) Safety stripes	87	145	____
	(B) No safety stripes	50	110	____
635	UP NW2 Switcher, *65 u*	60	118	____
637	2-6-4 Locomotive, 2046 736W Tender, *59–63*			
	(A) 2046W Lionel Lines Tender	55	158	____
	(B) 736W Pennsylvania Tender	70	178	____
638-2361	Van Camp's Pork & Beans Boxcar, *62 u*	21	38	____

			Good	Exc
___ 645	Union Pacific NW2 Switcher, *69*		60	148
___ 646	4-6-4 Locomotive, 2046W Tender, *54–58*		123	252
665 ___	4-6-4 Locomotive, 2046W, 6026W, or 736W Tender, *54–59, 66*		100	225
671 ___	6-8-6 Steam Turbine Locomotive, smoke bulb, *46*		133	258
671	6-8-6 Steam Turbine Locomotive, *47–49*			
___	(A) 671W Tender		74	207
___	(B) 2671W Tender, backup lights		250	453
___	(C) 2671W Tender, no backup lights		160	279
___ 671-75	Smoke Lamp, 12 volt, *46*		10	20
671R ___	6-8-6 Steam Turbine Locomotive, 4424W or 4671 Tender, *46–49*		137	280
671RR ___	6-8-6 Steam Turbine Locomotive, 2046W-50 Tender, *52*		90	204
___ 671S	Smoke Conversion Kit		20	82
___ 671W	Whistle Tender, *46–48*		28	70
675	2-6-2 Locomotive, 2466WX or 6466WX Tender, *47–49*			
___	(A) Aluminum smokestack, *47*		86	219
___	(B) Black smokestack, *48–49*		90	186
___ 675	2-6-4 Locomotive, 2046W Tender, *52*		80	189
681 ___	6-8-6 Steam Turbine Locomotive, 2046W-50 or 2671W Tender, *50–51, 53*		115	202
682 ___	6-8-6 Steam Turbine Locomotive, 2046W-50 Tender, *54–55*		167	360
___ 685	4-6-4 Hudson Locomotive, 6026W Tender, *53*		103	206
___ 703-10	Smoke Lamp, 18 volt, *46*		7	24
726	2-8-4 Berkshire, *46–49*			
___	(A) 2426W Tender, smoke lamp, *46*		293	581
___	(B) 2426W Tender, *47–49*		240	472
726RR ___	2-8-4 Berkshire Locomotive, 2046W Tender, *52*		140	264
___ 726S	Smoke Conversion Kit		42	167
736 ___	2-8-4 Berkshire Locomotive, 2671WX, 2046W, or 736W Tender, *50–66*		179	307
___ 736W	Whistle Tender			69
746	N&W 4-8-4 Class J Northern, *57–60*			
___	(A) Tender with long stripe		501	874
___	(B) Tender with short stripe		350	868
___ 760	Curved Track, 16 sections (O72), *54–57*		20	41
773	4-6-4 Hudson Locomotive, 2426W Tender, *50*		846	1495
773	4-6-4 Hudson Locomotive, *64–66*			
___	(A) 773W NYC Tender		697	1177
___	(B) 736W PRR Tender		467	873
___ 902	Elevated Trestle Set, *60*		24	125
909 ___	Smoke Fluid, large or small bottle, *57–66, 68–69*		6	27
B909 ___	Smoke Capsules, pack of three, *57–66, 68–69*		5	30

		Good	Exc	
919	Artificial Grass, *46–64*	5	15	____
920	Scenic Display Set, *57–58*	55	95	____
920-2	Tunnel Portals, pair, *58–59*	19	38	____
920-3	Green Grass, *57*	3	13	____
920-4	Yellow Grass, *57*	5	16	____
920-5	Artificial Rock, *57–58*	3	11	____
920-6	Dry Glue, *57–58*	3	10	____
920-8	Dyed Lichen, *57–58*	3	15	____
925	Lubricant, large tube, *46–69*	3	17	____
926	Lubricant, small tube, *55*	1	3	____
926-5	Instruction Booklet, *46–48*	1	5	____
927	Lubricating Kit, *50–59*	13	23	____
928	Maintenance and Lubricating Kit, *60–63*	24	55	____
943	Ammo Dump, *59–61*	19	49	____
950	U.S. Railroad Map, *58–66*	19	57	____
951	Farm Set, 13 pieces, *58*	52	100	____
952	Figure Set, 30 pieces, *58*	33	57	____
953	Figure Set, 32 pieces, *59–62*	40	78	____
954	Swimming Pool and Playground Set, 30 pieces, *59*	41	73	____
955	Highway Set, 22 pieces, *58*	32	70	____
956	Stockyard Set, 18 pieces, *59*	41	87	____
957	Farm Building and Animal Set, 35 pieces, *58*	59	108	____
958	Vehicle Set, 24 pieces, *58*	51	88	____
959	Barn Set, 23 pieces, *58*	36	63	____
960	Barnyard Set, 29 pieces, *59–61*	36	77	____
961	School Set, 36 pieces, *59*	41	85	____
962	Turnpike Set, 24 pieces, *58*	59	143	____
963	Frontier Set, 18 pieces, *59–60*	61	99	____
963-100	Frontier Set, 18 pieces, *60*	133	245	____
964	Factory Site Set, 18 pieces, *59*	56	328	____
965	Farm Set, 36 pieces, *59*	49	97	____
966	Firehouse Set, 45 pieces, *58*	50	206	____
967	Post Office Set, 25 pieces, *58*	48	95	____
968	TV Transmitter Set, 28 pieces, *58*	51	94	____
969	Construction Set, 23 pieces, *60*	61	114	____
970	Ticket Booth, *58–60*	39	139	____
971	Lichen with box, *60–64*	29	95	____
972	Landscape Tree Assortment, *61–64*	25	92	____
973	Complete Landscaping Set, *60–64*	37	126	____
974	Scenery Set, *58*	68	262	____
980	Ranch Set, 14 pieces, *60*	51	85	____
981	Freight Yard Set, 10 pieces, *60*	50	173	____
982	Suburban Split Level Set, 18 pieces, *60*	33	99	____
983	Farm Set, 7 pieces, *60–61*	33	86	____
984	Railroad Set, 22 pieces, *61–62*	33	78	____
985	Freight Area Set, 32 pieces, *61*	36	78	____

		Good	Exc
____ **986**	Farm Set, 20 pieces, *62*	44	65
____ **987**	Town Set, 24 pieces, *62*	42	65
____ **988**	Railroad Structure Set, 16 pieces, *62*	39	98
1001	2-4-2 Scout Locomotive, plastic body, 1001T Tender, *48*		
____	(A) Silver rubber-stamped cab number	30	78
____	(B) White heat-stamped cab number	16	41
____ **1001T**	Tender	9	19
1002	Gondola, *48–52*		
____	(A) Black, white lettering	5	9
____	(B) Blue, white lettering	5	10
____	(C) Silver, black lettering	127	424
____	(D) Yellow, black lettering	121	424
____	(E) Red, white lettering	121	424
____ **X1004**	PRR Baby Ruth Boxcar, *48–52*	6	12
____ **1005**	Sunoco 1-D Tank Car, *48–50*	7	12
1007	LL SP-type Caboose, *48–52*		
____	(A) Red body	5	14
____	(B) Red body, raised board on catwalk	10	33
____	(C) Tuscan body	215	998
____ **1008**	Uncoupling Unit (027), *57–62*		5
____ **1008-50**	Uncoupling Track Section (027), *57–62*		5
____ **1010**	Transformer, 35 watts, *61–66*	5	12
____ **1011**	Transformer, 25 watts, *48–49*	4	11
____ **1012**	Transformer, 35 watts, *50–54*	5	12
____ **1013**	Curved Track (027), *45–69*		1
____ **1013-17**	Steel Pins, dozen (027), *46–60*		1
____ **1013-42**	Steel Pins, dozen (027), *61–68*		2
____ **1014**	Transformer, 40 watts, *55*	5	12
____ **1015**	Transformer, 45 watts, *56–60*	5	12
____ **1016**	Transformer, 35 watts, *59–60*	5	11
____ **1018**	Half Straight Track (027), *55–69*		1
____ **1018**	Straight Track (027), *45–69*		1
____ **1019**	Remote Control Track Set (027), *46–48*	2	8
____ **1020**	90-degree Crossing (027), *55–69*	2	5
____ **1021**	90-degree Crossing (027), *45–54*	2	4
____ **1022**	Manual Switches, pair (027), *53–69*	8	15
____ **1023**	45-degree Crossing (027), *56–69*	3	5
____ **1024**	Manual Switches, pair (027), *46–52*	7	15
____ **1025**	Illuminated Bumper (027), *46–47*	10	15
____ **1025**	Transformer, 45 watts, *61–69*	6	12
____ **1026**	Transformer, 25 watts, *61–64*	3	7
____ **1032**	Transformer, 75 watts, *48*	14	30
____ **1033**	Transformer, 90 watts, *48–56*	21	43
____ **1034**	Transformer, 75 watts, *48–54*	15	27
____ **1035**	Transformer, 60 watts, *47*	12	22
____ **1037**	Transformer, 40 watts, *46–47*	7	16

		Good	Exc	
1041	Transformer, 60 watts, *45–46*	15	23	___
1042	Transformer, 75 watts, *47–48*	16	29	___
1043	Transformer, 50 watts, *53–57*	7	16	___
1043-500	Transformer, 60 watts, ivory, *57–58*	62	174	___
1044	Transformer, 90 watts, *57–69*	25	46	___
1045	Operating Watchman, *46–50*	19	48	___
1045C	Contactor		15	___
1047	Operating Switchman, *59–61*	36	120	___
1050	0-4-0 Scout Locomotive, 1050T Tender, *59 u*	56	192	___
1050T	Tender		22	___
1053	Transformer, 60 watts, *56–60*	8	16	___
1055	Texas Special Alco Diesel A Unit, *59–60*	27	65	___
1060	2-4-2 Locomotive, 1050T or 1060T Tender, *60–62*	13	32	___
1060T	Tender	13	20	___
1061	0-4-0 or 2–4–2 Scout Locomotive, 1061T Tender, *64, 69*			
	(A) Slope-back Lionel Lines tender	15	34	___
	(B) Paper number labels	50	228	___
	(C) No number stamped on cab	35	105	___
1061T	Tender		17	___
1062	0-4-0 or 2-4-2 Scout Locomotive, *63–64*			
	(A) Streamlined Southern Pacific Tender	15	43	___
	(B) Other tenders	13	31	___
1063	Transformer, 75 watts, *60–64*	13	32	___
1065	Union Pacific Alco Diesel A Unit, *61*	32	68	___
1066	Union Pacific Alco Diesel A Unit, *64 u*	35	80	___
1073	Transformer, 60 watts, *61–66*	13	30	___
1101	Transformer, 25 watts, *48*	4	8	___
1101	2-4-2 Scout Locomotive, 1001T Tender, *48 u*			
	(A) Cab correctly marked "1101"	18	42	___
	(B) Cab marked "1001"	147	325	___
1110	2-4-2 Locomotive, 1001T Tender, *49, 51–52*	15	27	___
1120	2-4-2 Scout Locomotive, 1001T Tender, *50*	19	35	___
1121	Remote Control Switches, pair (O27), *46–51*	14	22	___
1122	Remote Control Switches, pair (O27), *52–53*	14	28	___
1122-34	Remote Control Switches, pair, *52–53*	14	26	___
1122-500	Gauge Adapter (O27), *57–66*		10	___
1122E	Remote Control Switches, pair (O27), *53–69*	12	26	___
1130	2-4-2 Locomotive, 6066T or 1130T Tender, *53–54*			
	(A) Plastic body	18	36	___
	(B) Die-cast body	37	98	___
1130T	Tender			
	(A) Black-painted shell	30	100	___
	(B) Black plastic shell	7	18	___
1130T-500	Tender, pink, from Girls Set		125	___
1144	Transformer, 75 watts, *61–66*	8	21	___

			Good	Exc
__ 1232	Transformer, 75 watts, made for export, *48*		18	50
1615	0-4-0 Locomotive, 1615T Tender, *55–57*			
__	(A) No grab irons		73	164
__	(B) Grab irons on locomotive and tender		162	318
__ 1615T	Tender		7	18
__ 1625	0-4-0 Locomotive, 1625T Tender, *58*		155	411
__ 1625T	Tender			29
__ 1640-100	Presidential Kit, *60*		58	198
__ 1654	2-4-2 Locomotive, 1654W Tender, *46–47*		34	70
__ 1654T	Tender		8	14
__ 1654W	Whistling Tender		11	30
__ 1655	2-4-2 Locomotive, 6654W Tender, *48–49*		40	70
1656	0-4-0 Locomotive, 6403B Tender, *48–49*			
__	(A) Large silver cab number		118	265
__	(B) Small silver cab number		128	262
__ 1665	0-4-0 Locomotive, 2403B Tender, *46*		183	358
1666	2-6-2 Locomotive, 2466W or 2466WX Tender, *46–47*			
__	(A) Number plate and two-piece bell		57	131
__	(B) Rubber-stamped number and one-piece bell		30	150
__ 1666T	Tender		20	
1862	4-4-0 Civil War General, 1862T Tender, *59–62*			
__	(A) Gray smokestack		85	180
__	(B) Black smokestack		90	200
__ 1862T	Tender			30
__ 1865	Western & Atlantic Coach, *59–62*		28	58
__ 1866	Western & Atlantic Mail-Baggage Car, *59–62*		33	62
1872	4-4-0 Civil War General, 1872T Tender, *59–62*		95	293
__ 1872T	Tender		24	35
__ 1875	Western & Atlantic Coach, *59–62*		92	241
__ 1875W	Western & Atlantic Coach, whistle, *59–62*		53	169
__ 1876	Western & Atlantic Baggage Car, *59–62*		28	88
__ 1877	Flatcar with fence and horses, *59–62*		45	102
__ 1882	4-4-0 Civil War General, 1882T Tender, *60 u*		199	427
__ 1885	Western & Atlantic Coach, *60 u*		100	305
__ 1887	Flatcar with fences and horses, *60 u*		72	174
__ 2001	Track Make-up Kit (O27), *63*			500
__ 2002	Track Make-up Kit (O27), *63*			NRS
__ 2003	Track Make-up Kit (O27), *63*			NRS
__ 2016	2-6-4 Locomotive, 6026W Tender, *55–56*		52	105
2018	2-6-4 Locomotive, *56–59, 61*			
__	(A) 6026T Tender		38	72
__	(B) 6026W Tender		60	111
__	(C) 1130T Tender		35	65
2020	6-8-6 Steam Turbine Locomotive, 2020W or 2466WX Tender, smoke lamp, *46*		95	198

		Good	Exc	
2020	6-8-6 Steam Turbine Locomotive, 2020W or 6020W Tender, *47–49*	72	176	___
2020W	Whistling Tender	40	62	___
2023	Union Pacific Alco Diesel AA Units, *50–51*			
	(A) Yellow body	99	226	___
	(B) Gray nose and side frames	907	2950	___
	(C) Silver body	73	222	___
2024	C&O Alco Diesel A Unit, *69*	30	63	___
2025	2-6-2 Locomotive, 2466WX or 6466WX Tender, *47–49*			
	(A) Black smokestack, *48–49*	80	177	___
	(B) Aluminum smokestack, *47*	95	199	___
2025	2-6-4 Locomotive, 6466W Tender, *52*	88	170	___
2026	2-6-2 Locomotive, 6466WX Tender, *48–49*	63	105	___
2026	2-6-4 Locomotive, 6466W, 6466T, or 6066T Tender, *51–53*	40	95	___
2028	Pennsylvania GP7 Diesel, *55*			
	(A) Gold lettering	150	274	___
	(B) Yellow lettering	138	271	___
	(C) Tan frame	245	508	___
2029	2-6-4 Locomotive, *64–69*			
	(A) 234W Lionel Lines Tender	50	120	___
	(B) LL Tender with "Hagerstown" on bottom	60	135	___
	(C) 234W Pennsylvania Tender	139	227	___
2031	Rock Island Alco Diesel AA Units, *52–54*	69	243	___
2032	Erie Alco Diesel AA Units, *52–54*	126	175	___
2033	Union Pacific Alco Diesel AA Units, *52–54*	90	242	___
2034	2-4-2 Scout Locomotive, 6066T Tender, *52*	25	65	___
2035	2-6-4 Locomotive, 6466W Tender, *50–51*	70	174	___
2036	2-6-4 Locomotive, 6466W Tender, *50*	58	115	___
2037	2-6-4 Locomotive, *54–55, 57–63*			
	(A) 6026T or 1130T Tender	45	80	___
	(B) 6026W, 233W, or 234W whistle Tender	64	128	___
2037-500	2-6-4 Locomotive, pink, 1130T-500 Tender, *57–58*	276	866	___
2041	Rock Island Alco Diesel AA Units, *69*	70	150	___
2046	4-6-4 Locomotive, 2046W Tender, *50–51, 53*	95	186	___
2046T	Tender, for export	35	115	___
2046W	Whistle Tender	25	61	___
2046W-50	PRR Whistle Tender	33	53	___
2055	4-6-4 Locomotive, 2046W or 6026W Tender, *53–55*	88	170	___
2056	4-6-4 Locomotive, 2046W Tender, *52*	93	257	___
2065	4-6-4 Locomotive, 2046W or 6026W Tender, *54–56*	96	167	___
2203B	Tender		120	___
2224W	Whistle Tender		112	___
2240	Wabash F3 AB Units, *56*	253	612	___

			Good	Exc
	2242	New Haven F3 AB Units, *58–59*	400	874
	2243	Santa Fe F3 AB Units, *55–57*		
___		(A) Gray body mold, raised molded cab door ladder	150	287
___		(B) Typical molded cab door ladder	113	285
___	**2243C**	Santa Fe F3 B Unit, *55–57*	64	181
	2245	Texas Special F3 AB Units, *54–55*		
___		(A) B Unit with portholes, *54*	262	517
___		(B) B Unit without portholes, *55*	288	725
	2257	SP-type caboose, *47*		
___		(A) Red body, no smokestack	8	16
___		(B) Tuscan body and smokestack	83	319
___		(C) Red body and smokestack	118	493
	2321	Lackawanna FM Train Master Diesel, *54–56*		
___		(A) Gray roof	211	349
___		(B) Maroon roof	237	462
	2322	Virginian FM Train Master Diesel, *65–66*		
___		(A) Unpainted blue body, yellow stripes	270	533
___		(B) Blue or black body, painted blue and yellow stripes	346	672
___	**2328**	Burlington GP7 Diesel, *55–56*	111	255
___	**2329**	Virginian GE E-33 or EL-C Electric Locomotive, *58–59*	169	525
___	**2330**	Pennsylvania GG1 Electric Locomotive, green, *50*	422	1324
	2331	Virginian FM Train Master Diesel, *55–58*		
___		(A) Black and yellow stripes, gray mold, *55*	342	712
___		(B) Yellow stripes, blue mold, *56–58*	227	640
___		(C) Blue and yellow stripes, gray mold	603	1213
	2332	Pennsylvania GG1 Electric Locomotive, *47–49*		
___		(A) Black	615	1494
___		(B) Dark green	254	467
	2333	NYC F3 Diesel AA Units, *48–49*		
___		(A) Rubber-stamped lettering	264	594
___		(B) Heat-stamped lettering	243	519
___	**2333**	Santa Fe F3 Diesel AA Units, *48–49*	226	483
___	**2337**	Wabash GP7 Diesel, *58*	113	285
	2338	Milwaukee Road GP7 Diesel, *55–56*		
___		(A) Orange band around shell	507	1160
___		(B) Interrupted orange band	123	230
___	**2339**	Wabash GP7 Diesel, *57*	116	286
	2340	Pennsylvania GG1 Electric Locomotive, *55*		
___		(A) Tuscan	457	1253
___		(B) Dark green	315	675
	2341	Jersey Central FM Train Master Diesel, *56*		
___		(A) High-gloss orange	912	2174
___		(B) Dull orange	925	1985
___	**2343**	Santa Fe F3 Diesel AA Units, *50–52*	155	471

		Good	Exc	
2343C	Santa Fe F3 B Unit, *50–55*			
	(A) Screen roof vents	106	272	____
	(B) Louver roof vents	93	189	____
2344	NYC F3 Diesel AA Units, *50–52*	197	512	____
2344C	NYC F3 B Unit, *50–55*	119	241	____
2345	Western Pacific F3 Diesel AA Units, *52*	491	886	____
2346	B&M GP9 Diesel, *65–66*	168	365	____
2347	C&O GP7 Diesel, *65 u*	1400	2850	____
2348	M&StL GP9 Diesel, *58–59*	115	384	____
2349	Northern Pacific GP9 Diesel, *59–60*	174	406	____
2350	New Haven EP-5 Electric Locomotive, *56–58*			
	(A) Painted nose trim, white N and orange H	274	577	____
	(B) Decaled nose trim, white N and orange H	191	337	____
	(C) Painted nose trim, orange N and black H	775	1600	____
	(D) Decaled nose trim, orange N and black H	459	911	____
	(E) Orange and white stripes go through doorjambs	345	750	____
2351	Milwaukee Road EP-5 Electric Locomotive, *57–58*	163	432	____
2352	Pennsylvania EP-5 Electric Locomotive, *58–59*			
	(A) Tuscan body	236	458	____
	(B) Chocolate brown body	195	373	____
2353	Santa Fe F3 Diesel AA Units, *53–55*	246	468	____
2354	NYC F3 Diesel AA Units, *53–55*	272	477	____
2355	Western Pacific F3 Diesel AA Units, *53*	492	939	____
2356	Southern F3 Diesel AA Units, *54–56*	368	646	____
2356C	Southern F3 B Unit, *54–56*	166	253	____
2357	SP-type Caboose, *47–48*			
	(A) Red body and smokestack	174	564	____
	(B) Tuscan body and smokestack	13	29	____
	(C) Tile red, no smokestack, "6357" stamped on bottom	75	229	____
2358	Great Northern EP-5 Electric Locomotive, *59–60*	271	733	____
2359	Boston & Maine GP9 Diesel, *61–62*	123	294	____
2360	Pennsylvania GG1 Electric Locomotive, *56–58, 61–63*			
	(A) Tuscan, 5 gold stripes	571	1288	____
	(B) Dark green, 5 gold stripes	442	872	____
	(C) Tuscan, gold stripe, heat-stamped letters	443	865	____
	(D) Tuscan, gold stripe, decaled lettering	398	725	____
2363	Illinois Central F3 Diesel AB Units, *55–56*			
	(A) Black lettering	340	785	____
	(B) Brown lettering	384	872	____
2365	C&O GP7 Diesel, *62–63*	116	259	____
2367	Wabash F3 Diesel AB Units, *55*	318	689	____
2368	B&O F3 Diesel AB Units, *56*	514	1436	____
2373	CP F3 Diesel AA Units, *57*	675	1791	____

			Good	Exc
	2378	Milwaukee Road F3 Diesel AB Units, *56*		
___		(A) Yellow roof line stripes	585	1340
___		(B) No roof line stripes	544	1199
___	2379	Rio Grande F3 Diesel AB Units, *57–58*	373	779
___	2383	Santa Fe F3 Diesel AA Units, *58–66*	220	452
___	2400	Maplewood Pullman Car, green, *48–49*	47	126
___	2401	Hillside Observation Car, green, *48–49*	48	126
___	2402	Chatham Pullman Car, green, *48–49*	46	128
___	2404	Santa Fe Vista Dome Car, *64–65*	29	70
___	2405	Santa Fe Pullman Car, *64–65*	33	75
___	2406	Santa Fe Observation Car, *64–65*	26	60
___	2408	Santa Fe Vista Dome Car, *66*	43	80
___	2409	Santa Fe Pullman Car, *66*	38	82
___	2410	Santa Fe Observation Car, *66*	34	74
	2411	Lionel Lines Flatcar, *46–48*		
___		(A) With pipes, *46*	38	77
___		(B) With logs, *47–48*	16	36
___	2412	Santa Fe Vista Dome Car, *59–63*	35	87
___	2414	Santa Fe Pullman Car, *59–63*	36	91
___	2416	Santa Fe Observation Car, *59–63*	29	74
___	2419	DL&W Work Caboose, *46–47*	23	60
	2420	DL&W Work Caboose with searchlight, *46–48*		
___		(A) Light or dark gray, heat-stamped lettering	46	103
___		(B) Light or dark gray, rubber-stamped lettering	75	199
	2421	Maplewood Pullman Car, *50–53*		
___		(A) Gray roof	32	68
___		(B) Silver roof	27	54
	2422	Chatham Pullman Car, *50–53*		
___		(A) Gray roof	35	69
___		(B) Silver roof	28	59
	2423	Hillside Observation Car, *50–53*		
___		(A) Gray roof	30	63
___		(B) Silver roof	25	54
___	2426W	Whistle Tender, *50*	123	220
___	2429	Livingston Pullman Car, *52–53*	52	105
___	2430	Pullman Car, blue, *46–47*	29	95
___	2431	Observation Car, blue, *46–47*	26	89
___	2432	Clifton Vista Dome Car, *54–58*	33	79
___	2434	Newark Pullman Car, *54–58*	33	78
___	2435	Elizabeth Pullman Car, *54–58*	41	113
___	2436	Mooseheart Observation Car, *57–58*	31	78
___	2436	Summit Observation Car, *54–56*	20	57

		Good	Exc	
2440	Pullman Car, green, *46–47*			
	(A) Silver lettering	53	85	____
	(B) White lettering	38	75	____
2441	Observation Car, green, *46–47*			
	(A) Silver lettering	53	85	____
	(B) White lettering	30	63	____
2442	Clifton Vista Dome Car, *56*	50	107	____
2442	Pullman Car, brown, *46–48*			
	(A) Silver lettering	52	102	____
	(B) White lettering	38	75	____
2443	Observation Car, brown, *46–48*			
	(A) Silver lettering	49	101	____
	(B) White lettering	37	75	____
2444	Newark Pullman Car, *56*	43	99	____
2445	Elizabeth Pullman Car, *56*	95	240	____
2446	Summit Observation Car, *56*	46	98	____
2452	Pennsylvania Gondola, *45–47*			
	(A) Whirly wheels, *45*	21	44	____
	(B) Regular wheels	10	20	____
	(C) Early flying shoe trucks, two holes in floor, *45*	30	160	____
2452X	Pennsylvania Gondola, *46–47*	6	14	____
X2454	Baby Ruth Boxcar, PRR logo, *46–47*	18	40	____
X2454	Pennsylvania Boxcar, *46*			
	(A) Brown door	95	200	____
	(B) Orange door	165	291	____
2456	Lehigh Valley Hopper, *48*			
	(A) Flat black, 2 lines of data, *48*	10	39	____
	(B) Flat black, 3 lines of data, *48*	107	429	____
2457	PRR N5-type Caboose "477618," tintype, *45–47*			
	(A) Red, white lettering	21	44	____
	(B) Brown, offset white lettering	133	582	____
	(C) Brown, centered white lettering	28	117	____
X2458	PRR Automobile Boxcar, *46–48*	20	54	____
2460	Bucyrus Erle Crane Car, 12-wheel, *46–50*			
	(A) Gray cab	92	267	____
	(B) Black cab	45	93	____
2461	Transformer Car, die-cast, *47–48*			
	(A) Red transformer	36	95	____
	(B) Black transformer	30	78	____

			Good	Exc
	2465	Sunoco 2-D Tank Car, *46–48*		
____		(A) "Gas, Sunoco, and Oils" in diamond, centered	59	235
____		(B) "Sunoco" in diamond	9	18
____		(C) "Sunoco" extends beyond diamond	9	17
____	**2466T**	Tender		72
____	**2466WX**	Whistle Tender, *45–48*	28	62
____	**2472**	PRR N5-type Caboose, tintype, *46–47*	13	29
____	**2481**	Plainfield Pullman Car, yellow, *50*	140	279
____	**2482**	Westfield Pullman Car, yellow, *50*	131	275
____	**2483**	Livingston Observation Car, yellow, *50*	109	245
____	**2521**	President McKinley Observation Car, *62–66*	71	140
____	**2522**	President Harrison Vista Dome Car, *62–66*	82	171
____	**2523**	President Garfield Pullman Car, *62–66*	74	151
	2530	REA Baggage Car, *54–60*		
____		(A) Large doors	213	501
____		(B) Small doors	73	169
	2531	Silver Dawn Observation Car, *52–60*		
____		(A) Ribbed channels, round rivets	39	120
____		(B) Ribbed channels, hex rivets	58	140
____		(C) Ribbed channels, hex rivets, red center taillight	58	180
____		(D) Flat channels, glued nameplates	78	175
____	**2532**	Silver Range Vista Dome Car, *52–60*	55	117
____	**2533**	Silver Cloud Pullman Car, *52–59*	51	109
____	**2534**	Silver Bluff Pullman Car, *52–59*	62	130
____	**2541**	Alexander Hamilton Observation Car, *55–56**	58	175
____	**2542**	Betsy Ross Vista Dome Car, *55–56**	45	160
____	**2543**	William Penn Pullman Car, *55–56**	65	178
____	**2544**	Molly Pitcher Pullman Car, *55–56**	61	178
____	**2550**	B&O Baggage-Mail Rail Diesel Car, *57–58*	201	422
____	**2551**	Banff Park Observation Car, *57**	132	248
____	**2552**	Skyline 500 Vista Dome Car, *57**	150	264
____	**2553**	Blair Manor Pullman Car, *57**	237	451
____	**2554**	Craig Manor Pullman Car, *57**	212	450
____	**2555**	Sunoco 1-D Tank Car, *46–48*	21	58
____	**2559**	B&O Passenger Rail Diesel Car, *57–58*	131	285
	2560	Lionel Lines Crane Car, 8-wheel, *46–47*		
____		(A) Black boom	23	74
____		(B) Brown boom	23	77
____		(C) Green boom	28	88
____		(D) Black boom from 2460 crane, *47*	22	68
____	**2561**	Vista Valley Observation Car, *59–61**	115	282
____	**2562**	Regal Pass Vista Dome Car, *59–61**	134	314

		Good	Exc	
2563	Indian Falls Pullman Car, *59–61**	126	314	___
2625	Irvington Pullman Car, *46–50**			
	(A) No silhouettes	84	174	___
	(B) Silhouettes	116	265	___
2625	Madison Pullman Car, *46–47**	105	186	___
2625	Manhattan Pullman Car, *46–47**	107	185	___
2627	Madison Pullman Car, *48–50**			
	(A) No silhouettes	80	164	___
	(B) Silhouettes	120	243	___
2628	Manhattan Pullman Car, *48–50**			
	(A) No silhouettes	83	167	___
	(B) Silhouettes	130	251	___
2666T	Tender		40	___
2666W	Whistle Tender		70	___
2671T	PRR Tender, for export	43	131	___
2671W	Whistle Tender	45	95	___
2671WX	Whistle Tender	50	74	___
2755	Sunoco 1-D Tank Car, *45*	38	79	___
X2758	PRR Automobile Boxcar, *45–46*	30	67	___
2855	Sunoco 1-D Tank Car, *46–47*			
	(A) Black	96	217	___
	(B) Black, decal without "Gas" and "Oils"	72	234	___
	(C) Gray	51	188	___
3309	Turbo Missile Launch Car, red body, *63–64*	23	50	___
3309-50	Turbo Missile Launch Car, olive body, *63–64*	165	719	___
3330	Flatcar with submarine kit, *60–62*	47	159	___
3330-100	Operating Submarine Kit with box, *60–61*	108	341	___
3349	Turbo Missile Launch Car, *62–65*			
	(A) Red body	16	49	___
	(B) Olive drab body	137	585	___
3356	Operating Horse Car and Corral Set, *56–60, 64–66*	62	124	___
3356	Operating Horse Car only, *56–60, 64–66*			
	(A) Built date, bar-end trucks, *56–60*	31	71	___
	(B) No built date, AAR trucks, *64–66*	43	156	___
3356-100	Black Horses, 9 pieces, *56–59*	14	30	___
3356-150	Horse Car Corral, *57–60*	30	75	___
3357	Hydraulic Maintenance Car, *62–64*	23	70	___
3357	Hydraulic Maintenance Car, *62*		37	___
3359	Lionel Lines Twin-bin Coal Dump Car, *55–58*	27	40	___
3360	Operating Burro Crane, self-propelled, *56–57*	115	211	___
3361	Operating Log Dump Car, *55–58*	16	41	___
3362	Helium Tank Unloading Car, *61–63, 69*	22	48	___

		Good	Exc
3362/64	Operating Dump Car with 2 helium tanks, *65–66, 68*	28	68
____ 3364	Operating Dump Car with 3 logs, *65–66, 68*	17	36
____ 3366	Circus Car Corral Set, *59–62*	122	267
____ 3366	Circus Car only, *59–62*	72	149
____ 3366-100	White Horses, 9 pieces, *59–62*	42	65
3370	W&A Sheriff and Outlaw Car, *61–64*		
____	(A) AAR trucks	10	50
____	(B) Archbar trucks	20	75
3376	Bronx Zoo Car, *60–66, 69*		
____	(A) Blue, white lettering	19	48
____	(B) Green, yellow lettering	35	83
____	(C) Blue, yellow lettering	88	209
____ 3386	Bronx Zoo Car, *60*	27	64
____ 3409	Helicopter Car, *61*	37	90
3410	Helicopter Car, *61–63*		
____	(A) 2 operating couplers, gray Navy helicopter	28	85
____	(B) Single operating coupler, yellow helicopter, *63*	62	170
____ 3413	Mercury Capsule Car, *62–64*	62	166
____ 3419	Helicopter Car, *59–65*	38	81
____ 3424	Wabash Operating Boxcar, *56–58*	38	60
____ 3424-75	Low Bridge Signal, *56–57*	84	183
____ 3424-100	Low Bridge Signal Set, *56–58*	18	56
____ 3428	U.S. Mail Operating Boxcar, *59–60*	44	83
3429	USMC Helicopter Car, *60*		
____	(A) USMC helicopter	210	482
____	(B) Navy helicopter	58	218
____ 3434	Poultry Dispatch Car, *59–60, 64–66*	21	49
____	(A) Gray man	53	98
____	(B) Blue man	60	155
3435	Traveling Aquarium Car, *59–62*		
____	(A) Gold lettering, tank designations, and circle around L	428	1060
____	(B) Gold lettering, tank designations, no circle around L	258	652
____	(C) Gold lettering, no tank designations, no circle around L	128	251
____	(D) Yellow lettering, no tank designations, no circle around L	58	146
____ 3444	Erie Operating Gondola, *57–59*	39	61
3451	Operating Log Dump Car, *46–48*		
____	(A) Heat-stamped lettering	13	40
____	(B) Rubber-stamped lettering	22	82

		Good	Exc	
3454	PRR Operating Merchandise Car, *46–47*			
	(A) Red lettering	988	4130	___
	(B) Blue lettering	29	138	___
3456	N&W Operating Hopper, *50–55*	21	56	___
3459	LL Operating Coal Dump Car, *46–48*			
	(A) Aluminum bin	87	252	___
	(B) Black bin	21	75	___
	(C) Green bin	20	97	___
3460	Flatcar with trailers, *55–57*	27	75	___
3461	LL Operating Log Car, *49–55*			
	(A) Black car, heat-stamped lettering	21	39	___
	(B) Black car, rubber-stamped lettering	136	335	___
	(C) Green car	27	59	___
3462	Automatic Milk Car, *47–48*			
	(A) Flat white or cream, steel base mechanism	17	65	___
	(B) Flat white or cream, brass base mechanism	18	70	___
	(C) Glossy cream	92	303	___
3462-70	Magnetic Milk Cans, *52–59*	12	22	___
3462P	Milk Car Platform, *47–48*	8	17	___
X3464	ATSF Operating Boxcar, *49–52*	13	27	___
X3464	NYC Operating Boxcar, *49–52*	13	27	___
3469	LL Operating Coal Dump Car, *49–55*	22	42	___
3470	Target Launching Car, dark blue, *62–64*	30	70	___
3470-100	Target Launching Car, light blue, *63*	65	183	___
3472	Automatic Milk Car, *49–53*	35	57	___
3474	Western Pacific Operating Boxcar, *52–53*	19	68	___
3482	Automatic Milk Car, *54–55*			
	(A) "RT3472" on right	40	114	___
	(B) "RT3482" on right	28	72	___
3484	Pennsylvania Operating Boxcar, *53*	17	54	___
3484-25	ATSF Operating Boxcar, *54*			
	(A) White lettering	23	70	___
	(B) Black lettering	321	1144	___
3494-1	NYC Operating Boxcar, *55*	42	113	___
3494-150	MP Operating Boxcar, *56*	65	133	___
3494-275	State of Maine Operating Boxcar, *56–58*			
	(A) "3494275" on side	38	123	___
	(B) No number on side	57	192	___
3494-550	Monon Operating Boxcar, *57–58*	200	362	___
3494-625	Soo Operating Boxcar, *57–58*	202	449	___
3509	Satellite Launching Car, *61*			
	(A) Chrome satellite cover	20	69	___
	(B) Gray satellite cover	50	160	___
3510	Satellite Launching Car, *62*	40	120	___

		Good	Exc
3512	Fireman and Ladder Car, *59–61*		
___	(A) Black extension ladder	58	138
___	(B) Silver extension ladder	78	213
___ **3519**	Satellite Launching Car, *61–64*	22	59
3520	Searchlight Car, *52–53*		
___	(A) Serif lettering	22	71
___	(B) Sans serif lettering	20	40
3530	GM Generator Car, *56–58*		
___	(A) Blue fuel tank	60	119
___	(B) Black fuel tank	56	116
___	(C) 3530 underscored	413	1533
___ **3530-50**	Searchlight with pole and base, *56–56*	20	65
___ **3535**	Security Car with searchlight, *60–61*	38	95
___ **3540**	Operating Radar Car, *59–60*	44	142
___ **3545**	Operating TV Monitor Car, *61–62*	55	170
___ **3559**	Operating Coal Dump Car, *46–48*	20	42
3562-1	ATSF Operating Barrel Car, *54*		
___	(A) Black, black unloading trough	67	203
___	(B) Black, yellow unloading trough	63	195
___	(C) Gray, red lettering	800	2838
3562-25	ATSF Operating Barrel Car, gray, *54*		
___	(A) Red lettering, no bracket tab	193	416
___	(B) Blue lettering, no bracket tab	18	60
___	(C) Blue lettering, bracket tab	15	75
3562-50	ATSF Operating Barrel Car, yellow, *55–56*		
___	(A) Painted	45	115
___	(B) Unpainted	24	59
___ **3562-75**	ATSF Operating Barrel Car, orange, *57–58*	40	88
3619	Helicopter Reconnaissance Car, *62–64*		
___	(A) Light yellow	41	114
___	(B) Dark yellow	53	175
3620	Searchlight Car, orange generator, *54–56*		
___	(A) Unpainted gray plastic searchlight	29	41
___	(B) Gray-painted gray plastic searchlight	30	47
___	(C) Unpainted orange plastic searchlight	60	150
___	(D) Gray-painted orange plastic searchlight	80	263
3650	Extension Searchlight Car, *56–59*		
___	(A) Light gray	43	80
___	(B) Dark gray	63	137
___	(C) Olive gray	97	267

		Good	Exc	
3656	Armour Operating Cattle Car, some with an open coil, *49–55*			
	(A) Black letters, Armour sticker	94	243	___
	(B) White letters, Armour sticker	34	69	___
	(C) Black letters, no Armour sticker	74	182	___
	(D) White letters, no Armour sticker	30	70	___
3656	Stockyard with cattle, *49–55*	28	75	___
3656-34	Cattle, black, 9 pieces, *49–58*			
	(A) Rounded ridge on base, *49*	55	108	___
	(B) Plain base	12	25	___
3656-150	Corral Platform, yellow tray	217	533	___
3662	Automatic Milk Car, *55–60, 64–66*	40	70	___
3662-79	Nonmagnetic Milk Cans, 7, white envelope	15	65	___
3662-80	Nonmagnetic Milk Cans, 7, manila envelope	20	83	___
3665	Minuteman Operating Car, *61–64*			
	(A) Medium blue roof	82	199	___
	(B) Dark blue roof	50	105	___
3666	Minuteman Boxcar with cannon, *64 u*	175	461	___
3672	Bosco Operating Milk Car, *59–60*			
	(A) Unpainted yellow body	85	201	___
	(B) Painted yellow body	143	305	___
3672-79	Bosco Can Set, 7 pieces, *59–60*		125	___
3820	USMC Operating Submarine Car, *60–62*	102	197	___
3830	Operating Submarine Car, *60–63*	38	99	___
3854	Automatic Merchandise Car, *46–47*	207	518	___
3927	Lionel Lines Track Cleaning Car, *56–60*	30	58	___
3927-38	Track Cleaning Fluid Bottle		20	___
3927-50	Track Wiping Cylinders, 25 pieces, *57–60*	6	35	___
3927-75	Track-Clean Detergent, can, *56–69*	4	15	___
4357	SP-type Caboose, electronic, die-cast stack, *48–49*			
	(A) Die-cast metal smokestack	63	200	___
	(B) Matching plastic smokestack	100	300	___
	(C) Matching plastic smokestack, raised board on catwalk	100	300	___
4452	PRR Gondola, electronic, *46–49*	49	112	___
4454	Baby Ruth PRR Boxcar, electronic, *46–49*	60	180	___
4457	PRR N5-type Caboose, tintype, electronic, *46–47*	45	150	___
4671W	Whistle Tender	40		___
5102	Railroad and Roadway Crossing	15	65	___
5159	Maintenance Kit, *63–65*	28	80	___
5159-50	Maintenance and Lube Kit, *66–69*	28	80	___
5160	Viewing Stand, *63*	50	190	___
5459	LL Coal Dump Car, electronic, *46–49*	57	138	___
6001T	Tender		24	___

		Good	Exc
6002	NYC Gondola, *50*	5	11
X6004	Baby Ruth PRR Boxcar, *50*	4	7
6007	Lionel Lines SP-type Caboose, *50*	3	7
6009	Remote Control Uncoupling Track, *53–54*	1	5
6012	Gondola, *51–56*	2	6
6014	Airex Boxcar, *60 u*	22	43
6014	Bosco PRR Boxcar, *58*		
	(A) White body	23	48
	(B) Red body	4	8
	(C) Orange body	4	7
6014	Chun King Boxcar, *57 u*	60	148
6014	Frisco Boxcar, *57, 63–69*		
	(A) White body	5	12
	(B) Red body	4	7
	(C) White body, coin slot	25	45
	(D) Orange body, *57*	19	62
	(E) Orange body, *69*	22	39
X6014	Baby Ruth PRR Boxcar, *51–56*		
	(A) White body	5	9
	(B) Red body	7	16
6014-150	Wix Boxcar, *59 u*	95	197
6015	Sunoco 1-D Tank Car, *54–55*		
	(A) Painted tank	79	308
	(B) Unpainted tank	4	12
6017	Lionel Lines SP-type Caboose, *51–62*		
	(A) Glossy tuscan-painted orange mold	28	97
	(B) Semigloss tuscan-painted, orange mold	10	40
	(C) Tile red-painted, blue mold	10	40
	(D) Common red, tuscan, and brown bodies	3	8
6017	SP-type Caboose, maroon, "Lionel" only, *56*	14	34
6017-50	U.S. Marine Corps SP-type Caboose, *58*	29	68
6017-85	LL SP-type Caboose, gray, *58*	27	90
6017-100	B&M SP-type Caboose, *59, 62, 65–66*		
	(A) Purple-blue	183	494
	(B) Medium or light blue	13	60
6017-185	ATSF SP-type Caboose, *59–60*	13	33
6017-200	U.S. Navy SP-type Caboose, *60*	52	179
6017-225	ATSF SP-type Caboose, *61–62*	15	50
6017-235	ATSF SP-type Caboose, *62*	14	49
6019	Remote Control Track (O27), *48–66*	2	8
6020W	Whistle Tender	30	69
6024	Nabisco Shredded Wheat Boxcar, *57*	13	30
6024	RCA Whirlpool Boxcar, *57 u*	28	60
6025	Gulf 1-D Tank Car, *56–58*		
	(A) Gray body, blue lettering	5	14
	(B) Orange body, blue lettering	5	13
	(C) Black body, red-orange Gulf emblem	5	13

		Good	Exc	
6026T	Tender	16	30	___
6026W	Whistle Tender	25	45	___
6027	Alaska SP-type Caboose, *59*	24	58	___
6029	Remote Control Uncoupling Track, *55–63*	2	10	___
6032	Short Gondola, black (027), *52–54*	2	7	___
X6034	Baby Ruth PRR Boxcar, *53–54*			
	(A) Orange, blue lettering	5	10	___
	(B) Red, white lettering	5	10	___
	(C) Orange, black lettering	5	13	___
6035	Sunoco 1-D Tank Car, *52–53*	3	8	___
6037	Lionel Lines SP-type Caboose, *52–54*			
	(A) Tuscan	3	6	___
	(B) Red	5	12	___
6042	Short Gondola, *59–61, 62–64 u*	3	13	___
6044	Airex Boxcar, orange lettering, *59–60 u*			
	(A) Medium blue	8	21	___
	(B) Teal blue	32	65	___
	(C) Purple-blue	90	333	___
6044-1X	Nestles/McCall's Boxcar, *62–63 u*	287	828	___
6045	Lionel Lines 2-D Tank Car, *59–64*			
	(A) Gray	10	21	___
	(B) Orange	13	34	___
	(C) Beige	10	30	___
6045	Cities Service 2-D Tank, *60 u*	13	36	___
6047	Lionel Lines SP-type Caboose, *62*			
	(A) Unpainted, medium red	2	5	___
	(B) Painted, brown	78	263	___
	(C) Unpainted, coral pink	14	54	___
6050	Lionel Savings Bank Boxcar, *61*			
	(A) Blt by Lionel	22	50	___
	(B) Built by Lionel	78	194	___
6050	Swift Boxcar, *62–63*			
	(A) Red body	11	24	___
	(B) Dark red body, 2 open holes in roof walk	43	184	___
6050	Libby's Tomato Juice Boxcar, *63 u*			
	(A) Green stems on tomatoes	18	38	___
	(B) Green stems missing	21	52	___
6057	LL SP-type Caboose, *59–62*			
	(A) Unpainted red plastic	3	8	___
	(B) Red-painted	36	103	___
	(C) Unpainted coral pink plastic	19	65	___
6057-50	LL SP-type Caboose, orange, *62*	16	51	___
6058	C&O SP-type Caboose, *61*			
	(A) Blue lettering	19	57	___
	(B) Black lettering	34	94	___

			Good	Exc
6059		M&StL SP-type Caboose, *61–69*		
____		(A) Painted, red	13	39
____		(B) Unpainted, red	4	13
____		(C) Unpainted, maroon	9	15
6062		NYC Gondola with 3 cable reels, *59–62*		
____		(A) No metal undercarriage	9	29
____		(B) Metal undercarriage	27	75
____	**6062-50**	NYC Gondola with 2 canisters, *69*	6	19
____	**6066T**	Tender	17	27
6067		SP-type Caboose, unmarked, *61–62*		
____		(A) Red	3	8
____		(B) Yellow	6	16
____		(C) Brown	9	20
____	**6076**	ATSF Hopper, *63 u*	11	31
6076		Lehigh Valley Hopper, short, *63*		
____		(A) Gray body	8	14
____		(B) Black body	7	14
____		(C) Red body	9	14
____		(D) Yellow body, painted	273	771
____	**6076-100**	Hopper, gray, unmarked, *63*	10	27
____	**6110**	2-4-2 Locomotive, 6001T Tender, *50–51*	16	35
6111		Flatcar with logs, *55–57*		
____		(A) Yellow with black lettering	10	35
____		(B) Yellow with white lettering	90	400
6112		Short Gondola with 4 canisters, *56–58*		
____		(A) Black body	7	18
____		(B) Blue body	8	16
____		(C) White body	17	39
6112-5		Canister, *56–58*		
____		(A) Red or white	1	3
____		(B) Red with black letters	20	84
____	**6112-25**	Canister Set, 4 pieces, red or white, with box, *56–58*	30	65
____	**6119**	DL&W Work Caboose, red, *55–56*	14	29
____	**6119-25**	DL&W Work Caboose, orange, *56–59*	16	37
____	**6119-50**	DL&W Work Caboose, brown, *56*	22	57
6119-75		DL&W Work Caboose, *57*		
____		(A) Heat-stamped letters on frame	14	33
____		(B) Closely spaced rubber-stamped letters on frame	53	200
____		(C) Widely spaced rubber-stamped letters on frame	40	163
6119-100		DL&W Work Caboose, red cab, gray tool tray, *57–66, 69*		
____		(A) Black frame, white letters	9	27
____		(B) "Built By Lionel" builders plate, *66*	27	84
____		(C) Black frame, white letters, red-painted cab	61	244
____		(D) Santa Fe cab, gray tool box	10	35

		Good	Exc	
6119-125	Rescue Caboose, olive, black frame, *64*	85	180	___
6120	Work Caboose, yellow, unmarked, *61–62*	7	22	___
6121	Flatcar with pipes, *56–57*			
	(A) Yellow, peach, red, or gray	10	34	___
	(B) Maroon	21	67	___
6130	ATSF Work Caboose, *61, 65–69*			
	(A) Red painted, no builders plate	12	36	___
	(B) Red unpainted, builders plate	10	30	___
	(C) Red painted, builders plate	48	224	___
6139	Remote Control Uncoupling Track (O27), *63*	1	4	___
6142	Short Gondola, green, blue, or black, with 2 canisters, *63–66, 69*	5	13	___
6142-75	Short Gondola, olive drab, with 2 canisters	39	125	___
6149	Remote Control Uncoupling Track (O27), *64–69*	1	5	___
6151	Flatcar with patrol truck, *58*			
	(A) Yellow frame	34	85	___
	(B) Orange frame	27	78	___
	(C) Cream frame	34	85	___
6162	NYC Gondola with 3 white canisters, *59–68*			
	(A) Blue body	5	29	___
	(B) Red body	70	323	___
6162-60	Alaska Gondola with 3 red canisters, *59*	38	80	___
6167	LL SP-type Caboose, red, *63–64*			
	(A) Unpainted	3	9	___
	(B) Painted	52	209	___
6167	SP-type Caboose, unmarked, no end rails, *63–64*			
	(A) Red body	3	8	___
	(B) Brown body	9	23	___
6167-50	SP-type Caboose, unmarked, yellow	11	26	___
6167-85	Union Pacific SP-type Caboose, *69*	10	37	___
6167-175	SP-type Caboose, unmarked, olive	97	363	___
6175	Flatcar with rocket, *58–61*			
	(A) Black frame	25	65	___
	(B) Red frame	25	66	___
6176	Hopper, unmarked, *63–69*			
	(A) Dark yellow	13	49	___
	(B) Gray	8	14	___
	(C) Red	15	30	___
	(D) Bright yellow	23	68	___
6176	Lehigh Valley Hopper, *64–66, 69*			
	(A) Dark yellow	6	9	___
	(B) Gray	7	12	___
	(C) Black	3	8	___
	(D) Red	25	55	___
	(E) Bright yellow	25	75	___

			Good	Exc
6176-100	Olive Drab Hopper, unmarked		40	97
6219	C&O Work Caboose, *60*		23	53
6220	Santa Fe NW2 Switcher, *49–50*			
		(A) Large GM decal on cab	135	292
		(B) Small GM decal on side	115	229
6250	Seaboard NW2 Switcher, *54–55*			
		(A) Seaboard decal	117	279
		(B) Widely spaced rubber-stamped letters	137	265
		(C) Closely spaced rubber-stamped letters	184	558
6257	SP-type Caboose, *48–52*			
		(A) Dark red, matching plastic smokestack	180	578
		(B) All other variations	4	14
6257-25	SP-type Caboose, circled-L logo, *53–55*			
		(A) Red painted	5	18
		(B) Unpainted red plastic	4	12
6257-50	SP-type Caboose, *56*		4	12
6257-100	Lionel Lines SP-type Caboose, smokestack, *63–64*		9	27
6257X	SP-type Caboose, red, 2 couplers, with box, *48*		11	45
6262	Flatcar with wheel load, *56–57*			
		(A) Black frame, *56–57*	30	65
		(B) Red frame, *56*	240	653
6264	Flatcar with lumber for 264 Fork Lift Platform, *57–60*			
		(A) Bar-end trucks	28	61
		(B) Plastic trucks	30	75
		(C) Separate-sale box and envelope	101	253
6311	Flatcar with 3 pipes, *55*		22	54
6315	Gulf 1-D Chemical Tank Car, *56–59, 68–69*			
		(A) Early, painted	38	78
		(B) Late, unpainted	29	57
		(C) Late, unpainted, built date	49	138
6315	Lionel Lines 1-D Tank Car, *63–66*			
		(A) Unpainted orange body	15	23
		(B) Painted orange body	115	346
6342	NYC Gondola with culvert channel and 7 pipes, *56–58, 64–66*		16	38
6343	Barrel Ramp Car with 6 barrels, *61–62*		18	41
6346	Alcoa Quad Hopper, *56*		31	65
6352-1	PFE Ice Car from 352 Ice Depot, *55–57*			
		(A) 3 lines of data	64	178
		(B) 4 lines of data	59	115
		(C) Separate-sale box	488	1267
6356	NYC Stock Car, 2-level, *54–55*			
		(A) Heat-stamped lettering	22	42
		(B) Rubber-stamped lettering	38	87

		Good	Exc	
6357	SP-type Caboose, SP logo, *48–53*			
	(A) Tile red, tuscan, or maroon	13	41	___
	(B) Tile red, extra board on catwalk	165	592	___
6357	SP-type Caboose, no logo, *57–61*			
	(A) Number to left	10	29	___
	(B) Number to right	12	46	___
6357-25	SP-type Caboose, circle L logo, *53–56*			
	(A) Maroon or tuscan body, black metal smokestack	9	27	___
	(B) Maroon body, maroon metal smokestack	113	492	___
6357-50	ATSF SP-type Caboose, lighted, *60*	313	1241	___
6361	Timber Transport Car, *60–61, 64–69*			
	(A) White lettering	27	78	___
	(B) No lettering	75	150	___
6362	Truck Car with 3 trucks, *55–56*			
	(A) Shiny orange	22	51	___
	(B) Dull orange	51	116	___
6376	LL Circus Stock Car, *56–57*	39	70	___
6401	Flatcar, no load, gray, *60*	3	10	___
6401-25	Gray flatcar with load, *64–67*			
	(A) Jeep and cannon	117	295	___
	(B) Tank	69	150	___
	(C) Payton automobile		49	___
	(D) Logs		29	___
6402	Flatcar with orange or gray reels, *62, 64–66*	11	27	___
6402	Flatcar with blue boat, *69*	35	63	___
6402-150	Maroon Flatcar with white trailer	12	36	___
6403B	Tender		87	___
6404	Black Flatcar with auto, *60*			
	(A) Red auto	28	83	___
	(B) Yellow auto	42	134	___
	(C) Brown auto	73	233	___
	(D) Green auto	80	250	___
6405	Flatcar with piggyback van, *61*	16	50	___
6406	Flatcar with auto, *61*			
	(A) Maroon frame, red auto	24	63	___
	(B) Maroon frame, yellow auto	54	133	___
	(C) Gray frame, dark brown auto	78	225	___
	(D) Gray frame, green auto	90	245	___
	(E) Gray frame, yellow auto	49	98	___
6407	Flatcar with rocket, *63*	104	362	___
6408	Flatcar with pipes, *63*	14	43	___
6408	Flatcar with 2 orange cable reels, *67*	13	48	___
6409-25	Flatcar with pipes, *63*	14	44	___
6410-25	Flatcar with 2 automobiles, *63*			
	(A) Yellow autos	117	473	___
	(B) Brown autos	155	609	___

			Good	Exc
____ **6411**	Flatcar with logs, *48–50*		16	33
6413	Mercury Capsule Carrying Car, *62–63*			
____	(A) Medium blue frame		57	142
____	(B) Aquamarine frame		89	214
____	(C) Teal frame		81	220
6414	Evans Auto Loader with 4 cars, *55–66*			
____	(A) Premium cars (chrome bumpers, windows, rubber wheels): red, yellow, blue-green, and white		56	119
____	(B) Cheapie cars (no wheels): 2 red and 2 yellow		180	356
____	(C) Red cars with gray bumpers		69	161
____	(D) Yellow cars with gray bumpers		160	346
____	(E) Brown cars with gray bumpers		338	788
____	(F) Green cars with gray bumpers		373	878
____	(G) Metal trucks, number right of Lionel, premium cars		50	147
____ **6415**	Sunoco 3-D Tank Car, *53–55, 64–66, 69*		12	32
____ **6416**	Boat Transport Car, 4 boats, *61–63*		119	260
6417	PRR N5c Porthole Caboose, *53–57*			
____	(A) New York Zone		13	35
____	(B) Without New York Zone		118	230
____ **6417-25**	Lionel Lines N5c Porthole Caboose, *54*		15	37
6417-50	LV N5c Porthole Caboose, *54*			
____	(A) Tuscan		467	1241
____	(B) Gray		60	141
6418	Machinery Car with 2 steel girders, *55–57*			
____	(A) Black girders, "Lionel" in raised letters		80	123
____	(B) Orange girders, "Lionel" in raised letters		62	100
____	(C) Pinkish orange girders, U.S. Steel		70	112
____	(D) Black girders, U.S. Steel		68	120
____ **6419**	DL&W Work Caboose, *48–50, 52–55*		20	39
____ **6419-25**	DL&W Work Caboose, one coupler, *54–55*		16	33
6419-50	DL&W Work Caboose, short smokestack, *56–57*		17	48
____ **6419-75**	DL&W Work Caboose, one coupler, *56–57*		17	46
____ **6419-100**	N&W Work Caboose, *57–58*		47	107
6420	DL&W Work Caboose with searchlight, *48–50*			
____	(A) Heat-stamped serif lettering		40	81
____	(B) Rubber-stamped sans serif lettering		72	178
6424	Twin Auto Flatcar, *56–59*			
____	(A) Black frame, premium cars		23	60
____	(B) 6805 slots and rail stops, *58–59*		87	221
____	(C) 6805 slots, no rail stops		53	170
____	(D) AAR trucks, number on right		20	100
____ **6425**	Gulf 3-D Tank Car, *56–58*		17	37
____ **6427**	Lionel Lines N5c Porthole Caboose, *54–60*		14	35
____ **6427-60**	Virginian N5c Porthole Caboose, *58*		175	471

		Good	Exc	
6427-500	PRR N5c Porthole Caboose, sky blue, from Girls Set, *57–58**	150	343	___
6428	U.S. Mail Boxcar, *60–61, 65–66*	21	52	___
6429	DL&W Work Caboose, AAR trucks, *63*	130	265	___
6430	Flatcar with 2 trailers, *56–58*			
	(A) Gray Cooper-Jarrett trailers	31	70	___
	(B) White Cooper-Jarrett trailers	32	78	___
	(C) Green Fruehauf trailers	24	62	___
	(D) Gray Cooper-Jarrett trailers with Fruehauf stickers	35	88	___
6431	Flatcar with 2 vans and Midge tractor, *66*	70	205	___
6434	Poultry Dispatch Stock Car, *58–59*	40	76	___
6436-1	LV Open Quad Hopper, black, *55*			
	(A) Spreader brace with holes	15	29	___
	(B) No spreader brace holes	52	202	___
6436-25	LV Open Quad Hopper, maroon, *55–57*			
	(A) Spreader brace with holes	14	47	___
	(B) No spreader brace holes	65	176	___
6436-110	LV Quad Hopper, red, *63–68*			
	(A) No built date	18	42	___
	(B) Built date "New 3-55"	32	99	___
6436-500	LV Open Quad Hopper, lilac, from Girls Set, *57–58**			
	(A) Spreader brace with holes	80	320	___
	(B) No spreader brace holes	153	500	___
6437	PRR N5c Porthole Caboose, *61–68*	13	41	___
6440	Flatcar with gray vans, *61–63*	34	90	___
6440	Green Pullman Car, *48–49*	35	102	___
6441	Green Observation Car, *48–49*	31	92	___
6442	Brown Pullman Car, *49*	33	75	___
6443	Brown Observation Car, *49*	31	65	___
6445	Fort Knox Gold Reserve Boxcar with coin slot, *61–63*	53	130	___
6446	N&W Covered Quad Hopper, black or gray, *54–55*	25	56	___
6446-25	N&W Covered Quad Hopper, *55–57*			
	(A) Black, white lettering	21	67	___
	(B) Gray, black lettering	29	68	___
	(C) Gray, plastic trucks, spreader brace holes	50	200	___
6446-60	LV Covered Quad Hopper, *63*	100	297	___
6447	PRR N5c Porthole Caboose, *63*	82	334	___
6448	Exploding Target Range Boxcar, *61–64*			
	(A) Red sides, white roof and ends	20	38	___
	(B) White sides, red roof and ends	23	42	___
6452	Pennsylvania Gondola, black, *48–49*			
	(A) Numbered "6462", *48*	27	53	___
	(B) Numbered "6452", *49*	10	23	___
X6454	Baby Ruth PRR Boxcar, *48*	73	314	___
X6454	Santa Fe Boxcar, *48*	12	39	___

		Good	Exc
X6454	NYC Boxcar, *48*		
____	(A) Brown body	19	52
____	(B) Orange body	65	133
____	(C) Tan body	22	56
____ **X6454**	Erie Boxcar, *49–52*	19	44
____ **X6454**	PRR Boxcar, *49–52*	26	45
X6454	SP Boxcar, *49–52*		
____	(A) Break in herald circle between R and N, *49*	34	91
____	(B) Complete herald circle	15	42
6456	Lehigh Valley Short Hopper, *48–55*		
____	(A) Black	10	20
____	(B) Maroon	7	19
____	(C) Gray	21	38
____	(D) Enamel red, yellow lettering	60	137
____	(E) Enamel red, white lettering	240	590
____ **6457**	SP-type Caboose, *49–52*	18	27
6460	Bucyrus Erie Crane Car, black cab, 8-wheel, *52–54*	21	47
6460-25	Bucyrus Erie Crane Car, red cab, 8-wheel, *54*	38	110
____ **6461**	Transformer Car, *49–50*	33	70
____ **6462**	NYC Gondola, black, with 6 barrels, *49–54*	9	17
6462-25	NYC Gondola, green, with 6 barrels, *54–57*		
____	(A) N in second panel, 2 lines of data	12	35
____	(B) N in third panel, 3 lines of data	17	55
6462-75	NYC Gondola, red-painted, with 6 barrels, *52–55*	12	29
6462-125	NYC Gondola, red plastic, with 6 barrels, *55–57*	10	25
6462-500	NYC Gondola, pink, from Girls Set, with 4 canisters, *57–58**	75	175
____ **6463**	Rocket Fuel 2-D Tank Car, *62–63*	21	69
6464-1	WP Boxcar, *53–54*		
____	(A) Blue lettering	28	57
____	(B) Red lettering	425	1175
____ **6464-25**	GN Boxcar, *53–54*	32	91
____ **6464-50**	M&StL Boxcar, *53–56*	21	91
6464-75	RI Boxcar, green, *53–54, 69*		
____	(A) Built date, *53–54*	31	57
____	(B) No built date, *69*	38	88
6464-100	Western Pacific Boxcar, *54–55*		
____	(A) Silver body, yellow feather	37	167
____	(B) Orange body, blue feather	234	760
____ **6464-125**	NYC Pacemaker Boxcar, *54–56*	46	86
____ **6464-150**	MP Boxcar, *54–55, 57*	48	132
6464-175	Rock Island Boxcar, *54–55*		
____	(A) Blue lettering	40	130
____	(B) Black lettering	374	954

		Good	Exc	
6464-200	Pennsylvania Boxcar, *54–55, 69*	65	136	___
6464-225	SP Boxcar, *54–56*	56	122	___
6464-250	WP Boxcar, *66*	61	229	___
6464-275	State of Maine Boxcar, *55, 57–59*			
	(A) Striped doors	40	75	___
	(B) Solid doors	55	138	___
6464-300	Rutland Boxcar, *55–56*			
	(A) Rubber-stamped lettering	49	83	___
	(B) Split door with bottom painted green	270	446	___
	(C) Rubber-stamped lettering with solid shield	1575	3900	___
	(D) Heat-stamped lettering	74	153	___
	(E) Painted yellow body	300	725	___
6464-325	B&O Sentinel Boxcar, *56*	146	462	___
6464-350	MKT Boxcar, *56*	124	323	___
6464-375	Central of Georgia Boxcar, *56–57, 66*			
	(A) Unpainted maroon body	44	78	___
	(B) Painted red body	775	4085	___
6464-400	B&O Time-Saver Boxcar, *56–57, 69*			
	(A) BLT 5-54	39	87	___
	(B) BLT 2-56	72	324	___
	(C) No built date	35	125	___
6464-425	New Haven Boxcar, *56–58*	21	58	___
6464-450	Great Northern Boxcar, *56–57, 66*	71	155	___
6464-475	B&M Boxcar, *57–60, 65–66, 68*			
	(A) Medium blue-painted or unpainted plastic	33	74	___
	(B) Dark purple-painted, gray or blue mold	68	250	___
6464-500	Timken Boxcar, white side band and charcoal lettering, *57–59, 69*			
	(A) Unpainted yellow body	66	164	___
	(B) Painted yellow body	80	200	___
6464-510	NYC Pacemaker Boxcar, *57–58*	260	660	___
6464-515	MKT Boxcar, *57–58*	260	608	___
6464-525	M&StL Boxcar, *57–58, 64–66*			
	(A) Red, white lettering	28	75	___
	(B) Maroon, white lettering	115	503	___
6464-650	D&RGW Boxcar, *57–58, 66*			
	(A) Yellow body, silver roof, black stripe	54	121	___
	(B) Yellow body, silver roof, no black stripe	150	195	___
	(C) Painted yellow body and yellow roof	500	2359	___
6464-700	Santa Fe Boxcar, *61, 66*	66	180	___
6464-725	New Haven Boxcar, *62–66, 68*			
	(A) Orange body	23	52	___
	(B) Black body	63	237	___
6464-825	Alaska Boxcar, *59–60*	143	390	___
6464-900	NYC Boxcar, *60–66*	49	101	___

		Good	Exc
6465	Sunoco 2-D Tank Car, *48–56*		
____	(A) Silver tank, rubber-stamped "6465"	6	12
____	(B) Silver tank, rubber-stamped "6455"	22	77
____	(C) Silver tank, no number	7	18
____	(D) Glossy gray tank	10	50
6465-60	Gulf 2-D Tank Car, *58*		
____	(A) Black tank	23	48
____	(B) Gray tank	9	23
____ **6465-85**	LL 2-D Tank Car, black, *59*	16	52
____ **6465-110**	Cities Service 2-D Tank, *60–62*	20	80
6465-160	LL 2-D Tank Car, orange with black ends,		
____	*63–64*	10	23
____ **6466T**	Tender, *49–53*	11	25
____ **6466W**	Whistle Tender, *49–53*	22	44
____ **6466WX**	Whistle Tender, *49–53*	24	40
____ **6467**	Miscellaneous Car, *56*	23	56
6468	B&O Auto Boxcar, *53–55*		
____	(A) Tuscan	135	370
____	(B) Blue	21	41
6468-25	NH Auto Boxcar, *56–58*		
____	(A) Black N over white H, black doors	24	88
____	(B) White N over black H, black doors	94	276
	(C) Black N over white H, painted Tuscan		
____	doors	43	115
____ **6469**	Liquified Gas Tank Car, *63*	50	150
____ **6470**	Explosives Boxcar, *59–60*	15	40
____ **6472**	Refrigerator Car, *50–53*	16	29
____ **6473**	Horse Transport Car, *62–69*	13	27
____ **6475**	Libby's Crushed Pineapple Vat Car, *63 u*	33	83
____ **6475**	Pickles Vat Car, *60–62*	26	67
6476	LV Short Hopper, *57–63*		
____	(A) Red body	7	18
____	(B) Gray body	9	20
____	(C) Black body	7	20
____ **6476-75**	LV Short Hopper, black, Type VI body, *63*	7	23
____ **6476-135**	LV Short Hopper, yellow, *64–66, 68*	7	18
____ **6476-160**	LV Short Hopper, black, *69*	7	16
____ **6476-185**	LV Short Hopper, yellow, *69*	7	18
____ **6477**	Miscellaneous Car with pipes, *57–58*	24	63
____ **6480**	Explosives Boxcar, red, *61*	26	49
____ **6482**	Refrigerator Car, *57*	16	41
6500	Flatcar with Bonanza airplane, *62, 65*		
____	(A) Plane, red top and wings	333	637
____	(B) Plane, white top and wings	358	700
____ **6501**	Flatcar with jet boat, *62–63*	70	163

		Good	Exc	
6502	Flatcar with bridge girder, *62*			
	(A) Black flatcar	22	83	___
	(B) Red flatcar	33	100	___
6502-50	Flatcar, blue or teal, no lettering, with bridge girder, *62*	13	37	___
6511	Flatcar with pipes, *53–56*			
	(A) Die-cast truck plates, *53*	22	53	___
	(B) Stamped metal truck plates	19	40	___
6511-24	Set of 6 pipes with box, *55–58*	33	150	___
6512	Cherry Picker Car, *62–63*	33	95	___
6517	LL Bay Window Caboose, *55–59*			
	(A) Built date underscored	30	68	___
	(B) Built date not underscored	23	48	___
6517-75	Erie Bay Window Caboose, *66*	180	469	___
6518	Transformer Car, *56–58*	34	80	___
6519	Allis-Chalmers Flatcar, *58–61*			
	(A) Dark or medium orange base	35	70	___
	(B) Dull light orange base	36	119	___
6520	Searchlight Car, *49–51*			
	(A) Tan generator	550	1257	___
	(B) Green generator	180	287	___
	(C) Maroon generator	15	48	___
	(D) Orange generator	15	42	___
6530	Firefighting Instruction Car, *60–61*			
	(A) Red body, white lettering	34	80	___
	(B) Black body, white lettering	103	415	___
6536	M&StL Open Quad Hopper, *58–59, 63*	29	75	___
6544	Missile Firing Car, 4 missiles, *60–64*			
	(A) White-lettered console	40	162	___
	(B) Black-lettered console	109	322	___
6555	Sunoco 1-D Tank Car, *49–50*	22	52	___
6556	MKT Stock Car, *58*	102	298	___
6557	SP-type Caboose, smoke, *58–59*			
	(A) Tuscan, with number on left	88	183	___
	(B) Brown, with number on right	225	650	___
6560	Bucyrus Erie Crane Car, smokestack, *55–58, 68–69*			
	(A) Black frame, red-orange cab	55	133	___
	(B) Black frame, gray cab	35	73	___
	(C) Black frame, red cab	29	41	___
	(D) Dark blue frame, red cab	40	85	___
	(E) Black frame, red cab, rubber-stamped "6560"	65	270	___
	(F) Black frame, black cab	30	150	___
6560-25	Bucyrus Erie Crane Car, 8-wheel, *56*	39	85	___
6561	Cable Car, 2 reels, *53–56*			
	(A) Orange reels	29	58	___
	(B) Gray reels	31	67	___

			Good	Exc
6562		NYC Gondola with 4 red canisters, *56–58*		
____		(A) Gray body, *56*	21	46
____		(B) Red body, *56, 58*	13	32
____		(C) Black body, *57*	13	31
6572		REA Refrigerator Car, *58–59, 63*		
____		(A) Passenger trucks	72	268
____		(B) Bar-end trucks	41	122
____		(C) AAR trucks, *63*	33	85
____ **6630**		Missile Launching Car, *61*	27	77
____ **6636**		Alaska Open Quad Hopper, *59–60*	40	97
____ **6640**		USMC Missile Launching Car, *60*	98	220
____ **6646**		Lionel Lines Stock Car, *57*	19	43
6650		IRBM Rocket Launcher, *59–63*		
____		(A) "6650" stamped on left	23	47
____		(B) "6650" stamped on right	75	206
____ **6650-80**		Missile, *60*	3	9
____ **6651**		USMC Cannon Car, *64 u*	88	194
____ **6654W**		Whistle Tender	22	36
6656		Lionel Lines Stock Car, *49–55*		
____		(A) Brown Armour decal	28	73
____		(B) No decal	10	30
6657		Rio Grande SP-type Caboose, *57–58*		
____		(A) With ladder slots	75	185
____		(B) Without ladder slots	180	459
____ **6660**		Boom Car, *58*	33	80
____ **6670**		Derrick Car, *59–60*	15	60
____		(A) "6670" stamped on left	25	67
____		(B) "6670" stamped on right	70	258
6672		Santa Fe Refrigerator Car, *54–56*		
____		(A) Blue lettering, 2 lines of data	27	60
____		(B) Black lettering, 2 lines of data	28	65
____		(C) Blue lettering, 3 lines of data	85	220
6736		Detroit & Mackinac Open Quad Hopper, *60–62*	18	40
6800		Flatcar with airplane, *57–60*		
____		(A) Plane, black top and wings	41	97
____		(B) Plane, yellow top and wings	45	121
6801		Flatcar with boat, white hull, brown deck, *57*	35	69
6801-50		Flatcar with boat, yellow hull, white deck, *58–60*	45	87
6801-75		Flatcar with boat, blue hull, white deck, *58–60*	45	86
____ **6802**		Flatcar with 2 U.S. Steel girders, *58–59*	14	43
6803		Flatcar with USMC tank and sound truck, *58–59*	87	192
____ **6804**		Flatcar with 2 USMC trucks, *58–59*	89	185
____ **6805**		Atomic Energy Disposal Flatcar, *58–59*	36	150

		Good	Exc	
6806	Flatcar with 2 USMC trucks, *58–59*	81	195	____
6807	Flatcar with boat, *58–59*	55	125	____
6808	Flatcar with USMC tank and truck, *58–59*	94	210	____
6809	Flatcar with 2 USMC trucks, *58–59*	81	197	____
6810	Flatcar with trailer, *58*	25	50	____
6812	Track Maintenance Car, *59*			
	(A) Dark yellow superstructure	18	57	____
	(B) Black base, gray platform and crank handle	18	65	____
	(C) Gray base, black platform and crank handle	18	65	____
	(D) Cream superstructure	32	187	____
	(E) Light yellow superstructure	24	75	____
6814	Rescue Caboose, *59–61*	39	117	____
6816	Flatcar with Allis-Chalmers bulldozer, *59–60*			
	(A) Red car	204	430	____
	(B) Black car	500	1033	____
6816-100	Allis-Chalmers Bulldozer, *59–60*			
	(A) No box	87	287	____
	(B) Separate-sale box	250	850	____
6817	Flatcar with Allis-Chalmers motor scraper, *59–60*			
	(A) Red car	209	485	____
	(B) Black car	475	1160	____
6817-100	Allis-Chalmers Motor Scraper, *59–60*			
	(A) No box	128	283	____
	(B) Separate-sale box	250	700	____
6818	Flatcar with transformer, *58*	23	34	____
6819	Flatcar with helicopter, *59–60*	19	60	____
6820	Aerial Missile Transport Car with helicopter, *60–61*			
	(A) Light blue frame	107	228	____
	(B) Medium blue frame	78	192	____
6821	Flatcar with crates, *59–60*	19	29	____
6822	Searchlight Car, *61–69*			
	(A) Black base, gray light	20	32	
	(B) Gray base, black light	23	52	____
6823	Flatcar with 2 IRBM missiles, *59–60*	33	70	____
6824	USMC Work Caboose, *60*	80	225	____
6824-50	Rescue Caboose, white, *64*	35	113	____
6825	Flatcar with arch trestle bridge, *59–62*	22	36	____
6826	Flatcar with Christmas trees, *59–60*	24	80	____
6827	Flatcar with Harnischfeger power shovel, *60–63*	68	217	____
6827-100	Harnischfeger Tractor Shovel, *60*			
	(A) No box	55	105	____
	(B) Separate-sale box	113	203	____

		Good	Exc
6828	Flatcar with Harnischfeger crane, *60–63, 66*		
____	(A) Black flatcar, light yellow crane cab	67	230
____	(B) Black flatcar, dark yellow crane cab	75	244
____	(C) Red flatcar, dark yellow crane cab	288	1138
6828-100	Harnischfeger Construction Crane, *60*		
____	(A) No box	33	105
____	(B) Separate-sale box	79	202
____ **6830**	Flatcar with submarine, *60–61*	60	143
6844	Missile Carrying Car, 6 missiles, *59–60*		
____	(A) Black frame	28	82
____	(B) Red frame	348	1026

Other Track, Transformers, and Assorted Items

		Good	Exc
____ **A**	Transformer, 90 watts, *47–48*	20	48
____ **CO-1**	Track Clips, dozen, with envelope (O), *49*	5	12
____ **CO-1**	Track Clips, box of 100 (O), *49*	40	150
____ **CTC**	Lockon (O and O27), *47–69*		2
____ **CTC-14**	Lockons, dozen, with envelope	15	60
____ **ECU-1**	Electronic Control Unit, *46*	30	82
____ **KW**	Transformer, 190 watts, *50–65*	44	87
____ **LTC**	Lockon (O and O27), *50–69*	2	12
____ **LW**	Transformer, 125 watts, *55–56*	35	68
____ **OC**	Curved Track (O), *45–61*	0	1
____ **OC½**	Half Section Curved Track (O), *45–66*	0	1
____ **OCS**	Curved Insulated Track (O), *46–50*	18	33
____ **OS**	Straight Track (O), *45–61*	0	2
____ **OSS**	Straight Insulated Track, *46–50*	5	24
____ **OTC**	Lockon Track (O and O27)	2	5
____ **Q**	Transformer, 75 watts, *46*	16	36
____ **R**	Transformer, 110 watts, *46–47*	33	49
____ **RCS**	Remote Control Track (O), *45–48*	4	12
____ **RW**	Transformer, 110 watts, *48–54*	17	44
____ **RX**	Transformer, 100 watts, *47–48*	15	39
____ **S**	Transformer, 80 watts, *47*	22	41
SP	Smoke Pellets, bottle, *48–69*		
____	(A) Tall, light amber bottle	7	35
____	(B) Tall, dark amber bottle	13	65
____	(C) Short, light amber bottle	7	25
____	(D) All other bottles	4	14
____	(E) Bottle on blister pack, *65*		50
____ **SP-12**	Dealer Display Box with 12 full smoke bottles	115	343

		Good	Exc	
ST-311	Wheel puller, service station item	38	95	____
ST-325	Screwdriver Set, service station item		850	____
ST-350	Rivet Press, service station item		945	____
ST-342	Track pliers, service station item	75	188	____
SW	Transformer, 130 watts, *61–66*	43	74	____
TW	Transformer, 175 watts, *53–60*	51	81	____
TOC	Curved Track (O), *62–66, 68–69*		1	____
TOC½	Half Section Straight Track (O), *62–66*		1	____
TOS	Straight Track (O), *62–69*		1	____
UCS	Remote Control Track (O), *45–69*	8	18	____
UTC	Lockon (O, O27, Standard), *45*		1	____
V	Transformer, 150 watts, *46–47*	75	102	____
VW	Transformer, 150 watts, *48–49*	45	95	____
Z	Transformer, 250 watts, *45–47*	83	128	____
ZW	Transformer, 250 watts, *48–49*	66	124	____
ZW	Transformer, 275 watts, *50–56*	87	164	____
ZW	Transformer, 275 watts, R type, *57–66*	90	190	____

		Exc	Mint
366	Menards C&NW 4-4-2 Locomotive with tender, *09*	45	75
____ **400**	Menards C&NW Chicago Combine Car, *09*	25	40
403	Menards C&NW Lake Superior Observation Car, *09*	25	40
____ **410**	Menards C&NW Lake Michigan Coach, *09*	40	65
____ **0512**	Toy Fair Reefer, *81 u*	60	70
____ **550C**	31" Diameter Curved Track (O), *70*	1	2
____ **550S**	Straight Track (O), *70*	1	2
665E	Johnny Cash Blue Train 4-6-4 Locomotive, *71 u*		NRS
____ **1050**	New Englander Set, *80–81*	155	205
____ **1052**	Chesapeake Flyer Set, *80*	140	150
____ **1053**	James Gang Set, *80–82*	155	195
____ **1070**	Royal Limited Set, *80*	285	350
____ **1071**	Mid Atlantic Limited Set, *80*	225	230
____ **1072**	Cross Country Express Set, *80–81*	240	385
____ **1081**	Wabash Cannonball Set, *70–72*	105	120
____ **1082**	Yard Boss Set, *70*	120	165
____ **1083**	Pacemaker Set, *70*	105	120
____ **1084**	Grand Trunk Western Freight Set, *70*	120	140
____ **1085**	Santa Fe Express Diesel Freight Set, *70*	175	190
____ **1091**	Sears Special Steam Freight Set, *70 u*	150	165
____ **1092**	Sears GTW Steam Freight Set, *70 u*	150	165
____ **1100**	Happy Huff n' Puff, *74–75 u*	55	70
____ **1150**	L.A.S.E.R. Train Set, *81–82*	155	195
____ **1151**	Union Pacific Thunder Freight Set, *81–82*	150	175
____ **1153**	JCPenney Thunderball Freight Set, *81 u*	165	180
____ **1154**	Reading Yard King Set, *81–82*	170	190
____ **1155**	Cannonball Freight Set, *82*	75	85
____ **1157**	Lionel Leisure Wabash Cannonball Set, *81 u*		250
____ **1158**	Maple Leaf Limited Set, *81*	405	435
____ **1159**	Toys "R" Us Midnight Flyer Set, *81 u*	130	140
____ **1160**	Great Lakes Limited Set, *81*	280	330
____ **T-1171**	CN Locomotive Set, *71 u*	240	275
____ **T-1172**	Yardmaster Set, *71 u*		200
____ **T-1173**	Grand Trunk Western Freight Set, *71–73 u*	175	195
____ **T-1174**	Canadian National Set, *71–73 u*	265	300
____ **1182**	Yardmaster Set, *71–72*	85	105
____ **1183**	Silver Star Set, *71–72*	65	80
____ **1184**	Allegheny Set, *71*	120	150
____ **1186**	Cross Country Express Set, *71–72*	210	260
____ **1187**	Illinois Central Set (SSS), *71*	400	485
____ **1190**	Sears Special #1 Set, *71 u*	85	100
____ **1195**	JCPenney Special Set, *71 u*	150	165
____ **1198**	Unnamed Set, *71 u*		175
____ **1199**	Ford-Autolite Allegheny Set, *71 u*	183	203
____ **1200**	Gravel Gus, *75 u*	75	100
____ **1250**	New York Central Set (SSS), *72*	315	380
____ **1252**	Heavy Iron Set, *82–83*	90	130
____ **1253**	Quicksilver Express Set, *82–83*	265	340

		Exc	Mint	
1254	Black Cave Flyer Set, *82*	75	105	____
1260	Continental Limited Set, *82*	290	385	____
1261	Sears Black Cave Flyer Set, *82 u*	165	195	____
1262	Toys "R" Us Heavy Iron Set, *82 u*	150	165	____
1263	JCPenney Overland Freight Set, *82 u*	150	165	____
1264	Nibco Express Set, *82 u*	190	195	____
1265	Tappan Special Set, *82 u*	130	155	____
T-1272	Yardmaster Set, *72–73 u*	150	165	____
T-1273	Silver Star Set, *72–73 u*	90	115	____
1280	Kickapoo Valley & Northern Set, *72*	60	75	____
1284	Allegheny Set, *72*	140	165	____
1285	Santa Fe Twin Diesel Set, *72*	95	140	____
1287	Pioneer Dockside Switcher Set, *72*	95	100	____
1290	Sears Steam Freight Set, *72 u*	150	165	____
1291	Sears Steam Freight Set, *72 u*	150	165	____
1300	Gravel Gus Junior, *75 u*	70	90	____
1350	Canadian Pacific Set (SSS), *73*	460	620	____
1351	Baltimore & Ohio Set, *83–84*	205	280	____
1352	Rocky Mountain Freight Set, *83–84*	75	95	____
1353	Southern Streak Set, *83–85*	75	95	____
1354	Northern Freight Flyer Set, *83–85*	230	280	____
1355	Commando Assault Train, *83–84*	175	248	____
1359	Display Case for Set 1355, *83 u*	75	95	____
1361	Gold Coast Limited Set, *83*	390	400	____
1362	Lionel Leisure BN Express Set, *83 u*	200	300	____
1380	U.S. Steel Industrial Switcher Set, *73–75*	60	75	____
1381	Cannonball Set, *73–75*	70	75	____
1382	Yardmaster Set, *73–74*	110	135	____
1383	Santa Fe Freight Set, *73–75*	100	125	____
1384	Southern Express Set, *73–76*	75	120	____
1385	Blue Streak Freight Set, *73–74*	100	120	____
1386	Rock Island Express Set, *73–74*	120	140	____
1387	Milwaukee Road Special Set, *73*	185	285	____
1388	Golden State Arrow Set, *73–75*	215	240	____
1390	Sears 7-unit Steam Freight Set, *73 u*	170	190	____
1392	Sears 8-unit Steam Freight Set, *73 u*	150	165	____
1393	Sears 6-unit Diesel Freight Set, *73 u*	150	165	____
1395	JCPenney Set, *73 u*	150	165	____
1400	Happy Huff n' Puff Junior, *75 u*	130	140	____
1402	Chessie System Set, *84–85*	125	150	____
1403	Redwood Valley Express Set, *84–85*	170	205	____
1450	D&RGW Set (SSS), *74*	335	415	____
1451	Erie-Lackawanna Limited Set, *84*	415	465	____
1460	Grand National Set, *74*	300	330	____
1461	Black Diamond Set, *74 u, 75*	100	120	____
1463	Coca-Cola Special Set, *74 u, 75*	202	250	____
1487	Broadway Limited Set, *74–75*	160	255	____
1489	Santa Fe Double Diesel Set, *74–76*	140	165	____
1492	Sears 7-unit Steam Freight Set, *74 u*	150	165	____
1493	Sears 7-unit Steam Freight Set, *74 u*	150	165	____
1499	JCPenney Great Express Set, *74 u*	150	165	____
1501	Midland Freight Set, *85–86*	75	95	____
1502	Yard Chief Set, *85–86*	205	230	____

			Exc	Mint
____	1506	Sears Centennial Chessie System Set, *85 u*	165	195
____	1512	JCPenney Midland Freight Set, *85 u*	90	115
____	1549	Toys "R" Us Heavy Iron Set, *85–89 u*	180	215
____	1552	Burlington Northern Limited Set, *85*	500	570
____	1560	North American Express Set, *75*	275	365
____	1562	Fast Freight Flyer Set, *85 u*	120	140
____	1577	Liberty Special Set, *75 u*	213	215
____	1579	Milwaukee Road Set (SSS), *75*	325	410
____	1581	Thunderball Freight Set, *75–76*	90	100
____	1582	Yard Chief Set, *75–76*	115	155
____	1584	N&W "Spirit of America" Set, *75*	160	180
____	1585	75th Anniversary Special Set, *75–77*	203	218
____	1586	Chesapeake Flyer Set, *75–77*	160	190
____	1587	Capitol Limited Set, *75*	270	300
____	1593	Sears Set, *75 u*		100
____	1595	Sears 6-unit Diesel Freight Set, *75 u*	150	165
____	1602	Nickel Plate Special Set, *86–91*	120	125
____	1606	Sears Centennial Nickel Plate Set, *86 u*	165	195
____	1608	American Express General Set, *86 u*	205	320
____	1615	Cannonball Express Set, *86–90*	65	75
____	1632	Santa Fe Work Train (SSS), *86*	220	255
____	1652	B&O Freight Set, *86*	140	185
____	1658	Town House TV and Appliances Set, *86 u*	80	95
____	1660	Yard Boss Set, *76*	100	115
____	1661	Rock Island Line Set, *76–77*	80	100
____	1662	Black River Freight Set, *76–78*	75	95
____	1663	Amtrak Lake Shore Limited Set, *76–77*	215	265
____	1664	Illinois Central Freight Set, *76–77*	265	355
____	1665	NYC Empire State Express Set, *76*	310	435
____	1672	Northern Pacific Set (SSS), *76*	215	280
____	1685	True Value Freight Flyer Set, *86–87 u*	60	75
____	1686	Kay Bee Toys Freight Flyer Set, *86 u*	150	165
____	1687	Freight Flyer Set, *87–90*	39	47
____	1693	Toys "R" Us Rock Island Line Set, *76 u*	110	130
____	1694	Toys "R" Us Black River Freight Set, *76 u*	110	130
____	1696	Sears Steam Freight Set, *76 u*	110	130
____	1698	True Value Rock Island Line Set, *76 u*	125	145
____	1760	Trains n' Truckin' Steel Hauler Set, *77–78*	105	110
____	1761	Trains n' Truckin' Cargo King Set, *77–78*	95	165
____	1762	Wabash Cannonball Set, *77*	135	190
____	1764	Heartland Express Set, *77*	185	240
____	1765	Rocky Mountain Special Set, *77*	210	315
____	1766	B&O Budd Car Set (SSS), *77*	335	390
____	1776	Seaboard U36B Diesel, *74–76*	175	260
____	1790	Lionel Leisure Steel Hauler Set, *77 u*	150	200
____	1791	Toys "R" Us Steel Hauler Set, *77 u*	130	175
____	1792	True Value Rock Island Line Set, *77 u*	100	135
____	1793	Toys "R" Us Black River Freight Set, *77 u*	120	155
____	1796	JCPenney Cargo Master Set, *77 u*		200
____	1860	"Workin' on the Railroad" Timberline Set, *78*	65	85
	1862	"Workin' on the Railroad" Logging Empire		
____		Set, *78*	85	110
____	1864	Santa Fe Double Diesel Set, *78–79*	155	190

		Exc	Mint
1865	Chesapeake Flyer Set, *78–79*	155	180 ___
1866	Great Plains Express Set, *78–79*	195	285 ___
1867	Milwaukee Road Limited Set, *78*	230	275 ___
1868	M&StL Set (SSS), *78*	215	255 ___
1892	JCPenney Logging Empire Set, *78 u*	95	125 ___
1893	Toys "R" Us Logging Empire Set, *78 u*	175	225 ___
1960	Midnight Flyer Set, *79–81*	55	75 ___
1962	Wabash Cannonball Set, *79*	90	105 ___
1963	Black River Freight Set, *79–81*	75	85 ___
1965	Smokey Mountain Line Set, *79*	65	85 ___
1970	Southern Pacific Limited Set, *79 u*	340	365 ___
1971	Quaker City Limited Set, *79*	315	335 ___
1990	Mystery Glow Midnight Flyer Set, *79 u*	75	90 ___
1991	JCPenney Wabash Cannonball Deluxe Express Set, *79 u*	150	165 ___
1993	Toys "R" Us Midnight Flyer Set, *79 u*	110	130 ___
2110	Graduated Trestle Set, 22 pieces, *70–88*	9	13 ___
2111	Elevated Trestle Set, 10 pieces, *70–88*	8	11 ___
2113	Tunnel Portals, pair, *84–87*	11	17 ___
2115	Dwarf Signal, *84–87*	12	13 ___
2117	Block Target Signal, *84–87*	23	29 ___
2122	Extension Bridge, rock piers, *76–87*	24	34 ___
2125	Whistling Freight Shed, *71*	36	43 ___
2126	Whistling Freight Shed, *76–87*	25	26 ___
2127	Diesel Horn Shed, *76–87*	25	30 ___
2128	Operating Switchman, *83–86*	26	29 ___
2129	Illuminated Freight Station, *83–86*	30	33 ___
2133	Lighted Freight Station, *72–78, 80–84*	34	38 ___
2140	Automatic Banjo Signal, *70–84*	17	21 ___
2145	Automatic Gateman, *72–84*	31	47 ___
2151	Operating Semaphore, *78–82*	15	19 ___
2152	Automatic Crossing Gate, *70–84*	21	25 ___
2154	Automatic Highway Flasher, *70–87*	19	24 ___
2156	Illuminated Station Platform, *70–71*	26	34 ___
2162	Automatic Crossing Gate and Signal "262," *70–87, 94, 96–98, 05*	16	27 ___
2163	Block Target Signal, *70–78*	14	19 ___
2170	Street Lamps, set of 3, *70–87*	13	19 ___
2171	Gooseneck Street Lamps, set of 2, *80–81, 83–84*	15	18 ___
2175	"Sandy Andy" Gravel Loader Kit, *76–79*	34	55 ___
2180	Road Signs, 16 pieces, *77–98*		6 ___
2181	Telephone Pole Set "150," *77–98*		5 ___
2195	Floodlight Tower, *70–71*	38	50 ___
2199	Microwave Tower, *72–75*	30	39 ___
2214	Girder Bridge, *70–71, 72 u, 73–87*	5	9 ___
2256	Station Platform, *73–81*	17	18 ___
2260	Illuminated Bumper, *70–71, 72 u, 73*	23	35 ___
2280	Nonilluminated Bumpers, set of 3, *73–84*	2	4 ___
2282	Die-cast Bumpers, pair, *83 u*	17	18 ___
2283	Die-cast Illuminated Bumpers "260," *84–99*	15	16 ___
2290	Illuminated Bumpers, pair, *75 u, 76–86*	10	11 ___
2292	Station Platform, *85–87*	5	9 ___
2300	Operating Oil Drum Loader, *83–87*	80	90 ___

			Exc	Mint
____	2301	Operating Sawmill, *80–84*	60	65
____	2302	Union Pacific Manual Gantry Crane, *80–82*	24	31
____	2303	Santa Fe Manual Gantry Crane, *80–81, 83 u*	17	21
____	2305	Getty Operating Oil Derrick, *81–84*	105	115
____	2306	Operating Ice Station with 6700 Ice Car, *82–83*	90	105
____	2307	Lighted Billboard, *82–86*	12	13
____	2308	Animated Newsstand, *82–83*	105	120
____	2309	Mechanical Crossing Gate, *82–92*	4	7
____	2310	Mechanical Crossing Gate, *73–77*	2	4
____	2311	Mechanical Semaphore, *82–92*	4	7
____	2312	Mechanical Semaphore, *73–77*	2	4
____	2313	Floodlight Tower, *75–86*	22	27
____	2314	Searchlight Tower, *75–84*	22	27
____	2315	Operating Coaling Station, *83–84*	80	83
____	2316	N&W Operating Gantry Crane, *83–84*	90	125
____	2317	Operating Drawbridge, *75 u, 76–81*	100	130
____	2318	Operating Control Tower, *83–86*	40	50
____	2319	Illuminated Watchtower, *75–78, 80*	29	56
____	2320	Flagpole Kit, *83–87*	10	14
____	2321	Operating Sawmill, *84, 86–87*	115	133
____	2323	Operating Freight Station, *84–87*	43	47
____	2324	Operating Switch Tower, *84–87*	60	65
____	2390	Lionel Mirror, *82 u*	70	110
____	2494	Rotary Beacon, *72–74*	37	44
____	2709	Rico Station Kit, *81–98*		42
____	2710	Billboards, set of 5, *70–84*	4	10
____	2714	Tunnel, *75 u, 76–77*	36	43
____	2716	Short Extension Bridge, *88–98*	3	8
____	2717	Short Extension Bridge, *77–87*	2	4
____	2718	Barrel Platform Kit, *77–84*	3	5
____	2719	Watchman's Shanty Kit, *77–87*	3	5
____	2720	Lumber Shed Kit, *77–84, 87*	3	5
____	2721	Operating Log Mill Kit, *78*	2	4
____	2722	Barrel Loader Kit, *78*	2	4
____	2783	Freight Station Kit, *84*	6	10
____	2784	Freight Platform Kit, *81–90*	5	8
____	2785	Engine House Kit, *73–77*	31	39
____	2786	Freight Platform Kit, *73–77*	4	6
____	2787	Freight Station Kit, *73–77, 83*	7	10
____	2788	Coal Station Kit, *75 u, 76–77*	18	30
____	2789	Water Tower Kit, *75–77, 80*	19	24
____	2791	Cross Country Set, *70–71*	22	30
____	2792	Whistle Stop Set, *70–71*	24	34
____	2792	Layout Starter Pack, *80–84*	9	21
____	2793	Alamo Junction Set, *70–71*	22	30
____	2796	Grain Elevator Kit, *76 u, 77*	43	47
____	2797	Rico Station Kit, *76–77*	23	37
____	2900	Lockon, *70–98*		1
____	2901	Track Clips, dozen (027), *71–98*		6
____	2905	Lockon and Wire, *74–00*		3
____	2909	Smoke Fluid, *70–98*		4
____	2910	OTC Contactor, *84–86, 88*	4	7

		Exc	Mint
2911	Smoke Pellets, *70–73*	18	35 ___
2925	Lubricant, *70–71, 72 u, 73–75*		2 ___
2927	Maintenance Kit, *70, 78–98*		11 ___
2928	Oil, *71*		2 ___
2951	Track Layout Book, *70–86*	1	2 ___
2952	Train and Accessory Manual, *70–74*	1	2 ___
2953	Train and Accessory Manual, *75–86*	1	2 ___
2960	Lionel 75th Anniversary Book, *75 u, 76*	14	26 ___
2980	Magnetic Conversion Coupler, *70–71*	1	2 ___
2985	The Lionel Train Book, *86–98*		11 ___
3100	Great Northern 4-8-4 (FARR 3), *81*	335	388 ___
4044	Transformer, 45-watt, *70–71*	2	4 ___
4045	Safety Transformer, *70–71*	2	3 ___
4050	Safety Transformer, *72–79*	2	3 ___
4060	Power Master Transformer, *80–93*		13 ___
4065	DC Hobby Transformer, *81–83*	2	3 ___
4090	Power Master Transformer, *70–84*	47	65 ___
4125	Transformer, 25-watt, *72*	2	3 ___
4150	Trainmaster Transformer, *72–73, 75–77*	6	15 ___
4250	Trainmaster Transformer, *74*	5	10 ___
4651	Trainmaster Transformer, *78–79*	1	2 ___
4690	MW Transformer, *86–89*	60	80 ___
4851	DC Transformer, *85–91, 94–96*	5	10 ___
4870	DC Hobby Transformer and Throttle Controller, *77–78*	2	3 ___
5012	27" Diameter Curved Track, card of 4 (O27), *70–96*		17 ___
5013	27" Diameter Curved Track (O27), *70–78*		1 ___
5014	Half Curved Track (O27), *70–98*		1 ___
5016	36" Straight Track (O27), *87–88*	1	2 ___
5017	Straight Track, card of 4 (O27), *70–96*		4 ___
5018	Straight Track (O27), *70–78*		1 ___
5019	Half Straight Track (O27), *70–98*		1 ___
5020	90-degree Crossover (O27), *70–98*		7 ___
5021	27" Manual Switch, left hand (O27), *70–98*		15 ___
5022	27" Manual Switch, right hand (O27), *70–98*		15 ___
5023	45-degree Crossover (O27), *70–98*		6 ___
5024	35" Straight Track (O27), *88–98, 05*		3 ___
5025	Manumatic Uncoupler, *71–72*	1	2 ___
5027	27" Manual Switches, pair (O27), *74–84*	13	21 ___
5030	Track Expander Set (O27), *71–84*	18	26 ___
5031	Ford-Autolite Layout Expander Set, *71 u*	50	65 ___
5033	27" Diameter Curved Track (O27), *79–98*		1 ___
5038	Straight Track (O27), *79–98*		1 ___
5041	Insulator Pins, dozen (O27), *70–98*		1 ___
5042	Steel Pins, dozen (O27), *70–98*		1 ___
5045	54" Diameter Curved Track Ballast (O27), *87–88*	1	2 ___
5046	27" Diameter Curved Track Ballast (O27), *87–88*	1	2 ___
5047	Straight Track Ballast (O27), *87–88*	1	2 ___
5049	42" Diameter Curved Track (O27), *88–98*	1	2 ___
5090	27" Manual Switches, 3 pair (O27), *78–84*	55	70 ___
5113	54" Diameter Curved Track (O27), *79–98*	1	2 ___

		Exc	Mint
_____ 5121	27" Remote Switch, left hand (027), _70–98_	18	22
_____ 5122	27" Remote Switch, right hand (027), _70–98_	20	22
_____ 5125	27" Remote Switches, pair (027), _71–83_	20	30
_____ 5132	31" Remote Switch, right hand (0), _80–94_	29	30
_____ 5133	31" Remote Switch, left hand (0), _80–94_	22	30
_____ 5149	Remote Uncoupling Section (027), _70–98_		7
_____ 5165	72" Remote Switch, right hand (0), _87–98_	23	65
_____ 5166	72" Remote Switch, left hand (0), _87–98_	23	75
_____ 5167	42" Remote Switch, right hand (027), _88–98_	25	37
_____ 5168	42" Remote Switch, left hand (027), _88–98_	25	37
_____ 5193	27" Remote Switches, 3 pair (027), _78–83_	80	95
_____ 5500	10" Straight Track (0), _71–98_		1
_____ 5501	31" Diameter Curved Track (0), _71–98_		1
_____ 5502	Remote Uncoupling Section (0), _71–72_	7	9
_____ 5504	Half Curved Track (0), _83–98_		1
_____ 5505	Half Straight Track (0), _83–98_		1
_____ 5520	90-degree Crossover (0), _71–72_	6	9
_____ 5522	36" Straight, _87–88_		3
_____ 5523	40" Straight Track (0), _88–98_		4
_____ 5530	Remote Uncoupling Section (0), _81–98_	10	19
_____ 5540	90-degree Crossover (0), _81–98_		10
_____ 5543	Insulator Pins, dozen (0), _70–98_		1
_____ 5545	45-degree Crossover (0), _83–98_		11
_____ 5551	Steel Pins, dozen (0), _70–98_		1
_____ 5554	54" Diameter Curved Track (0), _90–98_		2
_____ 5560	72" Diameter Curved Track Ballast (0), _87–88_	1	2
_____ 5561	31" Diameter Curved Track Ballast (0), _87–88_	1	2
_____ 5562	Straight Track Ballast (0), _87–88_	1	2
_____ 5572	72" Diameter Curved Track (0), _79–98_	2	3
_____ 5600	Curved Track (Trutrack), _73–74_	1	2
_____ 5601	Curved Track, card of 4 (Trutrack), _73–74_	6	10
5602	Curved Track Ballast, card of 4 (Trutrack), _73–74_	5	9
_____ 5605	Straight Track (Trutrack), _73–74_	1	2
_____ 5606	Straight Track, card of 4 (Trutrack), _73–74_	5	9
5607	Straight Track Ballast, card of 4 (Trutrack), _73–74_	5	9
_____ 5620	Manual Switch, left hand (Trutrack), _73–74_	4	13
_____ 5625	Remote Switch, left hand (Trutrack), _73–74_	9	17
_____ 5630	Manual Switch, right hand (Trutrack), _73–74_	4	13
_____ 5635	Remote Switch, right hand (Trutrack), _73–74_	9	17
5640	Left Switch Ballast, card of 2 (Trutrack), _73–74_	5	9
5650	Right Switch Ballast, card of 2 (Trutrack), _73–74_	5	9
_____ 5655	Lockon (Trutrack), _73–74_	1	2
_____ 5660	Terminal Track with lockon (Trutrack), _74_	1	3
_____ 5700	Oppenheimer Reefer, _81_	30	38
_____ 5701	Dairymen's League Reefer, _81_	21	23
_____ 5702	National Dairy Despatch Reefer, _81_	16	21
_____ 5703	North American Despatch Reefer, _81_	22	26
_____ 5704	Budweiser Reefer, _81–82_	64	70
_____ 5705	Ball Glass Jars Reefer, _81–82_	30	35
_____ 5706	Lindsay Brothers Reefer, _81–82_	26	27

		Exc	Mint	
5707	American Refrigerator Transit Reefer, *81–82*	17	20	___
5708	Armour Reefer, *82–83*	16	21	___
5709	REA Reefer, *82–83*	22	26	___
5710	Canadian Pacific Reefer, *82–83*	22	25	___
5711	Commercial Express Reefer, *82–83*	13	15	___
5712	Lionel Lines Reefer, *82 u*	67	108	___
5713	Cotton Belt Reefer, *83–84*	19	22	___
5714	Michigan Central Reefer, *83–84*	17	24	___
5715	Santa Fe Reefer, *83–84*	19	26	___
5716	Vermont Central Reefer, *83–84*	20	23	___
5717	Santa Fe Bunk Car, *83*	22	30	___
5719	Canadian National Reefer, *84*	15	16	___
5720	Great Northern Reefer, *84*	75	90	___
5721	Soo Line Reefer, *84*	21	23	___
5722	NKP Reefer, *84*	16	18	___
5724	PRR Bunk Car, *84*	15	23	___
5726	Southern Bunk Car, *84 u*	22	27	___
5727	USMC Bunk Car, *84–85*	25	30	___
5728	Canadian Pacific Bunk Car, *86*	18	23	___
5730	Strasburg Reefer, *85–86*	20	27	___
5731	L&N Reefer, *85–86*	19	24	___
5732	Jersey Central Reefer, *85–86*		24	___
5733	Lionel Lines Bunk Car, *86 u*	18	24	___
5735	NYC Bunk Car, *85–86*	33	35	___
5739	B&O Tool Car, *86*	32	37	___
5745	Santa Fe Bunk Car (SSS), *86*	39	45	___
5760	Santa Fe Tool Car (SSS), *86*	30	35	___
5900	AC/DC Converter, *79–83*	3	5	___
6076	LV Hopper (O27), *70 u*	17	21	___
6100	Ontario Northland Covered Quad Hopper, *81–82*	30	34	___
6101	BN Covered Quad Hopper, *81–82*	17	31	___
6102	GN Covered Quad Hopper (FARR 3), *81*	26	28	___
6103	Canadian National Covered Quad Hopper, *81*	35	38	___
6104	Southern Quad Hopper with coal (FARR 4), *83*	50	60	___
6105	Reading Operating Hopper, *82*	34	39	___
6106	N&W Covered Quad Hopper, *82*	30	40	___
6107	Shell Covered Quad Hopper, *82*	22	26	___
6109	C&O Operating Hopper, *83*	29	41	___
6110	MP Covered Quad Hopper, *83–84*	17	27	___
6111	L&N Covered Quad Hopper, *83–84*	13	20	___
6113	Illinois Central Hopper (O27), *83–85*	15	25	___
6114	C&NW Covered Quad Hopper, *83*	63	80	___
6115	Southern Hopper (O27), *83–86*	15	19	___
6116	Soo Line Ore Car, *84*	21	27	___
6117	Erie Operating Hopper, *84*	29	39	___
6118	Erie Covered Quad Hopper, *84*	31	45	___
6122	Penn Central Ore Car, *84*	20	25	___
6123	PRR Covered Quad Hopper (FARR 5), *84–85*	55	105	___
6124	D&H Covered Quad Hopper, *84*	19	32	___
6126	Canadian National Ore Car, *86*	18	24	___
6127	Northern Pacific Ore Car, *86*	20	24	___
6131	Illinois Terminal Covered Quad Hopper, *85–86*	15	21	___

		Exc	Mint
6134	BN 2-bay ACF Hopper (std O), *86 u*	95	115
6135	C&NW 2-bay ACF Hopper (std O), *86 u*	65	80
6137	NKP Hopper (O27), *86–91*	13	17
6138	B&O Quad Hopper with coal, *86*	21	28
6142	Gondola, black, *70*	20	33
6150	Santa Fe Hopper (O27), *85–86, 92 u*	10	15
6177	Reading Hopper (O27), *86–90*	14	19
6200	FEC Gondola with canisters, *81–82*	13	24
6201	Union Pacific Animated Gondola, *82–83*	19	25
6202	WM Gondola with coal, *82*	34	36
6203	Black Cave Gondola (O27), *82*	2	4
6205	CP Gondola with canisters, *83*	18	26
6206	C&IM Gondola with canisters, *83–85*	18	26
6207	Southern Gondola with canisters (O27), *83–85*	6	8
6208	Chessie System Gondola with canisters, *83 u*	21	24
6209	NYC Gondola with coal (std O), *84–85*	42	46
6210	Erie-Lackawanna Gondola with canisters, *84*	21	30
6211	C&O Gondola with canisters, *84–85*		10
6214	Lionel Lines Gondola with canisters, *84 u*	38	45
6230	Erie-Lackawanna Reefer (std O), *86 u*	95	120
6231	Railgon Gondola with coal (std O), *86 u*	66	76
6232	Illinois Central Boxcar (std O), *86 u*	65	80
6233	CP Flatcar with stakes (std O), *86 u*	47	50
6234	Burlington Northern Boxcar (std O), *85*	55	75
6235	Burlington Northern Boxcar (std O), *85*	33	43
6236	Burlington Northern Boxcar (std O), *85*	33	43
6237	Burlington Northern Boxcar (std O), *85*	32	47
6238	Burlington Northern Boxcar (std O), *85*	33	43
6239	Burlington Northern Boxcar (std O), *86 u*	37	55
6251	NYC Coal Dump Car, *85*	25	42
6254	NKP Gondola with canisters, *86–91*	10	11
6258	Santa Fe Gondola with canisters (O27), *85–86, 92 u*		3
X6260	NYC Gondola with canisters, *85–86*	13	15
6272	Santa Fe Gondola with cable reels (SSS), *86*	20	25
6300	Corn Products 3-D Tank Car, *81–82*	19	25
6301	Gulf 1-D Tank Car, *81*	20	26
6302	Quaker State 3-D Tank Car, *81*	42	46
6304	GN 1-D Tank Car (FARR 3), *81*	44	55
6305	British Columbia 1-D Tank Car, *81*	55	76
6306	Southern 1-D Tank Car (FARR 4), *83*	45	50
6307	PRR 1-D Tank Car (FARR 5), *84–85*	70	75
6308	Alaska 1-D Tank Car (O27), *82–83*	27	35
6310	Shell 2-D Tank Car (O27), *83–84*	19	24
6312	C&O 2-D Tank Car (O27), *84–85*	18	26
6313	Lionel Lines 1-D Tank Car, *84 u*	43	50
6314	B&O 3-D Tank Car, *86*	31	38
6317	Gulf 2-D Tank Car (O27), *84–85*	18	22
6357	Frisco 1-D Tank Car, *83*	42	50
6401	Virginian Bay Window Caboose, *81*	37	47
6403	Amtrak Vista Dome Car (O27), *76–77*	30	31
6404	Amtrak Passenger Coach (O27), *76–77*	24	31
6405	Amtrak Passenger Coach (O27), *76–77*	24	31

		Exc	Mint
6406	Amtrak Observation Car (027), *76–77*	22	29 ____
6410	Amtrak Passenger Coach (027), *77*	28	48 ____
6411	Amtrak Passenger Coach (027), *77*	24	35 ____
6412	Amtrak Vista Dome Car (027), *77*	22	33 ____
6420	Reading Transfer Caboose, *81–82*	20	28 ____
6421	Joshua L. Cowen Bay Window Caboose, *82*	34	40 ____
6422	DM&IR Bay Window Caboose, *81*	32	38 ____
6425	Erie-Lackawanna Bay Window Caboose, *83–84*	35	43 ____
6426	Reading Transfer Caboose, *82–83*	14	24 ____
6427	BN Transfer Caboose, *83–84*	12	21 ____
6428	C&NW Transfer Caboose, *83–85*	22	25 ____
6430	Santa Fe SP-type Caboose, *83–89*	4	14 ____
6431	Southern Bay Window Caboose (FARR 4), *83*	42	55 ____
6432	Union Pacific SP-type Caboose, *81–82*	9	10 ____
6433	Canadian Pacific Bay Window Caboose, *81*	60	70 ____
6435	U.S. Marines Transfer Caboose, *83–84*	9	17 ____
6438	GN Bay Window Caboose (FARR 3), *81*	48	65 ____
6439	Reading Bay Window Caboose, *84–85*	22	30 ____
6441	Alaska Bay Window Caboose, *82–83*	45	50 ____
6446-25	N&W Covered Quad Hopper, *70 u*	203	340 ____
6449	Wendy's N5c Caboose, *81–82*	59	69 ____
6464-500	Timken Boxcar, orange, *70 u*	208	290 ____
6464-500	Timken Boxcar, yellow, *70 u*	210	350 ____
6476-135	LV Hopper "25000" (027), *70–71 u*	6	11 ____
6478	Black Cave SP-type Caboose, *82*	5	9 ____
6482	Nibco Express SP-type Caboose, *82 u*	26	34 ____
6485	Chessie System SP-type Caboose, *84–85*	6	10 ____
6486	Southern SP-type Caboose, *83–85*	5	7 ____
6490	NKP N5c Caboose, *84 u*		NRS ____
6491	Erie-Lackawanna Transfer Caboose, *85–86*	9	17 ____
6493	L&C Bay Window Caboose, *86–87*	21	36 ____
6494	Santa Fe Bobber Caboose, *85–86*	7	9 ____
6496	Santa Fe Work Caboose (SSS), *86*	21	29 ____
6504	L.A.S.E.R. Flatcar with helicopter (027), *81–82*	18	26 ____
6505	L.A.S.E.R. Radar Car, *81–82*	17	25 ____
6506	L.A.S.E.R. Security Car, *81–82*	18	26 ____
6507	L.A.S.E.R. Flatcar with cruise missile, *81–82*	21	30 ____
6508	Canadian Pacific Crane Car, *81*	50	70 ____
6509	Depressed Center Flatcar with girders, *81*	60	85 ____
6510	Union Pacific Crane Car, *82*	55	60 ____
6515	Union Pacific Flatcar (027), *83–84, 86*	5	9 ____
6521	NYC Flatcar with stakes (std 0), *84–85*	29	35 ____
6522	C&NW Searchlight Car, *83–85*	27	30 ____
6524	Erie Crane Car, *84*	55	60 ____
6526	Searchlight Car, *84–85*	23	25 ____
6529	NYC Searchlight Car, *85–86*	21	27 ____
6531	Express Mail Flatcar with trailers, *85–86*	23	32 ____
6560	Bucyrus Erie Crane Car, *71*	100	130 ____
6561	Flatcar with cruise missile (027), *83–84*	13	26 ____
6562	Flatcar with fences (027), *83–84*	13	21 ____
6564	U.S. Marines Flatcar with 2 tanks (027), *83–84*	13	21 ____

		Exc	Mint
6573	Redwood Valley Express Log Dump Car (027), 84–85	8	13
6574	Redwood Valley Express Crane Car (027), 84–85	7	13
6575	Redwood Valley Express Flatcar with fences (027), 84–85	7	13
6576	Santa Fe Crane Car (027), 85–86, 92 u	7	10
6579	NYC Crane Car, 85–86	36	44
6585	PRR Flatcar with fences (027), 86–90	5	9
6587	W&ARR Flatcar with horses, 86 u	18	26
6593	Santa Fe Crane Car (SSS), 86	41	48
6700	PFE Ice Car, 82–83		70
6900	N&W Extended Vision Caboose, 82	60	65
6901	Ontario Northland Extended Vision Caboose, 82 u	44	55
6903	Santa Fe Extended Vision Caboose, 83	80	95
6904	Union Pacific Extended Vision Caboose, 83	115	135
6905	NKP Extended Vision Caboose, 83 u	50	65
6906	Erie-Lack. Extended Vision Caboose, 84	75	90
6907	NYC Wood-sided Caboose (std O), 86 u	90	92
6908	PRR N5c Caboose (FARR 5), 84–85	43	47
6910	NYC Extended Vision Caboose, 84 u	55	60
6912	Redwood Valley Express SP-type Caboose, 84–85	9	16
6913	Burlington Northern Extended Vision Caboose, 85	70	90
6916	NYC Work Caboose, 85–86	16	22
6917	Jersey Central Extended Vision Caboose, 86	36	50
6918	B&O SP-type Caboose, 86	10	15
6919	Nickel Plate Road SP-type Caboose, 86–91	5	9
6920	B&A Wood-sided Caboose (std O), 86 u	65	80
6921	PRR SP-type Caboose, 86–90	5	9
7200	Quicksilver Passenger Coach (027), 82–83	26	34
7201	Quicksilver Passenger Coach (027), 82–83	26	34
7202	Quicksilver Observation Car (027), 82–83	26	34
7203	N&W Diner "491," 82 u	130	180
7204	Southern Pacific Diner, 82 u	190	235
7207	NYC Diner, 83 u	70	140
7208	PRR Diner, 83 u	80	90
7210	Union Pacific Diner, 84	85	110
7211	Southern Pacific Vista Dome Car, 83 u	145	185
7215	B&O Passenger Coach, 83–84	43	50
7216	B&O Passenger Coach, 83–84	43	50
7217	B&O Baggage Car, 83–84	43	50
7220	Illinois Central Baggage Car, 85, 87	105	135
7221	Illinois Central Combination Car, 85, 87	85	105
7222	Illinois Central Passenger Coach, 85, 87	85	105
7223	Illinois Central Passenger Coach, 85, 87	85	105
7224	Illinois Central Diner, 85, 87	75	90
7225	Illinois Central Observation Car, 85, 87	95	115
7227	Wabash Diner (FF 1), 86–87	115	130
7228	Wabash Baggage Car (FF 1), 86–87	90	100
7229	Wabash Combination Car (FF 1), 86–87	90	100
7230	Wabash Passenger Coach (FF 1), 86–87	90	100

		Exc	Mint
7231	Wabash Passenger Coach (FF 1), *86–87*	90	100 ____
7232	Wabash Observation Car (FF 1), *86–87*	85	95 ____
7241	W&ARR Passenger Coach, *86 u*	43	50 ____
7242	W&ARR Baggage Car, *86 u*	43	50 ____
7301	Norfolk & Western Stock Car, *82*	44	45 ____
7302	Texas & Pacific Stock Car (O27), *83–84*	11	14 ____
7303	Erie Stock Car, *84*	41	50 ____
7304	Southern Stock Car (FARR 4), *83 u*	41	45 ____
7309	Southern Stock Car (O27), *85–86*	12	16 ____
7312	W&ARR Stock Car (O27), *86 u*	25	30 ____
7401	Chessie System Stock Car (O27), *84–85*	13	17 ____
7404	Jersey Central Boxcar, *86*	26	40 ____
7500	Lionel 75th Anniversary U36B Diesel, *75–77*	124	144 ____
7501	Lionel 75th Anniversary Boxcar, *75–77*	24	34 ____
7502	Lionel 75th Anniversary Reefer, *75–77*	27	36 ____
7503	Lionel 75th Anniversary Reefer, *75–77*	29	40 ____
7504	Lionel 75th Anniversary Covered Quad Hopper, *75–77*	28	40 ____
7505	Lionel 75th Anniversary Boxcar, *75–77*	29	41 ____
7506	Lionel 75th Anniversary Boxcar, *75–77*	16	21 ____
7507	Lionel 75th Anniversary Reefer, *75–77*	27	39 ____
7508	Lionel 75th Anniversary N5c Caboose, *75–77*	24	29 ____
7509	Kentucky Fried Chicken Reefer, *81–82*	64	73 ____
7510	Red Lobster Reefer, *81–82*	55	64 ____
7511	Pizza Hut Reefer, *81–82*	55	64 ____
7512	Arthur Treacher's Reefer, *82*	55	60 ____
7513	Bonanza Reefer, *82*	54	61 ____
7514	Taco Bell Reefer, *82*	58	76 ____
7515	Denver Mint Car, *81*	64	81 ____
7517	Philadelphia Mint Car, *82*	38	39 ____
7518	Carson City Mint Car, *83*	34	43 ____
7519	Toy Fair Reefer, *82 u*	35	42 ____
7520	Nibco Express Boxcar, *82 u*	265	440 ____
7521	Toy Fair Reefer, *83 u*	50	65 ____
7522	New Orleans Mint Car, *84 u*	33	38 ____
7523	Toy Fair Reefer, *84 u*	44	49 ____
7524	Toy Fair Reefer, *85 u*	55	60 ____
7525	Toy Fair Boxcar, *86 u*	65	80 ____
7530	Dahlonega Mint Car, *86 u*	37	48 ____
7600	Frisco "Spirit of '76" N5c Caboose, *74–76*	33	39 ____
7601	Delaware Boxcar, *74–76*	16	19 ____
7602	Pennsylvania Boxcar, *74–76*	23	27 ____
7603	New Jersey Boxcar, *74–76*	23	24 ____
7604	Georgia Boxcar, *74 u, 75–76*	22	26 ____
7605	Connecticut Boxcar, *74 u, 75–76*	22	32 ____
7606	Massachusetts Boxcar, *74 u, 75–76*	25	29 ____
7607	Maryland Boxcar, *74 u, 75–76*	22	34 ____
7608	South Carolina Boxcar, *75 u, 76*	38	50 ____
7609	New Hampshire Boxcar, *75 u, 76*	38	46 ____
7610	Virginia Boxcar, *75 u, 76*	155	200 ____
7611	New York Boxcar, *75 u, 76*	50	65 ____
7612	North Carolina Boxcar, *75 u, 76*	35	60 ____
7613	Rhode Island Boxcar, *75 u, 76*	36	50 ____

			Exc	Mint
____	7700	Uncle Sam Boxcar, *75 u*	44	51
____	7701	Camel Boxcar, *76–77*	54	64
____	7702	Prince Albert Boxcar, *76–77*	59	76
____	7703	Beechnut Boxcar, *76–77*	30	48
____	7704	Toy Fair Boxcar, *76 u*	110	120
____	7705	Canadian Toy Fair Boxcar, *76 u*	130	145
____	7706	Sir Walter Raleigh Boxcar, *77–78*	52	62
____	7707	White Owl Boxcar, *77–78*	52	64
____	7708	Winston Boxcar, *77–78*	53	69
____	7709	Salem Boxcar, *78*	54	62
____	7710	Mail Pouch Boxcar, *78*	56	68
____	7711	El Producto Boxcar, *78*	52	68
____	7712	Santa Fe Boxcar (FARR 1), *79*	25	44
____	7800	Pepsi Boxcar, *76 u, 77*	69	72
____	7801	A&W Boxcar, *76 u, 77*	43	57
____	7802	Canada Dry Boxcar, *76 u, 77*	44	57
____	7803	Trains n' Truckin' Boxcar, *77 u*	20	26
____	7806	Season's Greetings Boxcar, *76 u*	70	95
____	7807	Toy Fair Boxcar, *77 u*	70	95
____	7808	Northern Pacific Stock Car, *77*	37	44
____	7809	Vernors Boxcar, *77 u, 78*	50	65
____	7810	Orange Crush Boxcar, *77 u, 78*	40	55
____	7811	Dr Pepper Boxcar, *77 u, 78*	45	61
____	7813	"Season's Greetings" Boxcar, *77 u*	65	90
____	7814	"Season's Greetings" Boxcar, *78 u*	70	95
____	7815	Toy Fair Boxcar, *78 u*	65	85
____	7816	Toy Fair Boxcar, *79 u*	65	85
____	7817	Toy Fair Boxcar, *80 u*	95	105
____	7900	D&RGW Operating Cowboy Car (027), *82–83*	22	26
____	7901	LL Cop and Hobo Car (027), *82–83*	24	27
____	7902	Santa Fe Boxcar (027), *82–85*	5	9
____	7903	Rock Island Boxcar (027), *83*	8	13
____	7904	San Diego Zoo Giraffe Car (027), *83–84*	44	55
____	7905	Black Cave Boxcar (027), *82*	6	9
____	7908	Tappan Boxcar (027), *82 u*	39	55
____	7909	L&N Boxcar (027), *83–84*	40	49
____	7910	Chessie System Boxcar (027), *84–85*	18	23
____	7912	Toys "R" Us Giraffe Car (027), *82–84 u*	70	80
____	7913	Turtleback Zoo Giraffe Car (027), *85–86*	50	60
____	7914	Toys "R" Us Giraffe Car (027), *85–89 u*	70	90
____	7920	Sears Centennial Boxcar (027), *85–86 u*	39	44
____	7925	Erie-Lackawanna Boxcar (027), *86–90*	10	18
____	7926	NKP Boxcar (027), *86–91*	8	10
____	7930	True Value Boxcar (027), *86–87 u*	34	50
____	7931	Town House TV and Appliances Boxcar (027), *86 u*	31	39
____	7932	Kay Bee Toys Boxcar (027), *86–87 u*	40	49
____	8001	NKP 2-6-4 Locomotive, *80 u*	55	65
____	8002	Union Pacific 2-8-4 Locomotive (FARR 2), *80*	310	345
____	8003	Chessie System 2-8-4 Locomotive, *80*	360	540
____	8004	Rock Island 4-4-0 Locomotive, *80–82*	190	220
____	8005	Santa Fe 4-4-0 Locomotive, *80–82*	65	75
____	8006	ACL 4-6-4 Locomotive, *80 u*	245	340

		Exc	Mint
8007	NYNH&H 2-6-4 Locomotive, *80–81*	65	75 ____
8008	Chessie System 4-4-2 Locomotive, *80*	65	75 ____
8010	Santa Fe NW2 Switcher, *70, 71 u*	55	89 ____
8020	Santa Fe Alco Diesel A Unit, *70–72, 74–76*	65	85 ____
8020	Santa Fe Alco Diesel A Unit, dummy, *70*	45	60 ____
8021	Santa Fe Alco Diesel B Unit, *71–72, 74–76*	47	70 ____
8022	Santa Fe Alco Diesel A Unit, *71 u*	80	105 ____
8025	CN Alco Diesel A Unit, *71–73 u*	85	105 ____
8025	CN Alco Diesel A Unit, dummy, *71–73 u*	45	65 ____
8030	Illinois Central GP9 Diesel, *70–72*	125	145 ____
8031	Canadian National GP7 Diesel, *71–73 u*	80	150 ____
8031	Illinois Central GP9 Diesel Dummy Unit, *70*		NRS ____
8040	Canadian National 2-4-2 Locomotive, *71 u*	43	85 ____
8040	NKP 2-4-2 Locomotive, *70–72*	26	34 ____
8041	NYC 2-4-2 Locomotive, *70*	55	65 ____
8041	PRR 2-4-2 Locomotive, *71 u*	55	65 ____
8042	GTW 2-4-2 Locomotive, *70, 71–73 u*	26	34 ____
8043	NKP 2-4-2 Locomotive, *70 u*	45	65 ____
8050	D&H U36C Diesel, *80*	105	220 ____
8051	D&H U36C Diesel Dummy Unit, *80*	95	115 ____
8054/55	Burlington F3 Diesel AA Set, *80*	360	385 ____
8056	C&NW FM Train Master Diesel, *80*	175	225 ____
8057	Burlington NW2 Switcher, *80*	100	115 ____
8059	Pennsylvania F3 Diesel B Unit, *80 u*	190	290 ____
8060	Pennsylvania F3 Diesel B Unit, *80 u*	335	420 ____
8061	Chessie System U36C Diesel, *80*	110	140 ____
8062	Burlington F3 Diesel B Unit, *80 u*	205	255 ____
8063	Seaboard SD9 Diesel, *80*	80	100 ____
8064	Florida East Coast GP9 Diesel, *80*	150	200 ____
8065	Florida East Coast GP9 Diesel Dummy Unit, *80*	95	120 ____
8066	TP&W GP20 Diesel, *80–81, 83 u*	65	80 ____
8071	Virginian SD18 Diesel, *80 u*	135	155 ____
8072	Virginian SD18 Diesel Dummy Unit, *80 u*	75	110 ____
8100	Norfolk & Western 4-8-4 "611," *81*	360	402 ____
8101	Chicago & Alton 4-6-4 Locomotive "659," *81*	275	445 ____
8102	Union Pacific 4-4-2 Locomotive, *81–82*	49	65 ____
8104	Union Pacific 4-4-0 Locomotive "3," *81 u*	180	235 ____
8111	DT&I NW2 Switcher, *71–74*	55	65 ____
8140	Southern 2-4-0 Locomotive, *71 u*	22	30 ____
8141	PRR 2-4-2 Locomotive, *71–72*	41	43 ____
8142	C&O 4-4-2 Locomotive, *71–72*		55 ____
8150	PRR GG1 Electric Locomotive "4935," *81*	330	395 ____
8151	Burlington SD28 Diesel, *81*	120	145 ____
8152	Canadian Pacific SD24 Diesel, *81*	170	180 ____
8153	Reading NW2 Switcher, *81–82*	100	155 ____
8154	Alaska NW2 Switcher, *81–82*	120	160 ____
8155	Monon U36B Diesel, *81–82*	110	135 ____
8156	Monon U36B Diesel Dummy Unit, *81–82*		65 ____
8157	Santa Fe FM Train Master, *81*	280	325 ____
8158	DM&IR GP35 Diesel, *81–82*	90	150 ____
8159	DM&IR GP35 Diesel Dummy Unit, *81–82*	55	75 ____
8160	Burger King GP20 Diesel, *81–82*	97	120 ____
8161	L.A.S.E.R. Switcher, *81–82*	23	55 ____

			Exc	Mint
___	8162	Ontario Northland SD18 Diesel, *81 u*	150	210
	8163	Ontario Northland SD18 Diesel Dummy Unit,		
___		*81 u*	95	140
___	8164	Pennsylvania F3 Diesel B Unit, *81 u*	340	370
___	8182	Nibco Express NW2 Switcher, *82 u*	90	130
___	8190	Diesel Horn Kit, *81 u*		30
___	8200	Kickapoo Dockside 0-4-0T, *72*	30	39
___	8203	PRR 2-4-2 Locomotive, *72, 74 u, 75*	26	34
___	8204	C&O 4-4-2 Locomotive, *72*	55	60
___	8206	NYC 4-6-4 Locomotive, *72–75*	140	155
___	8209	Pioneer Dockside 0-4-0T with tender, *72*	45	65
___	8209	Pioneer Dockside 0-4-0T, no tender, *73–76*	42	55
___	8210	Joshua L. Cowen 4-6-4 Locomotive, *82*	245	350
___	8212	Black Cave 0-4-0 Locomotive, *82*	30	49
___	8213	D&RGW 2-4-2 Locomotive, *82–83, 84–91 u*	65	70
___	8214	Pennsylvania 2-4-2 Locomotive, *82–83*	55	65
	8215	Nickel Plate Road 2-8-4 Locomotive "779,"		
___		*82 u*	245	285
___	8250	Santa Fe GP9 Diesel, *72, 74–75*	120	145
___	8251-50	Horn/Whistle Controller, *72–74*	1	2
___	8252	D&H Alco Diesel A Unit, *72*	85	125
___	8253	D&H Alco Diesel B Unit, *72*	50	70
___	8254	Illinois Central GP9 Diesel Dummy Unit, *72*	60	65
___	8255	Santa Fe GP9 Diesel Dummy Unit, *72*	60	65
	8258	Canadian National GP7 Diesel Dummy Unit,		
___		*72–73 u*	65	85
___	8260/62	Southern Pacific F3 Diesel AA Set, *82*	490	520
___	8261	Southern Pacific F3 Diesel B Unit, *82 u*	435	445
___	8263	Santa Fe GP7 Diesel, *82*	65	80
___	8264	CP Vulcan Switcher Snowplow, *82*	80	100
___	8265	Santa Fe SD40 Diesel, *82*	205	225
___	8266	Norfolk & Western SD24 Diesel, *82*	150	225
___	8268	Quicksilver Alco Diesel A Unit, *82–83*	85	105
___	8269	Quicksilver Alco Diesel A Unit, dummy, *82–83*	55	65
___	8272	Pennsylvania EP-5 Electric Locomotive, *82 u*	205	265
___	8300	Santa Fe 2-4-0 Locomotive, *73–74*	22	25
___	8302	Southern 2-4-0 Locomotive, *73–76*	29	30
___	8303	Jersey Central 2-4-2 Locomotive, *73–74*	55	59
___	8304	B&O 4-4-2 Locomotive, *75*	75	105
___	8304	C&O 4-4-2 Locomotive, *75–77*	75	105
___	8304	Pennsylvania 4-4-2 Locomotive, *74–75*	75	105
___	8304	Rock Island 4-4-2 Locomotive, *73–75*	85	105
___	8305	Milwaukee Road 4-4-2 Locomotive, *73*	95	120
___	8307	Southern Pacific 4-8-4 Locomotive "4449," *83*	490	560
___	8308	Jersey Central 2-4-2 Locomotive, *73–74 u*	36	43
	8309	Southern 2-8-2 Locomotive "4501"		
___		(FARR 4), *83*	385	495
___	8310	Jersey Central 2-4-0 Locomotive, *74–75 u*	26	50
___	8310	Nickel Plate Road 2-4-0 Locomotive, *73 u*	26	50
___	8310	Santa Fe 2-4-0 Locomotive, *74–75 u*	26	34
___	8311	Southern 0-4-0 Locomotive, *73 u*	26	34
___	8313	Santa Fe 0-4-0 Locomotive, *83–84*	13	17
___	8314	Southern 2-4-0 Locomotive, *83–85*	17	21
___	8315	B&O 4-4-0 Locomotive, *83–84*	85	120

		Exc	Mint	
8341	ACL SP-type Caboose, *86 u, 87–90*	6	8	___
8350	U.S. Steel Switcher, *73–75*	18	26	___
8351	Santa Fe Alco Diesel A Unit, *73–75*	60	65	___
8352	Santa Fe GP20 Diesel, *73–75*	65	105	___
8353	Grand Trunk Western GP7 Diesel, *73–75*	90	120	___
8354	Erie NW2 Switcher, *73, 75*	80	105	___
8355	Santa Fe GP20 Diesel Dummy Unit, *73–74*	65	90	___
8356	Grand Trunk Western GP7 Diesel Dummy Unit, *73–75*	65	75	___
8357	PRR GP9 Diesel, *73–75*	100	120	___
8358	PRR GP9 Diesel Dummy Unit, *73–75*	55	100	___
8359	Chessie System GP7 Diesel "GM50," *73*	95	120	___
8360	Long Island GP20 Diesel, *73–74*	70	105	___
8361	Western Pacific Alco Diesel A Unit, *73–75*	50	70	___
8362	Western Pacific Alco Diesel B Unit, *73–75*	45	65	___
8363	B&O F3 Diesel A Unit, *73–75*	280	310	___
8364	B&O F3 Diesel A Unit, dummy, *73–75*	120	160	___
8365/66	CP F3 Diesel AA Set (SSS), *73*	355	405	___
8367	Long Island GP20 Diesel Dummy Unit, *73–75*	80	100	___
8368	Alaska Vulcan Switcher, *83*	120	129	___
8369	Erie-Lackawanna GP20 Diesel, *83–85*	125	140	___
8370/72	NYC F3 Diesel AA Set, *83*	330	435	___
8371	NYC F3 Diesel B Unit, *83*	105	150	___
8374	Burlington Northern NW2 Switcher, *83–85*	105	110	___
8375	C&NW GP7 Diesel, *83–85*	135	165	___
8376	Union Pacific SD40 Diesel, *83*	175	200	___
8377	U.S. Marines Switcher, *83–84*	55	65	___
8378	Wabash FM Train Master Diesel "550," *83 u*	500	690	___
8379	PRR Fire Car, *83 u*	80	100	___
8380	Lionel Lines SD28 Diesel, *83 u*	235	315	___
8402	Reading 4-4-2 Locomotive, *84–85*	47	55	___
8403	Chessie System 4-4-2 Locomotive, *84–85*	55	65	___
8404	PRR 6-8-6 "6200" (FARR 5), *84–85*	360	460	___
8406	NYC 4-6-4 Locomotive "783," *84*	445	571	___
8410	Redwood Valley Express 4-4-0 Locomotive, *84–85*	34	50	___
8452	Erie Alco Diesel A Unit, *74–75*	75	95	___
8453	Erie Alco Diesel B Unit, *74–75*	55	75	___
8454	D&RGW GP7 Diesel, *74–75*	80	110	___
8455	D&RGW GP7 Diesel Dummy Unit, *74–75*	50	85	___
8458	Erie-Lackawanna SD40 Diesel, *84*	160	190	___
8459	D&RGW Vulcan Rotary Snowplow, *84*	125	146	___
8460	MKT NW2 Switcher, *74–75*	45	65	___
8463	Chessie System GP20 Diesel, *74 u*	130	190	___
8464/65	D&RGW F3 Diesel AA Set (SSS), *74*	220	325	___
8466	Amtrak F3 Diesel A Unit, *74–76*	225	250	___
8467	Amtrak F3 Diesel A Unit, dummy, *74–76*	80	90	___
8468	B&O F3 Diesel B Unit, *74–75*	95	100	___
8469	CP F3 Diesel B Unit (SSS), *74*	85	110	___
8470	Chessie System U36B Diesel, *74*	80	110	___
8471	Pennsylvania NW2 Switcher, *74–76*	170	195	___
8473	Coca-Cola NW2 Switcher, *74 u, 75*	109	128	___
8474	D&RGW F3 Diesel B Unit (SSS), *74*	95	110	___

			Exc	Mint
8475	Amtrak F3 Diesel B Unit, *74*		85	105
8477	NYC GP9 Diesel, *84 u*		150	205
8480/82	Union Pacific F3 Diesel AA Set, *84*		280	365
8481	Union Pacific F3 Diesel B Unit, *84*		150	155
8485	USMC NW2 Switcher, *84–85*		105	135
8500	Pennsylvania 2-4-0 Locomotive, *75–76*		17	21
8502	Santa Fe 2-4-0 Locomotive, *75*		17	21
8506	PRR 0-4-0 Locomotive, *75–77*		75	90
8507	Santa Fe 2-4-0 Locomotive, *75 u*		25	30
8512	Santa Fe 0-4-0T Locomotive, *85–86*		22	30
8516	NYC 0-4-0 Locomotive, *85–86*		115	140
8550	Jersey Central GP9 Diesel, *75–76*		120	155
8551	Pennsylvania EP-5 Electric Locomotive, *75–76*		115	120
8552/53/54	SP Alco Diesel ABA Set, *75–76*		200	245
8555/57	Milwaukee Road F3 Diesel AA Set (SSS), *75*		240	315
8556	Chessie System NW2 Switcher, *75–76*		160	200
8558	Milwaukee Road EP-5 Electric Locomotive, *76–77*		160	195
8559	N&W GP9 Diesel "1776," *75*		115	145
8560	Chessie System U36B Diesel Dummy Unit, *75*		85	130
8561	Jersey Central GP9 Diesel Dummy Unit, *75–76*		70	95
8562	Missouri Pacific GP20 Diesel, *75–76*		130	145
8563	Rock Island Alco Diesel A Unit, *75–76 u*		65	90
8564	Union Pacific U36B Diesel, *75*		110	155
8565	Missouri Pacific GP20 Diesel Dummy Unit, *75–76*		55	70
8566	Southern F3 Diesel A Unit, *75–77*		220	370
8567	Southern F3 Diesel A Unit, dummy, *75–77*		105	135
8568	Preamble Express F3 Diesel A Unit, *75 u*		90	115
8569	Soo Line NW2 Switcher, *75–77*		60	65
8570	Liberty Special Alco Diesel A Unit, *75 u*		75	90
8571	Frisco U36B Diesel, *75–76*		75	95
8572	Frisco U36B Diesel Dummy Unit, *75–76*			55
8573	Union Pacific U36B Diesel Dummy Unit, *75 u*		145	190
8575	Milwaukee Road F3 Diesel B Unit (SSS), *75*		105	160
8576	Penn Central GP7 Diesel, *75 u, 76–77*		90	120
8578	NYC Ballast Tamper, *85, 87*		85	90
8580/82	Illinois Central F3 Diesel AA Set, *85, 87*		420	485
8581	Illinois Central F3 Diesel B Unit, *85, 87*		130	155
8585	Burlington Northern SD40 Diesel, *85*		355	385
8587	Wabash GP9 Diesel "484," *85 u*		250	280
8600	NYC 4-6-4 Locomotive, *76*		175	195
8601	Rock Island 0-4-0 Locomotive, *76–77*		17	21
8602	D&RGW 2-4-0 Locomotive, *76–78*		22	26
8603	C&O 4-6-4 Locomotive, *76–77*		135	190
8604	Jersey Central 2-4-2 Locomotive, *76 u*		39	44
8606	B&A 4-6-4 Locomotive "784," *86 u*		720	760
8610	Wabash 4-6-2 "672" (FF 1), *86–87*		435	610
8615	L&N 2-8-4 Locomotive "1970," *86 u*		540	630
8616	Santa Fe 4-4-2 Locomotive, *86*		60	65
8617	Nickel Plate Road 4-4-2 Locomotive, *86–91*		60	65
8625	Pennsylvania 2-4-0 Locomotive, *86–90*		21	34
8630	W&ARR 4-4-0 Locomotive "3," *86 u*		125	150

		Exc	Mint	
8635	Santa Fe 0-4-0 (SSS), *86*	80	100	___
8650	Burlington Northern U36B Diesel, *76–77*	120	170	___
8651	Burlington Northern U36B Diesel Dummy Unit, *76–77*	70	90	___
8652	Santa Fe F3 Diesel A Unit, *76–77*	260	510	___
8653	Santa Fe F3 Diesel A Unit, dummy, *76–77*	135	160	___
8654	Boston & Maine GP9 Diesel, *76–77*	155	195	___
8655	Boston & Maine GP9 Diesel Dummy Unit, *76–77*	90	110	___
8656	Canadian National Alco Diesel A Unit, *76*	150	195	___
8657	Canadian National Alco Diesel B Unit, *76*	60	75	___
8658	CN Alco Diesel A Unit, dummy, *76*	85	170	___
8659	Virginian Electric Locomotive, *76–77*	125	137	___
8660	CP Rail NW2 Switcher, *76–77*	100	135	___
8661	Southern F3 Diesel B Unit, *76*	165	170	___
8662	B&O GP7 Diesel, *86*	120	130	___
8664	Amtrak Alco Diesel A Unit, *76–77*	85	120	___
8665	BAR Jeremiah O'Brien GP9 Diesel "1776," *76 u*	100	170	___
8666	Northern Pacific GP9 Diesel (SSS), *76*	125	175	___
8667	Amtrak Alco Diesel B Unit, *76–77*	60	80	___
8668	Northern Pacific GP9 Diesel Dummy Unit (SSS), *76*	100	130	___
8669	Illinois Central Gulf U36B Diesel, *76–77*	125	165	___
8670	Chessie System Switcher, *76*	30	55	___
8679	Northern Pacific GP20 Diesel, *86*	90	105	___
8687	Jersey Central FM Train Master Diesel, *86*	198	276	___
8690	Lionel Lines Trolley, *86*	105	115	___
8701	W&ARR 4-4-0 Locomotive "3," *77–79*	175	238	___
8702	Southern 4-6-4 Locomotive, *77–78*	280	398	___
8703	Wabash 2-4-2 Locomotive, *77*	22	30	___
8750	Rock Island GP7 Diesel, *77–78*	110	125	___
8751	Rock Island GP7 Diesel Dummy Unit, *77–78*	50	70	___
8753	Pennsylvania GG1 Electric Locomotive, *77 u*	290	315	___
8754	New Haven Electric Locomotive, *77–78*	100	115	___
8755	Santa Fe U36B Diesel, *77–78*	130	150	___
8756	Santa Fe U36B Diesel Dummy Unit, *77–78*	75	95	___
8757	Conrail GP9 Diesel, *76 u, 77–78*	110	140	___
8758	Southern GP7 Diesel Dummy Unit, *77 u, 78*	75	95	___
8759	Erie-Lackawanna GP9 Diesel, *77–79*	115	175	___
8760	Erie-Lackawanna GP9 Diesel Dummy Unit, *77–79*	95	115	___
8761	GTW NW2 Switcher, *77–78*	95	130	___
8762	Great Northern EP-5 Electric Locomotive, *77–78*	130	140	___
8763	Norfolk & Western GP9 Diesel, *76 u, 77–78*	110	120	___
8764	B&O Budd RDC Passenger (SSS), *77*	110	135	___
8765	B&O Budd RDC Baggage Dummy Unit (SSS), *77*	80	100	___
8766	B&O Budd RDC Baggage (SSS), *77*		310	___
8767	B&O Budd RDC Passenger Dummy Unit (SSS), *77*	85	105	___
8768	B&O Budd RDC Passenger Dummy Unit (SSS), *77*	85	105	___
8769	Republic Steel Switcher, *77–78*	22	39	___

		Exc	Mint
8770	NW2 Switcher, 77–78		65
8771	Great Northern U36B Diesel, 77	110	140
8772	GM&O GP20 Diesel, 77	85	95
8773	Mickey Mouse U36B Diesel, 77–78	485	640
8774	Southern GP7 Diesel, 77 u, 78	110	135
8775	Lehigh Valley GP9 Diesel, 77 u, 78	85	105
8776	C&NW GP20 Diesel, 77 u, 78	87	129
8777	Santa Fe F3 Diesel B Unit (SSS), 77	160	175
8778	Lehigh Valley GP9 Diesel Dummy Unit, 77 u, 78	90	110
8779	C&NW GP20 Diesel Dummy Unit, 77 u, 78	73	109
8800	Lionel Lines 4-4-2 Locomotive, 78–81	75	105
8801	Blue Comet 4-6-4 Locomotive, 78–80	380	500
8803	Santa Fe 0-4-0 Locomotive, 78	14	24
8850	Penn Central GG1 Electric Locomotive, 78 u, 79	250	305
8851/52	New Haven F3 Diesel AA Set, 78 u, 79	320	430
8854	CP Rail GP9 Diesel, 78–79	100	120
8855	Milwaukee Road SD18 Diesel, 78		115
8857	Northern Pacific U36B Diesel, 78–80	140	180
8858	Northern Pacific U36B Diesel Dummy Unit, 78–80	55	85
8859	Conrail Electric Locomotive, 78–82	105	150
8860	Rock Island NW2 Switcher, 78–79	85	100
8861	Santa Fe Alco Diesel A Unit, 78–79	65	85
8862	Santa Fe Alco Diesel B Unit, 78–79	36	43
8864	New Haven F3 Diesel B Unit, 78	85	105
8866	M&StL GP9 Diesel (SSS), 78	85	120
8867	M&StL GP9 Diesel Dummy Unit (SSS), 78	65	95
8868	Amtrak Budd RDC Baggage, 78, 80	195	235
8869	Amtrak Budd RDC Passenger Dummy Unit, 78, 80	75	95
8870	Amtrak Budd RDC Passenger Dummy Unit, 78, 80	85	115
8871	Amtrak Budd RDC Baggage Dummy Unit, 78, 80	85	105
8872	Santa Fe SD18 Diesel, 78 u	125	155
8873	Santa Fe SD18 Diesel Dummy Unit, 78 u	60	85
8900	Santa Fe 4-6-4 Locomotive (FARR 1), 79	270	310
8902	ACL 2-4-0 Locomotive, 79–82, 86 u, 87–90	13	17
8903	D&RGW 2-4-2 Locomotive, 79–81	17	21
8904	Wabash 2-4-2 Locomotive, 79, 81 u	30	34
8905	Smokey Mountain Dockside 0-4-0T Locomotive, 79	9	17
8950	Virginian FM Train Master Diesel, 79	230	285
8951	Southern Pacific FM Train Master Diesel, 79	237	335
8952/53	PRR F3 Diesel AA Set, 79	350	500
8955	Southern U36B Diesel, 79	120	195
8956	Southern U36B Diesel Dummy Unit, 79	80	125
8957	Burlington Northern GP20 Diesel, 79	120	150
8958	Burlington Northern GP20 Diesel Dummy Unit, 79	85	90
8960	Southern Pacific U36C Diesel, 79 u	130	180
8961	Southern Pacific U36C Diesel Dummy Unit, 79 u	70	80

		Exc	Mint
8962	Reading U36B Diesel, *79*	115	130 ____
8970/71	PRR F3 Diesel AA Set, *79 u, 80*	330	425 ____
9001	Conrail Boxcar (027), *86–87 u, 88–90*	5	10 ____
9010	GN Hopper (027), *70–71*	6	8 ____
9011	GN Hopper (027), *70 u, 75–76, 78–83*	8	10 ____
9012	TA&G Hopper (027), *71–72*	7	8 ____
9013	Canadian National Hopper (027), *72–76*	5	8 ____
9015	Reading Hopper (027), *73–75*	17	21 ____
9016	Chessie System Hopper (027), *75–79, 87–88, 89 u*	4	6 ____
9017	Wabash Gondola with canisters (027), *78–82*	3	5 ____
9018	DT&I Hopper (027), *78–79, 81–82*	6	7 ____
9019	Flatcar (027), *78*	2	3 ____
9020	Union Pacific Flatcar (027), *70–78*	3	5 ____
9021	Santa Fe Work Caboose, *70–71, 73–75*	9	13 ____
9022	Santa Fe Bulkhead Flatcar (027), *70–72, 75–79*	7	13 ____
9023	MKT Bulkhead Flatcar (027), *73–74*	7	10 ____
9024	C&O Flatcar (027), *73–75*	3	6 ____
9025	DT&I Work Caboose, *71–74, 77–78*	8	10 ____
9026	Republic Steel Flatcar (027), *75–82*	5	7 ____
9027	Soo Line Work Caboose, *75–76*	7	9 ____
9030	Kickapoo Gondola (027), *72, 79*	5	9 ____
9031	NKP Gondola with canisters (027), *73–75, 82–83, 84–91 u*	4	7 ____
9032	SP Gondola with canisters (027), *75–78*		3 ____
9033	PC Gondola with canisters (027), *76–78, 82, 86 u, 87–90, 92 u*		3 ____
9034	Lionel Leisure Hopper (027), *77 u*	30	34 ____
9035	Conrail Boxcar (027), *78–82*	5	9 ____
9036	Mobilgas 1-D Tank Car (027), *78–82*	7	19 ____
9037	Conrail Boxcar (027), *78 u, 80*	7	10 ____
9038	Chessie System Hopper (027), *78 u, 80*	15	19 ____
9039	Mobilgas 1-D Tank Car (027), *78 u, 80*	10	15 ____
9040	General Mills Wheaties Boxcar (027), *70–72*	9	13 ____
9041	Hershey's Boxcar (027), *70–71, 73–76*	16	25 ____
9042	Ford-Autolite Boxcar (027), *71 u, 72 74–76*	13	21 ____
9043	Erie-Lackawanna Boxcar (027), *73–75*	13	20 ____
9044	D&RGW Boxcar (027), *75–76*	5	8
9045	Toys "R" Us Boxcar (027), *75 u*	35	42 ____
9046	True Value Boxcar (027), *76 u*	26	34 ____
9047	Toys "R" Us Boxcar (027), *76 u*	40	43 ____
9048	Toys "R" Us Boxcar (027), *76 u*	33	41 ____
9049	Toys "R" Us Boxcar (027), *78 u*		NRS ____
9050	Sunoco 1-D Tank Car (027), *70–71*	17	23 ____
9051	Firestone 1-D Tank Car (027), *74–75, 78*	15	19 ____
9052	Toys "R" Us Boxcar (027), *77 u*	26	34 ____
9053	True Value Boxcar (027), *77 u*	28	40 ____
9054	JCPenney Boxcar (027), *77 u*	14	19 ____
9055	Republic Steel Gondola with canisters, *78 u*	9	10 ____
9057	CP Rail SP-type Caboose, *78–79*	10	15 ____
9058	Lionel Lines SP-type Caboose, *78–79, 83*	5	7 ____
9059	Lionel Lines SP-type Caboose, *79 u, 81 u*	7	9 ____
9060	Nickel Plate Road SP-type Caboose, *70–72*	5	7 ____

			Exc	Mint
____	**9061**	Santa Fe SP-type Caboose, *70–76*	5	8
____	**9062**	Penn Central SP-type Caboose, *70–72, 74–76*	5	9
____	**9063**	GTW SP-type Caboose, *70, 71–73 u*	15	19
____	**9064**	C&O SP-type Caboose, *71–72, 75–77*	7	10
____	**9065**	Canadian National SP-type Caboose, *71–73 u*	19	24
____	**9066**	Southern SP-type Caboose, *73–76*	7	9
____	**9067**	Kickapoo Valley Bobber Caboose, *72*	6	9
____	**9068**	Reading Bobber Caboose, *73–76*	5	7
____	**9069**	Jersey Central SP-type Caboose, *73–74, 75–76 u*	5	8
____	**9070**	Rock Island SP-type Caboose, *73–74*	13	17
____	**9071**	Santa Fe Bobber Caboose, *74 u, 77–78*	7	9
____	**9073**	Coca-Cola SP-type Caboose, *74 u, 75*	20	26
____	**9075**	Rock Island SP-type Caboose, *75–76 u*	13	17
____	**9076**	"We The People" SP-type Caboose, *75 u*	19	28
____	**9077**	D&RGW SP-type Caboose, *76–83, 84–91 u*	7	8
____	**9078**	Rock Island Bobber Caboose, *76–77*	5	7
____	**9079**	GTW Hopper (O27), *77*	28	32
____	**9080**	Wabash SP-type Caboose, *77*	9	10
____	**9085**	Santa Fe Work Caboose, *79–82*	4	5
____	**9090**	General Mills Mini-Max Car, *71*	27	32
____	**9106**	Miller Vat Car, *84–85*	31	49
____	**9107**	Dr Pepper Vat Car, *86–87*	30	36
____	**9110**	B&O Quad Hopper, *71*	25	30
____	**9111**	N&W Quad Hopper, *72–75*	15	20
____	**9112**	D&RGW Covered Quad Hopper, *73–75*	20	23
____	**9113**	Norfolk & Western Quad Hopper (SSS), *73*	27	32
____	**9114**	Morton Salt Covered Quad Hopper, *74–76*	20	27
____	**9115**	Planter's Covered Quad Hopper, *74–76*	21	33
____	**9116**	Domino Sugar Covered Quad Hopper, *74–76*	22	29
____	**9117**	Alaska Covered Quad Hopper (SSS), *74–76*	29	33
____	**9119**	Detroit & Mackinac Covered Hopper, *75 u*		20
____	**9120**	Northern Pacific Flatcar with trailers, *70–71*	33	38
____	**9121**	L&N Flatcar with bulldozer and scraper, *71–79*	47	50
____	**9122**	Northern Pacific Flatcar with trailers, *72–75*	19	32
____	**9123**	C&O Auto Carrier, 3-tier, *72 u, 73–74*	18	27
____	**9124**	P&LE Flatcar with logs, *73–74*	18	25
____	**9125**	Norfolk & Western Auto Carrier, 2-tier, *73–77*	23	28
____	**9126**	C&O Auto Carrier, 3-tier, *73–75*	23	34
____	**9128**	Heinz Vat Car, *74–76*	23	30
____	**9129**	N&W Auto Carrier, 3-tier, *75–76*	17	19
____	**9130**	B&O Quad Hopper, *70*	23	24
____	**9131**	D&RGW Gondola with canisters, *73–77*	5	8
____	**9132**	Libby's Vat Car (SSS), *75–77*	16	23
____	**9133**	BN Flatcar with trailers, *76–77, 80*	20	28
____	**9134**	Virginian Covered Quad Hopper, *76–77*		32
____	**9135**	N&W Covered Quad Hopper, *70 u, 71, 75*	19	27
____	**9136**	Republic Steel Gondola with canisters, *72–76, 79*	8	11
____	**9138**	Sunoco 3-D Tank Car (SSS), *78*	33	37
____	**9139**	PC Auto Carrier, 3-tier, *76–77*	21	29
____	**9140**	Burlington Gondola with canisters, *70, 73–82, 87–89*	7	9

		Exc	Mint
9141	BN Gondola with canisters, *70–72*	8	10 ____
9143	CN Gondola with canisters, *71–73 u*	30	34 ____
9144	D&RGW Gondola with canisters (SSS), *74–76*	9	13 ____
9145	ICG Auto Carrier, 3-tier, *77–80*	21	29 ____
9146	Mogen David Vat Car, *77–81*	21	26 ____
9147	Texaco 1-D Tank Car, *77–78*	39	55 ____
9148	Du Pont 3-D Tank Car, *77–81*	25	28 ____
9149	CP Rail Flatcar with trailers, *77–78*	22	35 ____
9150	Gulf 1-D Tank Car, *70 u, 71*	22	28 ____
9151	Shell 1-D Tank Car, *72*	27	31 ____
9152	Shell 1-D Tank Car, *73–76*	25	34 ____
9153	Chevron 1-D Tank Car, *74–76*	25	30 ____
9154	Borden 1-D Tank Car, *75–76*	33	47 ____
9156	Mobilgas 1-D Tank Car, *76–77*	30	40 ____
9157	C&O Crane Car, *76–78, 81–82*	35	44 ____
9158	PC Flatcar with shovel, *76–77, 80*	40	55 ____
9159	Sunoco 1-D Tank Car, *76*	35	50 ____
9160	Illinois Central N5c Caboose, *70–72*	17	23 ____
9161	CN N5c Caboose, *72–74*	14	25 ____
9162	PRR N5c Caboose, *72–76*	25	30 ____
9163	Santa Fe N5c Caboose, *73–76*	17	24 ____
9165	Canadian Pacific N5c Caboose (SSS), *73*	21	30 ____
9166	D&RGW SP-type Caboose (SSS), *74–75*	20	25 ____
9167	Chessie System N5c Caboose, *74–76*	24	31 ____
9168	Union Pacific N5c Caboose, *75–77*	17	19 ____
9169	Milwaukee Road SP-type Caboose (SSS), *75*	16	19 ____
9170	N&W N5c Caboose "1776," *75*	27	30 ____
9171	MP SP-type Caboose, *75 u, 76–77*	19	20 ____
9172	Penn Central SP-type Caboose, *75 u, 76–77*	23	31 ____
9173	Jersey Central SP-type Caboose, *75 u, 76–77*	22	33 ____
9174	NYC (P&E) Bay Window Caboose, *76*	65	70 ____
9175	Virginian N5c Caboose, *76–77*	24	26 ____
9176	BAR N5c Caboose, *76 u*	18	30 ____
9177	Northern Pacific Bay Window Caboose (SSS), *76*	25	35 ____
9178	ICG SP-type Caboose, *76–77*	19	24 ____
9179	Chessie System Bobber Caboose, *76*	7	11 ____
9180	Rock Island N5c Caboose, *77–78*	12	23 ____
9181	B&M N5c Caboose, *76 u, 77*	39	49 ____
9182	N&W N5c Caboose, *76 u, 77–80*	20	26 ____
9183	Mickey Mouse N5c Caboose, *77–78*	32	50 ____
9184	Erie Bay Window Caboose, *77–78*	24	30 ____
9185	GTW N5c Caboose, *77*	21	28 ____
9186	Conrail N5c Caboose, *76 u, 77–78*	27	29 ____
9187	Gulf, Mobile & Ohio SP-type Caboose, *77*	10	16 ____
9188	GN Bay Window Caboose, *77*	22	27 ____
9189	Gulf 1-D Tank Car, *77*	40	60 ____
9193	Budweiser Vat Car, *83–84*	85	111 ____
9200	Illinois Central Boxcar, *70–71*	19	25 ____
9201	Penn Central Boxcar, *70*	17	25 ____
9202	Santa Fe Boxcar, *70*	20	24 ____
9203	Union Pacific Boxcar, *70*		21 ____
9204	Northern Pacific Boxcar, *70*		21 ____

			Exc	Mint
____	9205	Norfolk & Western Boxcar, *70*	22	25
____	9206	Great Northern Boxcar, *70–71*		20
____	9207	Soo Line Boxcar, *71*	11	18
____	9208	CP Rail Boxcar, *71*	21	23
____	9209	Burlington Northern Boxcar, *71–72*	16	21
____	9210	B&O DD Boxcar, *71*	16	20
____	9211	Penn Central Boxcar, *71*	17	28
____	9213	M&StL Covered Quad Hopper (SSS), *78*	20	29
____	9214	Northern Pacific Boxcar, *71–72*	16	21
____	9215	Norfolk & Western Boxcar, *71*	19	24
____	9216	Great Northern Auto Carrier, 3-tier, *78*	25	39
____	9217	Soo Line Operating Boxcar, *82–84*	29	36
____	9218	Monon Operating Boxcar, *81*	25	30
____	9219	Missouri Pacific Operating Boxcar, *83*	27	33
____	9220	Borden Operating Milk Car, *83–86*	95	113
____	9221	Poultry Dispatch Operating Chicken Car, *83–85*	45	50
____	9222	L&N Flatcar with trailers, *83–84*	38	60
____	9223	Reading Operating Boxcar, *84*	33	40
____	9224	Churchill Downs Operating Horse Car, *84–86*	85	110
____	9225	Conrail Operating Barrel Car, *84*	42	55
____	9226	Delaware & Hudson Flatcar with trailers, *84–85*	31	34
____	9228	Canadian Pacific Operating Boxcar, *86*	24	37
____	9229	Express Mail Operating Boxcar, *85–86*	21	27
____	9230	Monon Boxcar (SSS), *71, 72 u*	17	24
____	9231	Reading Bay Window Caboose, *79*	24	32
____	9232	Allis-Chalmers Condenser Car, *80–81, 83 u*	42	50
____	9233	Depressed Center Flatcar with transformer, *80*	55	65
____	9234	Radioactive Waste Car, *80*	53	78
____	9235	Union Pacific Derrick Car, *83–84*	16	22
____	9236	C&NW Derrick Car, *83–85*	22	30
____	9238	Northern Pacific Log Dump Car, *84*	16	24
____	9239	Lionel Lines N5c Caboose, *83 u*	50	60
____	9240	NYC Hopper (O27), *87 u*	20	29
____	9240	NYC Operating Hopper, *86*	32	39
____	9241	PRR Log Dump Car, *85–86*	21	27
____	9250	WaterPoxy 3-D Tank Car, *70–71*	23	34
____	9260	Reynolds Aluminum Covered Quad Hopper, *75–77*	19	22
____	9261	Sun-Maid Raisins Covered Quad Hopper, *75 u, 76*	21	27
____	9262	Ralston Purina Covered Quad Hopper, *75 u, 76*	36	58
____	9263	PRR Covered Quad Hopper, *75 u, 76–77*	23	30
____	9264	Illinois Central Covered Quad Hopper, *75 u, 76–77*	28	39
____	9265	Chessie System Covered Quad Hopper, *75 u, 76–77*	21	27
____	9266	Southern "Big John" Covered Quad Hopper, *76*	46	65
____	9267	Alcoa Covered Quad Hopper (SSS), *76*	20	25
____	9268	Northern Pacific Bay Window Caboose, *77 u*	33	40
____	9269	Milwaukee Road Bay Window Caboose, *78*	34	47
____	9270	Northern Pacific N5c Caboose, *78*	14	27

		Exc	Mint
9271	M&StL Bay Window Caboose (SSS), *78–79*	18	30 ____
9272	New Haven Bay Window Caboose, *78–80*	20	34 ____
9273	Southern Bay Window Caboose, *78 u*	36	45 ____
9274	Santa Fe Bay Window Caboose, *78 u*	40	47 ____
9276	Peabody Quad Hopper, *78*	19	28 ____
9277	Cities Service 1-D Tank Car, *78*	41	45 ____
9278	Life Savers 1-D Tank Car, *78–79*	112	152 ____
9279	Magnolia 3-D Tank Car, *78, 79 u*	13	19 ____
9280	Santa Fe Operating Stock Car (O27), *77–81*	20	24 ____
9281	Santa Fe Auto Carrier, 3-tier, *78–80*	21	27 ____
9282	GN Flatcar with trailers, *78–79, 81–82*	22	28 ____
9283	Union Pacific Gondola with canisters, *77*	15	21 ____
9284	Santa Fe Gondola with canisters, *77*	16	27 ____
9285	ICG Flatcar with trailers, *77*	47	48 ____
9286	B&LE Covered Quad Hopper, *77*	14	26 ____
9287	Southern N5c Caboose, *77 u, 78*	18	30 ____
9288	Lehigh Valley N5c Caboose, *77 u, 78, 80*	25	31 ____
9289	C&NW N5c Caboose, *77 u, 78, 80*	25	36 ____
9290	Union Pacific Operating Barrel Car, *83*	65	75 ____
9300	PC Log Dump Car, *70–75, 77*	18	24 ____
9301	U.S. Mail Operating Boxcar, *73–84*	32	42 ____
9302	L&N Searchlight Car, *72 u, 73–78*	21	24 ____
9303	Union Pacific Log Dump Car, *74–78, 80*	17	22 ____
9304	C&O Coal Dump Car, *74–78*	12	23 ____
9305	Santa Fe Operating Cowboy Car (O27), *80–82*	16	23 ____
9306	Santa Fe Flatcar with horses, *80–82*	18	26 ____
9307	Erie Animated Gondola, *80–84*	55	70 ____
9308	Aquarium Car, *81–84*	125	129 ____
9309	TP&W Bay Window Caboose, *80–81, 83 u*	19	25 ____
9310	Santa Fe Log Dump Car, *78 u, 79–83*	13	24 ____
9311	Union Pacific Coal Dump Car, *78 u, 79–82*	13	24 ____
9312	Conrail Searchlight Car, *78 u, 79–83*	18	27 ____
9313	Gulf 3-D Tank Car, *79 u*	43	50 ____
9315	Southern Pacific Gondola with canisters, *79 u*	16	23 ____
9316	Southern Pacific Bay Window Caboose, *79 u*	47	50 ____
9317	Santa Fe Bay Window Caboose, *79*	21	36 ____
9320	Fort Knox Mint Car, *79 u*	110	135 ____
9321	Santa Fe 1-D Tank Car (FARR 1), *79*	25	31 ____
9322	Santa Fe Covered Quad Hopper (FARR 1), *79*	30	38 ____
9323	Santa Fe Bay Window Caboose (FARR 1), *79*	39	49 ____
9324	Tootsie Roll 1-D Tank Car, *79–81*	67	96 ____
9325	Norfolk & Western Flatcar with fences, *79–81 u*	6	10 ____
9326	Burlington Northern Bay Window Caboose, *79–80*	34	44 ____
9327	Bakelite 3-D Tank Car, *80*	19	29 ____
9328	Chessie System Bay Window Caboose, *80*	33	42 ____
9329	Chessie System Crane Car, *80*	40	47 ____
9330	Kickapoo Dump Car, *72, 79*	3	7 ____
9331	Union 76 1-D Tank Car, *79*	39	44 ____
9332	Reading Crane Car, *79*	37	50 ____
9333	Southern Pacific Flatcar with trailers, *79–80*	33	47 ____
9334	Humble 1-D Tank Car, *79*	21	26 ____

			Exc	Mint
____	**9335**	B&O Log Dump Car, *86*	16	22
____	**9336**	CP Rail Gondola with canisters, *79*	20	29
____	**9338**	Pennsylvania Power & Light Quad Hopper, *79*	60	75
____	**9339**	GN Boxcar (027), *79–83, 85 u, 86*	7	10
____	**9340**	Illinois Central Gondola with canisters (027), *79–81, 82 u, 83*	5	9
____	**9341**	ACL SP-type Caboose, *79–82, 86 u 87–90*	6	8
____	**9344**	Citgo 3-D Tank Car, *80*	23	38
____	**9345**	Reading Searchlight Car, *84–85*	20	25
____	**9346**	Wabash SP-type Caboose, *79*	6	10
____	**9348**	Santa Fe Crane Car (FARR 1), *79 u*	60	70
____	**9349**	San Francisco Mint Car, *80*	55	70
____	**9351**	PRR Auto Carrier, 3-tier, *80*	23	40
____	**9352**	Trailer Train Flatcar with C&NW trailers, *80*	29	55
____	**9353**	Crystal Line 3-D Tank Car, *80*	18	26
____	**9354**	Pennzoil 1-D Tank Car, *80, 81 u*	60	85
____	**9355**	Delaware & Hudson Bay Window Caboose, *80*	37	45
____	**9357**	Smokey Mountain Bobber Caboose, *79*	8	10
____	**9359**	National Basketball Association Boxcar (027), *79–80 u*	19	24
____	**9360**	National Hockey League Boxcar (027), *79–80 u*	21	26
____	**9361**	C&NW Bay Window Caboose, *80*	47	50
____	**9362**	Major League Baseball Boxcar (027), *79–80 u*	17	21
____	**9363**	N&W Log Dump Car "9325" (027), *79*	4	7
____	**9364**	N&W Crane Car "9325" (027), *79*	7	9
____	**9365**	Toys "R" Us Boxcar (027), *79 u*	30	37
____	**9366**	UP Covered Quad Hopper (FARR 2), *80*	19	23
____	**9367**	Union Pacific 1-D Tank Car (FARR 2), *80*	21	30
____	**9368**	Union Pacific Bay Window Caboose (FARR 2), *80*	30	36
____	**9369**	Sinclair 1-D Tank Car, *80*	60	85
____	**9370**	Seaboard Gondola with canisters, *80*	19	21
____	**9371**	Atlantic Sugar Covered Quad Hopper, *80*	19	22
____	**9372**	Seaboard Bay Window Caboose, *80*	30	41
____	**9373**	Getty 1-D Tank Car, *80–81, 83 u*	31	42
____	**9374**	Reading Covered Quad Hopper, *80–81, 83 u*	39	40
____	**9376**	Soo Line Boxcar (027), *81 u*	40	50
____	**9378**	Derrick Car, *80–82*	18	22
____	**9379**	Santa Fe Gondola with canisters, *80–81, 83 u*	22	30
____	**9380**	NYNH&H SP-type Caboose, *80–81*	9	10
____	**9381**	Chessie System SP-type Caboose, *80*	7	9
____	**9382**	Florida East Coast Bay Window Caboose, *80*	34	48
____	**9383**	UP Flatcar with trailers (FARR 2), *80 u*	27	34
____	**9384**	Great Northern Operating Hopper, *81*	50	55
____	**9385**	Alaska Gondola with canisters, *81*	27	34
____	**9386**	Pure Oil 1-D Tank Car, *81*	38	50
____	**9387**	Burlington Bay Window Caboose, *81*	46	52
____	**9388**	Toys "R" Us Boxcar (027), *81 u*	38	45
____	**9389**	Radioactive Waste Car, *81–82*	63	78
____	**9398**	PRR Coal Dump Car, *83–84*	28	38
____	**9399**	C&NW Coal Dump Car, *83–85*	17	22
____	**9400**	Conrail Boxcar, *78*	14	20
____	**9401**	Great Northern Boxcar, *78*	18	23

		Exc	Mint
9402	Susquehanna Boxcar, *78*	30	33 ___
9403	Seaboard Coast Line Boxcar, *78*	12	17 ___
9404	NKP Boxcar, *78*	19	21 ___
9405	Chattahoochee Boxcar, *78*	14	19 ___
9406	D&RGW Boxcar, *78–79*	17	21 ___
9407	Union Pacific Stock Car, *78*	24	25 ___
9408	Lionel Lines Circus Stock Car (SSS), *78*	31	40 ___
9411	Lackawanna Phoebe Snow Boxcar, *78*	35	43 ___
9412	RF&P Boxcar, *79*	21	27 ___
9413	Napierville Junction Boxcar, *79*	18	24 ___
9414	Cotton Belt Boxcar, *79*	19	23 ___
9415	Providence & Worcester Boxcar, *79*	17	25 ___
9416	MD&W Boxcar, *79, 81*	13	19 ___
9417	CP Rail Boxcar, *79*	45	50 ___
9418	FARR Boxcar, *79 u*	50	60 ___
9419	Union Pacific Boxcar (FARR 2), *80*	15	17 ___
9420	B&O Sentinel Boxcar, *80*	21	26 ___
9421	Maine Central Boxcar, *80*	10	17 ___
9422	EJ&E Boxcar, *80*	12	20 ___
9423	NYNH&H Boxcar, *80*	14	22 ___
9424	TP&W Boxcar, *80*	17	21 ___
9425	British Columbia DD Boxcar, *80*	27	35 ___
9426	Chesapeake & Ohio Boxcar, *80*	19	30 ___
9427	Bay Line Boxcar, *80–81*	12	17 ___
9428	TP&W Boxcar, *80–81, 83 u*		23 ___
9429	"The Early Years" Boxcar, *80*	20	27 ___
9430	"The Standard Gauge Years" Boxcar, *80*	22	25 ___
9431	"The Prewar Years" Boxcar, *80*	20	25 ___
9432	"The Postwar Years" Boxcar, *80*	50	55 ___
9433	"The Golden Years" Boxcar, *80*	33	43 ___
9434	Joshua Lionel Cowen "The Man" Boxcar, *80 u*	29	37 ___
9436	Burlington Boxcar, *81*	25	30 ___
9437	Northern Pacific Stock Car, *81*	22	36 ___
9438	Ontario Northland Boxcar, *81*	25	31 ___
9439	Ashley Drew & Northern Boxcar, *81*	11	19 ___
9440	Reading Boxcar, *81*	50	65 ___
9441	Pennsylvania Boxcar, *81*	32	42 ___
9442	Canadian Pacific Boxcar, *81*	13	21 ___
9443	Florida East Coast Boxcar, *81*	19	24 ___
9444	Louisiana Midland Boxcar, *81*	14	18 ___
9445	Vermont Northern Boxcar, *81*	14	17 ___
9446	Sabine River & Northern Boxcar, *81*	15	21 ___
9447	Pullman Standard Boxcar, *81*	16	21 ___
9448	Santa Fe Stock Car, *81–82*	34	40 ___
9449	Great Northern Boxcar (FARR 3), *81*	27	31 ___
9450	Great Northern Stock Car (FARR 3), *81 u*	50	60 ___
9451	Southern Boxcar (FARR 4), *83*	26	32 ___
9452	Western Pacific Boxcar, *82–83*	12	16 ___
9453	MPA Boxcar, *82–83*	14	19 ___
9454	New Hope & Ivyland Boxcar, *82–83*	21	27 ___
9455	Milwaukee Road Boxcar, *82–83*	15	19 ___
9456	PRR DD Boxcar (FARR 5), *84–85*	24	30 ___
9461	Norfolk & Southern Boxcar, *82*	25	43 ___

			Exc	Mint
____	**9462**	Southern Pacific Boxcar, *83–84*	18	23
____	**9463**	Texas & Pacific Boxcar, *83–84*	15	19
____	**9464**	NC&StL Boxcar, *83–84*	16	22
____	**9465**	Santa Fe Boxcar, *83–84*	12	19
____	**9466**	Wanamaker Boxcar, *82 u*	60	70
____	**9467**	Tennessee World's Fair Boxcar, *82 u*	26	31
____	**9468**	Union Pacific DD Boxcar, *83*	31	34
____	**9469**	NYC Pacemaker Boxcar (std O), *84–85*	37	53
____	**9470**	Chicago Beltline Boxcar, *84*	15	20
____	**9471**	Atlantic Coast Line Boxcar, *84*	13	20
____	**9472**	Detroit & Mackinac Boxcar, *84*	22	26
____	**9473**	Lehigh Valley Boxcar, *84*	24	28
____	**9474**	Erie-Lackawanna Boxcar, *84*	31	35
____	**9475**	D&H "I Love NY" Boxcar, *84 u*	28	37
____	**9476**	PRR Boxcar (FARR 5), *84–85*	27	36
____	**9480**	MN&S Boxcar, *85–86*	15	18
____	**9481**	Seaboard System Boxcar, *85–86*	15	18
____	**9482**	Norfolk & Southern Boxcar, *85–86*	13	17
____	**9483**	Manufacturers Railway Boxcar, *85–86*	14	19
____	**9484**	Lionel 85th Anniversary Boxcar, *85*	22	26
____	**9486**	GTW "I Love Michigan" Boxcar, *86*	23	34
____	**9490**	Christmas Boxcar for Lionel Employees, *85 u*		1750
____	**9491**	Christmas Boxcar, *86 u*	26	37
____	**9492**	Lionel Lines Boxcar, *86*	23	29
____	**9500**	Milwaukee Road Passenger Coach, *73*	28	75
____	**9501**	Milwaukee Road Passenger Coach, *73 u, 74–76*	33	37
____	**9502**	Milwaukee Road Observation Car, *73*	30	48
____	**9503**	Milwaukee Road Passenger Coach, *73*	33	48
____	**9504**	Milwaukee Road Passenger Coach, *73 u, 74–76*	33	37
____	**9505**	Milwaukee Road Passenger Coach, *73 u, 74–76*	35	38
____	**9506**	Milwaukee Road Combination Car, *74 u, 75–76*	32	37
____	**9507**	PRR Passenger Coach, *74–75*	34	55
____	**9508**	PRR Passenger Coach, *74–75*	32	50
____	**9509**	PRR Observation Car, *74–75*	41	60
____	**9510**	PRR Combination Car, *74 u, 75–76*	30	47
____	**9511**	Milwaukee Road Passenger Coach, *74 u*	33	48
____	**9513**	PRR Passenger Coach, *75–76*	25	44
____	**9514**	PRR Passenger Coach, *75–76*	23	36
____	**9515**	PRR Passenger Coach, *75–76*	22	34
____	**9516**	B&O Passenger Coach, *76*	27	42
____	**9517**	B&O Passenger Coach, *75*	45	65
____	**9518**	B&O Observation Car, *75*	45	65
____	**9519**	B&O Combination Car, *75*	55	85
____	**9521**	PRR Baggage Car, *75 u, 76*	65	95
____	**9522**	Milwaukee Road Baggage Car, *75 u, 76*	65	80
____	**9523**	B&O Baggage Car, *75 u, 76*	60	70
____	**9524**	B&O Passenger Coach, *76*	27	37
____	**9525**	B&O Passenger Coach, *76*	30	43
____	**9527**	Milwaukee Road Campaign Observation Car, *76 u*	50	75

		Exc	Mint	
9528	PRR Campaign Observation Car, *76 u*	65	95	___
9529	B&O Campaign Observation Car, *76 u*	44	70	___
9530	Southern Baggage Car, *77–78*	45	65	___
9531	Southern Combination Car, *77–78*	29	37	___
9532	Southern Passenger Coach, *77–78*	33	47	___
9533	Southern Passenger Coach, *77–78*	27	38	___
9534	Southern Observation Car, *77–78*	31	47	___
9536	Blue Comet Baggage Car, *78–80*	39	55	___
9537	Blue Comet Combination Car, *78–80*	35	50	___
9538	Blue Comet Passenger Coach, *78–80*	35	47	___
9539	Blue Comet Passenger Coach, *78–80*	35	48	___
9540	Blue Comet Observation Car, *78–80*	27	40	___
9541	Santa Fe Baggage Car, *80–82*	21	30	___
9545	Union Pacific Baggage Car, *84*	135	200	___
9546	Union Pacific Combination Car, *84*	85	105	___
9547	Union Pacific Observation Car, *84*	85	105	___
9548	UP Placid Bay Passenger Coach, *84*	90	110	___
9549	UP Ocean Sunset Passenger Coach, *84*	85	105	___
9551	W&ARR Baggage Car, *77 u, 78–80*	36	48	___
9552	W&ARR Passenger Coach, *77 u, 78–80*	46	60	___
9553	W&ARR Flatcar with horses, *77 u, 78–80*	32	50	___
9554	Chicago & Alton Baggage Car, *81*	55	85	___
9555	Chicago & Alton Combination Car, *81*	50	75	___
9556	Chicago & Alton Wilson Passenger Coach, *81*	50	75	___
9557	Chicago & Alton Webster Groves Passenger Coach, *81*	45	65	___
9558	Chicago & Alton Observation Car, *81*	50	75	___
9559	Rock Island Baggage Car, *81–82*	42	65	___
9560	Rock Island Passenger Coach, *81–82*	43	65	___
9561	Rock Island Passenger Coach, *81–82*	42	65	___
9562	N&W Baggage Car "577," *81*	80	110	___
9563	N&W Combination Car "578," *81*	80	105	___
9564	N&W Passenger Coach "579," *81*	90	100	___
9565	N&W Passenger Coach "580," *81*	85	100	___
9566	N&W Observation Car "581," *81*	90	95	___
9567	N&W Vista Dome Car "582," *81 u*	160	255	___
9569	PRR Combination Car, *81 u*	115	160	___
9570	PRR Baggage Car, *79*	85	115	___
9571	PRR Passenger Coach, *79*	125	145	___
9572	PRR Passenger Coach, *79*	110	125	___
9573	PRR Vista Dome Car, *79*	95	120	___
9574	PRR Observation Car, *79*	75	100	___
9575	PRR Passenger Coach, *79–80 u*	100	135	___
9576	Burlington Baggage Car, *80*	145	175	___
9577	Burlington Passenger Coach, *80*	95	105	___
9578	Burlington Passenger Coach, *80*	105	110	___
9579	Burlington Vista Dome Car, *80*	95	110	___
9580	Burlington Observation Car, *80*	95	110	___
9581	Chessie System Baggage Car, *80*	55	62	___
9582	Chessie System Combination Car, *80*	47	55	___
9583	Chessie System Passenger Coach, *80*	40	47	___
9584	Chessie System Passenger Coach, *80*	31	37	___
9585	Chessie System Observation Car, *80*	55	65	___

			Exc	Mint
____	9586	Chessie System Diner, *86 u*	85	90
____	9588	Burlington Vista Dome Car, *80 u*	110	120
____	9589	Southern Pacific Baggage Car, *82–83*	110	135
____	9590	Southern Pacific Combination Car, *82–83*	90	105
____	9591	Southern Pacific Pullman Passenger Coach, *82–83*	85	105
____	9592	Southern Pacific Pullman Passenger Coach, *82–83*	85	105
____	9593	Southern Pacific Observation Car, *82–83*	100	130
____	9594	NYC Baggage Car, *83–84*	105	130
____	9595	NYC Combination Car, *83–84*	75	85
____	9596	NYC Wayne County Passenger Coach, *83–84*	80	95
____	9597	NYC Hudson River Passenger Coach, *83–84*	70	85
____	9598	NYC Observation Car, *83–84*	75	85
____	9599	Chicago & Alton Diner, *86 u*	80	90
____	9600	Chessie System Hi-Cube Boxcar, *75 u, 76–77*	19	25
____	9601	ICG Hi-Cube Boxcar, *75 u, 76–77*	20	21
____	9602	Santa Fe Hi-Cube Boxcar, *75 u, 76–77*	17	20
____	9603	Penn Central Hi-Cube Boxcar, *76–77*	17	18
____	9604	Norfolk & Western Hi-Cube Boxcar, *76–77*	23	26
____	9605	NH Hi-Cube Boxcar, *76–77*	17	21
____	9606	Union Pacific Hi-Cube Boxcar, *76 u, 77*	16	17
____	9607	Southern Pacific Hi-Cube Boxcar, *76 u, 77*	12	15
____	9608	Burlington Northern Hi-Cube Boxcar, *76 u, 77*	21	23
____	9610	Frisco Hi-Cube Boxcar, *77*	25	34
____	9620	NHL Wales Boxcar, *80*	27	35
____	9621	NHL Campbell Boxcar, *80*	27	34
____	9622	NBA Western Boxcar, *80*	24	30
____	9623	NBA Eastern Boxcar, *80*	26	34
____	9624	National League Baseball Boxcar, *80*	27	34
____	9625	American League Baseball Boxcar, *80*	27	35
____	9626	Santa Fe Hi-Cube Boxcar, *82–84*	10	14
____	9627	Union Pacific Hi-Cube Boxcar, *82–83*	15	21
____	9628	Burlington Northern Hi-Cube Boxcar, *82–84*	14	19
____	9629	Chessie System Hi-Cube Boxcar, *83–84*	23	34
____	9660	Mickey Mouse Hi-Cube Boxcar, *77–78*	28	40
____	9661	Goofy Hi-Cube Boxcar, *77–78*	53	61
____	9662	Donald Duck Hi-Cube Boxcar, *77–78*	38	49
____	9663	Dumbo Hi-Cube Boxcar, *77 u, 78*	43	58
____	9664	Cinderella Hi-Cube Boxcar, *77 u, 78*	56	86
____	9665	Peter Pan Hi-Cube Boxcar, *77 u, 78*	49	77
____	9666	Pinocchio Hi-Cube Boxcar, *78*	106	157
____	9667	Snow White Hi-Cube Boxcar, *78*	348	461
____	9668	Pluto Hi-Cube Boxcar, *78*	149	193
____	9669	Bambi Hi-Cube Boxcar, *78 u*	67	105
____	9670	Alice In Wonderland Hi-Cube Boxcar, *78 u*	61	91
____	9671	Fantasia Hi-Cube Boxcar, *78 u*	56	91
____	9672	Mickey Mouse 50th Anniversary Hi-Cube Boxcar, *78 u*	357	422
____	9700	Southern Boxcar, *72–73*	22	30
____	9701	B&O DD Boxcar, *72*	14	19
____	9702	Soo Line Boxcar, *72–73*	15	21
____	9703	CP Rail Boxcar, *72*	34	44
____	9704	Norfolk & Western Boxcar, *72*	10	17

		Exc	Mint	
9705	D&RGW Boxcar, *72*	13	20	___
9706	C&O Boxcar, *72*	17	19	___
9707	MKT Stock Car, *72–75*	14	22	___
9708	U.S. Mail Boxcar, *72–75*	18	23	___
9708	U.S. Mail Toy Fair Boxcar, *73 u*	85	95	___
9709	BAR State of Maine Boxcar (SSS), *72–74*	29	32	___
9710	Rutland Boxcar (SSS), *72–74*	24	28	___
9711	Southern Boxcar, *74–75*	19	25	___
9712	B&O DD Boxcar, *73–74*	31	34	___
9713	CP Rail Boxcar, *73–74*	24	30	___
9713	CP Rail "Season's Greetings" Boxcar, *74 u*	95	120	___
9714	D&RGW Boxcar, *73–74*	16	20	___
9715	C&O Boxcar, *73–74*	17	22	___
9716	Penn Central Boxcar, *73–74*	15	20	___
9717	Union Pacific Boxcar, *73–74*	21	25	___
9718	Canadian National Boxcar, *73–74*	23	31	___
9719	New Haven DD Boxcar, *73 u*	23	32	___
9723	Western Pacific Boxcar (SSS), *73–74*	27	29	___
9723	Western Pacific Toy Fair Boxcar, *74 u*	20	60	___
9724	Missouri Pacific Boxcar (SSS), *73–74*	21	24	___
9725	MKT Stock Car (SSS), *73–75*	15	18	___
9726	Erie-Lackawanna Boxcar (SSS), *78*	25	30	___
9729	CP Rail Boxcar, *78*		34	___
9730	CP Rail Boxcar, *74–75*	23	27	___
9731	Milwaukee Road Boxcar, *74–75*	16	21	___
9732	Southern Pacific Boxcar, *79 u*	24	31	___
9734	Bangor & Aroostook Boxcar, *79*	30	38	___
9735	Grand Trunk Western Boxcar, *74–75*	15	21	___
9737	Vermont Central Boxcar, *74–76*	27	34	___
9738	Illinois Terminal Boxcar, *82*	43	45	___
9739	D&RGW Boxcar (SSS), *74–76*	17	25	___
9740	Chessie System Boxcar, *74–75*	15	19	___
9742	M&StL Boxcar, *73 u*	17	19	___
9742	M&StL "Season's Greetings" Boxcar, *73 u*	85	105	___
9743	Sprite Boxcar, *74 u, 75*	19	27	___
9744	Tab Boxcar, *74 u, 75*	17	24	___
9745	Fanta Boxcar, *74 u, 75*	19	29	___
9747	Chessie System DD Boxcar, *75–76*	24	28	___
9748	CP Rail Boxcar, *75–76*	16	20	___
9749	Penn Central Boxcar, *75–76*	16	21	___
9750	DT&I Boxcar, *75–76*	13	15	___
9751	Frisco Boxcar, *75–76*	21	23	___
9752	L&N Boxcar, *75–76*	20	23	___
9753	Maine Central Boxcar, *75–76*	16	22	___
9754	NYC Pacemaker Boxcar (SSS), *75–77*	20	30	___
9755	Union Pacific Boxcar, *75–76*	20	24	___
9757	Central of Georgia Boxcar, *74 u*	16	19	___
9758	Alaska Boxcar (SSS), *75–77*	24	31	___
9759	Paul Revere Boxcar, *75 u*	36	43	___
9760	Liberty Bell Boxcar, *75 u*	30	40	___
9761	George Washington Boxcar, *75 u*	36	43	___
9762	Toy Fair Boxcar, *75 u*	125	170	___
9763	D&RGW Stock Car, *76–77*	15	20	___

			Exc	Mint
____	9764	GTW DD Boxcar, *76–77*	40	55
____	9767	Railbox Boxcar, *76–77*	15	20
____	9768	B&M Boxcar, *76–77*	18	27
____	9769	B&LE Boxcar, *76–77*	17	21
____	9770	Northern Pacific Boxcar, *76–77*	14	18
____	9771	Norfolk & Western Boxcar, *76–77*	16	24
____	9772	Great Northern Boxcar, *76*	60	85
____	9773	NYC Stock Car, *76*	32	39
____	9775	M&StL Boxcar (SSS), *76*	19	23
____	9776	SP Overnight Boxcar (SSS), *76*	32	34
____	9777	Virginian Boxcar, *76–77*	22	25
____	9778	"Season's Greetings" Boxcar, *75 u*	165	185
____	9780	Johnny Cash Boxcar, *76 u*	54	58
____	9781	Delaware & Hudson Boxcar, *77–78*	19	23
____	9782	Rock Island Boxcar, *77–78*	14	17
____	9783	B&O Time-Saver Boxcar, *77–78*	25	27
____	9784	Santa Fe Boxcar, *77–78*	13	17
____	9785	Conrail Boxcar, *77–78*	20	23
____	9786	C&NW Boxcar, *77–79*	18	27
____	9787	Jersey Central Boxcar, *77–79*	18	19
____	9788	Lehigh Valley Boxcar, *77–79*	17	21
____	9789	Pickens Boxcar, *77*	25	33
____	9801	B&O Sentinel Boxcar (std O), *73–75*	18	26
____	9802	Miller High Life Reefer (std O), *73–75*	28	33
____	9803	Johnson Wax Boxcar (std O), *73–75*	27	33
____	9805	Grand Trunk Western Reefer (std O), *73–75*	30	31
____	9806	Rock Island Boxcar (std O), *74–75*	38	46
____	9807	Stroh's Beer Reefer (std O), *74–76*	67	79
____	9808	Union Pacific Boxcar (std O), *75–76*	36	50
____	9809	Clark Reefer (std O), *75–76*	33	41
____	9811	Pacific Fruit Express Reefer (FARR 2), *80*	26	33
____	9812	Arm & Hammer Reefer, *80*	24	30
____	9813	Ruffles Reefer, *80*	18	26
____	9814	Perrier Reefer, *80*	21	30
____	9815	NYC "Early Bird" Reefer (std O), *84–85*	34	40
____	9816	Brach's Candy Reefer, *80*	21	26
____	9817	Bazooka Bubble Gum Reefer, *80*	24	31
____	9818	Western Maryland Reefer, *80*	18	23
____	9819	Western Fruit Express Reefer (FARR 3), *81*	22	29
____	9820	Wabash Gondola with coal (std O), *73–74*	24	38
____	9821	SP Gondola with coal (std O), *73–75*	28	32
____	9822	GTW Gondola with coal (std O), *74–75*	24	29
____	9823	Santa Fe Flatcar with crates (std O), *75–76*	34	44
____	9824	NYC Gondola with coal (std O), *75–76*	41	56
____	9825	Schaefer Reefer (std O), *76–77*	45	60
____	9826	P&LE Boxcar (std O), *76–77*	34	39
____	9827	Cutty Sark Reefer, *84*	34	44
____	9828	J&B Reefer, *84*	31	44
____	9829	Dewar's White Label Reefer, *84*	33	42
____	9830	Johnnie Walker Red Label Reefer, *84*	23	41
____	9831	Pepsi Cola Reefer, *82*	74	85
____	9832	Cheerios Reefer, *82*	153	177
____	9833	Vlasic Pickles Reefer, *82*	23	29

		Exc	Mint
9834	Southern Comfort Reefer, *83–84*	32	44 ____
9835	Jim Beam Reefer, *83–84*	41	58 ____
9836	Old Grand-Dad Reefer, *83–84*	35	48 ____
9837	Wild Turkey Reefer, *83–84*	60	90 ____
9840	Fleischmann's Gin Reefer, *85*	38	43 ____
9841	Calvert Gin Reefer, *85*	35	41 ____
9842	Seagram's Gin Reefer, *85*	38	43 ____
9843	Tanqueray Gin Reefer, *85*	41	44 ____
9844	Sambuca Reefer, *86*	37	49 ____
9845	Baileys Irish Cream Reefer, *86*	56	83 ____
9846	Seagram's Vodka Reefer, *86*	37	43 ____
9847	Wolfschmidt Vodka Reefer, *86*	34	39 ____
9849	Lionel Lines Reefer, *83 u*	30	32 ____
9850	Budweiser Reefer, *72 u, 73–75*	52	62 ____
9851	Schlitz Reefer, *72 u, 73–75*	29	35 ____
9852	Miller Reefer, *72 u, 73–77*	32	38 ____
9853	Cracker Jack Reefer, *72 u, 73–75*		
	(A) Caramel-colored body	29	34 ____
	(B) White body, black logo border	23	28 ____
9854	Baby Ruth Reefer, *72 u, 73–76*	22	26 ____
9855	Swift Reefer, *72 u, 73–77*	23	28 ____
9856	Old Milwaukee Reefer, *75–76*	33	40 ____
9858	Butterfinger Reefer, *73 u, 74–76*	22	28 ____
9859	Pabst Reefer, *73 u, 74–75*	38	45 ____
9860	Gold Medal Reefer, *73 u, 74–76*	12	21 ____
9861	Tropicana Reefer, *75–77*	23	35 ____
9862	Hamm's Reefer, *75–76*	35	42 ____
9863	REA Reefer (SSS), *74–76*	24	28 ____
9866	Coors Reefer, *76–77*	41	56 ____
9867	Hershey's Reefer, *76–77*	71	81 ____
9869	Santa Fe Reefer (SSS), *76*	32	37 ____
9870	Old Dutch Cleanser Reefer, *77–78, 80*	15	21 ____
9871	Carling Black Label Reefer, *77–78, 80*	33	45 ____
9872	Pacific Fruit Express Reefer, *77–79*	24	28 ____
9873	Ralston Purina Reefer, *78*	30	38 ____
9874	Miller Lite Beer Reefer, *78–79*	52	59 ____
9875	A&P Reefer, *78–79*	23	31 ____
9876	Vermont Central Reefer, *78*	26	31 ____
9877	Gerber Reefer, *79–80*	68	78 ____
9878	Good and Plenty Reefer, *79*	24	31 ____
9879	Hills Bros. Reefer, *79–80*	23	29 ____
9880	Santa Fe Reefer (FARR 1), *79*	27	31 ____
9881	Rath Packing Reefer, *79 u*	23	31 ____
9882	NYC "Early Bird" Reefer, *79*	25	29 ____
9883	Nabisco Oreo Reefer, *79*	83	88 ____
9884	Fritos Reefer, *81–82*	26	34 ____
9885	Lipton Tea Reefer, *81–82*	30	38 ____
9886	Mounds Reefer, *81–82*	24	30 ____
9887	Fruit Growers Express Reefer (FARR 4), *83*	29	38 ____
9888	Green Bay & Western Reefer, *83*	42	49 ____
11000	Holiday Express Freight Set, *08*		280 ____
11004	NASCAR Diesel Freight Set, *06–07*		300 ____
11005	Dale Earnhardt Jr. Diesel Freight Set, *06–07*		240 ____

		Exc	Mint
___ 11006	Kasey Kahne Expansion Pack, *06–07*		130
___ 11006	Lionel Lion Set, *03 u*		230
___ 11007	Dale Earnhardt Sr. Expansion Pack, *06–07*		130
___ 11008	Dale Earnhardt Jr. Expansion Pack, *06–07*		130
___ 11009	Tony Stewart Expansion Pack, *06–07*		130
___ 11010	Jimmie Johnson Expansion Pack, *06–07*		130
___ 11011	Jeff Gordon Expansion Pack, *06–07*		130
___ 11020	Harry Potter Hogwarts Express Steam Passenger Set, *08–13*		330
___ 11025	Jimmie Johnson 2006 Champion Boxcar, *07*		45
___ 11038	Snow-covered Straight Track 4-pack, *08*		14
___ 11041	Holiday Calliope Car, *08*		45
___ 11067	Lionel Bear, *08*		25
___ 11077	Harry Potter Figures, *08*		27
___ 11096	Engineer Hat, *08*		18
___ 11098	Holiday Toy Soldier Car, *08*		50
___ 11100	PRR 2-8-2 Mikado Locomotive "9631," CC, *07*		370
___ 11101	LL 2-8-4 Berkshire Locomotive "737," CC, *06*		350
___ 11103	Southern PS-4 4-6-2 Pacific Locomotive "1403," CC, *06*		1000
___ 11104	UP Big Boy Locomotive "4014," CC, *06*		1700
___ 11105	NYC L-2A 4-8-2 Mohawk Locomotive "2770," CC, *06*		1100
___ 11107	LionMaster SP Cab Forward Locomotive "4276," RailSounds, *06–07*		850
___ 11108	C&O F-19 4-6-2 Pacific Locomotive "494," CC, *06–07*		1160
___ 11109	C&O 0-8-0 Locomotive "79," TrainSounds, *06*		420
___ 11110	NYC 0-8-0 Locomotive "7805," TrainSounds, *06*		420
___ 11116	UP 4-8-4 FEF-3 Locomotive "844," gray, CC, *08–09*		1160
___ 11117	Santa Fe E6 4-4-2 Atlantic Locomotive "1484," CC, *07–09*		600
___ 11119	Southern 0-8-0 Locomotive "6535," TrainSounds, *07*		420
___ 11122	UP Big Boy Locomotive "4024," CC, *06*		1700
___ 11123	UP Big Boy Locomotive "4023," CC, *06*		1700
___ 11126	UP Big Boy Locomotive "4012," CC, *06*		1700
___ 11127	SP GS-4 4-8-4 Northern Locomotive "4436," CC, *07–09*		1200
___ 11128	C&O F-19 4-6-2 Pacific Locomotive "490," CC, *07*		1160
___ 11131	UP 4-8-4 FEF-3 Locomotive "844," black, CC, *08–09*		1160
___ 11132	Reading 2-8-0 Consolidation Locomotive "1914," RailSounds, *08*		450
___ 11133	NYC 2-8-0 Consolidation Locomotive "1149," RailSounds, *08*		450
___ 11134	WM 2-8-0 Consolidation Locomotive "729," RailSounds, *08*		450
___ 11135	B&O 2-8-0 Consolidation Locomotive "2784," RailSounds, *08*		450
___ 11136	WP 2-8-2 Mikado Locomotive "322," CC, *08*		800
___ 11137	UP 2-8-2 Mikado Locomotive "1925," CC, *08*		800
___ 11138	ATSF 2-8-2 Mikado Locomotive "3156," CC, *08*		800

		Exc	Mint
11139	MILW 2-8-2 Mikado Locomotive "462," CC, *08*		800 ___
11140	Cass Scenic Shay Locomotive "7," CC, *07*		800 ___
11141	Birch Valley Lumber Shay Locomotive "5," CC, *07*		800 ___
11142	Hogwarts Express Add-on 2-pack, *09–10*		120 ___
11143	SP AC-4 Cab Forward Locomotive "4100," CC, *08*		1670 ___
11146	Pere Marquette 2-8-4 Berkshire Locomotive "1225," CC, *08*		1290 ___
11147	PRR 4-8-2 Mib Locomotive "6750," CC, *08*		1290 ___
11148	NYC Dreyfuss J-3a 4-6-4 Hudson Locomotive "5448," CC, *08*		1130 ___
11149	LionMaster UP Big Boy 4-8-8-4 Locomotive "4006," CC, *08*		860 ___
11150	NYC F-12e 4-6-0 10-wheel Locomotive "827," CC, *08*		700 ___
11151	Polar Express Tender, RailSounds, *08–10*		440 ___
11152	D&RGW LionMaster 4-6-6-4 Challenger Locomotive "3805," CC, *09*		900 ___
11153	Stourbridge Lion Steam Locomotive, *09–10*		430 ___
11154	PRR CC2s 0-8-8-0 Mallet Locomotive "8183," CC, *09–10*		2000 ___
11155	ATSF 2-10-10-2 Mallet Locomotive "3000," CC, *09–10*		2500 ___
11156	C&O 4-6-0 Ten-Wheeler Locomotive, CC, *10*		740 ___
11157	WM Shay Locomotive "6," CC, *10*		800 ___
11162	Lone Ranger Add-on 3-pack, *10*		165 ___
11164	Dewitt Clinton Passenger Set, *10*		630 ___
11165	Dewitt Clinton Add-on Coach, *10*		70 ___
11166	CSX Merger Freight 2-pack #1, *10–11*		130 ___
11167	CSX Merger Freight 2-pack #2, *10–11*		105 ___
11168	CSX Merger Freight 2-pack #3, *10–11*		130 ___
11169	Strasburg Freight Add-on 2-pack, *10*		100 ___
11170	Three Rivers Fast Freight Set, *10–12*		400 ___
11172	Santa Fe 4-4-2 Steam Freight Set, *13*		200 ___
11173	Texan Freight Add-on 2-pack, *10–11*		130 ___
11174	Maple Leaf Freight Add-on 2-pack, *10–11*		110 ___
11175	Operation Eagle Justice Add-on 2-pack, *10–11*		125 ___
11180	Motor City Express Diesel Freight Train Set, CC, *12–13*		1150 ___
11181	CN GP9 Diesel Piggyback Train Set, CC, *12*		850 ___
11182	Dixie Special FT Diesel Freight Set, *11*		700 ___
11183	Lincoln Funeral Train, *13*		1140 ___
11194	Texas Special Diesel Passenger Set, CC, *13–14*		1110 ___
11195	PRR Diesel Passenger Set, CC, *13–14*		1110 ___
11199	UP NW2 Diesel Switcher Work Train Set, CC, *12*		600 ___
11200	UP LionMaster Challenger Locomotive "3985," CC, *10*		900 ___
11201	WM LionMaster Challenger Locomotive "1204," CC, *10*		900 ___
11202	CP 4-6-0 Ten-Wheeler Locomotive "914," CC, *10*		740 ___
11203	Pere Marquette Berkshire Locomotive "1225," CC, *09*		980 ___

Exc Mint

		Exc	Mint
____ 11204	Pere Marquette Tender, RailSounds, *09*		440
11207	PRR LionMaster T1 Duplex Locomotive "5511," CC, *10*		800
11208	UP LionMaster Big Boy Locomotive "4011," CC, *10*		900
11209	Vision NYC Hudson Locomotive "5344," CC, *10*		1600
____ 11210	UP Challenger Locomotive "3967," CC, *10*		1825
11211	UP 4-6-6-4 Challenger Locomotive "3976," CC, *10*		1825
____ 11212	NKP Berkshire Locomotive "765," CC, *10*		1400
11215	LV 4-6-0 Camelback Locomotive "1598," CC, *10*		550
11216	Jersey Central 4-6-0 Camelback Locomotive, CC, *10*		550
11217	PRR 4-6-0 Camelback Locomotive "822," CC, *10*		550
11218	Vision NYC Hudson Locomotive "5331," CC, *10*		1600
11219	Clinchfield Challenger Locomotive "672," CC, *10*		1825
____ 11220	UP Challenger Locomotive "3989," CC, *10*		1825
____ 11221	UP Challenger Locomotive "3983," CC, *10*		1825
____ 11224	PRR Atlantic Locomotive "460," CC, *10–11*		700
____ 11225	B&O Atlantic Locomotive "1440," CC		700
____ 11226	UP Water Tender, black, CC, *11*		300
____ 11227	UP Water Tender, gray, CC, *11*		300
____ 11228	Clinchfield Water Tender, CC, *11*		300
11229	MILW 4-8-4 Northern Locomotive "261," CC, *11*		995
11230	MILW 4-8-4 Northern Locomotive "267," CC, *11*		995
____ 11232	Reading Atlantic Locomotive "351," CC, *11*		700
11233	Pennsylvania Power & Light 2-Truck Shay Locomotive, CC, *11*		900
11234	Pennsylvania Power & Light 2-Truck Shay Locomotive, *11*		750
11235	West Side Lumber 2-Truck Shay Steam Locomotive, CC, *11*		900
11236	West Side Lumber 2-Truck Shay Steam Locomotive, *11*		750
11237	Sugar Pine Lumber Shay Locomotive "4," CC, *11*		900
____ 11238	Sugar Pine Lumber Shay Locomotive "5," *11*		750
11239	Merrill & Ring Lumber 2-Truck Shay Steam Locomotive, CC, *11*		900
11240	Merrill & Ring Lumber 2-Truck Shay Steam Locomotive, *11*		750
11247	Erie USRA 0-8-0 Steam Switcher "121," CC, *11–12*		700
11248	Erie USRA 0-8-0 Steam Switcher "127," *11–12*		550
11249	L&N USRA 0-8-0 Steam Switcher "2119," CC, *11–12*		700
11250	L&N USRA 0-8-0 Steam Switcher "2121," *11–12*		550
11251	Pere Marquette USRA 0-8-0 Steam Switcher "1300," CC, *11–12*		700

Exc Mint

		Exc	Mint
11252	Pere Marquette USRA 0-8-0 Steam Switcher "1307," 11–12		550 ___
11253	NH 0-8-0 Steam Switcher "3603," CC, 11–13		700 ___
11254	NH 0-8-0 Steam Switcher "3606," 11–13		550 ___
11255	C&O 2-8-2 Mikado Steam Locomotive "1062," CC, 12		900 ___
11256	NH 2-8-2 Mikado Steam Locomotive "3021," CC, 12		900 ___
11257	PRR 2-8-2 Mikado Steam Locomotive "8631," CC, 12		900 ___
11258	Southern 2-8-2 Mikado Steam Locomotive "4501," CC, 12		900 ___
11259	UP 2-8-2 Mikado Steam Locomotive "2840," CC, 12		900 ___
11260	Rio Grande 2-8-2 Mikado Steam Locomotive "1207," CC, 12		900 ___
11261	DM&I 2-8-2 Mikado Steam Locomotive "1305," CC, 12		900 ___
11262	Erie 2-8-2 Mikado Steam Locomotive "3007," CC, 12		900 ___
11264	PRR K4 4-6-2 Pacific Steam Locomotive "1361," CC, 11		900 ___
11265	PRR K4 4-6-2 Pacific Steam Locomotive "1330," CC, 11		900 ___
11266	PRR K4 4-6-2 Pacific Steam Locomotive "1361," 11		750 ___
11268	Strasburg 2-6-0 Mogul Steam Locomotive "89," 11		550 ___
11269	RI 2-6-0 Mogul Steam Locomotive "750," 11–13		550 ___
11270	GN 2-6-0 Mogul Steam Locomotive "453," 11		550 ___
11271	C&O 2-6-0 Mogul Steam Locomotive "49," 11–12		550 ___
11272	ATSF 2-6-0 Mogul Steam Locomotive "573," 11		550 ___
11273	Central Pacific 2-6-0 Mogul Steam Locomotive "1470," 11–13		550 ___
11274	MKT USRA 0-8-0 Steam Switcher "46," CC, 11–12		700 ___
11275	MKT 0-8-0 Steam Switcher "51," CC, 11		550 ___
11276	Lionelville & Western 0-8-0 Steam Switcher "1," CC, 11–13		700 ___
11277	Lionelville & Western 0-8-0 Steam Switcher "2," 11–13		550 ___
11278	WP 2-8-2 Mikado Steam Locomotive "322," CC, 11		900 ___
11279	WP 2-8-2 Mikado Steam Locomotive "327," 11		750 ___
11280	B&O 2-8-2 Mikado Steam Locomotive "4507," CC, 11		900 ___
11281	B&O 2-8-2 Mikado Steam Locomotive "451," 11		750 ___
11282	GN 2-8-2 Mikado Steam Locomotive "3125," CC, 11		900 ___
11284	MP 2-8-2 Mikado Steam Locomotive "1310," CC, 11		900 ___
11286	RI 2-8-2 Mikado Steam Locomotive "2302," CC, 11		900 ___

Exc Mint

		Exc	Mint
11287	RI 2-8-2 Mikado Steam Locomotive "2305," *11*		750
11288	T&P 2-8-2 Mikado Steam Locomotive "552," CC, *11*		900
11289	T&P 2-8-2 Mikado Steam Locomotive "557," *11*		750
11290	Bethlehem Steel 2-6-0 Mogul Steam Locomotive "28," *11*		550
11291	Weyerhaeuser 2-6-0 Mogul Locomotive "288," *11–13*		550
11295	Elk River Lumber 2-Truck Shay Locomotive "1," CC, *11*		900
11296	Elk River Lumber 2-Truck Shay Locomotive "2," *11*		750
11297	P. Bunyan Lumber 2-Truck Shay Locomotive "18," CC, *11*		900
11298	P. Bunyan Lumber 2-Truck Shay Locomotive "23," *11*		750
11299	C&O 2-6-6-2 Mallet Steam Locomotive "875," CC, *12*		1300
11300	PRR 2-10-4 Texas Steam Locomotive "6479," CC, *11*		1300
11301	PRR 2-10-4 Texas Steam Locomotive "6498," CC, *11*		1300
11303	C&O 2-10-4 Texas Steam Locomotive "3011," CC, *11*		1300
11304	C&O 2-10-4 Texas Steam Locomotive "3025," CC, *11*		1300
11306	NKP 2-10-4 Texas Steam Locomotive "801," CC, *11*		1300
11308	Erie 2-10-4 Texas Steam Locomotive "3405," CC, *11*		1300
11310	Pere Marquette 2-10-4 Texas Locomotive "1241," CC, *11*		1300
11312	MILW S3 4-8-4 Northern Steam Locomotive "265," CC, *11*		995
11315	Pennsylvania-Reading Seashore Atlantic Locomotive, *11*		550
11316	PRR 4-4-2 Atlantic Steam Locomotive "272," *11*		550
11317	Southern 4-4-2 Atlantic Steam Locomotive "1910," *11*		550
11318	CN 4-4-2 Atlantic Steam Locomotive "1630," *11*		550
11319	PRR K4 4-6-2 Pacific Locomotive "5409," *13*		900
11320	PRR K4 4-6-2 Pacific Locomotive, "5436," *13*		750
11321	C&O 2-6-6-2 Mallet Steam Locomotive "1525," CC, *12*		1300
11322	NKP 2-6-6-2 Mallet Steam Locomotive "943," CC, *12*		1300
11323	W&LE 2-6-6-2 Mallet Steam Locomotive "8002," CC, *12*		1300
11327	PRR Prewar K4 4-6-2 Pacific Locomotive "3667," CC, *11*		900
11328	PRR Prewar K4 4-6-2 Pacific Locomotive "3672," CC, *11*		900
11329	PRR Prewar K4 4-6-2 Pacific Locomotive "3678," *11*		750
11330	Polar K4 4-6-2 Pacific Locomotive, CC, *11–13*		900

Exc Mint

		Exc	Mint
11331	Polar K4 4-6-2 Pacific Locomotive, *11*		750 ___
11332	ATSF 4-8-4 Northern Steam Locomotive "3751," CC, *12*		1300 ___
11333	ATSF 4-8-4 Northern Steam Locomotive "3759," CC, *12*		1300 ___
11334	Southern Crescent Limited 4-6-2 Pacific Locomotive, CC, *12*		1100 ___
11335	Blue Comet 4-6-2 Pacific Steam Locomotive "832," CC, *12*		1100 ___
11337	B&O 2-8-8-4 Steam Locomotive "7621," CC, *12*		1300 ___
11338	Alton Limited 4-6-2 Pacific Steam Locomotive "657," CC, *12*		1100 ___
11339	N&W 2-6-6-2 Mallet Steam Locomotive "1409," CC, *12*		1300 ___
11340	B&O 2-8-8-4 Steam Locomotive "659," CC, *12*		1300 ___
11341	Pilot 4-12-2 Locomotive, CC, *13*		1300 ___
11342	UP 4-12-2 Steam Locomotive "9004," CC, *12–13*		1300 ___
11343	UP 4-12-2 Steam Locomotive, black, "9000," CC, *12–13*		1300 ___
11344	UP 4-12-2 Steam Locomotive, greyhound, "9000," CC, *12*		1300 ___
11363	Cass Scenic RR 2-Truck Shay Steam Locomotive "3," CC, *12*		900 ___
11364	Meadow River 2-Truck Shay Steam Locomotive "1," CC, *12–13*		900 ___
11365	Weyerhaeuser 2-Truck Shay Steam Locomotive "3," CC, *12–13*		900 ___
11366	Pickering Lumber 2-Truck Shay Locomotive "3," CC, *12–13*		900 ___
11367	CP 2-Truck Shay Steam Locomotive "111," CC, *12–13*		900 ___
11368	WM 2-Truck Shay Steam Locomotive "2," CC, *12*		900 ___
11369	Bethlehem Steel 2-Truck Shay Steam Locomotive "5," CC, *12–13*		900 ___
11374	DM&I 2-8-8-4 Steam Locomotive "223," CC, *12*		1300 ___
11375	WP 2-8-8-4 Steam Locomotive "258," CC, *12*		1300 ___
11376	NP 2-8-8-4 Steam Locomotive "5000," CC, *12*		1300
11377	GN 2-8-8-4 Steam Locomotive "2060," CC, *12*		1300 ___
11379	PRR 0-4-0 Shifter Steam Locomotive "112," *12*		450 ___
11380	PRR 0-4-0 Shifter Steam Locomotive "94," *12*		450 ___
11381	North Pole Central 0-4-0 Switcher (std O), *12*		450 ___
11382	Transylvania 0-4-0 Shifter Steam Locomotive "13," *12*		450 ___
11383	Bethlehem Steel 0-4-0 Shifter Steam Locomotive "134," *12*		450 ___
11384	ATSF 0-4-0 Shifter Steam Locomotive "2301," *13*		450 ___
11385	UP 0-4-0 Shifter Steam Locomotive "206," *13*		450 ___
11386	B&M 2-8-4 Berkshire Steam Locomotive "4018," CC, *12–13*		1250 ___
11387	ATSF 2-8-4 Berkshire Steam Locomotive "4199," CC, *12–13*		1250 ___

		Exc	Mint
11388	SP 2-8-4 Berkshire Steam Locomotive "3505," CC, *12–13*		1250
11389	B&A 2-8-4 Berkshire Steam Locomotive "1404," CC, *12–13*		1250
11390	Lima Demonstrator 2-8-4 Berkshire Locomotive "1," CC, *12–13*		1250
11391	IC 2-8-4 Berkshire Steam Locomotive "7020," CC, *12–13*		1250
11392	Michigan Central 2-8-4 Berkshire Locomotive "1420," CC, *12–13*		1250
11399	UP H7 Class 2-8-8-2 Steam Locomotive "3595," CC, *13–14*		1350
11400	C&O H7 Class 2-8-8-2 Steam Locomotive "1578," CC, *13–14*		1350
11401	Pilot H7 Class 2-8-8-2 Locomotive, CC, *14*		1350
11402	Virginian USRA Y3 2-8-8-2 Locomotive, CC, *13–14*		1350
11403	Pilot USRA 2-8-8-2 Locomotive, CC, *13–14*		1350
11404	ATSF USRA Y3 2-8-8-2 Locomotive, CC, *13–14*		1350
11405	N&W USRA Y3 2-8-8-2 Locomotive, CC, *13–14*		1350
11410	Pilot 4-8-2 Mohawk Locomotive, CC, *13–14*		1300
11411	NYC 4-8-2 Mohawk Locomotive "2854," CC, *12–13*		1300
11412	NYC 4-8-2 Mohawk Locomotive "2867," CC, *12–13*		1300
11413	Pilot 4-8-4 J-Class Locomotive, CC, *13–14*		1300
11414	N&W 4-8-4 Steam Locomotive "612," CC, *12–13*		1300
11415	Pilot S2 6-8-6 Turbine Locomotive, CC, *14*		1300
11416	PRR S2 6-8-6 Steam Turbine Locomotive "6200," CC, *12–14*		1300
11417	PRR S2 6-8-6 Steam Turbine Locomotive "6200," CC, *12–13*		1300
11418	Pilot GS-6 Locomotive, CC, *13–14*		1300
11419	SP 4-8-4 GS-2 Locomotive, black, CC, *12–13*		1300
11420	SP 4-8-4 GS-2 Locomotive, Daylight, CC, *12*		1300
11421	SP 4-8-4 GS-6 Locomotive, black, CC, *12*		1300
11422	WP 4-8-4 GS-64 Locomotive "482," CC, *12*		1300
11423	CNJ Blue Comet Locomotive "833," CC, *12–13*		1100
11425	Alaska 0-4-0 Locomotive, RailSounds, *12–13*		1100
11426	Rio Grande 0-4-0 Locomotive, RailSounds, *12–13*		450
11427	SP 0-4-0 Locomotive "14," RailSounds, *12–13*		450
11428	MILW 0-4-0 Locomotive, RailSounds, *12–13*		450
11429	Southern 0-4-0 Locomotive, RailSounds, *12–13*		450
11430	GN 0-4-0 Locomotive "1066," RailSounds, *12–13*		450
11431	N&W 4-8-4 Locomotive "611," CC, *12*		1300
11432	LL S2 6-8-6 Steam Turbine Locomotive, CC, *13–14*		1300
11433	PRR S2 6-8-6 Steam Turbine Locomotive CC, *13–14*		1300
11434	UP Big Boy Locomotive "4006," CC, *14*		2700

		Exc	Mint
11435	UP Big Boy Locomotive "4018," CC, *14*		2700 ____
11436	UP Big Boy Locomotive "4005," CC, *14*		2700 ____
11437	UP Big Boy Locomotive "4014," CC, *14*		2700 ____
11438	UP Big Boy Locomotive "4017," CC, *14*		2700 ____
11446	UP USRA Y3 2-8-8-2 Locomotive "3671," CC, *13–14*		1350 ____
11447	PRR USRA Y3 2-8-8-2 Locomotive "376," CC, *13–14*		1350 ____
11448	UP Big Boy Locomotive "4012," CC, *14*		2700 ____
11449	UP Big Boy Locomotive "4004," CC, *14*		2700 ____
11450	Polar Express Berkshire Scale Locomotive, gold, CC, *14*		1500 ____
11451	Polar Express Berkshire Scale Locomotive, black, CC, *14*		1500 ____
11452	C&O 2-8-4 Berkshire Locomotive "2687," CC, *14*		1500 ____
11453	Erie 2-8-4 Berkshire Locomotive "3321," CC, *14*		1500 ____
11454	NKP 2-8-4 Berkshire Locomotive "765," CC, *14*		1500 ____
11455	Pere Marquette 2-8-4 Berkshire Locomotive "1225," CC, *14*		1500 ____
11456	Pere Marquette 2-8-4 Berkshire Locomotive "1227," CC, *14*		1500 ____
11462	SP AC-12 Cab-Forward Locomotive "4291," CC, *14*		1700 ____
11463	SP AC-12 Cab-Forward Locomotive "4286," CC, *14*		1700 ____
11464	SP AC-12 Cab-Forward Locomotive "4294," CC, *14*		1700 ____
11465	SP AC-12 Cab-Forward Locomotive "4275," CC, *14*		1700 ____
11469	Pilot AC-12 Cab-Forward Locomotive, CC, *14*		1700 ____
11650	Alderney Dairy General American Milk Car 2-pack (std O), *07*		130 ____
11651	Freeport General American Milk Car 2-pack (std O), *07*		130 ____
11652	BNSF Mechanical Reefer 2-pack (std O), *07–09*		140 ____
11653	SPFE Mechanical Reefer 2-pack (std O), *07*		140 ____
11654	UPFE Mechanical Reefer 2-pack (std O), *07*		140 ____
11655	GN WFE Mechanical Reefer 2-pack (std O), *07*		140 ____
11657	PFE Wood-sided Reefer 3-pack (std O), *06*		190 ____
11658	John Bull Add-on Coach, *08*		80 ____
11700	Conrail Limited Set, *87*	320	370 ____
11701	Rail Blazer Set, *87–88*		60 ____
11702	Black Diamond Set, *87*	195	265 ____
11703	Iron Horse Freight Set, *88–91*	100	105 ____
11704	Southern Freight Runner Set (SSS), *87*	210	285 ____
11705	Chessie System Unit Train, *88*	360	450 ____
11706	Dry Gulch Line Set (SSS), *88*	190	260 ____
11707	Silver Spike Set, *88–89*	175	245 ____
11708	Midnight Shift Set, *88 u, 89*	60	75 ____
11710	CP Rail Freight Set, *89*	375	447 ____
11711	Santa Fe F3 Diesel ABA Set, *91*	480	590 ____
11712	Great Lakes Express Set (SSS), *90*	260	280 ____

			Exc	Mint
____	**11713**	Santa Fe Dash 8-40B Set, *90*	395	480
____	**11714**	Badlands Express Set, *90–91*	49	60
____	**11715**	Lionel 90th Anniversary Set, *90*	336	358
____	**11716**	Lionelville Circus Special Set, *90–91*	155	190
____	**11717**	CSX Freight Set, *90*	230	240
____	**11718**	Norfolk Southern Dash 8-40C Unit Train, *92*	445	481
____	**11719**	Coastal Freight Set (SSS), *91*	165	215
____	**11720**	Santa Fe Special Set, *91*	49	60
____	**11721**	Mickey's World Tour Train Set, *91, 92 u*	118	158
____	**11722**	Girls Train Set, *91*	547	817
____	**11723**	Amtrak Maintenance Train, *91, 92 u*	210	245
____	**11724**	GN F3 Diesel ABA Set, *92*	730	840
____	**11726**	Erie-Lackawanna Freight Set, *91 u*	225	275
____	**11727**	Coastal Limited Set, *92*	90	110
____	**11728**	High Plains Runner Set, *92*	120	130
____	**11733**	Feather River Set (SSS), *92*	285	330
____	**11734**	Erie Alco Diesel ABA Set (FF 7), *93*	250	305
____	**11735**	NYC Flyer Freight Set "1735WS," *93–99*	125	160
____	**11736**	Union Pacific Express Set, *93–95*	110	130
____	**11738**	Soo Line Set (SSS), *93*	250	280
____	**11739**	Super Chief Set, *93–94*	135	155
____	**11740**	Conrail Consolidated Set, *93*	200	240
____	**11741**	Northwest Express Set, *93*	130	155
____	**11742**	Coastal Limited Set, *93 u*	90	115
____	**11743**	Chesapeake & Ohio Freight Set, *94*	240	280
____	**11744**	NYC Passenger/Freight Set (SSS), *94*	295	335
____	**11745**	U.S. Navy Set, *94–95*	248	286
____	**11746**	Seaboard Freight Set, *94, 95 u*	90	115
____	**11747**	Lionel Lines Steam Set, *95*	310	340
____	**11748**	Amtrak Alco Diesel Passenger Set, *95–96*	130	185
____	**11749**	Western Maryland Set (SSS), *95*	275	300
____	**11750**	McDonald's Nickel Plate Special Set, *87 u*	143	153
____	**11751**	Sears PRR Passenger Set, *87 u*	120	155
____	**11752**	JCPenney Timber Master Set, *87 u*	75	115
____	**11753**	Kay Bee Toys Rail Blazer Set, *87 u*	80	100
____	**11754**	Key America Set, *87 u*	150	165
____	**11755**	Timber Master Set, *87 u*	150	165
____	**11756**	Hawthorne Freight Flyer Set, *87–88 u*	65	85
____	**11757**	Chrysler Mopar Express Set, *88 u*	315	362
____	**11758**	Desert King Set (SSS), *89*	195	250
____	**11759**	JCPenney Silver Spike Set, *88 u*	175	250
____	**11761**	JCPenney Iron Horse Freight Set, *88 u*	120	125
____	**11762**	True Value Cannonball Express Set, *89 u*	95	145
____	**11763**	United Model Freight Hauler Set, *88 u*	135	145
____	**11764**	Sears Iron Horse Freight Set, *88 u*	155	190
____	**11765**	Spiegel Silver Spike Set, *88 u*	175	250
____	**11767**	Shoprite Freight Flyer Set, *88 u*	80	125
____	**11769**	JCPenney Midnight Shift Set, *89 u*	100	175
____	**11770**	Sears Circus Set, *89 u*	185	220
____	**11771**	K-Mart Microracers Set, *89 u*	80	110
____	**11772**	Macy's Freight Flyer Set, *89 u*	170	220
____	**11773**	Sears NYC Passenger Set, *89 u*	175	200
____	**11774**	Ace Hardware Cannonball Express Set, *89 u*	145	175

		Exc	Mint	
11775	Anheuser-Busch Set, *89–92 u*	241	339	____
11776	Pace Iron Horse Freight Set, *89 u*	115	135	____
11777	Sears Lionelville Circus Set, *90 u*	175	190	____
11778	Sears Badlands Express Set, *90 u*	49	60	____
11779	Sears CSX Freight Set, *90 u*	190	230	____
11780	Sears NP Passenger Set, *90 u*	155	190	____
11781	True Value Cannonball Express Set, *90 u*	75	115	____
11783	Toys "R" Us Heavy Iron Set, *90–91 u*	135	160	____
11784	Pace Iron Horse Freight Set, *90 u*	115	135	____
11785	Costco Union Pacific Express Set, *90 u*	200	230	____
11789	Sears Illinois Central Passenger Set, *91 u*	170	200	____
11793	Santa Fe Set, *91 u*	49	60	____
11794	Mickey's World Tour Set, *91 u*	80	100	____
11796	Union Pacific Express Set, *91 u*	150	160	____
11797	Sears Coastal Limited Set, *92 u*	80	100	____
11800	Toys "R" Us Heavy Iron Thunder Limited Set, *92–93 u*	235	295	____
11803	Nickel Plate Special Set, *92 u*	135	145	____
11804	K-Mart Coastal Limited Set, *92 u*	80	100	____
11809	Village Trolley Set, *95–97*	55	85	____
11810	Budweiser Modern Era Set, *93–94 u*	198	206	____
11811	United Auto Workers Set, *93 u*	189	447	____
11812	Coastal Limited Special Set, *93 u*	95	115	____
11813	Crayola Activity Train Set, *94 u, 95*	103	127	____
11814	Ford Limited Edition Set, *94 u*	205	251	____
11818	Chrysler Mopar Set, *94 u*	221	255	____
11819	Georgia Power Set, *95 u*	511	535	____
11820	Red Wing Shoes NYC Flyer Set, *95 u*	256	310	____
11821	Sears Zenith Set, *95 u*		770	____
11822	Chevrolet Set, *96 u*	270	315	____
11825	Bloomingdale's Set, *96 u*		316	____
11826	Sears Freight Set, *95–96 u*		758	____
11827	Zenith Employees Set, *96 u*		790	____
11828	NJ Transit Passenger Set, *96 u*		180	____
11833	NJ Transit GP38 Diesel Passenger Set, *97*	275	300	____
11837	Union Pacific GP9 Diesel Set, *97*		520	____
11838	ATSF Warhorse Hudson Freight Set, *97*		810	____
11839	SP&S 4-6-2 Steam Freight Set, *97*		280	____
11841	Bloomingdale's Set, *97 u*		287	____
11843	Boston & Maine GP9 Diesel ABA Set, *98*		510	____
11844	Union Pacific Die-cast Ore Cars 4-pack, *98*		225	____
11846	Kal Kan Pet Care Train Set, *97 u*		792	____
11849	Lionel Centennial Series Reefer 4-pack, *98*		115	____
11850	Rice A Roni Trolley Set, *02 u*		260	____
11851	PFE Reefer 6-pack (std O), *02*	225	255	____
11852	Clinchfield PS-2 2-bay Hopper, *04*		70	____
11853	B&M PS-2 2-bay Hopper 2-pack, *05*		128	____
11854	N&W PS-2 Covered Hopper 2-pack, *04*		70	____
11855	GN Offset Hopper with coal, 2-pack, *05*		120	____
11856	Green Bay & Western Offset Hopper 2-pack, *05*		120	____
11857	Baltimore & Ohio Offset Hopper 2-pack, *05*		120	____
11858	PRR PS-4 Flatcar with trailers, 2-pack (std O), *05*		160	____

Exc Mint

		Exc	Mint
____ **11859**	GN PS-4 Flatcar with trailers (std O), *05*		160
____ **11860**	SP PS-4 Flatcar with trailers (std O), *05*		160
____ **11861**	C&O PS-4 Flatcar with trailers (std O), *05*		160
____ **11863**	Southern Pacific GP9 Diesel "2383," *98*		225
____ **11864**	New York Central GP9 Diesel "2383," *98*		275
____ **11865**	Alaska GP7 Diesel "1802," *98–99*		90
11866 ____	Govt. of Canada Cylindrical Hopper 2-pack (std O), *05*		120
____ **11867**	CN Cylindrical Hopper 2-pack (std O), *05*		120
____ **11868**	BN Husky Stack Car 2-pack (std O), *05*		160
____ **11869**	SP Husky Stack Car 2-pack (std O), *05*		160
____ **11870**	CSX Husky Stack Car 2-pack (std O), *05*		220
____ **11871**	TTX Trailer Train Stack Car 2-pack (std O), *05*		160
11872 ____	PFE Orange Steel-sided Reefer 3-pack (std O), *05*		130
____ **11873**	C&O Offset Hopper 3-pack (std O), *05*		130
11874 ____	PFE Orange Steel-sided Reefer 3-pack (std O), *05*		130
____ **11875**	NP Steel-sided Reefer 3-pack (std O), *05*		130
11876 ____	PFE Silver Steel-sided Reefer 3-pack (std O), *05*		130
____ **11877**	C&NW Steel-sided Reefer 3-pack (std O), *05*		130
11878 ____	Santa Fe PS-2 2-bay Covered Hopper 3-pack (std O), *06*		125
11879 ____	MKT PS-2 2-bay Covered Hopper 3-pack (std O), *06*		125
11880 ____	Boraxo PS-2 2-bay Covered Hopper 3-pack (std O), *06*		125
11881 ____	PRR PS-2 2-bay Covered Hopper 3-pack (std O), *06*		125
11882 ____	RI Offset Hopper with gravel, 3-pack (std O), *06*		125
____ **11883**	CNJ Offset Hopper 3-pack (std O), *06*		145
11884 ____	Maine Central Offset Hopper 3-pack (std O), *06*		145
____ **11891**	Pennsylvania 3-bay Hopper 3-pack (std O), *06*		155
____ **11892**	Conrail ACF 3-bay Hopper 3-pack (std O), *06*		155
____ **11893**	N&W 3-bay Hopper 3-pack (std O), *06*		155
____ **11894**	UP 3-bay Hopper 3-pack (std O), *06*		155
____ **11895**	GN Steel-sided Reefer 3-pack (std O), *06*		145
11896 ____	Santa Fe Steel-sided Reefer 3-pack (std O), *06*		145
11897 ____	Pepper Packing Steel-sided Reefer 3-pack (std O), *06*		145
____ **11900**	SF Steam Freight Set, *96–01*		130
____ **11903**	ACL F3 Diesel ABA Set, *96*		716
____ **11905**	U.S. Coast Guard Set, *96*	160	180
____ **11906**	Factory Selection Special Set, *95 u*		85
____ **11909**	N&W J 4-8-4 Warhorse Set, *96*	560	720
____ **11910**	Lionel Lines Set (O27), *96*	140	160
____ **11912**	"57" Switcher Service Exclusive, *96*		310
____ **11913**	SP GP9 Diesel Freight Set, *97*		440
____ **11914**	NYC GP9 Diesel Freight Set, *97*		370
11918 ____	Conrail SD20 Service Exclusive "X1144" (SSS), *97*		255
____ **11919**	Docksider Set, *97*		70

		Exc	Mint
11920	Port of Lionel City Dive Team Set, *97*		185 ____
11921	Lionel Lines Freight Set, *97*		130 ____
11929	ATSF Warbonnet Passenger Set, *97–99*		132 ____
11930	ATSF Warbonnet Passenger Car 2-pack, *97–99*		80 ____
11931	Chessie Flyer Freight Set "1931S," *97–99*		165 ____
11933	Dodge Motorsports Freight Set, *96 u*		275 ____
11934	Virginian Electric Locomotive Freight Set, *97–99*		260 ____
11935	NYC Flyer Freight Set, *97*		155 ____
11936	Little League Baseball Steam Set, *97*	222	287 ____
11939	SP&S 4-6-2 Steam Freight Set, *97*		220 ____
11940	Southern Pacific SD40 Warhorse Coal Set, *98*		600 ____
11944	Lionel Lines 4-4-2 Steam Freight Set, *98*		175 ____
11956	UP GP9 Diesel Set, *97*	325	375 ____
11957	Mobil Oil Steam Special Set, *97*		381 ____
11971	D&H 4-4-2 Steam Freight Set, *98*	125	155 ____
11972	Alaska GP7 Diesel Set, *98–99*	180	215 ____
11974	Station Accessory Set, *98*		22 ____
11975	Freight Accessory Pack, *98*		23 ____
11977	NP Freight Cars 4-pack, *98*		170 ____
11979	N&W 4-4-2 Steam Freight Set, *98*		75 ____
11981	1998 Holiday Trolley Set, *98*		75 ____
11982	New Jersey Transit Ore Car Set, *98*		250 ____
11983	Farmrail Agricultural Set, *99*		451 ____
11984	Corvette GP7 Diesel Set, *99*		447 ____
11988	NYC Firecar "18444" and Instruction Car "19853," *99*		210 ____
12000	NY Yankees Berkshire Passenger Set, *13*		380 ____
12004	Philadelphia Phillies Berkshire Passenger Set, *13*		380 ____
12008	Boston Red Sox Berkshire Passenger Set, *13*		380 ____
12012	Chicago Cubs Berkshire Passenger Set, *13*		380 ____
12013	NY Mets and Yankees Subway Series Set, *13*		400 ____
12014	10" Straight Track (FasTrack), *03–14*		5 ____
12015	O36 Curved Track (FasTrack), *03–14*		4 ____
12016	10" Terminal Track (FasTrack), *03–14*		6 ____
12017	O36 Manual Switch, left hand (FasTrack), *03–14*		50 ____
12018	O36 Manual Switch, right hand (FasTrack), *03–14*		50 ____
12019	90-degree Crossover (FasTrack), *03–14*		26 ____
12020	5" Uncoupling Track (FasTrack), *03–14*		45 ____
12022	O36 Half Curved Track (FasTrack), *03–14*		5 ____
12023	O36 Quarter Curved Track (FasTrack), *03–14*		5 ____
12024	5" Straight Track (FasTrack), *03–14*		5 ____
12025	4" Straight Track (FasTrack), *03–14*		5 ____
12026	1" Straight Track (FasTrack), *03–14*		5 ____
12027	10" Insulated Track (FasTrack), *03–14*		5 ____
12028	Inner Passing Loop Track Pack (FasTrack), *03–14*		115 ____
12029	Accessory Activator Pack (FasTrack), *03–14*		21 ____
12030	Figure 8 Track Pack (FasTrack), *03–14*		75 ____
12031	Outer Passing Loop Track Pack (FasTrack), *03–14*		145 ____

		Exc	Mint
____ **12032**	10" Straight Track 4-pack (FasTrack), *03–14*		22
12033	O36 Curved Track, card of 4 (FasTrack), *03–14*		
____			22
____ **12035**	FasTrack Lighted Bumper 2-pack, *05–14*		33
____ **12036**	Grade Crossing (FasTrack), *05–14*		14
____ **12037**	Graduated Trestle Set (FasTrack), *05–14*		185
____ **12038**	Elevated Trestle Set (FasTrack), *05–14*		45
____ **12039**	Railer (FasTrack), *04–14*		9
____ **12040**	O Gauge Transition Piece (FasTrack), *04–14*		9
____ **12041**	O72 Curved Track (FasTrack), *04–14*		7
____ **12042**	30" Straight Track (FasTrack), *04–14*		15
____ **12043**	O48 Curved Track (FasTrack), *04–14*		5
12044	Siding Track Add-on Track Pack (FasTrack), *04–14*		
____			120
12045	O36 Remote Switch, left hand (FasTrack), *04–14*		
____			95
12046	O36 Remote Switch, right hand (FasTrack), *04–14*		
____			95
12047	O72 Wye Remote Switch (FasTrack), *04–14*		97
12048	O72 Remote Switch, left hand (FasTrack), *04–14*		
____			104
12049	O72 Remote Switch, right hand (FasTrack), *04–14*		
____			104
____ **12050**	22½-degree Crossover (FasTrack), *04–14*		46
____ **12051**	45-degree Crossover (FasTrack), *04–14*		24
12052	Grade Crossing with flashers (FasTrack), *05–14*		
____			92
____ **12053**	Accessory Power Wire (FasTrack), *04–14*		6
12054	Operating Track with half straight (FasTrack), *05–14*		
____			45
____ **12055**	O72 Half Curved Track (FasTrack), *04–14*		6
____ **12056**	O60 Curved Track (FasTrack), *05–14*		7
____ **12057**	O60 Remote Switch, left hand, *05–14*		104
12058	O60 Remote Switch, right hand (FasTrack), *05–14*		
____			104
____ **12059**	Earthen Bumper (FasTrack), *04–14*		9
____ **12060**	Block Section (FasTrack), *05–14*		9
____ **12061**	O84 Curved Track (FasTrack), *05–14*		7
12062	Grade Crossing with gates and flashers (FasTrack), *06–14*		
____			160
12065	O48 Remote Switch, left hand (FasTrack), *07–14*		
____			104
12066	O48 Remote Switch, right hand (FasTrack), *07–14*		
____			104
____ **12073**	1⅜" Track Section (FasTrack), *07–14*		5
12074	1⅜" Track Section, no roadbed (FasTrack), *07–14*		
____			5
____ **12080**	42" Path Remote Switch, right hand, *07–12*		80
____ **12081**	42" Path Remote Switch, left hand, *07–12*		80
____ **12700**	Erie Magnetic Gantry Crane, *87*	125	150
____ **12701**	Operating Fueling Station, *87*	60	74
____ **12702**	Control Tower, *87*	60	75
____ **12703**	Icing Station, *88–89*	60	65
____ **12704**	Dwarf Signal, *88–93*	9	11
____ **12705**	Lumber Shed Kit, *88–99*		9
____ **12706**	Barrel Loader Building Kit, *87–99*		10

		Exc	Mint
12707	Billboards, set of 3, *87–99*		5 ___
12708	Street Lamps, set of 3, *88–93*	6	9 ___
12709	Banjo Signal, *87–91, 95–00*		29 ___
12710	Engine House Kit, *87–91*	21	25 ___
12711	Water Tower Kit, *87–99*		13 ___
12712	Automatic Ore Loader, *87–88*	17	21 ___
12713	Automatic Gateman, *87–88, 94–00*	30	40 ___
12714	Crossing Gate, *87–91, 93–14*		50 ___
12715	Illuminated Bumpers, set of 2, *87–14*		13 ___
12716	Searchlight Tower, *87–89, 91–92*	19	22 ___
12717	Nonilluminated Bumpers, set of 3, *87–14*		7 ___
12718	Barrel Shed Kit, *87–99*		10 ___
12719	Animated Refreshment Stand, *88–89*	65	70 ___
12720	Rotary Beacon, *88–89*	40	45 ___
12721	Illuminated Extension Bridge, rock piers, *89*	26	38 ___
12722	Roadside Diner, smoke, *88–89*	27	38 ___
12723	Microwave Tower, *88–91, 94–95*	14	19 ___
12724	Double Signal Bridge, *88–90*	39	50 ___
12725	Lionel Tractor and Trailer, *88–89*	16	18 ___
12726	Grain Elevator Kit, *88–91, 94–99*		36 ___
12727	Operating Semaphore, *89–99*		26 ___
12728	Illuminated Freight Station, *89*	29	38 ___
12729	Mail Pickup Set, *88–91, 95*	12	16 ___
12730	Girder Bridge, *88–03, 08–14*		21 ___
12731	Station Platform, *88–00*		8 ___
12732	Coal Bag, *88–14*		7 ___
12733	Watchman Shanty Kit, *88–99*		5 ___
12734	Passenger/Freight Station, *89–99*		18 ___
12735	Diesel Horn Shed, *88–91*	19	24 ___
12736	Coaling Station Kit, *88–91*	21	31 ___
12737	Whistling Freight Shed, *88–99*		28 ___
12739	Lionel Gas Company Tractor and Tanker, *89*	20	25 ___
12740	Genuine Wood Logs, set of 3, *88–92, 94–95, 97–99*		5 ___
12741	Union Pacific Intermodal Crane, *89*	165	185 ___
12742	Gooseneck Lamps, set of 2, *89–00*		21 ___
12743	Track Clips, dozen (O), *89–14*		12 ___
12744	Rock Piers, set of 2, *89–92, 94–05, 08, 11–14*		15 ___
12745	Barrel Pack, set of 6, *89–14*		8 ___
12746	Operating/Uncoupling Track (O27), *89–14*		10 ___
12748	Illuminated Passenger Platform, *89–99*		18 ___
12749	Rotary Radar Antenna, *89–92, 95*	28	38 ___
12750	Crane Kit, *89–91*	8	10 ___
12751	Shovel Kit, *89–91*	8	10 ___
12752	History of Lionel Trains Video, *89–92, 94*	19	21 ___
12753	Ore Load, set of 2, *89–91, 95*	1	2 ___
12754	Graduated Trestle Set, 22 pieces, *89–14*		27 ___
12755	Elevated Trestle Set, 10 pieces, *89–14*		27 ___
12756	The Making of the Scale Hudson Video, *91–94*	20	22 ___
12759	Floodlight Tower, *90–00*		25 ___
12760	Automatic Highway Flasher, *90–91*	23	27 ___
12761	Animated Billboard, *90–91, 93, 95*	22	23 ___
12763	Single Signal Bridge, *90–91, 93*	31	35 ___

		Exc	Mint
12767	Steam Clean and Wheel Grind Shop, *92–93, 95*	240	290
12768	Burning Switch Tower, *90, 93*	85	90
12770	Arch-Under Bridge, *90–03, 08–14*		30
12771	Mom's Roadside Diner, smoke, *90–91*	34	50
12772	Truss Bridge, flasher and piers, *90–14*		70
12773	Freight Platform Kit, *90–98*		32
12774	Lumber Loader Kit, *90–99*		19
12777	Chevron Tractor and Tanker, *90–91*	9	15
12778	Conrail Tractor and Trailer, *90*	9	16
12779	Lionelville Grain Company Tractor and Trailer, *90*	11	19
12780	RS-1 50-watt Transformer, *90–93*	95	130
12781	N&W Intermodal Crane, *90–91*	145	160
12782	Lift Bridge, *91–92*	428	518
12783	Monon Tractor and Trailer, *91*	11	19
12784	Intermodal Containers, set of 3, *91*	12	17
12785	Lionel Gravel Company Tractor and Trailer, *91*	9	15
12786	Lionel Steel Company Tractor and Trailer, *91*	10	16
12791	Animated Passenger Station, *91*	45	60
12794	Lionel Tractor, *91*	7	13
12795	Cable Reels, pair, *91–98*	3	5
12798	Forklift Loader Station, *92–95*	33	44
12800	Scale Hudson Replacement Pilot Truck, *91 u*	13	17
12802	Chat & Chew Roadside Diner, smoke and lights, *92–95*	41	50
12804	Highway Lights, set of 4, *92–99, 02–04, 13–14*	9	27
12805	Intermodal Containers, set of 3, *92*	10	14
12806	Lionel Lumber Company Tractor and Trailer, *92*	10	15
12807	Little Caesars Tractor and Trailer, *92*	9	14
12808	Mobil Tractor and Tanker, *92*	8	13
12809	Animated Billboard, *92–93*	20	22
12810	American Flyer Tractor and Trailer, *94*	12	18
12811	Alka Seltzer Tractor and Trailer, *92*	11	19
12812	Illuminated Freight Station, *93–00*		27
12818	Animated Freight Station, *92, 94–95*	50	60
12819	Inland Steel Tractor and Trailer, *92*	9	16
12821	Lionel Catalog Video, *92*	13	17
12826	Intermodal Containers, set of 3, *93*	10	16
12831	Rotary Beacon, *93–95*	22	32
12832	Block Target Signal, *93–98*		25
12833	RoadRailer Tractor and Trailer, *93*	9	15
12834	Pennsylvania Magnetic Gantry Crane, *93*	130	170
12835	Operating Fueling Station, *93*	55	60
12836	Santa Fe Quantum Tractor and Trailer, *93*	8	14
12837	Humble Oil Tractor and Tanker, *93*	9	16
12838	Crate Load, set of 2, *93–97*		3
12839	Grade Crossings, set of 2, *93–14*		7
12840	Insulated Straight Track (O), *93–14*		8
12841	Insulated Straight Track (O27), *93–14*		5
12842	Dunkin' Donuts Tractor and Trailer, *92 u*	23	25
12843	Die-cast Sprung Trucks, pair, *93–99*		10
12844	Coil Covers, pair (O), *93–98*		3

		Exc	Mint
12847	Animated Ice Depot, 94–99		65 ____
12848	Lionel Oil Company Derrick, 94	55	75 ____
12849	Lionel Controller with wall pack, 94, 95 u		NRS ____
12852	Die-cast Intermodal Trailer Frame, 94–01		6 ____
12853	Coil Covers, pair (std O), 94–98		7 ____
12854	U.S. Navy Tractor and Tanker, 94–95		33 ____
12855	Intermodal Containers, set of 3, 94–95	9	13 ____
12860	Lionel Visitor's Center Tractor and Trailer, 94 u	10	14 ____
12861	Lionel Leasing Company Tractor, 94	8	13 ____
12862	Oil Drum Loader, 94–95	75	85 ____
12864	Little Caesars Tractor and Trailer, 94	8	14 ____
12865	Wisk Tractor and Trailer, 94	12	55 ____
12866	TMCC 135-watt PowerHouse Power Supply, 94 u, 95–03		46 ____
12867	TMCC 135 PowerMaster Power Distribution Center, 94 u, 95–04		49 ____
12868	TMCC CAB-1 Remote Controller, 94 u, 95–09		115 ____
12869	Marathon Oil Tractor and Tanker, 94	15	22 ____
12873	Operating Sawmill, 95–97		70 ____
12874	Classic Street Lamps, set of 3, 94–00		13 ____
12877	Operating Fueling Station, 95	75	85 ____
12878	Control Tower, 95	49	60 ____
12881	Chrysler Mopar Tractor and Trailer, 94 u	41	52 ____
12882	Lighted Billboard, 95	9	14 ____
12883	Dwarf Signal, 95–14		27 ____
12884	Truck Loading Dock Kit, 95–98		16 ____
12885	40-watt Control System, 94 u, 95–05		35 ____
12886	Floodlight Tower, 95–98		31 ____
12888	Railroad Crossing Flasher, 95–14		56 ____
12889	Operating Windmill, 95–98		34 ____
12890	Big Red Control Button, 94 u, 95–00		43 ____
12891	Lionel Refrigerator Lines Tractor and Trailer, 95	12	16 ____
12892	Automatic Flagman, 92–98		25 ____
12893	TMCC PowerMaster Power Adapter Cable, 94 u, 95–13		20 ____
12894	Signal Bridge, 95–01		22 ____
12895	Double-track Signal Bridge, 95–00		44 ____
12896	Tunnel Portals, pair, 95–14		20 ____
12897	Engine House Kit, 96–98		29 ____
12898	Flagpole, 95–97		8 ____
12899	Searchlight Tower, 95–98		25 ____
12900	Crane Kit, 95–98		8 ____
12901	Shovel Kit, 95–98		7 ____
12902	Marathon Oil Derrick, 94 u, 95	103	156 ____
12903	Diesel Horn Shed, 95–98		29 ____
12904	Coaling Station Kit, 95–98		19 ____
12905	Factory Kit, 95–98		20 ____
12906	Maintenance Shed Kit, 95–98		20 ____
12907	Intermodal Containers, set of 3, 95	9	14 ____
12911	TMCC Command Base, 95–09		80 ____
12912	Oil Pumping Station, 95–98	38	65 ____
12914	SC-1 Switch and Accessory Controller, 95–98		35 ____
12915	Log Loader, 96		115 ____

			Exc	Mint
___	**12916**	Water Tower, *96–97*		56
___	**12917**	Animated Switch Tower, *96–98*		29
___	**12922**	NYC Operating Gantry Crane, coil covers, *96*	75	90
___	**12923**	Red Wing Shoes Tractor and Trailer, *95 u*	34	38
___	**12925**	42" Diameter Curved Track Section (O), *96–14*		4
___	**12926**	Globe Street Lamps, set of 3, *96–03, 08–09*		10
___	**12927**	Yard Light, set of 3, *96–14*		27
___	**12929**	Rail-truck Loading Dock, *96*		44
___	**12930**	Lionelville Oil Company Derrick, *95 u, 96*	55	75
___	**12931**	Electrical Substation, *96*		22
___	**12932**	Laimbeer Packaging Tractor and Trailer Set, *96*		14
___	**12933**	GM Parts Tractor and Trailer, *95*		NRS
___	**12935**	Zenith Tractor and Trailer, *96*		24
___	**12936**	SP Intermodal Crane, *97*		195
___	**12937**	NS Intermodal Crane, *97*		200
___	**12938**	PowerStation Controller and PowerHouse 135-watt Power Supply, *97–00*		150
___	**12943**	Illuminated Station Platform, *97–00*		24
___	**12944**	Sunoco Oil Derrick, *97*		85
___	**12945**	Sunoco Pumping Oil Station, *97*		80
___	**12948**	Bascule Bridge, *97*		315
___	**12949**	Billboards, set of 3, *97–00*		7
___	**12951**	Airplane Hangar Kit, *97–98*		29
___	**12952**	Big L Diner Kit, *97*		24
___	**12953**	Linex Gas Tall Oil Tank, *97*		9
___	**12954**	Linex Gas Wide Oil Tank, *97*		10
___	**12955**	Road Runner and Wile E. Coyote Ambush Shack, *97*		93
___	**12958**	Industrial Water Tower, *97–98*		50
___	**12960**	Rotary Radar Antenna, *97*		26
___	**12961**	Newsstand with diesel horn, *97*		30
___	**12962**	LL Passenger Service Train Whistle, *97–99*		30
___	**12964**	Donald Duck Radar Antenna, *97*		61
___	**12965**	Goofy Rotary Beacon, *97*		52
___	**12966**	Rotary Aircraft Beacon, *97–00*		35
___	**12968**	Girder Bridge Building Kit, *97*		22
___	**12969**	TMCC Command Set, *97–09*		148
___	**12974**	Blinking Light Billboard, *97–00*		15
___	**12975**	Steiner Victorian Building Kit, *97–98*		33
___	**12976**	Dobson Victorian Building Kit, *97–98*		24
___	**12977**	Kindler Victorian Building Kit, *97–98*		35
___	**12982**	Culvert Loader, conventional, *98–00*		190
___	**12983**	Culvert Unloader, conventional, *99*		185
___	**12987**	Intermodal Contianers, set of 3, *98*		15
___	**12989**	Lionel Tractor and Trailer, *98*		16
___	**12991**	Linex Gas Tractor-Tanker, *98*		16
___	**13113**	Electric Trolley and Trail Car (std), *07*		450
___	**14000**	Operating Forklift Platform, *00*		160
___	**14001**	Operating Belt Lumber Loader, *00*		95
___	**14002**	ZW Amp/Volt Meter, *00–04*		80
___	**14003**	80-watt Transformer/Controller, *00–03*		70
___	**14004**	Operating Coal Loader, *00*		135
___	**14005**	Operating Coal Ramp, *00*		130

		Exc	Mint
14018	ElectroCoupler Kit for Command Upgradeable GP9s, *00*		20 ____
14062	31" Path Remote Switch, left hand, *01–14*		55 ____
14063	31" Path Remote Switch, right hand, *01–14*		75 ____
14065	Nuclear Reactor, *00*		233 ____
14071	Yard Light, *00–14*		35 ____
14072	Haunted House, *01*		181 ____
14073	History of Lionel, The First 90 Years Video, *00*		15 ____
14075	A Century of Lionel, 1900-1969 Video, *00*		15 ____
14076	A Century of Lionel, 1970-2000 Video, *00*		15 ____
14077	ZW Amp/Volt Meter, *00–03*		70 ____
14078	Die-cast Sprung Trucks, *00–05, 07–14*		24 ____
14079	Operating North Pole Pylon, *01*		70 ____
14080	Hobo Hotel, *01*	30	65 ____
14081	Shell Oil Derrick, *01*		100 ____
14082	Pedestrian Walkover, speed sensor, *01–03*		50 ____
14083	Pedestrian Walkover, *01–03, 08, 12–14*		55 ____
14084	Lionel Heliport, *01*		85 ____
14085	Newsstand, *01*		75 ____
14086	Water Tower, *00*		105 ____
14087	Lighthouse, *01*		95 ____
14090	Banjo Signal, *01–14*		60 ____
14091	Automatic Gateman, *01–03, 07–09*		45 ____
14092	Floodlight Tower, *01–05, 08–14*		48 ____
14093	Single Signal Bridge, *01–04, 08*		22 ____
14094	Double Signal Bridge, *01–04, 08*		30 ____
14095	Illuminated Station Platform, *01–04*		20 ____
14096	Station Platform, *01–04*		10 ____
14097	Rotary Aircraft Beacon, *01–04, 07–10*		40 ____
14098	Auto Crossing Gate, *01–14*		100 ____
14099	Block Target Signal, *01–04, 07–08*		22 ____
14100	Blinking Light Billboard, *01–03*		23 ____
14101	Red Baron Pylon, *01*		85 ____
14102	Rocket Launcher, *01*		250 ____
14104	Burning Switch Tower, *00*		70 ____
14105	Aquarium, *01*		175 ____
14106	Operating Freight Station, *00*		70 ____
14107	Coaling Station, *01–03*		95 ____
14109	Carousel, *01*		230 ____
14110	Operating Ferris Wheel, *01–02, 04*		170 ____
14111	1531R Controller, *00–14*		45 ____
14112	Lighted Lockon, *01–10, 13–14*		6 ____
14113	Engine Transfer Table, *01*		210 ____
14114	Engine Transfer Table Extension, *01*		75 ____
14116	PRR Die-cast Girder Bridge, *01*		20 ____
14117	NYC Die-cast Girder Bridge, *01*		20 ____
14119	Gooseneck Lamps, set of 2, *01–04, 07*		22 ____
14121	Classic Billboards, set of 3, *01–03*		10 ____
14124	ZW Controller with 2 transformers, *01*		300 ____
14125	Christmas Tree with 400E Train, *00*		65 ____
14126	Exploding Ammo Dump		55 ____
14133	Madison Hobby Shop, *01*		290 ____
14134	Triple Action Magnetic Crane, *01*		230 ____

____	**14135**	NS Black Die-cast Girder Bridge, *02*	15
____	**14137**	Die-cast Girder Bridge, *01–07*	25
____	**14138**	Snap-On Tool Animated Billboard, *01 u*	NRS
____	**14142**	Industrial Smokestack, *02–04*	50
____	**14143**	Industrial Tank, *02–04*	40
____	**14145**	Operating Lumberjacks, *02–03*	65
____	**14147**	Die-cast Old Style Clock Tower, *02–04, 08–14*	47
____	**14148**	Operating Billboard Signmen, *02–03*	60
____	**14149**	Scale-sized Banjo Signal, *02–05*	40
____	**14151**	Mainline Dwarf Signal, *02–08*	43
____	**14152**	Passenger Station, *02–04*	37
____	**14153**	Lion Oil Derrick, *02–03*	50
____	**14154**	Water Tower, *01–02*	65
____	**14155**	Floodlight Tower, *02–03*	55
____	**14156**	Lion Oil Diesel Fueling Station, *02–03*	70
____	**14157**	Coal Loader, *01–03*	120
____	**14158**	Icing Station, *01–02*	75
____	**14159**	Animated Billboard, *02–04*	20
____	**14160**	Frank's Hotdog Stand, *03–04*	55
____	**14161**	Smoking Hobo Shack, *02*	60
____	**14162**	Missile Launching Platform, *02–03*	48
____	**14163**	Industrial Power Station, *02–03*	550
____	**14164**	Lionelville Bandstand, *02*	140
____	**14166**	Train Orders Building, *04–05*	49
____	**14167**	Operating Lift Bridge, *02*	380
____	**14168**	Operating Harry's Barber Shop, *02–04*	100
____	**14170**	Amusement Park Swing Ride, *03–04*	150
____	**14171**	Pirate Ship Ride, *02–04*	130
____	**14172**	NYC Railroad Tugboat, *02*	180
____	**14173**	Drawbridge, *02–04*	70
____	**14175**	Santa Fe Die-cast Girder Bridge, *01–03*	17
____	**14176**	Norfolk Southern Die-cast Girder Bridge, *02–03*	18
____	**14178**	TMCC Direct Lockon, *02–03*	25
____	**14179**	TMCC Track Power Controller, *02–13*	230
____	**14180**	B&O Railroad Tugboat, *02–03*	155
____	**14181**	TMCC Action Recorder Controller, *02–13*	115
____	**14182**	TMCC Accessory Switch Controller, *02–13*	115
____	**14183**	TMCC Accessory Motor Controller, *02–13*	115
____	**14184**	TMCC Block Power Controller, *02–12*	90
____	**14185**	TMCC Operating Track Controller, *02–13*	100
____	**14186**	TMCC Accessory Voltage Controller, *02–13*	160
____	**14187**	TMCC How-to Video, *02–04*	11
____	**14189**	TMCC Track Power Controller, *02–13*	175
____	**14190**	The Lionel Train Book, *04–14*	30
____	**14191**	TMCC Command Base Cable, 6 feet, *02–13*	14
____	**14192**	TMCC 3-wire Command Base Cable, *02–13*	15
____	**14193**	TMCC Controller to Controller Cable, 1 foot, *02–13*	6
____	**14194**	TMCC TPC Cable Set, *02–13*	16
____	**14195**	TMCC Command Base Cable, 20 feet, *02–07*	12
____	**14196**	TMCC Controller to Controller Cable, 6 feet, *02–13*	9

		Exc	Mint
14197	TMCC Controller to Controller Cable, 20 feet, *02–07*		9 ___
14198	CW-80 80-watt Transformer, *03–14*		150 ___
14199	Playground Swings, *03–04, 08–09*		50 ___
14201	Burning Switch Tower, *05*		70 ___
14202	Water Tower, *05*		140 ___
14203	Amusement Park Swing Ride, *06–07*		230 ___
14209	U.S. Steel Gantry Crane, *05*		180 ___
14210	Pony Ride, *06–07*		70 ___
14211	Road Crew, *07–08*		90 ___
14214	Lionelville Mini Golf, *06*		80 ___
14215	Tug-of-War, *06–08*		60 ___
14217	Helicopter Pylon, *06–09*		140 ___
14218	Downtown People Pack, *06–14*		27 ___
14219	Ice Rink, *06–08*		80 ___
14220	Lionelville Water Tower, *06–08*		21 ___
14221	Witches Cauldron, *06–08*		70 ___
14222	Die-cast Girder Bridge, *06–09*		30 ___
14225	Sunoco Industrial Tank, *06–09*		70 ___
14227	Yard Tower, *06–08*		45 ___
14229	Crossing Shanty, *06–09*		20 ___
14230	Milk Bottle Toss Midway Game, *06*		20 ___
14231	Cotton Candy Midway Booth, *06*		20 ___
14236	Operating Freight Station, *06–07*		105 ___
14237	Rocket Launcher, *06–07*		320 ___
14240	Ice Block Pack, *06–14*		6 ___
14241	Work Crew People Pack, *06–14*		27 ___
14242	Hard Rock Cafe, *06*		50 ___
14243	U.S. Army Water Tower, *06–08*		95 ___
14244	Ammo Loader, *06–07*		105 ___
14251	Die-cast Sprung Trucks, rotating bearing caps, *07–14*		25 ___
14255	Sand Tower, *06–14*		35 ___
14257	Passenger Station, *06–13*		60 ___
14258	North Pole Passenger Station, *06–10*		53 ___
14259	Christmas People Pack, *06–12*		23 ___
14260	Christmas Tractor and Trailer, *06–08*		25 ___
14261	Christmas Tree Lot, *06*		70 ___
14262	Elevated Tank, *07*		70 ___
14265	Sawmill with sound, *08*		130 ___
14267	Sir Topham Hatt Gateman, *07–12*		80 ___
14273	Polar Express Add-on Figures, *06–07, 12–13*		30 ___
14289	Operating Santa Gateman, *08*		80 ___
14290	UPS Store, *06*		30 ___
14291	Operating Milk Loading Depot, K-Line, *08*		100 ___
14294	993 Legacy Expansion Set, *07–14*		290 ___
14295	990 Legacy Command Set, *07–14*		400 ___
14297	Halloween Witch Pylon, *07–08*		140 ___
14500	KCS F3 Diesel AA Set, Railsounds, CC, *01*	380	660 ___
14512	F3 Diesel ABA Demonstrator "291," CC, *01*	360	425 ___
14517	Santa Fe F3 Diesel B Unit "2343C," powered, *01*		280 ___
14518	CP F3 Diesel B Unit "2373C," RailSounds, CC, *01*		345 ___

			Exc	Mint
___	**14520**	Texas Special F3 Diesel B Unit, RailSounds, *01*		360
___	**14521**	Rock Island E6 Diesel AA Set, *01*		530
___	**14524**	Atlantic Coast Line E6 Diesel AA Set, *01*		630
___	**14536**	Santa Fe F3 Diesel AA Set, RailSounds, CC, *03–04*		800
___	**14539**	Santa Fe F3 Diesel B Unit, *03*		300
___	**14540**	D&RGW F3 Diesel B Unit, RailSounds, CC, *01*		315
___	**14541**	C&O F3 Diesel B Unit, RailSounds, CC, *01*		300
___	**14542**	KCS F3 Diesel B Unit "2388C," RailSounds, CC, *01*		375
___	**14543**	SP F3 Diesel B Unit, RailSounds, CC, *01*		282
___	**14544**	Southern E6 AA Diesel Set, CC, *02*		560
___	**14547**	Burlington E5 AA Diesel Set, CC, *02*		570
___	**14552**	NYC F3 Diesel AA Set, RailSounds, CC, *03–04*		740
___	**14555**	NYC F3 Diesel B Unit, *03*		200
___	**14557**	WP F3 Diesel B Unit, nonpowered, *03–04*		190
___	**14558**	B&O F3 Diesel B Unit, nonpowered, *03–04*		155
___	**14559**	D&RGW F3 Diesel AA Set, *01*		620
___	**14560**	NP F3 Diesel A Unit "2390B," freight, *02*		175
___	**14561**	NP F3 Diesel A Unit "2390B," passenger, *02*		190
___	**14562**	Milwaukee Road F3 Diesel A Unit "75C," *02*		190
___	**14563**	Erie-Lackawanna F3 Diesel A Unit "7094," *02*		175
___	**14564**	CP F3 Diesel B Unit "237C," CC, *02*		350
___	**14565**	B&O F3 Diesel AA Set, *03–04*		650
___	**14568**	WP F3 Diesel AA Set, *03–04*		780
___	**14571**	Santa Fe PA Diesel AA Set, CC, *03*		660
___	**14574**	D&H PA Diesel AA Set, CC, *03*		580
___	**14584**	Wabash F3 Diesel A Unit, nonpowered, *03*		180
___	**14586**	D&H PB Unit, *03*		125
___	**14587**	Santa Fe PB Unit, *03*		125
___	**14588**	Santa Fe F3 Diesel ABA Set, CC, *04–05*		980
___	**14592**	PRR F3 Diesel ABA Set, CC, *04–05*		750
___	**14596**	NH Alco PA Diesel AA Set, *04–05*		700
___	**14599**	NH Alco PB Diesel B Unit "0767-B," *04–05*		150
___	**15000**	D&RGW Waffle-sided Boxcar, *95*	16	18
___	**15001**	Seaboard Waffle-sided Boxcar, *95*	14	19
___	**15002**	Chesapeake & Ohio Waffle-sided Boxcar, *96*	16	20
___	**15003**	Green Bay & Western Waffle-sided Boxcar, *96*	16	20
___	**15004**	Bloomingdale's Boxcar, *97 u*		40
___	**15005**	"I Love NY" Boxcar, *97 u*		65
___	**15008**	CP Rail Boxcar		30
___	**15013**	L&N Waffle-sided Boxcar "102402," *00*		29
___	**15014**	Seaboard Waffle-sided Boxcar "125925," *00*		25
___	**15015**	C&NW Waffle-sided Boxcar "161013," *03*		18
___	**15016**	IC Waffle-sided Boxcar "12981," *04*		20
___	**15017**	CSX Waffle-sided Boxcar, *05*		27
___	**15018**	D&H Waffle-sided Boxcar "24052," *06*		30
___	**15020**	NH Waffle-sided Boxcar, *07*		30
___	**15021**	MKT Waffle-sided Boxcar, *08*		35
___	**15024**	UP Waffle Boxcar "960860," *09–11*		40
___	**15028**	Southern Waffle-sided Boxcar "539889," *10*		40
___	**15029**	Western & Atlantic Wood-sided Reefer, *10*		53
___	**15033**	MTK Stock Car, *10*		65

Exc Mint

		Exc	Mint
15038	CSX Hi-Cube Boxcar, 11–12	40	___
15039	NS Waffle-sided Boxcar, 11–12	40	___
15041	BNSF Hi-Cube Boxcar, 10	50	___
15042	CSX Waffle-sided Boxcar, 11	40	___
15051	Lionel Lines Boxcar, 11–12	40	___
15052	Amtrak Hi-Cube Boxcar, 11–12	40	___
15053	REA Waffle-sided Boxcar, 11–12	40	___
15054	C&NW Wood-sided Reefer, 11–12	40	___
15060	K-Line Boxcar, 06	40	___
15063	U.S.A.F. Minuteman Boxcar, 11	55	___
15069	Coke Wood-sided Reefer #1, 09–14	55	___
15071	Coca-Cola Christmas Boxcar, 12	70	___
15072	Halloween Boxcar, 09–11	55	___
15074	Mr. Goodbar Wood-sided Reefer, 09-11	55	___
15075	Boy Scouts of America Eagle Scout Boxcar, 11–14	60	___
15077	ATSF Stock Car, 11	55	___
15078	Pabst Wood-sided Reefeer, 11	58	___
15079	Schlitz Wood-sided Reefer, 11	55	___
15080	C&O 40' Boxcar, 11	55	___
15083	CP Rail Waffle-sided Boxcar, 13	43	___
15084	GN Hi-Cube Boxcar, 13–14	43	___
15086	Alaska Wood-Sided Reefer, 12	40	___
15091	Angela Trotta Thomas "High Hopes" Hi-Cube Boxcar, 12	55	___
15094	Sleepy Hollow Halloween Reefer, 14	55	___
15095	1953 Lionel Catalog Art Reefer, 13	55	___
15096	Hershey's Kisses Christmas Boxcar, 12	65	___
15097	Peanuts Christmas Boxcar, 12–13	70	___
15098	Lone Ranger Boxcar, 12–14	60	___
15100	Amtrak Passenger Coach, 95–97	35	___
15101	Reading Baggage Car (027), 96	34	___
15102	Reading Combination Car (027), 96	23	___
15103	Reading Passenger Coach (027), 96	23	___
15104	Reading Vista Dome Car (027), 96	26	___
15105	Reading Full Vista Dome Car (027), 96	26	___
15106	Reading Observation Car (027), 96	23	___
15107	Amtrak Vista Dome Car, 96	38	___
15108	Northern Pacific Vista Dome Car, 96	34	___
15109	ATSF Combine Car "2407," 97	35	___
15110	ATSF Vista Dome Car 2404," 97	35	___
15111	ATSF Observation Car "2406," 97	35	___
15112	ATSF Albuquerque Coach "2405," 97	34	___
15113	ATSF Culebra Vista Dome Car "2404," 97	34	___
15114	NJ Transit Coach "5610," 96 u	45	___
15115	NJ Transit Coach "5611," 96 u	45	
15116	NJ Transit Coach "5612," 96 u	45	___
15117	Annie Passenger Coach, 97	26	___
15118	Clarabel Passenger Coach, 97	26	___
15122	NJ Transit Passenger Coach "5613," 97 u	45	___
15123	NJ Transit Passenger Coach "5614," 97 u	45	___
15124	NJ Transit Passenger Coach "5615," 97 u	45	___
15125	Amtrak Observation Car, 97 u	50	___

Exc Mint

			Exc	Mint
____	15126	Stars & Stripes Abraham Lincoln General Coach, *99*		60
____	15127	Stars & Stripes Ulysses S. Grant General Coach, *99*		60
____	15128	Pride of Richmond Robert E. Lee General Coach, *99*		60
____	15129	Pride of Richmond Jefferson Davis General Coach, *99*		60
____	15136	Custom Series Short Observation Car, blue, *99*		40
____	15137	Custom Series Short Observation Car, red, *99*		34
____	15138	Pratt's Hollow Baggage Car, *98*		100
____	15139	Pratt's Hollow Vista Dome Car, *98*		100
____	15140	Pratt's Hollow Coach, *98*		100
____	15141	Pratt's Hollow Observation, *98*		100
____	15142	U.S. Army Baby Heavyweight Coach, *00*		50
____	15143	U.S. Army Baby Heavyweight Coach, *00*		50
____	15153	Pullman Baby Madison Set 4-pack, *01*		190
____	15163	T&P Baby Heavyweight Coach, *01*		30
____	15166	Union Pacific Whistling Baggage Car, *04*		41
____	15169	C&O Streamliner Car 4-pack, *03*		140
____	15170	L&N Streamliner Car 4-pack, *03*		140
____	15180	NYC Streamliner Car 4-pack, *04*		340
____	15185	UP Streamliner Car 4-pack, *04*		340
____	15300	NYC Superliner Aluminum Passenger Car 4-pack, *02*		360
____	15301	NYC Manhattan Superliner Passenger Coach, *02*		90
____	15302	NYC Queens Superliner Passenger Coach, *02*		90
____	15304	NYC Staten Island Superliner Passenger Coach, *02*		90
____	15305	NYC Brooklyn Superliner Passenger Coach, *02*		90
____	15311	CB&Q California Zephyr Aluminum Passenger Car 4-pack, *03*		350
____	15312	Santa Fe Super Chief Aluminum Passenger Car 4-pack, *03*		275
____	15313	D&H Aluminum Passenger Car 4-pack, *03*		415
____	15314	Amtrak Superliner 2-pack, *03*		220
____	15315	Santa Fe Superliner 2-pack, *03*		200
____	15316	NYC Superliner 2-pack, *03*		195
____	15317	Southern Aluminum Passenger Car 4-pack, *03*		350
____	15318	Lionel Lines Aluminum Passenger Car 2-pack, *03*		125
____	15319	Santa Fe Superliner Aluminum Passenger Car 2-pack, *03*		145
____	15326	NYC 20th Century Limited Aluminum Passenger Car 6-pack, *02*		485
____	15333	N&W Powhatan Arrow Aluminum Passenger Car 6-pack, *02*		435
____	15340	PRR South Wind Aluminum Passenger Car 6-pack, *02*		435
____	15379	Lionel Lines Silver Valley Aluminum Combination Car, *03*		100
____	15380	Lionel Lines Silver Spoon Aluminum Diner, *03*		100
____	15381	Santa Fe Aluminum Baggage Car "2571," *03*		100
____	15382	Santa Fe Regal Dome Aluminum Vista Dome Car, *03*		100

Exc Mint

15383	NYC 20th Century Limited Diner, StationSounds, *03*	195 ____
15384	N&W Powhatan Arrow Diner, StationSounds, *03*	190 ____
15385	Pennsylvania South Wind Diner, StationSounds, *03*	190 ____
15394	Amtrak Streamliner Car 4-pack, *03–04*	450 ____
15395	Alaska Streamliner Car 4-pack, *03–04*	355 ____
15396	Amtrak Superliner Diner, StationSounds, *03*	220 ____
15397	Santa Fe Superliner Diner, StationSounds, *03*	200 ____
15398	NYC Superliner Diner, StationSounds, *03*	200 ____
15405	50th Anniversary Hillside Heavyweight Diner, StationSounds, *02*	195 ____
15406	Blue Comet Giacobini Heavyweight Diner, StationSounds, *02*	300 ____
15504	Alton Limited Diner, StationSounds, *03*	230 ____
15507	Phantom III Passenger Car 4-pack (15508 Baggage, 15509 Vista Dome, 15510 Coach, 15511 Observation), *02*	245 ____
15512	Phantom II Passenger Car 4-pack, *02*	250 ____
15517	Southern Crescent Limited Heavyweight Passenger Car 2-pack, *03–04*	205 ____
15520	Southern Crescent Limited Heavyweight Diner, StationSounds, *03–04*	220 ____
15521	NYC 20th Century Limited Heavyweight Passenger Car 4-pack, *04*	345 ____
15526	Santa Fe Chief Heavyweight Passenger Car 4-pack, *04*	370 ____
15538	NYC 20th Century Limited Heavyweight Passenger Car 2-pack, *04*	200 ____
15541	NYC 20th Century Limited Heavyweight Diner, StationSounds, *04*	200 ____
15542	Santa Fe Chief Heavyweight Passenger Car 2-pack, *04*	195 ____
15545	Santa Fe Chief Heavyweight Diner, StationSounds, *04*	200 ____
15546	Napa Valley Wine Train Heavyweight 2-pack, *05*	250 ____
15549	Napa Valley Wine Train Diner, StationSounds, *05*	280 ____
15554	Pennsylvania Heavyweight Car 3-pack (std O), *05*	375 ____
15558	Pennsylvania Heavyweight Add-on Coach (std O), *05*	140 ____
15559	PRR Reading Seashore Heavyweight Car 3-pack (std O), *05*	370 ____
15563	PRR Reading Seashore Heavyweight Add-on Coach, *05*	130 ____
15564	LIRR Heavyweight Car 3-pack (std O), *05*	370 ____
15568	LIRR Heavyweight Add-on Coach (std O), *05*	130 ____
15570	LIRR Heavyweight Car 3-pack (std O), *06*	230 ____
15574	LIRR Heavyweight Car Add-on (std O), *06*	140 ____
15575	C&O Heavyweight Diner, StationSounds (std O), *06–07*	295 ____
15576	C&O Heavyweight Passenger Car 2-pack (std O), *06–07*	265 ____
15577	NYC Heavyweight 3-pack (std O), *05–06*	370 ____

		Exc	Mint
15581	NYC Heavyweight Add-on Coach (std O), _05–06_		130
15584	Amtrak Acela Passenger Car 3-pack (std O), _06_		580
15588	Southern Heavyweight Passenger Car 4-pack, _06_		495
15593	Southern Heavyweight Passenger Car 2-pack, _06_		265
15596	Southern Heavyweight Diner, StationSounds, _06_		295
15597	C&O Heavyweight Passenger Car 4-pack (std O), _06–07_		495
15906	RailSounds Trigger Button, _90–95_		12
16000	PRR Vista Dome Car (027), _87–88_	37	55
16001	PRR Passenger Coach (027), _87–88_	33	41
16002	PRR Passenger Coach (027), _87–88_	24	29
16003	PRR Observation Car (027), _87–88_	24	29
16009	PRR Combination Car (027), _88_	36	38
16010	Virginia & Truckee Passenger Coach (SSS), _88_	36	47
16011	Virginia & Truckee Passenger Coach (SSS), _88_	36	47
16012	Virginia & Truckee Baggage Car (SSS), _88_	36	47
16013	Amtrak Combination Car (027), _88–89_	21	34
16014	Amtrak Vista Dome Car (027), _88–89_	21	34
16015	Amtrak Observation Car (027), _88–89_	21	34
16016	NYC Baggage Car (027), _89_	36	55
16017	NYC Combination Car (027), _89_	21	29
16018	NYC Passenger Coach (027), _89_	21	29
16019	NYC Vista Dome Car (027), _89_	21	29
16020	NYC Passenger Coach (027), _89_	23	33
16021	NYC Observation Car (027), _89_	20	28
16022	Pennsylvania Baggage Car (027), _89_	27	38
16023	Amtrak Passenger Coach (027), _89_	21	30
16024	Northern Pacific Diner (027), _92_	39	44
16027	LL Combination Car (027, SSS), _90_	39	48
16028	LL Passenger Coach (SSS, 027), _90_	35	42
16029	LL Passenger Coach (SSS, 027), _90_	35	42
16030	LL Observation Car (SSS, 027), _90_	35	42
16031	Pennsylvania Diner (027), _90_	35	39
16033	Amtrak Baggage Car (027), _90_	28	38
16034	NP Baggage Car (027), _90–91_	30	45
16035	NP Combination Car (027), _90–91_	18	26
16036	NP Passenger Coach (027), _90–91_	21	30
16037	NP Vista Dome Car (027), _90–91_	18	26
16038	NP Passenger Coach (027), _90–91_	17	25
16039	NP Observation Car (027), _90–91_	21	30
16040	Southern Pacific Baggage Car, _90–91_	22	30
16041	NYC Diner (027), _91_	37	47
16042	Illinois Central Baggage Car (027), _91_	24	34
16043	Illinois Central Combination Car (027), _91_	22	30
16044	Illinois Central Passenger Coach (027), _91_	24	34
16045	Illinois Central Vista Dome Car (027), _91_	22	30
16046	Illinois Central Passenger Coach (027), _91_	24	34
16047	Illinois Central Observation Car (027), _91_	24	34
16048	Amtrak Diner (027), _91–92_	33	40

		Exc	Mint
16049	Illinois Central Diner (027), *92*	27	38 ____
16050	C&NW Baggage Car "6620," *93*	44	55 ____
16051	C&NW Combination Car "6630," *93*	40	50 ____
16052	C&NW Passenger Coach "6616," *93*	34	42 ____
16053	C&NW Passenger Coach "6602," *93*	37	46 ____
16054	C&NW Observation Car "6603," *93*	38	47 ____
16055	Santa Fe Passenger Coach (027), *93–94*	29	38 ____
16056	Santa Fe Vista Dome Car (027), *93–94*	25	32 ____
16057	Santa Fe Passenger Coach (027), *93–94*	30	40 ____
16058	Santa Fe Combination Car (027), *93–94*	27	35 ____
16059	Santa Fe Vista Dome Car (027), *93–94*	26	34 ____
16060	Santa Fe Observation Car (027), *93–94*	25	31 ____
16061	N&W Baggage Car "6061," *94*	60	85 ____
16062	N&W Combination Car "6062," *94*	38	50 ____
16063	N&W Passenger Coach "6063," *94*	43	55 ____
16064	N&W Passenger Coach "6064," *94*	43	55 ____
16065	N&W Observation Car "6065," *94*	36	48 ____
16066	NYC Combination Car "6066" (SSS), *94*	55	70 ____
16067	NYC Passenger Coach "6067" (SSS), *94*	38	47 ____
16068	UP Baggage Car "6068" (027), *94*	50	65 ____
16069	UP Combination Car "6069" (027), *94*	36	43 ____
16070	UP Passenger Coach "6070" (027), *94*	36	43 ____
16071	UP Diner "6071" (027), *94*	36	46 ____
16072	UP Vista Dome Car "6072" (027), *94*	36	43 ____
16073	UP Passenger Coach "6073" (027), *94*	36	42 ____
16074	UP Observation Car "6074" (027), *94*	36	43 ____
16075	Missouri Pacific Baggage Car "6620," *95*	44	55 ____
16076	Missouri Pacific Combination Car "6630," *95*	34	41 ____
16077	Missouri Pacific Passenger Coach "6616," *95*	34	41 ____
16078	Missouri Pacific Passenger Coach "7805," *95*	34	39 ____
16079	Missouri Pacific Observation Car "6609," *95*	34	41 ____
16080	New Haven Baggage Car "6080" (027), *95*	35	44 ____
16081	New Haven Combination Car "6081" (027), *95*	28	37 ____
16082	New Haven Passenger Coach "6082" (027), *95*	28	37 ____
16083	New Haven Vista Dome Car "6083" (027), *95*	30	39 ____
16084	New Haven Full Vista Dome Car "6084" (027), *95*	33	39 ____
16086	New Haven Observation Car "6086" (027), *95*	31	40 ____
16087	NYC Baggage Car "6087" (SSS), *95*	48	65 ____
16088	NYC Passenger Coach "6088" (SSS), *95*	36	43 ____
16089	NYC Diner "6089" (SSS), *95*	36	43 ____
16090	NYC Observation Car "6090" (SSS), *95*	38	46 ____
16091	NYC Passenger Cars, set of 4 (SSS), *95*	140	165 ____
16092	Santa Fe Full Vista Dome Car (027), *95*	30	38 ____
16093	Illinois Central Full Vista Dome Car (027), *95*	29	38 ____
16094	Pennsylvania Full Vista Dome Car (027), *95*	30	39 ____
16095	Amtrak Combination Car (027), *95*	19	23 ____
16096	Amtrak Vista Dome Car (027), *95*	19	23 ____
16097	Amtrak Observation Car (027), *95*	19	23 ____
16098	Amtrak Passenger Coach, *95–97*	20	33 ____
16099	Amtrak Vista Dome Car, *95–97*	20	33 ____
16102	Southern 3-D Tank Car (SSS), *87*	23	30 ____

			Exc	Mint
____	**16103**	Lehigh Valley 2-D Tank Car (027), *88*	19	25
____	**16104**	Santa Fe 2-D Tank Car (027), *89*	19	23
____	**16105**	D&RGW 3-D Tank Car (SSS), *89*	48	65
____	**16106**	Mopar Express 3-D Tank Car, *88 u*	98	169
____	**16107**	Sunoco 2-D Tank Car (027), *90*	16	20
____	**16108**	Racing Fuel 1-D Tank Car "6108" (027), *89 u, 92 u*	9	13
____	**16109**	B&O 1-D Tank Car (SSS), *91*	29	34
____	**16110**	Circus Animals Operating Stock Car "1989" (027), *89 u*	24	34
____	**16111**	Alaska 1-D Tank Car (027), *90–91*	22	27
____	**16112**	Dow Chemical 3-D Tank Car, *90*	20	26
____	**16113**	Diamond Shamrock 2-D Tank Car (027), *91*	20	25
____	**16114**	Hooker Chemicals 1-D Tank Car (027), *91*	13	17
____	**16115**	MKT 3-D Tank Car, *92*	13	16
____	**16116**	U.S. Army 1-D Tank Car, *91 u*	36	42
____	**16119**	MKT 2-D Tank Car (027), *92, 93 u*	14	19
____	**16121**	C&NW Stock Car (SSS), *92*	33	43
____	**16123**	Union Pacific 3-D Tank Car, *93–95*	16	22
____	**16124**	Penn Salt 3-D Tank Car, *93*	21	26
____	**16125**	Virginian Stock Car, *93*	19	24
____	**16126**	Jefferson Lake 3-D Tank Car, *93*	22	26
____	**16127**	Mobil 1-D Tank Car, *93*	28	33
____	**16128**	Alaska 1-D Tank Car, *94*	24	29
____	**16129**	Alaska 1-D Tank Car (027), *93 u, 94*	21	28
____	**16130**	SP Stock Car (027), *93 u, 94*	10	13
____	**16131**	T&P Reefer, *94*	19	24
____	**16132**	Deep Rock 3-D Tank Car, *94*	25	30
____	**16133**	Santa Fe Reefer, *94*	22	28
____	**16134**	Reading Reefer, *94*	17	21
____	**16135**	C&O Stock Car, *94*	23	27
____	**16136**	B&O 1-D Tank Car, *94*	28	32
____	**16137**	Ford 1-D Tank Car "12," *94 u*	34	39
____	**16138**	Goodyear 1-D Tank Car, *95*	28	34
____	**16140**	Domino Sugar 1-D Tank Car, *95*	24	29
____	**16141**	Erie Stock Car, *95*	22	30
____	**16142**	Santa Fe 1-D Tank Car, *95*	26	30
____	**16143**	Reading Reefer, *95*	18	23
____	**16144**	San Angelo 3-D Tank Car, *95*	22	25
____	**16146**	Dairy Despatch Reefer, *95*	15	20
____	**16147**	Clearly Canadian 1-D Tank Car (027), *94 u*	25	40
____	**16149**	Zep Chemical 1-D Tank Car (027), *95 u*	54	67
____	**16150**	Sunoco 1-D Tank Car "6315," *97*	35	38
____	**16152**	Sunoco 3-D Tank Car "6415," *97*		26
____	**16153**	AEC Reactor Fluid 1-D Tank Car "6515-1," *97*		82
____	**16154**	AEC Reactor Fluid 1-D Tank Car "6515-2," *97*		94
____	**16155**	AEC Reactor Fluid 1-D Tank Car "6515-3," *97*		96
____	**16157**	Gatorade Little League Baseball 1-D Tank Car "6315," *97 u*		52
____	**16160**	AEC Tank Car "6515" with reactor fluid, *98*		74
____	**16162**	Hooker 1-D Tank Car "6315-1," *97*		50
____	**16163**	Hooker 1-D Tank Car "6315-2," *97*		50
____	**16164**	Hooker 1-D Tank Car "6315-3," *97*		50
____	**16165**	Mobilfuel 3-D Tank Car "6415," *97 u*		50

		Exc	Mint
16171	Alaska 1-D Tank Car "6171," *98–99*		33 ____
16173	Harold the Helicopter Flatcar, *98*	45	60 ____
16175	NJ Transit Port Morris Ore Car "9125," *98*		45 ____
16176	NJ Transit Raritan Yard Ore Car "9126," *98 u*		45 ____
16177	NJ Transit Gladstone Yard Ore Car "9127," *98 u*		45 ____
16178	NJ Transit Bay Head Yard Ore Car "9128," *98 u*		45 ____
16179	NJ Transit Dover Yard Ore Car "9129," *98 u*		45 ____
16180	Tabasco 1-D Tank Car, *98*	60	74 ____
16181	Biohazard Tank Car with Lights, *98*		76 ____
16182	Gatorade 1-D Tank Car "6315," *98 u*		62 ____
16187	Linex 3-D Tank Car "6425," *99*		30 ____
16188	Kodak 1-D Tank Car "6515," *99*	71	86 ____
16199	UP 1-D Tank Car "6035," *99–00*		25 ____
16200	Rock Island Boxcar (O27), *87–88*	7	10 ____
16201	Wabash Boxcar (O27), *88–91*	7	10 ____
16203	Key America Boxcar (O27), *87 u*	45	65 ____
16204	Hawthorne Boxcar (O27), *87 u*	50	85 ____
16205	Mopar Express Boxcar "1987" (O27), *87–88 u*	50	60 ____
16206	D&RGW Boxcar (SSS), *89*	37	42 ____
16207	True Value Boxcar (O27), *88 u*	32	47 ____
16208	PRR Auto Carrier, 3-tier, *89*	24	37 ____
16209	Disney Magic Boxcar (O27), *88 u*	90	110 ____
16211	Hawthorne Boxcar (O27), *88 u*	45	65 ____
16213	Shoprite Boxcar (O27), *88 u*	55	80 ____
16214	D&RGW Auto Carrier, *90*	24	32 ____
16215	Conrail Auto Carrier, *90*	27	38 ____
16217	Burlington Northern Auto Carrier, *92*	24	36 ____
16219	True Value Boxcar (O27), *89 u*	55	75 ____
16220	Ace Hardware Boxcar (O27), *89 u*	55	80 ____
16221	Macy's Boxcar (O27), *89 u*	55	80 ____
16222	Great Northern Boxcar (O27), *90–91*	8	15 ____
16223	Budweiser Reefer, *89–92 u*	55	76 ____
16224	True Value "Lawn Chief" Boxcar (O27), *90 u*	45	60 ____
16225	Budweiser Vat Car, *90–91 u*	120	157 ____
16226	Union Pacific Boxcar "6226" (O27), *90–91 u*	15	19 ____
16227	Santa Fe Boxcar (O27), *91*	13	17 ____
16228	Union Pacific Auto Carrier, *92*	26	33 ____
16229	Erie-Lackawanna Auto Carrier, *91 u*	45	55 ____
16232	Chessie System Boxcar, *92, 93 u, 94, 95 u*	25	30 ____
16233	MKT DD Boxcar, *92*	20	29 ____
16234	ACY Boxcar (SSS), *92*	34	41 ____
16235	Railway Express Agency Reefer, *92*	19	23 ____
16236	NYC Pacemaker Boxcar, *92 u*	18	24 ____
16237	Railway Express Agency Boxcar, *92 u*	21	23 ____
16238	NYNH&H Boxcar, *93–95*		3 ____
16239	Union Pacific Boxcar, *93–95*	15	20 ____
16241	Toys "R" Us Boxcar, *92–93 u*	35	45 ____
16242	Grand Trunk Western Auto Carrier, *93*	35	40 ____
16243	Conrail Boxcar, *93*	26	34 ____
16244	Duluth, South Shore & Atlantic Boxcar, *93*	20	24 ____
16245	Contadina Boxcar, *93*	16	20 ____

			Exc	Mint
____	16247	ACL Boxcar, *94*	15	19
____	16248	Budweiser Boxcar, *93–94 u*	38	53
____	16249	United Auto Workers Boxcar, *93 u*		55
____	16250	Santa Fe Boxcar (027), *93 u, 94*	8	10
____	16251	Columbus & Greenville Boxcar, *94*	14	15
____	16252	U.S. Navy Boxcar "6106888," *94–95*		30
____	16253	Santa Fe Auto Carrier, *94*	32	38
____	16255	Wabash DD Boxcar, *95*	20	26
____	16256	Ford DD Boxcar, *94 u*	30	34
____	16257	Crayola Boxcar, *94 u, 95*	17	23
____	16258	Lehigh Valley Boxcar, *95*	17	22
____	16259	Chrysler Mopar Boxcar, *97 u*	33	43
____	16260	Chrysler Mopar Auto Carrier, *96 u*	54	64
____	16261	Union Pacific DD Boxcar, *95*	26	29
____	16263	ATSF Boxcar, *96–99*		25
____	16264	Red Wing Shoes Boxcar, *95*	24	28
____	16265	Georgia Power "Atlanta '96" Boxcar, *95 u*	183	225
____	16266	Crayola Boxcar, *95*	17	23
____	16267	Sears Zenith Boxcar, *95–96 u*		55
____	16268	GM/AC Delco Boxcar, *95 u*		51
____	16269	Lionel Lines Boxcar, *96*		10
____	16272	Christmas Boxcar, *97*		36
____	16273	Lionel Employee Christmas Boxcar, *97*		55
____	16274	Marvin the Martian Boxcar, *97*		44
____	16279	Dodge Motorsports Boxcar, *96 u*	130	172
____	16284	Galveston Wharves Boxcar, *98*		28
____	16285	Savannah State Docks Boxcar, *98*		26
____	16291	Christmas Boxcar, *98*		34
____	16292	Lionel Employee Christmas Boxcar, *98*	309	369
____	16293	JCPenney Boxcar, *97*		100
____	16294	Pedigree Boxcar, *97*	139	159
____	16295	Kal Kan Boxcar, *97*	138	159
____	16296	Whiskas Boxcar, *97*	129	154
____	16297	Sheba Boxcar, *97*	127	150
____	16298	Mobil Boxcar, *97*		50
____	16300	Rock Island Flatcar with fences (027), *87–88*	8	10
____	16301	Lionel Barrel Ramp Car, *87*	14	19
____	16303	PRR Flatcar with trailers, *87*	26	33
____	16304	RI Gondola with cable reels (027), *87–88*	5	9
____	16305	Lehigh Valley Ore Car, *87*	80	130
____	16306	Santa Fe Barrel Ramp Car, *88*	12	16
____	16307	NKP Flatcar with trailers, *88*	30	40
____	16308	Burlington Northern Flatcar with trailer, *88–89*	20	25
____	16309	Wabash Gondola with canisters, *88–91*	9	13
____	16310	Mopar Express Gondola with canisters, *87–88 u*	35	39
____	16311	Mopar Express Flatcar with trailers, *87–88 u*	113	158
____	16313	PRR Gondola with cable reels (027), *88 u, 89*	9	10
____	16314	Wabash Flatcar with trailers, *89*	26	30
____	16315	PRR Flatcar with fences (027), *88 u, 89*	7	9
____	16317	PRR Barrel Ramp Car, *89*	18	22
____	16318	LL Depressed Center Flatcar with cable reels, *89*	22	26

		Exc	Mint
16320	Great Northern Barrel Ramp Car, *90*	13	19 ____
16321/22	Sealand TTUX Flatcar Set with trailers, *90*	65	73 ____
16323	Lionel Lines Flatcar with trailers, *90*	21	25 ____
16324	PRR Depressed Center Flatcar with cable reels, *90*	16	20 ____
16325	Microracers Exhibition Ramp Car, *89 u*	21	28 ____
16326	Santa Fe Depressed Center Flatcar with cable reels, *91*	16	21 ____
16327	"The Big Top" Circus Gondola with canisters, *89 u*	19	24 ____
16328	NKP Gondola with cable reels, *90–91*	17	23 ____
16329	SP Flatcar with horses (027), *90–91*	19	24 ____
16330	MKT Flatcar with trailers, *91*	25	30 ____
16332	LL Depressed Center Flatcar with transformer, *91*	28	33 ____
16333	Frisco Bulkhead Flatcar with lumber, *91*	17	22 ____
16334	C&NW Flatcar Set ("16337, 16338") with trailers, *91*	55	60 ____
16335	NYC Pacemaker Flatcar with trailer (SSS), *91*	46	65 ____
16336	UP Gondola "6336" with canisters, *90–91 u*	17	21 ____
16339	Mickey's World Tour Gondola with canisters (027), *91, 92 u*	17	21 ____
16341	NYC Depressed Center Flatcar with transformer, *92*	29	32 ____
16342	CSX Gondola with coil covers, *92*	18	23 ____
16343	Burlington Gondola with coil covers, *92*	20	23 ____
16345/46	SP TTUX Flatcar Set with trailers, *92*	55	65 ____
16347	Ontario Northland Bulkhead Flatcar with pulp load, *92*	22	26 ____
16348	Erie Liquefied Petroleum Car, *92*	23	25 ____
16349	Allis Chalmers Condenser Car, *92*	28	35 ____
16350	CP Rail Bulkhead Flatcar with lumber, *91 u*	20	29 ____
16351	Flatcar with U.S. Navy submarine, *92*	27	33 ____
16352	U.S. Military Flatcar with cruise missile, *92*	33	43 ____
16353	B&M Gondola with coil covers, *91 u*	33	39 ____
16355	Burlington Gondola, *92, 93 u, 94–95*	11	17 ____
16356	MKT Depressed Center Flatcar with cable reels, *92*	17	21 ____
16357	L&N Flatcar with trailer, *92*	24	31 ____
16358	L&N Gondola with coil covers, *92*	17	21 ____
16359	Pacific Coast Gondola with coil covers (SSS), *92*	33	38 ____
16360	N&W Maxi-Stack Flatcar Set ("16361" and "16362") with containers, *93*	44	55 ____
16363	Southern TTUX Flatcar Set ("16364" and "16365") with trailers, *93*	38	49 ____
16367	Clinchfield Gondola with coil covers, *93*	18	21 ____
16368	MKT Liquid Oxygen Car, *93*	21	22 ____
16369	Amtrak Flatcar with wheel load, *92 u*	19	28 ____
16370	Amtrak Flatcar with rail load, *92 u*	19	28 ____
16371	BN I-Beam Flatcar with load, *92 u*	24	29 ____
16372	Southern I-Beam Flatcar with load, *92 u*	24	34 ____
16373	Erie-Lackawanna Flatcar with stakes, *93*	19	23 ____
16374	D&RGW Flatcar with trailer, *93*	25	28 ____
16375	NYC Bulkhead Flatcar, *93–95*	21	25 ____
16376	UP Flatcar with trailer, *93–95*	31	37 ____

			Exc	Mint
____	16378	Toys "R" Us Flatcar with trailer, *92–93 u*	60	95
____	16379	NP Bulkhead Flatcar with pulp load, *93*	16	23
____	16380	UP I-Beam Flatcar with load, *93*	20	26
____	16381	CSX I-Beam Flatcar with load, *93*	20	25
____	16382	Kansas City Southern Bulkhead Flatcar, *93*	14	18
____	16383	Conrail Flatcar with trailer, *93*	50	58
____	16384	Soo Line Gondola with cable reels, *93*	14	19
____	16385	Soo Line Ore Car, *93*	65	75
____	16386	SP Flatcar with lumber, *94*	15	19
____	16387	KCS Gondola with coil covers, *94*	13	16
____	16388	LV Gondola with canisters, *94*	16	20
____	16389	PRR Flatcar with wheel load, *94*	27	32
____	16390	Flatcar with water tank, *94*	24	27
____	16391	Lionel Lines Gondola, *93 u*		15
____	16392	Wabash Gondola with canisters (027), *93 u, 94*	7	9
____	16393	Wisconsin Central Bulkhead Flatcar, *94*	13	19
____	16394	Vermont Central Bulkhead Flatcar, *94*	20	30
____	16395	CP Flatcar with rail load, *94*	18	23
____	16396	Alaska Bulkhead Flatcar, *94*	17	22
____	16397	Milwaukee Road I-Beam Flatcar with load, *94*	30	34
____	16398	C&O Flatcar with trailer, *94*	80	85
____	16399	Western Pacific I-Beam Flatcar with load, *94*	31	35
____	16400	PRR Hopper (027), *88 u, 89*	15	18
____	16402	Southern Quad Hopper with coal (SSS), *87*	30	42
____	16406	CSX Quad Hopper with coal, *90*	29	34
____	16407	B&M Covered Quad Hopper (SSS), *91*	28	37
____	16408	UP Hopper "6408" (027), *90–91 u*	17	21
____	16410	MKT Hopper (027), *92, 93 u*	19	24
____	16411	L&N Quad Hopper with coal, *92*	28	32
____	16412	C&NW Covered Quad Hopper, *94*	16	21
____	16413	Clinchfield Quad Hopper with coal, *94*	16	22
____	16414	CCC&StL Hopper (027), *94*	18	25
____	16416	D&RGW Covered Quad Hopper, *95*	16	20
____	16417	Wabash Quad Hopper with coal, *95*	19	21
____	16418	C&NW Hopper with coal (027), *95*	15	21
____	16419	Tennessee Central Hopper, *96*		17
____	16420	WM Quad Hopper with coal (SSS), *95*	30	34
____	16421	WM Quad Hopper with coal (SSS), *95*	30	33
____	16422	WM Quad Hopper with coal (SSS), *95*		33
____	16423	WM Quad Hopper with coal (SSS), *95*		30
____	16424	WM Covered Quad Hopper (SSS), *95*	34	39
____	16425	WM Covered Quad Hopper (SSS), *95*	25	29
____	16426	WM Covered Quad Hopper (SSS), *95*	24	27
____	16427	WM Covered Quad Hopper (SSS), *95*	27	30
____	16429	WM Quad Hopper with coal, set of 2		70
____	16430	Georgia Power Quad Hopper "82947" with coal, *95 u*		109
____	16431	Lionel Corporation 2-bay Hopper "6456-1," *96*		30
____	16432	Lionel Corporation 2-bay Hopper "6456-2," *96*		64
____	16433	Lionel Corporation 2-bay Hopper "6456-3," *96*		18
____	16434	LV 2-bay Hopper "6456," "TLDX," *97*		25
____	16435	Virginian 2-bay Hopper "6456-1," *97*		30

		Exc	Mint
16436	N&W 2-bay Hopper "6456-2," *97*		33 ____
16437	C&O 2-bay Hopper "6456-3," *97*		33 ____
16438	Frisco 4-bay Covered Hopper "87538," *98*		34 ____
16439	Southern 4-bay Covered Hopper "77836," *98*		34 ____
16440	Alaska 2-bay Hopper "7100," *98–99*		35 ____
16441	New York Central 4-bay Hopper, *99*		26 ____
16442	Bethlehem Gondola "6462" (SSS), *99*		40 ____
16443	GN 2-bay Hopper "172364," *99–00*		20 ____
16444	CNJ 2-bay Hopper "643," *00*		20 ____
16445	Frisco 2-bay Hopper "93108," *00*		20 ____
16446	Burlington 2-bay Hopper, *00*		20 ____
16447	PRR Tuscan 2-bay Hopper, *00 u*		30 ____
16448	PRR Gray 2-bay Hopper, *00 u*		30 ____
16449	PRR Black 2-bay Hopper, *00 u*		30 ____
16450	PRR Green 2-bay Hopper, *00 u*		30 ____
16451	Lionel Mines 2-bay Hopper, *00 u*		50 ____
16453	SP 2-bay Hopper "460604," *01*		15 ____
16454	Bethlehem Steel Hopper "41025," *U1*		37 ____
16455	Pioneer Seed 2-bay Hopper, *00 u*		50 ____
16456	B&O 2-bay Hopper, *01*		20 ____
16459	LV 2-bay Hopper "51102," *01*		23 ____
16460	Reading 2-bay Hopper "79636," *02*		25 ____
16463	Rio Grande Icebreaker Tunnel Car "18936," *02*		32 ____
16464	NYC Icebreaker Tunnel Car "X3200," *02*		32 ____
16465	WP 2-bay Hopper "100340," *03*		19 ____
16466	Pennsylvania Icebreaker Tunnel Car, *03*		33 ____
16467	"Naughty and Nice" Hopper 2-pack, *02*		60 ____
16469	B&O Hopper "435351," *02*		22 ____
16470	"Naughty and Nice" Ore Car 2-pack, *03*		43 ____
16473	Rock Island Ore Car "99122," *03*		18 ____
16474	Alaska Ore Car "16474," *04*		21 ____
16475	Santa Fe Hopper "16475," *04*		18 ____
16480	Lionelville Snow Transport Quad Hopper, *04*		45 ____
16482	Norfolk Southern Hopper, traditional, *05*		27 ____
16489	BNSF Ore Car, traditional, *05*		15 ____
16490	Sodor Mining Hopper, *05, 13*		35 ____
16491	CNJ Hopper "60714," *06*		30 ____
16492	C&NW Ore Car "114023," *06*		30 ____
16493	Christmas Ice Breaker Car, *06*		55 ____
16500	Rock Island Bobber Caboose, *87–88*	9	13 ____
16501	Lehigh Valley SP-type Caboose, *87*	19	24 ____
16503	NYC Transfer Caboose, *87*	16	22 ____
16504	Southern N5c Caboose (SSS), *87*	17	30 ____
16505	Wabash SP-type Caboose, *88–91*	10	15 ____
16506	Santa Fe Bay Window Caboose, *88*	18	28 ____
16507	Mopar Express SP-type Caboose, *87–88 u*	42	54 ____
16508	Lionel Lines SP-type Caboose "6508," *89 u*	13	17 ____
16509	D&RGW SP-type Caboose (SSS), *89*	19	24 ____
16510	New Haven Bay Window Caboose, *89*	25	30 ____
16511	PRR Bobber Caboose, *88 u, 89*	9	13 ____
16513	Union Pacific SP-type Caboose, *89*	14	21 ____
16515	Lionel Lines SP-type Caboose, RailScope, *89*	20	23 ____
16516	Lehigh Valley SP-type Caboose, *90*	15	26 ____

			Exc	Mint
____	16517	Atlantic Coast Line Bay Window Caboose, *90*	22	26
____	16518	Chessie System Bay Window Caboose, *90*	41	50
____	16519	Rock Island Transfer Caboose, *90*	13	17
____	16520	"Welcome to the Show" Circus SP-type Caboose, *89 u*	13	21
____	16521	PRR SP-type Caboose, *90–91*	8	11
____	16522	"Chills & Thrills" Circus N5c Caboose, *90–91*	10	15
____	16523	Alaska SP-type Caboose, *91*	24	31
____	16524	Anheuser-Busch SP-type Caboose, *89–92 u*	31	41
____	16525	D&H Bay Window Caboose (SSS), *91*	30	39
____	16526	Kansas City Southern SP-type Caboose, *91*	17	21
____	16528	UP SP-type Caboose "6528," *90–91 u*	17	21
____	16529	Santa Fe SP-type Caboose "16829," *91*	9	13
____	16530	Mickey's World Tour SP-type Caboose "16830," *91, 92 u*	13	17
____	16531	Texas & Pacific SP-type Caboose, *92*	18	23
____	16533	C&NW Bay Window Caboose, *92*	29	40
____	16534	Delaware & Hudson SP-type Caboose, *92*	14	19
____	16535	Erie-Lackawanna Bay Window Caboose, *91 u*	42	50
____	16536	Chessie System SP-type Caboose, *92, 93 u, 94, 95 u*		23
____	16537	MKT SP-type Caboose, *92, 93 u*	17	21
____	16538	L&N Bay Window Caboose "1041," *92 u*	29	33
____	16539	WP Steelside Caboose "539," smoke, SSS (std O), *92*	50	55
____	16541	Montana Rail Link Extended Vision Caboose "10131" with smoke, *93*	55	65
____	16543	NYC SP-type Caboose, *93–95*		20
____	16544	Union Pacific SP-type Caboose, *93–95*	22	26
____	16546	Clinchfield SP-type Caboose, *93*	22	26
____	16547	"Happy Holidays" SP-type Caboose, *93–95*	46	55
____	16548	Conrail SP-type Caboose, *93*	15	20
____	16549	Soo Line Work Caboose, *93*	18	26
____	16550	U.S. Navy Searchlight Caboose, *94–95*	17	21
____	16551	Budweiser SP-type Caboose, *93–94 u*	27	31
____	16552	Frisco Searchlight Caboose, *94*	23	26
____	16553	United Auto Workers SP-type Caboose, *93 u*		40
____	16554	GT Extended Vision Caboose "79052," smoke, *94*	40	47
____	16555	C&O SP-type Caboose, *94*	22	26
____	16557	Ford SP-type Caboose, *94 u*	19	24
____	16558	Crayola SP-type Caboose, *94 u, 95*	17	21
____	16559	Seaboard Center Cupola Caboose "5658," *95*	23	24
____	16560	Chrysler Mopar Caboose, *94 u*	24	26
____	16561	UP Center Cupola Caboose "25766," *95*	27	31
____	16562	Reading Center Cupola Caboose, *95*	25	29
____	16563	Lionel Lines SP-type Caboose, *95*	22	26
____	16564	Western Maryland Center Cupola Caboose (SSS), *95*	30	34
____	16565	Milwaukee Road Bay Window Caboose, *95*	50	60
____	16566	U.S. Army SP-type Caboose "907," *95*		28
____	16568	ATSF SP-type Caboose, *96–99*		23
____	16571	Georgia Power SP-type Caboose "52789," *95 u*		68
____	16575	Sears Zenith SP-type Caboose, *95*		38

		Exc	Mint
16577	U.S. Coast Guard Work Caboose, *96*		26 ___
16578	Lionel Lines SP-type Caboose, *95 u*		20 ___
16579	GM/AC Delco, SP-type Caboose, *95*		35 ___
16580	SP-type Caboose, *96–99*		11 ___
16581	UP Illuminated Caboose, *96*		30 ___
16586	SP Illuminated Caboose "6357," *97*		42 ___
16590	Dodge Motorsports SP-type Caboose "6950," *96*		52 ___
16591	Little League Baseball SP-type Caboose "6397," *97*		38 ___
16593	Lionel Belt Line Caboose "6257," *98*		32 ___
16594	Caboose "6357," *98*		29 ___
16600	Illinois Central Coal Dump Car, *88*	14	23 ___
16601	Canadian National Searchlight Car, *88*	19	24 ___
16602	Erie-Lackawanna Coal Dump Car, *87*	16	26 ___
16603	Detroit Zoo Giraffe Car (O27), *87*	40	49 ___
16604	NYC Log Dump Car, *87*	15	27 ___
16605	Bronx Zoo Giraffe Car (O27), *88*	39	44 ___
16606	Southern Searchlight Car, *87*	13	21 ___
16607	Southern Coal Dump Car "16707" (SSS), *87*	18	26 ___
16608	Lehigh Valley Searchlight Car, *87*	22	30 ___
16609	Lehigh Valley Derrick Car, *87*	22	30 ___
16610	Track Maintenance Car, *87–88*	15	25 ___
16611	Santa Fe Log Dump Car, *88*	15	23 ___
16612	Soo Line Log Dump Car, *89*	14	24 ___
16613	MKT Coal Dump Car, *89*	17	26 ___
16614	Reading Cop and Hobo Car (O27), *89*	24	25 ___
16615	Lionel Lines Extension Searchlight Car, *89*	20	28 ___
16616	D&RGW Searchlight Car (SSS), *89*	22	30 ___
16617	C&NW Boxcar with ETD, *89*	23	34 ___
16618	Santa Fe Track Maintenance Car, *89*	11	19 ___
16619	Wabash Coal Dump Car, *90*	14	25 ___
16620	C&O Track Maintenance Car, *90–91*	16	19 ___
16621	Alaska Log Dump Car, *90*	24	31 ___
16622	CSX Boxcar with ETD, *90–91*	20	28 ___
16623	MKT DD Boxcar with ETD, *91*	16	23 ___
16624	NH Cop and Hobo Car (O27), *90–91*	23	31 ___
16625	NYC Extension Searchlight Car, *90*	22	30 ___
16626	CSX Searchlight Car, *90*	18	26 ___
16627	CSX Log Dump Car, *90*	19	23 ___
16628	Cop and Hobo Circus Gondola, *90–91*	36	43 ___
16629	Operating Circus Elephant Car (O27), *90–91*	38	50 ___
16630	SP Operating Cowboy Car (O27), *90–91*	22	26 ___
16631	RI Boxcar, steam RailSounds, *90*	110	130 ___
16632	BN Boxcar, diesel RailSounds, *90*	90	100 ___
16634	WM Coal Dump Car, *91*	26	32 ___
16636	D&RGW Log Dump Car, *91*	19	25 ___
16637	WP Extension Searchlight Car, *91*	27	30 ___
16638	Operating Circus Animal Car (O27), *91*	50	55 ___
16639	B&O Boxcar, steam RailSounds, *91*	100	120 ___
16640	Rutland Boxcar, diesel RailSounds, *91*	100	120 ___
16641	Toys "R" Us Giraffe Car (O27), *90–91 u*	45	65 ___
16642	Mickey's World Tour Goofy Car (O27), *91, 92 u*	33	41 ___

			Exc	Mint
____	**16644**	Amtrak Crane Car, *91, 92 u*	36	42
____	**16645**	Amtrak Searchlight Caboose, *91*	27	30
____	**16649**	Railway Express Agency Boxcar, steam RailSounds, *92*	110	140
____	**16650**	NYC Pacemaker Boxcar, diesel RailSounds, *92*	100	135
____	**16651**	Operating Circus Clown Car (027), *92*	24	30
____	**16652**	Radar Car, *92*	25	29
____	**16653**	Western Pacific Crane Car (SSS), *92*	44	60
____	**16655**	Steam Tender "1993," RailSounds, *93*	115	140
____	**16656**	Burlington Log Dump Car, *92 u*	18	25
____	**16657**	Lehigh Valley Coal Dump Car, *92 u*	22	29
____	**16658**	Erie-Lackawanna Crane Car, *93*	47	65
____	**16659**	Union Pacific Searchlight Car, *93–95*	15	18
____	**16660**	Fire Car with ladders, *93–94*	28	33
____	**16661**	Flatcar with boat, *93*	20	22
____	**16662**	Bugs Bunny and Yosemite Sam Outlaw Car (027), *93–94*	28	30
____	**16663**	Missouri Pacific Searchlight Car, *93*	16	19
____	**16664**	L&N Coal Dump Car, *93*	22	25
____	**16665**	Maine Central Log Dump Car, *93*	23	27
____	**16666**	Toxic Waste Car, *93–94*	25	32
____	**16667**	Conrail Searchlight Car, *93*	27	30
____	**16668**	Ontario Northland Log Dump Car, *93*	20	24
____	**16669**	Soo Line Searchlight Car, *93*	17	21
____	**16670**	TV Car, *93–94*	20	22
____	**16673**	Lionel Lines Tender, whistle, *94–97*	33	42
____	**16674**	Pinkerton Animated Gondola, *94*	28	32
____	**16675**	Great Northern Log Dump Car, *94*	21	25
____	**16676**	Burlington Coal Dump Car, *94*	23	28
____	**16677**	NATO Flatcar with Royal Navy submarine, *94*	34	44
____	**16678**	Rock Island Searchlight Car, *94*	21	23
____	**16679**	U.S. Mail Operating Boxcar, *94*	45	50
____	**16680**	Cherry Picker Car, *94*	25	28
____	**16681**	Aquarium Car, *95*	35	44
____	**16682**	Lionelville Farms Operating Stock Car (027), *94*	23	27
____	**16683**	Los Angeles Zoo Elephant Car (027), *94*	22	26
____	**16684**	U.S. Navy Crane Car, *94–95*	35	40
____	**16685**	Erie Extension Searchlight Car, *95*	30	34
____	**16686**	Mickey Mouse Animated Boxcar, *95*	28	35
____	**16687**	U.S. Mail Operating Boxcar, *94*	29	37
____	**16688**	Fire Car with ladders, *94*	35	43
____	**16689**	Toxic Waste Car, *94*	29	32
____	**16690**	Bugs Bunny and Yosemite Sam Outlaw Car (027), *94*	30	34
____	**16701**	Southern Tool Car (SSS), *87*	43	55
____	**16702**	Amtrak Bunk Car, *91, 92 u*	25	27
____	**16703**	NYC Tool Car, *92*	24	31
____	**16704**	TV Car, *94*	27	29
____	**16705**	Chesapeake & Ohio Cop and Hobo Car, *95*	28	34
____	**16706**	Animal Transport Service Giraffe Car, *95*	27	30
____	**16708**	C&NW Track Maintenance Car, *95*	24	31
____	**16709**	New York Central Derrick Car, *95*	22	28
____	**16710**	U.S. Army Operating Missile Car, *95*	40	42

		Exc	Mint
16711	Pennsylvania Searchlight Car, *95*	27	31 ____
16712	Pinkerton Animated Gondola, *95*	34	39 ____
16715	ATSF Log Dump Car, *96–99*		24 ____
16717	Jersey Central Crane Car, *96*		41 ____
16718	USMC Missile Launching Flatcar, *96*	26	31 ____
16719	Exploding Boxcar, *96*		38 ____
16720	Lionel Lines Searchlight Car "3650," *96–97*		50 ____
16724	Mickey and Friends Submarine Car, *96*		39 ____
16725	Rhino Transport Car, *97*		31 ____
16726	U.S. Army Fire Ladder Car, *96*		43 ____
16734	U.S. Coast Guard Searchlight Car, *96*		30 ____
16735	U.S. Coast Guard Flatcar with radar, *96*	28	35 ____
16736	U.S. Coast Guard Derrick Car, *96*		34 ____
16737	Road Runner and Wile E. Coyote Gondola "3444," *96*		60 ____
16738	Pepe LePew Boxcar "3370," *96*		40 ____
16739	Foghorn Leghorn Poultry Car "6434," *96*		44 ____
16740	Lionel Corporation Mail Car "3428," *96*		37 ____
16741	Union Pacific Illuminated Bunk Car, *97*		25 ____
16742	Trout Ranch Aquarium Car "3435," *96*		32 ____
16744	Port of Lionel City Searchlight Car, *97*		30 ____
16745	Port of Lionel City Flatcar with radar, *97*		30 ____
16746	Port of Lionel City Derrick Car, *97*		30 ____
16747	Breyer Animated Horse Car "6473," *97*		34 ____
16748	U.S. Forest Service Log-Dump Car "3361," *97*		30 ____
16749	Midget Mines Ore-Dump Car "3479," *97*		36 ____
16750	Lionel City Aquarium Car "3436," *97*		32 ____
16751	AIREX Sports Channel TV Car "3545," *97*		25 ____
16752	Marvin the Martian Missile Launching Flatcar "6655," *97*	118	129 ____
16754	Porky Pig and Instant Martians Flatcar "6805," *97*	122	168 ____
16755	Daffy Duck Animated Balloon Car "3470," *97*	117	158 ____
16760	Pluto and Cats Animated Gondola "3444," *97*		55 ____
16765	Bureau of Land Management Log Car "3351," *98*		30 ____
16766	Bureau of Land Management Ore Car "3479," *98*		31 ____
16767	New York Central Ice Docks Ice Car "6352," *98*		47 ____
16776	Holiday Boxcar, RailSounds, *98*		68 ____
16777	Animated Cola Car and Platform, *98*		100 ____
16782	Bethlehem Ore Dump Car "3479," *99*		95 ____
16783	Westside Lumber Log Dump Car "3351," *99*		32 ____
16784	Pratt's Hollow Seed Dump Car "3479," *99*		36 ____
16785	"Happy Holidays" Music Reefer "5700," *99*		100 ____
16789	Easter Operating Boxcar, *99*		39 ____
16790	UP Stock Car "3356," Crowsounds, *99*		90 ____
16791	New York City Lights Boxcar, *99*		44 ____
16792	Constellation Boxcar "9600," *99*		37 ____
16793	Animated Glow-in-the-Dark Alien Boxcar, *99*		44 ____
16794	Wicked Witch Halloween Boxcar, *99*		46 ____
16795	Elf Chasing Rudolph Gondola "6462," *99*		55 ____
16796	Snowman Loading Ice Car "6352," *99*		55 ____

		Exc	Mint
16805	Budweiser Malt Nutrine Reefer "3285," 91–92 u	76	102
____ **16806**	Toys "R" Us Boxcar, 92 u	21	26
____ **16807**	H.J. Heinz Reefer "301," 93	23	27
____ **16808**	Toys "R" Us Boxcar, 93 u	28	30
____ **16817**	Ambassador 1-D Tank Car, 00 u		165
____ **16818**	Engineer Award Tank Car, 00 u		704
____ **16819**	JLC Award Tank Car, 00 u		754
____ **16820**	Ambassador Boxcar, 00 u	309	505
____ **16822**	CSX Water Tower, 08		23
16824	036 Command Control Switch, left hand (FasTrack), 09–14		110
16825	036 Command Control Switch, right hand (FasTrack), 09–14		110
16826	072 Command Control Switch, left hand (FasTrack), 09–14		120
16827	072 Command Control Switch, right hand (FasTrack), 09–14		120
16828	060 Command Control Switch, left hand (FasTrack), 09–14		120
16829	060 Command Control Switch, right hand (FasTrack), 09–14		120
16830	048 Command Control Switch, left hand (FasTrack), 09–14		120
16831	048 Command Control Switch, right hand (FasTrack), 09–14		120
16832	072 Command Control Wye Switch (FasTrack), 09–14		115
____ **16834**	048 Half-Curved Track (FasTrack), 09–14		5
____ **16835**	048 Quarter-Curved Track (FasTrack), 09–14		5
____ **16836**	Christmas Girder Bridge, 09		21
____ **16837**	Christmas Operating Billboard, 09		45
____ **16841**	Halloween Gateman, 09		80
____ **16842**	Big Moe Crane, 10		70
____ **16843**	City and Western Diorama, 10–11		15
____ **16845**	Bookstore, 09–10		60
____ **16846**	Burning Hobo Depot, 09		90
____ **16847**	Legacy Hotel, 10–11		70
____ **16848**	Creature Comforts Pet Store, sound, 09–10		80
____ **16849**	Rotary Dumper with coal conveyor, CC, 10		600
____ **16850**	Operating Wind Turbine, 3-pack, 09–11		225
____ **16851**	Sunoco Cylindrical Oil Tank, gray, 10–11		100
____ **16852**	Sunoco Cylindrical Oil Tank, yellow, 10–11		90
____ **16853**	Polar Express Diorama, 09–11, 13		18
____ **16854**	MTA LIRR Blinking Billboard, 09		30
____ **16855**	MTA LIRR Illuminated Station Platform, 09		37
____ **16856**	MTA LIRR Passenger Station, 09		60
____ **16857**	Thomas & Friends Diorama, 10–14		18
____ **16859**	Grand Central Terminal, 09		1500
____ **16861**	50,000-gallon Water Tank, 09–11		150
____ **16863**	Santa's Christmas Wish Station, 09–11		125
____ **16868**	Straight O Gauge Tunnel, 09–14		55
____ **16871**	Winter Wonderland Diorama, 09–11		15
____ **16872**	Illuminated Christmas Station Platform, 09		35
____ **16873**	Bathtub Gondola Coal Load 3-pack, 10–14		20

Exc Mint

		Exc	Mint
16874	Coaling Station, *10–11*		80 ____
16880	Freight Platform, *10–12*		30 ____
16881	Barrel Shed, *10–11*		30 ____
16882	12" Covered Bridge, *10–14*		50 ____
16883	Neil's Guitar Shop, *10–11*		60 ____
16889	Coal Tipple Pack, *11–14*		15 ____
16891	Tank Car Accident, *10–11*		130 ____
16896	Flagpole with lights, *10–14*		28 ____
16897	75th Anniversary Gateman, *10*		75 ____
16903	CP Bulkhead Flatcar with pulp load (SSS), *94*	22	25 ____
16904	NYC Pacemaker Flatcar Set with trailers, *94*	55	60 ____
16907	Flatcar with farm tractors, *94*	27	33 ____
16908	U.S. Navy Flatcar "04039" with submarine, *94–95*	39	46 ____
16909	U.S. Navy Gondola "16556" with canisters, *94–95*	16	22 ____
16910	Missouri Pacific Flatcar with trailer, *94*	22	27 ____
16911	B&M Flatcar with trailer, *94*	28	34 ____
16912	CN Maxi-Stack Flatcar Set with containers, *94*	70	75 ____
16915	Lionel Lines Gondola (O27), *93–94 u*	7	10 ____
16916	Ford Flatcar with trailer, *94 u*	38	45 ____
16917	Crayola Gondola with crayons, *94 u, 95*	8	9 ____
16919	Chrysler Mopar Gondola with coil covers, *94–96*	33	36 ____
16922	Chesapeake & Ohio Flatcar with trailer, *95*	25	31 ____
16923	Intermodal Service Flatcar with wheel chocks, *95*	15	22 ____
16924	Lionel Corporation Flatcar "6424" with trailer, *96*		24 ____
16925	New York Central Flatcar with trailer, *95*	65	85 ____
16926	Frisco Flatcar with trailers, *95*	24	31 ____
16927	New York Central Flatcar with gondola, *95*	17	22 ____
16928	Soo Line Flatcar with dump bin (O27), *95*	12	15 ____
16929	BC Rail Gondola with cable reels, *95*	21	25 ____
16930	Santa Fe Flatcar with wheel load, *95*	20	25 ____
16932	Erie Flatcar with rail load, *95*	17	22 ____
16933	Lionel Lines Flatcar with autos, *95*	23	25 ____
16934	Pennsylvania Flatcar with Ertl road grader, *95*	28	39 ____
16935	UP Depressed Center Flatcar with Ertl bulldozer, *95*	22	35 ____
16936	Sealand Maxi-Stack Flatcar Set with containers, *95*	70	85 ____
16939	U.S. Navy Flatcar "04040" with boat, *95*	25	30 ____
16940	ATSF Flatcar with trailer, *96–99*		40 ____
16941	ATSF Flatcar with autos, *96–99*		25 ____
16943	Jersey Central Gondola, *96*		18 ____
16944	Georgia Power Depressed Center Flatcar "31438" with transformer, *95 u*		50 ____
16945	Georgia Power Depressed Center Flatcar "31950" with cable reels, *95 u*		53 ____
16946	C&O F9 Well Car "3840," *96*		31 ____
16951	Southern I-Beam Flatcar "9823" with load, *97*		25 ____
16952	U.S. Navy Flatcar with Ertl helicopter, *96*		25 ____
16953	NYC Flatcar with Red Wing Shoes trailer, *95 u*	39	45 ____
16954	NYC Flatcar "6424" with Ertl scraper, *96*		30 ____

			Exc	Mint
____	**16955**	ATSF Flatcar with Ertl Challenger, *96*		30
____	**16956**	Zenith Flatcar with trailer, *95 u*		134
____	**16957**	Depressed Center Flatcar "6461" with Ertl Case tractor, *96*		29
____	**16958**	Flatcar with Ertl New Holland loader, *96*		26
____	**16960**	U.S. Coast Guard Flatcar with boat, *96*		40
____	**16961**	GM/AC Delco Flatcar with trailer, *95*		73
____	**16963**	Lionel Corporation Flatcar "6411," *96–97*		34
____	**16964**	Lionel Corporation Gondola "6462," *97*		22
____	**16965**	Scout Flatcar "6424" with stakes, *96–97*		20
____	**16967**	Depressed Center Flatcar "6461" with transformer, *96*		21
____	**16968**	Depressed Center Flatcar "6461" with Ertl Helicopter, *96*		35
____	**16969**	Flatcar "6411" with Beechcraft Bonanza, *96*		33
____	**16970**	LA County Flatcar "6424" with motorized powerboat, *96*		20
____	**16971**	Port of Lionel City Flatcar with boat, *97*		35
____	**16972**	P&LE Gondola "6462," *97*		22
____	**16975**	Well Car Doublestack Set, *97*		75
____	**16978**	MILW Flatcar "6424" with P&H shovel, *97*		43
____	**16980**	Speedy Gonzales Missile Flatcar "6823," *97*		43
____	**16982**	BC Rail Bulkhead Flatcar "9823" with lumber, *97*		28
____	**16983**	PRR F9 Well Car "6983" with cable reels, *97*		39
____	**16986**	Sears Zenith Bulkhead Flatcar, *96 u*		45
____	**16987**	Musco Lighting Bulkhead Flatcar, *97 u*		35
____	**16997**	Lionel Lines Recovery Crane Car, *99*		50
____	**17002**	Conrail 2-bay ACF Hopper (std O), *87*	42	47
____	**17003**	Du Pont 2-bay ACF Hopper (std O), *90*	39	45
____	**17004**	MKT 2-bay ACF Hopper (std O), *91*	23	27
____	**17005**	Cargill 2-bay ACF Hopper (std O), *92*	29	37
____	**17006**	Soo Line 2-bay ACF Hopper (std O, SSS), *93*	31	36
____	**17007**	GN 2-bay ACF Hopper "173872" (std O), *94*	26	31
____	**17008**	D&RGW 2-bay ACF Hopper "10009" (std O), *95*		31
____	**17009**	New York Central 2-bay ACF Hopper, *96*		35
____	**17010**	Govt. of Canada ACF 2-bay Covered Hopper "7000," *98*		32
____	**17011**	NP ACF 2-bay Covered Hopper "75052," *98*		44
____	**17012**	Govt. of Canada ACF 2-bay Covered Hopper "7001," *98*		30
____	**17013**	NYC Graffiti 2-bay Covered Hopper "7000," *99*		55
____	**17014**	Graffiti 2-bay Covered Hopper "7000" (std O), *99*		45
____	**17015**	Corning 2-bay Hopper "90409" (std O), *01*		40
____	**17016**	C&NW 2-bay Hopper "96644" (std O), *01*		46
____	**17017**	Chessie System 2-bay Hopper "605527" (std O), *02*		32
____	**17018**	Nickel Plate Road Offset Hopper "33074," *02*		43
____	**17019**	Santa Fe Offset Hopper "78299," *02*		43
____	**17020**	Frisco Offset Hopper "92092," *02*		43
____	**17021**	NYC Offset Hopper "867999," *02*		43
____	**17022**	Burlington 2-bay ACF Hopper "183925" (std O), *03*		30

		Exc	Mint
17023	BNSF 2-bay Hopper "409038" (std O), *04*		30 ____
17024	Reading Offset Hopper "81089" (std O), *03–04*		43 ____
17025	C&O Offset Hopper "300027" (std O), *03–04*		43 ____
17026	D&H Offset Hopper "7215" (std O), *03–04*		41 ____
17027	IC Offset Hopper "92142" (std O), *03–04*		49 ____
17028	GE PS-2 2-bay Covered Hopper "326" (std O), *03–04*		35 ____
17029	CNJ PS-2 2-bay Covered Hopper "803" (std O), *03–04*		35 ____
17030	MILW PS-2 2-bay Covered Hopper "99708" (std O), *03–04*		35 ____
17031	SP PS-2 2-bay Covered Hopper "401306" (std O), *03–04*		38 ____
17038	Clinchfield PS-2 Covered Hopper, *05*		70 ____
17039	Boston & Maine PS-2 2-bay Covered Hopper, *05*		55 ____
17040	Norfolk & Western PS-2 2-bay Covered Hopper, *05*		55 ____
17041	Great Northern Offset Hopper, *05*		60 ____
17042	Green Bay & Western Offset Hopper, *05*		60 ____
17043	Baltimore & Ohio Offset Hopper, *05*		60 ____
17063	Santa Fe PS-2 2-bay Covered Hopper "82297" (std O), *06*		55 ____
17064	MKT PS-2 2-bay Covered Hopper "1311" (std O), *06*		55 ____
17065	Boraxo PS-2 2-bay Covered Hopper "31062" (std O), *06*		55 ____
17066	PRR PS-2 2-bay Covered Hopper "256177" (std O), *06*		55 ____
17067	Rock Island Offset Hopper "89500" with gravel (std O), *06*		65 ____
17068	CNJ Offset Hopper "61261" (std O), *06*		65 ____
17069	Maine Central Offset Hopper "3785" (std O), *06*		65 ____
17070	P&LE Offset Hopper "4990" (std O), *06*		65 ____
17083	C&O Offset Hopper "47386" (std O), *05*		40 ____
17100	Chessie System 3-bay ACF Hopper	49	85 ____
17101	Chessie System 3-bay ACF Hopper (std O), *88*	37	45 ____
17102	Chessie System 3-bay ACF Hopper (std O), *88*	35	41 ____
17103	Chessie System 3-bay ACF Hopper (std O), *88*	31	34 ____
17104	Chessie System 3-bay ACF Hopper (std O), *88*	38	46 ____
17105	Chessie System 3-bay ACF Hopper (std O), *88*	39	46 ____
17107	Sinclair 3-bay ACF Hopper (std O), *89*	40	48 ____
17108	Santa Fe 3-bay ACF Hopper (std O), *90*	42	48 ____
17109	N&W 3-bay ACF Hopper (std O), *91*	24	31 ____
17110	UP Hopper with coal (std O), *91*	24	30 ____
17111	Reading Hopper with coal (std O), *91*	23	28 ____
17112	Erie-Lack. 3-bay ACF Hopper (std O), *92*	24	34 ____
17113	LV Hopper with coal (std O), *92–93*	25	32 ____
17114	Peabody Hopper with coal (std O), *92–93*	26	30 ____
17118	Archer Daniels Midland 3-bay ACF Hopper "60029" (std O), *93*	28	35 ____
17120	CSX Hopper "295110" with coal (std O), *94*	28	30 ____
17121	ICG Hopper "72867" with coal (std O), *94*	26	33 ____
17122	RI 3-bay ACF Hopper "800200" (std O), *94*	32	39 ____

			Exc	Mint
	17123	Cargill Covered Grain Hopper "844304" (std O), *95*	25	34
	17124	Archer Daniels Midland 3-bay ACF Hopper "50224" (std O), *95*	24	30
___	**17127**	Delaware & Hudson 3-bay Hopper, *96*		34
___	**17128**	Chesapeake & Ohio 3-bay Hopper, *96*		30
	17129	WM 3-bay Hopper "9300" with coal (std O), *97*		34
___	**17132**	PRR 3-bay ACF Hopper "260815," *98*		40
	17133	BNSF ACF 3-bay Covered Hopper "403698," *98*		38
	17134	BNSF 3-bay Covered Hopper "403698" (std O), *01*		38
	17135	BNSF ACF 3-bay Covered Hopper with ETD, *98*		39
	17137	Cargill 3-bay Covered Hopper "1219" (std O), *99*		45
	17138	Farmers Elevator 3-bay Covered Hopper (std O), *99*		45
	17139	"Grain Train" 3-bay Hopper "BLMR 1025," *99–00*		39
	17140	Virginian 3-bay Hopper 6-pack, "5260-5265," *99*		230
	17147	C&O 3-bay Hopper 6-pack, "156330-156335," *99*		230
___	**17154**	Alberta Cylindrical Hopper "628373" (std O), *01*		40
___	**17155**	Shell Cylindrical Hopper "3527" (std O), *01*		40
	17156	ACF Pressureaide 3-bay Hopper "59267" (std O), *01*		27
	17157	Wonder Bread "56670" 3-bay Hopper (std O), *01*		40
___	**17158**	Conrail Coal Hopper "487739" (std O), *01*		42
___	**17159**	N&W Coal Hopper "1776" (std O), *01*		45
___	**17163**	C&O 3-bay Hopper (std O), *01*		30
	17170	General Mills 3-bay Covered Hopper (std O), *00 u*		60
	17171	Lionel Lion Cylindrical Hopper (std O), *01*		45
	17172	CP Rail Cylindrical Hopper "385206" (std O), *02*		37
	17173	Govt. of Canada Cylindrical Hopper "111031" (std O), *02*		33
___	**17174**	GN 3-bay Hopper "171250" (std O), *02*		29
	17175	IC PS-2CD 4427 Covered Hopper "57031" (std O), *02*		40
	17176	Cargill PS-2CD 4427 Covered Hopper "2514" (std O), *02*		46
	17177	PS-2CD 4427 Covered Hopper "2500" (std O), *02*		40
	17178	Santa Fe PS-2CD 4427 Covered Hopper "304774" (std O), *02*		40
	17179	Indianapolis Power & Light Coal Hopper "10074" (std O), *02*		40
___	**17180**	Rock Island Coal Hopper "700665" (std O), *02*		40
	17181	NYC 4-bay ACF Centerflow Hopper "892138" (std O), *03*		45
	17182	Sigco Hybrids 4-bay ACF Centerflow Hopper "1100" (std O), *03*		46

		Exc	Mint
17183	C&O Hopper "156341" (std O), *01*		30 ____
17184	Virginian Hopper "5271" (std O), *01*		30 ____
17185	LLCX Bathtub Gondola "877900" (std O), *01*		36 ____
17186	Cannonaide 4-bay ACF Centerflow Hopper "96169" (std O), *03*		40 ____
17187	Rio Grande 4-bay ACF Centerflow Hopper "15521" (std O), *03*		40 ____
17188	Govt. of Canada 3-bay Cylindrical Hopper (std O), *03*		48 ____
17189	Saskatchewan Grain 3-bay Cylindrical Hopper (std O), *03*		48 ____
17190	Soo/CP 3-bay ACF Hopper "119303" (std O), *03*		37 ____
17191	BN PS-2CD 4427 Hopper "450669" (std O), *03–04*		45 ____
17192	Lehigh Valley PS-2CD 4427 Hopper "51118" (std O), *03–04*		40 ____
17193	Chessie System/WM PS-2CD 4427 Hopper "4673" (std O), *03–04*		30 ____
17194	MKT PS-2CD 4427 Hopper "1122" (std O), *03–04*		40 ____
17195	L&N 3-bay Hopper "240850" (std O), *04*		40 ____
17196	Firestone 4-bay Hopper "53240" (std O), *04*		40 ____
17197	Diamond Chemicals 4-bay Hopper "53286" (std O), *04*		40 ____
17198	Hercules 4-bay Hopper "50503" (std O), *04*		40 ____
17199	Conrail 4-bay Hopper "888367" (std O), *04*		46 ____
17200	Canadian Pacific Boxcar (std O), *89*	26	32 ____
17201	Conrail Boxcar (std O), *87*	33	38 ____
17202	Santa Fe Boxcar (std O), diesel RailSounds, *90*	80	85 ____
17203	Cotton Belt DD Boxcar (std O), *91*	33	38 ____
17204	Missouri Pacific DD Boxcar (std O), *91*	27	30 ____
17207	C&IM DD Boxcar (std O), *92*	36	42 ____
17208	Union Pacific DD Boxcar (std O), *92*	35	40 ____
17209	B&O DD Boxcar "296000" (std O), *93*	37	43 ____
17210	Chicago & Illinois Midland Boxcar "16021" (std O), *92 u*	30	39 ____
17211	Chicago & Illinois Midland Boxcar "16022" (std O), *92 u*	30	39 ____
17212	Chicago & Illinois Midland Boxcar "16023" (std O), *92 u*	24	31 ____
17213	Susquehanna Boxcar "501" (std O), *93*	28	31 ____
17214	Railbox Boxcar (std O), diesel RailSounds, *93*	75	85 ____
17216	PRR DD Boxcar "60155" (std O), *94*	34	38 ____
17217	New Haven State of Maine Boxcar "45003" (std O), *95*	28	35 ____
17218	BAR State of Maine Boxcar "2184" (std O), *95*	23	36 ____
17219	Tazmanian Devil 40th Birthday Boxcar (std O), *95*	40	50 ____
17220	Pennsylvania Boxcar (std O), *96*		23 ____
17221	NYC Boxcar (std O), *96*		34 ____
17222	Western Pacific Boxcar (std O), *96*	28	34 ____
17223	Milwaukee Road DD Boxcar (std O), *96*		34 ____
17224	Central of Georgia Boxcar "9464-197" (std O), *97*	15	29 ____
17225	Penn Central Boxcar "9464-297" (std O), *97*	13	26 ____

			Exc	Mint
	17226	Milwaukee Road Boxcar "9464-397" (std O), *97*		23
____	**17227**	UP DD Boxcar "9200" (std O), *97*		35
	17231	Wisconsin Central DD Boxcar "9200" with auto frames, *98*		40
____	**17232**	SP/UP Merger DD Boxcar "9200," *98*		33
____	**17233**	Western Pacific Boxcar "9464-198," *98*		27
____	**17234**	Port Huron & Detroit Boxcar "9464-298," *98*		33
____	**17235**	Boston & Maine Boxcar "9464-398," *98*		41
____	**17239**	ATSF "Texas Chief" Boxcar "9464-1," *97*		50
____	**17240**	ATSF "Super Chief" Boxcar "9464-2," *97*		50
____	**17241**	ATSF" El Capitan" Boxcar "9464-3," *97*		50
____	**17242**	ATSF "Grand Canyon" Boxcar "9464-4," *97*		60
____	**17243**	NP Boxcar "8722," *98*		48
____	**17244**	Santa Fe "Chief" Boxcar, *98*		37
____	**17245**	C&O Boxcar with Chessie kitten, *98*		44
____	**17246**	NYC Pacemaker Rolling Stock 4-pack, *98*		200
____	**17247**	NYC 9464 Boxcar "174940," *98*		135
____	**17248**	NYC 9464 Boxcar "174945," *98*		115
____	**17249**	NYC 9464 Boxcar "174949," *98*		60
____	**17250**	UP Boxcar "507406" (std O), *99*		45
____	**17251**	BNSF Boxcar "103277," *99*		41
____	**17252**	NS Boxcar "564824" (std O), *99*		41
____	**17253**	CSX Boxcar "141756" (std O), *99*		35
____	**17254**	UP Boxcar "551967" (std O), *99*		42
____	**17255**	Chevy DD Boxcar "9200" (std O), *99*		38
____	**17257**	Atlantic Coast Line Boxcar "28809" (std O), *99*		36
____	**17258**	D&H 9464 Boxcar "29055" std O, *99*		41
____	**17259**	MKT 9464 Boxcar "1422" (std O), *99*		34
	17260	CP Rail 9464 Boxcar "286138" (std O), silver, *00*		45
____	**17261**	CP Rail 9464 Boxcar "85154," green, *00*		44
____	**17262**	CP Rail 9464 Boxcar "56776," red (std O), *00*		48
____	**17263**	NYC Boxcar "45725" (std O), *00*		46
____	**17264**	C&O Boxcar "6054" (std O), *00*		44
____	**17265**	U.S. Army Boxcar (std O), *00*		35
____	**17266**	Monon Boxcar "911" (std O), *00*		45
____	**17268**	C&O 9464 Boxcar "12700" (std O), *01*		44
	17269	Western Maryland 9464 Boxcar "29140" (std O), *01*		44
	17270	B&O Time-Saver 9464 Boxcar "467439" (std O), *01*		42
____	**17271**	"The Rock" Boxcar "300324" (std O), *01*		37
____	**17272**	Railbox Boxcar "15150" (std O), *01*		27
____	**17273**	DT&I DD Boxcar "26852" (std O), *01*		44
____	**17274**	Soo Line DD Boxcar "177587" (std O), *01*		42
____	**17275**	NYC PS-1 Boxcar "175008" (std O), *02*		43
____	**17276**	Cotton Belt PS-1 Boxcar "75000" (std O), *02*		44
____	**17277**	Rio Grande PS-1 Boxcar "69676" (std O), *02*		40
____	**17278**	WP PS-1 Boxcar "1953" (std O), *02*		44
____	**17279**	Ontario Northland Boxcar "7428" (std O), *02*		40
	17280	Santa Fe Boxcar "600194" with auto frames (std O), *02*		45
____	**17281**	PRR DD Boxcar "83158" (std O), *04*		42

		Exc	Mint
17282	UP DD Boxcar "160300" (std O), *04*		42 ___
17283	GM&O DD Boxcar "9077" (std O), *04*		41 ___
17284	Erie DD Boxcar "66000" (std O), *04*		41 ___
17285	CSX Big Blue Boxcar "151296" (std O), *03*		36 ___
17287	BAR Boxcar "5976" (std O), *03*		35 ___
17288	NYC PS-1 Boxcar "175012" (std O), *03–04*		38 ___
17289	GN PS-1 Boxcar "18485" (std O), *03*		40 ___
17290	Seaboard PS-1 Boxcar "24452" (std O), *03–04*		42 ___
17291	RI PS-1 Boxcar "21110" (std O), *03–04*		42 ___
17292	B&M PS-1 Boxcar "76182" (std O), *04*		34 ___
17293	IC PS-1 Boxcar "400666" (std O), *04*		40 ___
17294	TP&W PS-1 Boxcar "5036" (std O), *04*		36 ___
17295	Santa Fe PS-1 Boxcar "276749" (std O), *04*		40 ___
17297	UP PS-1 Boxcar, *03*		100 ___
17300	Canadian Pacific Reefer (std O), *89*	28	33 ___
17301	Conrail Reefer (std O), *87*	35	42 ___
17302	Santa Fe Reefer with ETD (std O), *90*	35	41 ___
17303	C&O Reefer "7890" (std O), *93*	23	30 ___
17304	Wabash Reefer "26269" (std O), *94*	29	37 ___
17305	Pacific Fruit Express Reefer "459400" (std O), *94*	27	40 ___
17306	Pacific Fruit Express Reefer "459401" (std O), *94*	19	27 ___
17307	Tropicana Reefer "300" (std O), *95*	44	65 ___
17308	Tropicana Reefer "301" (std O), *95*	22	35 ___
17309	Tropicana Reefer "302" (std O), *95*	21	29 ___
17310	Tropicana Reefer "303" (std O), *95*	20	27 ___
17311	REA Reefer (std O), *96*	28	30 ___
17314	PFE Reefer "9800-198," *98*		42 ___
17315	PFE Reefer "9800-298," *98*		39 ___
17316	NP Reefer "98583," *98*		50 ___
17317	PRR Reefer FGE "91904," *98*		36 ___
17318	UP Reefer "170650" (std O), *99*		47 ___
17319	PFE Reefer 6-pack (std O), *01*		300 ___
17331	Hood's General American Milk Car "802" (std O), *02*		100 ___
17332	Pfaudler General American Milk Car "501" (std O), *02*		70 ___
17334	REA General American Milk Car "1741" (std O), *02*		100 ___
17335	New Haven General American Milk Car "102" (std O), *02*		75 ___
17336	PFE Steel-sided Reefer "17760" (std O), *03*		45 ___
17337	CN Steel-sided Reefer "209712" (std O), *03*		38 ___
17338	Merchants Dispatch Transit Steel-sided Reefer "12322" (std O), *03*		39 ___
17339	Burlington Steel-sided Reefer "74825" (std O), *03*		45 ___
17340	White Bros. General American Milk Car "891" (std O), *03*		44 ___
17341	Dairymen's League General American Milk Car "779" (std O), *03*		43 ___
17342	Miller Beer Steel-sided Reefer (std O), *03 u*		58 ___
17343	Miller Beer Steel-sided Reefer (std O), *03 u*		64 ___

			Exc	Mint
____	**17349**	NYC General American Milk Car "6581" (std O), *03 u*		42
____	**17350**	Hood's General American Milk Car "503" (std O), *03 u*		45
____	**17351**	Santa Fe Steel-sided Reefer "3526" (std O), *04*		43
____	**17352**	PFE Steel-sided Reefer "20043" (std O), *04*		41
____	**17353**	Needham Packing Steel-sided Reefer "60507" (std O), *04*		44
____	**17354**	Swift Steel-sided Reefer "15392" (std O), *04*		42
____	**17355**	Hood's Steel-sided Reefer "550" (std O), *04*		40
____	**17356**	Nestle Nesquik Steel-sided Reefer (std O), *04*		44
____	**17357**	Borden's Steel-sided Reefer "522" (std O), *04*		47
____	**17358**	Fairfield Farms Steel-sided Reefer (std O), *04*		44
____	**17360**	Hood's General American Milk Car "810" (std O), *03*		46
____	**17361**	Hood's General American Milk Car "811" (std O), *03*		43
____	**17362**	Pfaudler General American Milk Car "502" (std O), *03*		47
____	**17363**	Pfaudler General American Milk Car "503" (std O), *03*		40
____	**17364**	REA General American Milk Car "1742" (std O), *03*		38
____	**17365**	REA General American Milk Car "1743" (std O), *03*		44
____	**17366**	NH General American Milk Car "103" (std O), *03*		43
____	**17367**	NH General American Milk Car "104" (std O), *03*		47
____	**17368**	White Brothers General American Milk Car "892" (std O), *03*		43
____	**17369**	White Brothers General American Milk Car "893" (std O), *03*		47
____	**17370**	Dairymen's League General American Milk Car "780" (std O), *03*		47
____	**17371**	Dairymen's League Milk Car "781" (std O), *03*		47
____	**17372**	NYC General American Milk Car "6582" (std O), *03*		47
____	**17373**	NYC General American Milk Car "6583" (std O), *03*		40
____	**17374**	Hood's General American Milk Car "504" (std O), *03*		43
____	**17375**	Hood's General American Milk Car "505" (std O), *03*		47
____	**17377**	Railway Express Operating Milk Car "302" (std O), *05*		172
____	**17378**	Supplee General American Milk Car (std O), *05*		63
____	**17379**	NP Steel-sided Reefer "91353" (std O), *05*		60
____	**17380**	PFE Silver Steel-sided Reefer "45698" (std O), *05*		60
____	**17381**	North Western Steel-sided Reefer "751" (std O), *05*		40
____	**17397**	PFE Steel-sided Reefer "47767" (std O), *05*		45
____	**17398**	A&P General American Milk Car "737" (std O), *06*		65
____	**17399**	Bowman Dairy General American Milk Car "117" (std O), *06*		65

		Exc	Mint
17400	CP Rail Gondola with coal (std O), *89*	30	34 ____
17401	Conrail Gondola with coal (std O), *87*	24	26 ____
17402	Santa Fe Gondola with coal (std O), *90*	19	25 ____
17403	Chessie System Gondola "371629" with coil covers (std O), *93*	24	25 ____
17404	ICG Gondola "245998" with coil covers (std O), *93*	26	32 ____
17405	Reading Gondola "24876" with coil covers (std O), *94*	27	31 ____
17406	PRR Gondola "385405" with coil covers (std O), *95*	37	42 ____
17407	NKP Gondola with scrap load, *96*		24 ____
17408	Cotton Belt Gondola "9820" with scrap load (std O), *97*		32 ____
17410	UP Gondola "903004" with scrap load (std O), *99*		30 ____
17412	Gondola, blue, online store, *98*		20 ____
17413	Service Center Gondola with parts load (SSS), *00*		24 ____
17414	Nickel Plate PS-5 Gondola "44801" (std O), *01–02*		40 ____
17415	Frisco PS-5 Gondola "61878" (std O), *01–02*		35 ____
17416	D&H Gondola "14011" with scrap load (std O), *01*		33 ____
17417	BN Rotary Bathtub Gondola 3-pack, *01*		140 ____
17421	CSX Rotary Bathtub Gondola 3-pack, *01*		135 ____
17425	Western Maryland PS-5 Gondola "354903" (std O), *01–02*		36 ____
17426	Maine Central PS-5 Gondola "1116" (std O), *01–02*		40 ____
17427	CSX Rotary Bathtub Gondola Add-on Unit (std O), *02*		47 ____
17428	BN Rotary Bathtub Gondola Add-on Unit (std O), *02*		42 ____
17429	Conrail Rotary Bathtub Gondola 3-pack (std O), *02–03*		115 ____
17433	BNSF Rotary Bathtub Gondola 3-pack (std O), *02–03*		145 ____
17439	UP PS-5 Gondola "229606" (std O), *03*		35 ____
17440	Algoma Central PS-5 Gondola "801" (std O), *03*		32 ____
17441	Conrail Rotary Bathtub Gondola "507673" (std O), *03*		39 ____
17442	BNSF Rotary Bathtub Gondola "668330" (std O), *03*		46 ____
17443	NS Rotary Bathtub Gondola 3-pack (std O), *03*		90 ____
17447	UP Rotary Bathtub Gondola 3-pack (std O), *03*		100 ____
17457	GN PS-5 Gondola "72839" (std O), *03*		35 ____
17458	Reading PS-5 Gondola "33267" (std O), *03*		35 ____
17459	CP Rail PS-5 Gondola "338966" (std O), *04*		35 ____
17460	NYC PS-5 Gondola "749592" (std O), *04*		40 ____
17461	Pennsylvania PS-5 Gondola "374256" (std O), *04*		36 ____
17462	Santa Fe PS-5 Gondola "167340" (std O), *04*		35 ____
17463	NS Bathtub Gondola "10303" (std O), *04*		40 ____
17464	UP Bathtub Gondola "28100" (std O), *04*		35 ____
17465	CP Rail Bathtub Gondola 3-pack (std O), *04*		105 ____

		Exc	Mint
____ 17470	CP Rail Bathtub Gondola, *05*		50
17471	Burlington PS-5 Gondola with covers (std O), *05*		
____			44
17472	New Haven PS-5 Gondola with covers (std O), *05*		
____			53
____ 17473	NYC PS-5 Gondola "502351" (std O), *06–07*		65
____ 17474	D&H PS-5 Gondola "13816" (std O), *06–07*		65
____ 17475	Koppers PS-5 Gondola "213" (std O), *06–07*		65
____ 17477	L&N PS-5 Gondola "170012" (std O), *06–07*		46
17478	N&W PS-5 Gondola "275005" with containers (std O), *08*		
____			70
17479	LV PS-5 Gondola "33455" with containers (std O), *08*		
____			70
17480	RI PS-5 Gondola with coke containers (std O), *08–09*		
____			70
____ 17488	UP Bathtub Gondola 3-pack (std O), *09*		190
____ 17500	CP Flatcar with logs (std O), *89*	27	29
____ 17501	Conrail Flatcar with stakes (std O), *87*	37	45
____ 17502	Santa Fe Flatcar with trailer (std O), *90*	70	75
____ 17503	NS Flatcar with trailer (std O), *92*	55	65
____ 17504	NS Flatcar with trailer (std O), *92*	55	65
____ 17505	NS Flatcar with trailer (std O), *92*	50	55
____ 17506	NS Flatcar with trailer (std O), *92*	46	55
____ 17507	NS Flatcar with trailer (std O), *92*	50	55
____ 17510	NP Flatcar "61200" with logs (std O), *94*	31	36
____ 17511	WM Flatcar with logs, set of 3 (std O), *95*		145
____ 17512	WM Flatcar with logs (std O), *95*	35	41
____ 17513	WM Flatcar with logs (std O), *95*	43	50
____ 17514	WM Flatcar with logs (std O), *95*	39	45
17515	Norfolk Southern Flatcar with tractors (std O), *95*		
____		24	42
17516	T&P Flatcar "9823" with 2 Beechcraft Bonanzas (std O), *97*		
____			50
17517	WP Flatcar "9823" with Ertl Caterpillar frontloader (std O), *97*		
____			39
17518	PRR Flatcar "9823" with 2 Corgi Mack trucks (std O), *97*		
____		49	50
____ 17522	Flatcar with Plymouth Prowler, *98*		41
____ 17527	Flatcar with 2 Dodge Vipers, *98*		38
____ 17529	ATSF Flatcar "90010" with Ford milk truck, *99*		55
____ 17533	MTTX Ford Flatcar with auto frames, *99*		38
17534	Diamond T Flatcar with Mack trucks "9823," *99*		
____			55
17536	Route 66 Flatcar "9823-3" with 2 luxury coupes, *99*		
____			37
17537	Route 66 Flatcar "9823-4" with 2 touring coupes, *99*		
____			32
____ 17538	NYC Flatcar with Ford tow truck, *99*		43
____ 17539	Flatcar "9823" with 2 Corvettes (std O), *99*		70
____ 17540	Flatcar "9823" with 2 Corvettes (std O), *99*		70
____ 17546	LL Recovery Flatcar "6424" with rail load, *99*		50
17547	Lionel Lines Recovery Flatcar "6429" with machinery, *99*		
____			50
17548	Route 66 Flatcar "9823-6" with 2 luxury coupes, *99*		
____			42

		Exc	Mint
17549	Route 66 Flatcar "9823-5" with station wagon and trailer, *99*		42 ____
17550	BN Center Beam Flatcar "6216" with lumber (std O), *99*		39 ____
17551	NYC Flatcar with NYC pickups "499," *99*		49 ____
17553	Trailer Train Flatcar "98102" with combine (std O), *99*		125 ____
17554	GN Flatcar "61042" with logs, *00*		32 ____
17555	Ford Mustang Flatcar with 2 cars (std O), *01*		NRS ____
17556	Ford Mustang Flatcar with 2 cars (std O), *01*		NRS ____
17557	Route 66 Flatcar "9823-7" with black sedans, *99–00*		39 ____
17558	Route 66 Flatcar "9823-8" with brown sedans, *99*		39 ____
17559	Route 66 Flatcar "9823-9" with 2 wagons (std O), *01*		40 ____
17560	Route 66 Flatcar "9823-10" with 2 sedans (std O), *01*		40 ____
17563	Santa Fe Flatcar "90011" with pickup trucks (std O), *01*		49 ____
17564	West Side Lumber Shay Log Car 3-pack #2 (std O), *01*		95 ____
17568	PRR Flatcar "470333" with pickup trucks (std O), *02*		50 ____
17571	UP Flatcar "909231" with pickup trucks (std O), *03*		50 ____
17572	Pioneer Seed Flatcar with pedal cars, *02 u*		190 ____
17573	WM PS-4 Flatcar "2631" (std O), *03*		35 ____
17574	Santa Fe PS-4 Flatcar "90081" (std O), *03*		35 ____
17575	NYC PS-4 Flatcar "506098" (std O), *03*		40 ____
17576	Ontario Northland PS-4 Flatcar "2020" (std O), *03*		35 ____
17577	B&O PS-4 Flatcar "8651" (std O), *04*		35 ____
17578	B&M PS-4 Flatcar "34007" (std O), *04*		35 ____
17579	Milwaukee Road PS-4 Flatcar "64073" (std O), *04*		35 ____
17580	UP PS-4 Flatcar "54603" (std O), *04*		35 ____
17581	GN Flatcar "X4168" with pickup trucks (std O), *04*		42 ____
17582	PRR PS-4 Flatcar "469617" with trailers (std O), *05*		110 ____
17583	GN PS-4 Flatcar with trailers, *05*		80 ____
17584	SP PS-4 Flatcar with trailers, *05*		80 ____
17585	C&O PS-4 Flatcar "81000" with trailers (std O), *05*		80 ____
17586	BN Husky Stack Car "63322" (std O), *05*		80 ____
17587	SP Husky Stack Car "513915" (std O), *05*		80 ____
17588	CSX Husky Stack Car "620350" (std O), *05*		80 ____
17589	TTX Trailer Train Husky Stack Car "456249" (std O), *05*		65 ____
17600	NYC Wood-sided Caboose (std O), *87 u*	35	45 ____
17601	Southern Wood-sided Caboose (std O), *88*	35	44 ____
17602	Conrail Wood-sided Caboose (std O), *87*	65	75 ____
17603	RI Wood-sided Caboose (std O), *88*	19	34 ____
17604	Lackawanna Wood-sided Caboose (std O), *88*	42	53 ____
17605	Reading Wood-sided Caboose (std O), *89*	34	37 ____
17606	NYC Steel-sided Caboose, smoke (std O), *90*	49	65 ____

		Exc	Mint
___ 17607	Reading Steel-sided Caboose, smoke (std O), *90*	55	65
___ 17608	C&O Steel-sided Caboose, smoke (std O), *91*	46	55
___ 17610	Wabash Steel-sided Caboose, smoke (std O), *91*	39	55
___ 17611	NYC Wood-sided Caboose "6003" (std O), *90 u*	40	55
___ 17612	NKP Steel-sided Caboose, smoke (FF 6), *92*	60	65
___ 17613	Southern Steel-sided Caboose "7613," smoke (std O), *92*	60	65
___ 17615	NP Wood-sided Caboose, smoke (std O), *92*	65	70
___ 17617	D&RGW Steel-sided Caboose (std O), *95*	50	55
___ 17618	Frisco Wood-sided Caboose (std O), *95*	65	75
___ 17620	NP Wood-sided Caboose "1746," *98*		70
___ 17623	Farmrail Extended Vision Caboose, *99*		74
___ 17624	Conrail Extended Vision Caboose "6900," *99*		43
___ 17625	Burlington Northern Steel-sided Caboose "7606," *99*		65
___ 17626	Service Center Extended Vision Caboose (SSS), *00*		29
___ 17627	C&O Extended Vision Caboose, *01*		65
___ 17628	BNSF Extended Vision Caboose, *01*		65
___ 17629	Santa Fe Extended Vision Caboose, *01*		80
___ 17630	UP Extended Vision Caboose, *01*		85
___ 17631	Virginian Bay Window Caboose, *01*		85
___ 17632	CSX Bay Window Caboose, *01*		75
___ 17633	NYC Bay Window Caboose, *01*		90
___ 17634	Delaware & Hudson Bay Window Caboose, *01*		75
___ 17635	100th Anniversary Die-cast Gold Caboose, *00*		345
___ 17636	NYC Die-cast Caboose "18096," *00–01*		100
___ 17637	NYC "Quicker via Peoria" Die-cast Caboose, *00*		135
___ 17638	RI Extended Vision Caboose "17011" (std O), *02*		55
___ 17639	Chessie Extended Vision Caboose "3322" (std O), *02*		55
___ 17640	CP Extended Vision Caboose "434604" (std O), *02*		57
___ 17641	Soo Line Extended Vision Caboose "2" (std O), *02*		55
___ 17642	Conrail Bay Window Caboose "21023" (std O), *02*		65
___ 17643	NKP Bay Window Caboose "480" (std O), *02*		60
___ 17644	Erie Bay Window Caboose "C307," (std O), *02*		55
___ 17645	N&W Bay Window Caboose "C-6," (std O), *02*		55
___ 17646	UP Bay Window Caboose "24555," (std O), *02*		65
___ 17647	B&O Caboose "C-2820" (std O), *03–04*		65
___ 17648	Chessie System Caboose "C-2800" (std O), *03–04*		75
___ 17649	Lionel Lines Caboose "7649" (std O), *03–04*		65
___ 17650	Rio Grande Extended Vision Caboose "01500" (std O), *03*		65
___ 17651	BN Extended Vision Caboose "10531" (std O), *03–05*		80
___ 17652	NYC Bay Window Caboose "20200" (std O), *03*		75
___ 17653	SP Bay Window Caboose "1337" (std O), *03*		65

		Exc	Mint
17654	Alaska Extended Vision Caboose "989" (std O), *03*		75 ____
17655	WP Bay Window Caboose "448" (std O), *03–04*		75 ____
17657	Norman Rockwell Holiday Caboose, *03*		30 ____
17658	Burlington Extended Vision Caboose "13611" (std O), *04*		70 ____
17659	CN Extended Vision Caboose "79646" (std O), *04*		70 ____
17660	Seaboard Extended Vision Caboose "5700" (std O), *04*		65 ____
17661	C&NW Bay Window Caboose "10871" (std O), *04*		65 ____
17662	PC Bay Window Caboose "21001" (std O), *04*		65 ____
17663	Southern Bay Window Caboose "X546" (std O), *04*		65 ____
17664	B&O Caboose "C-2824" (std O), *03–04*		65 ____
17665	Chessie System Caboose "C-2802" (std O), *03–04*		75 ____
17669	NYC Bay Window Caboose, smoke, *05*		85 ____
17670	CP Rail Bay Window Caboose, smoke, *05*		85 ____
17671	BN Extended Vision Caboose, *05*		85 ____
17672	GN Extended Vision Caboose "X-106" (std O), *05*		85 ____
17673	Santa Fe Extended Vision Caboose, *05*		85 ____
17674	Reading Extended Vision Caboose "94119" (std O), *05*		75 ____
17675	Rio Grande Extended Vision Caboose "01507" (std O), *06*		90 ____
17676	NYC Bay Window Caboose "20300," *07*		60 ____
17677	Erie-Lack. Bay Window Caboose "C359" (std O), *06*		90 ____
17678	B&O I-12 Caboose "C2421" (std O), *06*		90 ____
17679	Long Island Bay Window Caboose "C-62" (std O), *06*		90 ____
17682	Reading Northeastern Caboose "92841" (std O), *06–07*		85 ____
17683	Chessie System Northeastern Caboose "1893" (std O), *07*		85 ____
17684	Conrail Northeastern Caboose "18873" (std O), *07*		85 ____
17685	Jersey Central Northeastern Caboose "91533" (std O), *07*		85 ____
17690	UP CA-4 Caboose "3826" (std O), *06*		90 ____
17691	UP CA-4 Caboose "25103" (std O), *06*		90 ____
17692	LL CA-4 B22 Caboose "7629" (std O), *06*		90 ____
17693	Chessie Extended Vision Caboose "3285" (std O), *06*		90 ____
17694	NS Extended Vision Caboose "555582" (std O), *06*		90 ____
17695	Alaska I-12 Caboose "1001" (std O), *06*		90 ____
17696	CP Bay Window Caboose "437266" (std O), *06*		90 ____
17697	CN Extended Vision Caboose "78128" (std O), *06*		90 ____
17699	UP Ca-4 Caboose "25193" (std O), *07*		90 ____
17700	UP ACF 40-ton Stock Car "47456" (std O), *01–02*		85 ____

		Exc	Mint
17701	Rio Grande ACF 40-ton Stock Car "39269" (std O), *01–02*		60
17702	CP ACF 40-ton Stock Car "277083" (std O), *01–02*		75
17703	NYC ACF 40-ton Stock Car "23334" (std O), *01–02*		85
17704	B&O ACF 40-ton Stock Car "110234" (std O), *02*		40
17705	CB&Q ACF 40-ton Stock Car "52886" (std O), *02*		40
17707	PRR ARF 40-ton Stock Car "128994" (std O), *03*		35
17708	CP Rail ACF 40-ton Stock Car "277313" (std O), *03*		38
17709	UP Stock Car "48154" (std O), *04*		45
17710	Great Northern Stock Car "56385" (std O), *04*		40
17711	C&O ACF 40-ton Stock Car "95237" (std O), *06*		60
17712	N&W ACF 40-ton Stock Car "33000" (std O), *06*		60
17713	MKT ACF 40-ton Stock Car "47150" (std O), *06*		60
17714	CN 40-ton Stock Car "172755" (std O), *06*		60
17715	MP 40-ton Stock Car "52428" (std O), *06*		60
17716	CGW 40-ton Stock Car "838," *08*		60
17717	UP 40-ton Stock Car "48217," *08*		60
17718	NS Heritage 3-bay Hopper 2-pack (std O), *12*		160
17719	C&BQ ACF Stock Car "52925" (std O), *09*		70
17720	UP ACF Stock Car (std O), *10*		70
17721	Postwar Scale Stock Car 2-pack, *10–11*		140
17724	CN Scale Steel-sided Reefer "210552," (std O), *11*		80
17725	NP Scale Steel-sided Reefer "98528," (std O), *11*		80
17726	IC Scale Steel-sided Reefer "16644," (std O), *11*		80
17727	Mopac/Wabash Scale Steel-sided Reefer "30790," (std O), *11*		80
17729	C&O Scale PS-1 Boxcar "2992" (std O), *12*		70
17730	Seaboard Scale Round-roof Boxcar "19293" (std O), *11*		70
17731	Pere Marquette Scale Boxcar "81805" (std O), *12*		70
17732	L&N Scale PS-1 Boxcar "4798" (std O), *12*		70
17733	PRR Scale Round-roof Boxcar "78948" (std O), *11*		70
17734	PRR Scale Round-roof Boxcar "76644" (std O), *11*		70
17735	PRR Round-roof DD Boxcar "77851" (std O), *12*		70
17736	PRR Round-roof DD Boxcar "60156" (std O), *12*		70
17737	N&W Scale Round-roof Boxcar "46494" (std O), *11*		70
17738	NP Round-roof DD Boxcar "39300" (std O), *12*		70
17739	DT&I Round-roof DD Boxcar "12250" (std O), *12*		70

Exc Mint

		Exc	Mint
17740	Alaska Scale Round-roof Boxcar "27781" (std O), 11		70 ___
17741	Santa Fe Scale Slogan Reefer 5-Car Set (std O), 12		320 ___
17747	Santa Fe Scale Boxcar "39009" (std O), 12		70 ___
17748	Grave's Mortuary Supply Scale PS-1 Boxcar (std O), 12-13		70 ___
17749	Erie Scale PS-1 Boxcar "90300" (std O), 12		70 ___
17750	NYC Round-roof DD Boxcar "77147" (std O), 12		70 ___
17751	NKP Scale PS-1 Boxcar "6605" (std O), 12		70 ___
17752	Polar Round-roof Boxcar "1202" (std O), 12–13		70 ___
17753	LV Scale PS-1 Boxcar "65124" (std O), 12		70 ___
17754	EL DD Boxcar "65000" (std O), 12		75 ___
17755	D&H DD Boxcar "25025" (std O), 12		75 ___
17756	CP Rail DD Boxcar "42630" (std O), 12		75 ___
17757	Milwaukee Road DD Boxcar "13441" (std O), 12		75 ___
17758	ATSF Map and Slogan Reefer 3-pack, 12		190 ___
17762	BN 57' Mechanical Reefer "9618" (std O), 12		85 ___
17763	NYC 57' Mechanical Reefer "6762" (std O), 12		85 ___
17764	ATSF 57' Mechanical Reefer "56244" (std O), 12		85 ___
17765	Virginian Round-roof Boxcar "3131" (std O), 13–14		80 ___
17766	NH Round-roof Boxcar "39303" (std O), 13		70 ___
17767	SP Round-roof Boxcar "166052" (std O), 13		70 ___
17768	Grave's Mortuary Supply Round-roof Boxcar (std O), 13		70 ___
17769	D&RGW PS-1 Boxcar "60046" (std O), 13		70 ___
17770	MILW PS-1 Boxcar "8777" (std O), 13		70 ___
17771	CNJ PS-1 Boxcar "23522" (std O), 13		70 ___
17772	Central of Georgia PS-1 Boxcar (std O), 13		70 ___
17773	D&M Round-roof Boxcar "3148" (std O), 13–14		80 ___
17774	D&M PS-1 Boxcar "2833" (std O), 13		70 ___
17775	NS Heritage 3-bay Hopper 3-pack (std O), 13–14		240 ___
17779	NS Herltage 3-bay Hopper 3-pack (std O), 13–14		240 ___
17783	NS Heritage 3-bay Hopper 3-pack (std O), 13–14		240 ___
17787	NS Heritage 3-bay Hopper 3-pack (std O), 13		240 ___
17791	NS Heritage 3-bay Hopper 3-pack (std O), 13		240 ___
17795	NS Heritage 3-bay Hopper 3-pack (std O), 13		240 ___
17800	Ontario Northland Ore Car "6126," 00		30 ___
17801	CN Ore Car "345165," 00		37 ___
17802	CP Ore Car "377249," 00		28 ___
17803	DMIR Ore Car "51456," 00		30 ___
17804	UP Ore Car "8023," 01		29 ___
17805	CP Rail Ore Car "377238," 01		29 ___
17806	UP Ore Car "27250," 03		30 ___
17807	BN Ore Car "95887," 02		28 ___
17900	Santa Fe Unibody Tank Car (std O), 90	37	46 ___
17901	Chevron Unibody Tank Car (std O), 90	26	32 ___

		Exc	Mint
____ **17902**	NJ Zinc Unibody Tank Car (std O), *91*	26	34
____ **17903**	Conoco Unibody Tank Car (std O), *91*	24	29
____ **17904**	Texaco Unibody Tank Car (std O), *92*	34	43
____ **17905**	Archer Daniels Midland Unibody Tank Car (std O), *92*	24	33
____ **17906**	SCM Unibody Tank Car "78286" (std O), *93*	47	55
____ **17908**	Marathon Oil Unibody Tank Car (std O), *95*	47	52
____ **17909**	Hooker Chemicals Unibody Tank Car (std O), *96*		55
____ **17910**	Sunoco Unibody Tank Car "7900," *97*		37
____ **17913**	J.M. Huber Tank Car, *98*		29
____ **17914**	Englehard Tank Car, *98*		36
____ **17915**	Gulf Unibody Tank Car "8438," *00*		43
____ **17916**	Burlington Unibody Tank Car "130000," *00*	24	38
____ **17918**	Southern Unibody Tank Car, *01*		32
____ **17919**	Koppers Unibody Tank Car, *01*		39
____ **17924**	Safety Kleen Unibody Tank Car "77603" (std O), *02*		40
____ **17925**	Beefmaster Unibody Tank Car "120021" (std O), *02*		38
____ **17926**	Cargill Unibody 1-D Tank Car "5836" (std O), *03*		40
____ **17927**	Union Starch Unibody 1-D Tank Car "59137" (std O), *03*		35
____ **17928**	Merck 1-D Tank Car "25421" (std O), *03*		35
____ **17929**	Wyandotte Chemicals 1-D Tank Car "1325" (std O), *03*		34
____ **17930**	CSX Unibody Tank Car "993369" (std O), *04*		35
____ **17931**	UP Unibody Tank Car "6" (std O), *04*		35
____ **17932**	CIBRO TankTrain Intermediate Car "26263" (std O), *04*		35
____ **17933**	GATX TankTrain Intermediate Car 3-pack (std O), *04*		100
____ **17946**	Candy Cane Unibody Tank Car, *04*		60
____ **17948**	Philadelphia Quartz 1-D Tank Car "806" (std O), *06*		55
____ **17949**	Skelly Oil 1-D Tank Car "2293" (std O), *06*		55
____ **17950**	ADM Unibody Tank Car "19020" (std O), *06*		60
____ **17951**	Cerestar Unibody Tank Car "190177" (std O), *06*		60
____ **17959**	Dow 1-D Tank Car "310101" (std O), *07*		55
____ **17960**	Amaizo 1-D Tank Car "15440" (std O), *07*		55
____ **17962**	Domino Sugar 1-D Tank Car "3008" (std O), *07*		60
____ **17966**	Procor 1-D Tank Car "82607" (std O), *07*		60
____ **17972**	Union Starch 1-D Tank Car "724" (std O), *08*		60
____ **17973**	UP 1-D Tank Car "907838" (std O), *08*		60
____ **17975**	Cargill Foods Unibody Tank Car 3-pack (std O), *08–09*		195
____ **17976**	Huber Unibody Tank Car 3-pack (std O), *08–09*		195
____ **17983**	GATX TankTrain Intermediate Car 3-pack, *08*		195
____ **18000**	PRR 0-6-0 Locomotive "8977," *89, 91*	258	405
____ **18001**	Rock Island 4-8-4 Locomotive "5100," *87*	305	315
____ **18002**	NYC 4-6-4 Locomotive "785," *87 u*	510	576
____ **18003**	DL&W 4-8-4 Locomotive "1501," *88*	235	294

		Exc	Mint	
18004	Reading 4-6-2 Locomotive "8004," *89*	185	205	___
18005	NYC 4-6-4 Locomotive "5340," display case, *90*	705	799	___
18006	Reading 4-8-4 Locomotive "2100," *89 u*	490	528	___
18007	Southern Pacific 4-8-4 Locomotive "4410," *91*	374	392	___
18008	Disneyland 35th Anniversary 4-4-0 Locomotive, display case, *90*	239	294	___
18009	NYC 4-8-2 Locomotive "3000," *90 u, 91*	370	561	___
18010	PRR 6-8-6 Steam Turbine Locomotive "6200," *91–92*	900	1041	___
18011	Chessie System 4-8-4 Locomotive "2101," *91*	440	536	___
18012	NYC 4-6-4 Locomotive "5340," *90*	710	900	___
18013	Disneyland 35th Anniversary 4-4-0 Locomotive, *90*	235	275	___
18014	Lionel Lines 2-6-4 Locomotive "8014," *91*	145	190	___
18016	Northern Pacific 4-8-4 Locomotive "2626," *92*	385	440	___
18018	Southern 2-8-2 Locomotive "4501," *92*	640	650	___
18022	Pere Marquette 2-8-4 Locomotive "1201," *93*	550	650	___
18023	Western Maryland Shay Locomotive "6," *92*	1050	1350	___
18024	Sears T&P 4-8-2 Locomotive "907," display case, *92 u*	750	790	___
18025	T&P 4-8-2 Locomotive "907," *92 u*		640	___
18026	NYC 4-6-4 Dreyfuss Hudson Locomotive, 2-rail, *92 u*		2350	___
18027	NYC 4-6-4 Dreyfuss Hudson Locomotive, 3-rail, *93 u*		1450	___
18028	Smithsonian PRR 4-6-2 Locomotive "3768," 2-rail, *93 u*		2150	___
18029	NYC 4-6-4 Dreyfuss Hudson Locomotive, 3-rail, *93 u*	1900	2150	___
18030	Frisco 2-8-2 Locomotive "4100," *93 u*	530	625	___
18031	2-10-0 Bundesbahn BR-50 Locomotive, 2-rail, *93 u*		NRS	___
18034	Santa Fe 2-8-2 Locomotive "3158," *94*	540	620	___
18035	2-10-0 Reichsbahn BR-50 Locomotive, 2-rail, *93 u*		NRS	___
18036	2-10-0 French BR-50 Locomotive, 2-rail, *93 u*		NRS	___
18040	N&W 4-8-4 Locomotive "612," *95*	640	710	___
18042	Boston & Albany 4-6-4 Locomotive "618," *95*		250	___
18043	Chesapeake & Ohio 4-6-4 Locomotive "490," *95*	680	750	___
18044	Southern 4-6-2 Locomotive "1390," *96*		255	___
18045	Commodore Vanderbilt Locomotive "777," *96*		678	___
18046	Wabash 4-6-4 Locomotive "700," *96*	190	375	___
18049	N&W Warhorse 4-8-4 Locomotive "600," *96*		490	___
18050	JCPenney 4-6-2 Locomotive "2055," *96*	235	245	___
18052	Pennsylvania Torpedo Locomotive "238E," *97*		455	___
18054	NYC 0-4-0 Switcher "1665," black, *97*		145	___
18056	NYC J1-e Hudson Locomotive "763E," Vanderbilt tender, *97*		603	___
18062	ATSF 4-6-4 Hudson Locomotive "3447," *97*		680	___
18063	NYC 4-6-4 Commodore Vanderbilt Locomotive, *99*		952	___
18064	NYC 4-8-2 Mohawk L-3A Locomotive "3000," tender, *98*	540	740	___

			Exc	Mint
____	18067	NYC Weathered Commodore Vanderbilt Scale Hudson Locomotive, *97*		840
____	18071	SP Daylight Locomotive "4449," *98*		680
____	18072	Lionel Lines Torpedo Locomotive, tender, *98*		360
____	18079	NYC 2-8-2 Mikado Locomotive "1967," *99*		710
____	18080	D&RGW 2-8-2 Mikado Locomotive "1210," *99*		720
____	18082	NYC 4-6-4 Hudson Locomotive "5404," *99*		230
____	18083	C&O 4-6-4 Hudson Locomotive "305," *99*		205
____	18084	Santa Fe 4-6-4 Hudson Locomotive "305," *99*		225
____	18085	NH 4-6-2 Pacific Locomotive "1334," *99*		275
____	18086	NYC 4-6-2 Pacific Locomotive "4929," *99*		235
____	18087	Santa Fe 4-6-2 Pacific Locomotive "3448," *99*		265
____	18088	SP 4-6-2 Pacific Locomotive "1407," *99*		350
____	18089	CNJ 4-6-0 Camelback Locomotive "771," *99*		405
____	18091	PRR 4-6-0 Camelback Locomotive "821," *99*		405
____	18092	SP 4-6-0 Camelback Locomotive "2283," *99*		395
____	18093	C&NW 4-6-0 Camelback Locomotive "3006," *99*		285
____	18094	B&O 4-4-2 E6 Atlantic Locomotive, CC, *99–00*		345
____	18095	PRR 4-4-2 E6 Atlantic Locomotive, CC, *99–00*	275	455
____	18096	ATSF 4-4-2 E6 Atlantic Locomotive, CC, *99–00*		370
____	18097	CNJ 4-6-0 Camelback Locomotive "770," *99*		330
____	18098	PRR 4-6-0 Camelback Locomotive "820," *99*		355
____	18099	SP 4-6-0 Camelback Locomotive "2282," *99*		360
____	18100	Santa Fe F3 Diesel A Unit "8100" (see 11711)		NRS
____	18101	Santa Fe F3 Diesel B Unit "8101" (see 11711)		NRS
____	18102	Santa Fe F3 Diesel A Unit "8102," dummy (see 11711)		NRS
____	18103	Santa Fe F3 Diesel B Unit "8103," dummy, *91 u*	180	190
____	18104	GN F3 Diesel A Unit "366A," dummy (see 11724)		500
____	18105	GN F3 Diesel B Unit "370B," dummy (see 11724)		NRS
____	18106	GN F3 Diesel A Unit "351C," dummy (see 11724)		NRS
____	18107	D&RGW Alco PA1 Diesel ABA Set, *92*	640	740
____	18108	Great Northern F3 Diesel B Unit "371B," *93*	85	105
____	18109	Erie Alco Diesel A Unit "725A" (see 11734)		NRS
____	18110	Erie Alco Diesel B Unit "725B" (see 11734)		160
____	18111	Erie Alco Diesel A Unit "736A," dummy (see 11734)		NRS
____	18115	Santa Fe F3 Diesel B Unit, *93*	90	115
____	18116	Erie-Lackawanna Alco PA1 Diesel AA Set, *93*	450	490
____	18117/18	Santa Fe F3 Diesel AA Set "200," *93*	330	410
____	18119/20	UP Alco Diesel AA Set, *94*	200	235
____	18121	Santa Fe F3 Diesel B Unit "200A," *94*	75	95
____	18122	Santa Fe F3 Diesel B Unit "200B," *95*	140	150
____	18123	ACL F3 Diesel A Unit "342" (see 11903)		NRS
____	18124	ACL F3 Diesel B Unit "342B" (see 11903)		NRS
____	18125	ACL F3 Diesel A Unit "343," dummy (see 11903)		NRS
____	18128	Santa Fe F3 Diesel A Unit "2343," *96*		435
____	18129	Santa Fe F3 Diesel B Unit "2343C," *96*		245

		Exc	Mint
18130	Santa Fe F3 Diesel AB Set, *96*		580 ___
18131	NP F3 Diesel AB Set, "2390A, 2390C," *97*	295	360 ___
18132	NP F3 Diesel A Unit, powered		300 ___
18133	NP F3 Diesel B Unit, dummy		150 ___
18134	Santa Fe F3 Diesel A Unit "2343," dummy, *97*		195 ___
18136	Santa Fe F3 Diesel B Unit "2343C,," *97*	135	240 ___
18138	Milwaukee Road F3 Diesel A Unit "75A," *98*		400 ___
18139	Milwaukee Road F3 Diesel B Unit "2378B," *98*		250 ___
18140	Milwaukee Road F3 Diesel AB Set, *98*	390	600 ___
18145	NP F3 Diesel A Unit "2390A," *97*	300	360 ___
18146	NP F3 Diesel B Unit "2390C," *97*		170 ___
18147	NP F3 Diesel AB Set, *97*	450	580 ___
18149	UP Veranda Gas Turbine Locomotive "61," *98*	860	900 ___
18154	Deluxe Santa Fe FT Diesel AA Set, *98–00*		375 ___
18155	Deluxe Santa Fe FT Diesel A Unit, powered (see 18154)		NRS ___
18156	Deluxe Santa Fe FT Diesel A Unit, dummy (see 18154)		NRS ___
18157	Santa Fe FT Diesel AA Set, *98–00*		240 ___
18158	Santa Fe FT Diesel A Unit, powered (see 18157)		NRS ___
18159	Santa Fe FT Diesel A Unit, dummy (see 18157)		NRS ___
18160	NYC Deluxe FT Diesel AA Set, "1602, 1603," *98–00*		500 ___
18163	NYC FT Diesel AA Set, "1600, 2400," *98–00*		300 ___
18166	B&O FT Diesel AA Set, CC, *99–00*		340 ___
18169	B&O FT Diesel AA Set, traditional, *99–00*		240 ___
18189	Army of Potomac Operating Stock Car, *99*		45 ___
18190	McNeil's Rangers Operating Stock Car "2," *99*		45 ___
18191	WP F3 Diesel AA Set, *98*	153	570 ___
18192	WP F3 Diesel A Unit, powered, *98*		485 ___
18193	WP F3 Diesel A Unit, dummy, *98*		495 ___
18197	WP F3 Diesel B Unit "2355C," *99*	88	255 ___
18198	WP F3 Diesel B Unit "2345C" CC, *99*		360 ___
18200	Conrail SD40 Diesel "8200," *87*	180	200 ___
18201	Chessie System SD40 Diesel "8201," *88*	245	340 ___
18202	Erie-Lack. SD40 Diesel Unit "8459," dummy, *89 u*	90	140 ___
18203	CP Rail SD40 Diesel "8203," *89*	195	250 ___
18204	Chessie SD40 Diesel Unit "8204," dummy, *90 u*	135	190 ___
18205	Union Pacific Dash 8-40C Diesel "9100," *89*	275	335 ___
18206	Santa Fe Dash 8-40B Diesel "8206," *90*	195	235 ___
18207	Norfolk Southern Dash 8-40C Diesel "8689," *92*	230	270 ___
18208	BN SD40 Diesel Dummy Unit "8586," *91 u*	115	165 ___
18209	CP Rail SD40 Diesel Dummy Unit "8209," *92 u*	135	165 ___
18210	Illinois Central SD40 "6006," *93*	220	250 ___
18211	Susquehanna Dash 8-40B Diesel "4002," *93*	145	165 ___
18212	Santa Fe Dash 8-40B Diesel Dummy Unit "8212," *93*	155	180 ___
18213	Norfolk Southern Dash 8-40C Diesel "8688," *94*	225	240 ___

			Exc	Mint
____	18214	CSX Dash 8-40C Diesel "7500," *94*	235	255
____	18215	CSX Dash 8-40C Diesel "7643," *94*	240	260
____	18216	Conrail SD-60M Diesel "5500," *94*	355	380
____	18217	Illinois Central SD40 Diesel "6007," *94*	170	175
____	18218	Susquehanna Dash 8-40B Diesel "4004," *94*	205	225
____	18219	C&NW Dash 8-40C Diesel "8501," *95*	325	330
____	18220	C&NW Dash 8-40C Diesel "8502," *95*	215	315
____	18221	D&RGW SD50 Diesel "5512," *95*	455	520
____	18222	D&RGW SD50 Diesel "5517," *95*	280	325
____	18223	Milwaukee Road SD40 Diesel "154," *95*	375	380
____	18224	Milwaukee Road SD40 Diesel "155," *95*	240	265
	18226	GE Dash 9 Diesel, *97*		295
	18228	SP Dash 9 Diesel "8228," gray with red nose, *97*		340
____	18229	SP SD40 Diesel "7333," *98*	300	425
____	18231	BNSF Dash 9 Diesel "739," *98*		435
____	18232	Soo Line SD60 Diesel "5500," *97*		350
____	18233	BNSF Dash 9 Diesel "745," *98*		330
____	18234	BNSF Dash 9 Diesel "740," CC, *98–99*		405
____	18235	BNSF Dash 9 Diesel 2-pack, "739, 740," *98*		710
____	18238	Conrail SD70 Diesel "4145," *99–00*		300
____	18240	Conrail Dash 8-40B Diesel "5065" CC, *98*		260
____	18241	BN SD70 Diesel "9413," *99–00*		345
____	18245	PRR Alco PA1 Diesel AA Set, *99*		495
____	18248	PRR Alco PB-1 Diesel "5750B," *99*		215
____	18249	Erie Alco PB-1 Diesel "850B," *00*		250
____	18250	BNSF SD70 Diesel "9870," *99–00*		365
____	18251	CSX SD60 Diesel "8701," *99–00*		300
____	18252	Amtrak Dash 9 Diesel, CC, *99*		285
____	18253	BNSF Dash 9 Diesel, CC, *99*		305
____	18254	ATSF Dash 9 Diesel, CC, *99*		340
____	18255	NS Dash 9 Diesel, CC, *99*		315
____	18256	Amtrak Dash 9 Diesel, traditional, *99*		200
____	18257	BNSF Dash 9 Diesel, traditional, *99*		190
____	18258	ATSF Dash 9 Diesel, traditional, *99*		205
____	18259	NS Dash 9 Diesel, traditional, *99*		215
____	18260	Conrail SD70 Diesel "4144," *99–00*		280
____	18261	BN SD60 Diesel "9412," *99–00*		255
____	18262	BNSF SD70 Diesel "9869," *99–00*		250
____	18263	CSX SD60 Diesel "8700," *99–00*		255
	18264	Southern Pacific SD70M Diesel "8238," *99–00*		245
	18265	Southern Pacific SD70M Diesel "9803," *99–00*		340
	18266	Norfolk Southern SD60 Diesel "6552," CC, *01–02*		400
	18268	Lionel Centennial SD90MAC Diesel, CC, *00*		389
____	18269	UP SD90MAC Diesel "8006," CC, *00*		405
____	18271	CP SD90MAC Diesel "9129," CC, *00*		440
____	18273	UP SD40 Diesel "8071," *99–00*		330
____	18274	Burlington U30C Diesel "891," CC, *01*		370
____	18276	Seaboard U30C Diesel "7274," CC, *01*		325
____	18278	UP U30C Diesel "2938," CC, *01*		330
____	18280	Maersk SD70 Diesel, CC, *00*		345

		Exc	Mint
18281	BNSF Dash 9-44CW Diesel "788," CC, *00*		340 ___
18282	BNSF Dash 9-44CW Diesel "789," traditional, *00*		225 ___
18283	CSX Dash 9-44CW Diesel "9019," CC, *00*		340 ___
18284	CSX Dash 9-44CW Diesel "9020," traditional, *00*		300 ___
18285	UP Dash 9-44C Diesel "9659," CC, *01*		325 ___
18286	UP Dash 9-44CW Diesel "9717," CC, *01*		355 ___
18287	CN Dash 9-44C Diesel "2529," CC, *01*		460 ___
18288	Odyssey System SD70 Diesel, CC, *00 u*		400 ___
18290	Amtrak Dash 8-32BWH Diesel "509," CC, *01*		325 ___
18291	BNSF Dash 8-32BWH Diesel "580," CC, *02*		340 ___
18292	Chessie GE U30C Diesel "3312," CC, *02*		340 ___
18293	Santa Fe U30C Diesel, CC, *03*		395 ___
18294	Alaska SD70MAC Diesel "4005," CC, *01–02*		435 ___
18295	Conrail SD80MAC Diesel "7200," CC, *02–03*		365 ___
18296	CSX SD80MAC Diesel "801," CC, *02–03*		405 ___
18297	NYC SD80MAC Diesel "9914," CC, *02–03*		405 ___
18298	UP "Desert Victory" SD40-2 Diesel "3593," CC, *02–03*		380 ___
18299	CP Rail SD40-2 Diesel "5420," CC, *02–03*		375 ___
18300	PRR GG1 Electric Locomotive "8300," *87*	285	335 ___
18301	Southern FM Train Master Diesel "8301," *88*	150	204 ___
18302	GN EP-5 Electric Locomotive "8302" (FF 3), *88*	190	250 ___
18303	Amtrak GG1 Electric Locomotive "8303," *89*	275	338 ___
18304	Lackawanna MU Commuter Car Set, *91*	380	435 ___
18305	Lackawanna MU Commuter Car Dummy Set, *92*	230	255 ___
18306	PRR MU Commuter Car Set, *92*	260	330 ___
18307	PRR FM Train Master Diesel "8699," *94*	170	202 ___
18308	PRR GG1 Electric Locomotive "4866," *92*	193	278 ___
18309	Reading FM Train Master Diesel "863," *93*	173	212 ___
18310	PRR MU Commuter Car Dummy Set, *93*	265	345 ___
18311	Disney EP-5 Electric Locomotive "8311," *94*	293	394 ___
18313	Pennsylvania GG1 Electric Locomotive "4907," *96*	75	297 ___
18314	PRR GG1 Electric Locomotive "2332," 5 gold stripes, *97*	500	507 ___
18315	Virginian E33 Electric Locomotive "2329," *97*		240 ___
18319	New Haven EP-5 Electric Locomotive, *99*	300	365 ___
18321	CNJ Train Master Diesel "2341," *99*		405 ___
18322	Lackawanna Train Master Diesel "2321," *99*		465 ___
18326	PRR Congressional GG1 Electric Locomotive, *00*		600 ___
18327	Virginian FM Train Master Diesel "2331," *99–00*		410 ___
18328	NH MU Commuter Car Set, CC, *00*		385 ___
18331	Reading MU Commuter Car Set, CC, *00*		460 ___
18334	NH MU Commuter Car Dummy Set, CC, *01*		180 ___
18337	Reading MU Commuter Car Dummy Set, CC, *01*		200 ___
18343	PRR GG1 Electric Locomotive "2332," CC, *01*		610 ___
18344	LIRR MU Commuter Car Set, powered, CC, *01*		470 ___
18347	IC MU Commuter Car Set, powered, CC, *01*		470 ___

			Exc	Mint
____	**18351**	NYC S1 Electric Locomotive, *03*		400
	18352	JCPenney SP MU Commuter Car, display case, *02*		140
____	**18353**	Pennsylvania E33 Electric Locomotive "4403," CC, *02*		280
____	**18354**	PRR GG1 Electric Locomotive "4918," tuscan, CC, *04*		790
____	**18355**	PRR GG1 Electric Locomotive "4876," green, CC, *04*		900
____	**18356**	Penn Central GG1 Electric Locomotive "4901," CC, *04*		1050
____	**18364**	PRR BB1 Electric Locomotive "3900," CC, *05–07*		530
____	**18367**	LIRR BB3 Electric Locomotive "328 A," CC, *05*		530
____	**18371**	PRR GG1 Electric Locomotive "4912," tuscan, 5 stripes, CC, *05–07*		780
____	**18372**	PRR GG1 Electric Locomotive "4925," green, 1 stripe, CC, *05–07*		780
____	**18373**	NYC S2 Electric Locomotive "125," CC, *05–07*		410
____	**18374**	PRR GG1 Electric Locomotive "4866," silver, CC, *06–08*		900
____	**18375**	Lackawanna FM Train Master Diesel "850," CC, *06*		400
____	**18376**	Lackawanna FM Train Master Diesel "851," nonpowered (std O), *06*		130
____	**18378**	New York City R27 Subway Car 2-pack, *07*		360
____	**18384**	MILW EP-2 Electric Locomotive, CC, *07–08*		950
____	**18385**	NYC H-16-44 Diesel "7001," *07–09*		202
____	**18386**	NYC H-16-44 Diesel "7002," nonpowered (std O), *07–09*		123
____	**18389**	MILW EP-2 Electric Locomotive "E-1," CC, *07–08*		950
____	**18399**	NH EF-4 Rectifier Locomotive "306," CC, *09*		360
____	**18400**	Santa Fe Vulcan Rotary Snowplow "8400," *87*	135	170
____	**18401**	Workmen Handcar, *87–88*	30	37
____	**18402**	Lionel Lines Burro Crane, *88*	65	80
____	**18403**	Santa Claus Handcar, *88*	26	29
____	**18404**	San Francisco Trolley "8404," *88*	55	85
____	**18405**	Santa Fe Burro Crane, *89*	70	83
____	**18406**	Track Maintenance Car, *89, 91*	34	49
____	**18407**	Snoopy and Woodstock Handcar, *90–91*	87	101
____	**18408**	Santa Claus Handcar, *89*	26	35
____	**18410**	PRR Burro Crane, *90*	100	115
____	**18411**	Canadian Pacific Fire Car, *90*	70	98
____	**18413**	Charlie Brown and Lucy Handcar, *91*	39	69
____	**18416**	Bugs Bunny and Daffy Duck Handcar, *92–93*	112	159
____	**18417**	Section Gang Car, *93*	65	80
____	**18419**	Lionelville Electric Trolley "8419," *94*	75	90
____	**18421**	Sylvester and Tweety Handcar, *94*	44	50
____	**18422**	Santa and Snowman Handcar, *94*	32	37
____	**18423**	On-track Step Van, *95*	23	28
____	**18424**	On-track Pickup Truck, *95*	20	25
____	**18425**	Goofy and Pluto Handcar, *95*	36	50
____	**18426**	Santa and Snowman Handcar, *95*	25	30
____	**18427**	Tie-Jector Car "55," *97*		60
____	**18429**	Workmen Handcar, *96*	28	34

		Exc	Mint
18430	Crew Car, *96*		28 ____
18431	Trolley Car, *96–97*		46 ____
18433	Mickey and Minnie Handcar, *96–97*	41	79 ____
18434	Porky and Petunia Handcar, *96*		35 ____
18436	Dodge Ram Track Inspection Vehicle, *97*		39 ____
18438	PRR High-rail Inspection Vehicle, *98*		50 ____
18439	Union Pacific High-rail Inspection Vehicle, *98*		42 ____
18440	NJ Transit High-rail Inspection Vehicle, *98*		50 ____
18444	Lionelville Fire Car (SSS), *98*		150 ____
18445	NYC Fire Car, *98*		90 ____
18446	Postwar "58" GN Rotary Snowplow, *99*		181 ____
18447	Executive Inspection Vehicle, *99*		125 ____
18452	Boston Trolley "3321," *99–00*		65 ____
18454	Executive Inspection Vehicle, blue, *00*		105 ____
18455	NYC Tie-Jector Car "X-2," *00–01*		74 ____
18456	Postwar "59" Minuteman Motorized Unit, *01–02*		290 ____
18457	Postwar "65" Handcar, *00–01*		45 ____
18458	Postwar "53" D&RGW Snowplow, *00*		160 ____
18459	Christmas Handcar, *01*		35 ____
18461	Track Cleaning Car, *02–03*		90 ____
18463	Hot Rod Inspection Vehicle, *01–02*		100 ____
18464	Postwar "54" Track Ballast Tamper, *02–03*		170 ____
18465	Postwar "50" Gang Car, *03*		78 ____
18466	UP Rotary Snow Plow, *01–02*		150 ____
18467	Train Robbery Handcar, *02*		45 ____
18468	CN Railroad Speeder, *03–04*		49 ____
18469	Chessie System Railroad Speeder, *03–04*		49 ____
18470	Postwar "52" Fire Car, *02*		105 ____
18471	UP GP20 Diesel "1977," *03*		105 ____
18473	Lehigh Valley GP38 Diesel "310," *03*		160 ____
18474	Postwar "41" U.S. Army Switcher, *03–04*		145 ____
18475	Toy Story Handcar, *03*		55 ____
18476	Mickey and Minnie Mouse Handcar, *03–04*		55 ____
18480	Hobo Motorized Handcar, *03–04*		35 ____
18481	Christmas Yuletide Trolley, *03*		50 ____
18482	New Haven Rail Bonder "16," *04*		35 ____
18483	C&O Ballast Tamper "48," *04*		55 ____
18484	NS Dodge Inspection Vehicle, *04–05*		50 ____
18485	NYC Gang Car, *04–05*		100 ____
18486	Donald and Daisy Duck Handcar, *04–05*		63 ____
18487	Postwar "56" M&StL Mine Transport Car, *04–05*		230 ____
18489	Great Northern Rail Bonder "HR-73," *04*		35 ____
18490	UP Ballast Tamper, *04–05*		150 ____
18491	MOW Ballast Tamper "325," *04*		44 ____
18492	MOW Rail Bonder "58," *04*		35 ____
18493	Santa's Speeder, *05*		60 ____
18497	N&W Speeder "541005," traditional, *05*		65 ____
18498	New York Central Rotary Snowplow, *05*		210 ____
18500	Milwaukee Road GP9 Diesel "8500" (FF 2), *87*	175	230 ____
18501	WM NW2 Switcher "8501" (FF 4), *89*	185	215 ____
18502	LL 90th Anniversary GP9 Diesel "1900," *90*	146	171 ____

			Exc	Mint
____	**18503**	Southern Pacific NW2 Switcher "8503," *90*	250	280
____	**18504**	Frisco GP7 Diesel "504" (FF 5), *91*	155	240
____	**18505**	NKP GP7 Diesel Set "400, 401" (FF 6)	295	365
____	**18506**	CN Budd RDC Set, "D202, D203"	210	261
____	**18507**	CN Budd RDC Baggage Car "D202," powered, *92*	50	75
____	**18508**	CN Budd RDC Passenger Dummy Unit "D203," *92*	125	150
____	**18510**	CN Budd RDC Passenger Dummy Unit "D200"	50	75
____	**18511**	CN Budd RDC Passenger Dummy Unit "D250"	50	75
____	**18512**	CN Budd RDC Dummy Set, "D200, D250," *93*	125	195
____	**18513**	NYC GP7 Diesel "7420," *94*	90	125
____	**18514**	Missouri Pacific GP7 Diesel "4124," *95*	245	310
____	**18515**	Lionel Steel Vulcan Diesel "57" (SSS), *96*		190
____	**18516**	Phantom III Locomotive, CC, *02*		345
____	**18550**	JCPenney MILW GP9 Diesel "8500," display case, *87 u*	180	245
____	**18551**	JCPenney Susquehanna RS3 Diesel "8809," display case, *89 u*	180	195
____	**18552**	JCPenney DM&IR SD18 Diesel "8813," display case, *90 u*	170	195
____	**18553**	Sears UP GP9 Diesel "150," display case, *91 u*	150	151
____	**18554**	JCPenney GM&O RS3 "721," display case, *92–93 u*	160	180
____	**18555**	Sears C&IM SD9 Diesel "52," *92 u*	165	190
____	**18556**	Sears Chicago & Illinois Midland Freight Car Set, *92 u*	110	120
____	**18557**	Chessie System 4-8-4 Locomotive "2101," display case, export, *92 u*		NRS
____	**18558**	JCPenney MKT GP9 Diesel "91," display case, *94 u*	160	180
____	**18562**	SP GP9 Diesel "2380," *96*		195
____	**18563**	NYC GP9 Diesel "2380," *96*		230
____	**18564**	CP GP9 Diesel "2380," *97*		265
____	**18565**	Milwaukee Road GP9 Diesel "2338," *97*		220
____	**18566**	CR SD20 Diesel "8495" (SSS), *97*		150
____	**18567**	PRR GP9 Diesel "2028," *97*		225
____	**18569**	CB&Q GP9 Diesel "2380," *98*		190
____	**18573**	Santa Fe GP9 Diesel "2380," *98*		155
____	**18574**	Milwaukee Road GP20 Diesel "975," *98*		250
____	**18575**	Custom Series I GP9 Diesel "2398," *98*		350
____	**18576**	SP GP9 Diesel B Unit "2385," nonpowered, *98*		135
____	**18577**	NYC GP9 Diesel B Unit "2385," nonpowered, *98*		145
____	**18579**	MILW GP9 Diesel "2384," nonpowered, *99*		135
____	**18580**	Pennsylvania GP9 Diesel B Unit "2027," *98*		165
____	**18582**	Seaboard NW2 Switcher, *98*	450	455
____	**18583**	AEC Switcher "57," *98*		213
____	**18585**	Centennial SD40 Diesel, *99*		443
____	**18587**	NKP Alco C420 Switcher "577," CC, *99–01*	215	255
____	**18588**	D&H Alco C420 Switcher "412," CC, *99–01*	250	275
____	**18589**	LV Alco C420 Switcher "409," CC, *99–01*	255	300
____	**18590**	NKP Alco C420 Switcher "578," traditional, *99–01*		170
____	**18591**	D&H Alco C420 Switcher "411," traditional, *99–01*		215

		Exc	Mint
18592	LV Alco C420 Switcher "410," traditional, *99–01*		175 ____
18596	D&H Alco RS-11 Switcher "5001," CC, *99–01*		370 ____
18598	NYC Alco RS-11 Switcher "8010," CC, *99–01*		380 ____
18599	C&O GP38 Diesel "3855," *99–00*		145 ____
18600	ACL 4-4-2 Locomotive "8600," *87 u*	65	75 ____
18601	Great Northern 4-4-2 Locomotive "8601," *88*	80	95 ____
18602	PRR 4-4-2 Locomotive "8602," *87*	75	85 ____
18604	Wabash 4-4-2 Locomotive "8604," *88–91*	65	75 ____
18605	Mopar Express 4-4-2 Locomotive "1987," *87–88 u*	75	120 ____
18606	NYC 2-6-4 Locomotive "8606," *89*	170	190 ____
18607	Union Pacific 2-6-4 Locomotive "8607," *89*	130	155 ____
18608	D&RGW 2-6-4 Locomotive "8608" (SSS), *89*	90	105 ____
18609	Northern Pacific 2-6-4 Locomotive "8609," *90*	170	195 ____
18610	Rock Island 0-4-0 Locomotive "8610," *90*	105	115 ____
18611	Lionel Lines 2-6-4 Locomotive (SSS), *90*	125	140 ____
18612	C&NW 4-4-2 Locomotive "8612," *89*	75	100 ____
18613	NYC 4-4-2 Locomotive "8613," *89 u*	75	95 ____
18614	Circus Train 4-4-2 Locomotive "1989," *89 u*	95	125 ____
18615	GTW 4-4-2 Locomotive "8615," *90*	70	85 ____
18616	Northern Pacific 4-4-2 Locomotive "8616," *90 u*	85	110 ____
18617	Adolphus III 4-4-2 Locomotive, *89–92 u*	100	125 ____
18620	Illinois Central 2-6-2 Locomotive "8620," *91*	165	190 ____
18622	Union Pacific 4-4-2 Locomotive "8622," *90–91 u*	65	80 ____
18623	Texas & Pacific 4-4-2 Locomotive "8623," *92*	80	110 ____
18625	Illinois Central 4-4-2 Locomotive "8625," *91 u*	70	95 ____
18626	Delaware & Hudson 2-6-2 Locomotive "8626," *92*	105	115 ____
18627	C&O 4-4-2 Locomotive "8627" or "8633," *92, 93 u, 94, 95 u*	75	95 ____
18628	MKT 4-4-2 Locomotive "8628," *92, 93 u*	70	85 ____
18630	C&NW 4-6-2 Locomotive "2903," *93*	325	370 ____
18632	C&O Columbia 4-4-2 Locomotive "8632," *97–99*	75	95 ____
18632	NYC 4-4-2 Locomotive "8632," *93–95*	75	95 ____
18633	C&O 4-4-2 Locomotive "8633," *94–95*	65	85 ____
18633	UP 4-4-2 Locomotive "8633," *93–95*	65	85 ____
18635	Santa Fe 2-6-4 Locomotive "8625," *93*	135	155 ____
18636	B&O 4-6-2 Locomotive "5300," *94*	295	315 ____
18637	United Auto Workers 4-4-2 Locomotive "8633," *93 u*		90 ____
18638	Norfolk & Western 2-6-4 Locomotive "638," *94*	170	220 ____
18639	Reading 4-6-2 Locomotive "639," *95*	145	170 ____
18640	Union Pacific 4-6-2 Locomotive "8640," *95*	110	130 ____
18641	Ford 4-4-2 Locomotive "8641," *94 u*	65	85 ____
18642	Lionel Lines 4-6-2 Locomotive, *95*	110	130 ____
18644	ATSF 4-4-2 Columbia Locomotive "8644," *96–99*	75	90 ____
18648	Sears Zenith 4-4-2 Locomotive "8632," *96 u*		132 ____
18649	Chevrolet 4-4-2 Locomotive "USA-1," *96 u*		112 ____

		Exc	Mint
18650	LL 4-4-2 Columbia Locomotive "X-1110," *96–99*	95	120
18653	B&A 4-6-2 Pacific Locomotive "2044," *97*		140
18654	SP 4-6-2 Pacific Locomotive "2044," *97*		140
18656	Bloomingdale's 4-4-2 Columbia Locomotive "8632," *96*		108
18657	Sears Zenith 4-4-2 Columbia Locomotive "8632," *96*		109
18658	LL Little League 4-4-2 Columbia Locomotive "X-1110," *97*		90
18660	CN 4-6-2 Locomotive "2044," tender, *98*		175
18661	N&W 4-6-2 Locomotive "2044," tender, *98*		160
18662	Pennsylvania 0-4-0 Switcher, *98*	165	230
18666	SP&S 4-6-2 Pacific Locomotive "2044," *97*		200
18668	Bloomingdale's 4-4-2 Columbia Locomotive "8632," *97*		130
18669	JCPenney IC 4-6-2 Pacific Locomotive "2099," *98*		205
18670	D&H Columbia 4-4-2 Locomotive "1400," *98*		80
18671	N&W Columbia 4-4-2 Locomotive "1201," *98*		70
18678	Quaker Oats Columbia 4-4-2 Locomotive "8632," *98*		158
18679	JCPenney T&P 4-6-2 Locomotive "2000," traditional, *99, 00 u*		250
18681	PRR 4-4-2 Locomotive "460," *99*		75
18682	Santa Fe 4-4-2 Columbia Locomotive "524," traditional, *00–01*		70
18696	ACL 4-6-4 Locomotive "1800," *01*		120
18697	Santa Fe 4-6-4 Locomotive "3465," *01*		100
18699	Alaska 4-4-2 Locomotive "64," *01*		105
18700	Rock Island 0-4-0T Locomotive "8700," *87–88*	36	43
18702	V&TRR 4-4-0 Locomotive "8702" (SSS), *88*	160	195
18704	Lionel Lines 2-4-0 Locomotive, *89 u*	36	43
18705	Neptune 0-4-0T Locomotive "8705," *90–91*	35	42
18706	Santa Fe 2-4-0 Locomotive "8706," *91*	36	43
18707	Mickey's World Tour 2-4-0 Locomotive "8707," *91, 92 u*	58	68
18709	Lionel Employee Learning Center 0-4-0T Locomotive, *92 u*		139
18710	SP 2-4-0 Locomotive "2000," *93*	30	38
18711	Southern 2-4-0 Locomotive "2000," *93*	30	38
18712	Jersey Central 2-4-0 Locomotive "2000," *93*	30	38
18713	Chessie System 2-4-0 Locomotive "1993," *94–95*	30	38
18716	Lionelville Circus 4-4-0 Locomotive, *90–91*	90	110
18718	LL 0-4-0 Dockside Switcher "8200," *97–98*		40
18719	Thomas the Tank Engine "1," *97*		158
18720	Union 4-4-0 General Locomotive "1865," *99*		175
18721	Confederate 4-4-0 General Locomotive "1861," *99*		175
18722	Percy the Tank Engine "6," *99*		170
18723	Union Pacific 4-4-0 General Locomotive, *05*		100
18730	Transylvania RR 4-4-0 Locomotive "13," traditional, *05*		105
18732	North Pole Central 4-4-0 Locomotive "25," *06*		110

		Exc	Mint
18733	Percy the Tank Engine "6," *05–12*		120 ____
18734	James the Tank Engine "5," *06–12*		120 ____
18741	Thomas the Tank Engine, *08–13*		120 ____
18745	Hallow's Eve 4-6-0 Steam Locomotive, *11–12*		190 ____
18753	Route of the Reindeer RS3 Diesel, *11*		190 ____
18754	Polar Express 2-8-4 Berkshire Steam Locomotive, *11, 13*		300 ____
18755	C&O Berkshire Steam Locomotive "2751," with TrainSounds, *11*		290 ____
18771	Percy, remote system, *13–14*		150 ____
18774	James, remote system, *13–14*		150 ____
18775	Diesel, remote system, *13–14*		150 ____
18799	Bethlehem Steel Switcher "44," *99*		100 ____
18800	Lehigh Valley GP9 Diesel "8800," *87*	80	95 ____
18801	Santa Fe U36B Diesel "8801," *87*	100	120 ____
18802	Southern GP9 Diesel "8802" (SSS), *87*	100	115 ____
18803	Santa Fe RS3 Diesel "8803," *88*	90	105 ____
18804	Soo Line RS3 Diesel "8804," *88*	95	115 ____
18805	Union Pacific RS3 Diesel "8805," *89*	100	125 ____
18806	New Haven SD18 Diesel "8806," *89*	100	115 ____
18807	Lehigh Vallcy RS3 Diesel "8807," *90*	90	120 ____
18808	ACL SD18 Diesel "8808," *90*	85	105 ____
18809	Susquehanna RS3 Diesel "8809," *89 u*		130 ____
18810	CSX SD18 Diesel "8810," *90*	95	130 ____
18811	Alaska SD9 Diesel "8811," *91*	95	135 ____
18812	Kansas City Southern GP38 Diesel "4000," *91*	120	140 ____
18813	DM&IR SD18 Diesel "8813," *90 u*	90	145 ____
18814	D&H RS3 Diesel "8814" (SSS), *91*	90	120 ____
18815	Amtrak RS3 Diesel "1815," *91, 92 u*	100	130 ____
18816	C&NW GP38-2 Diesel "4600," *92*	105	130 ____
18817	UP GP9 Diesel "150" (see 18553), *91 u*		135 ____
18819	L&N GP38-2 Diesel "4136," *92*	115	145 ____
18820	WP GP9 Diesel "8820" (SSS), *92*	120	140 ____
18821	Clinchfield GP38-2 Diesel "6005," *93*	125	150 ____
18822	Gulf, Mobile & Ohio RS3 Diesel "721," *92–93 u*		NRS ____
18823	Chicago & Illinois Midland SD9 Diesel "52," *92 u*		235 ____
18824	Montana Rail Link SD9 Diesel "600," *93*	185	230 ____
18825	Soo Line GP38-2 Diesel "4000" (SSS), *93*	120	145 ____
18826	Conrail GP7 Diesel "5808," *93*	100	120 ____
18827	"Happy Holidays" RS3 Diesel "8827," *93*	165	220 ____
18830	Budweiser GP9 Diesel "1947," *93–94 u*	118	158 ____
18831	SP GP20 Diesel "4060," *94*	105	120 ____
18832	PRR RSD-4 Diesel "8446," *95*	110	135 ____
18833	Milwaukee Road RS3 Diesel "2487," *94*	100	110 ____
18834	C&O SD28 Diesel "8834," *94*	110	140 ____
18835	NYC RS3 Diesel "8223" (SSS), *94*	135	195 ____
18836	CN (Grand Trunk) GP38-2 Diesel "5800," *94*	135	160 ____
18837	"Happy Holidays" RS3 Diesel "8837," *94–95*	150	190 ____
18838	Seaboard RSC-3 Diesel "1538," *95*	110	140 ____
18840	U.S. Army GP7 Diesel "1821," *95*	85	124 ____
18841	Western Maryland GP20 Diesel "27" (SSS), *95*	120	150 ____
18842	JCPenney B&LE SD38 Diesel "868," *95 u*		265 ____

		Exc	Mint
____ **18843**	Great Northern RS3 Diesel "197," *96*		145
____ **18845**	D&RGW RS3 Diesel "5204," *97*		100
____ **18846**	Lionel Centennial Series GP9 Diesel, *98*		410
____ **18847**	Santa Fe H-12-44 Switcher "602," *99*		385
____ **18848**	PRR H-12-44 Switcher "9087," *99*		420
____ **18853**	JCPenney Santa Fe GP9 Diesel "2370," *97 u*		150
____ **18854**	UP GP9 Diesel Dummy Set, "2380, 2387," *97*		450
____ **18856**	NJ Transit GP38-2 Diesel "4303," *99*		315
____ **18857**	Union Pacific GP9 Diesel "2397," *97*		240
____ **18858**	Lionel Centennial GP20 Diesel, *98*		430
____ **18859**	Phantom II, *99*		360
____ **18860**	Pratt's Hollow Collection I: Phantom, *98*		400
____ **18864**	Southern Pacific GP9 Diesel B Unit, *98*		140
____ **18865**	New York Central GP9 Diesel B Unit, *98*		170
____ **18866**	Milwaukee Road GP7 Diesel "2383," *98*		205
____ **18868**	NJ Transit GP38-2 Diesel "4300," *98 u*		140
____ **18870**	Pennsylvania GP9 Diesel "2029," *98*		180
____ **18872**	Wabash GP7 Diesel Set, "453, 454, 455," *99*		560
____ **18876**	C&NW H-12-44 Switcher "1053," *99*	125	363
____ **18877**	Union Pacific GP9 Diesel "2399," nonpowered, *99*		175
____ **18878**	Alaska GP7 Diesel "1803," *99*		115
____ **18879**	B&O GP9 Diesel "5616," *99*		260
____ **18881**	Custom GP9 Diesel "5616," *99*		350
____ **18892**	Burlington GP9 Diesel "2328," *99*		205
____ **18897**	Christmas GP7 Diesel "1999," *99*		200
____ **18900**	PRR Switcher "8900," *88 u, 89*	26	34
____ **18901/02**	PRR Alco Diesel AA Set, *88*	110	130
____ **18903/04**	Amtrak Alco Diesel AA Set, *88–89*	90	130
____ **18903**	Amtrak "Mopar Express," *99*		500
____ **18905**	PRR 44-ton Switcher "9312," *92*	80	116
____ **18906**	Erie-Lackawanna RS3 Diesel "8906," *91 u*	70	90
____ **18907**	Rock Island 44-ton Switcher "371," *93*	95	110
____ **18908/09**	NYC Alco Diesel AA Set, *93*	105	115
____ **18910**	CSX Switcher "8910," *93*	40	46
____ **18911**	UP Switcher "8911," *93*	33	37
____ **18912**	Amtrak Switcher "8912," *93*	37	43
____ **18913**	Santa Fe Alco Diesel A Unit "8913," *93–94*	55	65
____ **18915**	WM Alco Diesel A Unit "8915," *93*	65	80
____ **18916**	WM Alco Diesel A Unit "8916," dummy, *93*	38	42
____ **18917**	Soo Line NW2 Switcher, *93*	65	75
____ **18918**	B&M NW2 Switcher "8918," *93*	75	90
____ **18919**	Santa Fe Alco Diesel A Unit "8919," dummy, *93–94*	36	55
____ **18920**	Frisco NW2 Switcher "254," *94*	70	75
____ **18921**	C&NW NW2 Switcher "1017," *94*	60	80
____ **18922**	New Haven Alco Diesel A Unit "8922," *94*	75	105
____ **18923**	New Haven Alco Diesel A Unit "8923," dummy, *94*	50	55
____ **18924**	IC Switcher "8924," *94–95*	37	44
____ **18925**	D&RGW Switcher "8925," *94–95*	32	37
____ **18926**	Reading Switcher "8926," *94–95*	31	39
____ **18927**	U.S. Navy NW2 Switcher "65-00637," *94–95*	65	85
____ **18928**	C&NW NW2 Switcher Calf Unit, *95*	50	55

		Exc	Mint
18929	B&M NW2 Switcher Calf Unit, *95*	44	49 ____
18930	Crayola Switcher, *94 u, 95*	27	30 ____
18931	Chrysler Mopar NW2 Switcher "1818," *94 u*	73	88 ____
18932	Jersey Central NW2 Switcher "8932," *96*		65 ____
18933	Jersey Central NW2 Switcher Calf Unit "8933," *96*		55 ____
18934/35	Reading Alco Diesel AA Set, *95*	75	95 ____
18936	Amtrak Alco Diesel A Unit "8936," *95*		65 ____
18937	Amtrak FA2 Alco Diesel, nonpowered, *95–97*		50 ____
18938	U.S. Navy NW2 Switcher Calf Unit, *95*	55	65 ____
18939	Union Pacific NW2 Switcher Set, *96*		145 ____
18943	Georgia Power NW2 Switcher "1960," *95 u*		170 ____
18946	U.S. Coast Guard NW2 Switcher "8946," *96*		80 ____
18947	Port of Lionel City Alco FA2 Diesel "2030," *97*		70 ____
18948	Port of Lionel City Alco FB2 Diesel "2030B," *97*		45 ____
18952	ATSF Alco PA1 Diesel "2000," *97*		345 ____
18953	NYC Alco PA1 Diesel "2000," *97*		260 ____
18954	ATSF Alco FA2 Diesel "212," powered, *97–99*		80 ____
18955	NJ Transit NW2 Switcher "500," *96 u*		110 ____
18956	Dodge Motorsports NW2 Switcher "8956," *96 u*		163 ____
18959	New York Central NW2 Switcher "622," *97*		475 ____
18961	Erie Alco PA1 Diesel "850," *98*		315 ____
18965	Santa Fe Alco PB1 Diesel, *98*		255 ____
18966	New York Central Alco BP1 Diesel "2008," *98*		250 ____
18971	Alco Diesel A Unit, nonpowered, *98*		60 ____
18973	RI Alco FA2 Diesel "2031," powered, *98–99*		NRS ____
18974	RI Alco FA2 Diesel Dummy Unit, *98–99*		NRS ____
18975	Southern 44-ton Switcher "1955," *99*		190 ____
18978	C&O NW2 Switcher "624," *99–00*		410 ____
18981	Pennsylvania Railroad Speeder "16," *04*		45 ____
18982	Santa Fe Railroad Speeder "122," *04–05*		65 ____
18988	MP15 Diesel, K-Line, *06*		140 ____
18989	Bethlehem Steel Plymouth Switcher, traditional, K-Line, *06*		100 ____
18992	SP S2 Diesel Switcher "1440," CC, *08*		410 ____
18993	C&NW S2 Diesel Switcher "1031," CC, *08*		410 ____
18994	Lionel Lines FA Diesel, traditional, *08–09*		90 ____
19000	Blue Comet Diner, *87 u*	60	75 ____
19001	Southern Diner, *87 u*	55	65 ____
19002	Pennsylvania Diner, *88 u*	29	41 ____
19003	Milwaukee Road Diner, *88 u*	29	44 ____
19010	B&O Diner, *89 u*	36	55 ____
19011	Lionel Lines Baggage Car, *93*	268	398 ____
19015	Lionel Lines Passenger Coach, *91*	125	180 ____
19016	Lionel Lines Passenger Coach, *91*	100	135 ____
19017	Lionel Lines Passenger Coach, *91*	85	110 ____
19018	Lionel Lines Observation Car, *91*	95	120 ____
19019	SP Baggage Car "9019," *93*	120	153 ____
19023	SP Passenger Coach "9023," *92*	125	160 ____
19024	SP Passenger Coach "9024," *92*	85	100 ____
19025	SP Passenger Coach "9025," *92*	100	115 ____
19026	SP Observation Car "9026," *92*	85	100 ____

		Exc	Mint
____ 19038	Adolphus Busch Observation Car, *92–93 u*		85
____ 19039	Pere Marquette Baggage Car, *93*		75
____ 19040	Pere Marquette Passenger Coach "1115," *93*		75
____ 19041	Pere Marquette Passenger Coach "1116," *93*		75
____ 19042	Pere Marquette Observation Car "36," *93*		75
____ 19047	Baltimore & Ohio Combination Car "9047," *96*		55
____ 19048	Baltimore & Ohio Passenger Coach "9048," *96*		50
____ 19049	Baltimore & Ohio Diner "9049," *96*		42
____ 19050	Baltimore & Ohio Observation Car "9050," *96*		42
____ 19056	NYC Heavyweight Baggage Car, *96*		105
____ 19057	NYC Willow Run Heavyweight Coach, *96*		95
____ 19058	NYC Willow Trail Heavyweight Coach, *96*		90
____ 19059	NYC Seneca Valley Heavyweight Observation Car, *96*		100
____ 19060	Pullman Heavyweight Set, *96*		473
____ 19061	Wabash Passenger Set, *97*		235
____ 19062	Wabash City of Columbia Coach "2361," *97*		90
____ 19063	Wabash City of Danville Coach "2362," *97*		75
____ 19064	Wabash REA Baggage Car "2360," *97*		47
____ 19065	Wabash Windy City Observation Car "2363," *97*		90
____ 19066	Commodore Vanderbilt Pullman Heavyweight 2-pack, *97*		190
____ 19067	Commodore Vanderbilt Willow River Pullman "2543," *97*		115
____ 19068	Commodore Vanderbilt Willow Valley Pullman "2544," *97*		100
____ 19069	Pullman Baby Madison Set "9500-02," *97*		155
____ 19070	Baby Madison Combination Car "9501," *97*		40
____ 19071	Laurel Gap Baby Madison Coach "9500," *97*		34
____ 19072	Laurel Summit Baby Madison Coach "9500," *97*		40
____ 19073	Catskill Valley Baby Madison Observation Car "9502," *97*		34
____ 19074	Legends of Lionel Madison Set, *97*		385
____ 19075	Mazzone Lionel Legends Coach "2621," *97*		105
____ 19076	Caruso Lionel Legends Coach "2624," *97*		90
____ 19077	Raphael Lionel Legends Coach "2652," *97*		90
____ 19078	Cowen Lionel Legends Observation Car "2600," *97*		95
____ 19079	NYC Heavyweight Passenger Car Set, *97*		275
____ 19080	NYC Heavyweight REA Baggage Car "2564," *97*		100
____ 19081	NYC Park Place Heavyweight Coach "2565," *97*		100
____ 19082	NYC Star Beam Heavyweight Coach "2566," *97*		100
____ 19083	NYC Hudson Valley Heavyweight Observation Car "2567," *97*		100
____ 19087	C&O Heavyweight Passenger Car 4-pack, "2571-74," *97*		290
____ 19088	C&O Heavyweight Baggage Car "2571," *97*		100
____ 19089	C&O Heavyweight Sleeper Car "2572," *97*		100
____ 19090	C&O Heavyweight Diner "2573," *97*		110
____ 19091	C&O Heavyweight Observation Car "2574," *97*		100

		Exc	Mint
19093	Commodore Vanderbilt Heavyweight Sleeper Car 2-pack, *98*		170 ____
19094	Commodore Vanderbilt Niagara Falls Sleeper, *98*		75 ____
19095	Commodore Vanderbilt Highland Falls Sleeper, *98*		75 ____
19096	Legends of Lionel Madison Car 2-pack, *98*		130 ____
19097	Bonnano Lionel Legends Coach "2653," *98*		80 ____
19098	Pagano Lionel Legends Coach "2654," *98*		105 ____
19099	PRR Liberty Gap Baggage Car "2623," *99*		80 ____
19100	Amtrak Baggage Car "9100," *89*	125	165 ____
19101	Amtrak Combination Car "9101," *89*	75	85 ____
19102	Amtrak Passenger Coach "9102," *89*	75	85 ____
19103	Amtrak Vista Dome "9103," *89*	70	90 ____
19104	Amtrak Diner "9104," *89*	65	80 ____
19105	Amtrak Full Vista Dome Car "9105," *89 u*	70	80 ____
19106	Amtrak Observation Car "9106," *89*	75	90 ____
19107	SP Full Vista Dome Car, *90 u*	70	88 ____
19108	N&W Full Vista Dome Car "576," *91 u*	75	85 ____
19109	Santa Fe Baggage Car "3400," *91*	225	300 ____
19110	Santa Fe Combination Car "3500," *91*	80	110 ____
19111	Santa Fe Diner "601," *91*	100	135 ____
19112	Santa Fe Passenger Coach, *91*	125	175 ____
19113	Santa Fe Vista Dome Car, *91*	100	135 ____
19116	Great Northern Baggage Car "1200," *92*	135	165 ____
19117	Great Northern Combination Car "1240," *92*	65	80 ____
19118	Great Northern Passenger Coach "1212," *92*	75	95 ____
19119	Great Northern Vista Dome Car "1322," *92*	75	95 ____
19120	Great Northern Observation Car "1192," *92*	75	95 ____
19121	Union Pacific Vista Dome Car "9121," *92 u*	90	100 ____
19122	D&RGW California Zephyr Baggage Car, *93*	170	210 ____
19123	D&RGW California Zephyr Silver Bronco Vista Dome Car, *93*	95	115 ____
19124	D&RGW California Zephyr Silver Colt Vista Dome Car, *93*	95	115 ____
19125	D&RGW California Zephyr Silver Mustang Vista Dome Car, *93*	100	125 ____
19126	D&RGW California Zephyr Silver Pony Vista Dome Car, *93*	95	115 ____
19127	D&RGW California Zephyr Vista Dome Car, *93*	85	100 ____
19128	Santa Fe Full Vista Dome Car "507," *92 u*	175	185 ____
19129	IC Full Vista Dome Car "9129," *93*	75	85 ____
19130	Lackawanna Passenger Cars, set of 4, *94*	280	350 ____
19131	Lackawanna Baggage Car "2000" (see 19130)		150 ____
19132	Lackawanna Diner "469" (see 19130)		100 ____
19133	Lackawanna Passenger Coach "260" (see 19130)		100 ____
19134	Lackawanna Observation Car "789" (see 19130)		85 ____
19135	Lackawanna Combination Car "425," *94*	85	100 ____
19136	Lackawanna Passenger Coach "211," *94*	65	75 ____
19137	New York Central Roomette Car, *95*	90	105 ____
19138	Santa Fe Roomette Car, *95*	75	95 ____
19139	N&W Baggage Car "577," *95*	150	200 ____

			Exc	Mint
___	19140	N&W Combination Car "494," *95*	60	80
___	19141	N&W Diner "495," *95*	105	135
___	19142	N&W Passenger Coach "538," *95*	75	95
___	19143	N&W Passenger Coach "537," *95*	75	95
___	19144	N&W Observation Car "582," *95*	80	95
___	19145	C&O Combination Car "1403," *96*		65
___	19146	C&O Passenger Coach "1623," *96*		60
___	19147	C&O Passenger Coach "1803," *96*		55
___	19148	C&O Chessie Club Coach "1903," *96*		55
___	19149	C&O Coach/Diner "1950," *96*		50
___	19150	C&O Observation Car "2504," *96*		55
___	19151	Norfolk & Western Duplex Roomette car, *96*		108
___	19152	Union Pacific Duplex Roomette Car, *96*		75
___	19153	C&O Passenger Cars, set of 4, *96*		340
___	19154	Atlantic Coast Line Passenger Car Set, *96*		340
___	19155	ACL Combination Car "101," *96*		90
___	19156	ACL Talladega Diner, *96*		90
___	19157	ACL Moultrie Coach, *96*		95
___	19158	ACL Observation Car "256," *96*		90
___	19159	N&W Passenger Cars, set of 4, *95 u*	300	385
___	19160	LL REA Baggage Car, *96*		90
___	19161	LL Silver Mesa Coach, *96*		80
___	19162	LL Silver Sky Vista Dome Car, *96*		75
___	19163	LL Silver Rail Observation Car, *96*		75
___	19164	Chesapeake & Ohio Passenger Cars, *96*		160
___	19165	ATSF Super Chief Set, *96*		305
___	19166	NP Vista Dome Car Set, *97*		305
___	19167	NP Pullman Coach "2571," *97*		105
___	19168	NP Pullman Coach "2571," *97*		105
___	19169	NP Pullman Coach "2570," *97*		95
___	19170	NP Pullman Coach "2571," *97*		100
___	19171	NYC Streamliner Car 4-pack, *97*		285
___	19172	NYC Aluminum Passenger/Baggage Car "2570," *97*		95
___	19173	NYC Manhattan Island Aluminum Passenger Diner, *97*		100
___	19174	NYC Queensboro Bridge Aluminum Passenger Coach, *97*		100
___	19175	NYC Windgate Brook Aluminum Observation Car, *97*		90
___	19176	ATSF Indian Arrow Diner "2572," *97*		90
___	19177	ATSF Grass Valley Coach "2573," *97*		90
___	19178	ATSF Citrus Valley Coach "2574," *97*		90
___	19179	ATSF Vista Heights Coach "2575," *97*		90
___	19180	ATSF Surfliner Passenger Car 4-pack, *97*		250
___	19181	GN Empire Builder Prairie View Full Vista Dome Car, *98*		75
___	19182	GN Empire Builder River View Full Vista Dome Car, *98*		75
___	19183	GN Empire Builder Vista Dome Car 2-pack, *98*		125
___	19184	Milwaukee Road Passenger Car 4-pack, *99*		390
___	19185	MILW Red River Valley Aluminum Passenger Coach "194," *99*		125
___	19186	MILW Aluminum Coach/Diner "170," *99*		110

		Exc	Mint
19187	MILW Cedar Rapids Aluminum Observation Car "186," *99*		120 ____
19188	MILW Aluminum REA Passenger/Baggage Car "1336," *99*		95 ____
19194	KCS Aluminum Passenger Car 4-pack, *00*		380 ____
19200	Tidewater Southern Boxcar, *87*	13	21 ____
19201	Lancaster & Chester Boxcar, *87*	23	37 ____
19202	PRR Boxcar, *87*	22	30 ____
19203	D&TS Boxcar, *87*	11	18 ____
19204	Milwaukee Road Boxcar (FF 2), *87*	29	41 ____
19205	Great Northern DD Boxcar (FF 3), *88*	20	24 ____
19206	Seaboard System Boxcar, *88*	18	23 ____
19207	CP Rail DD Boxcar, *88*	17	22 ____
19208	Southern DD Boxcar, *88*	11	13 ____
19209	Florida East Coast Boxcar, *88*	15	19 ____
19210	Soo Line Boxcar, *89*	19	23 ____
19211	Vermont Railway Boxcar, *89*	18	21 ____
19212	PRR Boxcar, *89*	21	25 ____
19213	SP&S DD Boxcar, *89*	16	19 ____
19214	Western Maryland Boxcar (FF 4), *89*	23	27 ____
19215	Union Pacific DD Boxcar, *90*	17	21 ____
19216	Santa Fe Boxcar, *90*	17	22 ____
19217	Burlington Boxcar, *90*	16	21 ____
19218	New Haven Boxcar, *90*	16	20 ____
19219	Lionel Lines 1900-1906 Boxcar, diesel RailSounds, *90*	120	145 ____
19220	Lionel Lines 1926-1934 Boxcar, *90*	27	30 ____
19221	Lionel Lines 1935-1937 Boxcar, *90*	27	30 ____
19222	Lionel Lines 1948-1950 Boxcar, *90*	27	30 ____
19223	Lionel Lines 1979-1989 Boxcar, *90*	23	25 ____
19228	Cotton Belt Boxcar, *91*	21	22 ____
19229	Frisco Boxcar, diesel RailSounds (FF 5), *91*	75	90 ____
19230	Frisco DD Boxcar (FF 5), *91*	21	26 ____
19231	TA&G DD Boxcar, *91*	13	16 ____
19232	Rock Island DD Boxcar, *91*	17	20 ____
19233	Southern Pacific Boxcar, *91*	15	19 ____
19234	NYC Boxcar, *91*	60	65 ____
19235	MKT Boxcar, *91*	55	65 ____
19236	NKP DD Boxcar (FF 6), *92*	22	30 ____
19237	C&IM Boxcar, *92*	17	24 ____
19238	Kansas City Southern Boxcar, *92*	18	23 ____
19239	Toronto, Hamilton & Buffalo DD Boxcar, *92*	15	20 ____
19240	Great Northern DD Boxcar, *92*	15	20 ____
19241	Mickey Mouse 60th Anniversary Hi-Cube Boxcar, *91 u*	130	170 ____
19242	Donald Duck 50th Anniversary Hi-Cube Boxcar, *91 u*	130	137 ____
19243	Clinchfield Boxcar "9790," *91 u*	35	41 ____
19244	L&N Boxcar "9791," *92*	35	38 ____
19245	Mickey's World Tour Hi-Cube Boxcar, *92 u*	35	40 ____
19246	Disney World 20th Anniversary Hi-Cube Boxcar, *92 u*	33	40 ____
19247	Postwar "6464" Series Boxcar Set I, 3 cars, *93*	445	610 ____

		Exc	Mint
____ 19248	Western Pacific Boxcar "6464," *93*	75	95
____ 19249	Great Northern Boxcar "6464," *93*	75	95
____ 19250	M&StL Boxcar "6464," *93*	80	105
____ 19251	Montana Rail Link DD Boxcar "10001," *93*	21	27
____ 19254	Erie Boxcar (FF 7), *93*	21	25
____ 19255	Erie DD Boxcar (FF 7), *93*	22	26
____ 19256	Goofy Hi-Cube Boxcar, *93*	23	26
19257	Postwar "6464" Series Boxcar Set II, 3 cars, *94*	80	97
____ 19258	Rock Island Boxcar "6464," *94*	25	34
____ 19259	Western Pacific Boxcar "6464100," *94*	33	46
____ 19260	Western Pacific Boxcar "6464100," *94*	35	49
____ 19261	Perils of Mickey Hi-Cube Boxcar #1, *93*	28	30
____ 19262	Perils of Mickey Hi-Cube Boxcar #2, *93*	20	28
____ 19263	NYC DD Boxcar (SSS), *94*	36	42
____ 19264	Perils of Mickey Hi-Cube Boxcar #3, *94*	28	31
19265	Mickey Mouse 65th Anniversary Hi-Cube Boxcar, *94*	42	44
19266	Postwar "6464" Series Boxcar Set III, 3 cars, *95*	75	90
____ 19267	NYC Pacemaker Boxcar "6464125," *95*	37	42
____ 19268	Missouri Pacific Boxcar "6464150," *95*	25	29
____ 19269	Rock Island Boxcar "6464," *95*	25	26
19270	Donald Duck 60th Anniversary Hi-Cube Boxcar, *95*	30	34
____ 19271	Minnie Mouse Hi-Cube Boxcar, *95*	41	43
19272	Postwar "6464" Series Boxcar Set IV, 3 cars, *96*	70	85
____ 19273	BAR State of Maine Boxcar "6464275," *96*		35
____ 19274	SP Overnight Boxcar "6464225," *96*		28
____ 19275	Pennsylvania Boxcar "6464," *96*		44
19276	Postwar "6464" Series Boxcar Set V, 3 cars, *96*	65	85
____ 19277	Rutland Boxcar "6464-300," *96*		26
____ 19278	B&O Boxcar "6464-325," *96*		30
____ 19279	Central of Georgia Boxcar "6464-375," *96*		29
____ 19280	Mickey's Wheat Hi-Cube Boxcar, *96*		32
____ 19281	Mickey's Carrots Hi-Cube Boxcar, *96*		40
19282	Santa Fe "Super Chief" Boxcar "6464-196," *96*		24
____ 19283	Erie Boxcar "6464-296," *96*		22
____ 19284	Northern Pacific Boxcar "6464-396," *96*		29
____ 19285	B&A State of Maine Boxcar "6464-275," *96*		27
____ 19286	Tweety and Sylvester Boxcar, *96*		46
19287	NYC/PC Merger Boxcar "6464-125X" (SSS), *97*	50	75
19288	PRR/CR Merger Boxcar "6464-200X" (SSS), *97*	43	56
____ 19289	Monon "Hoosier Line" Boxcar "6464," *97*		27
____ 19290	Seaboard "Silver Meteor" Boxcar "6464," *97*		24
____ 19291	GN Boxcar "6464-397," *97*		26
19292	Postwar "6464" Series Boxcar Set VI, 3 cars, *97*		90
____ 19293	MKT Boxcar "6464-350," *97*	28	32
____ 19294	B&O Boxcar "6464-400," *97*	27	34

		Exc	Mint
19295	NH Boxcar "6464-425," *97*	25	34 ___
19300	PRR Ore Car, *87*	15	23 ___
19301	Milwaukee Road Ore Car, *87*	20	25 ___
19302	Milwaukee Road Quad Hopper with coal (FF 2), *87*	24	35 ___
19303	Lionel Lines Quad Hopper with coal, *87 u*	20	31 ___
19304	GN Covered Quad Hopper (FF 3), *88*	24	25 ___
19305	Chessie System Ore Car, *88*	18	23 ___
19307	B&LE Ore Car with load, *89*	19	25 ___
19308	GN Ore Car with load, *89*	18	23 ___
19309	Seaboard Covered Quad Hopper, *89*	16	19 ___
19310	L&C Quad Hopper with coal, *89*	16	30 ___
19311	SP Covered Quad Hopper, *90*	14	19 ___
19312	Reading Quad Hopper with coal, *90*	21	36 ___
19313	B&O Ore Car with load, *90–91*	20	25 ___
19315	Amtrak Ore Car with load, *91*	22	30 ___
19316	Wabash Covered Quad Hopper, *91*	18	23 ___
19317	Lehigh Valley Quad Hopper with coal, *91*	47	55 ___
19318	NKP Quad Hopper with coal (FF 6), *92*	30	34 ___
19319	Union Pacific Covered Quad Hopper, *92*	19	23 ___
19320	PRR Ore Car with load, *92*	21	30 ___
19321	B&LE Ore Car with load, *92*	21	30 ___
19322	C&NW Ore Car with load, *93*	27	34 ___
19323	Detroit & Mackinac Ore Car with load, *93*	20	29 ___
19324	Erie Quad Hopper with coal (FF 7), *93*	25	33 ___
19325	N&W 4-bay Hopper "6446-1" with coal, *97*		65 ___
19326	N&W 4-bay Hopper with coal, *96*		60 ___
19327	N&W 4-bay Hopper "6446-3" with coal, *96*		60 ___
19328	N&W 4-bay Hopper "6446-4" with coal, *96*		60 ___
19329	N&W 4-bay Hopper "6436" with coal, *97*		55 ___
19330	Cotton Belt 4-bay Hopper "64661" with coal, *98*		45 ___
19331	Cotton Belt 4-bay Hopper "64662" with coal, *98*		45 ___
19332	Cotton Belt 4-bay Hopper "64663" with coal, *98*		45 ___
19333	Cotton Belt 4-bay Hopper "64664" with coal, *98*		45 ___
19338	Cotton Belt 4-bay Hopper 2-pack, *99*		120 ___
19339	Cotton Belt 4-bay Hopper "64469," *99*		NRS ___
19340	Cotton Belt 4-bay Hopper "64470," *99*		NRS ___
19341	LV 2-bay Hopper "6456," *99*		30 ___
19344	D&RGW 3-bay Cylindrical Hopper "15990," *99–00*		42 ___
19345	CN 3-bay Cylindrical Hopper "370708," *99–00*		95 ___
19346	PRR 4-bay Hopper with coal "744433," *01*		40 ___
19347	LV 2-bay Hopper "643657," *01*		40 ___
19348	Duluth, Missabe & Iron Range Ore Car "28000," *03*		25 ___
19349	U.S. Steel Ore Car "19349," *03*		29 ___
19350	Postwar "6636" Alaska Quad Hopper, *03*		34 ___
19357	N&W Hopper "6446-25," Archive Collection, *07*		50 ___
19361	Twizzlers Quad Hopper, *10*		55 ___
19362	Coursers Christmas Hopper with gifts, *10*		60 ___

			Exc	Mint
____	**19364**	Milk Duds Covered Hopper, *11*		55
____	**19365**	Coca-Cola Quad Hopper, *10*		60
____	**19366**	Santa's Little Hopper, *10–11*		55
____	**19367**	ATSF Quad Hopper, *11*		60
____	**19368**	Southern Offset Hopper "106723," (std O), *11*		70
____	**19369**	Alaska Quad Hopper "20756," *12*		60
____	**19371**	Burlington Northern I-Beam Car, *04*		60
____	**19383**	UP PS-4 Flatcar "57125" (std O), *13*		70
____	**19384**	ATSF PS-4 Flatcar "90088" (std O), *13*		70
____	**19385**	CNJ PS-4 Flatcar "339" (std O), *13*		70
____	**19386**	BN PS-4 Flatcar "613200" (std O), *13*		70
____	**19388**	BN 89' Auto Carrier (std O), *13–14*		110
____	**19389**	SP 89' Auto Carrier (std O), *13–14*		110
____	**19390**	CP 89' Auto Carrier (std O), *13–14*		110
____	**19391**	Soo Line 89' Auto Carrier (std O), *13–14*		110
____	**19393**	BNSF Auto Carrier 2-pack (std O), *12*		220
____	**19394**	UP Auto Carrier 2-pack (std O), *12*		220
____	**19395**	Grand Trunk Auto Carrier 2-pack (std O), *12*		220
____	**19396**	CSX Auto Carrier 2-pack (std O), *12*		220
____	**19397**	CN Auto Carrier 2-pack (std O), *12*		220
____	**19398**	Conrail Auto Carrier 2-pack (std O), *12*		220
____	**19400**	Milwaukee Road Gondola with cable reels (FF 2), *87*	23	31
____	**19401**	GN Gondola with coal (FF 3), *88*	14	16
____	**19402**	GN Crane Car (FF 3), *88*	47	65
____	**19403**	WM Gondola with coal (FF 4), *89*	20	25
____	**19404**	Trailer Train Flatcar with WM trailers (FF 4), *89*	29	33
____	**19405**	Southern Crane Car, *91*	42	65
____	**19406**	West Point Mint Car, *91 u*	38	50
____	**19408**	Frisco Gondola with coil covers (FF 5), *91*	26	31
____	**19409**	Southern Flatcar with stakes, *91*	18	22
____	**19410**	NYC Gondola with canisters, *91*	47	55
____	**19411**	NKP Flatcar with Sears trailer (FF 6), *92*	50	59
____	**19412**	Frisco Crane Car, *92*	49	65
____	**19413**	Frisco Flatcar with stakes, *92*	16	21
____	**19414**	Union Pacific Flatcar with stakes (SSS), *92*	19	26
____	**19415**	Erie Flatcar with trailer "7200" (FF 7), *93*	28	39
____	**19416**	ICG TTUX Flatcar Set with trailers (SSS), *93*	70	75
____	**19419**	Charlotte Mint Car, *93*	25	32
____	**19420**	Lionel Lines Vat Car, *94*	18	22
____	**19421**	Hirsch Brothers Vat Car, *95*	20	21
____	**19423**	Circle L Racing Flatcar "6424" with stock cars, *96*		27
____	**19424**	Edison Electric Depressed Center Flatcar "6461" with transformer, *97*		31
____	**19427**	Evans Auto Loader "6414," *99*		55
____	**19428**	Evans Boat Loader "6414," *99*		70
____	**19429**	Culvert Gondola "6342," *98–99*		48
____	**19430**	ATSF Flatcar "6411" with Beechcraft Bonanza, *98*		47
____	**19438**	Christmas Gondola (std O), *98*		42
____	**19439**	Flatcar with safes, *98*		35
____	**19440**	Flatcar with FedEx trailer, *98*		34
____	**19441**	Lobster Vat Car, *98*		35

		Exc	Mint
19442	Water Supply Flatcar with tank (SSS), *98*		31 ____
19444	Flatcar with VW Bug, *98*		38 ____
19445	Borden Milk Tank Car "520," *99*		38 ____
19446	Pittsburgh Paint Vat Car, *99*		43 ____
19447	Mama's Baked Beans Vat Car, *99*		35 ____
19448	Easter Gondola "6462" with candy, *99*		27 ____
19449	Liquified Gas Tank Car "6469," *99*		31 ____
19450	Barrel Ramp Car "6343," *99*		31 ____
19451	Wheel Car "6262," *99*		32 ____
19454	PRR Flatcar "6424" with gondola, *99*		25 ____
19455	Lionel Lines Flatcar "6430" with Cooper-Jarrett trailers, *99*		60 ____
19457	Lionel Lines Extension Searchlight Car, *99*		40 ____
19459	Valentine Gondola "6462" with candy, *99*		50 ____
19471	Mobil Flatcar with 2 trailers, *00 u*		96 ____
19472	Mobil Bulkhead Flatcar with tank, *00 u*		68 ____
19474	L&N Flatcar "6424" with trailer frames, *99*		26 ____
19476	Zoo Gondola "6462" with animals, *99–00*		43 ____
19477	Monday Night Football Flatcar with trailer, *01*		30 ____
19478	Culvert Gondola "6342," *99*		45 ____
19479	Borden Milk Car "521," *00*		38 ____
19480	Valentine's Vat Car "6475," *99–00*		30 ____
19481	Easter Vat Car, *99–00*		38 ____
19482	NYC Flat with trailer "6424," *00*		50 ____
19483	VW Beetle Flatcar, *00*		48 ____
19484	Flatcar "6264" with timber, *00*		34 ____
19485	PRR Culvert Gondola "347004," *01*		41 ____
19486	NYC Lumber Flatcar, *01*		34 ____
19487	Flatcar "6800" with airplane, *00*		41 ____
19489	Evans Auto Loader "500085," *00*		50 ____
19490	Postwar "6475" Libby's Vat Car, *01–02*		36 ____
19491	Christmas Vat Car, *01*		30 ____
19492	WM Skeleton Log Car 3-pack, *01*		95 ____
19496	Westside Lumber Skeleton Log Car 3-pack, *01*		112 ____
19500	Milwaukee Road Reefer (FF 2), *87*	30	39 ____
19502	C&NW Reefer, *87*	30	33 ____
19503	Bangor & Aroostook Reefer, *87*	22	25 ____
19504	Northern Pacific Reefer, *87*	20	22 ____
19505	Great Northern Reefer (FF 3), *88*	29	35 ____
19506	Thomas Newcomen Reefer, *88*	18	23 ____
19507	Thomas Edison Reefer, *88*	21	27 ____
19508	Leonardo da Vinci Reefer, *89*	19	27 ____
19509	Alexander Graham Bell Reefer, *89*	17	20 ____
19510	PRR Stock Car (FARR 5), *89 u*	25	26 ____
19511	WM Reefer (FF 4), *89*	22	28 ____
19512	Wright Brothers Reefer, *90*	17	21 ____
19513	Ben Franklin Reefer, *90*	17	20 ____
19515	Milwaukee Road Stock Car (FF 2), *90 u*	33	41 ____
19516	George Washington Reefer, *89 u, 91*	14	19 ____
19517	Civil War Reefer, *89 u, 91*	14	19 ____
19518	Man on the Moon Reefer, *89 u, 91*	13	17 ____
19519	Frisco Stock Car (FF 5), *91*	26	31 ____

			Exc	Mint
___	19520	CSX Reefer, *91*	18	23
___	19522	Guglielmo Marconi Reefer, *91*	19	23
___	19523	Dr. Robert Goddard Reefer, *91*	19	23
___	19524	Delaware & Hudson Reefer (SSS), *91*	29	32
___	19525	Speedy Alka Seltzer Reefer, *91 u*	31	32
___	19526	Jolly Green Giant Reefer, *91 u*	21	33
___	19527	Nickel Plate Road Reefer (FF 6), *92*	20	29
___	19528	Joshua L. Cowen Reefer, *92*	23	28
___	19529	A.C. Gilbert Reefer, *92*	18	23
___	19530	Rock Island Stock Car, *92 u*	34	38
___	19531	Rice Krispies Reefer, *92 u*	23	33
___	19532	Hormel Reefer "901," *92 u*	18	24
___	19535	Erie Reefer (FF 7), *93*	23	26
___	19536	Soo Line REA Reefer (SSS), *93*	25	30
___	19538	Hormel Reefer "102," *94*	22	25
___	19539	Heinz Reefer, *94*	38	47
___	19540	Broken Arrow Ranch Stock Car "3356," *97*		28
___	19552	Rutland Reefer "395" (std O), *00*		32
___	19553	ATSF Stock Car "23003," *00*		37
___	19554	Postwar Celebration Milk Car "36621," *00*		125
___	19555	Swift Reefer "5839," red, *01*		33
___	19556	Swift Reefer "1020," silver, *01*		31
___	19557	Circus Stock Car "6376," *00*		32
___	19558	Postwar "6556" MKT Stock Car, *02*		27
___	19559	MKT Stock Car, girls set add-on, *02*		95
	19560	NP 2-door Stock Car "6356," Archive Collection, *02*		
___				33
___	19561	Norman Rockwell Holiday Reefer, *03*		25
___	19562	Norman Rockwell Holiday Reefer, *03*		25
___	19563	Norman Rockwell Holiday Reefer, *03*		25
___	19564	Postwar "6672" Santa Fe Reefer, *03*		35
	19565	Burlington Reefer "6672," Archive Collection, *03*		
___				35
	19567	Postwar "6572" Railway Express Agency Reefer, *05*		
___				45
___	19568	GN Reefer, Archive Collection, *05*		45
___	19569	Pillsbury Reefer, traditional, *05*		53
___	19570	Nestle Nesquik Reefer, traditional, *05*		53
___	19572	NYC Reefer "6672," Archive Collection, *06*		45
___	19573	Postwar "6356" NYC Stock Car, *06–07*		50
___	19574	GN Stock Car, *08*		50
___	19575	REA Reefer "6721," *08–09*		50
___	19576	Alaska Reefer, *08*		50
___	19577	Krey's Reefer, *10–11*		60
	19578	Granny Smith Apples Wood-sided Reefer, *10–11*		
___				53
___	19585	NS Transparent Instruction Car, *10–11*		75
___	19586	Alaska Husky Transport Car, *10–11*		75
___	19587	Hershey's Chocolate Wood-sided Reefer, *10*		68
___	19588	Santa's Wish Transparent Gift Car, *10*		75
___	19589	Blood Transfusion Bunk Car, *10–11*		60
___	19590	Wood-sided Reefer 2-pack, *10*		110
___	19593	Hershey's Kisses Wood-sided Reefer, *11–14*		55

		Exc	Mint
19594	York Peppermint Patty Wood-sided Reefer, *10–11*		55 ___
19599	Old Glory Reefers, set of 3, *89 u, 91*	37	43 ___
19600	Milwaukee Road 1-D Tank Car (FF 2), *87*	33	40 ___
19601	North American 1-D Tank Car (FF 4), *89*	27	29 ___
19602	Johnson 1-D Tank Car (FF 5), *91*	24	30 ___
19603	GATX 1-D Tank Car (FF 6), *92*	32	41 ___
19604	Goodyear 1-D Tank Car (SSS), *93*	33	36 ___
19605	Hudson's Bay 1-D Tank Car (SSS), *94*	25	29 ___
19607	Sunoco 1-D Tank Car "6315," *96*		23 ___
19608	Sunoco Aviation Services 1-D Tank Car "6315" (SSS), *97*		38 ___
19611	Gulf Oil 1-D Tank Car "6315," *98*		33 ___
19612	Gulf Oil 3-D Tank Car "6425," *98*		30 ___
19614	BASF 1-D Tank Car "UTLX 78252," *99–00*		25 ___
19615	Vulcan Chemicals 1-D Tank Car, *99–00*		25 ___
19621	Centennial 1-D Tank Car "6015-1," *99*		51 ___
19622	Centennial 1-D Tank Car "6015-2," *99*		58 ___
19623	Centennial 1-D Tank Car "6015-3," *99*		56 ___
19624	Centennial 1-D Tank Car "6015-4," *99*		50 ___
19625	Ethyl Tank Car " 6236," *01*		31 ___
19626	Diamond Chemical Tank Car "19419," *01*		29 ___
19627	Shell 1-D Tank Car "1227," *01*		37 ___
19628	Lion Oil 1-D Tank Car "2256," *01*		35 ___
19634	General American 1-D Tank Car, *01*		30 ___
19635	U.S. Army 1-D Tank Car "10936," *01*		31 ___
19636	Hooker Chemicals 1-D Tank Car "6180," *01*		36 ___
19637	GATX TankTrain Intermediate Car "44589" (std O), *02*		55 ___
19638	CN TankTrain Intermediate Car "75571" (std O), *02*		65 ___
19639	GATX TankTrain Intermediate Car 3-pack (std O), *02*		140 ___
19644	Union Texas 1-D Tank Car "9922," *02*		33 ___
19645	Penn Salt 1-D Tank Car "4730," *02*		33 ___
19646	CN TankTrain Intermediate Car "75571" (std O), *03*		45 ___
19647	GATX TankTrain Intermediate Car "44589" (std O), *03*		45 ___
19649	Scrooge McDuck Mint Car, *05*		192 ___
19651	Santa Fe Tool Car, *87*	30	35 ___
19652	Jersey Central Bunk Car, *88*	25	33 ___
19653	Jersey Central Tool Car, *88*	26	28 ___
19654	Amtrak Bunk Car, *89*	22	25 ___
19655	Amtrak Tool Car, *90–91*	23	30 ___
19656	Milwaukee Road Bunk Car, smoke, *90*	40	50 ___
19657	Wabash Bunk Car, smoke, *91–92*	36	42 ___
19658	Norfolk & Western Tool Car, *91*	24	29 ___
19660	Mint Car, *98*		40 ___
19663	Pratt's Hollow Bunk Car "5717," *99*		40 ___
19664	Ambassador Award Bunk Car, bronze, *99 u*		378 ___
19665	Ambassador Engineer Bunk Car, silver, *99 u*		573 ___
19666	Ambassador Cowen Bunk Car, gold, *99 u*		403 ___
19667	Wellspring Gold Bullion Car, *99*		54 ___

			Exc	Mint
____	**19669**	King Tut Museum Car "9660," *99*		70
____	**19670**	NY Federal Reserve Bullion Car "6445," *00*		44
____	**19671**	Lionel Model Shop Display Car "6445-01," *99–00*		50
____	**19672**	Lionel Mines Mint Car, *00 u*		250
____	**19673**	Wellspring Capital Management Mint Car, *99 u*		212
____	**19674**	Lionel Lines Platinum Car, *00*		43
____	**19675**	Lionel Model Shop Display "6445-2," *01*		42
____	**19676**	Philadelphia Mint Car, *01*		40
____	**19677**	Fort Knox Mint Car "6445," *00*		50
____	**19678**	U.S. Army Bunk Car, *02*		45
____	**19679**	St. Louis Federal Reserve Mint Car, *02*		38
____	**19681**	Area 51 Alien Suspension Car, *02*		47
____	**19682**	Alaska Klondike Mining Mint Car, *02*		40
____	**19683**	Pony Express Mint Car, *02*		50
____	**19686**	Chicago Federal Reserve Mint Car "6445," *03–04*		45
____	**19687**	UP Bunk Car "3887," smoke, *03*		40
____	**19688**	Postwar "6445" Fort Knox Mint Car, *02–03*		39
____	**19689**	CIBRO TankTrain Intermediate Car 3-pack (std O), *03*		100
____	**19694**	Pony Express Mint Car, *03*		50
____	**19696**	U.S. Savings Bond Mint Car, *00*		150
____	**19697**	U.S. Bureau of Engraving and Printing Mint Car "19697," *04*		40
____	**19698**	San Francisco Federal Reserve Mint Car, *04*		40
____	**19700**	Chessie System Extended Vision Caboose, *88*	43	50
____	**19701**	Milwaukee Road N5c Caboose (FF 2), *88*	50	65
____	**19702**	PRR N5c Caboose, *87*	44	55
____	**19703**	GN Extended Vision Caboose (FF 3), *88*	42	49
____	**19704**	WM Extended Vision Caboose, smoke (FF 4), *89*	42	49
____	**19705**	CP Rail Extended Vision Caboose, smoke, *89*	43	47
____	**19706**	UP Extended Vision Caboose "9706," smoke, *89*	40	56
____	**19707**	SP Work Caboose with searchlight, smoke, *90*	55	60
____	**19708**	Lionel Lines Bay Window Caboose, *90*	43	46
____	**19709**	PRR Work Caboose, smoke, *89, 91*	55	70
____	**19710**	Frisco Extended Vision Caboose, smoke (FF 5), *91*	43	47
____	**19711**	NS Extended Vision Caboose, smoke, *92*	47	65
____	**19712**	PRR N5c Caboose, *91*	44	47
____	**19714**	NYC Work Caboose with searchlight, smoke, *92*	100	130
____	**19715**	DM&IR Extended Vision Caboose "C-217," *92 u*	50	60
____	**19716**	IC Extended Vision Caboose "9405," smoke, *93*	105	135
____	**19717**	Susquehanna Bay Window Caboose "0121," *93*	44	55
____	**19718**	C&IM Extended Vision Caboose "74," *92 u*	38	45
____	**19719**	Erie Bay Window Caboose "C-300" (FF 7), *93*	47	55
____	**19720**	Soo Line Extended Vision Caboose (SSS), *93*	32	41
____	**19721**	GM&O Extended Vision Caboose "2956," *93 u*	47	50
____	**19723**	Disney Extended Vision Caboose, *94*	36	45

		Exc	Mint	
19724	JCPenney MKT Extended Vision Caboose "125," *94 u*	38	43	___
19726	NYC Bay Window Caboose (SSS), *95*	50	60	___
19727	Pennsylvania N5c Caboose "477938," *96*		30	___
19728	N&W Bay Window Caboose, *96*		70	___
19732	ATSF Bay Window Caboose "6517," *96*		43	___
19733	New York Central Caboose "6357," *96*		30	___
19734	Southern Pacific Caboose "6357," *96*		26	___
19736	PRR N5c Caboose "6417," *97*		27	___
19737	Lackawanna Searchlight Caboose "2420," *97*		75	___
19738	Conrail N5c Caboose "6417" (SSS), *97*		55	___
19739	NYC Wood-sided Caboose "6907," *97*		60	___
19740	Virginian N5c Caboose "6427," *97 u*		65	___
19741	Pennsylvania N5c Caboose "6417," *98*		50	___
19742	Erie Bay Window Caboose "C301," Caboose Talk, *98*		95	___
19748	SP&S Bay Window Caboose "6517," *97 u*		50	___
19749	SP Bay Window Caboose "6517," *98*		100	___
19750	Holiday Music Bay Window Caboose, *98*		160	___
19751	PRR N5c Caboose "492418," *98*		30	___
19752	NP Bay Window Caboose "407," *98*		50	___
19753	UP Extended Vision Caboose "25641," *98*		55	___
19754	NYC Caboose "20112," *98*		55	___
19755	Centennial Porthole Caboose, *99*		54	___
19756	Lionel Lines Bay Window Caboose, *99*		50	___
19758	DL&W Work Caboose "6419," *99*		55	___
19759	Corvette N5c Caboose, *99*		60	___
19772	Lionel Visitor's Center Vat Car, *99 u*		40	___
19773	Lionel Kids Club Barrel Ramp Car "6343," *96 u*		48	___
19778	Case Cutlery Wood-sided Caboose "1889" (std O), *99 u*		NRS	___
19779	SP Bay Window Caboose "1908," *99*		65	___
19780	LV Porthole Caboose "641751," *99–00*		43	___
19781	Vapor Records Holiday Porthole Caboose "6417," *99–00*		50	___
19782	NYC Bay Window Caboose "21719," *00*		65	___
19783	Ford Mustang Extended Vision Caboose, *01*		50	___
19785	SP Bay Window Caboose "6517," *00*		55	___
19786	PRR Extended Vision Caboose, *00 u*		40	___
19787	PRR Extended Vision Caboose "477927," *01*		40	___
19790	Postwar "6417" Lehigh Valley Caboose, *02*		41	___
19792	Postwar "C301" Erie Bay Window Caboose, *03*		45	___
19796	C&O Bay Window Caboose, *03*		50	___
19800	Circle L Ranch Operating Cattle Car, *88*	75	95	___
19801	Poultry Dispatch Chicken Car, *87*	20	27	___
19802	Carnation Milk Car, *87*	87	102	___
19803	Reading Ice Car, *87*	38	44	___
19804	Wabash Operating Hopper, *87*	25	34	___
19805	Santa Fe Operating Boxcar, *87*	28	36	___
19806	PRR Operating Hopper, *88*	28	32	___
19807	PRR Extended Vision Caboose, smoke, *88*	39	47	___
19808	NYC Ice Car, *88*	38	49	___
19809	Erie-Lackawanna Operating Boxcar, *88*	27	35	___

			Exc	Mint
___	**19810**	Bosco Milk Car, *88*	80	89
___	**19811**	Monon Brakeman Car, *90*	50	55
___	**19813**	Northern Pacific Ice Car, *89 u*	41	46
___	**19815**	Delaware & Hudson Brakeman Car, *92*	49	60
___	**19816**	Madison Hardware Operating Boxcar "190991," *91 u*	80	102
___	**19817**	Virginian Ice Car, *94*	31	35
___	**19818**	Dairymen's League Milk Car "788," *94*	65	80
___	**19819**	Poultry Dispatch Car (SSS), *94*	36	43
___	**19820**	Die-cast Tender, RailSounds II, *95–96*		175
___	**19821**	UP Operating Boxcar, *95*	31	36
___	**19822**	Pork Dispatch Car, *95*	29	39
___	**19823**	Burlington Ice Car, *94 u, 95*	39	49
___	**19824**	U.S. Army Target Launcher, *96*		30
___	**19825**	Generator Car, *96*		48
___	**19827**	NYC Operating Boxcar, *97*		37
___	**19828**	C&NW Animated Stock Car "3356" and Stockyard, *96–97*		100
___	**19830**	U.S. Mail Operating Boxcar "3428," *97*		39
___	**19831**	GM Generator Car "3530," power pole and wire, *97*		46
___	**19832**	Cola Ice Car "6352," *97*		47
___	**19833**	Tender "2426RS," RailSounds II, *97*		240
___	**19834**	LL 6-wheel Crane Car "2460," *97*		60
___	**19835**	FedEx Animated Boxcar "3464X," *97*		38
___	**19837**	Bucyrus 6-wheel Crane Car "2460," *99*		49
___	**19845**	Aquarium Car "3435," CC, *98*		151
___	**19846**	Animated Giraffe Car "3376C," *98*		105
___	**19850**	Stock Car "33760," RailSounds, *00*		130
___	**19853**	Firefighting Instruction Generator Car (SSS), *98*		60
___	**19854**	Lionelville Fire Car (SSS), *98*		55
___	**19855**	Christmas Aquarium Car, *98*		60
___	**19856**	Mermaid Transport, *98*		65
___	**19857**	NYC Firefighting Instruction Car "19853," *98–99*		175
___	**19858**	Lionelville Operating Searchlight Car "19854," *99*		65
___	**19859**	REA Boxcar "6267," steam RailSounds, *99*		170
___	**19860**	Conrail Boxcar "169671," diesel RailSounds, *99*		140
___	**19864**	Animated Ostrich Boxcar, *99*		37
___	**19867**	Operating Poultry Dispatch Car "3434," *99*		48
___	**19868**	Shark Aquarium Car "3435," *99*		190
___	**19869**	Alien Aquarium Car "3435," *99*		49
___	**19877**	ATSF Operating Barrel Car, *99*		55
___	**19878**	Operating Helium Tank Flatcar "3362," *99*		40
___	**19880**	Lionel Lines Extension Searchlight Car, *00*		50
___	**19882**	Sanderson Farms Poultry Car "3434," *99*		41
___	**19883**	LL Bucyrus Erie Crane Car "64608," *99*		45
___	**19884**	Atlantis Travel Aquarium Car, *00 u*		95
___	**19885**	N&W Operating Hopper Car, *00*		31
___	**19886**	Seaboard Boxcar "16126," steam RailSounds, *00*		140
___	**19887**	SP Boxcar "651663," diesel RailSounds, *00*		140

		Exc	Mint
19888	Christmas Music Boxcar, *01*		65 ____
19889	PRR Bay Window Caboose "477719," Crewtalk, *00*		140 ____
19890	Santa Fe Bay Window Caboose "999211," Crewtalk, *00*		100 ____
19894	Hood's Operating Milk Car with platform, *03–04*		95 ____
19894	Pony Express Mint Car, *03*		50 ____
19895	3356 Santa Fe Horse Car with corral, *04*		120 ____
19896	USMC Missile Launch Sound Car "45," *03–04*		165 ____
19897	NYC Crane Car, TMCC, *04*		255 ____
19898	Nestle Nesquik Operating Milk Car with platform, *04*		95 ____
19899	Pennsylvania Crane Car "19899" CC, *03–05*		260 ____
19900	Toy Fair Boxcar, *87 u*	65	80 ____
19901	"I Love Virginia" Boxcar, *87*	25	35 ____
19902	Toy Fair Boxcar, *88 u*	55	80 ____
19903	Christmas Boxcar, *87 u*	32	34 ____
19904	Christmas Boxcar, *88 u*	32	43 ____
19905	"I Love California" Boxcar, *88*	20	24 ____
19906	"I Love Pennsylvania" Boxcar, *89*	26	32 ____
19907	Toy Fair Boxcar, *89 u*	38	55 ____
19908	Christmas Boxcar, *89 u*	30	39 ____
19909	"I Love New Jersey" Boxcar, *90*	19	25 ____
19910	Christmas Boxcar, *90 u*	35	38 ____
19911	Toy Fair Boxcar, *90 u*	75	95 ____
19912	"I Love Ohio" Boxcar, *91*	21	28 ____
19913	Christmas Boxcar, *91*	34	52 ____
19913	Lionel Employee Christmas Boxcar, *91 u*	150	200 ____
19914	Toy Fair Boxcar, *91 u*	38	50 ____
19915	"I Love Texas" Boxcar, *92*	35	60 ____
19916	Lionel Employee Christmas Boxcar, *92 u*	190	220 ____
19917	Toy Fair Boxcar, *92 u*	45	53 ____
19918	Christmas Boxcar, *92 u*	49	70 ____
19919	"I Love Minnesota" Boxcar, *93*	40	60 ____
19920	Lionel Visitor's Center Boxcar, *92 u*	26	28 ____
19921	Lionel Employee Christmas Boxcar, *93 u*	140	185 ____
19922	Christmas Boxcar, *93*	33	41 ____
19923	Toy Fair Boxcar, *93 u*	65	95 ____
19925	Lionel Employee Learning Center Boxcar, *93 u*	55	63 ____
19926	"I Love Nevada" Boxcar, *94*	21	26 ____
19927	Lionel Visitor's Center Boxcar, *93 u*	26	33 ____
19928	Lionel Employee Christmas Boxcar, *94 u*	205	230 ____
19929	Christmas Boxcar, *94*	30	40 ____
19931	Toy Fair Boxcar, *94 u*	49	65 ____
19932	Lionel Visitor's Center Boxcar, *94 u*	26	33 ____
19933	"I Love Illinois" Boxcar, *95*	21	27 ____
19934	Lionel Visitor's Center Boxcar, *95 u*	18	22 ____
19937	Toy Fair Boxcar, *95 u*	55	75 ____
19938	Christmas Boxcar, *95*	26	34 ____
19939	Lionel Employee Christmas Boxcar, *95 u*	100	128 ____
19941	"I Love Colorado" Boxcar, *95*	23	30 ____
19942	"I Love Florida" Boxcar, *96*	19	27 ____
19943	"I Love Arizona" Boxcar, *96*	20	25 ____

		Exc	Mint
___ **19944**	Lionel Visitor's Center Tank Car, *96 u*		35
___ **19945**	Holiday Boxcar, *96*		29
___ **19946**	Lionel Employee Christmas Boxcar, *96 u*		195
___ **19947**	Lionel Toy Fair Boxcar, *96 u*		200
___ **19948**	Visitor's Center Flatcar with trailer, *96 u*		34
___ **19949**	"I Love NY" Boxcar, *97*		50
___ **19950**	"I Love Montana" Boxcar, *97*		30
___ **19951**	"I Love Massachusetts" Boxcar, *98*		26
___ **19952**	"I Love Indiana" Boxcar, *98*		31
19955	Lionel Visitor's Center Gondola with coil		
___	covers, *98 u*		20
___ **19956**	Toy Fair Boxcar "777," *98 u*		65
___ **19957**	Ambassador Caboose, *97 u*		478
___ **19958**	Ambassador Caboose, silver (std O), *98 u*		553
___ **19959**	Ambassador Caboose, gold (std O), *98 u*		744
___ **19964**	U.S. JCI Senate Boxcar, *92 u*	55	63
___ **19968**	"I Love Maine" Boxcar, *99*		40
___ **19969**	"I Love Vermont" Boxcar, *99*		40
___ **19970**	"I Love New Hampshire" Boxcar, *99*		34
___ **19971**	"I Love Rhode Island" Boxcar, *99*		34
___ **19976**	Lionel Employee Holiday Boxcar, *99 u*		150
___ **19977**	Toy Fair Boxcar, *99 u*		50
___ **19981**	Lionel Centennial Boxcar, *99*		36
___ **19982**	Lionel Centennial Boxcar, *99*		36
___ **19983**	Lionel Centennial Boxcar, *99*		36
___ **19984**	Lionel Centennial Boxcar, *99*		36
___ **19985**	"I Love Georgia" Boxcar, *99–00*		45
___ **19986**	"I Love North Carolina" Boxcar, *99–00*		40
___ **19987**	"I Love South Carolina" Boxcar, *99–00*		40
___ **19988**	"I Love Tennessee" Boxcar, *99–00*		55
___ **19989**	Toy Fair Boxcar, *00 u*		55
___ **19996**	Toy Fair Boxcar, *01 u*		50
___ **19997**	Lionel Employee Boxcar, *01 u*		120
___ **19998**	Christmas Boxcar, *01*		33
___ **19999**	Lionel Visitor's Center 4-bay Hopper, *02 u*		153
___ **20000**	PRR Senator Coach 4-pack (std O), *13*		640
___ **20005**	SP Sunset Limited Coach 4-pack (std O), *13*		640
20010	UP City of Los Angeles Coach 4-pack		
___	(std O), *13*		640
___ **20015**	B&O Capitol Limited Coach 4-pack (std O), *13*		640
___ **20020**	FEC City of Miami Coach 4-pack (std O), *13*		640
___ **20025**	KCS Southern Belle Coach 4-pack (std O), *13*		640
___ **20030**	MILW Olympian Coach 4-pack (std O), *13*		640
___ **21029**	World of Little Choo Choo Set, *94u, 95*	36	43
___ **21141**	North Dakota State Quarter Gondola Bank, *07*		60
___ **21142**	South Dakota State Quarter Hopper Bank, *07*		60
___ **21163**	SuperStreets FasTrack Grade Crossing, *08–10*		20
21164	SuperStreets 10" Transition to FasTrack,		
___	*08–10*		9
21165	SuperStreets Transition to FasTrack, 2 pieces,		
___	*08–10*		17
___ **21168**	City Traction Trolley Add-on, *08*		75
___ **21169**	City Traction Speeder Add-on, *08*		75

		Exc	Mint
21170	NYC 15" Heavyweight Passenger Car 4-pack, *07*		250 ___
21175	NYC 15" Heavyweight Passenger Car 2-pack, *07*		125 ___
21198	ATSF Alco Diesel AA Set, horn, *08*		200 ___
21199	ATSF Midnight Chief Streamliner Car 4-pack, *08*		200 ___
21204	ATSF Midnight Chief Streamliner Car 2-pack, *08*		100 ___
21207	SP Diesel Work Train, *07*		175 ___
21212	NH Diesel Freight Set, *07*		250 ___
21217	Southern Diesel Executive Inspection Train, *07*		175 ___
21229	Ringling Bros. S2 Diesel Switcher, horn, *07*		80 ___
21230	Ringling Bros. Porter Locomotive, *07*		105 ___
21231	Ringling Bros. Streamliner Car 4-pack, *07*		210 ___
21234	Ringling Bros. Streamliner Car 2-pack, *07*		105 ___
21237	Ringling Bros. Flatcar with 3 wagons, *07*		50 ___
21238	Ringling Bros. Flatcar with 3 wagons, *07*		50 ___
21239	Ringling Bros. Flatcar with crates, *07*		45 ___
21240	Ringling Bros. Flatcar with front end loader and poles, *07*		45 ___
21252	Boy Flying Kite, *08*		60 ___
21253	Operating Bunk Car Yard Office, *07*		80 ___
21261	SuperStreets 2.5" Straight-to-Curve Connector, 4 pieces, *08–10*		9 ___
21265	Operating Voltmeter Car, *07*		75 ___
21266	SuperStreets Intersection, 4 pieces, *08–10*		40 ___
21267	PRR Boxcab Electric Locomotive, horn, *07*		77 ___
21271	WP Operating Coal Dump Car with vehicle, *07*		33 ___
21276	Congressional Diner, smoke, *07*		110 ___
21277	Operating Flagman's Shanty, *08*		70 ___
21279	Roach Wranglers Pest Control Van, *08*		30 ___
21281	SuperStreets D21 Curve, *08–10*		3 ___
21282	SuperStreets 2.5" Curve-to-Curve Connector, 4 pieces, *08–10*		9 ___
21283	SuperStreets Tubular Track Grade Crossing, *08–10*		18 ___
21284	SuperStreets 10" Tubular Transition, *08–10*		8 ___
21285	SuperStreets 10" Tubular Transition, 2 pieces, *08–10*		14 ___
21286	SuperStreets Intersection, *08–10*		10 ___
21287	SuperStreets Y Roadway, *08–10*		12 ___
21288	SuperStreets O Gauge Conversion Pins, *08–10*		2 ___
21289	SuperStreets Connector Pins, *08–10*		2 ___
21290	SuperStreets Hookup Wires, 2 pieces, *08–10*		3 ___
21291	Dogbone Expander pack, *08–10*		25 ___
21296	City Traction Classic Truck, *07*		30 ___
21298	NYC 4-6-4 Hudson Locomotive "5279," CC, *07*		500 ___
21316	PE RS3 Diesel "2815," CC, *07*		350 ___
21324	Acrobats and Clowns Figures, 10 pieces, *08–10*		12 ___
21325	Ringmaster Circus Figures, 5, with accessories, *08–10*		12 ___
21326	PRR 15" Interurban Car 2-pack, *07*		200 ___
21354	Fresh Never Frozen Fish Transport Car, *07*		80 ___

		Exc	Mint
____ 21355	Dump Bin, *08–10*		20
____ 21358	Special Addition Boxcar, Girl, *08–10*		25
____ 21359	Special Addition Boxcar, Boy, *08–10*		25
____ 21368	Passenger Coach Figures, 9 pieces, *08–10*		11
____ 21369	Walking Figures, 8 pieces, *08–10*		11
____ 21370	Sitting Figures, 6, with benches, *08–10*		11
____ 21371	Standing Figures, 8 pieces, *08–10*		11
21372 ____	Railroad Station Figures, 6, with accessories, *08–10*		11
____ 21373	School Figures, 7, with accessories, *08–10*		11
21374 ____	Service Station Figures, 5, with accessories, *08–10*		11
____ 21375	Police Figures, 10, with dog, *08*		20
____ 21376	Seated Passenger Figures, 40 pieces, *08*		27
____ 21377	Mounted Police, 3, with horses, *08–10*		11
____ 21378	Factory, *08–10*		18
____ 21379	Police Station, *08–10*		16
____ 21380	Colonial House, *08–10*		16
____ 21381	Suburban Station, *08–10*		16
____ 21382	School, *08–10*		17
____ 21383	Suburban Ranch House, *08–10*		15
____ 21384	Service Station with gas pumps, *08–10*		17
____ 21385	Barn and Chicken Coop, *08–10*		20
____ 21386	Firehouse, *08–10*		17
____ 21387	Church, *08–10*		15
____ 21388	Country L-shaped Ranch House, *08–10*		16
____ 21389	Supermarket, *08–10*		12
____ 21390	Diner, *08–10*		15
____ 21394	Rotating Beacon, *08–09*		31
____ 21396	Single Tunnel Portals, pair, *08–10*		15
21397 ____	SuperSnap 31" Remote Switch, left hand, *08–09*		55
21398 ____	SuperSnap 31" Remote Switch, right hand, *08–09*		55
21399 ____	SuperSnap 72" Remote Switch, left hand, *08–09*		70
21400 ____	SuperSnap 72" Remote Switch, right hand, *08–09*		70
____ 21412	NYC Plymouth Switcher Freight Set, *07*		155
____ 21430	SuperStreets D16 Curve, *08–10*		2
____ 21431	SuperStreets 10" Straight Track, *08–10*		2
21432 ____	SuperStreets D16 Curved Track, 8 pieces, *08–10*		18
21433 ____	SuperStreets 5" Straight Track, 4 pieces, *08–10*		14
21434 ____	SuperStreets 10" Straight Track, 8 pieces, *08–10*		19
21435 ____	World War II Seated Soldiers, 9, with benches, *08–09*		20
____ 21436	Rings and Things Circus Accessories, *08–09*		10
____ 21438	Remote Controller, *07–10*		35
____ 21442	City Figures, 7, with scooter, *08–10*		11
____ 21443	Factory Figures, 6, with accessories, *08–10*		11
____ 21444	Church Figures, 5, with accessories, *08–10*		11

		Exc	Mint
21445	Firefighting Figures, 11, with accessories, *08–10*	20	
21449	Operating Loading Platform with flatcar, *07–08*	80	
21450	Unloading Station with dump bins, *07*	100	
21451	Girder Bridge with stone piers, *07*	40	
21452	Graduated Trestle Set, 26 pieces, *07*	50	
21453	Elevated Trestle Set, 10 pieces, *07*	40	
21454	Double Tunnel Portals, 2 pieces, *08–10*	20	
21456	UPS Step Van, *07*	30	
21466	Ringling Bros. 15" Aluminum Advertising Car, *07*	110	
21469	Ringling Bros. Flatcar, white, with container, *07*	45	
21470	Ringling Bros. Flatcar, blue, with container, *07*	45	
21471	Ringling Bros. Flatcar with 2 trailers, *08–10*	60	
21472	Ringling Bros. Flatcar with 2 trailers, *08–10*	60	
21476	Strasburg Plymouth Diesel Switcher, *07*	100	
21494	WM RS3 Diesel "189," CC, *07*	350	
21529	Montana State Quarter Boxcar Bank, *08*	45	
21542	Washington State Quarter Tank Car Bank, *08*	45	
21543	Boyd Bros. Ford Classic Truck, *08*	33	
21549	Ringling Bros. Crew Bus, *08*	33	
21552	S.W.A.T. Team Step Van, *08*	30	
21560	Reading Flatcar with rail load, *07*	25	
21567	School Bus SuperStreets Set, *08*	110	
21568	Dirty Dogz Van SuperStreets Set, *08*	100	
21569	Angelo's Pizza Delivery Van, *08*	30	
21570	Flying Colors Painting Van, *08*	30	
21571	SuperStreets 10" Insulated Roadway, 2 pieces, *08–10*	8	
21572	SuperStreets 5" Straight School, 2 pieces, *08–10*	8	
21573	SuperStreets 5" Straight Stop Ahead, 2 pieces, *08–10*	8	
21574	SuperStreets 5" Straight Crosswalk, 2 pieces, *08–10*	8	
21575	SuperStreets 10" Crossing, 2 pieces, *08–10*	10	
21576	SuperStreets Skid Mark Roadway Pack, *08–10*	13	
21577	Snack-On Step Van, *08*	30	
21582	Keystone Coal Porter Locomotive, *08*	100	
21583	Keystone Coal Freight Car 4-pack, *08*	100	
21590	ATSF "Midnight Chief" 2-bay Hopper "162277," *08*	25	
21591	ATSF "Midnight Chief" Flatcar "94468" with trailer, *08*	43	
21592	ATSF "Midnight Chief" Caboose, *08*	25	
21593	ATSF "Midnight Chief" Boxcar "621593," *08*	35	
21594	NYC Empire State Express 15" Aluminum Car 4-pack, *08–09*	420	
21599	SP flatcar with wheel load, *07*	35	
21600	B&M RS3 Diesel "1538," CC, *08–09*	350	
21607	Jack Frost Hopper "327" with sugar load, *08*	25	
21609	Elephants and Giraffes, 2 pair, *08–10*	13	
21610	Lions and Tigers, 2 pair, *08–10*	13	

			Exc	Mint
____	21611	Horses, 4 pieces, *08*		13
____	21621	ATSF Operating Boxcar "22658," *08–09*		90
____	21623	Rutland Operating Milk Car with platform, *08–10*		150
____	21626	Rath Wood-sided Reefer "622," *09*		45
____	21627	Greenlee Packing Wood-sided Reefer "3862," *10*		45
____	21628	CNJ Reefer "1438," *08–09*		35
____	21629	C&O Reefer "7783," *08–09*		35
____	21630	UP Stock Car "42005," *09*		45
____	21631	Reading Boxcar "107984," *08–09*		35
____	21632	GN Boxcar "34285," *08–09*		35
____	21633	RI "Route of the Rockets" Boxcar "21110," *09–10*		40
____	21634	Tidewater Flying A 1-D Tank Car "1367," *09*		40
____	21635	Southern Depressed Center Flatcar, 2 transformers, *09*		43
____	21636	NS Flatcar with bulkheads and stakes, *08–09*		35
____	21637	Ontario Northland Ribbed Hopper with coal, *09*		40
____	21639	Pan Am Boxcar "32126," *08–09*		55
____	21640	UP Modern Steel-sided Reefer "499030," *08–09*		55
____	21641	Ringling Bros. Merchandise Flatcar, *08*		50
____	21643	PRR Die-cast Gondola with covers, *09*		73
____	21644	PRR 16-wheel Flatcar with transformer, *08–09*		80
____	21646	DT&I Work Crane and Boom Car, *09*		85
____	21649	City Traction Trolley with Ringling Bros. banner, *08–09*		80
____	21651	Moo-Town Creamery Step Van, *08–09*		38
____	21656	Quikrete Step Van, *08–09*		42
____	21658	Ringling Bros. Vintage Truck, *08–09*		42
____	21659	DT&I Flatcar "90059" with Ford trailer, *08–09*		60
____	21662	Moo-Town Creamery Vending Machine, *08–09*		13
____	21663	Moo-Town Creamery Bunk Car Ice Cream Shop, *08–09*		115
____	21664	RI Operating Coal Dump Car with vehicle, *08–09*		40
____	21665	Alaska Operating Log Dump Car with vehicle, *09*		40
____	21667	Red River Lumber Boxcab Diesel with horn, *08–09*		100
____	21668	CP Operating Hopper "9628," *08–09*		45
____	21675	Mountain View Creamery Loading Depot, *08–10*		130
____	21676	Beaver Creek Logging Die-cast Porter Locomotive, *08–09*		120
____	21677	Ford Factory, *09*		22
____	21679	Assured Comfort HVAC Van, *08–09*		38
____	21680	Division of Prisons Bus SuperStreets Set, *08–09*		150
____	21688	Ringling Bros. Heavyweight Coach 2-pack, *08–11*		240
____	21691	Ringling Bros. Flatcar with 2 trailers, *08–10*		60
____	21692	C&NW MP15 Diesel with Ringling Bros. banner, *08–09*		140

		Exc	Mint
21693	Southern MP15 Diesel Pair, powered and dummy, *10*		200 ____
21696	Ford Flatcar with 2 trucks, *08–09*		53 ____
21698	Lionel Van SuperStreets Set, *08–10*		130 ____
21701	Star Spangled GG1 Electric Locomotive "4837," *08–10*		260 ____
21702	Milwaukee Road Girder Bridge, *08–09*		15 ____
21703	ATSF Black Mesa Aluminum Business Car, *09–10*		160 ____
21704	C&O Double Searchlight Car with vehicle, *08–09*		50 ____
21706	Chatham Police Van, *08–09*		38 ____
21707	NYC Aluminum Business Car, *09*		160 ____
21708	CN Operating Log Dump Car, *10*		120 ____
21709	PRR Girder Bridge, *08–09*		15 ____
21715	Ringling Bros. Stock Car, *08–09*		60 ____
21717	Pullman-Standard 1-D Tank Car, *08–09*		35 ____
21719	NYC Bay Window Caboose, *99*		70 ____
21720	Ringling Bros. Billboard Set #2, *08–09*		10 ____
21721	Warning Sign Pack, 12 pieces, *08–10*		25 ____
21730	Regulatory Sign Pack, 12 pieces, *08–10*		25 ____
21738	Railroad Crossing Sign Pack, 6 pieces, *08–10*		21 ____
21750	NKP Rolling Stock 4-pack, *98*		160 ____
21751	PRR Rolling Stock 4-pack, *98*		145 ____
21752	Conrail Unit Trailer Train, *98*		285 ____
21753	Service Station Fire Rescue Train, *98*	500	585 ____
21754	BNSF 3-bay Covered Hopper 2-pack (std O), *98*		65 ____
21755	4-bay Covered Hoppers 2-pack, *98*		65 ____
21756	6464-style Overstamped Boxcars 2-pack, *98*		65 ____
21757	UP Freight Car Set, *98*		188 ____
21758	Bethlehem Steel "44" (SSS), *99*		375 ____
21759	Canadian Pacific F3 Diesel Passenger Set, *99*		930 ____
21761	B&M Boxcar Set, 4-pack, *99*		180 ____
21763	New Haven Freight Set, *99*		265 ____
21766	ACL Passenger Car 2-pack, *99*		385 ____
21769	Centennial 1-D Tank Car Set, 4-pack, *99*		207 ____
21770	NYC Reefer Set, 4-pack, *99*		225 ____
21771	D&RGW Stock Car Set, 4-pack, *99*		230 ____
21774	Custom Series Consist I, 3-pack, *99*		150 ____
21775	Train Wreck Recovery Set, *99*		190 ____
21778	ATSF Train Master Diesel Freight Set, *99*		NRS ____
21779	Seaboard Freight Car Set, *99*		280 ____
21780	NYC Aluminum Passenger Car 2-pack, *99*		160 ____
21781	Case Cutlery Freight Set, *99 u*		965 ____
21782	PRR Congressional Set, *00*		930 ____
21783	Monday Night Football 2-pack, *01–02*		50 ____
21784	QVC PRR Coal Freight Steam Set, *00 u*		351 ____
21785	QVC Gold Mine Freight Steam Set, *00 u*		382 ____
21786	Santa Fe F3 Diesel ABBA Passenger Set, *00*		1500 ____
21787	Blue Comet Steam Passenger Set, *01–02*		1050 ____
21788	Postwar Missile Launch Freight Set, *02–03*		350 ____
21789	Norfolk Southern Piggyback Set, CC (SSS), *01*		370 ____
21790	CN TankTrain Dash 9 Diesel Freight Set, *02*		630 ____

		Exc	Mint
___	21791	Freedom Train Diesel Passenger Set, RailSounds, *03*		540
___ 21792	C&O Coal Hopper 6-pack #2 (std O), *01*		145
___ 21793	Virginian Coal Hopper 6-pack #2 (std O), *01*		160
___ 21794	Pioneer Seed GP7 Diesel Freight Set, *01 u*		840
___ 21795	Case Farmall Freight Set, *01 u*		965
___ 21796	NJ Medical Steam Freight Set, *01 u*		451
___ 21797	SP Daylight Passenger Set, *01*		670
___ 21852	MILW PS-2CD Hopper 3-pack (std O), *06*		155
___ 21853	BNSF PS-2CD Hopper 3-pack (std O), *06*		155
___ 21854	N&W PS-2CD Hopper 3-pack (std O), *06*		155
___ 21855	A&P Milk Car 3-pack, *06*		150
___ 21856	Bowman Dairy Milk Car 3-pack (std O), *06*		150
___ 21857	Western Dairy Milk Car 3-pack (std O), *06*		150
___ 21858	NP PS-4 Flatcar with trailers, 2-pack (std O), *06*		170
___ 21859	C&NW PS-4 Flatcar with trailers, 2-pack (std O), *06*		170
___ 21860	UP PS-4 Flatcar with trailers, 2-pack (std O), *06*		170
___ 21861	PRR PS-4 Flatcar with trailers (std O), *06*		170
___ 21863	ADM Unibody Tank Car 3-pack (std O), *06*		135
___ 21864	Cerestar Unibody Tank Car 3-pack (std O), *06*		135
___ 21865	Coe Rail Husky Stack Car 2-pack (std O), *06*		170
___ 21866	Santa Fe Husky Stack Car 2-pack (std O), *06*		170
___ 21872	C&O Offset Hopper 3-pack (std O), *05*		130
___ 21873	P&LE Offset Hopper 3-pack (std O), *06*		145
___ 21874	TTX Trailer Train 2-pack (std O), *06*		170
___ 21875	CSX Husky Stack Car 2-pack (std O), *06*		170
___ 21876	Disney Villain Hi-Cube Boxcar 3-pack, *05–06*		130
___ 21877	Domino Sugar 1-D Tank Car 3-pack (std O), *07*		135
___ 21878	Procor 1-D Tank Car 3-pack (std O), *07*		135
___ 21879	C&EI Offset Hopper 3-pack (std O), *07*		145
___ 21880	Erie Offset Hopper 3-pack (std O), *07*		145
___ 21881	Frisco Offset Hopper 3-pack (std O), *07–08*		200
___ 21882	Chessie System Offset Hopper 3-pack (std O), *07*		145
___ 21883	C&O 3-bay Hopper 2-pack (std O), *07–08*		140
___ 21884	Pennsylvania Power & Light 3-bay Hopper 2-pack (std O), *07*		140
___ 21885	Santa Fe 3-bay Hopper 2-pack (std O), *07*		140
___ 21886	C&NW 3-bay Hopper 2-pack (std O), *07–08*		140
___ 21888	IMC Canada Cylindrical Hopper 2-pack, *06*		130
___ 21893	Greenbrier Husky Stack Car 2-pack (std O), *07*		170
___ 21894	CSX Husky Stack Car 2-pack (std O), *07*		170
___ 21895	BN Husky Stack Car 2-pack (std O), *07*		170
___ 21896	Arizona & California Husky Stack Car 2-pack (std O), *07*		170
___ 21897	REA PS-4 Flatcar with trailers, 2-pack (std O), *07–08*		170
___ 21898	NYC PS-4 Flatcar with trailers, 2-pack (std O), *07–08*		170
___ 21899	Lackawanna PS-4 Flatcar with trailers, 2-pack (std O), *07*		170

		Exc	Mint
21900	Civil War Union Train Set, *99*		375 ___
21901	Civil War Confederate Train Set, *99*		375 ___
21902	Construction Zone Set, *99 u*		87 ___
21902	MILW PS-4 Flatcar with trailers, 2-pack (std O), *07–08*		170 ___
21904	Safari Adventure Set, *99 u*		90 ___
21904	UP PS-2 Covered Hopper 2-pack (std O), *07*		120 ___
21905	NYC Flyer Set, *99 u*		100 ___
21909	AGFA Film Steam Freight Set, *98 u*		1208 ___
21914	Lionel Lines Freight Set, *99*		120 ___
21916	Lionel Village Trolley, *99*		75 ___
21917	N&W Freight Set, *99*		70 ___
21918	Thomas Circus Play Set, *00*		100 ___
21918	PC PS-2 Covered Hopper 2-pack (std O), *07*		120 ___
21921	Imco PS-2 Covered Hopper 2-pack (std O), *07–08*		120 ___
21924	Holiday Trolley Set, *99*		65 ___
21925	Thomas the Tank Engine Island of Sodor Train Set, *99–00*		150 ___
21930	NYC PS-2 Covered Hopper 2-pack (std O), *07*		120 ___
21932	JCPenney NYC Freight Flyer Steam Set, *00 u*		170 ___
21934	Custom Series Consist II, 3-pack, *99*		140 ___
21936	Looney Tunes Train Set, *00 u*		370 ___
21937	NYC Steel-sided Reefer 2-pack (std O), *07*		130 ___
21939	Dubuque Steel-sided Reefer 2-pack (std O), *07–08*		130 ___
21940	ADM Steel-sided Reefer 2-pack (std O), *07*		130 ___
21941	National Car Steel-sided Reefer 2-pack (std O), *07*		130 ___
21944	"Celebrate a Lionel Christmas" Steam Set, *00–01*		165 ___
21945	Christmas Trolley Set, *00*		100 ___
21948	NYC Freight Flyer Set, air whistle, *00*		240 ___
21950	Maersk SD70 Diesel Maxi-Stack Set, *00*	560	700 ___
21951	World War II Troop Train, *00*		410 ___
21952	Lionel Lines Service Station Special Set, *00*		294 ___
21953	Ford Mustang GP7 Diesel Set, CC, *01*		345 ___
21955	D&RGW F3 Diesel AA Passenger Set, CC, *01*		740 ___
21956	New York Central Freight Set, *99–00*		355 ___
21969	Lionel Village Trolley Set, *00*		85 ___
21970	SP RS3 Diesel Freight Set, horn, *00–01*		110 ___
21971	Pennsylvania Flyer Steam Set, *00*		150 ___
21972	Frisco GP7 Diesel Freight Set, horn, *00*		150 ___
21973	ATSF Passenger Set, RailSounds, *00–01*		375 ___
21974	ATSF Passenger Set, SignalSounds, *00–01*		240 ___
21975	Burlington Steam Freight Set, SignalSounds, *00*		275 ___
21976	Centennial Steam Freight Starter Set, *00*		593 ___
21977	NYC Train Master Steam Freight Set, *99–00*		620 ___
21978	ATSF Train Master Diesel Freight Set, *99–00*		500 ___
21981	JCPenney NYC Flyer Set, *00 u*		150 ___
21988	NYC Freight Set, RailSounds, *00*		325 ___
21989	Burlington Steam Freight Set, RailSounds, *00*		300 ___
21990	NYC Flyer Freight Set, RailSounds, *00*		175 ___

			Exc	Mint
____	21999	Whirlpool Steam Freight Set, *00 u*		709
____	22103	PRR A5 Scale Switcher "411," CC, *08–09*		330
____	22104	PRR Freight Car 3-pack, *08*		135
	22105	NYC Empire State Express 4-6-4 Hudson Locomotive "5429," CC, *08–09*		
____				420
	22113	NYC Empire State Express 15" Aluminum Car 2-pack, *08–10*		
____				210
____	22116	Ringling Bros. Diesel Freight Set, *08–10*		245
____	22121	Ringling Bros. Freight Set, *08–10*		390
____	22126	Ringling Bros. Expansion Pack, *08–10*		135
____	22131	NH Streamliner Car 3-pack, *07*		150
____	22135	CB&Q S2 Diesel Switcher "9305," horn, *07*		80
____	22136	Erie S2 Diesel Switcher "522," horn, *07*		80
____	22137	Alaska MP15 Diesel "1552," horn, *07*		100
	22138	Astoria Heat & Power Porter Locomotive "4," *07*		
____				100
____	22139	LIRR Speeder, *08*		50
____	22140	CNJ Boxcab Diesel "1000," horn, *08*		90
____	22141	Lackawanna 15" Interurban Car 2-pack, *07*		200
____	22142	FEC Operating Dump Car, *07*		70
____	22143	B&A Operating Log Dump Car, *08–09*		70
	22144	Alaska Operating Coal Dump Car with vehicle, *08*		
____				33
____	22145	WM Operating Log Dump Car with vehicle, *08*		33
____	22146	PFE Operating Boxcar, *08*		80
____	22147	B&O Operating Hopper with coal, *08*		35
____	22148	GN Operating Hopper with coal, *08*		35
	22149	Dairymen's League Operating Milk Car, green, with platform, *08*		
____				140
____	22150	D&RGW Bunk Car, smoke, *08*		65
____	22151	Alaska Searchlight Car with vehicle, *08*		45
	22152	NKP 2-bay Outside-braced Hopper "31299," *08*		
____				50
____	22153	L&N 2-bay Offset Hopper "78660," *08*		50
____	22154	D&H 2-bay Rib Side Hopper "5737," *07*		50
	22155	Erie-Lack. 2-bay Aluminum Hopper "21353," *08*		
____				60
	22156	ACF Demonstrator 2-bay Aluminum Hopper "44586," *07*		
____				60
____	22157	GN Aluminum Tank Car "74787," *08*		60
	22158	MILW Bulkhead Flatcar "967116" with wood, *08–09*		
____				43
____	22159	BNSF Flatcar "585011" with trailer, *08*		43
____	22160	UP Flatcar "58059" with container, *08*		43
	22161	Conrail Flatcar "705910" with NS container, *08*		
____				43
____	22162	Foppiano Wine 3-D Tank Car "1112," *08*		45
____	22163	PRR Weed Control Car "6321226," *07*		45
____	22166	PRR Reefer "19492," *08*		25
____	22167	Seaboard Reefer "16622," *08*		25
____	22168	N&W Boxcar "645772," *08*		25
____	22169	ATSF Reefer "11744," *07*		25
____	22170	P&LE Reefer "22300," *07*		25
____	22171	B&O DD Boxcar "495289," *08*		25
____	22172	CB&Q Stock Car "52731," *08*		25

		Exc	Mint
22174	Erie-Lack. Transfer Caboose, *07*		25 ____
22176	PRR Caboose "478884," *07*		25 ____
22177	L&N Caboose "100," *07*		25 ____
22179	NYC Depressed Center Flatcar "66256" with 2 girders, *08*		25 ____
22180	IC Depressed Center Flatcar with 2 transformers, *07*		25 ____
22182	RI Gondola "180043" with coils, *08*		25 ____
22184	B&O Covered Hopper "604321," *08*		25 ____
22185	UP Covered Hopper "53186," *08*		25 ____
22186	P&LE (NYC) Gondola "17243," *08–09*		35 ____
22187	PRR 2-D Tank Car "6351815," *07*		25 ____
22188	Deep Rock 3-D Tank Car "2152," *08*		25 ____
22189	NP Java Diner, smoke, *08*		110 ____
22190	C&O Operating Billboard, *08*		65 ____
22191	Operating Passenger Station, *08–09*		105 ____
22192	Hot Box Operating BBQ Shack, *07*		80 ____
22193	Cold Drinks Vending Machine, *08*		12 ____
22194	Water Tower with light, *08–09*		20 ____
22199	City Traction Trolley Barn, *08–09*		65 ____
22202	Loading Ramp, *08–10*		20 ____
22203	Dairymen's League Operating Milk Car, white, with platform, *07*		140 ____
22204	Snacks Vending Machine, *08*		12 ____
22205	Soup and Sandwich Vending Machine, *08*		12 ____
22206	PRR Crew Bus, *08*		30 ____
22222	Ringling Bros. Speeder Chase Set, *08–10*		92 ____
22225	Ringling Bros. Jomar Heavyweight Private Car, *08–11*		120 ____
22226	Ringling Bros. 18" Caledonia Heavyweight Private Car, *08*		100 ____
22227	Ringling Bros. 18" Advertising Car, *08*		100 ____
22228	Ringling Bros. Flatcar with 3 wagons, *08*		50 ____
22231	Ringling Bros. Flatcar with 3 wagons, *08*		50 ____
22235	Ringling Bros. Flatcar with pole wagon and truck, *08*		75 ____
22238	Ringling Bros. Work Caboose with calliope wagon, *08*		40 ____
22240	Ringling Bros. Flatcar/Stock Car with wagon, *08*		50 ____
22243	Ringling Bros. Human Cannonball Car, *08*		45 ____
22244	Ringling Bros. Operating Searchlight Car with 3 spotlights, *08*		60 ____
22247	Ringling Bros. Stock Car "54," *08*		50 ____
22248	Ringling Bros. Stock Car "47," *08*		50 ____
22249	Ringling Bros. Dining Dept. Billboard Reefer, *08*		80 ____
22250	Ringling Bros. Dining Dept. Wood-sided Reefer, *08–09*		90 ____
22251	Ringling Bros. Dormitory Bunk Car "22," *08*		75 ____
22252	Ringling Bros. Operating Billboard, *08–09*		75 ____
22253	Ringling Bros. Vintage Billboard Set #1, *08*		9 ____
22255	Ringling Bros. Aluminum Coach "40010," *08–10*		165 ____
22257	Ringling Bros. Aluminum Shop Car "63002," *08–10*		165 ____

			Exc	Mint
____	22258	Ringling Bros. 18" Aluminum Large Animal Car, *08–10*		165
____	22259	Ringling Bros. Flatcar with trailer, *08*		53
____	22260	Ringling Bros. Tractor Trailer, *08*		30
____	22261	Idaho State Quarter Hopper Bank, *08*		65
____	22262	Wyoming State Quarter Tank Car Bank, *08*		50
____	22263	Utah State Quarter Boxcar Bank, *08*		45
____	22264	SuperStreets Figure-8 Expander Pack, *08–10*		35
____	22267	Mulligan Spring Water Step Van, *08*		30
____	22270	Quikrete Classic Truck with 2 pallets, *08*		33
____	22271	MILW EP-5 Electric Locomotive "E20," CC, *08–09*		460
____	22272	MILW Olympian Hiawatha 18" Aluminum Car 4-pack, *08*		480
____	22277	MILW Olympian Hiawatha 18" Aluminum Car 2-pack, *08*		250
____	22280	Erie-Lack. RS3 Diesel "933," CC, *08–09*		350
____	22281	Southern Train Master Diesel "6300," CC, *08–09*		420
____	22282	Southern Bay Window Caboose "X270," *08–09*		70
____	22283	UP S2 Diesel Switcher "1103" and Caboose "25384," *08*		130
____	22286	GN Boxcab Electric Locomotive "5008-A," horn, *08*		90
____	22287	North Shore Line 15" Interurban Car 2-pack, *08*		230
____	22288	Commuter Train Station, 6 road name stickers, *09*		25
____	22289	Ringling Bros. 18" Aluminum Passenger Car 2-pack, *08*		270
____	22290	Erie Boxcar "86448" with graffiti, *08*		46
____	22291	C&NW Stock Car "14303," *08*		46
____	22292	Land o' Lakes Butter Billboard Reefer, *08*		75
____	22293	PRR 4-bay Hopper "253776," *08*		65
____	22294	Montana Rail Link 3-bay Aluminum Hopper "50049," *08*		70
____	22295	Canada Wheat 4-bay Aluminum Hopper "606418," *08*		73
____	22296	Eaglebrook Aluminum Tank Car "19039," *08*		70
____	22297	Petri Wine 3-D Tank Car "904," *08–09*		45
____	22298	Cotton Belt Offset Cupola Wood-sided Caboose "2230," *08*		80
____	22299	MILW Bay Window Caboose "980502," *08–09*		70
____	22300	Detroit, Toledo & Ironton Coil Car "1352," *08*		60
____	22301	NYC Flatcar "506090" with freight kit, *08*		35
____	22302	C&O Flatcar "80951" with freight kit, *08*		35
____	22303	Extruded Aluminum I-Beam, 3 pieces, *08–09*		6
____	22304	Rails, 12 pieces, *08–09*		6
____	22305	Small Transformer Load, pair, *08–09*		15
____	22306	Large Transformer Load, *08*		19
____	22307	Forklifts, 3, with pallets, *08–09*		27
____	22308	Loaders with crates, pair, *08–09*		13
____	22309	Loaders with logs, pair, *08–09*		13
____	22310	KBL Logistics Container 2-pack, *08*		40

		Exc	Mint
22312	Commemorative Quarter Extended Vision Caboose, *09*	80	
22313	ATSF Boxcar "137460," *08*	25	
22314	Coastal King Seafood Wood-sided Reefer, *08*	25	
22315	Wisconsin & Southern "God Bless America" Boxcar, *09*	43	
22316	NP Depressed Center Flatcar "66130" with water tank, *08*	25	
22317	U.S. Air Force Hopper "55175" with ballast load, *08*	25	
22318	DM&IR Ore Car "29991," *08*	25	
22319	Celanese Chemicals 1-D Tank Car "12730," *08*	25	
22320	Baldwin Locomotives Works 1-D Tank Car "6809," *08*	25	
22321	B&O Operating Boxcar, *08*	45	
22322	PRR Operating Ballast Dump Car, *08*	75	
22323	FEMA Voltmeter Car, *08*	75	
22324	C&NW Cop and Robber Chase Gondola, *08–09*	55	
22325	White Milk Cans, 10 pieces, *08–10*	8	
22326	Twin Searchlight Tower, *08–10*	33	
22327	Tommy's Bunk Car Grill, *08–09*	100	
22328	Santa Fe Operating Freight Transfer Platform, *08–09*	130	
22329	Dual Track Signal Bridge, *08–10*	45	
22330	Stella's Heavyweight Diner, smoke, *08–09*	140	
22331	Coffee Vending Machine, *08*	12	
22332	Spring Water Vending Machine, *08*	12	
22333	Candy Vending Machine, *08*	12	
22334	Ford Plymouth Diesel Switcher and Ore Car 6-pack, *08*	200	
22335	NS Operating Paint Shop with boxcar, *08–09*	140	
22344	KBL Logistics ISO Tank, *08*	19	
22346	Tableau Circus Wagons, *08*	13	
22349	Forklift with 6 pallets, *08–09*	23	
22350	Twin Lamp Posts, 3 pieces, *08–09*	22	
22352	Lamp Posts, 4 pieces, *08–09*	20	
22354	Portable Spotlights, 3 pieces, *08–09*	15	
22356	High Tension Poles, 4 pieces, *08–09*	8	
22358	Rail Yard Signs, 12 pieces, *08–09*	10	
22360	Telephone Poles, 6 pieces, *08–09*	7	
22362	Girder Bridge, *08–09*	8	
22363	Stone Bridge Piers, pair, *08–10*	27	
22365	Heavyweight Passenger Coach 6-wheel Scale Trucks, pair, *08–09*	25	
22366	Aluminum Passenger Coach 4-wheel Scale Trucks, pair, *08–09*	25	
22367	Timkin Scale Sprung Trucks, pair, *08–09*	19	
22368	Bettendorf Scale Sprung Trucks, pair, *08–09*	19	
22369	Scale Couplers, pair, *08–09*	6	
22379	SuperStreets Barricade, 2 pieces, *08–10*	11	
22387	Kiosk with 3 vending machines, *08–09*	40	
22391	Ford MP15 Diesel "10021," horn, *08*	115	
22392	Ford Farming Boxcar "1681," *08*	30	
22393	Ford Stampings DD Boxcar "101," *08*	35	

			Exc	Mint
____	**22394**	Ford 2-bay Covered Hopper "1667," *08*		30
____	**22395**	Ford Speeder "14," *08*		65
____	**22396**	Ford Water Tower, *08*		25
____	**22397**	Ford Rotating Sign Tower, *08*		55
____	**22398**	Boyd Bros. and Ford Barn and Chicken Coop, *08*		25
____	**22399**	Ford ISO Tank, *08–09*		21
____	**22402**	PRR Streamlined K4 4-6-2 Pacific Locomotive, tender, *09–10*		500
____	**22408**	Ringling Bros. Tractor Trailer #1, *08–09*		35
____	**22411**	Tableau Wagon Set #2, *08–10*		18
____	**22412**	PRR Operating Flagman's Shanty, *08–09*		90
____	**22414**	Linde Union Carbide Boxcar with aluminum tank, *08–09*		70
____	**22415**	Ringling Bros. Flatcar with circus wagon, *08*		50
____	**22417**	Ringling Bros. Flatcar with container, *09*		55
____	**22420**	PRR Broadway Limited Aluminum Passenger Car 2-pack, *09–10*		300
____	**22423**	GN Aluminum Passenger Car 2-pack, *09–10*		360
____	**22426**	Ford Gondola "13447" with coils, *08–09*		43
____	**22427**	Ford Operating Billboard, *08–09*		75
____	**22428**	Ford Tin Sign Replica 4-pack, *08–09*		17
____	**22433**	PRR Broadway Limited Aluminum Passenger Car 4-pack, *09–10*		600
____	**22438**	Mail Crane, *08–10*		30
____	**22439**	Milwaukee Road Aluminum Passenger Car 2-pack, *09–11*		360
____	**22447**	Wabash Die-cast 2-bay Ribbed Hopper "37751," *08–09*		60
____	**22449**	UP Crew Bus, *08–09*		38
____	**22450**	Seaboard Die-cast Hopper with gravel, *10*		80
____	**22454**	Oklahoma State Quarter Die-cast Hopper Bank, *08–09*		75
____	**22455**	New Mexico State Quarter Die-cast Gondola Bank, *08–09*		74
____	**22456**	Arizona State Quarter Tank Car Bank, *08–09*		55
____	**22457**	Alaska State Quarter Boxcar Bank, *09*		55
____	**22458**	Hawaii State Quarter Die-cast Hopper Bank, *09*		75
____	**22459**	Southern Aluminum Passenger Car 2-pack #1, *09*		300
____	**22460**	Southern Aluminum Passenger Car 2-pack #2, *09*		300
____	**22461**	Scale Skeleton Log Car 4-pack, *08–09*		160
____	**22467**	Railroad Water Tower, *08–09*		23
____	**22468**	Fast Eddie's Used Car Lot with 2 die-cast vehicles, *08–09*		50
____	**22469**	Cola Illuminated Vending Machine, *08–09*		13
____	**22470**	SuperStreets Guard Rails, *08–10*		20
____	**22472**	Ringling Bros. Tin Sign Replica 4-pack, *08–09*		17
____	**22477**	Lionel Tin Sign Replica 4-pack, *08–09*		15
____	**22482**	Vintage Tin Sign Replica 4-pack, *08–09*		15
____	**22487**	Scooter Gang with scooters, *09–10*		13
____	**22492**	Airport Revolving Searchlight, *10*		40
____	**22493**	Ringling Bros. Lighted Clown Wood-sided Reefer, *09*		75

		Exc	Mint
22494	Ford Flatcar with 2 Thunderbird convertibles, *09*	53	___
22496	Vita O Flavored Water Vending Machine, *09*	13	___
22497	Top Pop Soda Illuminated Vending Machine, *09*	13	___
22498	Ringling Bros. Flatcar with 3 circus wagons, *09–10*	55	___
22500	Defense Dept. Flatcar with 2 jeeps and soldier, *09*	50	___
22501	C&NW Railroad Van, CC, *09–10*	100	___
22502	Ringling Bros. Flatcar with 3 circus wagons, *09–10*	55	___
22504	Ford Water Tower with vintage Ford logo, *09–10*	25	___
22505	Sparkling Springs Beverage Truck, *09*	45	___
22506	SuperStreets Fishtail Roadway, *09*	25	___
22507	Ringling Bros. Flatcar with boxcar and ticket wagon, *09*	60	___
22509	Pallet Pack with banded loads, *09*	20	___
22510	Lionel Step Van, CC, *09–10*	100	___
22511	BNSF Flatcar with helicopter, *09*	50	___
22513	Ringling Bros. Heavyweight Advertising Car, *09*	120	___
22514	NYC Girder Bridge, *09–10*	15	___
22515	Milwaukee Road/REA Scale Boxcar "6436," *09*	55	___
22516	BNSF MP15 Diesel "3704" with horn, *09*	120	___
22517	Quick Lane Ford Motorcraft Auto Parts Van, *09–10*	42	___
22518	Lionel Tank Container Leasing ISO Tank, *09–10*	23	___
22519	Roma Wine Wood-sided Billboard Reefer, *09–10*	70	___
22520	WWII Soldiers in Action, 10 pieces, *09–10*	20	___
22521	1959 Ford Billboard Set, *09*	10	___
22523	American Flyer Vintage Truck, *09*	38	___
22524	Ford Coil Car "749772," *09*	73	___
22525	Vermont Railway Operating Boxcar "177," *09*	50	___
22526	Crabby Matt's Smoking Heavyweight Diner, *09*	150	___
22527	Toledo, Peoria & Western Boxcar "5067," *09–10*	55	___
22528	GN Stock Car "55973," *09–10*	55	___
22529	U.S. Army 1-D Tank Car "11278," *09*	35	___
22530	Milwaukee Road Aluminum Coach "627," *09–11*	180	___
22531	Southern Girder Bridge, *09*	15	___
22532	Montana Rail Link 1-D Tank Car "100017," *09*	35	___
22533	GN Aluminum Coach "1377," *09–10*	180	___
22534	SuperStreets D16 Curve Guard Rails, *09–10*	20	___
22536	SuperStreets D21 Curve Guard Rails, *09–10*	22	___
22538	Ford Modern Aluminum Tank Car "30166," *09*	90	___
22539	BNSF Flatcar "922267" with Ford trailer, *09–10*	60	___
22542	PRR Flatcar "480227" with freight kit, *09*	40	___
22543	Biodiesel 2-D Tank Car "1544," *09*	40	___

		Exc	Mint
__ 22544	Ringling Bros. Wood-sided Gondola with equipment, *09*		63
__ 22548	Kiosk #2 with 3 illuminated vending machines, *09*		40
__ 22553	Convenience Mart, *09–10*		25
__ 22554	Auto Parts Store, *09–10*		20
__ 22555	Ringling Bros. Tractor with Gold Tour container, *09–10*		55
__ 22558	PRR Flatcar "469301" with milk containers, *09*		50
__ 22559	UP Gondola "229794" with freight kit, *09–10*		80
__ 22560	CB&Q Wood-sided Gondola "85150" with spools, *09–10*		60
__ 22561	Gondola Scrap Load, *09*		9
__ 22562	Operation Lifesaver Boxcar with flashing LEDs, *09*		65
__ 22563	Ringling Bros. Handcar and Trailer Set, *10–11*		70
__ 22566	SuperStreets 2.5" Straight Roadway, 4 pieces, *10*		12
__ 22568	Generators, 2 pieces, *09*		9
__ 22570	Large transformer, *09*		22
__ 22571	Cage Wagon Set, *09–10*		18
__ 22573	Display Base, *09*		20
__ 22574	Ringling Bros. Flatcar "39" with trailer, *09*		60
__ 22577	Biodiesel Storage Tank with 2 figures, *09–10*		40
__ 22578	Ringling Bros. Heavyweight Coach "70," *09*		120
__ 22579	Circus Horses, 4 pieces, *09–10*		15
__ 22580	Bollards and Chains, *09–10*		20
__ 22582	Pipe Stack Load, *09*		30
__ 22583	KBL Operating Wind Turbine, *09–10*		75
__ 22584	KBL Die-cast 16-wheel Flatcar "34807," *09*		85
__ 22587	Old Reading Flatcar Foot Bridge with stone piers, *09–10*		50
__ 22590	Roadside Fender Bender, *09–10*		75
__ 22592	SuperStreets D16 Turn Roadways, left and right, *10*		35
__ 22595	SuperStreets D21 Turn Roadways, left and right, *10*		39
__ 22598	SuperStreets Adjustable Straight Kit, *09–10*		20
__ 22600	Wire Spool Load, 6 pieces, *09*		20
__ 22610	Napa Valley Wine Train Alco FA Diesel AA Set, *10*		230
__ 22613	Napa Valley Wine Train 15" Passenger Car 4-pack, *10*		450
__ 22618	Signal Oil Co. 1-D Tank Car, *10*		40
__ 22619	PRR Paoli MU Commuter Train 2-pack, *10*		290
__ 22622	RR Paoli Motorized Combine, *10*		200
__ 22623	PRR Commuter Train Station, *10*		35
__ 22624	NH Die-cast Plymouth Switcher with snowplow, *10*		160
__ 22625	Ringling Bros. 18" Aluminum Generator Car, *10–11*		180
__ 22627	Ringling Bros. Lighted Clown Wood-sided Reefer, *10–11*		90
__ 22628	Ringling Bros. 18" Aluminum Advertising Car, *10–11*		180

		Exc	Mint
22629	Ringling Bros. Stock Car, *10–11*		60 ___
22630	Ringling Bros. Tractor and Trailer, *10–11*		35 ___
22633	Ringling Bros. 18" Aluminum Coach, *10–11*		180 ___
22634	Ringling Bros. 18" Heavyweight Advertising Car, *10–11*		146 ___
22635	Ringling Bros. Operating Dual Searchlight Car, *10–11*		60 ___
22637	Quikrete Step Van, *10*		48 ___
22638	PRR Crew Bus, *10*		45 ___
22639	B&O Boxcab Diesel "195," *10*		100 ___
22640	Central of Georgia Boxcar "5823," *10*		45 ___
22641	New Haven Boxcar "36438," *10*		45 ___
22642	Ringling Bros. Operating Large Animal Feed Car, *10–11*		150 ___
22643	Ford MP15 Diesel "10022," *10–11*		135 ___
22644	Ford Motorcraft 48' Aluminum Tank Car, *10–11*		95 ___
22645	Ringling Bros. Operating Tent Pole Dump Car, *10–11*		130 ___
22646	Ford Speeder, *10–11*		75 ___
22647	Rock Island Gondola "180044," *10*		35 ___
22648	PRR Gondola "353381," *10*		35 ___
22651	Central Vermont Operating Milk Car with platform, *10*		175 ___
22653	Starlite Diner with parking lot, *10*		200 ___
22654	Ringling Bros. Flatcar with 3 circus wagons, *10–11*		60 ___
22656	Ringling Bros. Flatcar with 3 circus wagons, *10–11*		60 ___
22658	Operating Flagman's Shanty, *10*		100 ___
22659	Union 76 1-D Tank Car "6322," *10*		40 ___
22660	Moose Pond Creamery Operating Loading Depot, *10*		140 ___
22661	WM 2-Bay Covered Hopper "5051," *10*		35 ___
22662	PRR Reefer "19494," *10*		45 ___
22663	New Haven Illuminated Caboose, *10*		40 ___
22667	Acme Scrap Platform Crane, *10*		60 ___
22670	ATSF Operating Boxcar, *10*		140 ___
22671	Smoking Southern Bay Window Caboose, *10*		90 ___
22672	Ringling Bros. 18" Sarasota Observation Car, *10–11*		146 ___
22673	Ford Water Tower with light, *10*		27 ___
22674	MILW 21" Aluminum Passenger Car 2-pack, *10–11*		400 ___
22679	Ringling Bros. Operating Billboard, *10–11*		100 ___
22902	Quonset Hut, *98–99*		22 ___
22907	Die-cast Girder Bridge, *98–01*		10 ___
22910	Gilbert Tractor Trailer, *98*		20 ___
22914	PowerHouse Lockon, *98–01*		24 ___
22915	Municipal Building, *98–99*		28 ___
22916	190-watt Power Accessory System, *98*		425 ___
22918	Locomotive Backshop, *98*	300	460 ___
22919	ElectroCouplers Kit for GP9 Diesel, *98–00*		20 ___
22922	Intermodal Crane, *98*		195 ___
22931	Die-cast Cantilever Signal Bridge, *98–06*		35 ___

			Mint
____	**22934**	Walkout Cantilever Signal, *98–03*	42
____	**22936**	Coaling Tower, 3 pieces, *98*	85
____	**22940**	Mast Signal, *98–00*	37
____	**22942**	Accessories Box, *98–01*	20
____	**22944**	Automatic Operating Semaphore, *98–03, 08*	35
____	**22945**	Block Target Signal, *98–00*	39
____	**22946**	Automatic Crossing Gate and Signal, *98–99*	45
____	**22947**	Auto Crossing Gate, *98–00*	36
____	**22948**	Gooseneck Street Lamps, set of 2, *98–00*	165
____	**22949**	Highway Lights, set of 4, *98–99*	20
____	**22950**	Classic Street Lamps, set of 3, *98–02*	20
____	**22951**	Dwarf Signal, *98–00*	24
____	**22952**	Classic Billboards, set of 3, *98–00*	15
____	**22953**	Linex Gasoline Tall Oil Tank, *98–99*	6
____	**22954**	Linex Gasoline Wide Oil Tank, *98–99*	6
____	**22955**	ElectroCouplers Kit for J Class and B&A tenders, *98–00*	20
____	**22956**	ElectroCouplers Kit for NW2 Switcher, *98*	20
____	**22957**	ElectroCouplers Kit for F3 Diesel, *98–01*	20
____	**22958**	ElectroCouplers Kit for Dash 9 Diesel, *98–01*	20
____	**22959**	ElectroCoupler Conversion Kit for Atlantic Locomotive, *98–01*	13
____	**22960**	Trainmaster Command Basic Upgrade Kit, *98–01*	34
____	**22961**	Standard GP9 Diesel B Unit Upgrade Kit, *98–01*	30
____	**22962**	Deluxe GP9 Diesel B Unit Upgrade Kit, black trucks, *98–01*	44
____	**22963**	RailSounds Upgrade Kit, steam RailSounds, *98–01*	55
____	**22964**	RailSounds Upgrade Kit, diesel RailSounds, *98–01*	55
____	**22965**	Culvert Loader, CC, *98–01*	255
____	**22966**	Figure-8 Add-on Track Pack (O27), *98–14*	17
____	**22967**	Double Loop Add-on Track Pack (O27), *98–14*	62
____	**22968**	Double Loop Track Pack (O27), *98–03*	65
____	**22969**	Deluxe Complete Track Pack (O), *98–14*	120
____	**22972**	Bascule Bridge, *98–99*	337
____	**22973**	Lionel Corporation Tractor and Trailer, *98*	15
____	**22975**	Culvert Unloader, CC, *99–00*	225
____	**22979**	GP9 Diesel B-Unit Deluxe Upgrade Kit, silver trucks, *98–01*	34
____	**22980**	TMCC SC-2 Switch Controller, *99–14*	130
____	**22982**	Postwar ZW Controller and Transformer Set, *98*	265
____	**22983**	180-watt PowerHouse Power Supply, *99–14*	100
____	**22990**	Flatcar with Route 66 autos, 4-pack, *99*	37
____	**22991**	Christmas Tree and Blue Comet Train, *99–00*	60
____	**22993**	Route 66 Sinclair Dino Cafe, *99–00*	210
____	**22997**	Oil Drum Loader, *99–00*	100
____	**22998**	Triple Action Magnetic Crane, *99*	220
____	**22999**	Sound Dispatching Station, *99–00*	90
____	**23000**	NYC Dreyfuss Hudson Operating Base, 2-rail, *92 u*	190

		Exc	Mint
23001	NYC Dreyfuss Hudson Operating Base, 3-rail, *93 u*		190 ____
23002	NYC Hudson Operating Base, *92 u, 93–94*		190 ____
23003	PRR B-6 Switcher Operating Base, *92 u, 93–94*		190 ____
23004	NP 4-8-4 Operating Base, *92 u, 93–94*		190 ____
23005	Reading T-1 Operating Base, *92 u, 93–94*		190 ____
23006	Chessie System T-1 Operating Base, *92 u, 93–94*		190 ____
23007	SP Daylight Operating Base, *92 u, 93–94*		190 ____
23008	NYC L-3 Mohawk Operating Base, *92 u, 93–94*		190 ____
23009	PRR S2 Turbine Locomotive Operating Base, *92 u, 93–94*		190 ____
23010	31" Remote Switch, left hand (O), *95–99*	30	37 ____
23011	31" Remote Switch, right hand (O), *95–99*	28	30 ____
23012	F3 Diesel ABA Operating Base, *92 u, 93–94*		190 ____
24018	PRR Boxcar, *05*		25 ____
24101	Mainline Color Position Signal, *04–08*		25 ____
24102	Industrial Water Tower, *03*		55 ____
24103	Double Floodlight Tower, *03, 05–09*		42 ____
24104	Hobo Tower, *03–05*		70 ____
24105	Track Gang, *03–06*		70 ____
24106	Exploding Ammunition Dump, *02*		25 ____
24107	Missile Firing Range Set, *02*		60 ____
24108	World War II Pylon, *03*		80 ____
24109	Santa Fe Railroad Tugboat, *03*		125 ____
24110	Pennsylvania Railroad Tugboat, *03*		118 ____
24111	Swing Bridge, *03*		215 ____
24112	Oil Field with bubble tubes, *03*		44 ____
24113	Lionelville Ford Auto Dealership, *03*		225 ____
24114	AMC/ARC Gantry Crane, CC, *03*		195 ____
24115	AMC/ARC Log Loader, CC, *03, 06–07*		140 ____
24117	Covered Bridge, *02–14*		60 ____
24119	Big Bay Lighthouse, *04–05*		170 ____
24122	Lionelville People Pack, *03, 08–09, 14*		27 ____
24123	Passenger Station People Pack, *03, 08–09, 14*		27 ____
24124	Carnival People Pack, *03, 08–11, 13–14*	5	27 ____
24130	TMCC 135/180 PowerMaster, *04–12*		79 ____
24131	Dumbo Pylon, *03*		70 ____
24134	Bethlehem Steel Gantry Crane, *02*		200 ____
24135	Lionel Lighthouse, *02–03*		100 ____
24137	Mr. Spiff and Puddles, *03, 08*		34 ____
24138	Playtime Playground, *03, 08*		50 ____
24139	Duck Shooting Gallery, *03*		110 ____
24140	Charles Bowdish Homestead, *03*		60 ____
24147	Lionel Sawmill, *03*		90 ____
24148	Coal Tipple Coal Pack, *02, 08–10, 13–14*		15 ____
24149	NYC Hobo Hotel, *02*		42 ____
24151	Hobo Campfire, *03*		25 ____
24152	Conveyor Lumber Loader, *03*		65 ____
24153	Railroad Control Tower, *03, 08–10*		40 ____
24154	Maiden Rescue, *03*		35 ____
24155	Blinking Light Billboard, *04–10*		21 ____

			Mint
	24156	Lionelville Street Lamps, set of 4, *04–05, 07–14*	30
	24159	Illuminated Station Platform, *04–08*	32
	24160	Rub-a-Dub-Dub, *04*	42
	24161	Test O' Strength, *04–06*	70
	24164	Summer Vacation, *04–05*	80
	24168	Tire Swing, *04–05*	70
	24170	Rover's Revenge, *04–05*	70
	24171	Campbell's Soup Water Tower, *04*	45
	24172	Balancing Man, *04–05*	70
	24173	Derrick Platform, *03–05*	60
	24174	Icing Station, *04–06*	100
	24176	Irene's Diner, *06–07*	65
	24177	Hot Air Balloon Ride, *04, 06*	95
	24179	Scrambler Amusement Ride, *04–07*	165
	24180	Choo Choo Barn Lionelville Zoo, *04–05*	105
	24182	Lionelville Firehouse, *04*	100
	24183	Lionelville Gas Station, *04, 06–09*	115
	24187	Classic Billboard Set: 3 stands and 5 inserts, *04–08*	10
	24190	Station Platform, *05–09*	17
	24191	Park People Pack, *04–14*	27
	24192	Park Benches People Pack, *04–09*	23
	24193	Railroad Yard People Pack, *04–08, 14*	27
	24194	Civil Servants People Pack, *04–14*	27
	24196	Farm People Pack, *04–09*	23
	24197	City Accessory Pack, *04–14*	27
	24200	Lionel FasTrack Book, *07–10, 13–14*	35
	24201	UPS Centennial Operating Billboard Signmen, *07*	100
	24203	Polar Express Original Figures, 4 pieces, *08–13*	27
	24204	Christmas Tractor Trailer with trees, *08*	25
	24205	Classic Billboard Set, *08–10*	20
	24206	MOW Gantry Crane, *08*	280
	24212	Lionel Art Blinking Billboard, *08–09*	23
	24213	Universal Lockon, *12–14*	4
	24214	Postwar "395" Floodlight Tower, *08*	75
	24215	MTA Metro-North Passenger Station, *07*	53
	24218	Sunoco Elevated Tank, *08–09*	75
	24219	PRR Plastic Girder Bridge, *08*	18
	24220	ATSF Girder Bridge, *08–09*	18
	24221	UP Die-cast Girder Bridge, *08*	30
	24222	UPS Die-cast Girder Bridge, *08*	30
	24223	Santa's Sleigh Pylon, *08*	150
	24224	Postwar "38" Water Tower, *08–09*	150
	24226	Christmas Toy Store, *08*	52
	24227	Halloween Animated Billboard, *08–09*	54
	24228	Christmas Operating Billboard, *08*	38
	24229	Pennsylvania Water Tower, *08–09*	23
	24230	Maiden Rescue, *08*	60
	24232	Burning Switch Tower, *08*	80
	24233	Exploding Ammunition Dump, *08*	36
	24234	Missile Firing Range, *08*	43

Exc Mint

Number	Description	Exc Mint
24235	UPS Water Tower, *08*	80 ____
24236	Wimpy's All-Star Burger Stand, *08*	97 ____
24238	Sunoco Oil Derrick, *08*	90 ____
24240	MTA Metro-North Blinking Billboard, *07*	21 ____
24242	Postwar "352" Icing Station, *08*	100 ____
24243	Rosie's Roadside Diner, *08*	85 ____
24244	Commuter People, *08, 13–14*	27 ____
24245	MTA Metro-North Illuminated Station Platform, *07*	32 ____
24248	Manual Crossing Gate, *08–14*	20 ____
24250	Mainline Gooseneck Lamps, pair, *08–09*	32 ____
24251	Polar Express Caribou, *08–13*	23 ____
24252	Polar Express Wolves and Rabbits, *08–13*	23 ____
24264	Halloween People, *08–12*	23 ____
24265	Trick or Treat People, *08–13*	23 ____
24270	Operating Forklift Platform, *08–09*	280 ____
24272	Train Orders Building, *08*	80 ____
24273	Christmas Water Tower, *08–10*	23 ____
24274	Christmas Girder Bridge, *08*	18 ____
24279	PowerMaster Bridge, *08–13*	55 ____
24283	NYC Girder Bridge, *09–10*	21 ____
24284	Halloween Girder Bridge, *09–11*	21 ____
24285	CP Rail Girder Bridge, *08–09*	30 ____
24286	Polar Express Girder Bridge, *09–12*	21 ____
24287	ATSF Blinking Light Water Tower, *09*	30 ____
24288	NYC Blinking Light Water Tower, *09*	30 ____
24293	Legacy Module Garage, *08–09*	50 ____
24294	AEC Nuclear Reactor, *09–10*	305 ____
24295	Cowen's Corner Hobby Shop, *09*	420 ____
24296	Engine House, *09–12, 14*	100 ____
24299	Main Street Ice Cream Parlor, *08*	37 ____
24500	D&RGW Alco PA Diesel AA Set, *04*	530 ____
24503	D&RGW Alco PB Diesel, *04*	150 ____
24504	Santa Fe E6 Diesel AA Set, CC, *03*	530 ____
24507	Milwaukee Road E6 Diesel AA Set, CC, *03*	530 ____
24511	Burlington FT Diesel AA Set, RailSounds, *03*	225 ____
24516	Santa Fe F3 Diesel B Unit, *03*	235 ____
24517	NYC F3 Diesel B Unit "2404," powered, CC, *03*	250 ____
24518	WP F3 Diesel B Unit, *03*	275 ____
24519	B&O F3 Diesel B Unit, *03*	270 ____
24520	Alaska F3 Diesel AA Set, *03*	650 ____
24521	Alaska F3 Diesel B Unit, nonpowered, *03*	200 ____
24522	Alaska F3 Diesel B Unit "1519," powered, CC, *03*	300 ____
24528	Postwar "2379T" Rio Grande F3 Diesel A Unit, nonpowered, *04*	175 ____
24529	Santa Fe F3 Diesel AA Set, CC, *04*	690 ____
24532	Santa Fe F3 Diesel B Unit "18A," nonpowered, *04*	150 ____
24533	Santa Fe F3 Diesel B Unit "18B," *04*	200 ____
24534	Erie-Lack. F3 Diesel ABA Set, CC, *05*	900 ____
24538	Erie-Lack. F3 Diesel B Unit "8042," powered, CC, *05*	225 ____
24544	NYC FA2 Diesel AA Set, CC, *05*	600 ____

Exc Mint

			Exc	Mint
____	24547	NYC FB2 Diesel B Unit "3330" (std O), *05*		150
____	24548	CN FPA-4 Diesel AA Set, CC, *05*		600
____	24551	CN FPB-4 Diesel B Unit "6865" (std O), *05*		150
____	24552	UP F3 Diesel ABA Set, CC, *05*		680
____	24556	UP F3 Diesel B Unit "900C," powered, CC, *05*		285
____	24562	Santa Fe F3 Diesel B Unit, powered, *04–05*		300
____	24563	PRR F3 Diesel B Unit, powered, *04–05*		195
____	24570	Santa Fe FT Diesel B Unit, nonpowered, *05*		85
____	24573	Postwar "2383C" Santa Fe F3 Diesel B Unit, nonpowered, *05*		180
____	24574	UP E7 Diesel AA Set, CC, *06*		700
____	24577	UP E7 Diesel B Unit "990," nonpowered (std O), *06*		150
____	24578	UP E7 Diesel B Unit "988," powered, *06*		300
____	24579	NYC E7 Diesel AA Set, CC, *06*		700
____	24582	NYC E7 Diesel B Unit "4105," nonpowered (std O), *06*		150
____	24583	NYC E7 Diesel B Unit "4104," powered, *06*		300
____	24584	Pennsylvania F7 Diesel ABA Set, CC, *06*		900
____	24588	Pennsylvania F7 Diesel B Unit "9643B," powered, *06–07*		300
____	24589	Santa Fe F7 Diesel ABA Set, CC, *06–07*		900
____	24593	Santa Fe F7 Diesel B Unit "332B," powered, *06–07*		300
____	24594	PRR F7 Diesel Breakdown B Unit, RailSounds, *06–07*		160
____	24595	Santa Fe F7 Diesel Breakdown B Unit, RailSounds, *06–07*		270
____	24596	UP E7 Diesel Breakdown B Unit, RailSounds, *06*		270
____	24597	NYC E7 Diesel Breakdown B Unit, RailSounds, *06*		270
____	24928	Franklin Mutual Bank, *08*		60
____	25003	WP Boxcar, orange with silver feather, *05*		30
____	25008	Holiday Boxcar, *06*		50
____	25009	Santa Fe Hi-Cube Boxcar "14064," *06*		30
____	25010	NP Boxcar "48189," *06*		30
____	25011	Angela Trotta Thomas "Santa's Break" Boxcar, *06*		50
____	25014	PRR Boxcar, silver, *10*		30
____	25016	ATSF Boxcar, *10*		35
____	25022	NYC Boxcar, *06*		35
____	25025	Reading Boxcar "106502," *07–08*		35
____	25026	RI Hi-Cube Boxcar, *07–08*		35
____	25030	Billboard Boxcar with catalog art, *06*		20
____	25033	Holiday Boxcar, *07*		50
____	25034	Angela Trotta Thomas "Santa's Workshop" Boxcar, *07*		50
____	25041	UPS Centennial Boxcar #1, *06*		55
____	25042	UPS Centennial Boxcar #2, *07*		55
____	25043	Macy's Parade Boxcar, *06*		40
____	25050	British Columbia Hi-Cube Boxcar "8008," *08*		35
____	25051	Seaboard Boxcar, *08*		35
____	25053	NYC DD Boxcar "75500," *08*		55
____	25054	Angela Trotta Thomas "Christmas Memories" Boxcar, *08*		55

		Exc	Mint
25057	PRR Boxcar "19751," *08*	20	___
25058	Santa Fe Boxcar, *10*	30	___
25059	Democrat 2008 Election Boxcar, *08*	50	___
25060	Republican 2008 Election Boxcar, *08*	50	___
25061	Holiday Boxcar, *08*	55	___
25063	Conrail Boxcar "25063," *09*	40	___
25064	CP Rail Hi-Cube Boxcar, *09–10*	40	___
25066	Holiday Boxcar, *09*	65	___
25067	Angela Trotta Thomas "General Delivery" Boxcar, *09*	65	___
25068	D&H Boxcar, *08 u*	60	___
25077	Milwaukee Road Boxcar "8484," *09–10*	40	___
25087	Wabash Boxcar "6439," *10–11*	40	___
25093	Seaboard Boxcar, *10*	30	___
25095	Texas Special Boxcar, *10*	100	___
25096	CN Boxcar, *10*	45	___
25103	Chessie "Steam Special" Madison Car 2-pack, *05*	100	___
25106	Pennsylvania Madison Car 4-pack, *05*	210	___
25111	Pennsylvania Madison Car 2-pack, *05*	120	___
25114	Lionel Lines Passenger Car 3-pack, *05*	120	___
25118	Lionel Lines Passenger Car 2-pack, *05*	80	___
25121	Southern Streamliner Car 4-pack, *05*	210	___
25126	Southern Streamliner Car 2-pack, *05–06*	120	___
25134	Polar Express Add-on Diner, *05–13*	47	___
25135	Polar Express Add-on Baggage Car, *05–13*	60	___
25148	B&O Madison Car 4-pack, *06–07*	220	___
25153	B&O Madison Car 2-pack, *06–07*	125	___
25156	California Zephyr Streamliner Car 4-pack (std O), *06–07*	220	___
25161	California Zephyr Streamliner Car 2-pack, *06–07*	125	___
25164	UP Madison Car 4-pack, *06–07*	220	___
25169	UP Madison Car 2-pack, *06–07*	125	___
25176	B&O Baggage Car, TrainSounds, *06–07*	160	___
25177	UP Baggage Car, TrainSounds, *06–07*	160	___
25178	California Zephyr Streamliner Baggage Car, TrainSounds, *06–07*	160	___
25186	Polar Express Hot Chocolate Car Add-on, *06–13*	60	___
25187	GN Streamliner Car 4-pack, *07*	220	___
25188	GN Streamliner Car 2-pack, *07*	125	___
25189	GN Streamliner Baggage Car, TrainSounds, *07*	160	___
25196	North Pole Central Vista Dome Car, *07–08*	45	___
25197	North Pole Central Baggage Car, *07–10*	45	___
25198	PRR Vista Dome Car "4058," *07–08*	45	___
25199	PRR Baggage Car "9359," *07–09*	45	___
25404	FEC Champion Aluminum Passenger Car 2-pack, *04–05*	290	___
25407	FEC Champion Aluminum Diner, StationSounds, *04–05*	290	___
25408	Santa Fe El Capitan Aluminum Passenger Car 2-pack, *05*	290	___
25411	Santa Fe El Capitan Aluminum Diner, StationSounds, *05*	290	___

		Exc	Mint
25412	B&O Columbian Aluminum Passenger Car 2-pack, *05*		275
25415	B&O Columbian Aluminum Diner, StationSounds, *05*		290
25416	SP Daylight Aluminum Passenger Car 2-pack, *04–05*		290
25419	SP Daylight Aluminum Diner, StationSounds, *04–05*		290
25420	PRR Trail Blazer Aluminum Passenger Car 2-pack, *04–05*		290
25423	PRR Trail Blazer Aluminum Diner, StationSounds, *04–05*		290
25433	UP City of Denver Aluminum Passenger Car 4-pack (std O), *05*		1000
25438	Union Pacific Aluminum Passenger Car 2-pack, *05*		250
25441	UP City of Denver 18" Aluminum Diner, StationSounds, *05*		290
25446	Santa Fe Super Chief Streamliner Car 2-pack, *05*		150
25450	PRR Congressional Aluminum Passenger Car 4-pack (std O), *06–07*		580
25455	PRR Congressional Aluminum Passenger Car 2-pack (std O), *06–07*		300
25458	PRR Congressional Diner, StationSounds (std O), *06–07*		300
25473	NYC Commodore Vanderbilt Aluminum Passenger Car 2-pack (std O), *06*		300
25476	NYC Commodore Vanderbilt Diner, StationSounds (std O), *06*		300
25496	Texas Special 21" Streamliner Diner, StationSounds (std O), *07*		300
25503	Santa Fe Heavyweight Passenger Car 4-pack (std O), *07–09*		495
25504	Santa Fe Heavyweight Passenger Car 2-pack (std O), *07–09*		265
25505	Santa Fe Heavyweight Diner, StationSounds (std O), *07–09*		295
25506	SP Heavyweight Passenger Car 4-pack (std O), *07*		495
25507	SP Heavyweight Passenger Car 2-pack (std O), *07–08*		265
25508	SP Heavyweight Diner, StationSounds (std O), *07–08*		295
25512	Texas Special Streamliner Car 2-pack (std O), *07*		300
25514	Best Friend of Charleston Coach, *08*		125
25515	MILW Heavyweight Passenger Car 4-pack (std O), *07*		495
25516	MILW Heavyweight Passenger Car 2-pack (std O), *07*		265
25517	MILW Heavyweight Diner, StationSounds (std O), *07–08*		295
25518	PRR Heavyweight Passenger Car 4-pack (std O), *07*		495
25519	PRR Heavyweight Passenger Car 2-pack (std O), *07*		265
25520	PRR Heavyweight Diner, StationSounds (std O), *07–08*		295

Exc   Mint

		Exc	Mint
25521	B&O Heavyweight Passenger Car 4-pack (std O), *07*	495	___
25522	B&O Heavyweight Passenger Car 2-pack (std O), *07*	265	___
25523	B&O Heavyweight Diner, StationSounds (std O), *07–08*	295	___
25559	Phantom IV Passenger Car 4-pack, *08*	380	___
25574	UP Streamlined Diner, StationSounds (std O), *08*	325	___
25575	Polar Express Heavyweight Car 2-pack, *09*	400	___
25576	Polar Express Scale Observation Car, *14*	210	___
25578	Polar Express Heavyweight Add-on Coach, *09*	200	___
25582	New York City Transit R30 Subway 2-pack, *10*	400	___
25586	Polar Express Heavyweight Baggage Car, *10, 12–14*	210	___
25587	Polar Express Abandoned Toy Car, *10, 13*	200	___
25595	New York City Transit R16 Subway 2-pack, *10*	400	___
25598	Polar Express Heavyweight Combination Car, *12–14*	210	___
25600	Postwar Scale CP 18" Aluminum Passenger Car 4-pack, *11*	640	___
25605	Postwar Scale CP 18" Aluminum Passenger Car 2-pack, *11*	320	___
25608	ATSF Super Chief 18" Aluminum Passenger Cars 4-pack, *11*	640	___
25613	ATSF Super Chief 18" Aluminum Passenger Cars 2-pack, *11*	320	___
25616	UP 18" Passenger Car 2-pack (std O), *11*	320	___
25619	PRR "Lindbergh Special" Passenger Car 2-pack, *11*	280	___
25622	Milwaukee Road 18" Passenger Car 4-pack, *11*	640	___
25623	Milwaukee Road 18" Passenger Car 2-pack, *11*	320	___
25630	Polar Express Heavyweight Diner, *12–14*	210	___
25631	Lionel Funeral Set Add-on 2-pack (std O), *13*	300	___
25635	PRR Red Arrow Heavyweight Coach 3-pack (std O), *13*	430	___
25639	PRR Red Arrow Heavyweight Diner (std O), *13*	150	___
25646	ATSF Scout Heavyweight Coach 4-pack (std O), *12–14*	550	___
25651	ATSF Scout Heavyweight Coach 2-pack (std O), *12–14*	280	___
25654	Southern Crescent Limited Heavyweight Passenger Car 2-pack, *12*	550	___
25655	Blue Comet Heavyweight Passenger Car 2-pack, *12–13*	550	___
25656	Alton Limited Heavyweight Passenger Car 2-pack, *12–14*	550	___
25665	Amtrak Acela Passenger Car 2-pack, *12*	500	___
25713	NYC 20th Century Limited Heavyweight Passenger Car 4-pack (std O), *12–14*	550	___
25714	NYC 20th Century Limited Van Twiller Combo Car (std O), *12*	140	___
25715	NYC 20th Century Limited Schuyler Mansion Sleeper Car (std O), *12*	140	___
25716	NYC 20th Century Limited Macomb House Sleeper Car (std O), *12*	140	___

		Exc	Mint
25717	NYC 20th Century Limited Catskill Valley Observation Car (std O), *12*		140
25718	NYC 20th Century Limited Heavyweight Passenger Car 2-pack, *12–14*		280
25719	NYC 20th Century Limited Baggage Car "4857" (std O), *12*		140
25720	NYC 20th Century Limited Poplar Highlands Sleeper Car (std O), *12*		140
25721	NYC 20th Century Limited Heavyweight Diner "655" (std O), *12*		280
25722	D&RGW California Zephyr 18" Aluminum Passenger Car 4-pack, *12*		640
25727	WP California Zephyr 18" Aluminum Passenger Car 2-pack, *12*		320
25731	CB&Q California Zephyr 18" Aluminum Passenger Car 2-pack, *12*		320
25757	Texas Special Passenger Car 2-pack, *13–14*		400
25760	PRR Passenger Car 2-pack, *13–14*		400
25773	SAL Round-roof Boxcar "19297" (std O), *14*		80
25790	NYC 20th Century Limited Heavyweight Diner (std O), *12*		140
25795	Polar Express 10th Anniversary Scale Coach, *14*		215
25796	Polar Express 10th Anniversary Scale Observation Car, *14*		215
25930	John Adams Boxcar, *13*		65
25931	Andrew Johnson Boxcar, *13*		65
25932	Calvin Coolidge Boxcar, *13*		65
25933	Harry S. Truman Boxcar, *13*		65
25934	Santa Fe Reefer 3-Pack, *14*		135
25938	PRR Freight Expansion 3-pack, *13*		155
25942	Western Freight Expansion 3-pack, *13–14*		155
25946	SP Hi-Cube Boxcar "128132," *13*		43
25947	North Pole Express Jack Frost Reefer, *13*		43
25958	Gingerbread Dough Vat Car, *13*		60
25959	Gingerbread 3-D Tank Car, *13*		55
25960	Christmas Tree Transparent Boxcar, *13*		75
25961	Thanksgiving on Parade Boxcar, *13*		60
25962	Thanksgiving Poultry Car, *13*		70
25963	A Christmas Story 30th Anniversary Boxcar, *13*		65
25964	Silver Bell Casting Co. Ore Car, *13*		55
25965	Polar Express 10th Anniversary Boxcar, *13*		65
25977	A Christmas Story Leg Lamp Mint Car, *13*		80
26000	C&O Flatcar with pipes, *01*		20
26001	BP Flatcar "6424" with trailers, *01 u*		150
26002	Monopoly Flatcar with airplane, *00 u*		NRS
26003	Lackawanna Flatcar with NH trailer, *01*		60
26004	Conrail Flatcar "71693" with trailer, *01*		50
26005	Nickel Plate Flatcar with trailer, *01*		55
26006	Southern Flatcar "50126" with trailer, *01*		50
26007	NW Flatcar "203029" with trailer, *01*		50
26008	Farmall Flatcar, *01 u*		NRS
26011	B&M Bulkhead Flatcar, *01 u*		NRS
26013	CN Flatcar with Zamboni ice resurfacing machine, *01*		48

Exc Mint

		Exc	Mint
26014	JCPenney Flatcar, *01 u*		145 ____
26016	Soo Line Flatcar with trucks, *01 u*		NRS ____
26017	Soo Line Flatcar with trailer, *01 u*		NRS ____
26018	Soo Line Flatcar with trailer, *01 u*		NRS ____
26019	Alaska Gondola "13801," *02*		30 ____
26020	Postwar "3830" Flatcar with submarine, *02*		46 ____
26021	CN Flatcar with trailer, *02*		44 ____
26022	PFE Flatcar with trailer, *02*		32 ____
26023	Postwar "6816" Flatcar with bulldozer, *02*		65 ____
26024	Postwar "6817" Flatcar with scraper, *02*		65 ____
26025	Postwar "6407" Flatcar with rocket, *02*		42 ____
26026	Postwar "6413" Flatcar with Mercury capsules, *02*		95 ____
26027	Flatcar "6425" with U.S. Army boat, *02*		30 ____
26028	Conrail Well Car "768121," *02*		40 ____
26030	NYC Flatcar "601172" with stakes and bulkheads, *02*		22 ____
26033	NYC Gondola "6462," *01*		30 ____
26035	LL Flatcar with traffic helicopter, *01*		50 ____
26039	Lions Flatcar with 2 Zamboni ice resurfacing machines, *02*		39 ____
26042	B&O Gondola "601272" with canisters, *03*		19 ____
26043	Seaboard Flatcar "48109" with trailer, *03*		30 ____
26044	NYC Flatcar "506089" with trailers, *03*		35 ____
26045	Postwar "2411" Flatcar with pipes, *03*		40 ____
26046	Postwar "6561" Flatcar with cable reels, *03*		30 ____
26047	Postwar "2461" Flatcar with transformer, *03*		25 ____
26048	Postwar "6801" Flatcar with boat, *02*		29 ____
26049	Speedboat Willie Flatcar with boat, *03*		29 ____
26053	PRR Gondola with canisters, *04 05*		20 ____
26056	Southern Bulkhead Flatcar "50125," *02*		19 ____
26057	SP Flatcar "599365" with tractors, *02*		37 ____
26058	SP Flatcar "599366" with trailer frames, *02*		35 ____
26061	Lionelville Tree Transport Gondola, *03*		40 ____
26062	NYC Gondola "26062" with cable reels, *03*		19 ____
26063	Pennsylvania Bulkhead Flatcar "26063," *03*		19 ____
26064	Rock Island Flatcar "90088" with trailer, *04*		34 ____
26065	REA Flatcar with trailers "TLCX2," *04*		35 ____
26066	Great Northern Bulkhead Flatcar "26066," *04*		20 ____
26067	Southern Gondola "60141" with cable reels, *04*		20 ____
26070	Nestle Nesquik Flatcar "26070" with trailer, *03*		70 ____
26077	LL Flatcar "6424" with autos, girls set add-on, *03*		44 ____
26078	LL Flatcar "6801" with boat, boys set add-on, *03*		40 ____
26080	NJ Medical School Flatcar with handcar, *03*		78 ____
26082	Frisco Auto Carrier, 2-tier, *04*		20 ____
26085	New York Auto Carrier, 2-tier, *05*		27 ____
26086	Alaska Bulkhead Flatcar, traditional, *05*		27 ____
26087	Rock Island Gondola with canisters, traditional, *05*		27 ____
26091	Elvis Flatcar with tractor and trailer, traditional, *05*		60 ____

			Mint
____	**26099**	PRR Auto Carrier "500423," 3-tier, *07*	30
____	**26100**	PRR 1-D Tank Car, *00*	27
____	**26101**	Lenoil 1-D Tank Car "6015," *00*	34
____	**26102**	AEC Glow-in-Dark 1-D Tank Car, *00*	48
____	**26103**	GATX Tank Train 1-D Tank Car "44588," *00*	34
____	**26107**	BP Petroleum 3-D Tank Car, *00 u*	99
____	**26108**	Lionel Visitor's Center Reefer "206482," *00 u*	38
____	**26109**	NYC (P&LE) 1-D Tank Car, *00*	42
____	**26110**	SP 3-D Tank Car "6415," *00–01*	15
____	**26111**	Frisco Tank Car, *00*	29
____	**26112**	Gulf Oil Tank Car, *00*	40
____	**26113**	U.S. Army 1-D Tank Car, *00*	35
____	**26114**	Service Station 1-D Tank Car (SSS), *00*	32
____	**26115**	Lionel Centennial Tank Car, *00 u*	86
____	**26116**	Pepe LePew 1-D Tank Car, *00 u*	90
____	**26118**	NYC Tank Car "101900," *01*	23
____	**26119**	Protex 3-D Tank Car "1054," *00*	29
____	**26120**	KCS Tank Car "1229," *00*	32
____	**26122**	Pioneer Seed Tank Car, *00 u*	NRS
____	**26123**	Santa Fe Stock Car "23002," *01*	35
____	**26124**	C&O 1-D Tank Car "X1019," *01*	30
	26125	Winter Wonderland Clear Tank Car with confetti, *00*	50
____	**26126**	Cheerios Boxcar, *98*	58
	26127	Wellspring Capital Management Tank Car with confetti, *00 u*	214
____	**26131**	Santa Fe 1-D Tank Car "335268," *02*	22
____	**26132**	UP 1-D Tank Car "69015, *02*	40
____	**26133**	Tootsie Roll 1-D Tank Car "26133," *02*	37
____	**26135**	Whirlpool Tank Car, *01*	NRS
____	**26136**	Southern 1-D Tank Car "8790011," *03*	20
____	**26137**	Jack Frost 1-D Tank Car "106," *03*	32
____	**26138**	Nestle Nesquik 1-D Tank Car "26138," *03*	40
	26139	Lionel Lines Stock Car "26139" with horses, *03*	39
____	**26141**	Whirlpool 1-D Tank Car, *03 u*	94
____	**26144**	Chessie System 1-D Tank Car "2233," *02*	22
____	**26145**	Do It Best 1-D Tank Car, *03 u*	80
____	**26146**	Do It Best 1-D Tank Car, *03 u*	95
	26147	Diamond Chemicals 1-D Tank Car "6315," Archive Collection, *02*	33
____	**26149**	Egg Nog 1-D Tank Car, *03*	43
____	**26150**	Alaska 3-D Tank Car "26150," *03*	23
____	**26151**	NP Wood-sided Reefer "26151," *03*	19
____	**26152**	Morton Salt 1-D Tank Car "26152," *04*	40
____	**26153**	Pillsbury 1-D Tank Car "26153," *04*	40
____	**26154**	NYC 3-D Tank Car "26154," *04*	25
____	**26155**	Pennsylvania 1-D Tank Car "26155," *04*	20
	26156	North Western Wood-sided Reefer "15356," *04*	20
	26157	Ballyhoo Brothers Circus Stock Car "26157," *04*	35
____	**26158**	Campbell's Soup 1-D Tank Car, *04*	35
____	**26164**	LL 1-D Tank Car "6315," girls set add-on, *03*	43

Exc Mint

		Exc	Mint
26167	New Haven 1-D Tank Car, traditional, *05*	27	
26168	Conrail 3-D Tank Car, traditional, *05*	27	
26169	Santa Fe Wood-sided Reefer, traditional, *05*	27	
26176	Tidmouth Milk 1-D Tank Car, *05*	35	
26179	GN 3-D Tank Car, *06*	30	
26180	DM&IR 1-D Tank Car "S15," *06*	30	
26181	NYC Wood-sided Reefer, *06*	30	
26193	UP 1-D Tank Car, *07*	15	
26196	Candy Cane 1-D Tank Car, *06*	60	
26197	D&H 1-D Tank Car "55," *07–08*	35	
26198	D&RGW 3-D Tank Car, *07*	30	
26199	WP PFE Wood-sided Reefer "55327," *07*	30	
26200	NKP Boxcar "18211," *98*	35	
26201	Operation Lifesaver Boxcar, *98*	29	
26203	D&H Boxcar "1829," *98*	25	
26204	Alaska Boxcar "10806," *98–99*	35	
26205	Rocky & Bullwinkle Boxcar, *99*	36	
26206	Curious George Boxcar, *99*	40	
26208	Vapor Records Boxcar #2, *98*	48	
26214	Celebrate the Century Stamp Boxcar, *98 u*	97	
26215	AEC Glow-in-the-Dark Boxcar, *98*	86	
26216	Cheerios Boxcar, *98 u*	74	
26218	Quaker Oats Boxcar, *98 u*	415	
26219	Ace Hardware Boxcar, *98 u*	NRS	
26220	Smuckers Boxcar, *98 u*	79	
26222	Penn Central Boxcar "125962," *99*	31	
26223	FEC Boxcar "5027," *99*	31	
26224	D&H Boxcar, *99*	24	
26228	Vapor Records Holiday Boxcar, *99 u*	110	
26230	AEC Glow-in-the-Dark Boxcar #2, *99*	45	
26232	Martin Guitar Lumber Boxcar "9823," *99*	41	
26234	NYC Boxcar, *99*	29	
26235	Valentine Boxcar, *99*	40	
26236	Aircraft Boxcar, *99*	28	
26237	Boy Scout Boxcar, *99*	85	
26238	Detroit Historical Museum Boxcar, *99*	29	
26239	M.A.D.D. Boxcar, *99*	19	
26240	RailBox Boxcar, *99–00*	24	
26241	Norfolk & Western Boxcar, *99–00*	17	
26242	D.A.R.E. Boxcar, *99*	30	
26243	Christmas Boxcar, *99*	35	
26244	Woody Woodpecker Boxcar, *99*	43	
26247	Lionel Lines Boxcar, *99*	38	
26253	Acme Explosives Boxcar, *99 u*	NRS	
26254	Keebler Boxcar, *99 u*	NRS	
26255	NYC Boxcar "200495," *99 u*	30	
26256	Salvation Army Charity Boxcar, *99*	29	
26257	Wheaties Boxcar, *99*	74	
26264	Lionel Station Boxcar, *99*	44	
26265	NYC Pacemaker Boxcar, *00*	30	
26271	AEC Glow-in-the-Dark Boxcar, *99*	55	
26272	Christmas Boxcar, *00*	42	
26275	Boy Scout Boxcar, *00*	55	

		Exc	Mint
____ **26276**	C&O Boxcar "23296," *99–00*		23
____ **26277**	UP Boxcar "491050," *00*		20
____ **26278**	Cap'n Crunch Christmas Boxcar, *99*		629
____ **26280**	Tinsel Town Express Boxcar, music, *00*		50
____ **26284**	Toy Fair Preview Boxcar, *99 u*		725
____ **26285**	NYC Pacemaker Boxcar, *00*		40
____ **26288**	AEC Glow-in-Dark Boxcar, *99*		44
____ **26290**	SP Boxcar, *00*		20
____ **26291**	Pennsylvania Boxcar "47158," *00*		20
____ **26292**	Frisco Boxcar "22015," *00*		20
____ **26293**	Burlington Boxcar, *00*		30
____ **26294**	Centennial Express Boxcar, *00*		NRS
____ **26295**	Trainmaster Boxcar, *99 u*		55
____ **26296**	Service Station Boxcar Set (SSS), *00*		105
____ **26298**	Taz Bobbing Boxcar, *00*		65
____ **26300**	UPS Flatcar with trailers, *04*		50
____ **26301**	UPS Flatcar with airplane, traditional, *05*		53
____ **26302**	Troublesome Truck #1, *05*		35
____ **26303**	Troublesome Truck #2, *05*		35
____ **26305**	SP Auto Carrier, 2-tier, *06*		30
____ **26306**	D&RGW Gondola "56135" with canisters, *06*		30
____ **26307**	Chessie System Bulkhead Flatcar, *06*		30
____ **26308**	Hard Rock Cafe Flatcar with billboards, *06*		55
____ **26309**	Alaska Flatcar with cable reels, *06*		55
____ **26310**	CGW Flatcar "3707" with trailer, *06*		55
____ **26311**	Santa Fe Flatcar with pickups, *06*		60
____ **26317**	AEC Gondola with toxic waste containers		30
____ **26318**	AEC Gondola with toxic waste containers		30
____ **26330**	Gondola with trees and presents, *06*		60
____ **26331**	Lionel Lines Bulkhead Flatcar, *07*		30
____ **26332**	CP Rail Gondola "337061" with canisters, *07*		30
____ **26335**	Domino Sugar Flatcar with trailer, *07–08*		60
____ **26357**	CSX Flatcar "600514" with pipes, *07–08*		50
____ **26366**	REA Flatcar with trailers, *07*		60
____ **26367**	Santa's Egg Nog Flatcar with container, *07*		60
____ **26368**	Gondola with trees and presents, *07*		60
____ **26378**	Conrail Auto Carrier "786414," 2-tier, *08*		35
____ **26379**	PRR Gondola with cable reels, *08–09*		35
____ **26380**	NYC Bulkhead Flatcar, *08*		35
____ **26389**	ATSF Flatcar "108477" with 2 pickups, *08*		60
____ **26390**	ATSF Flatcar with bulkheads, *09–10*		40
____ **26391**	NYC Gondola "263910" with containers, *09*		40
____ **26392**	BNSF Auto Carrier, *09*		40
____ **26400**	C&NW Hopper, *07–08*		35
____ **26401**	NP Ore Car "78540," *08*		35
____ **26410**	Chessie System Hopper "47806," *08*		35
____ **26411**	Lionel Lines Ore Car "2026," *08–09*		35
____ **26412**	Chessie System 4-bay Hopper "60573," *08*		35
____ **26418**	B&M Hopper, *09*		40
____ **26421**	PRR Ore Car, *11*		40
____ **26422**	White Pass Ice Breaker Car, *09*		50
____ **26423**	Soo Line Ore Car, *10*		40
____ **26424**	LV Hopper, *11*		30

		Exc	Mint
26425	UP Hopper, *11*		40 ____
26429	PRR Hopper, *11*		40 ____
26435	B&M Ice Breaker Hopper, *11*		50 ____
26437	CSX Hopper, *11*		40 ____
26439	Central of Georgia Hopper, *11–12*		40 ____
26443	M&StL Ore Car "6700," *11*		40 ____
26445	Polar Hopper with presents, *11–13*		60 ____
26446	Thomas & Friends Troublesome Trucks Christmas 2-pack, *11–13*		70 ____
26448	U.S. Army Gondola with reels, *11*		40 ____
26449	CN Hi-Cube Boxcar "799346," *13*		55 ____
26451	DM&IR Ore Car "28003," *13*		43 ____
26452	PRR Hopper "153935," *13*		43 ____
26457	PRR Ore Car, *12*		40 ____
26473	Lackawanna NS Heritage 2-bay Hopper, *13*		55 ____
26474	NYC NS Heritage Quad Hopper, *13*		55 ____
26477	Monopoly Electric Company Hopper, *13*		65 ____
26481	Boy Scouts of America Christmas Gondola, *13*		65 ____
26488	Hershey's Ice Breakers Hopper, *13*		63 ____
26489	Hershey's Chistmas Bells Boxcar, *13*		65 ____
26491	Pennsylvania Power & Light Gondola with canisters, *13*		43 ____
26492	Area 51 3-D Tank Car, *13*		43 ____
26493	Monopoly Water Works 3-D Tank Car, *13*		65 ____
26494	PRR Truss Rod Gondola with vats, *13*		60 ____
26495	C&NW Poultry Car, *13*		60 ____
26496	Lionelville Aquarium Co. Fish Food Vat Car, *13 14*		60 ____
26497	Bethlehem Steel Depressed Flatcar with reels, *13*		43 ____
26499	CN Hi-Cube Boxcar "799346," *14*		55 ____
26502	UP Bay Window Caboose "6517," *97*		47 ____
26503	ATSF High-Cupola Caboose "7606R," *97*		85 ____
26504	Mobil Oil Square Window Caboose "6257," *97 u*		37 ____
26505	Rescue Unit Caboose, *98*		50 ____
26506	N&W Square Window Caboose "562748," *98*		15 ____
26507	D&H Square Window Caboose "35707," *98*		20 ____
26508	Alaska Square Window Caboose "1081," *98*		28 ____
26511	Quaker Oats Square Window Caboose, *98 u*		48 ____
26513	NYC Emergency Caboose "26505," *99*		47 ____
26515	Lionel Lines Bobber Caboose, *99*		10 ____
26516	Safari Bobber Caboose, *99 u*		10 ____
26519	Christmas Work Caboose "6496," *99*		41 ____
26520	Bethlehem Steel Work Caboose "6130" (SSS), *99*		55 ____
26523	Keebler Cheezit Square Window Caboose, *99 u*		NRS ____
26524	NYC Square Window Caboose "295," *99 u*		20 ____
26526	Santa Fe Square Window Caboose "999471," *01*		30 ____
26527	Christmas Work Caboose with presents, *02*		27 ____
26528	PRR Square Window Caboose "6257," *99*		21 ____
26530	LL Square Window Caboose "6257," *99*		22 ____
26532	NYC Square Window Caboose "296," *00*		20 ____

___ 26533	SP Square Window Caboose, *00*	20
___ 26534	PRR Square Window Caboose "6257," *00*	20
___ 26535	Frisco Square Window Caboose "1700," *00*	20
26536	Centennial Express Square Window Caboose,	
___	*00*	NRS
___ 26537	Lionel Mines Square Window Caboose, *00 u*	45
___ 26539	Whirlpool Square Window Caboose, *00 u*	NRS
___ 26542	ACL Square Window Caboose "069," *01*	31
___ 26543	GN Square Window Caboose "X66," *00–01*	28
___ 26544	Alaska Square Window Caboose "1084," *01*	25
___ 26545	Snap-On Square Window Caboose, *00 u*	NRS
___ 26548	Pioneer Seed Square Window Caboose, *00 u*	NRS
___ 26549	PRR Square Window Caboose "4977947," *01*	20
___ 26550	NYC Square Window Caboose "19293," *01*	20
___ 26551	Chessie System Center Cupola Caboose, *01*	25
26552	Santa Fe Square Window Caboose "999472,"	
___	*01*	25
___ 26553	C&O Center Cupola Caboose "A918," *01*	30
26554	Monopoly Short Line Square Window Caboose,	
___	*00 u*	NRS
___ 26556	NH Center Cupola Caboose, *01*	35
___ 26557	Farmall Square Window Caboose, *01 u*	NRS
___ 26559	N&W Center Cupola Caboose "518408," *01*	20
___ 26560	B&M Square Window Caboose, *01 u*	20
___ 26564	Soo Line Center Cupola Caboose, *01 u*	20
26565	Lionel Employee Square Window Caboose,	
___	*01 u*	139
___ 26566	WP Square Window Caboose "731," *02*	25
___ 26568	NKP Square Window Caboose "1155," *02*	25
___ 26569	Southern Square Window Caboose "252," *02*	25
___ 26570	B&O Square Window Caboose "295," *02*	25
26572	Lionel 20th Century Square Window Caboose,	
___	*00 u*	25
___ 26580	Wabash Square Window Caboose "2805," *03*	22
___ 26581	C&O Square Window Caboose "C-1831," *03*	20
___ 26582	L&N Square Window Caboose "318," *03*	20
___ 26583	PRR Square Window Caboose "477814," *03*	25
___ 26594	Ontario Northland Work Caboose "26594," *03*	25
___ 26595	UP Caboose "26595," *03*	18
___ 26596	NYC Caboose "17716," *04*	25
___ 26597	Great Northern Caboose "X295," *04*	25
___ 26598	UP Caboose "26598," *04*	25
___ 26599	DM&IR Work Caboose "26599," *04*	25
26600	American Fire and Rescue Water Tank Car,	
___	*09–11*	55
___ 26603	LV Depressed Flatcar with reels, *09*	40
___ 26604	Halloween Spooky Grave Gondola, *09*	58
___ 26609	NYC Gondola with Pacemaker canisters	40
___ 26612	Christmas Gifts Gondola, *09*	60
___ 26614	Tupelo Dairy Farms Milk Car, *10–11*	60
___ 26616	UP Bulkhead Flatcar with pipes, *10*	40
26617	B&O Depressed Center Flatcar with	
___	generator, *10*	40
___ 26629	PRR Flatcar with generators	35

Exc   Mint

		Exc	Mint
26638	Pennsylvania Power & Light Flatcar with reels, *11*		40 ___
26639	Cities Service 3-Tier Auto Carrier, *11–12*		40 ___
26640	CN Maple Syrup Barrel Ramp Car, *11–12*		40 ___
26641	Coca-Cola Flatcar with trailer, *11*		70 ___
26642	CN Jet Snowblower, *11–12*		65 ___
26643	D&RGW Jet Snowblower, *11–13*		65 ___
26644	BNSF Flatcar with generator, *11*		40 ___
26645	BNSF Flatcar with trailer, *11*		40 ___
26646	Pennsylvania Power & Light Flatcar with transformer, *11–12*		40 ___
26647	IC Bulkhead Flatcar with pipes, *11*		40 ___
26649	Erie-Lack. Gondola with canisters, *11*		40 ___
26650	M&StL Flatcar with pipes, *11*		40 ___
26651	ATSF Scout Heavyweight Passenger Car 2-pack (std O), *12*		280 ___
26652	NYC Gondola with canisters, *11*		40 ___
26653	PC Flatcar with generator, *11*		35 ___
26654	Boy Scouts Flatcar with Pinewood Derby Kit, *11–13*		75 ___
26660	Coca-Cola Vat Car, *11–14*		60 ___
26661	Reindeer Feed Barrel Ramp Car, *09*		60 ___
26665	Hershey's Special Dark Flatcar with trailer, *11*		60 ___
26666	Boy Scouts Flatcar with trailer, *11*		70 ___
26667	Flatcar with Santa's sleigh, *12*		70 ___
26668	Strasburg Flatcar with wheels, *11*		55 ___
26669	U.S. Navy Flatcar with Shark submarine, *12–13*		60 ___
26673	B&M Flatcar with Milk Tank, *12*		60 ___
26675	Monopoly Auto Loader, *12*		80 ___
26676	Heinz Baked Beans Vat Car, *12*		60 ___
26677	LIRR Gondola with canisters, *12*		40 ___
26679	ATSF Gondola with reels, *12–13*		55 ___
26683	Christmas Track Maintenance Car, *12–13*		67 ___
26685	Flatcar with Santa's plane, *12*		55 ___
26686	Hershey's Cocoa Vat Car, *12–13*		63 ___
26687	Lone Ranger Gondola with gunpowder vats, *12–14*		65 ___
26693	Hershey's Krackel Piggyback Flatcar with trailer, *12–13*		70 ___
26694	Carnegie Science Center Flatcar with submarine, *3*		60 ___
26696	NJ Transit Gondola with wood ties, *12*		75 ___
26699	PRR Flatcar with wheel load," *12–14*		55 ___
26706	Lighted Christmas Boxcar, *00*		47 ___
26707	Lionel Steel Operating Welding Flatcar "1108," *00*		90 ___
26709	Flatcar "6511" with psychedelic submarine, *99*		32 ___
26710	Southern Stock Car, Carsounds, *99*		95 ___
26712	Churchill Downs Horse Car "6473," *99–00*		38 ___
26713	Shay Log Car 3-pack, *99*		105 ___
26714	Westside Lumber Flatcar with logs (std O), *99*		45 ___
26715	Westside Lumber Flatcar with logs (std O), *99*		45 ___
26716	Westside Lumber Flatcar with logs (std O), *99*		45 ___

			Exc	Mint
____	**26717**	Orion Star Boxcar 9600, *OO*		30
____	**26718**	Christmas Boxcar, RailSounds, *OO*		160
____	**26719**	Bobbing Ghost Halloween Boxcar, *OO*		46
____	**26721**	Lionel Lines Coal Dump Car "3379," *OO*		31
____	**26722**	Lionel Lines Log Dump Car "3351," *OO*		31
____	**26723**	Lion Chasing Trainer Gondola "3444," *OO*		49
____	**26724**	Veterans Day Boxcar, *OO*		70
____	**26725**	NYC Jumping Hobo Boxcar "88160," *OO*		38
____	**26726**	T. Rex Bobbing Boxcar, *OO*		41
____	**26727**	San Francisco City Lights Boxcar, *OO*		50
____	**26736**	Lionel Birthday Boxcar, *02 u*		40
____	**26737**	Operating Santa Gondola "6462," *OO u*		65
____	**26738**	Lionel Mines Gondola, *OO u*		NRS
____	**26739**	Santa and Snowman Boxcar, *OO*		46
____	**26740**	Reindeer Car, *OO*		43
____	**26741**	Operating Santa Boxcar, *OO*		50
____	**26743**	Christmas Reindeer Car, *01*		55
____	**26745**	Traveling Aquarium Car "506," *01*		70
____	**26746**	Bobbing Vampire Boxcar, *01*		46
____	**26747**	Halloween Bats Aquarium Car, *01*		75
____	**26748**	T&P Operating Hopper Car "9699," *01*		38
____	**26749**	Alaska Log Dump Car, *01*		29
____	**26751**	Chessie Coal Dump Car, *01*		27
____	**26752**	Christmas Aquarium Car, *01*		55
____	**26753**	Christmas Operating Dump Car, *01*		43
____	**26757**	Operating Barrel Car "35621," *OO*		55
____	**26758**	AEC Nuclear Gondola "719766," *01*		90
____	**26759**	Postwar "3459" Coal Dump Car, *02*		60
____	**26760**	Postwar "3461" Log Dump Car, *02*		60
____	**26761**	AEC Security Caboose 3535, *01*		63
____	**26762**	Postwar "3665" Minuteman Car, *01*		55
____	**26763**	Postwar "6448" Exploding Boxcar, *01*		40
____	**26764**	Bethlehem Steel Operating Welding Car, *01*		75
____	**26765**	Postwar "3370" Sheriff and Outlaw Car, *01–02*	40	49
____	**26766**	Priority Mail Operating Boxcar, *01–02*		32
____	**26768**	Postwar "6520" Searchlight Car, *02*		49
____	**26769**	Santa Fe Crane Car "199793," CC, *03*		255
____	**26770**	Wabash Brakeman Car "3424," *01*		70
____	**26773**	Chessie Searchlight Car, *01*		20
____	**26774**	Santa Fe Log Dump Car, *01*		25
____	**26775**	U.S. Army Searchlight Car, *OO*		50
____	**26776**	U.S. Army Operating Boxcar "26413," *OO*		55
____	**26777**	U.S. Flag Boxcar, *01 u*		250
____	**26779**	Burlington Operating Hopper "189312," *02*		40
____	**26780**	Postwar "3376" Bronx Zoo Giraffe Car, *02*	35	36
____	**26781**	Postwar "3540" Operating Radar Car, *02*		35
____	**26782**	Lenny the Lion Bobbing Head Car, *02*		38
____	**26784**	Stingray Express Aquarium Car, *02*		35
____	**26785**	Flatcar with powerboat, *02*		31
____	**26786**	Lionelville Operating Parade Car, *02*		40
____	**26787**	Erie Jumping Hobo Boxcar, *01–02*		43
____	**26788**	Christmas Music Boxcar, *02*		46

		Exc	Mint
26789	Kiss Kringle Chase Gondola, *02*		35 ___
26790	Lighted Christmas Boxcar, *02*		34 ___
26791	UP Animated Gondola, *02*	40	50 ___
26792	REA Operating Boxcar "6299," *03*		39 ___
26793	Alaska Extension Searchlight Car, *01*		44 ___
26794	Postwar "6352" PFE Ice Car, *01–02*		85 ___
26795	NYC Stock Car "3121," Cattle Sounds, *02*		50 ___
26796	Lionel Farms Poultry Dispatch Car, *01*		55 ___
26797	GN Log Dump Car "60011," *02*		48 ___
26798	Bethlehem Steel Coal Dump Car "26798," *02*		70 ___
26801	Jumping Bart Simpson Boxcar, *04*		44 ___
26802	Simpsons Animated Gondola, *04*		46 ___
26803	Santa Fe Derrick Car "26803," *04*		25 ___
26804	NYC Coal Dump Car "26804," *04*		22 ___
26805	Pennsylvania Log Dump Car "26805," *04*		24 ___
26806	Pillsbury Operating Boxcar "3428," Archive Collection, *04*		40 ___
26807	Blue Chip Line Motorized Animated Gondola, *04*		40 ___
26808	Egg Nog Barrel Car, *04*		55 ___
26809	Santa's Extension Searchlight Car, *04*		42 ___
26810	NYC Operating Searchlight Car, *05*		33 ___
26811	Pennsylvania Coal Dump Car, *05*		33 ___
26812	Santa Fe Log Dump Car, *05*		33 ___
26813	Lionel Lines Derrick Car, *05*		33 ___
26814	NYC Walking Brakeman Car "174226," *05*		40 ___
26815	PRR "Workin' on the Railroad" Boxcar "24255," *05*		42 ___
26816	REA Boxcar, steam TrainSounds, *05*		105 ___
26817	Alaska Boxcar, diesel TrainSounds, *05*		145 ___
26818	Christmas Music Boxcar, *05*		63 ___
26819	Holiday Animated Gondola, *05*		55 ___
26820	Penguin Transport Aquarium Car, *05*		60 ___
26821	NP Moe & Joe Lumber Flatcar, *05*		75 ___
26827	UPS Operating Boxcar "9237," Archive Collection, *05*		63 ___
26828	Tornado Chaser Radar Tracking Car, *05*		63 ___
26829	UPS Holiday Operating Boxcar, *05*		59 ___
26832	Lionel Lines Tender, TrainSounds, *07–08*		105 ___
26833	Wellspring Radar Car, *04*		65 ___
26834	PFE Ice Car "20042" (std O), *05–06*		63 ___
26835	MOW Track Cleaning Car, *05*		140 ___
26836	Halloween Boxcar, SpookySounds, *05*		105 ___
26841	PRR Log Dump Car, *05*		27 ___
26842	NYC Coal Dump Car, *05*		27 ___
26845	Southern Derrick Car, *06*		35 ___
26846	GN Coal Dump Car, *06*		38 ___
26847	C&O Coal Dump Car, *06–07*		80 ___
26848	Lionel Lines Moe & Joe Flatcar, *06*		80 ___
26849	SP Log Dump Car, *06–07*		80 ___
26850	D&RGW Searchlight Car, *06*		75 ___
26851	WM Log Dump Car, *06*		35 ___
26852	Postwar "3562-25" Santa Fe Barrel Car, *06*		75 ___
26853	SeaWorld Aquarium Car, *06*		75 ___

Exc Mint

			Exc	Mint
____	26854	UP Walking Brakeman Car, *06–07*		75
____	26855	Halloween Animated Gondola, *06*		65
____	26856	Christmas Chase Gondola, *06*		65
____	26857	Alien Radar Tracking Car, *06*		65
____	26858	Christmas Music Boxcar, *06*		65
____	26859	Christmas Parade Boxcar, *06*		75
____	26860	B&O Boxcar "466035," steam TrainSounds (std O), *06–07*		75
____	26861	Santa Fe Boxcar, diesel TrainSounds (std O), *06–07*		110
____	26862	Hard Rock Café Boxcar, *06*		35
____	26863	Railway Express Operating Milk Car with platform, *06*		140
____	26864	Domino Sugar Operating Boxcar, *06–07*		40
____	26865	CP Animated Caboose, *06–07*		80
____	26867	Boxcar, AlienSounds, *06–07*		110
____	26868	U.S. Steel Operating Welding Car, *06*		75
____	26869	REA Jumping Hobo Boxcar, *06–07*		70
____	26870	Christmas Dump Car with presents, *06*		80
____	26871	PRR Tender, steam TrainSounds (std O), *06*		105
____	26872	U.S. Army Security Car, *06*		75
____	26876	Missile Firing Trail Car, *06*		75
____	26877	U.S. Army Missile Launch Car, *06–07*		190
____	26888	Weyerhaeuser Timber Co. Log Car		40
____	26889	Weyerhaeuser Timber Co. Log Car		40
____	26891	PRR Coal Dump Car, *05*		30
____	26897	Great Western Flatcar with handcar, *07*		65
____	26898	NYC Log Dump Car, *05*		25
____	26905	Bethlehem Steel Gondola "6462" with canisters, *98*		29
____	26906	SP Flatcar "9823" with Corgi `57 Chevy, *98*		40
____	26908	TTUX Flatcar "6300" with Apple trailers, *98*		70
____	26913	East St. Louis Gondola "9820," *98*		29
____	26920	Union Pacific Die-cast Ore Car "64861," *97*		70
____	26921	Union Pacific Die-cast Ore Car "64862," *97*		55
____	26922	Union Pacific Die-cast Ore Car "64863," *97*		65
____	26923	Union Pacific Die-cast Ore Car "64864," *97*		55
____	26924	Union Pacific Die-cast Ore Car "64865," *97*		55
____	26925	Union Pacific Die-cast Ore Car "64866," *97*		60
____	26926	Union Pacific Die-cast Ore Car, *98*		55
____	26927	Union Pacific Die-cast Ore Car, *98*		55
____	26928	Union Pacific Die-cast Ore Car, *98*		55
____	26929	Union Pacific Die-cast Ore Car, *98*		40
____	26936	Die-cast Tank Car 4-pack, *98*		335
____	26937	Die-cast Hopper 4-pack, *98*		325
____	26938	NYC Reefer, *99*		80
____	26940	Rio Grande Stock Car "37710," *99*		80
____	26946	D&H Semi-Scale Hopper "9642"		85
____	26947	Gulf Die-cast Tank Car, *98*		120
____	26948	P&LE Die-cast Hopper, *98*		65
____	26949	NP Flatcar with trailer "6424-2017," *98*		47
____	26950	NP Flatcar with trailer "6424-2016," *98*		47
____	26951	TTX Flatcar "475185" with PRR trailer, *98*		55
____	26952	J.B. Hunt Flatcar with trailer, *98*		40

		Exc	Mint
26953	J.B. Hunt Flatcar with trailer, *98*		40 ____
26954	J.B. Hunt Flatcar with trailer, *98*		40 ____
26955	J.B. Hunt Flatcar with trailer, *98*		40 ____
26956	C&O Gondola (O27), *98–99*		15 ____
26957	Delaware & Hudson Flatcar with stakes, *98*		20 ____
26971	Lionel Steel 16-wheel Depressed Center Flatcar, *98*		135 ____
26972	Pony Express Animated Gondola, *98*		36 ____
26973	Getty Die-cast Tank Car 3-pack, *98*		270 ____
26974	Getty Die-cast 1-D Tank Car "4003," *98*		80 ____
26975	Getty Die-cast 1-D Tank Car "4004," *98*		90 ____
26976	Getty Die-cast 1-D Tank Car "4005," *98*		80 ____
26977	Sinclair Die-cast Tank Car 3-pack, *98*		275 ____
26978	Sinclair Tank Car UTLX "64026," *98*		105 ____
26979	Sinclair Tank Car UTLX "64027," *98*		85 ____
26980	Sinclair Tank UTLX "64028," *98*		90 ____
26981	Gulf Die-cast Tank Car 2-pack, *99*		165 ____
26985	B&O Die-cast Hopper 2-pack, *99*		160 ____
26987	Chessie System (B&O) Die-cast 4-bay Hopper "235154," *99*		90 ____
26991	Lionelville Ladder Fire Car, *99*		47 ____
26992	NYC Reefer, *99*		75 ____
26993	NYC Reefer, *99*		85 ____
26994	NYC Reefer, *99*		135 ____
26995	Rio Grande Stock Car "37714," *99*		80 ____
26996	Rio Grande Stock Car "37715," *99*		80 ____
26997	Rio Grande Stock Car "37716," *99*		80 ____
27000	C&EI Offset Hopper "97393" (std O), *07*		65 ____
27001	Erie Offset Hopper "28001" (std O), *07*		65 ____
27002	Frisco Offset Hopper "92399" (std O), *07*		65 ____
27003	Chessie System Offset Hopper "234355" (std O), *07*		65 ____
27016	UP PS-2 Covered Hopper "1312" (std O), *07–08*		60 ____
27019	Imco PS-2 Covered Hopper "41001" (std O), *07–08*		60 ____
27022	PC PS-2 Covered Hopper "74217" (std O), *07*		60 ____
27025	NYC PS-2 Covered Hopper "883180" (std O), *07*		60 ____
27029	ATSF Offset Hopper 3-pack (std O), *08–09*		200 ____
27030	Monon Offset Hopper 3-pack (std O), *08–09*		200 ____
27031	MoPac Offset Hopper 3-pack (std O), *08–09*		200 ____
27032	NYC Offset Hopper 3-pack (std O), *08–09*		200 ____
27033	Chessie System PS-2 Hopper 3-pack (std O), *08–09*		180 ____
27034	Nickel Plate Road PS-2 Hopper 3-pack (std O), *08–09*		180 ____
27053	CB&Q ACF 2-bay Covered Hopper "183925" (std O), *08–09*		55 ____
27059	Bakelite Plastics PS-2 Hopper "61445" (std O), *10–11*		70 ____
27061	Clinchfield Freight Car 2-pack (std O), *10*		150 ____
27064	PRR Flatcar with PRR piggyback trailers (std O), *12*		98 ____
27065	SP Flatcar with SP piggyback trailers (std O), *12*		98 ____

		Exc	Mint
____	**27066** IC Flatcar with IC piggyback trailers (std O), *12*		98
____	**27067** C&O Flatcar with REA piggyback trailers (std O), *12*		98
____	**27068** ATSF Flatcar with Santa Fe piggyback trailers (std O), *12*		98
____	**27069** Conrail PS-2 Hopper "878330" (std O), *12–13*		70
____	**27070** N&W Scale Offset Hopper "279850" (std O), *12*		70
____	**27071** CSX 4-Bay Covered Hopper "256300" (std O), *12*		90
____	**27072** C&NW Scale PS-1 Boxcar "7" (std O), *12–13*		70
____	**27073** PRR Scale Offset Hopper 3-pack (std O), *12*		200
____	**27077** L&N Scale Offset Hopper "88494" (std O), *12–13*		70
____	**27078** Frisco Scale 3-Bay Open Hopper "88299" (std O), *12–14*		75
____	**27079** NYC Boxcar, *09*		30
____	**27080** Lionel Vision Boxcar, *14*		55
____	**27081** BN PS-2 Hopper "424796" (std O), *12–13*		70
____	**27082** Grand Trunk 4-Bay Covered Hopper "38111" (std O), *12*		90
____	**27083** RI PS-2 Hopper "500751" (std O), *12–13*		70
____	**27084** Seaboard 8000-gallon 1-D Tank Car "27084" (std O), *12*		70
____	**27085** Wabash PS-2 Hopper "30425" (std O), *12–13*		70
____	**27086** Grand Trunk 60' Boxcar "383575" (std O), *12, 14*		85
____	**27087** CN 60' Boxcar "799424" (std O), *12, 14*		85
____	**27088** MKT PS-5 Gondola "12447" (std O), *12–13*		65
____	**27089** LIRR PS-5 Gondola "6053" (std O), *12*		65
____	**27090** NP 8000-gallon 1-D Tank Car "27090" (std O), *12*		70
____	**27091** WM Scale 3-Bay Open Hopper "85125" (std O), *12*		80
____	**27092** CSX Heritage 60' Boxcar "176740" (std O), *12*		85
____	**27093** Boy Scouts PS-2 Hopper "2013" (std O), *13*		70
____	**27094** BNSF PS-2 Hopper 2-pack (std O), *13–14*		130
____	**27095** KCS PS-2 Hopper 2-pack (std O), *13*		130
____	**27096** C&NW PS-2 Hopper 2-pack (std O), *13*		130
____	**27099** North Pole Central PS-1 Boxcar "125025" (std O), *13*		70
____	**27100** C&NW PS-2CD 4427 Hopper "450669" (std O), *04*		40
____	**27101** Morton Salt PS-2CD 4427 Hopper "504" (std O), *04*		43
____	**27102** Pillsbury PS-2CD 4427 Hopper "3980" (std O), *04*		42
____	**27103** Soo Line PS-2CD 4427 Hopper "70207" (std O), *04*		49
____	**27104** Wabash Cylindrical Hopper "33007" (std O), *03*		43
____	**27105** PC Cylindrical Hopper "884312" (std O), *03*		42
____	**27113** Govt. of Canada Cylindrical Hopper, *04–05*		60
____	**27114** Canadian National Cylindrical Hopper, *04–05*		60
____	**27115** D&H 3-bay ACF Hopper "3454" (std O), *05–06*		65

		Exc	Mint
27116	NYC 3-bay ACF Hopper "886270" (std O), *05–06*		65 ____
27117	DM&IR 3-bay ACF Hopper "5017" (std O), *05*		65 ____
27118	WP 3-bay ACF Hopper "11774" (std O), *05–06*		65 ____
27129	N&W 3-bay ACF Hopper "10717" (std O), *06*		70 ____
27130	PRR 3-bay ACF Hopper "180658" (std O), *06*		70 ____
27131	Conrail 3-bay ACF Hopper "473877" (std O), *06*		70 ____
27132	UP 3-bay ACF Hopper "18137" (std O), *06*		70 ____
27133	MILW PS-2CD Hopper "98606" (std O), *06*		70 ____
27134	BNSF PS-2CD Hopper "414367" (std O), *06*		70 ____
27135	N&W PS-2CD Hopper "71573" (std O), *06*		70 ____
27142	CP Rail 3-bay Hopper, *06*		48 ____
27146	CP Soo 3-bay Hopper, *06*		48 ____
27165	C&O 3-bay Hopper "86912" (std O), *07*		70 ____
27166	Pennsylvania Power & Light 3-bay Hopper "347" (std O), *07*		70 ____
27167	Santa Fe 3-bay Hopper "178558" (std O), *07–08*		70 ____
27168	C&NW 3-bay Hopper "135000" (std O), *07*		70 ____
27169	CN Cylindrical Hopper "370708" (std O), *06*		65 ____
27172	IMC Canada Cylindrical Hopper "45726" (std O), *06*		65 ____
27177	Union Starch Cylindrical Hopper 3-pack (std O), *08*		210 ____
27186	PRR Cylindrical Hopper 3-pack (std O), *08*		210 ____
27187	TH&B Cylindrical Hopper 3-pack (std O), *08*		210 ____
27188	KCS 3-bay Covered Hopper 3-pack, *08*		225 ____
27189	BNSF 3-bay Aluminum Covered Hopper 3-pack, *08*		225 ____
27190	C&NW PS-2CD Covered Hopper 3-pack (std O), *08*		225 ____
27191	RI PS-2CD Covered Hopper 3-pack, *08*		225 ____
27192	NP PS-2CD Covered Hopper 3-pack (std O), *08*		225 ____
27203	NYC DD Boxcar "75509" (std O), *05*		63 ____
27204	Grand Trunk Western DD Boxcar "596377" (std O), *05*		63 ____
27205	D&RGW DD Boxcar "63798" (std O), *05*		40 ____
27206	UP PS 60' Boxcar "960342" (std O), *08*		75 ____
27207	IC PS 60' Boxcar "44295" (std O), *08*		75 ____
27208	ATSF PS 60' Boxcar "37287" (std O), *08*		75 ____
27209	D&RGW PS 60' Boxcar "63835" (std O), *08*		75 ____
27210	PRR PS-1 Boxcar "47009" (std O), *05*		60 ____
27211	MKT PS-1 Boxcar "948" (std O), *05*		60 ____
27212	Rutland PS-1 Boxcar "358" (std O), *05*		60 ____
27213	N&W DD Boxcar, *05*		35 ____
27214	Chessie System PS-1 Boxcar "23770" (std O), *06*		60 ____
27215	Rock Island PS-1 Boxcar "57607" (std O), *06*		60 ____
27216	Erie-Lack. PS-1 Boxcar "84433" (std O), *06*		60 ____
27217	Frisco PS-1 Boxcar "17826" (std O), *06*		19 ____
27218	Santa Fe DD Boxcar "9870" (std O), *06–07*		70 ____
27219	GN DD Boxcar "35449" (std O), *06–07*		70 ____
27220	L&N DD Boxcar "41237" (std O), *06–07*		70 ____

		Exc	Mint
_____ **27221**	CB&Q DD Boxcar "48500" (std O), _06–07_		70
_____ **27224**	CGW PS-1 Boxcar "5180" (std O), _06_		60
_____ **27225**	WP PS-1 Boxcar "19528" (std O), _06_		60
_____ **27226**	NH PS-1 Boxcar "32196" (std O), _06_		60
_____ **27227**	UP PS-1 Boxcar "100306" (std O), _06_		60
_____ **27228**	UP DD Boxcar "454400" (std O), _07_		70
_____ **27229**	Nickel Plate Road DD Boxcar "87100" (std O), _08_		70
_____ **27230**	LV DD Boxcar "8505" (std O), _08_		70
_____ **27231**	GN USRA Double-sheathed Boxcar (std O), _07_		65
_____ **27232**	UP USRA Double-sheathed Boxcar (std O), _07_		65
_____ **27233**	Cotton Belt USRA Double-sheathed Boxcar (std O), _07_		65
_____ **27234**	C&NW USRA Double-sheathed Boxcar (std O), _07_		65
_____ **27235**	Railbox Boxcar "10011" (std O), _07_		55
_____ **27239**	SP DD Boxcar "232852" with auto rack (std O), _08_		75
_____ **27240**	Pere Marquette DD Boxcar with auto rack (std O), _08_		75
_____ **27241**	C&O PS-1 Boxcar "18719," _08_		60
_____ **27242**	LV PS-1 Boxcar "62080," _08_		60
_____ **27243**	SP PS-1 Boxcar "128131," _08_		60
_____ **27244**	GN PS-1 Boxcar "39404," _08_		60
_____ **27246**	SP Double-sheathed Boxcar "133" (std O), _08_		70
_____ **27247**	MP Double-sheathed Boxcar "45111" (std O), _08_		70
_____ **27249**	GN Express Boxcar "2500" (std O), _08_		65
_____ **27250**	CN Express Boxcar "11061" (std O), _08–09_		65
_____ **27251**	WP Express Boxcar "220116," _08–09_		65
_____ **27254**	Western Pacific UP Heritage Boxcar (std O), _09–11, 13_		85
_____ **27259**	PRR ACF Stock Car "128988" (std O), _10_		70
_____ **27260**	ATSF Tool Car "190021" (std O), _09–10_		80
_____ **27261**	D&RGW Double-sheathed Boxcar "3282," _09_		80
_____ **27263**	Polar Railroad PS-1 Boxcar, _09_		70
_____ **27264**	C&O Double-sheathed Boxcar "3502," _10_		80
_____ **27265**	Virginian PS-1 Boxcar "63300" (std O), _10_		70
_____ **27266**	PRR Express Boxcar "504141" (std O), _10_		70
_____ **27267**	SP UP Heritage 60' Boxcar "6991" (std O), _10_		85
_____ **27270**	B&O PS-1 Boxcar 2-pack (std O), _10–11_		140
_____ **27273**	Ann Arbor PS-1 Boxcar "1314" (std O), _11_		70
_____ **27274**	Polar Railroad Double-sheathed Boxcar "1201," _10_		70
_____ **27275**	SP Overnight PS-1 Boxcar "97938" (std O), _10_		70
_____ **27276**	NKP Double-sheathed Boxcar "10580" (std O), _10–11_		70
_____ **27277**	WP Scale PS-1 Boxcar "1925" (std O), _11_		70
_____ **27278**	Cryo-Trans Trans-Mechanical Reefer (std O), _10_		95
_____ **27282**	UP DD Boxcar "163100" (std O), _10_		70
_____ **27283**	Postwar Scale Boxcar 2-pack, _10_		140
_____ **27286**	Postwar Scale 6464 Boxcar 2-pack #2, _11–13_		140
_____ **27287**	LV Boxcar and Caboose Set (std O), _10–11_		160

		Exc	Mint
27289	Jersey Central Boxcar and Caboose Set (std O), *10–11*		160 ___
27291	PRR Double-sheathed Boxcar "539335" (std O), *10–11*		70 ___
27294	ATSF 57' Mechanical Reefer "3006" (std O), *10*		85 ___
27296	Cryo-Trans 57" Mechanical Reefer (std O), *11*		85 ___
27299	WM Steel-sided Reefer (std O), *11*		80 ___
27300	Western Dairy General American Milk Car (std O), *06*		65 ___
27305	GN Steel-sided Reefer "70290" (std O), *06*		65 ___
27306	Santa Fe Steel-sided Reefer "3494" (std O), *06*		42 ___
27307	Pepper Packing Steel-sided Reefer "2330" (std O), *06*		65 ___
27327	BNSF Mechanical Reefer "798870" (std O), *07*		70 ___
27328	SP Fruit Express Reefer "456465" (std O), *07–09*		70 ___
27329	UP Fruit Express Reefer "55962" (std O), *07*		70 ___
27330	Great Northern WFE Reefer "8873" (std O), *07–08*		70 ___
27331	Alderney Dairy General American Milk Car (std O), *07*		65 ___
27332	Freeport General American Milk Car (std O), *07*		65 ___
27345	Milwaukee Road 40' Steel-sided Reefer "5317" (std O), *12*		80 ___
27349	ADM Steel-sided Reefer "7019" (std O), *07*		65 ___
27350	National Car Steel-sided Reefer "2430" (std O), *07*		48 ___
27355	NYC Steel-sided Reefer "2570" (std O), *07–08*		65 ___
27358	Dubuque Steel-sided Reefer "63648" (std O), *07*		65 ___
27361	PFE Wood-sided Reefer "97680" (std O), *06*		65 ___
27364	Erie URTX Steel-sided Reefer (std O), *11*		80 ___
27365	Sheffield Farms Milk Car 2-pack (std O), *08*		140 ___
27368	CNJ 40' Steel-sided Reefer "1443" (std O), *12*		80 ___
27369	Borden's Milk Car 2-pack (std O), *08*		140 ___
27372	PFE Steel-sided Reefer 3-pack (std O), *08*		210 ___
27373	MILW Reefer 3-pack (std O), *08–09*		225 ___
27374	Alaska Reefer 3-pack (std O), *08–09*		225 ___
27375	NP Reefer 3-pack (std O), *08–09*		225 ___
27394	Detroit, Toledo & Ironton Steel-sided Reefer (std O), *09–10*		80 ___
27395	Amtrak ExpressTrak Baggage Car, *10*		75 ___
27396	C&NW UP Heritage Mechanical Reefer (std O), *10*		85 ___
27409	ATSF Water Tank Car "100844" (std O), *09–10*		70 ___
27410	30,000-gallon Ethanol Tank Car 3-pack, sound, *09*		270 ___
27411	30,000-gallon Ethanol Tank Car 3-pack, *09*		210 ___
27412	GATX TankTrain Car "53782" (std O), *10*		70 ___
27418	PRR NS Heritage Unibody Tank Car (std O), *10*		70 ___
27419	Pennsylvania Power & Light 3-bay Open Hopper, *08*		80 ___
27421	MoPac UP Heritage Cylindrical Hopper (std O), *09–11*		80 ___

		Exc	Mint
____ 27422	N&W 3-bay Open Hopper "1776" (std O), *09*		80
27424 ____	Penn Central PS-2 Hopper "440774" (std O), *10–11*		80
27425 ____	Saskatchewan Cylindrical Hopper "397015" (std O), *09*		80
27426 ____	Stourbridge Lion Anthracite Coal Car 2-pack, *09–10*		130
____ 27429	MKT UP Heritage PS2-CD Hopper (std O), *09*		80
____ 27431	CSX B&O Quad Hopper, *11*		50
____ 27432	UP 3-bay Open Hopper "78123" (std O), *10*		80
27433 ____	Conrail NS Heritage Cylindrical Hopper (std O), *10–11*		80
27434 ____	D&RGW UP Heritage PS2-CD Hopper (std O), *10*		80
____ 27435	Polar Railroad Tank Car, *09*		70
27436 ____	Alberta Cylindrical Hopper "396363" (std O), *10*		80
27438 ____	Virginian NS Heritage 3-bay Open Hopper std O), *10*		80
27439 ____	NS Heritage Unibody Tank Car "14098" (std O), *10*		70
____ 27440	BN Cylindrical Hopper "458456" (std O), *10*		80
____ 27441	D&M PS-2 Hopper "6133" (std O), *11*		70
____ 27445	N&W NS Heritage PS-2CD Hopper (std O), *10*		80
27446 ____	Southern NS Heritage Cylindrical Hopper (std O), *10*		80
27448 ____	PRR NS Heritage 3-Bay Open Hopper (std O), *11*		80
27449 ____	UP Boy Scouts 100th Anniversary Cylindrical Hopper (std O), *11*		80
27450 ____	NW NS Heritage 3-Bay Open Hopper (std O), *11*		80
27451 ____	Conrail NS Heritage Unibody 1-D Tank Car (std O), *11*		70
27452 ____	PRR NS Heritage PS-1 Boxcar "45540" (std O), *11*		70
____ 27453	NS Heritage PS-1 Boxcar "67850" (std O), *11*		70
____ 27454	CP Cylindrical Hopper (std O), *11*		80
____ 27455	Amtrak 57' Mechanical Reefer (std O), *11*		85
27456 ____	Soo Line PS2 Covered Hopper "70702" (std O), *11*		70
____ 27457	NS 3-Bay Open Hopper "148028" (std O), *11*		80
____ 27458	UP Mechanical Reefer "457244" (std O), *11*		85
____ 27459	WP DD Boxcar "19404" (std O), *11*		70
27460 ____	M&StL Double-sheathed Boxcar "26002" (std O), *11*		70
27461 ____	UP ACF 4-Bay Covered Hopper "91341" (std O), *11*		85
27462 ____	Chessie ACF 4-Bay Covered Hopper "601878" (std O), *11*		85
27463 ____	PRR ACF 3-Bay Covered Hopper "259900" (std O), *11–12*		80
27464 ____	BNSF ACF 3-Bay Covered Hopper "453403" (std O), *11*		80
27465 ____	CSX 89' Auto Rack Car "604540" (std O), *12–13*		150
____ 27466	UP 89' Auto Rack Car (std O), *12–13*		150

		Exc	Mint
27467	ATSF 89' Auto Rack Car (std O), *12–13*		150 ____
27468	Grand Truck 89' Auto Rack Car (std O), *12–13*		150 ____
27469	Frisco Cylindrical Hopper "81021" (std O), *11*		80 ____
27470	MKT Scale 1-D Tank Car (std O), *11*		70 ____
27471	DT&I 3-Bay Hopper "2070" (std O), *11*		80 ____
27472	CP Scale 1-D Tank Car "9943" (std O), *11*		70 ____
27473	Conrail 89' Auto Rack Car "456249" (std O), *12*		150 ____
27474	SP Cylindrical Hopper "491020" (std O), *11*		80 ____
27475	Lionelville & Western Scale 1-D Tank Car "2747" (std O), *11*		80 ____
27476	U.S. Army Scale 1-D Tank Car (std O), *11*		70 ____
27477	D&RGW 3-Bay Hopper "14901" (std O), *11*		80 ____
27478	NYC 3-Bay Hopper "922158" (std O), *11*		80 ____
27479	BN Scale 3-Bay Open Hopper "516400" (std O), *12*		80 ____
27480	NKP Scale Offset Hopper "33060" (std O), *12*		70 ____
27481	W&LE Scale Offset Hopper "62240" (std O), *12*		70 ____
27482	CP Scale Offset Hopper "354000" (std O), *12*		70 ____
27483	SP Unibody 1-D Tank Car "67200" (std O), *12*		70 ____
27484	D&H Unibody 1-D Tank Car "59" (std O), *12*		70 ____
27485	KCS Unibody 1-D Tank Car "996" (std O), *12*		70 ____
27488	Clinchfield CSX Heritage 3-Bay Open Hopper (std O), *12*		80 ____
27489	Chessie System CSX Heritage 3-Bay Open Hopper (std O), *12*		80 ____
27490	ATSF 3-Bay Covered Hopper "314000" (std O), *12–13*		85 ____
27491	GN 3-Bay Covered Hopper "171400" (std O), *12*		85 ____
27492	CN 89' Auto Rack Car "710833" (std O), *12*		150 ____
27493	CN PS-4 Flatcar with piggyback trailers (std O), *12*		98 ____
27494	CN PS-4 Flatcar with piggyback trailers (std O), *12*		98 ____
27495	CN PS-4 Flatcar with piggyback trailers (std O), *12*		98 ____
27496	Polar PS-2 Covered Hopper "1245" (std O), *12*		70 ____
27497	UP Offset Hopper "74556" (std O), *12*		80 ____
27498	DM&I 8000-gallon 1-D Tank Car "819" (std O), *12*		70 ____
27499	Monon Scale PS-1 Boxcar "916" (std O), *12*		70 ____
27510	WP PS-4 Flatcar "2001" (std O), *05–06*		53 ____
27511	P&LE PS-4 Flatcar "1154" (std O), *05–06*		35 ____
27512	Reading PS-4 Flatcar "9314" (std O), *05*		53 ____
27513	UP 40' Flatcar "51219" (std O), *06*		55 ____
27514	CP 40' Flatcar "307401" (std O), *06*		55 ____
27515	Pennsylvania 40' Flatcar "473567" (std O), *06*		55 ____
27516	N&W 40' Flatcar "32900" (std O), *06*		55 ____
27517	NP PS-4 Flatcar "62829" with trailers (std O), *06*		85 ____
27518	C&NW PS-4 Flatcar "44503" with trailers (std O), *06*		85 ____
27519	UP PS-4 Flatcar "53007" with trailers (std O), *06*		85 ____

Exc Mint

		Exc	Mint
____ 27520	Coe Rail Husky Stack Car "5540" (std O), *06*		85
27521	Santa Fe Husky Stack Car "254220"		
____	(std O), *06*		85
____ 27537	UP Flatcar with wood load, *06*		39
27541	NYC 40' Flatcar "496299" with load		
____	(std O), *07*		63
27542	NH 40' Flatcar "17808" with load (std O),		
____	*07–08*		70
27543	ATSF 40' Flatcar "191549" with load (std O),		
____	*07–08*		70
27544	GT 40' Flatcar "64301" with load (std O),		
____	*07–08*		70
27545	REA PS-4 Flatcar "81003" with trailers		
____	(std O), *07–08*		85
27546	Greenbrier Husky Stack Car "1993"		
____	(std O), *07*		85
27552	Arizona & California Husky Stack Car		
____	(std O), *07*		85
27562	NYC PS-4 Flatcar "506075" with trailers		
____	(std O), *07–08*		85
27563	Lackawanna PS-4 Flatcar "16540" with		
____	trailers (std O), *07*		85
27564	Milwaukee Road PS-4 Flatcar with trailers		
____	"64074" (std O), *07–08*		85
____ 27583	UP 40' Flatcar "59292" with load (std O), *08*		70
27584	Reading Flatcar with covered load (std O),		
____	*08–09*		70
27585	B&M 40' Flatcar "33773" with stakes (std O),		
____	*08–09*		65
____ 27586	Cass Scenic Skeleton Log Car 3-pack, *07*		170
27587	Birch Valley Lumber Skeleton Log Car		
____	3-pack, *07*		170
27594	Wabash PS-4 Flatcar with stakes (std O),		
____	*08–09*		65
____ 27600	RI Bay Window Caboose "17070" (std O), *07*		90
27601	MILW Extended Vision Caboose "992300"		
____	(std O), *07*		90
27603	MP UP Heritage Ca-4 Caboose "2891"		
____	(std O), *08*		95
____ 27604	UP Caboose "3881" (std O), *08*		90
27605	Pere Marquette Northeastern Caboose "A986"		
____	(std O), *08*		90
____ 27606	LL Northeastern Caboose "4679" (std O), *08*		90
____ 27607	Monongahela NS Heritage Caboose (std O), *12*		95
____ 27608	WM Caboose "1863" (std O), *08*		85
____ 27609	B&O Caboose "C-2445" (std O), *07*		90
____ 27612	WP Bay Window Caboose "446" (std O), *08*		90
____ 27615	NYC Bay Window Caboose "20383" (std O), *07*		90
27617	D&H Bay Window Caboose "35725"		
____	(std O), *08*		90
27618	MKT UP Heritage Ca-4 Caboose "8891"		
____	(std O), *08*		95
27619	WP UP Heritage Ca-4 Caboose "3891"		
____	(std O), *08*		95
27623	N&W Northeastern Caboose "500837"		
____	(std O), *09*		90
____ 27624	D&RGW UP Heritage CA-4 Caboose (std O), *09*		95
____ 27625	C&NW UP Heritage CA-4 Caboose (std O), *09*		95

		Exc	Mint
27626	SP UP Heritage CA-4 Caboose (std O), *09*		95 _____
27628	Wabash Northeastern Caboose "02222" (std O), *09–10*		90 _____
27629	C&O Northeastern Caboose (std O), *10*		90 _____
27630	Virginian NS Heritage CA-4 Caboose (std O), *10*		95 _____
27631	NS Heritage CA-4 Caboose (std O), *10*		95 _____
27633	UP CA-3 Caboose (std O), *10*		95 _____
27634	ATSF Extended Vision Caboose (std O), *10*		85 _____
27635	B&O I-12 Caboose (std O), *10*		85 _____
27636	NKP Northeastern Caboose (std O), *10–11*		85 _____
27638	Southern NS Heritage CA-4 Caboose (std O), *10–11*		95 _____
27639	N&W NS Heritage CA-4 Caboose (std O), *10*		95 _____
27640	Clinchfield Northeastern CA-3 Caboose, *10–11*		90 _____
27642	Virginian Scale Caboose with smoke, *10–13*		90 _____
27645	UP Boy Scouts 100th Anniversary Ca-3 Caboose (std O), *11*		95 _____
27648	PRR NS Heritage Ca-3 Caboose (std O), *11*		95 _____
27649	Baldwin Locomotive Works I-12 Caboose "6000" (std O), *12–13*		85 _____
27650	CSX Herltage Scale Bay Window Caboose "2510" (std O), *12*		90 _____
27651	B&O CSX Heritage I-12 Caboose (std O), *11*		90 _____
27652	CSX Heritage Chessie System Scale Caboose (std O), *12*		90 _____
27653	Family Lines CSX Heritage Ca-4 Caboose (std O), *11*		90 _____
27654	CSX/Clinchfield Scale Bay-Window Caboose (std O), *12*		90 _____
27655	WM CSX Heritage Extended Vision Caboose (std O), *11*		90 _____
27658	Pennsylvania Power & Light Work Caboose (std O), *11*		80 _____
27659	Bethlehem Steel Work Caboose (std O), *11*		80 _____
27660	UP George Bush Extended Vision Caboose (std O), *11*		90 _____
27661	KCS Extended Vision Caboose (std O), *11*		90 _____
27662	GTW Northeastern Caboose (std O), *11*		90 _____
27663	IC Extended Vision Caboose (std O), *11*		90 _____
27664	Lionel & Western Northeastern Caboose (std O), *11–12*		90 _____
27665	BN Bicentennial Extended Vision Caboose (std O), *11*		90 _____
27666	NH Scale Northeastern Caboose "C-666" (std O), *12*		90 _____
27667	UP Scale Ca-4 Caboose "3857" (std O), *12–13*		95 _____
27668	UP Scale Ca-3 Caboose "3779" (std O), *12–13*		95 _____
27669	PC Scale Northeastern Caboose "18420" with smoke (std O), *12–13*		90 _____
27670	CP Scale Northeastern Caboose "400501" (std O), *12–13*		90 _____
27671	West Side Lumber Scale Work Caboose "8" (std O), *12*		80 _____
27672	Weyerhaeuser Timber Scale Work Caboose "12" (std O), *12–13*		80 _____

		Exc	Mint
27673	NYC Scale Northeastern Caboose "20090" (std O), *12*		90
27674	Elk River Lumber Work Caboose "6" (std O), *12, 14*		80
27676	CN Wood-Sided Caboose (std O), *12*		90
27677	UP Work Caboose "907306" (std O), *12*		80
27678	ATSF Wood-Sided Caboose "1790" (std O), *12*		85
27679	NP Wood-Sided Caboose "1282" (std O), *12*		85
27680	GN Wood-Sided Caboose "X499" (std O), *12*		85
27681	Southern NS Heritage Caboose (std O), *12*		95
27682	Conrail NS Heritage Caboose (std O), *12*		95
27683	Erie NS Heritage Caboose (std O), *12, 14*		95
27684	Illinois Terminal NS Heritage Caboose (std O), *12, 14*		95
27685	Central of Georgia NS Heritage Caboose (std O), *12*		95
27686	LV NS Heritage Caboose (std O), *12*		95
27687	Reading NS Heritage Caboose (std O), *13–14*		95
27688	NYC NS Heritage Caboose (std O), *13*		95
27689	Wabash NS Heritage Caboose (std O), *13–14*		95
27690	Virginian NS Heritage Caboose (std O), *13*		95
27691	PRR NS Heritage Caboose (std O), *12*		95
27692	N&W NS Heritage Caboose (std O), *12*		95
27693	CNJ NS Heritage Caboose (std O), *13–14*		95
27694	NS Heritage Caboose (std O), *12*		95
27695	DL&W NS Heritage Caboose (std O), *13–14*		95
27696	Savannah & Atlanta NS Heritage Caboose (std O), *13–14*		95
27697	Nickel Plate Road NS Heritage Caboose (std O), *12*		95
27698	Interstate NS Heritage Caboose (std O), *12*		95
27699	PC NS Heritage Caboose (std O), *13*		95
27702	Maersk Husky Stack Car 2-pack (std O), *09*		225
27705	ATSF Wedge Plow Flatcar "191369" (std O), *09*		90
27706	ATSF Idler Flatcar "191852" with load (std O), *09*		75
27707	UP Husky Stack Car 2-pack (std O), *09–10*		225
27710	No. 6464 Variation Boxcar 2-pack #2, *09*		110
27767	Santa Fe Passenger 4-pack, *11–12*		240
27771	Postwar "6572" REA Reefer, *11–13*		60
27772	Santa Fe Baggage Car and Diner 2-pack, *11–12*		120
27775	Postwar "2414" Santa Fe Blue-stripe Coach, *11–13*		60
27776	No. 6464 Variation Boxcar 2-pack #3, *11*		105
27779	Postwar Archive UP Caboose "8561," *11–12*		48
27791	Archive 6464-50 M&StL Boxcar, *12*		55
27792	Archive Pastel Freight Car 3-pack, *12*		170
27800	B&M Gondola with coke containers, *09–11*		80
27816	D&RGW Flatcar "22177" with pipes, *09–10*		80
27820	Wabash PS-4 Flatcar with piggyback trailers (std O), *09–10*		98
27824	MILW 40' Flatcar with metal pipes (std O), *10*		80
27825	West Side Lumber Skeleton Log Car, *11*		70

		Exc	Mint
27826	CP Skeleton Log Car 2-pack (std O), *10*		133 ___
27827	UP Bathtub Gondola "28081" (std O), *10*		65 ___
27828	CN Bathtub Gondola "193140" (std O), *10*		65 ___
27829	WM Skeleton Log Car 2-pack, *10*		133 ___
27834	Pere Marquette PS-5 Gondola "18400," *11*		70 ___
27835	P. Bunyan Lumber Skeleton Log Car, *11–12*		70 ___
27836	Elk River Lumber Skeleton Log Car "11203" (std O), *11*		70 ___
27837	B&M PS-4 Flatcar with bulkheads (std O), *10–11*		80 ___
27838	PRR PS-4 Flatcar with bulkheads (std O), *10*		80 ___
27840	Polar Railroad PS-4 Flatcar with trailers, *10*		98 ___
27841	CSX Bathtub Gondola 2-pack (std O), *11*		130 ___
27842	UP Scale Flatcar with bulkheads "15775" (std O), *11*		70 ___
27843	WP Scale PS-5 Gondola "6774" (std O), *11*		70 ___
27844	BNSF Bathtub Gondola 3-pack (std O), *10*		200 ___
27848	Virginian NS Heritage 60' Boxcar (std O), *11*		85 ___
27849	Southern NS Heritage 60' Boxcar (std O), *11*		85 ___
27850	CSX 60' Boxcar "196911" (std O), *11*		85 ___
27851	BNSF Bathtub Gondola 2-pack, *11*		130 ___
27854	B&O Double-sheathed Boxcar "196500" (std O), *11*		70 ___
27855	NYC 60' DD Boxcar "53423" (std O), *11*		85 ___
27856	KCS PS-1 Boxcar "18741" (std O), *11*		70 ___
27857	PRR DD Boxcar "81919" (std O), *11, 14*		75 ___
27858	MP DD Boxcar "90103" (std O), *11*		70 ___
27860	Sugar Creek Lumber Skeleton Log Car "1749" (std O), *11*		70 ___
27863	Merrill & Ring Lumber Skeleton Log Car, *11–12*		70 ___
27868	NS Bathtub Gondola 2-pack (std O), *11*		130 ___
27871	NS 60' Boxcar "499646" (std O), *11*		85 ___
27872	Polar Hot Cocoa Milk Car, *11, 13*		70 ___
27873	Polar Reindeer Stock Car, *11, 13*		70 ___
27874	Grove's Mortuary Double-sheathed Boxcar (std O), *11*		70 ___
27875	NYC DD Boxcar "45395" (std O), *11*		70 ___
27876	State of Maine PS-1 Boxcar "5141" (std O), *11*		70 ___
27077	NH DD Boxcar "40510" (std O), *11*		70 ___
27882	Southern ACF 40-ton Stock Car "45655" (std O), *11*		70 ___
27883	T&P ACF 40-ton Stock Car "24042" (std O), *11*		70 ___
27884	RI ACF 40-ton Stock Car "77601" (std O), *11*		70 ___
27885	ATSF ACF 40-ton Stock Car "60390" (std O), *11*		70 ___
27886	GN PS-1 Boxcar "11310" (std O), *11*		70 ___
27887	D&RGW PS-5 Gondola "56316" with covers (std O), *11*		65 ___
27888	LIRR 40' Flatcar with wheels (std O), *11*		70 ___
27889	Erie 40' Flatcar "6361" with wheels (std O), *11*		70 ___
27890	L&N 40' Flatcar "22269" with wheels (std O), *11*		70 ___

			Exc	Mint
27891	NKP Heritage PS-4 Flatcar with trailers (std O), *11*			98
27892	Conrail PS-5 Gondola "612690" with covers (std O), *11*			65
27893	GTW PS-1 Boxcar "516650" (std O), *11*			70
27894	C&O PS-5 Gondola "362600" with covers (std O), *11*			65
27895	ATSF PS-4 Bulkhead Flatcar "90085" (std O), *11*			80
27896	CP 40' Flatcar with pipe load (std O), *11*			80
27899	UP Scale PS-1 Boxcar "196889" (std O), *12*			70
27903	Sager Place Observation Car, *09*			65
27912	Postwar "2445" Elizabeth Coach, *08*			60
27917	Postwar "2550" Baggage-Mail Rail Diesel Car, nonpowered, *13*			70
27928	UP Boy Scouts 100th Anniversary PS-1 Boxcar (std O), *11*			70
27929	Postwar Nos. 2484/2485 UP Passenger Car 2-pack, *12–13*			120
27935	Postwar "6820" Aerial Missile Transport Car, *13*			60
27941	Postwar "3854" Merchandise Car, *12*			75
27946	Postwar "6050-25" Christmas Savings Boxcar, *13*			55
27947	Postwar "6473-25" Reindeer Transport Car, *13*			60
27948	Postwar "6464-25" Great Northern Christmas Boxcar, *13*			60
27949	Postwar "3854-25" PRR Christmas Merchandise Car, *13*			75
27953	Reading PS-2 Hopper 2-pack (std O), *13–14*			140
27962	L&N PS-2 Hopper 2-pack (std O), *13–14*			140
27965	P&WV Offset Hopper 3-pack (std O), *13–14*			210
27969	N&W Offset Hopper 3-pack (std O), *13–14*			210
27973	C&O Offset Hopper 3-pack (std O), *13–14*			210
27977	GN Offset Hopper 3-pack (std O), *13–14*			210
27981	PRR USRA Double-sheathed Boxcar (std O), *13*			70
27982	SP USRA Double-sheathed Boxcar (std O), *13*			70
27983	UP USRA Double-sheathed Boxcar (std O), *13–14*			70
27984	Procor 30,000-gallon 1-D Tank Car 3-pack (std O), *13*			240
27988	UTLX 30,000-gallon 1-D Tank Car 3-pack (std O), *13*			240
27992	ADM 30,000-gallon 1-D Tank Car 3-pack (std O), *13*			240
27996	ACFX 30,000-gallon 1-D Tank Car 3-pack (std O), *13*			240
28000	C&NW 4-6-4 Hudson Locomotive "3005," *99*			205
28004	B&O 4-4-2 E6 Atlantic Locomotive, traditional, *99–00*			410
28005	PRR 4-4-2 E6 Atlantic Locomotive, traditional, *99–00*			345
28006	ATSF 4-4-2 E6 Atlantic Locomotive, traditional, *99–00*			285
28007	NYC 4-6-4 Hudson Locomotive "5406," *99*			380
28008	C&O 4-6-4 Hudson Locomotive "306," *99*			345

		Exc	Mint
28009	Santa Fe 4-6-4 Hudson Locomotive "3463," *99*		330 ____
28011	C&O 2-6-6-6 Allegheny Locomotive "1601," *99*		1800 ____
28012	4-6-4 Commodore Vanderbilt Locomotive, red, *00 u*		1700 ____
28013	NH 4-6-2 Pacific Locomotive "1335," *99*		325 ____
28014	NYC 4-6-2 Pacific Locomotive "4930," *99*		305 ____
28015	Santa Fe Pacific 4-6-2 Pacific Locomotive "3449," *99*		340 ____
28016	Southern 4-6-2 Pacific Locomotive "1407," *99*		345 ____
28017	Case Cutlery 4-6-2 Pacific Locomotive, *99 u*		313 ____
28018	Reading 4-6-0 Camelback Locomotive "571," CC, *01*		495 ____
28020	Lionel Lines 4-6-2 Pacific Locomotive "3344," *99*		250 ____
28022	West Side Lumber Shay Locomotive "800," *99*		810 ____
28023	PRR K4 4-6-2 Pacific Locomotive "3755," CC, *99*		375 ____
28024	4-6-4 Commodore Vanderbilt Locomotive, blue, *00 u*		1663 ____
28025	PRR K4 4-6-2 Pacific Locomotive, traditional, *99*		330 ____
28026	LL 4-6-2 Pacific Locomotive, CC, *99*		325 ____
28027	NYC 4-6-4 Hudson Locomotive "5413," *00*		590 ____
28028	Virginian 2-6-6-6 Allegheny Locomotive "1601," *99*		1318 ____
28029	UP 4-8-8-4 Big Boy Locomotive "4006," *99–00*		1500 ____
28030	NYC 4-6-4 Hudson Locomotive "5450," gray, CC, *00*		315 ____
28032	B&O 4-6-2 Pacific Locomotive, CC, *00*		315 ____
28033	B&O 4-6-2 Pacific Locomotive, traditional, *00*		195 ____
28034	UP 4-6-2 Pacific Locomotive, CC, *00*		310 ____
28035	UP 4-6-2 Pacific Locomotive, traditional, *00*		210 ____
28036	SP 2-8-0 Consolidation Locomotive "2685," CC, *00–01*		270 ____
28037	SP 2-8-0 Consolidation Locomotive "2686," traditional, *00–01*		295 ____
28038	UP 2-8-0 Consolidation Locomotive "324," CC, *00–01*		315 ____
28039	UP 2-8-0 Consolidation Locomotive "326," traditional, *00–01*		240 ____
28051	B&O 2-8-8-4 EM-1 Articulated Locomotive "7617," *00*		970 ____
28052	N&W 2-6-6-4 Class A Locomotive "1218," *00*		870 ____
28055	GN 4-6-4 Hudson Locomotive "1725," traditional, *00–01*		170 ____
28057	Southern 4-8-2 Mountain Locomotive "1491," CC, *00*		690 ____
28058	NH 4-8-2 Mountain Locomotive "3310," CC, *00*		670 ____
28059	WP 4-8-2 Mountain Locomotive "179," CC, *00*		630 ____
28062	LL Gold-plated 700E J-1E 4-6-4 Hudson Locomotive, display case, *00*		1050 ____
28063	PRR T-1 4-4-4-4 Duplex Locomotive "5511," CC, *00*		910 ____
28064	UP Challenger Coal Tender "3985," CC, *00 u*	1350	1800 ____

			Exc	Mint
____	**28065**	NYC Hudson 4-6-4 Locomotive "5412," RailSounds, *00*		290
____	**28066**	B&O President Polk 4-6-2 Locomotive, CC, *01*		750
____	**28067**	Erie 4-6-2 Locomotive "2934," CC, *01*		570
____	**28068**	D&RGW 4-6-4 Hudson Locomotive, traditional, *01 u*		300
____	**28070**	SP Daylight 4-4-2 Atlantic Locomotive "3000," CC, *01*		425
____	**28071**	NP 4-4-2 Atlantic Locomotive "604," CC, *01*		415
	28072	NYC 4-6-4 Hudson J3a Locomotive "5444," CC, *01*		790
____	**28074**	NP 2-8-4 Berkshire Locomotive "759," CC, *01*		640
	28075	C&O 2-6-6-2 Locomotive "1521," CC, *01*		930
	28076	NKP 2-6-6-2 Locomotive "921," CC, *01*		960
	28077	UP 4-6-6-4 Challenger Locomotive "3983," CC, *01*		680
____	**28078**	PRR 2-10-4 J1a Locomotive "6496," CC, *01*		880
____	**28079**	C&O 2-10-4 Class T Locomotive "3004," CC, *01*		882
____	**28080**	NYC 0-8-0 Locomotive "7745," CC, *01–02*		540
____	**28081**	C&O 0-8-0 Locomotive "75," CC, *01–02*		520
	28084	NYC Dreyfuss Hudson 4-6-4 Locomotive "5452," CC, *01–02*		790
	28085	N&W 2-8-8-2 Y6b Class Locomotive "2200," CC, *03*		1207
	28086	PRR H9 Consolidation Locomotive "1111," CC, *01*		480
____	**28087**	UP Auxiliary Tender, yellow, CC, *01*		210
____	**28088**	N&W Auxiliary Water Tender, CC, *01–02*		200
	28089	PRR 4-4-4-4 T-1 Duplex Locomotive "5511," 2-rail, *00*		1150
	28090	UP Challenger Oil Tender "3977," 2-rail, *00 u*		1800
	28098	NYC 4-6-0 10-wheel Locomotive "1916," CC, *01–02*		520
____	**28099**	UP Challenger Oil Tender "3977," CC, *00 u*		1700
____	**28200**	D&H U30C Diesel "702," CC (SSS), *02*		375
____	**28201**	UP SD90MAC Diesel "8049," *03*		345
____	**28202**	Conrail SD80MAC Diesel 7203," *03*		325
____	**28203**	CSX SD80MAC Diesel "803," *03*		325
____	**28204**	NS SD80MAC Diesel "7201," *03*		345
____	**28205**	Chessie System SD9 Diesel "1833," CC, *03*		230
____	**28207**	Erie-Lackawanna U33C Diesel "3304," CC, *02*		355
____	**28208**	BN U33C Diesel "5734," CC, *02*		355
____	**28211**	CP SD90MAC Diesel "9107," *03*		300
____	**28213**	Amtrak GE Dash 8 Diesel "516," CC, *02*		300
____	**28214**	BNSF GE Dash 8 Diesel "582," CC, *02*		325
____	**28215**	B&O GP30 Diesel "6939," CC, *02*		315
____	**28216**	Reading GP30 Diesel "5518," CC, *02*		315
____	**28217**	Rio Grande GP30 Diesel "3013," CC, *02*		315
	28218	Lehigh Valley Alco C420 Switcher "407," CC, *04*		325
____	**28219**	Seaboard Alco C420 Switcher "136," CC, *04*		300
____	**28222**	Santa Fe Dash 9 Diesel "605" CC, *05*		250
____	**28223**	BNSF SD70MAC Diesel "9433," CC, *05*		250
____	**28224**	Jersey Central SD40-2 Diesel "3067," CC, *04*		350
____	**28225**	SPSF SD40T-2 Diesel "8521," CC, *04–05*		430

		Exc	Mint
28226	NS SD80MAC Diesel "7204," CC, *04–05*	430	___
28227	UP SD70MAC Diesel "4979," CC, *04*	375	___
28228	C&NW Dash 9-44CW Diesel "8669," CC, *03*	350	___
28229	SP Dash 9-44CW Diesel "8132," CC, *03*	350	___
28230	Amtrak Dash 8 Diesel "505," CC, *04*	295	___
28235	Great Northern U33C Diesel "2543," CC, *05*	455	___
28237	Reading U30C Diesel "6301," CC, *05*	455	___
28239	Union Pacific SD70 Diesel, TMCC, *04*	360	___
28241	C&NW U30C Diesel "935," CC, *06*	455	___
28242	SP U33C Diesel "8773," CC, *06*	475	___
28243	LIRR Alco C420 Hi-nose Switcher "206," CC, *06*	420	___
28244	N&W Alco C420 Hi-nose Switcher "417," CC, *06–07*	420	___
28245	Chessie System SD40T-2 Diesel "7617," RailSounds, *06*	265	___
28246	Chessie System SD40T-2 Diesel "7618," nonpowered (std O), *06*	160	___
28247	Rio Grande SD40T-2 Diesel "5348," RailSounds, *06*	265	___
28248	Rio Grande SD40T-2 Diesel "5349," nonpowered (std O), *06*	160	___
28250	N&W Alco C420 Hi-nose Switcher "416," nonpowered (std O), *06–07*	160	___
28251	LIRR Alco C420 Hi-nose Switcher "206," nonpowered (std O), *06*	160	___
28252	SP U33C Diesel "8774," nonpowered (std O), *06*	160	___
28253	C&NW U30C Diesel "936," nonpowered (std O), *06*	160	___
28255	UP SD40T-2 Diesel "4551," traditional, CC, *07–08*	265	___
28256	UP SD40T-2 Diesel "4596," nonpowered (std O), *07*	170	___
28257	NS SD40-2 Diesel "3340," CC, *06*	430	___
28258	NS SD40-2 Diesel "3341," nonpowered (std O), *06*	170	___
28259	CN SD40-2 Diesel "5383," CC, *06*	430	___
28260	CN SD40-2 Diesel "5384," nonpowered (std O), *06*	170	___
28261	UP (MP) SD70ACe Diesel "1982," CC, *07*	450	___
28262	UP (WP) SD70ACe Diesel "1983," CC, *07*	450	___
28263	UP (MKT) SD70ACe Diesel "1988," CC, *07*	450	___
28264	UP "Building America" SD70ACe Diesel "8348," CC, *07*	450	___
28265	MILW U30C Diesel "5657," CC, *07*	455	___
28266	MILW U30C Diesel "5657," nonpowered (std O), *07–08*	170	___
28267	Conrail U30C Diesel "6837," CC, *07*	455	___
28268	Conrail U30C Diesel "6838," nonpowered (std O), *07–08*	170	___
28269	ATSF Dash 8-40BW Diesel "562," CC, *08*	500	___
28270	ATSF Dash 8-40CW Diesel "563," nonpowered, *08*	220	___
28272	"I Love USA" SD60 Diesel "1776," traditional, *06*	250	___
28279	UP SD70ACe Diesel "1989," CC, *07*	450	___

		Mint
28280	UP (C&NW) SD70ACe Diesel "1995," CC, 07	450
28281	UP (SP) SD70ACe Diesel "1996," CC, 07	450
28283	UP "Building America" SD70AC3 Diesel, nonpowered (std O), 07	170
28284	Ferromex SD70ACe Diesel "4011," CC, 08	495
28287	KCS SD70ACe Diesel "4050," CC, 08	495
28292	Chessie System U30C Diesel "3312," CC, 02	300
28293	Santa Fe U28CG Diesel "354," CC, 02	375
28295	Conrail LionMaster SD80MAC Diesel, nonpowered, 08	200
28296	UP AC6000 Diesel "7526," CC, 08	660
28297	SP GP9 Diesel "446," CC, 10	390
28298	CSX AC6000 Diesel "608," CC, 08	660
28299	CSX AC6000 Diesel "609," nonpowered, 08	220
28300	NS Dash 9 Diesel "9607," nonpowered, 08	220
28302	BNSF SD70ACe Diesel "9380," CC, 08	495
28305	CSX AC6000 Diesel "610," nonpowered, RailSounds, 08	430
28306	GE ES44AC Evolution Hybrid Diesel "2010," CC, 09–10	1000
28307	Wabash Train Master Diesel "550," CC, 09–10	495
28311	UP DD35A Diesel, CC, 11	600
28312	BN SD60 Diesel "8301," CC, 09	800
28314	UP 3GS21B Genset Switcher "2701," CC, 10	675
28316	PRR NS Heritage SD70ACe Diesel "1854," CC, 10	500
28318	Conrail NS Heritage SD70ACe Diesel "1209," CC, 10	500
28320	CP Evolution Hybrid Diesel, 10	875
28323	NS Genset Switcher, CC, 11	800
28327	UP AC6000 Diesel "7050," CC, 10	700
28328	UPAC6000 Diesel "7055," nonpowered, CC, 10	350
28330	UP SD70ACe Diesel "8444," CC, 10	500
28331	CSX AC6000 Diesel "618," CC, 10	700
28333	Virginian NS Heritage SD70ACe Diesel, CC, 10	500
28334	NS Heritage SD70ACe Diesel "1982," CC, 10	500
28338	PRR NS Heritage SD70ACe Diesel, CC, 11	500
28339	ATSF AC6000 Diesel "9876," CC, 10	550
28340	WP GP7 Diesel "705," CC, 10	450
28343	Amtrak Dash 9 Diesel "519," CC, 10	500
28344	Southern NS Heritage SD70ACe Diesel, CC, 10	500
28345	N&W NS Heritage SD70ACe Diesel "247," CC, 10	500
28347	UP Boy Scouts 100th Anniversary ES44AC Diesel, CC, 11	850
28350	BNSF ES44AC Diesel, CC, 11	850
28351	KCS ES44AC Diesel "4655," CC, 11	850
28353	Erie GP7 Diesel, CC, 11	450
28354	CSX Genset Switcher "1303," CC, 11	800
28355	BNSF Genset Switcher "1249," CC, 11	800
28356	CSX SD60 Diesel, CC, 11	500
28357	CSX SD60 Diesel, CC, 11	500
28358	Soo Line SD60 Diesel, CC, 11	500
28359	Soo Line SD60 Diesel, CC, 11	500

Exc Mint

		Exc	Mint
28360	WP GP7 Diesel "707," CC, *11*	450	___
28361	WM GP7 Diesel "21," CC, *11*	450	___
28362	WM GP7 Diesel "23," CC, *11*	450	___
28363	BN SD60 Diesel "8302," CC, *11*	500	___
28364	BNSF Dash-9 Diesel "4081," CC, *11*	500	___
28365	BNSF Dash-9 Diesel "5121," CC, *11*	500	___
28366	CN Dash-9 Diesel "2643," CC, *11*	500	___
28367	CN Dash-9 Diesel "2692," CC, *11*	500	___
28368	Amtrak Dash-9 Diesel, CC, *11*	500	___
28369	NYC DD35A Diesel "9950," CC, *11*	600	___
28370	UP DD35 Diesel "84," CC, *12*	600	___
28371	UP DD35A Diesel "72," CC, *11*	600	___
28372	NYC DD35A Diesel "9955," CC, *11*	600	___
28373	C&NW UP Heritage SD70ACe Diesel, CC, *11*	500	___
28374	SP UP Heritage SD70ACe Diesel, CC, *11*	500	___
28375	Katy UP Heritage SD70ACe Diesel, CC, *11*	500	___
28376	MoPac UP Heritage SD70ACe Diesel, CC, *11*	500	___
28377	Rio Grande UP Heritage SD70ACe Diesel, CC, *11*	500	___
28378	WP UP Heritage SD70ACe Diesel, CC, *11*	500	___
28380	NYC DD35A Diesel, nonpowered, *11*	440	___
28381	ATSF GP30 Diesel, CC, *11*	500	___
28382	U.S. Army Genset Switcher, CC, *11*	800	___
28383	Conrail Genset Switcher, CC, *11*	800	___
28384	CN Genset Switcher "7990," CC, *11–12*	800	___
28385	ATSF GP30 Diesel "1214," CC, *11*	500	___
28386	ATSF GP30 Diesel "2710," *11*	380	___
28387	ATSF GP30 Diesel "2715," nonpowered, *11*	240	___
28388	ICG GP30 Diesel "2268," CC, *11*	500	___
28389	ICG GP30 Diesel "2271," CC, *11*	500	___
28390	UP DD35 Diesel "79," nonpowered, *12*	440	___
28394	ICG GP30 Diesel "2277," *11*	380	___
28395	ICG GP30 Diesel "2279," nonpowered, *11*	240	___
28396	UP ES44AC Diesel "7454," CC, *11*	850	___
28397	UP ES44AC Diesel "7459," CC, *11*	850	___
28398	BNSF ES44AC Diesel "6436," CC, *11*	850	___
28399	KCS ES44AC Diesel "4682," CC, *11*	850	___
28400	Amtrak Rail Bonder, *05*	65	___
28403	Pennsylvania Ballast Tamper, traditional, *05–06*	105	___
28404	Maintenance Car, *05*	105	___
28405	Picatinny Arsenal Switcher, CC, *05*	290	___
28406	CSX Rail Bonder "92794," traditional, *05*	65	___
28407	UP Speeder, *05*	65	___
28408	CNJ Speeder "MW840," traditional, *06*	70	___
28409	Conrail Rail Bonder "X409," traditional, *06*	70	___
28411	U.S. Army Missile Launcher Locomotive, *06–07*	300	___
28412	Santa's Speeder, *06*	70	___
28413	Milwaukee Road Snowplow "X903," traditional, *06*	210	___
28414	Lionel Lines Burro Crane, traditional, *06*	160	___
28415	Third Avenue Trolley "1651," traditional, *06*	70	___
28416	Hobo Handcar, traditional, *06*	70	___

		Exc	Mint
____ 28417	Christmas Rotary Snowplow, *06*		180
____ 28418	Christmas Trolley, *06*		70
____ 28419	Lionel Lines Speeder, *07–08*		70
____ 28420	D&RGW Handcar, *07–08*		70
____ 28421	Fort Collins Trolley, *07*		73
____ 28422	PRR Burro Crane, *07–08*		160
____ 28423	Alaska Rotary Snowplow, *06–07*		220
____ 28424	Postwar "51" Navy Switcher, *07*		210
____ 28425	Polar Express Elf Handcar, *06–12*		85
____ 28427	Christmas Snowplow, *08–10*		210
____ 28428	Halloween Handcar, *07*		70
____ 28430	Wellspring Capital Management Trolley, *06*		79
____ 28432	Bethlehem Steel Switcher, traditional, *07*		210
____ 28434	Christmas Trolley, *07*		70
____ 28438	Portland Birney Trolley, *08–09*		65
____ 28440	PRR Inspection Vehicle, *08–09*		170
____ 28441	Transylvania Trolley, *08*		75
____ 28442	Postwar "50" Gang Car, *08*		120
____ 28444	NH Handcar, *08–09*		75
____ 28445	AEC Burro Crane Car		100
____ 28446	Silver Bell Trolley, *09*		90
____ 28447	4850TM Factory Trackmobile, CC, *10*		300
____ 28448	CSX 4850TM Trackmobile, CC, *10*		300
____ 28449	UP 4850TM Trackmobile, CC, *10*		300
____ 28450	CP Rail Trackmobile, CC, *11*		300
____ 28451	Christmas Track Cleaning Car, *10–13*		150
____ 28452	MOW Early Era Inspection Vehicle, *10*		130
____ 28453	PRR Early Era Inspection Vehicle, *10*		130
____ 28454	CP Early Era Inspection Vehicle, *10*		130
____ 28455	NYC Trackmobile, CC, *11–13*		300
____ 28456	Coca-Cola Trolley, *10*		90
____ 28457	B&M Rotary Snowplow "8457," *11*		250
____ 28466	U.S. Army Trackmobile, CC, *11*		300
____ 28467	PRR Trackmobile, CC, *11*		300
____ 28468	Amtrak Trackmobile, CC, *11*		300
____ 28469	BNSF Trackmobile, CC, *11*		300
____ 28470	NYC Early Era Inspection Vehicle, *11*		130
____ 28471	ATSF Early Era Inspection Vehicle, CC, *11*		130
____ 28472	Southern Early Era Inspection Vehicle, *11*		130
____ 28473	GN Early Era Inspection Vehicle, CC, *11*		130
____ 28474	North Pole Central Elf Handcar, *11*		80
____ 28475	UP Early Era Insprection Vehicle, *11*		130
____ 28476	IC Early Era Inspection Vehicle, *11*		130
____ 28478	Frisco Early Era Inspection Vehicle, CC, *11*		130
____ 28479	Christmas Early Era Inspection Vehicle, *11*		130
28480 ____	Grand Trunk Early Era Inspection Vehicle, CC, *11*		130
____ 28500	Mopac GP20 Diesel "2274," *99–00*		205
____ 28501	ATSF GP9 Diesel "2924," traditional, *99*		200
____ 28502	ATSF GP9 Diesel "2925," CC, *99–00*		255
____ 28503	ACL GP7 Diesel, CC, *00*		245
____ 28504	ACL GP7 Diesel, traditional, *00*		170
____ 28505	Monon Alco C420 Switcher "505," CC, *00–01*		230

		Exc	Mint
28506	Monon Alco C420 Switcher "506," traditional, *00–01*	170	___
28507	NH Alco C420 Switcher "2556," CC, *00–01*	275	___
28508	NH Alco C420 Switcher "2557," traditional, *00–01*	290	___
28509	FEC GP7 Diesel Set, *99*	560	___
28514	B&O GP9 Diesel "6590," *00*	85	___
28515	Lionel Service Station Alco C420 Switcher, CC, *00*	205	___
28516	Lehigh & Hudson River Alco C420 Diesel, *00*	160	___
28517	C&NW GP7 Diesel "1518," CC, *00–01*	275	___
28518	PRR EP-5 Electric Locomotive "2352," CC, *00*	410	___
28519	NP GP9 Diesel "2349," CC, *01*	290	___
28521	SP Alco RS-11 Switcher "5725," CC, *01–02*	280	___
28522	MP Alco RS-11 Switcher "4611," CC, *01–02*	305	___
28523	Soo SD40-2 Diesel "6622," CC, *01*	375	___
28524	Chessie SD40-2 Diesel "7616," CC, *01*	355	___
28527	AEC GP9 Diesel "2001," CC, *01*	378	___
28529	Norfolk Southern GP9 Diesel, CC, *02*	200	___
28530	NP Alco S4 Diesel "722," CC, *02*	285	___
28531	Santa Fe Alco S2 Switcher "2337," CC, *02*	285	___
28532	LV Alco S2 Switcher "150," CC, *02*	280	___
28533	Seaboard Air Line Alco S4 Diesel "1489," CC, *02*	290	___
28536	Rock Island GP7 Diesel "1274," CC, *02–03*	230	___
28538	WP Alco S2 Switcher "553," CC, *03*	340	___
28539	B&O Alco S2 Switcher "9045," CC, *03*	320	___
28540	UP SD40T-2 Diesel "4455," CC, *03*	390	___
28541	SP SD40T-2 Diesel "8239," CC, *03*	400	___
28542	Rio Grande SD40T-2 Diesel "5350," CC, *03*	400	___
28543	Ontario Northland RS3 Diesel "1308," *03*	80	___
28544	Pennsylvania Alco RS-11 Switcher "8618," CC, *04*	350	___
28545	NP Alco RS-11 Switcher "900," CC, *03*	325	___
28548	Chessie System S4 Diesel "9009," CC, *05*	400	___
28553	PRR Alco RS-11 Switcher "8620," traditional, *07–08*	285	___
28554	Pennsylvania Alco RS-11 Switcher "8618," nonpowered, CC, *07*	170	___
28554	PRR RS-11 Diesel "8621," nonpowered, *08*	170	___
28555	Alaska GP38-2 Diesel "2001," CC, *06*	400	___
28556	Alaska GP38-2 Diesel "2002," nonpowered (std O), *06*	160	___
28557	CP GP30 Diesel "5000," CC, *06–07*	400	___
28558	CP GP30 Diesel "5001," nonpowered (std O), *06–07*	150	___
28559	Chessie System GP30 Diesel "3044," CC, *06–07*	400	___
28560	Chessie System GP30 Diesel "3045," nonpowered (std O), *06–07*	150	___
28561	NYC GP7 Diesel "5628," CC, *07–08*	340	___
28562	NYC GP7 Diesel "5629," nonpowered (std O), *07*	170	___
28563	GN GP7 Diesel "626," CC, *07*	400	___
28564	GN GP7 Diesel "627," nonpowered (std O), *07*	170	___
28565	RI GP7 Diesel "1265," CC, *07*	400	___

			Exc	Mint
___	28566	RI GP7 Diesel "1266," nonpowered (std O), _07_		170
___	28567	UP GP7 Diesel "105," CC, _07_		400
___	28568	UP GP7 Diesel "106," nonpowered (std O), _07_		170
___	28570	D&RGW GP7 Diesel "5101," CC, _08_		440
___	28573	PRR GP7 Diesel "8512," CC, _08_		440
___	28578	D&H GP38-2 Diesel "7307," CC, _08_		440
___	28587	PRR GP7 Diesel "8510," CC, _10_		450
___	28592	N&W GP7 Diesel "2446," CC, _09_		500
___	28594	White Pass & Yukon NW2 Diesel Switcher, traditional, _09–10_		300
___	28595	ATSF SD40 Diesel "5004," CC, _09_		380
___	28596	Erie GP7 Diesel "1210," CC, _11_		450
___	28598	ATSF GP7 Diesel "2791," CC, _10_		450
___	28599	Erie GP9 Diesel "1261," CC, _10_		390
___	28612	WP 4-4-2 Atlantic Locomotive, traditional, _02_		80
___	28613	Reading 0-6-0 Dockside Switcher "1251," traditional, _04_		100
___	28615	B&O 4-6-4 Hudson Locomotive, traditional, _02_		225
___	28616	Nickel Plate 2-8-4 Berkshire Locomotive, traditional, _02_		190
___	28617	Southern 2-8-4 Berkshire Locomotive, traditional, _02_		235
___	28624	Santa Fe 0-6-0 Dockside Switcher "2174," traditional, _04_		175
___	28625	Wabash 4-4-2 Atlantic Locomotive "8625," traditional, _03_		85
___	28626	PRR 4-6-4 Hudson Locomotive "626," traditional, _03_		175
___	28627	C&O 2-8-4 Berkshire Locomotive "2755," traditional, _03_		200
___	28628	L&N 2-8-4 Berkshire Locomotive "1970," traditional, _03_	150	200
___	28633	JCPenney B&O 2-8-4 Berkshire Locomotive, _07_		135
___	28636	D&RGW 4-4-2 Atlantic Locomotive "8636," traditional, _04_		95
___	28637	UP 4-6-4 Hudson Locomotive "673," traditional, _04_		160
___	28638	GN 2-8-4 Berkshire Locomotive "3414," traditional, _04_		200
___	28639	NYC 2-8-4 Berkshire Locomotive "9401," traditional, _04_		200
___	28646	North Pole Central 2-8-4 Berkshire "1900," traditional, _04_		230
___	28649	Polar Express 2-8-4 Berkshire Locomotive, _03–10_		120
___	28650	NYC 0-6-0 Dockside Switcher "X-8688," traditional, _05_		80
___	28651	Bethlehem Steel 0-6-0 Dockside Switcher "72," traditional, _05_		80
___	28652	LL 4-4-2 Locomotive "8652," traditional, _05_		105
___	28655	Erie 2-8-4 Berkshire Locomotive "3338," traditional, _05_		240
___	28656	PRR 2-8-4 Berkshire Locomotive "56," traditional, _05_		240
___	28660	North Pole Central 0-6-0 Dockside Switcher "25," traditional, _05_		105

		Exc	Mint
28661	Santa Fe 0-4-0 Locomotive "2300" traditional, *05*		160 ___
28662	C&O 0-4-0 Locomotive "39," traditional, *05*		160 ___
28674	C&O 0-6-0 Dockside Switcher "67," traditional, *06–07*		110 ___
28675	SP 0-6-0 Dockside Switcher "675," traditional, *06–07*		110 ___
28676	U.S. Steel 0-6-0 Dockside Switcher "76," traditional, *06–07*		110 ___
28677	WM 4-4-2 Atlantic Locomotive "103," traditional, *06*		110 ___
28678	Rio Grande 0-4-0 Locomotive "55," traditional, *06–07*		170 ___
28679	U.S. Army Transportation Corps 0-4-0 Locomotive "40," traditional, *06*		170 ___
28680	Reading 0-4-0 Locomotive "1152," traditional, *06*		170 ___
28681	Virginian 2-8-4 Berkshire Locomotive "509," traditional, *06*		260 ___
28683	B&O 2-8-2 Mikado Locomotive "1520," TrainSounds, *06–07*		260 ___
28684	UP 2-8-2 Mikado Locomotive "2498," TrainSounds, *06–07*		260 ___
28693	B&O 4-4-2 Locomotive "28," traditional, *05*		105 ___
28694	NYC 4-4-2 Atlantic Locomotive "8637," traditional, *06*		100 ___
28695	Halloween 0-6-0 Dockside Switcher "X-131," traditional, *06–07*		85 ___
28699	Holiday 2-8-2 Mikado Locomotive "25," red, RailSounds, *08*		260 ___
28700	CB&Q 0-8-0 Locomotive "543," RailSounds, *05*		650 ___
28701	NP 0-8-0 Locomotive "1178," RailSounds, *05*		650 ___
28702	Boston & Albany 0-8-0 Locomotive "53," RailSounds, *05*		650 ___
28704	PRR 4-4-2 Atlantic Locomotive "68," CC, *05*		550 ___
28706	PRR Reading Seashore 4-4-2 Atlantic Locomotive "6064," CC, *05*		550 ___
28742	B&O 4-6-0 Camelback Locomotive "1630," CC, *03*		335 ___
28743	B&O 4-6-0 Camelback Locomotive "1632," traditional, *03*		300 ___
28744	D&H 4-6-0 Camelback Locomotive "548," CC, *03*		325 ___
28745	D&H 4-6-0 Camelback Locomotive "555," traditional, *03*		300 ___
28746	Erie 4-6-0 Camelback Locomotive "860," CC, *03*		375 ___
28747	Erie 4-6-0 Camelback Locomotive "878," traditional, *03*		300 ___
28748	Jersey Central 4-6-0 Camelback Locomotive "772," CC, *03*		300 ___
28749	Jersey Central 4-6-0 Camelback Locomotive "773," traditional, *03*		300 ___
28750	Lackawanna 4-6-0 Camelback Locomotive "690," CC, *03*		375 ___
28751	Lackawanna 4-6-0 Camelback Locomotive "1031," traditional, *03*		300 ___

		Exc	Mint
28752	LIRR 4-6-0 Camelback Locomotive "126," CC, *03*		300
28753	LIRR 4-6-0 Camelback Locomotive "127," traditional, *03*		300
28754	NYO&W 4-6-0 Camelback Locomotive "249," CC, *03*		300
28755	NYO&W 4-6-0 Camelback "253" Locomotive, traditional, *03*		300
28756	PRR Reading Seashore 4-6-0 Camelback Locomotive "6000," CC, *03*		325
28757	PRR Reading Seashore 4-6-0 Camelback Locomotive "6001," traditional, *03*		300
28758	Susquehanna 4-6-0 Camelback Locomotive "30," CC, *03*		305
28759	Susquehanna 4-6-0 Camelback Locomotive "36," traditional, *03*		300
28800	N&W GP7 Diesel "507," *99–00*		80
28801	Lionel Lines 44-ton Switcher, *99*		135
28806	Jersey Central FM H16-44 Diesel "1516," CC, *01*		335
28811	Santa Fe FM H16-44 Diesel "3003," CC, *01*		290
28813	Milwaukee Road FM H16-44 Diesel "406," CC, *01*		280
28815	B&O GP30 Diesel "6935," CC, *02*		295
28817	Reading GP30 Diesel "5513," CC, *02*		310
28819	Rio Grande GP30 Diesel "3013," CC, *02*		310
28821	GT GP7 Diesel "4438," *01*		100
28822	Southern RS3 Diesel "2127," *01*		70
28823	Virginian Electric Locomotive "234," *01*		122
28826	Pioneer Seed GP7 Diesel "2001," traditional, *00 u*		NRS
28827	Chessie GP38 Diesel, traditional, *01*		100
28830	Soo Line GP9 Diesel, traditional, *01 u*		NRS
28831	Conrail U36B Diesel "2971," traditional, *02*		100
28832	Santa Fe RS3 Diesel "2099," traditional, *02*		70
28836	NYC FM H-16-44 Diesel "7000," CC, *02*		330
28837	NH FM H-16-44 Diesel "591," CC, *02*		325
28838	UP FM H-16-44 Diesel "1340," CC, *02*		325
28839	Alaska GP 30 Diesel "2000," CC, *04*		315
28840	Burlington GP30 Diesel "945," CC, *03*		325
28841	Seaboard GP30 Diesel "1315," CC, *03*		220
28842	C&O GP9 Diesel, horn, *04*		160
28843	Southern GP38 Diesel, horn, *04*		140
28845	Amtrak RS3 Diesel "106," *03*		70
28846	Western Pacific U36B Diesel "3067," traditional, *04*		100
28847	DM & IR GP38 Diesel "203," traditional, *04*		170
28848	JCPenney Santa Fe GP38 Diesel, *04*		125
28849	Western Maryland GP7 Diesel, horn, *04*		185
28850	NYC GP30 Diesel "6115" CC, *04*		360
28851	Pennsylvania RS3 Diesel, *04*		75
28852	CSX U36B Diesel "1976," traditional, *05*		140
28853	Santa Fe GP38 Diesel "2371," traditional, *05*		210
28859	Pennsylvania GP30 Diesel "2206," nonpowered, *06*		160
28860	UP GP30 Diesel "844," CC, *06*		360

		Exc	Mint
28861	UP GP30 Diesel "845," nonpowered (std O), *06*		150 ___
28862	CSX GP30 Diesel "4249," CC, *06*		400 ___
28863	CSX GP30 Diesel "4250," nonpowered (std O), *06*		150 ___
28864	UP RS3 Diesel "1195," traditional, *06*		85 ___
28865	GN GP9 Diesel "688," traditional, *06*		210 ___
28866	NYC GP20 Diesel "6110," traditional, *06*		140 ___
28868	ATSF GP38 Diesel		140 ___
28873	NYC RS3 Diesel "8226," traditional, *06*		85 ___
28874	UP GP9 Diesel "178," traditional, *06–07*		210 ___
28875	Santa Fe GP20 "1107," traditional, *06*		140 ___
28876	GN FT Diesel "418," traditional, *07–08*		245 ___
28879	UPS Centennial GP38 Diesel, traditional, *06*		210 ___
28881	Conrail GP20 Diesel "2107," traditional, *07*		140 ___
28882	Alaska RS3 Diesel "1079," traditional, *07*		85 ___
28883	Diesel, *07–13*		120 ___
28884	PRR GP38 Diesel "2389," traditional, *08–09*		210 ___
28886	RI RS3 Diesel "492," traditional, *08*		95 ___
28887	Southern RS3 Diesel "2028," traditional, *08*		95 ___
28890	CN GP9 Diesel "4573," traditional, *08*		210 ___
28897	Seaboard U36B Diesel "1762," traditional, *08*		140 ___
28900	Iron 'Arry and Iron Bert 2-pack, *08–09*		240 ___
28905	ATSF FT Diesel "160," nonpowered, *09–10*		120 ___
29000	PRR Caleb Strong Madison Coach "2622," *99*		80 ___
29001	PRR Villa Royal Madison Coach "2621," *99*		80 ___
29002	PRR Philadelphia Madison Coach "2624," *99*	30	80 ___
29003	PRR Madison Car 4-pack, *98*		220 ___
29004	NYC Heavyweight Passenger Car 2-pack, *99*		170 ___
29007	NYC Pullman Passenger Car 2-pack, *98 u*		95 ___
29008	NYC Heavyweight Diner "383," *98*		95 ___
29009	NYC Van Twiller Heavyweight Combination Car, *98*		95 ___
29010	C&O Heavyweight Passenger Car 2-pack, *99*		150 ___
29039	Lionel Lines Recovery Combination Car "9501," *99*		NRS ___
29041	Alaska Streamliner Car 4-pack, *99–00*		230 ___
29042	Alaska Streamliner Baggage Car "6310," *99–00*		50 ___
29043	Alaska Streamliner Coach "5408," *99–00*		65 ___
29044	Alaska Streamliner Vista Dome Car "7014," *99–00*		65 ___
29046	B&O Streamliner Car 4-pack, *99–00*		165 ___
29047	B&O Streamliner Baggage Car, *99–00*		35 ___
29048	B&O Streamliner Coach, *99–00*		50 ___
29049	B&O Streamliner Vista Dome Car, *99–00*		50 ___
29050	B&O Streamliner Observation Car, *99–00*		40 ___
29051	ATSF Streamliner Car 4-pack, *99–00*		200 ___
29052	ATSF Streamliner Baggage Car, *99–00*		40 ___
29053	ATSF Streamliner Coach, *99–00*		60 ___
29054	ATSF Streamliner Vista Dome Car, *99–00*		60 ___
29055	ATSF Streamliner Observation Car, *99–00*		40 ___
29056	NYC Streamliner Car 4-pack, *99–00*		180 ___
29057	NYC Streamliner Baggage Car, *99–00*		40 ___

		Exc	Mint
___ **29058**	NYC Streamliner Coach, *99–00*		50
___ **29059**	NYC Streamliner Vista Dome Car, *99–00*		50
___ **29060**	NYC Streamliner Observation Car, *99–00*		45
___ **29061**	PRR Madison Passenger Car 4-pack, *99–00*		190
29062	PRR Indian Point Madison Baggage Car, *99–00*		50
29063	PRR Christopher Columbus Madison Coach, *99–00*		50
___ **29064**	PRR Andrew Jackson Madison Coach, *99–00*		50
29065	PRR Broussard Madison Observation Car, *99–00*		50
___ **29066**	CNJ Madison Passenger Car 4-pack, *99–00*		210
___ **29067**	CNJ Madison Baggage Car "420," *99–00*		50
___ **29068**	CNJ Beachcomber Madison Coach, *99–00*		50
___ **29069**	CNJ Echo Lake Madison Coach, *99–00*		50
___ **29070**	CNJ Madison Observation Car "1178," *99–00*		50
___ **29071**	NYC Baby Madison Car 4-pack, *00*		155
___ **29072**	NYC Baby Madison Baggage Car "1001," *00*		50
___ **29073**	NYC Baby Madison Coach "1005," *00*		50
___ **29074**	NYC Baby Madison Coach "1006," *00*		50
29075	NYC Detroit Baby Madison Observation Car "1019," *00*		40
___ **29076**	Southern Baby Madison Car 4-pack, *00*		155
29077	Southern Delaware Madison Baggage Car "702," *00*		30
29078	Southern North Carolina Madison Coach "800," *00*		50
___ **29079**	Southern Maryland Madison Coach "801," *00*		50
___ **29080**	Southern Madison Observation Car "1100," *00*		40
___ **29081**	ATSF Baby Madison Car 4-pack, *00*		160
___ **29082**	ATSF Baby Madison Baggage Car "1765," *00*		30
___ **29083**	ATSF Baby Madison Coach "3040," *00*		50
___ **29084**	ATSF Baby Madison Coach "1535," *00*		50
___ **29085**	ATSF Baby Madison Observation Car "10," *00*		45
___ **29086**	Madison Car 3-pack, *99*		280
___ **29090**	Lionel Liontech Madison Car "2656," *99*		75
29091	Lawrence Cowen Lionel Legends Madison Coach "2657," *99–00*		75
29105	PRR Trail Blazer Aluminum Passenger Car 4-pack, *04–05*		550
___ **29108**	Searchlight Car, *00*		30
29110	B&O Columbian Aluminum Passenger Car 4-pack, *04*		425
29115	SP Daylight Aluminum Passenger Car 4-pack, *04–05*		550
29122	Erie-Lack. F3 Diesel AB Passenger Set, *99*		840
29123	Erie-Lack. Aluminum Coach/Baggage Car "203," *99*		100
___ **29124**	Erie-Lack. Aluminum Coach/Diner "770," *99*		100
___ **29125**	Erie-Lack. Eleanor Lord Aluminum Coach, *99*		100
29126	Erie-Lack. Tavern Lounge Aluminum Observation Car "789," *99*		125
___ **29127**	ACL Aluminum Baggage Car "152," *99*		NRS
___ **29128**	ACL North Hampton Aluminum Coach, *99*		NRS
___ **29129**	Texas Special Passenger Car 4-pack, *99*	650	700

Exc Mint

		Exc	Mint
29130	Texas Special Edward Burleson Aluminum Coach "1200," *99*		115 ___
29131	Texas Special David G. Burnett Aluminum Coach "1201," *99*		115 ___
29132	Texas Special J. Pinckney Henderson Aluminum Coach "1202," *99*		115 ___
29133	Texas Special Stephen F. Austin Aluminum Observation Car "1203," *99*		100 ___
29135	California Zephyr Silver Poplar Aluminum Vista Dome Car, *99*		150 ___
29136	California Zephyr Silver Palm Aluminum Vista Dome Car, *99*		150 ___
29137	California Zephyr Silver Tavern Aluminum Vista Dome Car, *99*		150 ___
29138	California Zephyr Silver Planet Aluminum Vista Dome Car, *99*		150 ___
29139	Kughn Lionel Legends Madison Car "2655," *99*		113 ___
29140	NYC Castleton Bridge Aluminum Sleeper Car, *99*		120 ___
29141	NYC Martin Van Buren Aluminum Combination Car, *99*		120 ___
29142	CP Skyline Aluminum Vista Dome Car "596," *99*		125 ___
29143	CP Banff Park Aluminum Observation Car, *99*		125 ___
29144	Santa Fe El Capitan Aluminum Passenger Car 4-pack, *04*		400 ___
29149	CB&Q California Zephyr Aluminum Passenger Car 2-pack, *03*		300 ___
29152	Santa Fe Super Chief Aluminum Passenger Car 2-pack, *03*		190 ___
29155	D&H Aluminum Passenger Car 2-pack, *03*		190 ___
29158	Southern Aluminum Passenger Car 2-pack, *03*		205 ___
29165	Amtrak Superliner Passenger Car 2-pack, Phase IV, *04*		195 ___
29168	Amtrak Superliner Diner, StationSounds, Phase IV, *04*		200 ___
29169	Alaska Superliner Passenger Car 2-pack, *04*		200 ___
29172	Alaska Superliner Diner, StationSounds, *04*		200 ___
29182	N&W Powhatan Arrow Aluminum Passenger Car 4-pack (std O), *05*		550 ___
29187	N&W Powhatan Arrow Aluminum Passenger Car 2-pack (std O), *05*		290 ___
29190	N&W Powhatan Arrow Aluminum Diner, StationSounds, *05*		290 ___
29191	MILW Hiawatha Passenger Car 4-pack, *06*		370 ___
29196	MILW Hiawatha Passenger Car 2-pack, *06*		190 ___
29199	MILW Hiawatha Diner, StationSounds, *06*		190 ___
29202	Santa Fe Map Boxcar "6464," *97 u*		53 ___
29203	Maine Central Boxcar "6464-597," *97 u*		35 ___
29205	Mickey Mouse Hi-Cube Boxcar "9555," *97*		65 ___
29206	Vapor Records Boxcar #1, *97*		83 ___
29209	Postwar "6464" Boxcar Series VII, 3 cars, *98*		87 ___
29210	GN Boxcar "6464-450," *98*		33 ___
29211	B&M Boxcar "6464-475," *98*		27 ___
29212	Timken Boxcar "6464-500," *98*		28 ___

		Exc	Mint
____ 29213	ATSF Grand Canyon Route 6464 Boxcar "6464-198," *98*		26
____ 29214	Southern 6464 Boxcar "6464-298," *98*		27
____ 29215	Canadian Pacific 6464 Boxcar "6464-398," *98*		26
____ 29217	1997 Toy Fair Airex Boxcar, *97*		78
____ 29218	Vapor Records Boxcar "6464-496," *97 u*		74
29220	Lionel Centennial Series Hi-Cube Boxcar Set, 4 cars, *97*		204
29221	Centennial Series Hi-Cube Boxcar "9697-1," *97*		50
29222	Centennial Series Hi-Cube Boxcar "9697-2," *97*		59
29223	Centennial Series Hi-Cube Boxcar "9697-3," *97*		57
29224	Centennial Series Hi-Cube Boxcar "9697-4," *97*		59
____ 29225	H.O.R.D.E. Music Festival Boxcar, *97*	48	55
____ 29229	Vapor Records Holiday Car, *98*		152
____ 29231	Halloween Animated Boxcar, *98*		42
29233	Conrail PC Overstamped Boxcar "6464-598," *98*		38
29234	Conrail Erie Overstamped Boxcar "6464-698," *98*		32
____ 29235	NYC Boxcar "6464-510," *99*		47
____ 29236	MKT Boxcar "6464-515," *99*		40
____ 29237	M&StL Boxcar "6464-525," *99*		25
29247	Mainline Classic Street Lamps, 3 pieces, *08–14*		40
____ 29250	Phoebe Snow Boxcar "6464-199," *99*		41
____ 29251	BN Boxcar "6464-299," *99*		31
____ 29252	CP Boxcar "6464-399," *99*		33
____ 29253	B&M Boxcar "76032," *99*		50
____ 29254	B&M Boxcar "76033," *99*		50
____ 29255	B&M Boxcar "76034," *99*		50
____ 29256	B&M Boxcar "76035," *99*		50
____ 29257	Southern Boxcar "9464-199," *99*		38
____ 29258	Reading Boxcar "9464-299," *99*		36
____ 29259	NP Bicentennial Boxcar "9464-399," *99*		34
____ 29265	Maine Central Boxcar "8661," *99*		36
____ 29266	Frisco Boxcar "8722," *99*		36
____ 29267	No. 6464 Boxcar 3-pack, Series VIII, *99*		85
____ 29268	Rio Grande Boxcar "63067," *99*		40
____ 29271	Lionel Cola Tractor and Trailer, *98*		12
29279	Conrail Jersey Central Overstamped Boxcar "6464-28X," *99*		40
29280	Conrail LV Overstamped Boxcar "6464-31X," *99*		41
____ 29281	Conrail Overstamped Boxcar 2-pack, *99*		70
____ 29282	Postwar "6464" Boxcar 3-pack, *99*		130
____ 29283	NYC Boxcar, *99*		55
____ 29284	GN Boxcar, *99*		40
____ 29285	Seaboard Boxcar, *99*		36
____ 29286	Overstamped Boxcar 2-pack, *99*		65
____ 29287	NH PC Overstamped Boxcar "6464-29X," *99*	18	34
29288	Conrail Reading Overstamped Boxcar "6464-32X," *99*		38

Exc Mint

		Exc	Mint
29289	Postwar "6464" Series IX, 3 cars, *99–00*		70 ___
29290	D&RGW Boxcar "6464-650," *00*		41 ___
29291	ATSF Boxcar "6464-700," *00*		38 ___
29292	NH Boxcar "6464-725," *00*		39 ___
29293	NH Boxcar "6464-425," *99*		95 ___
29294	Hellgate Bridge Boxcar "1900-2000," *99 u*		38 ___
29295	PRR "Don't Stand Me Still" Boxcar "24018," *99–00*		65 ___
29296	PRR "Merchandise" Boxcar "29296," *99–00*		65 ___
29297	PRR "No Damage" Boxcar "47158," *99–00*		65 ___
29298	Lionel Boxcar "6464-2000," *00*		46 ___
29300	50th Anniversary Clear Shell Aquarium Car, *10*		85 ___
29301	Postwar "3662" Transparent Milk Car with platform, *11, 13*		155 ___
29302	Christmas Music Reefer, *10*		75 ___
29303	North Pole Central Crane Car, *10–11*		65 ___
29305	UP Chisholm Trail Stock Car, Cattle Sounds, *11, 13*		200 ___
29306	PRR Hi-Cube Lighted Garland Boxcar, *10–11*		70 ___
29309	GN Pullman-Standard Diesel Freight Set, CC, *13*		830 ___
29310	Marine Science Deep Sea Exhibition Aquarium Car, *11*		75 ___
29311	Strasburg Derrick Car, *11*		45 ___
29312	Santa's Operating Boxcar, *11–12*		75 ___
29314	SP DD Boxcar "214051" (std O), *13–14*		75 ___
29317	CN DD Boxcar "214051" (std O), *13–14*		75 ___
29320	CNJ DD Boxcar "214051" (std O), *13–14*		75 ___
29321	Ice Skating Aquarium Car, *12*		80 ___
29322	Koi Aquarium Car, *13–14*		80 ___
29323	UP DD Boxcar "500019" (std O), *13–14*		75 ___
29324	Walking Zombie Brakeman Car, *12*		80 ___
29326	NP "Pig Palace" Operating Stock Car "84144," *12*		200 ___
29327	Bethlehem Steel Operating Hopper "2025," *12*		60 ___
29328	Beatles "Nothing is Real" Aquarium Car, *12–13*		85 ___
29329	Peanuts Halloween Aquarium Car, *12–13*		85 ___
29333	ATSF 89' Auto Carrier 2-pack (std O), *13–14*		220 ___
29338	BN 89' Auto Carrier 2-pack (std O), *13–14*		220 ___
29344	C&NW DD Boxcar "57766" (std O), *13*		75 ___
29345	ATSF 89' Auto Carrier (std O), *13–14*		110 ___
29346	Soo Line 89' Auto Carrier 2-pack (std O), *13–14*		220 ___
29349	SP 89' Auto Carrier 2-pack (std O), *13–14*		220 ___
29364	NYC Water Level Steam Freight Set, CC, *12–13*		1600 ___
29365	N&W Pocahontas Steam Passenger Set, CC, *12*		1950 ___
29366	SP TankSet Diesel Set, CC, *12*		850 ___
29372	BNSF 89' Auto Carrier "300267" (std O), *13*		110 ___
29373	CN 89' Auto Carrier "710771" (std O), *13*		110 ___
29376	Conrail 89' Auto Carrier "964444" (std O), *13*		110 ___
29377	CP 89' Auto Carrier 2-pack (std O), *13–14*		220 ___
29380	CSX 89' Auto Carrier "604544" (std O), *13*		110 ___

			Exc	Mint
____	**29382**	UP 89' Auto Carrier "604545" (std O), *13*		110
____	**29384**	DL&W USRA Double-sheathed Boxcar "44153" (std O), *13*		70
____	**29385**	ATSF USRA Double-sheathed Boxcar "39012" (std O), *13*		70
____	**29386**	PRR PS-4 Flatcar with stakes "469614" (std O), *13*		70
____	**29387**	GN PS-4 Flatcar with stakes "629387" (std O), *13*		70
____	**29400**	Bethlehem Steel Slag Car 3-pack (std O), *03*		185
____	**29404**	Bethlehem Steel Hot Metal Car 3-pack (std O), *03*		210
____	**29408**	PRR Coil Car, *01*		40
____	**29411**	Sherwin-Williams Vat Car, *02*		35
____	**29412**	Tabasco Brand Vat Car, *02*		36
____	**29413**	Airex Boat Loader Car "29413," *02*		42
____	**29414**	PRR Evans Auto Loader "480123," *01*		56
____	**29415**	WM Skeleton Log Car 3-pack #2 (std O), *02*		90
____	**29419**	West Side Lumber Skeleton Log Car 3-pack #2 (std O), *02*		90
____	**29423**	Wellspring Capital Management Happy Holidays Vat Car, *03 u*		245
____	**29424**	Meadow River Lumber Skeleton Log Car 3-pack (std O), *03*		90
____	**29429**	Campbell's Soup Vat Car "29429," *03*		38
____	**29430**	Meadow River Lumber Skeleton Log Car 3-pack #2 (std O), *03*		90
____	**29434**	Weyerhauser Skeleton Log Car 3-pack, *05*		100
____	**29438**	Trailer Train Flatcar with 2 UP trailers, *03*		60
____	**29439**	Postwar "6414" Evans Auto Loader, *02*		43
____	**29441**	UP Flatcar "53471" with grader, *02*		43
____	**29442**	CSX Flatcar "600513" with backhoe, *02*		43
____	**29453**	Elk River Lumber Skeleton Log Car 3-pack #2 (std O), *03*		90
____	**29457**	NS Flatcar "157590" with Caterpillar loader, *03*		42
____	**29458**	BNSF Flatcar "922268" with Caterpillar truck, *03*		44
____	**29459**	Water Barrel Car "1878," Archive Collection, *03*		40
____	**29460**	LL Flatcar "3460" with trailers, Archive Collection, *03*		39
____	**29461**	Postwar "6500" Flatcar with red-and-white airplane, *03*		32
____	**29462**	Postwar "6500" Flatcar with white-and-red airplane, *03*		31
____	**29463**	Postwar "6414" Evans Auto Loader, *03*		30
____	**29464**	U.S. Army Vat Car "29464," *04*		35
____	**29465**	U.S. Steel Slag Car 3-pack (std O), *04–05*		160
____	**29469**	U.S. Steel Hot Metal Car 3-pack (std O), *04–05*		190
____	**29473**	Youngstown Sheet & Tube Slag Car 3-pack (std O), *03*		150
____	**29477**	Youngstown Sheet & Tube Hot Metal Car 3-pack (std O), *03*		170
____	**29481**	Cass Scenic Railroad Skeleton Log Car 3-pack (std O), *03*		80

Exc Mint

		Exc	Mint
29487	Boat-loader with 4 boats, *04*		65 ___
29488	Cass Scenic Railroad Skeleton Log Car 3-pack #2 (std O), *04*		90 ___
29492	Pickering Lumber Skeleton Log Car 3-pack #1 (std O), *04*		100 ___
29496	Pickering Lumber Skeleton Log Car 3-pack #2 (std O), *04*		90 ___
29602	Celanese Chemicals 1-D Tank Car, *05*		45 ___
29603	Comet 1-D Tank Car, traditional, *05*		53 ___
29604	Meadow Brook Molasses 1-D Tank Car, traditional, *05*		53 ___
29606	Elvis Presley Gold Record Transport Car, *04*		120 ___
29607	Las Vegas Mint Car, traditional, *05*		58 ___
29609	Alien Suspension Car, *06*		60 ___
29610	Dixie Honey 1-D Tank Car, *06*		60 ___
29611	Sunoco 1-D Tank Car, *06*		60 ___
29612	Las Vegas Poker Chip Car, *06*		40 ___
29613	Postwar "6463" Rocket Fuel 2-D Tank Car, *06*		75 ___
29617	Cities Service Tank Car, *06–07*		48 ___
29618	Hooker Chemicals 3-D Tank Car, *07*		60 ___
29619	Grave's Formaldehyde 1-D Tank Car, *07*		60 ___
29622	Fort Knox Mint Car, lilac, Archive Collection, *07*		60 ___
29624	Monopoly Mint Car with money, *08*		65 ___
29626	"Case Closed" Mint Car with shredded documents, *08*		109 ___
29628	Poinsettia Mint Car, *09*		70 ___
29629	AEC Glow-in-the-Dark Tank Car, *09–10*		54 ___
29633	Christmas Ornament Lighted Mint Car, *10*		70 ___
29634	Federal Reserve Bailout Mint Car, *10*		70 ___
29635	Monopoly "Go To Jail" Mint Car, *10*		70 ___
29636	Vampire Transport Mint Car, *10–11*		70 ___
29637	Candy Cane 2-D Tank Car, *10–11*		55 ___
29640	Coca-Cola Tank Car, *10*		58 ___
29642	Jolly Rancher 1-D Tank Car, *11*		55 ___
29643	Hershey's Syrup 1-D Tank Car, *11*		58 ___
29644	ATSF 1-D Tank Car, *11*		55 ___
29645	Atlantic City Casino Mint Car, *11*		70 ___
29646	Alaska Oil 2-D Tank Car, *11*		50 ___
29647	Gingerbread Man Mint Car, *11*		70 ___
29649	Lionel SP Smoke Pellets Mint Car, *12–13*		70 ___
29650	Cleveland Federal Reserve Mint Car, *11*		70 ___
29651	Richmond Federal Reserve Mint Car, *12*		70 ___
29654	Boston Federal Reserve Mint Car, *13*		70 ___
29655	PRR 16-wheel Flatcar with girders "469846," *12*		75 ___
29656	ATSF 16-wheel Flatcar with transformer "90096," *12*		75 ___
29671	Smoke Pellet Mint Car #2, *13–14*		70 ___
29694	Hershey's Mint Car, *14*		75 ___
29695	Trailer Set Maxi-Stack Pair "48," *13*		120 ___
29697	Santa's Flatcar with submarine, *13*		70 ___
29698	Tree Topper Star Transport Car, *13*		80 ___
29699	Silver and Gold Christmas Mint Car, *13*		70 ___
29703	PRR Porthole Caboose, *01*		45 ___

			Exc	Mint
___	**29708**	C&O Bay Window Caboose "8315," *04*		45
___	**29709**	Pennsylvania N5c Caboose "477938," *04*		40
___	**29711**	Santa Fe Bay Window Caboose, *05*		60
___	**29712**	Postwar "2420" Searchlight Caboose, *04*		50
___	**29718**	N&W Work Caboose, *06*		48
___	**29719**	Santa Fe Caboose "6427," Archive Collection, *06*		48
___	**29726**	Virginian Caboose "6427," Archive Collection, *06–07*		50
___	**29727**	"I Love U.S.A." Bay Window Caboose "1985," *06*		60
___	**29729**	Bethlehem Steel Searchlight Caboose, *06*		90
___	**29732**	PRR Caboose "477871," *08*		45
___	**29733**	White Pass & Yukon Extended Vision Caboose, *09–10*		90
___	**29734**	PRR NS Heritage CA-4 Caboose (std O), *10*		95
___	**29735**	Conrail NS Heritage CA-4 Caboose (std O), *10*		95
___	**29737**	ATSF Bay Window Caboose, traditional, *10–11*		70
___	**29739**	B&M Transfer Caboose, *11*		50
___	**29765**	TankSet Add-on 3-pack (std O), *12*		240
___	**29771**	CN TankSet 2-pack (std O), *12*		160
___	**29774**	GATX TankSet 2-pack (std O), *12*		160
___	**29777**	Cibro TankSet 2-pack (std O), *12*		160
___	**29786**	Bethlehem Steel PS-2 3-bay Hopper (std O), *13*		80
___	**29787**	PRR PS-2 3-bay Hopper (std O), *13*		80
___	**29791**	Wizard of Oz Anniversary Boxcar, *13–14*		70
___	**29792**	Angela Trotta Thomas "Toyland Express" Boxcar, *13*		65
___	**29792**	Where the Wild Things Are Boxcar, *13–14*		70
___	**29800**	MOW Crane Car, TMCC, *04*		250
___	**29804**	UP Crane Car "JPX 250," CC, *05*		320
___	**29805**	Conrail Crane Car "50202," CC, *05*		320
___	**29806**	Weyerhaeuser Log Dump Car, *05*		75
___	**29807**	DM&IR Coal Dump Car, *05*		75
___	**29808**	Candy Cane Dump Car, *05*		55
___	**29809**	Dump Car with presents, *05*		60
___	**29810**	Operating Egg Nog Car with platform, *05*		140
___	**29811**	Merchant's Despatch Transit Hot Box Reefer "12425," *05*		85
___	**29812**	Santa Fe Hot Box Reefer "20699," *05*		90
___	**29813**	Santa Fe Boom Car "19144," Crane Sounds, *05*		210
___	**29814**	Pennsylvania Boom Car "491063," Crane Sounds, *05*		210
___	**29815**	NYC Boom Car "X923," Crane Sounds, *05*		210
___	**29816**	MOW Boom Car "X-816," Crane Sounds, *05*		210
___	**29817**	UP Boom Car "909438," Crane Sounds, *05*		210
___	**29818**	Conrail Boom Car, Crane Sounds, *05*		210
___	**29821**	Postwar "2460" Lionel Lines Crane Car, gray cab, *05*		43
___	**29822**	Postwar "773W" NYC Tender, whistle, *05*		48
___	**29823**	Postwar "3484" Pennsylvania Operating Boxcar, *05*		38
___	**29827**	Postwar "3419" Helicopter Launching Car, *06*		49

		Exc	Mint
29828	Postwar "3666" Minuteman Car with cannon, *06*		85 ___
29829	Postwar "6905" Radioactive Waste Car, *06*		85 ___
29830	PFE Hot Box Reefer "5890" (std O), *06*		105 ___
29831	Swift Hot Box Reefer "15342" (std O), *06*		150 ___
29832	Chessie System Crane Car "940504," CC, *06*		320 ___
29833	Chessie System Boom Car "940561," CC, *06*		210 ___
29834	LL Bay Window Caboose "834," TrainSounds (std O), *06–07*		110 ___
29835	SP Bay Window Caboose "4667," TrainSounds (std O), *06–07*		160 ___
29839	Cherry Picker Car, *06*		63 ___
29849	Lionel Lines Crane Car, silver cab, *06*		60 ___
29850	N&W J Class Tender, air whistle, *06–07*		70 ___
29853	Postwar "6651" Big John Cannon Car, *08*		75 ___
29854	Satellite Launching Car, *07*		70 ___
29855	Lionel Lines Operating Milk Car with platform, *07*		140 ___
29856	Monon Operating Boxcar, *06–07*		65 ___
29857	Lionel Lines Boom Car, *06–07*		55 ___
29858	CP Rail Crane Car "414475," CC, *07*		320 ___
29859	CP Rail Boom Car "412567," CC, *07*		210 ___
29865	Southern Operating Barrel Car, *07–08*		75 ___
29866	Pirates Aquarium Car, *07*		75 ___
29867	NYC Jet Snow Blower "X27207," *07*		120 ___
29868	Alaska Jet Snow Blower, *07*		120 ___
29869	Bethlehem Steel Crane Car, *06*		60 ___
29870	MOW Jet Snow Blower "MWX-16," *07*		120 ___
29874	Peanuts Halloween Aquarium Car, *12*		85 ___
29877	Southern Crane Car "D76," CC, *08*		350 ___
29882	Witches Operating Brew Car, *08*		150 ___
29884	CNJ Twin Dump Car, *08*		85 ___
29885	BN Crane Car "S-104," CC, *10*		340 ___
29886	BN Boom Car "S-1040," CC, *10*		220 ___
29888	Postwar "3494-625" Soo Lines Operating Boxcar, *08*		70 ___
29893	PRR Operating Stock Car "129893," RailSounds, *09*		150 ___
29894	Christmas Chase Gondola, *09*		65 ___
29895	Christmas Operating Snow Globe Car, *10*		75 ___
29897	CSX Chessie System Research Car "3440," *11*		65 ___
29900	"I Love Wisconsin" Boxcar, *01*		35 ___
29901	"I Love Kentucky" Boxcar, *01*		30 ___
29902	"I Love Iowa" Boxcar, *01*		31 ___
29903	"I Love Missouri" Boxcar, *01*		31 ___
29904	2002 Toy Fair Boxcar, *02*		22 ___
29906	"I Love Connecticut" Boxcar, *02*		33 ___
29907	"I Love West Virginia" Boxcar, *02*		33 ___
29908	"I Love Delaware" Boxcar, *02*		33 ___
29909	"I Love Maryland" Boxcar, *02*		65 ___
29910	Toy Fair Centennial Boxcar, *03*		40 ___
29912	"I Love Alabama" Boxcar, *03*		30 ___
29913	"I Love Mississippi" Boxcar, *03*		35 ___
29914	"I Love Louisiana" Boxcar, *03*		35 ___

			Exc	Mint
____	**29915**	"I Love Arkansas" Boxcar, *03*		30
____	**29918**	2003 Toy Fair Boxcar, *03*		48
____	**29919**	2004 Toy Fair Boxcar, *04*		37
____	**29920**	"I Love North Dakota" Boxcar, *03*		35
____	**29921**	"I Love South Dakota" Boxcar, *03*		40
____	**29922**	"I Love Nebraska" Boxcar, *03*		30
____	**29923**	"I Love Kansas" Boxcar, *03*		30
____	**29925**	Toy Fair Polar Express Boxcar, *05*		250
____	**29927**	"I Love Washington" Boxcar, *05*		45
____	**29928**	"I Love Oregon" Boxcar, *05*		40
____	**29929**	"I Love Idaho" Boxcar, *05*		45
____	**29930**	"I Love Utah" Boxcar, *05*		45
____	**29932**	"I Love Oklahoma" Boxcar, *06*		45
____	**29933**	"I Love New Mexico" Boxcar, *06*		45
____	**29934**	"I Love Hawaii" Boxcar, *06*		45
____	**29935**	"I Love Alaska" Boxcar, *06*		45
____	**29936**	"I Love Wyoming" Boxcar, *06*		45
____	**29937**	2006 Toy Fair Boxcar, *06*		38
____	**29942**	Santa Fe Railroad Art Boxcar, *06*		50
____	**29943**	Texas Special Railroad Art Boxcar, *06*		50
____	**29944**	1957 Lionel Art Boxcar, *06*		50
____	**29945**	1947 Lionel Art Boxcar, *06*		50
____	**29949**	Weyerhaeuser Timber Skeleton Log Car 3-pack #2 (std O), *03*		90
____	**29950**	1948 Lionel Art Boxcar, *08*		50
____	**29951**	1954 Lionel Art Boxcar, *08*		50
____	**29952**	GN Art Boxcar, *08*		50
____	**29953**	SP Art Boxcar, *08*		50
____	**29954**	Dealer Christmas Boxcar, *07*		75
____	**29955**	Dealer Boxcar, *08*		75
____	**29958**	Dealer Boxcar, *09*		50
____	**29959**	1952 Lionel Art Boxcar, *09*		58
____	**29960**	Rock Island Art Boxcar, *09–10*		58
____	**29961**	Meet the Beatles Boxcar 2-pack, *10–14*		130
____	**29965**	Lionel Art Boxcar 2-pack, *10–11*		116
____	**29968**	Beatles "A Hard Day's Night" Boxcar, *11–14*		65
____	**29969**	Beatles "Something New" Boxcar, *11–14*		65
____	**29973**	NYC Pacemaker Boxcar "175005," *11*		60
____	**29974**	SP Boxcar "128133," *11*		60
____	**29975**	Holiday Boxcar, *11*		60
____	**29976**	Holiday Boxcar, *12–13*		65
____	**29978**	Railroad Museum of Pennsylvania Boxcar, *12*		65
____	**29979**	Angela Trotta Thomas "Christmas Morning" Boxcar, *12–13*		60
____	**29980**	Elvis Presley 35th Anniversary Boxcar, *12*		70
____	**29994**	U.S. Army Boxcar, *13–14*		65
____	**29995**	U.S. Navy Boxcar, *13–14*		65
____	**29996**	U.S. Marines Boxcar, *13–14*		65
____	**29997**	U.S. Air Force Boxcar, *13–14*		65
____	**29998**	U.S. National Guard Boxcar, *13–14*		65
____	**29999**	U.S. Coast Guard Boxcar, *13–14*		65
____	**30000**	PRR Keystone Super Freight Steam Train, TMCC, *05*		450

		Exc	Mint
30001	Santa Fe El Capitan Passenger Set, TrainSounds, *05–10*		370 ___
30002	Neil Young's Greendale Diesel Freight Set, *04*		420 ___
30003	Pennsylvania Flyer Operating Freight Expansion Pack, *05*		99 ___
30004	Pennsylvania Flyer Passenger Expansion Pack, *05–08*		120 ___
30007	NYC Flyer Operating Freight Expansion Pack, *05*		99 ___
30008	NYC Flyer Passenger Expansion Pack, *05–08*		120 ___
30011	Holiday Expansion Pack, *05*		100 ___
30012	Thomas the Tank Engine Expansion Pack, *05–13*		120 ___
30016	NYC Flyer Steam Freight Set, *06–08*		290 ___
30018	Pennsylvania Flyer Steam Freight Set, *06–07*		200 ___
30020	North Pole Central Christmas Steam Train, *06–07*		220 ___
30021	Cascade Range Steam Logging Train, *06–08*		190 ___
30022	Southwest Diesel Freight Set, TrainSounds, *06*		295 ___
30024	UP Fast Freight Steam Set, TrainSounds, *06–07*		340 ___
30025	Chesapeake Super Freight Steam Set, TMCC, *06–07*		475 ___
30026	CP Diesel Freight Set, TMCC, *06*		540 ___
30034	Great Western Train Set with Lincoln Logs, *07–09*		230 ___
30035	Sodor Freight Expansion Pack, *06–09*		120 ___
30036	Great Western Expansion Pack, *07–08*		120 ___
30037	Pennsylvania Flyer Operating Freight Expansion Pack, *06–08*		120 ___
30038	NYC Flyer Operating Freight Expansion Pack, *06–08*		120 ___
30039	North Pole Central Passenger Expansion Pack, *06–11*		110 ___
30040	North Pole Central Freight Expansion Pack, *06–11*		110 ___
30041	Southwest Diesel Freight Expansion Pack, *06*		110 ___
30042	Cascade Range Expansion Pack, *06*		110 ___
30044	NYC Empire Builder Steam Freight Set, TMCC, *06*		2800 ___
30045	Alaska Steam Work Train, *07–09*		270 ___
30046	Alaska Work Train Expansion Pack, *07–08*		110 ___
30047	Northwest Special Diesel Freight Set, TrainSounds, *07–08*		295 ___
30048	Northwest Special Freight Expansion Pack, *07–08*		110 ___
30049	D&RGW Fast Freight Set, TrainSounds, *08–09*		320 ___
30050	Pennsylvania Super Freight Set, CC, *08*		450 ___
30051	UP Diesel Freight Set, TMCC, *07*		500 ___
30056	Halloween Steam Freight Set, *07–10*		220 ___
30061	UPS Centennial Stream Freight Set, *07–08*		230 ___
30064	Pennsylvania Speeder Set, traditional, K-Line, *06*		75 ___
30065	Best Friend of Charleston Locomotive, *07*		425 ___
30066/67	C&O Empire Builder Steam Freight Set, CC, *07–09*		2700 ___
30068	North Pole Central Christmas Freight Set, *08*		220 ___

			Exc	Mint
_____	30069	Thomas & Friends Passenger Train, *08–12*		170
_____	30070	Lionel Lines 4-4-2 Steam Freight Set, *07*		300
_____	30081	UP Merger Special GP38 Freight Set, *08*		300
_____	30082	UP Heritage Freight Car 3-pack, *08*		100
_____	30084	British Great Western Shakespeare Express Passenger Train, *08*		300
_____	30085	MTA Metro-North M-7 Commuter Car Set, *07–08*		280
_____	30087	Alien Spaceship Recovery Freight Set, *08–09*		230
_____	30088	John Bull Passenger Train, *08*		430
_____	30089	Pennsylvania Flyer Freight Set, *08–10*		200
_____	30091	ATSF Steam Freight Set, *08–09*		270
_____	30094	Chicago & North Western Passenger Set, *08*		150
_____	30096	Pennsylvania Keystone Special Steam Freight Set, *09*		260
_____	30103	NYC 0-8-0 Steam Freight Set, *09–10*		300
_____	30108	American Fire and Rescue GP20 Freight Set, *09–10*		400
_____	30109	Nutcracker Route Christmas Train Set, *10–11*		270
_____	30111	Pullman Passenger Expansion Pack, *09–14*		155
_____	30112	Eastern Freight Expansion Pack, *09–14*		155
_____	30114	MTA LIRR M-7 Commuter Set, *09*		320
_____	30116	Lone Ranger Wild West Freight Set, *09–13*		400
_____	30118	A Christmas Story Steam Freight Set, *09–12*		330
_____	30120	Menards C&NW Steam Passenger Set, *09*		250
_____	30121	ATSF Baby Madison Car 3-pack, *10–11*		190
_____	30122	Wizard of Oz Steam Freight Set, *10–12*		310
_____	30123	Boy Scouts of America Steam Freight Set, *10*		305
_____	30124	Thunder Valley Quarry Steam Freight Set, *10–11*		300
_____	30125	Rio Grande Ski Train, TrainSounds, *10–11*		340
_____	30126	Pennsylvania Flyer Steam Freight Set, *10*		230
_____	30127	Scout Steam Freight Set, *10–12*		200
_____	30128	Western Freight Expansion Pack, *10–12*		138
_____	30131	Chessie System Merger Diesel Freight Set, *10*		300
_____	30133	Strasburg Steam Passenger Set, *10–13*		330
_____	30135	Scout Freight Expansion Pack, *11–14*		115
_____	30136	Thunder Valley Quarry Freight Car Add-on 2-pack, *10–11*		110
_____	30138	Chessie System Merger Freight Car Add-on 2-pack, *10–11*		120
_____	30139	Santa Fe Flyer Steam Freight Set, *10*		270
_____	30141	Sodor Tank and Wagon Expansion Pack, *10–14*		138
_____	30142	Texas Special Freight Set, TrainSounds, *10–11*		700
_____	30144	Operation Eagle Justice Diesel Freight Set, *10–11*		500
_____	30145	Maple Leaf Diesel Freight Set, *10–11*		550
_____	30146	Menards Soo Line Freight Set, *10*	175	275
_____	30147	MTA Long Island M-7 Commuter Set, *11*		320
_____	30153	CSX Diesel Freight Set, *11*		330
_____	30154	BNSF Diesel Freight Set, *11*		340
_____	30155	M&StL Diesel Freight Set, *11–12*		230
_____	30156	NYC Flyer Freight Set, TrainSounds, *11*		300
_____	30157	M&StL Diesel Freight 2-pack Add-on, *11–14*		110

		Exc	Mint
30158	Norfolk Southern GP38 Diesel Freight Train Set, *11*	320	___
30159	Wabash Blue Bird Passenger Set, *11–12*	360	___
30161	Boy Scouts Steam Freight Set, *11–13*	304	___
30162	Thomas & Friends Christmas Set, *13–14*	200	___
30164	Santa's Flyer Steam Freight Set, *11–13*	250	___
30165	Candy Cane Transit Commuter 2-pack, *11–13*	180	___
30166	Coca-Cola 125th Anniversary Steam Set, *11–12*	320	___
30167	SP Merger Steam Freight Train Set, *12*	400	___
30168	Rio Grande General Set, TrainSounds, *11–12*	300	___
30169	NJ Transit Train Set, *11*	350	___
30170	Sodor Freight 3-pack, *11–13*	100	___
30171	GG1 Electric Freight Train Set, *11–13*	550	___
30173	Santa Fe Flyer Freight Set, *11–12*	270	___
30174	Pennsylvania Flyer Freight Set, *11–13*	290	___
30178	ATSF Super Chief Diesel Passenger Train Set, *12–13*	400	___
30179	RI Rocket Diesel Freight Train Set, *12–13*	400	___
30180	Horseshoe Curve Steam Freight Train Set, *12–13*	440	___
30181	CP Diesel Passenger Set, RailSounds, *13*	440	___
30183	Scout Remote Steam Freight Set, *13*	200	___
30184	Polar Express Steam Freight Set, *13*	420	___
30185	NJ Transit Diesel MOW Train Set, *12–13*	350	___
30186	KCS Southern Belle Diesel Freight Train Set, *12–13*	350	___
30187	Titanic Centennial Diesel Freight Train Set, *12–13*	430	___
30188	UP Flyer Steam Freight Train Set, *12–13*	330	___
30189	LIRR Diesel Passenger Train Set, *12–13*	330	___
30190	Thomas & Friends, remote operating system, *12–14*	160	___
30191	Sodor Work Set 3-pack, *12–13*	100	___
30193	Peanuts Christmas Steam Freight Set, *12–14*	330	___
30194	North Pole Express Steam Freight Set, *12–13*	290	___
30195	Grand Central Express Diesel Passenger Train Set, *12–14*	440	___
30196	Hershey's Steam Freight Train Set, *12–13*	308	___
30200	NYC Flyer Steam Freight Train Set, *12–13*	350	___
30205	Silver Bells Christmas Steam Freight Set, *13–14*	240	___
30206	Area 51 RS3 Diesel Freight Set, *13*	250	___
30207	Santa Fe RS3 Diesel Freight Set, *13*	200	___
30210	CP Rail Grain Set Diesel Freight Set, *13*	390	___
30211	BNSF Maxi Stack Diesel Freight Set, *13*	440	___
30213	Northeast NS Heritage Diesel Freight Set, *13*	410	___
30214	Peanuts Halloween Steam Freight Set, *13*	300	___
30217	SP Black Widow Diesel Freight Set, *13*	440	___
30218	Polar Express Steam Passenger Set, *13–14*	400	___
30219	Gingerbread Junction Steam Freight Set, *13*	290	___
30220	Polar Express 10th Anniversary Passenger Set, *13*	470	___
30221	Diesel Remote Control Set, *13–14*	200	___
30222	Percy Remote Control Set, *13–14*	200	___

			Exc	Mint
___	**30223**	James Remote Control Set, *13–14*		200
___	**30224**	Pennsylvania Limited Steam Passenger Set, *13*		340
___	**30225**	Medal of Honor Train, *13*		430
___	**30226**	NS Diesel Freight Set, RailSounds, *13*		410
___	**30228**	Chattanooga Express Steam Passenger Set, *13*		250
___	**30233**	Pennsylvania Flyer Remote Steam Freight Set, *13–14*		250
___	**31569**	Western & Atlantic Passenger Car 2-pack, *08*		100
___	**31700**	Postwar Girls Freight Set, *01*		570
___	**31701**	Postwar Boys Freight Set, *02*		345
___	**31704**	Alton Limited Steam Passenger Set, *02*		870
___	**31705**	50th Anniversary Hudson Passenger Set, *02*		900
___	**31706**	UP Burro Crane Set, *02*		210
___	**31707**	C&O Diesel Freight Set, *03*		280
___	**31708**	Postwar "1805" Marines Missile Launch Train, *03*		400
___	**31710**	BN Diesel Coal Train, RailSounds, *03*		690
___	**31711**	Postwar "1563W" Wabash Diesel Freight Set, RailSounds, *03*		570
___	**31712**	UP Alco PA Diesel Passenger Set, RailSounds, *03*		1495
___	**31713**	Southern Crescent Limited Steam Passenger Set, RailSounds, *03*		1195
___	**31714**	Amtrak Acela Diesel Passenger Set, RailSounds, *04–05*		2000
___	**31715**	Fire Rescue Steam Freight Set, *02*		293
___	**31716**	Fire Rescue Steam Freight Set, *03*		275
___	**31717**	CP Rail Snow Removal Train, *03*		255
___	**31718**	SP "Oil Can" TankTrain Freight Set, *03*		1600
___	**31719**	Western Maryland Fireball Diesel Freight Set, *04*		290
___	**31720**	FEC Champion Diesel Passenger Set, RailSounds, *04*		900
___	**31721**	Postwar "13138" Majestic Electric Freight Set, RailSounds, *04*		580
___	**31724**	Nabisco 3-Car Passenger Set, *03*		110
___	**31727**	Postwar "2291W" Rio Grande Diesel Freight Set, RailSounds, *04*		640
___	**31728**	Elvis "He Dared to Rock" Steam Freight Set, *04*		325
___	**31730**	Norman Rockwell Boxcar 4-pack, *05*		95
___	**31733**	Jones & Laughlin Steel Slag Train, *05*		250
___	**31734**	Chessie Steam Special Passenger Set, TMCC, *05*		405
___	**31735**	Chessie Diesel Freight Set, TMCC, *05–06*		670
___	**31736**	CP Diesel Grain Train, TMCC, *05*		700
___	**31737**	Napa Valley Wine Train, TMCC, *05*		900
___	**31739**	Postwar "13150" Hudson Steam Freight Set, Super O, *05*		940
___	**31740**	Postwar "2519W" Virginian Diesel Freight Set, TMCC, *05–07*		620
___	**31742**	Postwar "2544W" Santa Fe Super Chief Diesel Passenger Set, *05*		700
___	**31746**	GN Mountain Mover Steam Freight Set, *12–13*		430
___	**31747**	Pennsylvania Electric Ballast Train, TMCC, *06*		550

		Exc	Mint
31748	Santa Fe U28CG Diesel Freight Set (std O), TMCC, *06–07*		770 ____
31749	Pennsylvania Diesel Coal Train, TMCC, *06*		770 ____
31750	NYC Hotbox Reefer Steam Freight Set, TMCC, *06–07*		530 ____
31751	New York City Transit Authority R27 Subway Train, CC, *07*		700 ____
31752	B&O Diesel Freight Set, TMCC, *06–07*		740 ____
31753	GN Diesel Freight Set, TMCC, *06–08*		740 ____
31754	Postwar "2545WS" N&W Space Freight Set, TMCC, *06–07*		960 ____
31755	Texas Special Diesel Passenger Set, CC, *07–08*		1280 ____
31757	Postwar "2289WS" Berkshire Freight Set, CC, *07*		750 ____
31758	Postwar "2270W" Jersey Central Diesel Passenger Car Set, CC, *08*		750 ____
31760	CSX SD40-2 Diesel Husky Stack Car Set, CC, *07–08*		770 ____
31765	Postwar "11268" C&O Diesel Freight Set, *08*		580 ____
31767	Bethlehem Steel Rolling Stock Set, K-Line, *06*		100 ____
31768	B&O Rolling Stock Set, K-Line, *06*		100 ____
31772	Conrail LionMaster Diesel Freight Set, CC, *08–09*		535 ____
31773	NS Dash 9 Diesel TankTrain Set, CC, *08*		785 ____
31774	AEC Burro Crane Set, traditional, *09–11*		260 ____
31775	"1562" Burlington GP Passenger Set, *08*		470 ____
31777	"2124W" GG1 Passenger Set, *08*		470 ____
31778	"1484WS" Steam Passenger Set, *08*		610 ____
31779	Amtrak HHP-8 Amfleet Passenger Set, CC, *09*		500 ____
31782	ATSF Crane Car and Boom Car, CC (std O), *09–10*		560 ____
31783	BNSF Ice Cold Express Diesel Freight Set, CC, *10*		1000 ____
31784	No. 1593 UP Work Train Set, *09*		470 ____
31787	CN SD70M-2 Diesel Coal Train, CC, *09*		800 ____
31790	PRR GG1 Passenger Set, *10*		500 ____
31791	NYC LionMaster Diesel Freight Set, CC, *10*		700 ____
31793	White Pass & Yukon Freight Car Add-on 3-pack, *10–11, 13*		195 ____
31795	Pere Marquette Freight Car 3-pack (std O), *10–11*		210 ____
31796	Feather Route Freight Car 3-pack (std O), *10–11*		210 ____
31797	New York City Transit R16 Subway Set, CC, *10*		800 ____
31799	GN Empire Steam Freight Express Set, *10*		430 ____
31901	Christmas Steam Freight Set, *02*		145 ____
31902	PRR K4 Freight Set, *01–02*		580 ____
31904	C&O Steam Freight Set, RailSounds, *01*		400 ____
31905	NH Diesel Freight Set, CC, *01*		660 ____
31907	PRR Atlantic Freight Set, *01 u*		400 ____
31908	Reading Hobo Express Freight Set, *01 u*		365 ____
31909	Santa Fe Shell Tank Car Freight Set, *01 u*		320 ____
31910	Soo Line Diesel Freight Set, *01 u*		350 ____
31911	Snap-On Anniversary Steam Freight Set, *00 u*		580 ____
31913	PRR Flyer Steam Freight Set, *01*		145 ____

		Exc	Mint
____ 31914	NYC Flyer Steam Freight Set, RailSounds, *01–02*		170
____ 31915	Chessie GP38 Diesel Freight Set, *01–02*		155
____ 31916	Santa Fe Steam Freight Set, *01*		300
____ 31918	C&O Steam Freight Set, SignalSounds, *01*		315
____ 31919	T&P Steam Passenger Set, RailSounds, *01*		210
____ 31920	L.L. Bean Freight Set, *01 u*		245
____ 31922	Snap-On Tool Diesel Freight Set, *01 u*		348
____ 31923	PRR Flyer Freight Set, *01 u*		130
____ 31924	Union Pacific RS3 Diesel Freight Set, *02*		95
____ 31926	Area 51 FA Diesel Freight Set, *02*		160
____ 31928	Great Train Robbery Set, *02*		180
____ 31931	Ballyhoo Brothers Circus Train, *02*		190
____ 31932	NYC Limited Passenger Set, RailSounds, *02*		285
____ 31933	Santa Fe Steam Freight Set, RailSounds, *02*		320
31934	Lionel 20th Century Express Steam Freight Set, *00 u*		285
____ 31936	Pennsylvania Flyer Steam Freight Set, *03–05*		190
____ 31938	Southern Diesel Freight Set, *03–04*		160
____ 31939	Great Train Robbery Steam Freight Set, *03*		185
____ 31940	NYC Flyer Steam Freight Set, RailSounds, *03*		225
31941	Winter Wonderland Railroad Christmas Train, *03*		150
____ 31942	Norman Rockwell Christmas Train, *03*		330
31944	NYC Limited Diesel Passenger Set, RailSounds, *03*		250
31945	Santa Fe Steam Super Freight Set, RailSounds, *03*		350
____ 31946	Disney Christmas Steam Train, *04–05*		310
____ 31947	World of Disney Steam Freight Set, *03*		215
____ 31950	Kraft Holiday UP RS3 Diesel Freight Set, *02 u*		149
31952	Great Northern Glacier Route Diesel Freight Set, *03–04*		110
____ 31953	"Riding the Rails" Hobo Train Set, *03–04*		225
____ 31956	Thomas the Tank Engine Set, *04–07*		195
31958	Santa Fe Flyer Steam Freight Set, RailSounds, *04*		205
____ 31960	Polar Express Steam Passenger Set, *04–13*		420
31961	Bloomingdale's Pennsylvania Flyer Steam Freight Set, *02 u*		159
31962	Nickel Plate Road Super Freight Set, RailSounds, *04*		350
31963	Southern Pacific Overnight Steam Freight Set, *04*		340
____ 31966	Holiday Tradition Steam Freight Set, *04–05*		210
____ 31969	NYC Flyer Steam Freight Set, RailSounds, *04*		205
____ 31976	Yukon Special Diesel Freight Set, *05*		225
____ 31977	New York Central Flyer Steam Freight Set, *05*		250
31985	Santa Fe Steam Fast Freight Set, TrainSounds, *05*		320
____ 31989	UP Overland Freight Express Set, *04*		880
____ 31990	Copper Range Steam Freight Mine Set, *05*		175
31993	NS Black Diamond Diesel Freight Set, TMCC, *05*		500
____ 32900	DC Billboard, *99*		24
____ 32902	Construction Zone Signs, set of 6, *99–14*		10

		Exc	Mint
32904	Hellgate Bridge, *99*	235	415 ___
32905	Irvington Factory, *99–00*		295 ___
32910	Rotary Coal Tipple with bathtub gondola, *02*		442 ___
32919	Animated Maiden Rescue, *99*		65 ___
32920	Animated Pylon with airplane, *99*		130 ___
32921	Electric Coaling Station, *99–01*		125 ___
32922	Highway Barrels, set of 6, *99–14*		10 ___
32923	Accessory Transformer, *99–03, 06–14*		46 ___
32929	Icing Station with Santa, *99*		90 ___
32930	Power Supply Set with ZW controller and 2 power supplies, *99–02, 06–09*		425 ___
32933	Christmas Stocking Hanger Set, 4-piece, *99–00*		50 ___
32934	Stocking Hanger, gondola, *99–00*		15 ___
32935	Stocking Hanger, boxcar, *99–00*		15 ___
32960	Hindenburger Cafe, *99*		195 ___
32961	Route 66 UFO Cafe, *99*		200 ___
32987	Hobo Campfire, *99–00*	25	45 ___
32988	Postwar "192" Railroad Control Tower, *99–00*		75 ___
32989	Postwar "464" Sawmill, *99–00*		75 ___
32990	Linex Oil Derrick, *99–00*		55 ___
32991	WLLC Radio Station, *99*		65 ___
32996	Postwar "362" Barrel Loader, *00*		125 ___
32997	Aluminum Rico Station, *00*		300 ___
32998	Hobby Shop, *99–00*		300 ___
32999	Hellgate Bridge, *99–00*		350 ___
33000	GP9 Diesel "3000," RailScope video camera system, *88–90*	125	170 ___
33002	RailScope Television Monitor, *88–90*	45	70 ___
34102	Amtrak Shelter, *04–08*		25 ___
34108	Lionelville Suburban House, *03*		20 ___
34109	Lionelville Large Suburban House, *03*		15 ___
34110	Lionelville Estate House, *03*		30 ___
34111	Lionelville Deluxe Fieldstone House, *03*		17 ___
34112	Lionelville Fieldstone House, *03*		17 ___
34113	Lionelville Large Suburban House, *03*		17 ___
34114	Late Illuminated Station and Terrace, red trim, *03*		475 ___
34117	Early Illuminated Station and Terrace, green trim, *03*		475 ___
34120	TMCC Direct Lockon, *04–14*		50 ___
34121	Lionelville Bungalow, *04*		20 ___
34122	Lionelville Bungalow with garage, *04*		20 ___
34123	Lionelville Bungalow with addition, *04*		20 ___
34124	Lionelville Anastasia's Bakery, *04*		20 ___
34125	Lionelville Cotton's Candy, *04*		20 ___
34126	Lionelville Market, *04*		20 ___
34127	Lionelville O'Grady's Tavern, *04*		22 ___
34128	Lionelville Pharmacy, *04*		15 ___
34129	Lionelville Kiddie City Toy Store, *04*		20 ___
34130	Lionelville Jim's 5&10, *04*		25 ___
34131	Lionelville Al's Hardware, *04*		30 ___
34144	Santa Fe Scrap Yard, *05–06*		80 ___
34145	New Haven Scrap Yard, *06*		100 ___

			Exc	Mint
____	34149	Sly Fox and the Hunter, *05–07*		80
____	34150	Reading Room, *05–06*		70
____	34158	Ring Toss Midway Game, *05–06*		20
____	34159	Camel Race Midway Game, *05–06*		20
____	34162	Operating Oil Pump, *04–09*		53
____	34163	Speeder Shed, *04–06*		30
____	34164	Nutcracker Operating Gateman, *05–08*		80
____	34190	Carousel, *04–06*		165
____	34191	Hobo Depot, *04–05*		70
____	34192	Operating Lumberjacks, *04–06*		60
____	34193	UPS Animated Billboard, *04*		30
____	34194	UPS Package Station, *05*		120
____	34195	UPS People Pack, *06–09, 11*		27
____	34210	TMCC Direct Lockon, *09*		52
____	34500	Rio Grande FT Diesel "5484," traditional, *06*		245
____	34501	Southern FT Diesel "4102," traditional, *06*		400
____	34504	B&O F3 Diesel A Unit "2368," nonpowered, *06–07*		200
____	34505	B&O E7 Diesel AA Set, CC, *07*		700
____	34508	PRR E7 Diesel AA Set, CC, *07*		700
____	34509	PRR E7 Diesel B Unit, nonpowered (std O), *07*		170
____	34510	PRR E7 Diesel B Unit, powered, CC, *07*		300
____	34511	NYC F7 Diesel ABA Set, CC, *07–08*		900
____	34512	NYC F7 Diesel B Unit "2439," powered, CC, *07–08*		300
____	34513	WP F7 Diesel ABA Set, CC, *07–08*		900
____	34514	WP F7 Diesel B Unit "918C," powered, CC, *07–08*		300
____	34515	NYC F7 Diesel Breakdown B Unit "2440," RailSounds, *07*		270
____	34518	PRR E7 Diesel Breakdown B Unit, RailSounds, *07*		270
____	34519	NYC Sharknose RF-16 Diesel AA Set, CC, *07–08*		630
____	34520	NYC Sharknose Diesel B Unit "3818," nonpowered (std O), *07–08*		160
____	34521	Santa Fe F3 Diesel A Unit "17," traditional, *07*		265
____	34522	Santa Fe F3 Diesel B Unit "17," nonpowered (std O), *07*		150
____	34544	ATSF F3 Diesel B Unit, CC, *08*		270
____	34545	D&RGW F3 Diesel B Unit, CC, *08*		270
____	34546	Southern F3 Diesel B Unit, CC, *08*		270
____	34547	Texas Special F3 Diesel B Unit, CC, *08*		270
____	34559	Archive New Haven F3 Diesel AA Set, *10*		500
____	34564	SP Alco PA Diesel AA Set, CC, *10–11*		750
____	34567	SP Alco PB B Unit, CC, *10–11*		400
____	34568	ATSF Alco PA AA Diesel Set, CC, *11*		750
____	34569	ATSF Alco PB Diesel, CC, *11*		400
____	34570	B&O FA Diesel AA Set, CC, *10*		650
____	34573	Postwar Scale ATSF F3 AA Diesel Set, CC, *11*		700
____	34576	Postwar Scale NYC F3 AA Diesel Set, CC, *11*		700
____	34579	Postwar Scale ATSF F3 B Unit, CC, *11*		380
____	34580	Postwar Scale NYC F3 B Unit, CC, *11*		380
____	34581	Postwar "2331" Virginian Train Master Diesel, CC, *10*		495

		Exc	Mint
34582	Postwar "2373" CP F3 Diesel AA Set, CC, *10*	700	___
34585	Postwar "2375" CP F3 B Unit, CC, *10*	380	___
34586	Postwar "2378" MILW F3 Diesel AB Set, CC, *10*	700	___
34589	Postwar "2377" MILW F3 A, powered, CC, *10*	425	___
34594	UP Alco PA AA Diesel Set, CC, *11*	750	___
34597	UP Alco PB Diesel, CC, *11*	400	___
34600	SP GP30 Diesel "5010," CC, *11*	500	___
34601	SP GP30 Diesel "5012," CC, *11*	500	___
34602	SP GP30 Diesel "5014," *11*	380	___
34603	SP GP30 Diesel "5017," nonpowered, *11*	240	___
34604	Conrail GP30 Diesel "2178," CC, *11*	500	___
34605	Conrail GP30 Diesel "2180," CC, *11*	500	___
34606	Conrail GP30 Diesel "2182," *11*	380	___
34607	Conrail GP30 Diesel "2185," nonpowered, *11*	240	___
34608	Lionelville & Western GP30 Diesel "1100," CC, *11*	450	___
34609	Lionelville & Western GP30 Diesel "1103," CC, *11*	450	___
34610	Lionelville & Western GP30 Diesel "1107," *11*	330	___
34611	Lionelville & Western GP30 Diesel "1112," nonpowered, *11*	190	___
34612	NS SD70M-2 Diesel "2658," CC, *11*	550	___
34613	NS SD70M-2 Diesel "2663," CC, *11*	550	___
34614	CN SD70M-2 Diesel "8020," CC, *11*	550	___
34615	CN SD70M-2 Diesel "8024," CC, *11*	550	___
34616	FEC SD70M-2 Diesel "101," CC, *11*	550	___
34617	FEC SD70M-2 Diesel "103," CC, *11*	550	___
34618	George Bush SD70ACe Diesel "4141," CC, *11*	550	___
34619	NH SD70ACe Diesel "8696," CC, *11*	550	___
34620	NH SD70ACe Diesel "8699," CC, *11*	550	___
34623	Texas Special SD70ACe Diesel "6340," CC, *11*	550	___
34624	Texas Special SD70ACe Diesel "6344," CC, *11*	550	___
34625	NP F3 AA Diesel Set, CC, *11*	700	___
34628	NP F3 Diesel B Unit "6005C," CC, *11*	380	___
34629	NP F3 Diesel B Unit "6006C," nonpowered, *11*	240	___
34630	Frisco F3 AA Diesel Set, CC, *11*	700	___
34633	Frisco F3 Diesel B Unit, CC, *11*	380	___
34634	Frisco F3 Diesel B Unit, nonpowered, *11*	260	___
34635	ATSF F3 AA Diesel Set, CC, *11*	700	___
34638	ATSF F3 Diesel B Unit, CC, *11*	380	___
34639	ATSF F3 Diesel B Unit, nonpowered, *11*	240	___
34640	GTW F3 AA Diesel Set, CC, *11*	700	___
34643	GTW F3 Diesel B Unit, CC, *11*	380	___
34644	GTW F3 Diesel B Unit, nonpowered, *11*	260	___
34645	CN F3 AA Diesel Set, CC, *11*	700	___
34648	CN F3 Diesel B Unit, CC, *11*	380	___
34649	CN F3 Diesel B Unit, nonpowered, *11*	260	___
34650	MILW DD35A Diesel "1535," CC, *11*	600	___
34651	MILW DD35A Diesel "1537," nonpowered, *11*	440	___
34662	RI GP9 Diesel "1331," CC, *12–13*	480	___
34663	RI GP9 Diesel "1327," CC, *12–13*	480	___
34664	GN GP9 Diesel "688," CC, *12–13*	480	___
34665	GN GP9 Diesel "695," CC, *12–13*	480	___

			Exc	Mint
____	34666	L&N GP9 Diesel "504," CC, *12–13*		480
____	34667	L&N GP9 Diesel "525," CC, *12–13*		480
____	34668	CN GP90 Diesel "4463," CC, *12*		480
____	34669	CN GP90 Diesel "4455," CC, *12*		480
____	34670	C&O GP9 Diesel "6240," CC, *12–13*		480
____	34671	C&O GP9 Diesel "6243," CC, *12*		480
____	34672	PRR Baldwin Centipede Diesel AA, CC, *12–13*		2200
____	34673	UP Baldwin Centipede Diesel AA, CC, *12*		2200
____	34676	PRR Baldwin Centipede Diesel "5821," CC, *12–14*		1100
____	34677	Seaboard Baldwin Centipede Diesel "4503," CC, *12–14*		1100
____	34680	NdeM Baldwin Centipede Diesel "6402," CC, *12–14*		1100
____	34681	UP GP9 Diesel "256," CC, *12*		480
____	34682	UP GP9 Diesel "261," CC, *12*		480
____	34683	PRR Baldwin Centipede Diesel AA, CC, *12–13*		2200
____	34686	Baldwin Demonstrator Centipede AA, CC, *12*		2200
____	34689	WM F7 AA Diesel Set, CC, *12–13*		730
____	34692	WM F7 B Unit "410," CC, *12–13*		400
____	34693	WM F7 B Unit, CC, *12–13*		250
____	34694	L&N F7 AA Diesel Set, CC, *12*		730
____	34697	L&N F7 B Unit "900," CC, *12–13*		400
____	34698	L&N F7 B Unit, CC, *12–13*		250
____	34701	PRR Baldwin RF-16 Diesel AA Set, CC, *12–14*		730
____	34704	PRR Baldwin RF-16 Diesel B Unit, CC, *12–14*		400
____	34705	PRR Baldwin RF-16 Diesel B Unit, nonpowered, *12–14*		250
____	34731	NH Alco RS-11 Diesel "1413," nonpowered, *12*		240
____	34732	LV Alco RS-11 Diesel "7640," CC, *12*		480
____	34733	LV Alco RS-11 Diesel "7642," CC, *12*		480
____	34734	LV Alco RS-11 Diesel "7643," nonpowered, *12*		240
____	34735	ATSF GP9 Diesel "726," CC, *12*		480
____	34736	ATSF GP9 Diesel "741," CC, *12*		480
____	34737	NP GP9 Diesel "202," CC, *12*		480
____	34738	NP GP9 Diesel "317," CC, *12–13*		480
____	34739	RI GP9 Diesel "1325," nonpowered, *12*		240
____	34740	GN GP9 Diesel "668," nonpowered, *12*		240
____	34741	L&N GP9 Diesel "531," nonpowered, *12*		240
____	34742	CN GP90 Diesel "4527," nonpowered, *12*		240
____	34743	C&O GP9 Diesel "6249," nonpowered, *12*		240
____	34744	UP GP9 Diesel "268," nonpowered, *12*		240
____	34745	Monon Alco C-420 Diesel "509," CC, *12–13*		530
____	34746	Monon Alco C-420 Diesel "512," CC, *12–13*		530
____	34747	Monon Alco C-420 Diesel "514," nonpowered, *12–13*		260
____	34748	LV Alco C-420 Diesel "404," CC, *12*		530
____	34749	LV Alco C-420 Diesel "412," CC, *12*		530
____	34750	LV Alco C-420 Diesel "414," nonpowered, *12*		260
____	34754	Alaska Alco C-420 Diesel "1210," CC, *12*		530
____	34755	Alaska Alco C-420 Diesel "1214," CC, *12*		530
____	34756	Alaska Alco C-420 Diesel "1217," nonpowered, *12*		260

		Exc	Mint
34757	Seaboard Alco C-420 Diesel "127," CC, *12–13*		530 ____
34758	Seaboard Alco C-420 Diesel "129," CC, *12–13*		530 ____
34759	Seaboard Alco C-420 Diesel "134," nonpowered, *12–13*		260 ____
34760	NKP Alco C-420 Diesel "578," CC, *12–13*		530 ____
34761	NKP Alco C-420 Diesel "575," CC, *12–13*		530 ____
34762	NKP Alco C-420 Diesel "572," nonpowered, *12–13*		260 ____
34763	CNJ Scale NW2 Diesel Switcher "1060," CC, *12*		470 ____
34764	CNJ Scale NW2 Diesel Switcher "1061," CC, *12*		470 ____
34765	KCS Scale NW2 Diesel Switcher "1221," CC, *12*		470 ____
34766	KCS Scale NW2 Diesel Switcher "1224," CC, *12*		470 ____
34767	L&N Scale NW2 Diesel Switcher "2203," CC, *12*		470 ____
34768	L&N Scale NW2 Diesel Switcher "2206," CC, *12*		470 ____
34769	MKT Scale NW2 Diesel Switcher "8," CC, *12*		470 ____
34770	MKT Scale NW2 Diesel Switcher "12," CC, *12*		470 ____
34771	Reading Scale NW2 Diesel Switcher "102," CC, *12*		470 ____
34772	Reading Scale NW2 Diesel Switcher "104," CC, *12*		470 ____
34773	PRR Scale NW2 Diesel Switcher "9163," CC, *12*		470 ____
34774	PRR Scale NW2 Diesel Switcher "9171," CC, *12*		470 ____
34775	N&W SD40-2 Diesel "6106," nonpowered, *12–13*		240 ____
34776	N&W SD40-2 Diesel "6121," CC, *12–13*		530 ____
34777	N&W SD40-2 Diesel "6109," CC, *12–14*		530 ____
34778	CSX SD40-2 Diesel "8023," nonpowered, *12–13*		240 ____
34779	CSX SD40-2 Diesel "8028," CC, *12–13*		530 ____
34780	CSX SD40-2 Diesel "8033," CC, *12–13*		530 ____
34781	BN SD40-2 Diesel "7140," nonpowered, *12–13*		240 ____
34782	BN SD40-2 Diesel "7153," CC, *12–13*		530 ____
34783	BN SD40-2 Diesel "7162," CC, *12–13*		530 ____
34784	Frisco SD40-2 Diesel "957," CC, *12–13*		530 ____
34785	Frisco SD40-2 Diesel "950," nonpowered, *12–13*		240 ____
34786	Frisco SD40-2 Diesel "952," CC, *12–13*		530 ____
34787	C&NW SD40-2 Diesel "6816," nonpowered, *12–13*		240 ____
34788	C&NW SD40-2 Diesel "6820," CC, *12–13*		530 ____
34789	C&NW SD40-2 Diesel "6832," CC, *12–13*		530 ____
34790	MKT SD40-2 Diesel "602," nonpowered, *12–13*		240 ____
34791	MKT SD40-2 Diesel "609," CC, *12–13*		530 ____
34792	MKT SD40-2 Diesel "620," CC, *12–13*		530 ____
35100	NYC Vista Dome Car "7012," *07–09*		45 ____
35101	NYC Baggage Car "5028," *07*		40 ____
35102	Santa Fe El Capitan Streamliner Diner, *07*		65 ____

		Exc	Mint
35124	Alton Limited Madison Passenger Car 4-pack, *08–10*		240
35128	ATSF El Capitan Baggage Car "2103," *08*		70
35129	ATSF El Capitan Vista Dome Car "3153," *08*		70
35130	Polar Express Disappearing Hobo Car, *08–12*		65
35133	MTA Metro-North M-7 Commuter Add-on 2-pack, *07–08*		85
35134	North Pole Central Vista Dome Car, *08*		45
35135	North Pole Central Diner, *08–10*		45
35167	PRR Diner "2044," *10*		52
35168	PRR Coach "4046," *09*		52
35173	North Pole Central Blitzen Coach, *09*		45
35174	MTA LIRR M-7 Add-on 2-pack, *09*		98
35184	Western & Atlantic Baggage Car, *09*		60
35185	Great Western Passenger Car 2-pack, *09*		100
35193	PRR Streamliner 4-pack, *10–11*		250
35200	Strasburg Observation Car, *10*		60
35205	D&RGW Pikes Peak Add-on Coach, *10–11*		70
35211	Strasburg Passenger Car Add-on 2-pack, *10*		100
35214	Rio Grande Winter Park Diner, *11*		70
35219	Hallow's Eve Express Passenger Car 2-pack, *11*		120
35229	Hogwarts Express Dementors Coach, *11–14*		60
35239	NJ Transit 2-pack Passenger Car Add-on, *11–14*		100
35247	Grand Central Express Passenger Car 2-pack, *12–13*		140
35250	North Pole Coach 2-pack, *12–13*		120
35256	Hallow's Eve Express Passenger Car 2-pack #2, *12*		120
35257	ATSF Vista Dome, *12*		70
35258	ATSF Baggage Car, *12–13*		70
35259	LIRR Passenger Car 2-pack, *12–14*		110
35281	ATSF Super Chief Diner "1495," *13*		70
35282	LIRR Jamaica Coach, *13–14*		60
35283	CP Baggage Car and Diner 2-pack, *13*		130
35286	Peanuts Coach 3-pack, *13*		165
35290	Polar Express Passenger Car Add-on 2-Pack, *13*		150
35294	Polar Express Snow Tower, *13*		28
35295	Christmas Billboard Set, *13*		13
35403	NYC 20th Century Limited 18" Aluminum Passenger Car 4-pack (std O), *08*		625
35408	NYC 20th Century Limited 18" Aluminum Passenger Car 2-pack (std O), *08*		325
35411	NYC 20th Century Limited Diner, StationSounds (std O), *08*		325
35412	Lenny Dean Passenger Coach, *08*		100
35413	LL Streamliner Car 2-pack, *08*		270
35415	UP 18" Streamliner Car 4-pack (std O), *08*		625
35423	UP 18" Streamliner Car 2-pack (std O), *08*		325
35430	Amtrak Coach		45
35431	Amtrak Coach		45
35432	Amtrak Coach		45
35433	Amfleet Phase IVB Coach 2-pack (std O), *10*		140

Exc Mint

		Exc	Mint
35445	SP Shasta Daylight 18" Passenger Car 4-pack (std O), *11*		640 ____
35446	SP Shasta Daylight 18" Passenger Car 2-pack (std O), *11*		320 ____
35454	Amfleet Cab Control End Car (std O), *10*		90 ____
35473	Amfleet Capstone Coach 3-pack (std O), *10*		180 ____
35481	NYC Add-on Passenger Car "M-498," *11*		120 ____
35490	Alaska Budd RDC Combination Car "702," nonpowered, *11*		130 ____
35497	RI Budd RDC Combination Car "751," nonpowered, *11*		130 ____
35498	RI Budd RDC Coach "750," nonpowered, *11*		130 ____
35499	Alaska Budd RDC Coach "712," nonpowered, *11*		130 ____
36000	Route 66 Flatcar with 2 red sedans, *98*		44 ____
36001	Route 66 Flatcar with 2 wagons, *98*		42 ____
36002	Pratt's Hollow Passenger Car 4-pack, *98*		445 ____
36006	Uranium Flatcar "6508," *99*		60 ____
36016	Flatcar with propellers, *98*		45 ____
36020	Flatcar "TT-6424" with auto frames, *99*		32 ____
36021	Alaska Flatcar "6424" with airplane, *99*		44 ____
36024	J.B. Hunt Flatcar "64245" with trailer, *99*		44 ____
36025	J.B. Hunt Flatcar "64246" with trailer, *99*		50 ____
36026	Flatcar with J.B. Hunt trailers 2-pack, *99*		85 ____
36027	Tredegar Iron Works Flatcar with cannon, *99*		45 ____
36028	Heavy Artillery Flatcar with cannon, *99*		45 ____
36029	SP Auto Carrier "516712," *99*		44 ____
36030	Troublesome Truck #1, *99*		35 ____
36031	Troublesome Truck #2, *99*		35 ____
36032	Christmas Gondola "6462" with presents, *99*		35 ____
36036	C&O Gondola, *99*		20 ____
36038	Construction Zone Gondola, *99 u*		NRS ____
36040	Bethlehem Flatcar with block (SSS), *99*		75 ____
36041	Bethlehem Ore Car (SSS), *99*		40 ____
36043	Custom Consist Flatcar with pickup truck, *99*		40 ____
36044	Custom Consist Flatcar with dragster, *99*		40 ____
36045	Flatcar with dragster, *04*		30 ____
36046	Flatcar with custom truck, *04*		30 ____
36047	Construction Zone Gondola, *99 u*		NRS
36048	Construction Zone Gondola, *99 u*		NRS ____
36054	Archaeological Expedition Gondola with eggs, *00 u*		55 ____
36055	Flatcar with dragster, *01 u*		30 ____
36056	Flatcar with roadster, *01 u*		30 ____
36059	"Season's Greetings" Gondola, *99 u*		50 ____
36062	NYC 6462 Gondola, *99–00*		22 ____
36063	Conrail Gondola "604768," *99–00*		20 ____
36064	Billboard Flatcar "6424," *00*		41 ____
36065	Wabash Flatcar "25536" with trailer, *00*		35 ____
36066	Christmas Gondola with presents, *00*		32 ____
36067	King Auto Sales Flatcar "6424" with pink Cadillac, *00*		40 ____
36068	Pine Peak Tree Transport Gondola, *00*		NRS ____
36079	Service Station Ltd. Flatcar with trailer, *00*		34 ____

			Exc	Mint
___	36082	Whirlpool Flatcar with trailer, *00 u*		NRS
___	36083	Santa Fe Gondola "168998," *01*		17
___	36084	Grand Trunk Western Coil Car, *00*		32
___	36085	FEC Coil Car, *00*		29
___	36086	SP Flatcar with trailer, *01*	34	35
___	36087	Flatcar "6424" with wooden whistle, *01*		25
___	36088	Allis Chalmers Condenser Car "6519," *00*		43
___	36089	Frisco Flatcar with airplane, *00*		35
___	36090	TT Flatcar "6424" with Pepsi truck, *01*		44
___	36091	Maersk Flatcar "250129" with die-cast tractors, *00*		55
___	36092	Maersk Flatcar "250130" with die-cast frames, *00*		55
___	36093	Soo TT Auto Carrier "906760," *00*		49
___	36094	PC F9 Well Car "768122," *01*		41
___	36095	Christmas Chase Gondola, *01*		37
___	36098	PRR Gondola "385186," *01*		20
___	36099	NYC Flatcar with stakes and bulkheads, *01*		25
___	36104	Area 51 3-D Tank Car, *07*		60
___	36108	Candy Cane 1-D Tank Car, *07*		60
___	36112	NP 3-D Tank Car, *08*		35
___	36113	IC 1-D Tank Car, *08*		35
___	36114	ART Wood-sided Reefer, *08*		35
___	36117	Lionel Lines 2-D Tank Car, *08*		50
___	36118	NYC Pastel Stock Car "63561," *08–09*		55
___	36128	Texas & Pacific 3-D Tank Car, *09*		40
___	36129	British Columbia 1-D Tank Car, *09*		40
___	36131	Lackawanna Wood-sided Reefer "7000," *09–10*		40
___	36145	Philadelphia Quartz 3-D Tank Car "606," *10*		40
___	36146	Cities Service 1-D Tank Car "11800," *10*		40
___	36149	Strasburg Wood-sided Reefer "105," *10*		55
___	36151	Grave's Blood Bank Tank Car, *10*		50
___	36156	Pennsylvania Power & Light 1-D Tank Car, *10*		40
___	36162	Diamond Chemicals 3-D Tank Car, *11*		40
___	36163	Celanese 2-D Tank Car, *11–12*		40
___	36166	Polar Express Reefer, *11–12*		55
___	36169	Coca-Cola 3-D Tank Car, *11*		55
___	36170	Partridge in a Pear Tree Reefer, *11–13*		55
___	36172	Bubble Yum 1-D Tank Car, *11*		55
___	36173	Santa's Flyer Hot Cocoa 3-D Tank Car, *11*		40
___	36176	C&O 1-D Tank Car, *13*		43
___	36177	WP 3-D Tank Car, *12*		40
___	36178	Frisco 2-D Tank Car, *12–13*		40
___	36182	Eggnog Unibody 1-D Tank Car, *12*		70
___	36191	GN Waffle-sided Boxcar, *13*		43
___	36195	PRR Flatcar with patrol helicopter, *13*		60
___	36200	Quaker Life Cereal Boxcar, *00*	410	452
___	36203	Whirlpool Boxcar, *00 u*		115
___	36205	eBay Boxcar, *00*		251
___	36206	REA Boxcar, *01*		25
___	36207	Vapor Records Christmas Boxcar, *01*		69
___	36208	Father's Day Boxcar, *00*		35
___	36210	Burlington Hi-Cube Boxcar "19825," *01*		40

		Exc	Mint
36211	NP Hi-Cube Boxcar "659999," *01*		33 ____
36212	Lionel Employee Christmas Boxcar, *00 u*		405 ____
36213	Vapor Records Christmas Boxcar, *00*		45 ____
36215	Train Station 25th Anniversary Boxcar, *00 u*		48 ____
36218	Snap-On Boxcar, *00 u*		125 ____
36219	UP Boxcar "183518," *02*		78 ____
36220	Pioneer Seed Boxcar, *00 u*		NRS ____
36221	PRR Boxcar "569356," *01*		20 ____
36222	NYC Boxcar "162440," *01*		20 ____
36223	Chessie System Boxcar, *01*		20 ____
36224	Santa Fe Boxcar "16263," *01*		20 ____
36225	C&O Boxcar "250549," *01*		20 ____
36226	E-Hobbies Boxcar, *01 u*		200 ____
36227	Monopoly Community Chest Boxcar, *00 u*		50 ____
36228	Lionel Visitor Center Boxcar, *01 u*		34 ____
36229	Island Trains 20th Anniversary Boxcar, *01 u*		29 ____
36232	Farmall Boxcar, *01 u*		NRS ____
36236	TM Books "I Love Lionel" Boxcar "7474-1," *01 u*		43 ____
36238	Snap-On Tool Team ASE Racing Boxcar, *01 u*		NRS ____
36239	L.L. Bean Boxcar, *01 u*		115 ____
36240	Do It Best Boxcar, *01 u*		100 ____
36242	Erie-Lackawanna Boxcar "73113," *02*		24 ____
36243	Christmas Boxcar "2002," *02*		31 ____
36244	Teddy Bear Centennial Boxcar, *02*		36 ____
36245	Lionel 20th Century Boxcar "1900-1925," *00 u*		30 ____
36246	Lionel 20th Century Boxcar "1926-1950," *00 u*		30 ____
36247	Lionel 20th Century Boxcar "1951-1975," *00 u*		30 ____
36248	Lionel 20th Century Boxcar "1976-2000," *00 u*		30 ____
36253	Christmas Boxcar (O), *03*		32 ____
36254	Goofy Hi-Cube Boxcar, *03*		37 ____
36255	Donald Duck Hi-Cube Boxcar, *03*		40 ____
36256	GN Boxcar "6341," *03*		23 ____
36261	PRR Boxcar, */03–05*		15 ____
36262	Southern Central of Georgia Boxcar, *03 04*		20 ____
36264	Santa Fe Boxcar "600196, *02*		18 ____
36265	Angela Trotta Thomas "Window Wishing" Boxcar, *02*		38 ____
36267	Mickey Mouse Hi-Cube Boxcar, *03*		50 ____
36270	Angela Trotta Thomas "Home for the Holidays" Boxcar, *02–03*		30 ____
36272	New Haven Boxcar "6501," *04*		20 ____
36273	Railbox Hi-Cube Boxcar "15000," *04*		21 ____
36275	Christmas Boxcar, *04*		35 ____
36276	Angela Trotta Thomas "Tis the Season" Boxcar, *04*		34 ____
36277	Pluto Hi-Cube Boxcar, *04–05*		50 ____
36278	Winnie the Pooh Hi-Cube Boxcar, *04–05*		50 ____
36281	B&O Boxcar, *04*		35 ____
36291	Simpsons Boxcar, *04–05*		44 ____
36294	UP Hi-Cube Boxcar, traditional, *05*		27 ____

		Mint
____ 36295	CN Boxcar, traditional, *05*	27
____ 36296	2005 Holiday Boxcar, *05*	48
36297	Angela Trotta Thomas "Christmas Eve" Boxcar,	
____	*05*	48
____ 36299	Hammacher Schlemmer Music Boxcar, *04*	65
____ 36305	eBay Boxcar, *00 u*	112
____ 36500	Western Pacific Caboose "36500," *04*	23
____ 36501	D&RGW Caboose "36501," *04*	22
____ 36502	Reading Caboose "36502," *04*	25
____ 36515	North Pole Central Lines Caboose "36515," *04*	36
____ 36519	Lionel Lines Caboose, *04*	22
____ 36520	Santa Fe Caboose "36520," *04*	22
____ 36525	CSX Work Caboose, lighted, *05*	35
____ 36526	Pennsylvania Work Caboose, traditional, *05*	27
____ 36527	Santa Fe Work Caboose, traditional, *05*	28
36528	Chesapeake & Ohio Work Caboose, traditional,	
____	*05*	40
36529	North Pole Central Work Caboose with	
____	presents, traditional, *05*	38
____ 36530	Pennsylvania Caboose, traditional, *05*	33
____ 36531	Erie Caboose "C150," traditional, *05*	33
____ 36532	SP Caboose "1097," traditional, *05*	48
____ 36533	Reading Caboose "92803," traditional, *05*	33
____ 36534	NYC Center Cupola Caboose, traditional, *05*	40
____ 36535	LL Center Cupola Caboose, traditional, *05*	28
36536	Southern Center Cupola Caboose, traditional,	
____	*05*	40
36547	Bethlehem Steel Transfer Caboose, traditional,	
____	*05*	40
____ 36548	Transylvania RR Work Caboose, traditional, *05*	45
36550	Halloween Transfer Caboose, traditional,	
____	*06–07*	45
____ 36551	Christmas Caboose, *06*	45
____ 36552	U.S. Steel Work Caboose, traditional, *06–07*	45
____ 36553	NYC Caboose, *08*	20
____ 36554	SP Work Caboose, traditional, *06*	45
____ 36555	Pennsylvania Transfer Caboose, *06*	45
____ 36556	Lionel Lines Work Caboose, *06–07*	30
____ 36557	Rio Grande Work Caboose, traditional, *06*	29
36558	Virginian Center Cupola Caboose "316,"	
____	traditional, *06*	45
36559	WM Center Cupola Caboose "1863,"	
____	traditional, *06*	45
36560	C&O Center Cupola Caboose "90876,"	
____	traditional, *06*	45
36562	Army Transportation Work Caboose,	
____	traditional, *06*	45
____ 36563	Reading Work Caboose, traditional, *06*	45
____ 36565	UP SP-type Caboose, traditional, *06*	48
____ 36566	NYC SP-type Caboose, traditional, *06*	48
____ 36567	GN SP-type Caboose, traditional, *06*	48
____ 36571	PRR Caboose, *08*	20
36580	B&O Center Cupola Caboose "C2047,"	
____	traditional, *05*	40
____ 36582	C&O Caboose, *05*	22

Exc Mint

		Exc	Mint
36583	Holiday Caboose, *07*		50 ___
36587	SP Caboose "1121," *07–09*		40 ___
36589	PRR Work Caboose, *07*		40 ___
36590	UP Work Caboose, *07*		45 ___
36591	Southern Caboose "X99," *08*		45 ___
36592	Santa Fe Caboose "999471," *06*		48 ___
36593	NYC Caboose, *06*		48 ___
36601	UP Caboose, *06*		48 ___
36602	UPS Centennial Caboose, *06*		45 ___
36604	Pennsylvania Caboose, *06*		25 ___
36607	K-Line Caboose, *06*		40 ___
36611	Conrail Caboose "19674," *07*		40 ___
36612	Alaska Caboose "1080," *07*		40 ___
36613	NYC Caboose, *07*		30 ___
36622	C&O Caboose "C-1838," *08–09*		40 ___
36623	ATSF Caboose, *07–09*		40 ___
36624	Lionel Lines Caboose, *08–09*		40 ___
36625	B&M Caboose, *08*		50 ___
36626	Erie Caboose "C101," *08–09*		45 ___
36634	Holiday Porthole Caboose, green, *08*		50 ___
36646	Monopoly Caboose, *10*		48 ___
36647	Strasburg Caboose, *10*		48 ___
36649	Pennsylvania Power & Light Work Caboose, *10*		45 ___
36657	Western & Atlantic Caboose, *10–11*		48 ___
36659	PRR Illuminated Porthole Caboose, *11*		35 ___
36668	CSX Illuminated Square Window Caboose, *10*		35 ___
36672	NS Caboose, *11*		25 ___
36674	Polar Caboose, *11–12*		53 ___
36701	Baldwin Locomotive Works Operating Welding Car "36701," *02*		60 ___
36702	Bosco Operating Milk Car with platform, *02*		115 ___
36703	Circus Horse Car with corral, *06*		150 ___
36704	Animated Reindeer Stock Car and Corral, *02*		145 ___
36718	AEC Security Caboose, *02*		42 ___
36719	Lionel Lion Bobbing Head Car, *02*		20 ___
36720	Aladdin Aquarium Car, *03*		40 ___
36721	101 Dalmatians Animated Gondola, *03*		45 ___
36722	Peter Pan Bobbing Head Boxcar, *03*		45 ___
36726	Santa Fe Searchlight Car "36726," *03*		50 ___
36727	Weyerhaeuser Moe & Joe Flatcar, *03*		65 ___
36728	SP Walking Brakeman Boxcar 163143," *03*		42 ___
36729	Lionel Lines Animated Caboose, *04–05*	12	68 ___
36730	U.S. Army Missile Launch Sound Car "44," *03*		175 ___
36731	Motorized Aquarium Car "3435," *03*		83 ___
36732	C&NW Jumping Hobo Car, *03*		41 ___
36733	Christmas Music Boxcar, *03*		45 ___
36734	Santa Fe Operating Searchlight Car "20611," *02*		25 ___
36735	WP Ice Car "7045," *02*		55 ___
36736	D&RGW Stock Car "39268," RailSounds, *04*		45 ___
36738	T&P Poultry Dispatch Car "36738," *02*		50 ___
36739	Postwar "3461" Lionel Lines Log Dump Car, *03*		50 ___

		Exc	Mint
____	**36740** Postwar "3469" Lionel Lines Coal Dump Car, *03*		49
____	**36743** Santa Claus Bobbing Head Boxcar, *03*		40
____	**36744** Little Mermaid Aquarium Car, *03*		55
____	**36745** Toy Story Animated Gondola, *03*		70
____	**36753** LFD Firecar with ladder, *02*		60
____	**36757** Southern Searchlight Car, *03–04*		NRS
____	**36758** Patriotic Lighted Boxcar, *02*		60
____	**36760** B&O Sentinel Operating Brakeman Boxcar "3424," Archive Collection, *02*		65
____	**36761** Wellspring Capital Management Lighted Boxcar, *02 u*		215
____	**36764** West Side Lumber Log Dump Car "36764," *03*		55
____	**36765** Alaska Coal Dump Car "401," *03*		50
____	**36766** Erie Chase Gondola, *03*		50
____	**36767** Santa's Radar Tracking Car, *03*		40
____	**36769** Fourth of July Lighted Boxcar, *03*		70
____	**36770** American Refrigerator Transit Ice Car "23701," *04*		42
____	**36771** CN Barrel Car "74208," *04*		48
____	**36772** Spokane, Portland & Seattle Log Dump Car "36772," *04*		46
____	**36773** Jersey Central Coal Dump Car "92926," *04*		45
____	**36774** PRR Moe & Joe Lumber Flatcar, *04*		50
____	**36775** Santa Fe Animated Caboose "999010," *05*		75
____	**36776** Santa Fe Walking Brakeman Car "19938," *04*		43
____	**36778** C&O Searchlight Car "216614," *04*		30
____	**36780** Sea-Monkeys Motorized Aquarium Car, *04*		45
____	**36781** Finding Nemo Aquarium Car, *04*		50
____	**36782** Goofy and Pete Jumping Boxcar, *05*		70
____	**36783** Disney Operating Boxcar, *04–05*		65
____	**36784** Monsters Inc. Bobbing Head Boxcar, *04*		40
____	**36786** Postwar "3494-150" MP Operating Boxcar, *03*		40
____	**36787** MOW Remote Control Searchlight Car, *04*		45
____	**36788** Lionel Lines Tender, TrainSounds, *04*		75
____	**36789** Railbox Boxcar, TrainSounds, *04–05*		105
____	**36790** Christmas Music Boxcar, *04*		70
____	**36793** Pennsylvania Derrick Car, *03*		22
____	**36794** NYC Log Dump Car, *03*		25
____	**36795** Southern Coal Dump Car, *03*		25
____	**36796** GN Searchlight Car, *03*		24
____	**36797** "Operation Iraqi Freedom" Minuteman Car, *03*		45
____	**36803** Santa Animated Caboose, *06*		75
____	**36804** Candy Cane Dump Car, *06*		80
____	**36805** Reindeer Jumping Boxcar, *06*		70
____	**36809** NYC Derrick Car, *07–08*		35
____	**36810** PRR Searchlight Car, *07*		35
____	**36811** UP Dump Coal Dump Car, *07*		35
____	**36812** British Columbia Log Dump Car, *07–08*		35
____	**36813** State of Maine Brakeman Car, *08*		80
____	**36814** D&RGW Animated Caboose "01415," *07–09*		80
____	**36815** Santa Fe Moe & Joe Flatcar, *07–08*		80
____	**36816** Virginian Coal Dump Car, *08*		80
____	**36818** U.S. Steel Searchlight Car, *07–08*		75

		Exc	Mint
36821	"Naughty or Nice" Dump Car, *07*		80 ____
36823	Halloween SpookySmoke Boxcar, *07*		110 ____
36824	AlienSmoke Boxcar, *07*		110 ____
36829	Alien Radioactive Car, *07*		70 ____
36830	Trick or Treat Aquarium Car, *07*		75 ____
36831	MOW Welding Car, *07–08*		75 ____
36833	Christmas Music Boxcar, *07*		65 ____
36834	Santa Fe Transparent Instruction Car, *07–08*		65 ____
36838	Lionel Power Co. Voltmeter Car, K-Line, *06*		75 ____
36839	Operating Milk Car with platform, K-Line, *06*		140 ____
36841	Visitor Center 15th Anniversary Lighted Boxcar, *06*		70 ____
36847	Polar Express Tender, TrainSounds, *08–12*		115 ____
36848	Candy Cane Dump Car, *07*		80 ____
36849	Tell-Tale Reindeer Car, *07*		53 ____
36850	Santa and Snowman Boxcar, *07*		75 ____
36851	Generator Car with Christmas tree, *07*		75 ____
36853	U.S. Army Exploding Boxcar, *08*		60 ____
36855	GW Horse Car and Corral, *08*		160 ____
36856	W&ARR Sheriff and Outlaw Car, *08*		75 ____
36857	Bobbing Ghost Boxcar, *08*		65 ____
36859	Lionel Lines Aquarium Car, *08*		80 ____
36861	PRR Poultry Dispatch Car, *08–09*		80 ____
36863	Alien Security Car, *08*		80 ____
36864	Bethlehem Steel Searchlight Car, *08*		40 ____
36866	WP Coal Dump Car "52369," *08*		40 ____
36868	NH Barrel Ramp Car, *08*		40 ____
36869	Bobbing Santa Boxcar, *08*		65 ____
36870	Postwar "6812" Track Maintenance Car, *08*		65 ____
36874	PRR Searchlight Car, *09*		35 ____
36875	Polar Express Coach, sound, *08–13*		115 ____
36878	NYC Track Cleaning Car, *08*		150 ____
36879	REA Ice Car "1221," *08*		65 ____
36880	Koi Fish Aquarium Car, *10*		75 ____
36881	Christmas Music Boxcar, *08*		70 ____
36887	Great Western Animated Gondola, *08–09*		65 ____
36888	Casper Aquarium Car, *09–10*		90 ____
36889	PRR Barrel Ramp Car, *09–10*		46 ____
36893	UP Transparent Instruction Car "195220," *09–10*		75 ____
36896	Christmas Music Boxcar, *09*		80 ____
36897	Pennsylvania Power & Light Coal Dump Car, *09–10*		46 ____
36898	Wisconsin Central Log Dump Car, *09*		46 ____
36900	Depressed Center Flatcar with backshop load, *99*		115 ____
36913	Allied Chemical 1-D Tank Car 2-pack, *00*		150 ____
36914	Allied Chemical 1-D Tank Car "68075," die-cast, white, *00*		90 ____
36915	Allied Chemical 1-D Tank Car "68076," die-cast, white, *00*		90 ____
36916	Allied Chemical 1-D Tank Car 2-pack, *00*		175 ____
36917	Allied Chemical 1-D Tank Car "65124," die-cast, black, *00*		95 ____

		Exc	Mint
36918	Allied Chemical 1-D Tank Car "65125," die-cast, black, *00*		90
36927	B&O DC Hopper 6-pack, "435040-45," *01*		520
36935	Maersk Maxi-Stack Car 2-pack, "250131-32," *00*		135
36937	SP Maxi-Stack Car "513957," *02*		65
36998	Gingerbread Man Gateman, *12–13*		80
37001	No. 3444 Erie Animated Gondola, *09*		70
37002	Operating Plutonium Car 2-pack, *10–11*		140
37003	PRR Jet Snow Blower "491252," *09–10*		138
37004	Area 51 Searchlight Car, *09*		46
37006	Lionel Flatcar with operating LCD billboard, *09*		180
37009	Smoking Mount St. Helens Boxcar, *10–11*		125
37010	Pennsylvania Power & Light Searchlight Car, *10*		46
37011	B&M Operating Milk Car with platform, *10*		155
37012	GN Jumping Hobo Boxcar, *10*		75
37015	Jack-o-Lantern Flatcar, *11–13*		75
37016	Radioactive Plutonium Flatcar, *11*		70
37017	Plutonium Boom Car, *11*		70
37022	ATSF Blinking Billboard, *12*		25
37032	Postwar "3562" Operating Barrel Car, *11*		75
37033	Casper Animated Gondola, *11*		70
37035	Santa's Operating Snow Globe Car, *11*		75
37036	Halloween Operating Globe Car, *11*		78
37038	Halloween Searchlight Car, *12–13*		45
37039	Minuteman Searchlight Car, *11*		45
37040	UP Derrick Car, *11–12*		46
37041	Pennsylvania Power & Light Coal Dump Car, *11*		80
37042	IC Coal Dump Car, *11*		46
37043	Seaboard Log Dump Car, *11*		46
37044	CP Rail Log Dump Car, *11, 13*		80
37045	Beatles Yellow Submarine Aquarium Car, *11*		85
37047	Santa's Flyer Animated Gondola, *11*		55
37053	EL Derrick Car, *12*		45
37054	CSX Coal Dump Car, *12*		46
37055	SP Log Dump Car, *12*		46
37056	Zombie Aquarium Car, *12*		80
37057	Bethlehem Steel Culvert Car, *12*		65
37058	Ghost Globe Halloween Car, *12–14*		75
37059	Christmas Snow Globe Car, *12*		85
37060	LIRR Derrick Car, *13–14*		50
37061	UP Railroad Speeder, CC, *12–14*		150
37062	NS Railroad Speeder, CC, *12–14*		150
37063	PRR Railroad Speeder, CC, *12–14*		150
37064	CSX Railroad Speeder, CC, *12–14*		150
37065	BNSF Railroad Speeder, CC, *12–14*		150
37066	MOW Railroad Speeder, CC, *12–14*		150
37067	NYC Railroad Speeder, CC, *12–14*		150
37068	CN Railroad Speeder, CC, *12–14*		150
37069	Strasburg RR Crane Car, *12*		65
37070	Gingerbread Man and Santa Animated Gondola, *12*		55

		Exc	Mint
37071	MOW Searchlight Car, *12*		46 ___
37073	U.S. Marine Corps Cannon Car, *12*		75 ___
37075	Boy Scouts of America Crane Car, *13*		75 ___
37076	Bethlehem Steel Coal Dump Car, *13*		50 ___
37078	RI Searchlight Car, *13*		50 ___
37079	Santa Fe Derrick Car, *13*		50 ___
37081	Peanuts Pumpkin Jack-O-Lantern Car, *13*		85 ___
37082	Peanuts Animated Trick or Treat Chase Gondola, *14*		70 ___
37083	Strasburg Coal Dump Car, *13*		50 ___
37084	PRR Cop and Hobo Animated Gondola, *13*		65 ___
37085	BN Log Dump Car, *13*		50 ___
37086	Lionelville Aquarium Co. Aquarium Car, *13*		80 ___
37087	NH Walking Brakeman Car, *13–14*		75 ___
37089	Santa's List Snow Globe Car, *13*		90 ___
37090	Polar Express Searchlight Car, *13*		60 ___
37094	Wizard of Oz Aquarium Car, *13–14*		85 ___
37095	North Pole Sleigh Repair Welding Car, *13*		85 ___
37097	Where the Wild Things Are Aquarium Car, *13–14*		85 ___
37099	North Pole Central EV Caboose "2510" (std O), *13*		95 ___
37100	Barrel Loader Building, *12–14*		43 ___
37101	Smiley Water Tower, *12–14*		23 ___
37102	Watchman Shanty, *12–14*		30 ___
37103	O31 Curved Track (FasTrack), *13–14*		5 ___
37110	LionChief FasTrack Terminal, *14*		9 ___
37112	Helicopter 2-pack, *13–14*		35 ___
37120	Railroad Crossing Signs, *13–14*		10 ___
37121	Christmas Station Platform, *13*		25 ___
37122	Santa Fe Blinking Billboard, *13*		25 ___
37123	Weyerhaeuser Timber Operating Sawmill, *12–13*		140 ___
37124	West Side Lumber Operating Sawmill, *12–13*		140 ___
37125	Legacy Writable Utility Mobile, *12–14*		20 ___
37127	Angela Trotta Thomas Gallery, *12*		75 ___
37129	Boy Scouts of America Girder Bridge, *13*		23 ___
37130	Boy Scouts of America Covered Bridge, *13*		60 ___
37139	Tis the Season Accessories, *12–13*		310 ___
37140	All Aboard Accessories, *12–13*		65 ___
37141	Rail Yard Accessories, *12–13*		277 ___
37142	Welcome Home Accessories, *12–13*		154 ___
37146	Legacy PowerMaster, *12–14*		100 ___
37147	CAB-1L/Base-1L Command Set, *12–14*		250 ___
37149	FasTrack Modular Layout Straight Section Kit, *13*		200 ___
37150	FasTrack Modular Layout Template, *13*		30 ___
37151	Christmas Classic Street Lamps, *14*		40 ___
37152	Operating Coaling Station, *13–14*		180 ___
37153	FasTrack Modular Layout 45-Degree Reversible Corner Kit, *13*		225 ___
37154	FasTrack Modular Layout 45-Degree Corner Kit, *13*		225 ___
37155	CAB-1L Remote Controller, *12–14*		150 ___

			Mint
____	37156	Base-1L, *12–14*	125
____	37158	Hershey's Water Tower, *13*	30
____	37159	Peanuts Figure Pack, *13*	30
____	37160	Strasburg Girder Bridge, *13*	21
____	37161	Container 4-pack, *13*	40
____	37162	Lionelville Water Tower, *13*	25
____	37163	LIRR Girder Bridge, *13*	21
____	37164	NS Girder Bridge, *13*	21
____	37165	CP Water Tower, *13*	25
____	37166	Crossing Shanty, *13–14*	25
____	37167	Freight Platform, *13*	30
____	37169	Peanuts Psychiatric Booth, *13*	40
____	37172	Gooseneck Lamp 2-pack, *13–14*	34
____	37173	Globe Lamp 3-pack, *13–14*	25
____	37174	Classic Street Lamp 3-pack, black, *13–14*	40
____	37176	Santa Fe Shanty, *13*	25
____	37183	Polar Express 10th Anniversary Pewter Snowman and Children Figure Pack, *13*	37
____	37184	Christmas Half Covered Bridge, *13*	43
____	37185	Christmas Railroad Signs, *13*	10
____	37187	Kris Kringle's Kloseout Shop, *13*	50
____	37191	LionChief 36-watt Power Supply, *14*	36
____	37195	Grand Central Terminal 100th Anniversary, *13–14*	280
____	37196	Christmas Extension Bridge, *13*	15
____	37197	North Pole Central Girder Bridge, *13*	30
____	37530	Santa Animated Caboose, *11*	80
____	37807	Station Platform, *10–14*	23
____	37808	Sunoco Spherical Oil Tank, *10–11*	100
____	37810	Curved O Gauge Tunnel, *11–14*	65
____	37813	Christmas Tractor and Trailer with trees, *10*	27
____	37814	Christmas Crossing Shanty, *10–13*	30
____	37816	Rockville Bridge, *11–12*	700
____	37820	Lionel Auto Loader Cars 4-pack, *12–13*	25
____	37821	Smoke Fluid Loader, *11*	250
____	37826	Classic Travel Billboard Set, *11–14*	13
____	37827	Coca-Cola Covered Bridge, *11*	45
____	37828	Vintage Boy Scouts Figure Pack, *11–14*	30
____	37829	Polar Express Station Platform, *11–13*	40
____	37831	NJ Transit Blinking Light Water Tower, *11–12*	30
____	37834	Lionel Boat 4-pack, *11–14*	25
____	37836	Monopoly Auto 4-pack, *12*	25
____	37837	Polar Express Straight Tunnel, *12–13*	80
____	37840	Santa Fe Diorama, *12–14*	15
____	37841	Premium Smoke Fluid, *12–14*	9
____	37842	CN Tractor with piggyback trailer, *12*	90
____	37846	PRR Tractor Trailer, *12*	90
____	37847	SP Tractor Trailer, *12*	90
____	37848	IC Tractor Trailer, *12*	90
____	37849	ATSF Tractor Trailer, *12*	90
____	37850	REA Tractor Trailer, *12*	90
____	37851	Scale Telephone Poles, *12–14*	37
____	37852	Christmas People Pack, *12–13*	25

		Exc	Mint
37853	Alien Billboard, *13*		13 ___
37854	Classic Christmas Billboard, *12*		11 ___
37855	Lionel Airplane 2-pack, *12–14*		37 ___
37900	Silver Truss Bridge, *11*		70 ___
37901	Lehigh Valley Tugboat, *10*		270 ___
37902	Illuminated Barge, *10*		180 ___
37903	Cell Tower, *10–14*		60 ___
37904	Boy Scouts Billboard Set, *10*		13 ___
37907	Christmas Street Lamps with wreaths, *10–13*		30 ___
37909	North Pole Central Jet Snowblower, *11–13*		138 ___
37910	Operating Lighthouse, *10*		180 ___
37911	D&RGW Blinking Light Water Tower, *10–11*		30 ___
37912	Lighted Coaling Tower, *10–14*		180 ___
37913	Hopper Shed, *10–14*		35 ___
37914	Work House, *10–14*		28 ___
37916	Beige Brick Suburban House, *10*		80 ___
37917	Red Brick Suburban House, *10*		80 ___
37919	Operating Sawmill, *10*		130 ___
37920	Bascule Bridge, *10*		350 ___
37921	ZW-L Transformer, *11–14*		675 ___
37923	Coca-Cola Blinking Light Water Tower, *11*		28 ___
37928	Passenger Station, sounds, *11*		90 ___
37929	Coca-Cola Diner, *11, 13*		75 ___
37930	Rotary Aircraft Beacon, *11–12*		81 ___
37933	MG Switch Tower, *11–13*		300 ___
37935	Operating Track Gang, *11*		100 ___
37939	Scale Telephone Poles, *11–14*		43 ___
37940	PRR Hobo Hotel, *12*		150 ___
37941	House Under Construction, *11*		90 ___
37942	Christmas Hobo Hotel, *12–13*		150 ___
37944	Weathered 50,000-gallon Water Tank, *11–12*		170 ___
37946	House Under Construction #2, *12–13*		90 ___
37947	GW-180 180-watt Transformer, *12–14*		280 ___
37948	Boy Scouts Flagpole with lights, *11*		30 ___
37951	Postwar "342" Culvert Loader, *11*		165 ___
37952	Postwar "345" Culvert Unloader, *11*		190 ___
37953	Jacobs Pharmacy, *11*		50 ___
37954	Halloween Station Platform, *11–13*		35 ___
37955	Sodor Station Platform, *11–14*		35 ___
37957	Deluxe Holiday House, *11*		85 ___
37958	SP Scrap Yard, *11–14*		110 ___
37959	Midway Basketball Shot Game, *11–13*		21 ___
37960	Burning Switch Tower, *11–13*		100 ___
37961	NYC Scrap Yard, *11–13*		110 ___
37962	NJ Transit Station Platform, *11*		37 ___
37964	Archive Operating Freight Terminal, *11–14*		150 ___
37965	Christmas Operating Freight Terminal, *11–13*		150 ___
37966	Lionel Cylindrical Oil Tank, *11–14*		100 ___
37967	Boy Scouts Troop Cabin, *12–13*		80 ___
37971	Bethlehem Steel Culvert Loader, *11*		165 ___
37972	Bethlehem Steel Culvert Unloader, *11*		190 ___
37973	Coca-Cola Station Platform, *12*		37 ___
37975	SP Operating Freight Terminal, *11–14*		150 ___

Exc Mint

		Exc	Mint
_____ 37977	Hooker Tank Car Accident, *11–14*		130
_____ 37978	Deluxe Suburban House, *11–13*		80
_____ 37979	Rotary Coal Tipple, *12*		540
_____ 37980	Operating Coal Conveyor, *12*		90
_____ 37984	Santa's Repair Work House, *12–13*		28
_____ 37985	Operating Wind Turbine, *12–14*		75
_____ 37986	NJ Transit Blinking Billboard, *12–13*		28
_____ 37989	Sodor Train Shed, *12–13*		40
_____ 37992	Coca-Cola Blinking Light Billboard, *10–11*		28
_____ 37993	Snoopy and the Red Baron Animated Pylon, *12*		160
_____ 37994	Deluxe Holiday House #2, *12–13*		120
_____ 37995	Illuminated Scale Telephone Poles, *12–14*		50
_____ 37996	Postwar 192 Control Tower, *12*		70
_____ 37997	Christmas Lawn Figure Pack, *12–13*		23
_____ 37998	Halloween Haunted Passenger Station, *12–13*		75
_____ 38004	Virginian 4-6-0 10-wheel Locomotive "203," CC, *01–02*		570
_____ 38005	Long Island 4-6-0 10-wheel Locomotive "138," CC, *01–02*		510
_____ 38007	UP Auxiliary tender, black, CC, *01*		200
_____ 38008	UP Auxiliary tender, gray, CC, *01*		205
_____ 38009	D&RGW 4-6-6-4 Challenger Locomotive "3803," CC, *01*		1550
_____ 38010	Clinchfield 4-6-6-4 Challenger Locomotive "673," CC, *01*		1400
_____ 38012	Wheeling & Lake Erie 2-6-6-2 Locomotive "8005," CC, *01*		610
_____ 38013	D&H 4-6-6-4 Challenger Locomotive "1527," CC, *01*		720
_____ 38014	D&RGW 4-6-6-4 Challenger Locomotive "3800," CC, *01*		710
_____ 38015	NYC 4-6-4 Hudson Locomotive "773," CC, *01*		900
_____ 38016	Southern 0-8-0 Yard Goat Locomotive "6536," CC, *01–02, 05*		530
_____ 38017	CN 2-6-0 Mogul Locomotive "86," CC, *03, 05*		600
_____ 38018	Wabash 2-6-0 Mogul Locomotive "826," CC, *03*		485
_____ 38019	B&M 2-6-0 Mogul Locomotive "1455," CC, *03, 05*		600
_____ 38020	PRR 4-4-4-4 T1 Duplex Locomotive "5514," *02–03*		630
_____ 38021	WP 4-6-6-4 Challenger Locomotive "402," CC, *02*		650
_____ 38022	WM 4-6-6-4 Challenger Locomotive "1206," CC, *02*		690
_____ 38023	UP 4-6-6-4 Challenger Locomotive "3976," CC, *02*		620
_____ 38024	PRR 6-4-4-6 S-1 Duplex Locomotive "6100," TMCC, *03*		1000
_____ 38025	PRR 4-6-2 K4 Pacific Locomotive "1361," CC, *02*		950
_____ 38026	N&W 4-8-4 J Class Northern Locomotive "606," CC, *02*		1450
_____ 38027	Meadow River Lumber Heisler Geared Locomotive "6," CC, *03*		880
_____ 38028	PRR 6-8-6 S2 Steam Turbine Locomotive, *01*		650

		Exc	Mint
38029	UP 4-12-2 Locomotive "9000," CC, *03*	570	____
38030	Santa Fe 2-8-8-2 Locomotive "1795," CC, *03*	920	____
38031	SP 2-8-8-4 AC-9 Locomotive "3809," CC, *04*	1100	____
38032	Virginian 2-8-8-2 Locomotive "741," CC, *03*	928	____
38036	Long Island 2-8-0 Consolidation Locomotive, *01*	500	____
38037	PRR Reading Seashore 2-8-0 Consolidation Locomotive "6072," CC, *01*	495	____
38038	D&RGW Auxiliary Water Tender, *01*	230	____
38039	Clinchfield Auxiliary Water Tender, *01*	220	____
38040	LV 4-6-0 Camelback Locomotive, *01*	405	____
38042	C&NW 4-6-0 10-wheel Locomotive "361," CC, *02*	450	____
38043	Frisco 4-6-0 10-wheel Locomotive "719," CC, *02*	525	____
38044	PRR 4-6-2 K4 Pacific Locomotive "5385," CC, *02*	920	____
38045	NYC Hudson J-3a 4-6-4 Locomotive "5418," CC, *03*	495	____
38046	GN 0-8-0 Locomotive "815," CC, *02*	530	____
38047	N&W 0-8-0 Locomotive "266," CC, *02*	550	____
38048	NPR 0-8-0 Locomotive "303," CC, *02*	530	____
38049	N&W 2-6-6-4 Locomotive "1234," CC, *02*	690	____
38050	Nickel Plate 2-8-4 Berkshire Locomotive "779," CC, *03*	925	____
38051	Erie 2-8-4 Berkshire Locomotive "3315," CC, *03*	810	____
38052	Pere Marquette 2-8-4 Berkshire Locomotive "1225," CC, *03*	1000	____
38053	NYC 4-8-2 Mohawk L-2a Locomotive "2793," CC, *03*	915	____
38055	Santa Fe 4-8-4 Northern Locomotive "3751" CC, *04*	1100	____
38056	PRR 4-8-2 Mountain M1a Locomotive "6759," CC, *03*	850	____
38057	Weyerhaeuser Shay Locomotive, CC, *03*	1000	____
38058	C&O 2-8-8-2 H7 Locomotive "1580," CC, *04*	1200	____
38060	UP 2-8-8-2 H7 Locomotive "3590," CC, *04*	1200	____
38061	Cass Scenic Heisler Geared Locomotive "6," CC, *03*	940	____
38062	Lionel Lines 4-6-2 Pacific Locomotive "8062," CC, *02–03*	275	____
38065	UP 2-8-8-2 Mallet Locomotive "3672," CC, *02*	1002	____
38066	Elk River Shay Locomotive, CC, *03*	1000	____
38067	MILW 4-6-2 Pacific Locomotive "6316," CC, *03*	300	____
38068	WM 4-6-2 Pacific Locomotive "204," CC, *03*	300	____
38069	Erie Hudson Locomotive, whistle, *05*	150	____
38070	C&O 4-6-2 Pacific Locomotive "489," CC, *04*	300	____
38071	SP Cab Forward AC-12 Locomotive "4294," CC, *05*	1550	____
38075	UP 4-8-8-4 Big Boy Locomotive "4024," LionMaster, *03*	800	____
38076	C&O 2-8-4 Berkshire Locomotive "2699," CC, *04*	860	____
38077	Virginian 2-8-4 Berkshire Locomotive "508," CC, *04*	1000	____

			Exc	Mint
_____	38079	SP 4-8-4 Northern GS-2 Locomotive "4410" CC, *04*		980
_____	38080	WP 4-8-4 Northern GS-64 Locomotive "485" CC, *04*		1000
_____	38081	C&O 2-6-6-6 Allegheny Locomotive "1650," CC, *05–07*		1700
_____	38082	Pennsylvania 2-8-8-2 Y3 Locomotive "374," CC, *04*		1000
_____	38083	N&W 2-8-8-2 Y3 Locomotive "2009," CC, *04*		910
_____	38085	NYC 4-6-4 Hudson J-3a Locomotive 5422," CC, *03*		495
_____	38086	B&A 4-6-4 Hudson Locomotive "607," CC, *03*		495
_____	38087	Nickel Plate 2-8-4 Berkshire Locomotive, RailSounds, *05*		190
_____	38088	NYC 2-6-0 Mogul Locomotive "1924," CC, *03, 05*		600
_____	38089	Pennsylvania 4-6-2 Pacific Locomotive "3678," CC, *04*		300
_____	38090	Clinchfield 4-6-6-4 Challenger Locomotive "672" CC, *04*		640
_____	38091	NP 4-6-6-4 Challenger Locomotive "5121" CC, *04*		660
_____	38092	Pickering Lumber Heisler Locomotive "5," CC, *04*		1000
_____	38093	UP 4-6-6-4 Challenger Locomotive "3980," CC, *04*		700
_____	38094	MILW Hiawatha 4-4-2 Atlantic Locomotive, CC, *06*		950
_____	38095	N&W 4-8-4 J Class Locomotive "611," CC, *05–06*		1250
_____	38100	Texas Special F3 Diesel AB Set, *99*	860	930
_____	38103	Texas Special F3 Diesel "2245," *99*	435	510
_____	38114	ATSF FT Diesel B Unit, *99–00*		170
_____	38115	NYC FT Diesel B Unit "2403," nonpowered, *99–00*		130
_____	38116	B&O FT Diesel B Unit, *99–00*		130
_____	38144	C&O F3 Diesel AA Set "7019, 7021," *00*		700
_____	38147	GN Alco FA2 AA Diesel Set, CC, *02*		405
_____	38150	Platinum Ghost "2333," *99*		495
_____	38153	"Spirit of the Century" F3 Diesel AA Set, *99*		800
_____	38160	Pennsylvania Alco FB2 Diesel, *02*		125
_____	38161	MKT Alco FB2 Diesel, *02*		125
_____	38162	Burlington FT Diesel B Unit, *01*		NRS
_____	38167	Burlington FT Diesel AA Set, *01*		225
_____	38176	Pennsylvania Alco FA2 AA Diesel Set, CC, *02*		405
_____	38182	MKT Alco FA2 AA Diesel Set, CC, *02*		360
_____	38188	Southern F3 Diesel ABA Set, *00*		557
_____	38194	GN Alco FB2 Diesel, *02*		125
_____	38196	Santa Fe FT Diesel A Unit "171," *00*		NRS
_____	38197	SP F3 Diesel ABA Set, *00*		640
_____	38202	Wild West Handcar, *10*		75
_____	38203	Holly Jolly Trolley 2-car Set, *10*		160
_____	38204	ATSF FT B Unit, nonpowered, *10*		120
_____	38210	PRR Alco Diesel AA Set, CC, *10*		400
_____	38214	Rio Grande Ski Train FT B Unit, nonpowered, *11*		120

Exc | Mint

		Exc	Mint
38215	ATSF FT Diesel "165," RailSounds, *10–11*		280 ____
38216	Rio Grande Ski Train FT A Unit, nonpowered, *11*		120 ____
38219	Texan FT B Unit Diesel, nonpowered, *11, 13–14*		120 ____
38221	CNJ Alco AA Diesel Set, *11*		300 ____
38224	Alaska Alco AA Diesel Set, *11*		300 ____
38234	Classic PRR GG1 Electric Locomotive "4866," *12*		330 ____
38235	Classic PC GG1 Electric Locomotive "4840," *12*		330 ____
38240	Elf Gang Car, *12*		120 ____
38241	MOW Gang Car, *12–13*		120 ____
38300	Postwar "2331" Virginian Train Master Diesel, *08*	190	210 ____
38303	Postwar "2340" GG1 Electric Locomotive, *08*		280 ____
38305	Postwar "2338" Milwaukee Road GP7 Diesel, *08*		220 ____
38308	Postwar 2146WS Berkshire Passenger Set, *12*		460 ____
38310	"2185W" NYC F3 Diesel Freight Set, *09*		600 ____
38311	"2276W" B&O RDC Commuter Set, *09*		470 ____
38312	"2343" Santa Fe F3 Diesel AA Set, *09*		500 ____
38313	B&O Budd RDC 2-pack, *09*		350 ____
38323	Postwar "2348" M&StL GP9 Diesel, CC, *10*		390 ____
38324	Postwar 2507W NH F3 Diesel Freight Set, *10*		600 ____
38328	Postwar 1623W NP GP9 Diesel Freight Set, *10*		750 ____
38329	Postwar 2261W Freight Hauler Set, *10*		610 ____
38334	Postwar 11288 Orbitor Diesel Freight Set, *10*		500 ____
38338	Postwar 2129WS Berkshire Freight Set, *12*		550 ____
38339	Postwar 2505W Virginian Rectifier Freight Set, *10*		470 ____
38340	Postwar 1587S Girl's Steam Freight Set, *10*		580 ____
38342	Postwar 1619W Santa Fe Freight Set, *10–11*		470 ____
38348	Postwar "2339" Transparent Wabash GP7 Diesel, *11*		290 ____
38349	Postwar 12885-500 C&O GP7 Freight Set, *11–12*		600 ____
38351	Postwar Archive UP GP7 Diesel, *11*		290 ____
38353	Postwar X-628 Promotional U.S. Navy Diesel Freight Set, *12–14*		600 ____
38354	Postwar 1464W UP Anniversary Alco Diesel Passenger Set, *12–14*		460 ____
38357	Postwar 221 U.S. Marine Corps Alco Diesel A Unit, *12–14*		300 ____
38358	Postwar 2239 IC F3 Freight Set, *12–14*		600 ____
38365	Archive ATSF Black Bonnet F3 AA Diesel Set, *12–14*		500 ____
38368	Archive NYC Red Lightning F3 AA Diesel Set, *12–14*		500 ____
38371	Postwar 2031 RI Alco Diesel AA Set, *12–13*		400 ____
38374	Postwar 221 U.S. Marine Corps Alco Diesel B Unit, *12–14*		120 ____
38377	Postwar 2363T F3 A Unit, nonpowered, *12–14*		170 ____
38379	Archive ATSF Black Bonnet F3 B Unit, *12–14*		170 ____
38380	Archive NYC Red Lightning F3 B Unit, *12–14*		170 ____

		Exc	Mint
38386	Postwar "2367" Wabash F3 Diesel AB Units, *12–14*		500
38388	Postwar "2367" Wabash F3 Diesel A Unit, nonpowered, *12–14*		170
38389	Postwar "2362" UP F3 Diesel AA Set, *14*		460
38392	Postwar "2362" F3 Diesel B Unit, nonpowered, *14*		170
38393	PRR Round-roof Boxcar "76648" (std O), *14*		80
38401	NYC M-497 Jet-Powered Rail Car, *10*		300
38402	Amtrak HHP-8 Electric Locomotive, RailSounds, *10*		400
38403	B&O CSX Heritage AC6000 Diesel "6607," CC, *11*		550
38404	B&O CSX Heritage AC6000 Diesel "7812," CC, *11*		550
38405	Chessie System CSX Heritage AC6000 Diesel, CC, *11–14*		550
38406	Chessie System CSX Heritage AC6000 Diesel, CC, *11–14*		550
38407	WM CSX Heritage AC6000 Diesel "2652," CC, *11*		550
38408	WM CSX Heritage AC6000 Diesel "2659," CC, *11*		550
38409	Clinchfield CSX Heritage AC6000 Diesel, CC, *11–13*		550
38410	Clinchfield CSX Heritage AC6000 Diesel, CC, *11–14*		550
38411	Family Lines CSX Heritage AC6000 Diesel "4825," CC, *11*		550
38412	Family Lines CSX Heritage AC6000 Diesel "4837," CC, *11*		550
38413	CSX Heritage AC6000 Diesel "607," CC, *11–13*		550
38414	CSX Heritage AC6000 Diesel "654," CC, *11–13*		550
38415	PRR U28C Diesel "6531," CC, *11–12*		530
38416	PRR U28C Diesel "6534," CC, *11–12*		530
38417	BN Bicentennial U30C Diesel "1776," CC, *11*		530
38418	BN Bicentennial U30C Diesel "1777," CC, *11*		530
38419	UP U30C Diesel "2918," CC, *11–12*		530
38420	UP U30C Diesel "2897," CC, *11–12*		530
38421	NP U33C Diesel "3305," CC, *11–12*		530
38422	NP U33C Diesel "3307," CC, *11–12*		530
38423	Southern U30C Diesel "3801," CC, *11–12*		530
38424	Southern U30C Diesel "3804," CC, *11–12*		530
38425	RI Budd RDC Jet Car, *11*		330
38428	Alaska Budd RDC Coach, *11*		300
38429	NYC Budd RDC M-497 Jet Car, *11*		330
38432	MKT H16-44 Diesel "1591," CC, *11*		500
38433	MKT H16-44 Diesel "1731," CC, *11*		500
38434	MKT H16-44 Diesel "1732," *11*		380
38435	MKT H16-44 Diesel "1733," nonpowered, *11*		240
38436	LIRR H-16-44 Diesel "1501," CC, *11*		500
38437	LIRR H-16-44 Diesel "1504," CC, *11*		500
38438	LIRR H-16-44 Diesel "1507," *11*		380
38439	LIRR H-16-44 Diesel "1509," nonpowered, *11*		240

		Exc	Mint
38440	UP H-16-44 Diesel "1341," CC, *11*	500	___
38441	UP H-16-44 Diesel "1342," CC, *11*	500	___
38442	UP H-16-44 Diesel "1343," *11*	380	___
38443	UP H-16-44 Diesel "1344," nonpowered, *11*	240	___
38444	PRR H16-44 Diesel "8807," CC, *11*	500	___
38445	PRR H16-44 Diesel "8810," CC, *11*	500	___
38446	PRR H16-44 Diesel "8812," *11*	380	___
38447	PRR H16-44 Diesel "8815," nonpowered, *11*	240	___
38452	PC Alco RS-11 Diesel "7605," CC, *12*	480	___
38453	PC Alco RS-11 Diesel "7608," CC, *12*	480	___
38454	PRR Alco RS-11 Diesel "9622," CC, *12*	480	___
38455	PC Alco RS-11 Diesel "7625," nonpowered, *12*	240	___
38456	N&W Alco RS-11 Diesel "308," CC, *12–13*	480	___
38457	N&W Alco RS-11 Diesel "318," CC, *12*	480	___
38458	PRR Alco RS-11 Diesel "8631," CC, *12*	480	___
38459	N&W Alco RS-11 Diesel "330," nonpowered, *12*	240	___
38460	NKP Alco RS-11 Diesel "855," CC, *12*	480	___
38461	NKP Alco RS-11 Diesel "859," CC, *12*	480	___
38462	PRR Alco RS-11 Diesel "8639," nonpowered, *12*	240	___
38463	NKP Alco RS-11 Diesel "863," nonpowered, *12*	240	___
38464	Alaska Alco RS-11 Diesel "3602," CC, *12*	480	___
38465	Alaska Alco RS-11 Diesel "3604," CC, *12*	480	___
38466	NH Alco RS-11 Diesel "1403," CC, *12*	480	___
38467	Alaska Alco RS-11 Diesel "3607," nonpowered, *12*	240	___
38468	Seaboard Alco RS-11 Diesel "101," CC, *12–13*	480	___
38469	Seaboard Alco RS-11 Diesel "102," CC, *12*	480	___
38470	NH Alco RS-11 Diesel "1405," CC, *12*	480	___
38471	Seaboard Alco RS-11 Diesel "104," nonpowered, *12*	240	___
38472	C&O Alco S2 Diesel Switcher "5001," CC, *11*	470	___
38473	C&O Alco S2 Diesel Switcher "5505," CC, *11*	480	___
38474	C&O Alco S2 Diesel Switcher "5020," *11*	360	___
38475	C&O Alco S2 Diesel Switcher "5027," nonpowered, *11*	220	___
38476	CN Alco S2 Diesel Switcher "7946," CC, *11*	480	___
38477	CN Alco S2 Diesel Switcher "7949," CC, *11*	480	___
38478	CN Alco S2 Diesel Switcher "7951," *11*	360	___
38479	CN Alco S2 Diesel Switcher "7954," *11*	360	___
38480	NYC Alco S2 Diesel Switcher "8504," CC, *11*	480	___
38481	NYC Alco S2 Diesel Switcher "8507," CC, *11*	480	___
38482	NYC Alco S2 Diesel Switcher "8514," *11*	360	___
38483	NYC Alco S2 Diesel Switcher "8521," nonpowered, *11*	220	___
38484	Southern Alco S2 Diesel Switcher "2209," CC, *11*	480	___
38485	Southern Alco S2 Diesel Switcher "2211," CC, *11*	480	___
38486	Southern Alco S2 Diesel Switcher "2215," *11*	360	___
38487	Southern Alco S2 Diesel Switcher "2218," nonpowered, *11*	220	___

		Exc	Mint
___ 38488	Mopac Alco S2 Diesel Switcher "9108," CC, *11*		480
___ 38489	Mopac Alco S2 Diesel Switcher "9113," CC, *11*		480
___ 38490	Mopac Alco S2 Diesel Switcher "9116," *11*		360
___ 38491	Mopac Alco S2 Diesel Switcher "9131," nonpowered, *11*		220
___ 38493	ATSF Early Era Inspection Vehicle, CC, *12*		150
___ 38494	CP DD35 Diesel "9864," CC, *12*		600
___ 38495	CP DD35 Diesel "9868," nonpowered, *12*		440
___ 38496	SP DD35A Diesel "9903," CC, *11*		600
___ 38497	SP DD35A Diesel "9914," nonpowered, *11*		440
___ 38498	PRR DD35A Diesel "2380," CC, *11*		600
___ 38499	PRR DD35A Diesel "2383," nonpowered, *11*		440
___ 38505	CSX GP-38 Diesel, *11*		140
___ 38521	PRR GG1 Electric "4839," *11*		330
___ 38522	Amtrak GG1 Electric "926," *11*		330
___ 38524	NYC GP35 Diesel "6131," CC, *12*		500
___ 38525	NYC GP35 Diesel "6138," CC, *12*		500
___ 38526	NYC GP35 Diesel "6147," nonpowered, *12*		260
___ 38527	UP GP35 Diesel "742," CC, *12*		500
___ 38528	UP GP35 Diesel "753," CC, *12*		500
___ 38529	UP GP35 Diesel "760," nonpowered, *12*		260
___ 38530	SP GP35 Diesel "7465," CC, *12*		500
___ 38531	SP GP35 Diesel "7474," CC, *12*		500
___ 38532	SP GP35 Diesel "7481," nonpowered, *12*		260
___ 38533	CP GP35 Diesel "5014," CC, *12*		500
___ 38534	CP GP35 Diesel "5018," CC, *12*		500
___ 38535	CP GP35 Diesel "5023," nonpowered, *12*		260
___ 38536	PRR GP35 Diesel "2297," CC, *12*		500
___ 38537	PRR GP35 Diesel "2302," CC, *12*		500
___ 38538	PRR GP35 Diesel "2305," nonpowered, *12*		260
___ 38539	N&W Alco RS-11 Diesel "308," CC, *12*		480
___ 38539	Conrail GP35 Diesel "2297," CC, *12*		500
___ 38540	Conrail GP35 Diesel "2302," CC, *12*		500
___ 38541	Conrail GP35 Diesel "2305," nonpowered, *12*		260
___ 38542	Milwaukee Road GP35 Diesel "361," CC, *12*		500
___ 38543	Milwaukee Road GP35 Diesel "363," CC, *12*		500
___ 38544	Milwaukee Road GP35 Diesel "366," nonpowered, *12*		260
___ 38545	Pacific Harbor Line Genset Switcher "31," CC, *11*		800
___ 38546	KCS Genset Switcher "1404," CC, *11–12*		800
___ 38547	Santa Fe Genset Switcher "9910," CC, *11*		800
___ 38548	EL GP35 Diesel "2555," CC, *12*		500
___ 38549	EL GP35 Diesel "2558," CC, *12*		500
___ 38550	EL GP35 Diesel "2561," nonpowered, *12*		260
___ 38558	D&H Baldwin RF-16 Diesel AA Set, CC, *12*		730
___ 38561	D&H Baldwin RF-16 Diesel B Unit, CC, *12*		400
___ 38562	D&H Baldwin RF-16 Diesel B Unit, nonpowered, *12*		250
___ 38563	B&O Baldwin RF-16 Diesel AA Set, CC, *12–14*		730
___ 38566	B&O Baldwin RF-16 Diesel B Unit, CC, *12–14*		400

		Exc	Mint
38567	B&O Baldwin RF-16 Diesel B Unit, nonpowered, *12–14*		250 ____
38568	NYC Baldwin RF-16 Diesel AA Set "3806-3808," CC, *12–14*		730 ____
38571	NYC Baldwin RF-16 Diesel B Unit, CC, *12–14*		400 ____
38572	NYC Baldwin RF-16 Diesel B Unit, nonpowered, *12–14*		250 ____
38573	SP Baldwin RF-16 Diesel AA Set, CC, *12–14*		730 ____
38576	SP Baldwin RF-16 Diesel B Unit, CC, *12–14*		400 ____
38577	SP Baldwin RF-16 Diesel B Unit, nonpowered, *12–14*		250 ____
38579	ATSF GP9 Diesel "744," nonpowered, *12*		240 ____
38580	NP GP9 Diesel "324," nonpowered, *12*		240 ____
38581	CSX SD80MAC Diesel "809," CC, *12–13*		530 ____
38582	CSX SD80MAC Diesel "812," CC, *12*		530 ____
38583	CSX SD80MAC Diesel "804," nonpowered, *12*		260 ____
38584	NS SD80MAC Diesel "7207," CC, *12*		530 ____
38585	NS SD80MAC Diesel "7203," CC, *12*		530 ____
38586	NS SD80MAC Diesel "7209," nonpowered, *12*		260 ____
38587	Conrail SD80MAC Diesel "4126," CC, *12*		530 ____
38588	Conrail SD80MAC Diesel "4129," CC, *12*		530 ____
38589	Conrail SD80MAC Diesel "4103," nonpowered, *12*		260 ____
38593	UP NW2 Diesel Switcher Locomotive "1028," CC, *12*		470 ____
38594	UP NW2 Diesel Switcher Locomotive "1043," CC, *12*		470 ____
38595	CB&Q Scale NW2 Diesel Switcher "9227," CC, *12*		470 ____
38596	CB&Q Scale NW2 Diesel Switcher "9245," CC, *12*		470 ____
38597	CB&Q F3 AA Diesel Set "9962A-9962C," CC, *12–13*		730 ____
38600	UP 0-6-0 Dockside Switcher "87," traditional, *07–09*		110 ____
38601	Lionel Lines 0-6-0 Dockside Switcher, traditional, *07–09*		110 ____
38605	PRR 0-4-0 Locomotive "94," traditional, *07*		170 ____
38606	SP 0-4-0 Locomotive "71," traditional, *07–08*		170 ____
38607	Southern 2-8-4 Berkshire Locomotive "2718," RailSounds, *07–08*		175 ____
38608	LL 2-8-2 Mikado Locomotive "57," RailSounds, *07*		260 ____
38609	NYC 2-8-2 Mikado Locomotive "1843," CC, *07*		370 ____
38610	NKP 2-8-4 Berkshire Locomotive "779," CC, *07–08*		370 ____
38619	Santa Fe 4-6-2 Pacific Locomotive "2037," traditional, K-Line, *06*		260 ____
38620	B&O Porter Locomotive "16," traditional, K-Line, *06*		100 ____
38621	4-6-2 Pacific Locomotive, traditional, K-Line, *06*		260 ____
38626	Holiday 2-8-2 Mikado Locomotive "25," green, RailSounds, *08*		260 ____
38627	GN 4-4-2 Atlantic Locomotive "1702," traditional, *08–09*		110 ____

		Exc	Mint
38630	U.S. Army 0-6-0 Dockside Switcher "486," traditional, *08–09*		110
38634	NYC 4-6-4 Hudson Locomotive "5417," TrainSounds, *07*		200
38635	C&O 4-6-4 Hudson Locomotive "309," TrainSounds, *08*		200
38636	ATSF 4-6-4 Hudson Locomotive "3459," TrainSounds, *07*		200
38637	LL 4-6-4 Hudson Locomotive "5242," TrainSounds, *08*		200
38638	UP 4-6-2 Pacific Locomotive "2888," RailSounds, *08*		300
38639	Erie 4-6-2 Pacific Locomotive "2939," RailSounds, *08*		300
38640	Southern 4-6-2 Pacific Locomotive "1317," RailSounds, *08*		300
38641	B&M 4-6-2 Pacific Locomotive "3713," RailSounds, *08*		300
38642	PRR 4-6-2 Pacific Locomotive "5385," RailSounds, *08*		300
38643	Alaska Mikado 2-8-2 Locomotive "701," CC, *08–09*		280
38644	T&P Mikado 2-8-2 Locomotive "810," CC, *08–09*		400
38649	Christmas 4-6-4 Hudson Locomotive, traditional, *08*		220
38651	Lionel Lines 0-8-0 Locomotive "100," traditional, *08–09*		120
38654	Bethlehem Steel 0-4-0 Locomotive, traditional, *08–09*		170
38657	Alton Limited Pacific 4-6-2 Locomotive "659," traditional, *08*		300
38658	W&ARR 4-4-0 General "1892," TrainSounds, *08–09*		165
38664	LL 4-4-2 Atlantic Locomotive "1058," traditional, *08–09*		110
38671	Santa Flyer 4-6-0 Locomotive, *09*		200
38677	Strasburg 0-6-0 Dockside Switcher "1252," *10*		130
38678	Monopoly Hudson Locomotive, TrainSounds, *10*		240
38679	ATSF 0-4-0 Switcher "1387," *10–11*		190
38684	Pennsylvania Power & Light Docksider Switcher, *10*		110
38687	Western & Atlantic 0-4-0 Locomotive "1897," *10–11*		190
38691	North Pole Central Santa Flyer "2," *10–11*		190
38692	Angela Trotta Thomas Signature Express, *10–11*		190
38700	CB&Q F3 B Unit "9962B," CC, *12–13*		400
38701	CB&Q F3 B Unit, *12–13*		250
38702	D&RGW F3 AA Diesel Set "5531-5533," CC, *12–14*		730
38705	D&RGW F3 B Unit "5532," CC, *12–14*		400
38706	D&RGW F3 B Unit, *12–14*		250
38707	WP F3 AB Diesel Set "803A-803B," CC, *12–14*		730
38710	WP F3 A Unit, nonpowered, *12–14*		380
38711	WP F3 B Unit "803C," CC, *12–14*		400

		Exc	Mint
38712	Wabash F7 AA Diesel Set "1102A-1102C," CC, *12–13*	730	___
38715	Wabash F7 B Unit "1102B," CC, *12–13*	400	___
38716	Wabash F7 B Unit, *12–13*	250	___
38717	Milwaukee Road F7 AA Diesel Set CC, *12*	730	___
38720	Milwaukee Road F7 B Unit "109B," CC, *12*	400	___
38721	Milwaukee Road F7 B Unit, *12*	250	___
38722	Grand Trunk SD80MAC Diesel "9085," CC, *12*	530	___
38723	Grand Trunk SD80MAC Diesel "9088," CC, *12*	530	___
38724	Grand Trunk SD80MAC Diesel "9079," nonpowered, *12*	260	___
38725	CB&Q SD80MAC Diesel "9654," CC, *12*	530	___
38726	CB&Q SD80MAC Diesel "9651," CC, *12*	530	___
38727	CB&Q SD80MAC Diesel "9660," nonpowered, *12*	260	___
38728	PRR SD80MAC Diesel "9942," CC, *12*	530	___
38729	PRR SD80MAC Diesel "9945," CC, *12*	530	___
38730	PRR SD80MAC Diesel "9947," nonpowered, *12–13*	260	___
38731	Polar SD80MAC Diesel, CC, *12*	530	___
38732	CB&Q BNSF Heritage SD70ACe Diesel "1848," CC, *12–13*	530	___
38733	CB&Q BNSF Heritage SD70ACe Diesel "1852," CC, *12–13*	530	___
38734	CB&Q BNSF Heritage SD70ACe Diesel "1856," nonpowered, *12–13*	260	___
38735	ATSF BNSF Heritage SD70ACe Diesel "1996," CC, *12–13*	530	___
38736	ATSF BNSF Heritage SD70ACe Diesel "1997," CC, *12–13*	530	___
38737	ATSF BNSF Heritage SD70ACe Diesel "1999," nonpowered, *12–13*	260	___
38738	Frisco BNSF Heritage SD70ACe Diesel "1876," CC, *12–13*	530	___
38739	Frisco BNSF Heritage SD70ACe Diesel "1896," CC, *12–14*	530	___
38740	Frisco BNSF Heritage SD70ACe Diesel "1916," nonpowered, *12–13*	260	___
38741	BN BNSF Heritage SD70ACe Diesel "1970," CC, *12–13*	530	___
38742	BN BNSF Heritage SD70ACe Diesel "1975," CC, *12–13*	530	___
38743	BN BNSF Heritage SD70ACe Diesel "1980," nonpowered, *12–13*	260	___
38744	GN BNSF Heritage SD70ACe Diesel "1889," CC, *12–13*	530	___
38745	GN BNSF Heritage SD70ACe Diesel "1891," CC, *12–13*	530	___
38746	GN BNSF Heritage SD70ACe Diesel "1893," nonpowered, *12–13*	260	___
38747	NP BNSF Heritage SD70ACe Diesel "1870," CC, *12–13*	530	___
38748	NP BNSF Heritage SD70ACe Diesel "1872," CC, *12–13*	530	___
38749	NP BNSF Heritage SD70ACe Diesel "1875," nonpowered, *12–13*	260	___
38750	EMD Demonstrator SD70ACe Diesel "2012," CC, *12–13*	530	___

			Exc	Mint
____	38751	CNJ F3 AA Diesel Set, CC, *13–14*		730
____	38752	Vision Centipede AA Pilot Diesels, CC, *13*		2200
____	38754	C&NW F7 AA Diesel Set, CC, *13–14*		730
____	38757	SP F7 AA Diesel Set, CC, *13–14*		730
____	38760	CNJ F3 B Unit, CC, *13–14*		400
____	38761	CNJ F3 B Unit, *13–14*		250
____	38762	C&NW F7 B Unit "410," CC, *13–14*		400
____	38763	C&NW F7 B Unit, *13–14*		250
____	38764	SP F7 B Unit "8219," CC, *13*		400
____	38765	SP F7 B Unit, *13*		250
____	38768	N&W GP35 Diesel "1306," CC, *13–14*		500
____	38769	N&W GP35 Diesel "1308," nonpowered, *13–14*		260
____	38770	RI GP35 Diesel "307," CC, *13–14*		500
____	38771	RI GP35 Diesel "309," CC, *13–14*		500
____	38772	RI GP35 Diesel "323," nonpowered, *13–14*		260
____	38773	WP GP35 Diesel "3002," CC, *13–14*		500
____	38774	WP GP35 Diesel "3009," CC, *13–14*		500
____	38775	WP GP35 Diesel "3014," nonpowered, *13–14*		260
____	38778	C&NW LionChief RS3 Diesel "1621," *14*		330
____	38779	NYC LionChief RS3 Diesel "8244," *14*		330
____	38782	C&BQ GP35 Diesel "990," CC, *13*		500
____	38783	C&BQ GP35 Diesel "996," nonpowered, *13*		500
____	38784	CN GP35 Diesel "4000," CC, *13*		500
____	38785	CN GP35 Diesel "4005," CC, *13*		500
____	38786	CN GP35 Diesel "4001," nonpowered, *13*		260
____	38787	D&RGW GP35 Diesel "3031," CC, *13*		500
____	38788	D&RGW GP35 Diesel "3034," CC, *13*		500
____	38789	D&RGW GP35 Diesel "3038," nonpowered, *13*		260
____	38790	DT&I GP35 Diesel "351," CC, *13*		500
____	38791	DT&I GP35 Diesel "353," CC, *13*		500
____	38792	DT&I GP35 Diesel "355," nonpowered, *13*		260
____	38794	GN GP35 Diesel "3018," CC, *13–14*		500
____	38795	GN GP35 Diesel "3036," nonpowered, *13–14*		260
____	38796	Chessie System GP35 Diesel "1125," CC, *13*		500
____	38797	Chessie System GP35 Diesel "1128," CC, *13*		500
____	38798	Chessie System GP35 Diesel "1113," nonpowered, *13*		260
____	38799	N&W GP35 Diesel "1302," CC, *13–14*		500
____	38800	B&M Early Era Inspection Vehicle, CC, *12*		150
____	38801	KCS Trackmobile, CC, *12–13*		300
____	38802	North Pole Central Trackmobile, CC, *12*		300
____	38803	MOW Trackmobile, CC, *12*		300
____	38804	LIRR Trackmobile, CC, *12*		300
____	38805	Conrail Trackmobile, CC, *12*		300
____	38806	NS Trackmobile, CC, *12*		300
____	38807	NP Trackmobile, CC, *12–13*		300
____	38808	Chessie System Trackmobile, CC, *12*		300
____	38809	CN Trackmobile, CC, *12*		300
____	38810	PRR Early Era Inspection Vehicle, CC, *12*		150
____	38811	D&RGW Early Era Inspection Vehicle, CC, *12*		150
____	38812	SP Early Era Inspection Vehicle, CC, *12–13*		150
____	38813	C&O Early Era Inspection Vehicle, CC, *12–13*		150

		Exc	Mint
38814	Milwaukee Road Early Era Inspection Vehicle, CC, *12*		150 ____
38815	Transylvania Early Era Inspection Vehicle, CC, *12*		150 ____
38816	LionChief PRR RS3 Diesel "5620," *14*		330 ____
38819	LionChief D&RGW RS3 Diesel "5202," *14*		330 ____
38821	LionChief AT&SF GP7 Diesel "2656," *14*		330 ____
38824	LionChief NP GP7 Diesel "563," *14*		330 ____
38825	LionChief UP GP7 Diesel "121," *14*		330 ____
38827	LionChief CB&Q GP7 Diesel "1596," *14*		330 ____
38848	Christmas Pioneer Zephyr Set, CC, *13–14*		1100 ____
38853	Santa and Mrs. Claus Handcar, *13*		90 ____
38855	GN GP35 Diesel "2519," CC, *13–14*		500 ____
38856	CB&Q Mark Twain Zephyr, CC, *13–14*		1100 ____
38860	CB&Q Pioneer Zephyr, CC, *13–14*		1100 ____
38864	Lionel Lines Zephyr, CC, *13–14*		1100 ____
38865	L&N GP35 Diesel "1105," CC, *13*		500 ____
38866	L&N GP35 Diesel "1109," CC, *13*		500 ____
38867	L&N GP35 Diesel "1114," nonpowered, *13*		260 ____
38868	C&BQ GP35 Diesel "978," CC, *13*		500 ____
38874	B&O GP9 Diesel "6448," CC, *13–14*		480 ____
38875	B&O GP9 Diesel "6456," CC, *13–14*		480 ____
38876	B&O GP9 Diesel "6461," nonpowered, *13–14*		240 ____
38877	B&M GP9 Diesel "1705," CC, *13*		480 ____
38878	B&M GP9 Diesel "1714," CC, *13*		480 ____
38879	B&M GP9 Diesel "1722," nonpowered, *13*		240 ____
38883	C&NW GP9 Diesel "701," CC, *13*		480 ____
38884	C&NW GP9 Diesel "704," CC, *13*		480 ____
38885	C&NW GP9 Diesel "712," nonpowered, *13*		240 ____
38886	Erie GP9 Diesel "1260," CC, *13*		480 ____
38887	Erie GP9 Diesel "1263," CC, *13*		480 ____
38888	Erie GP9 Diesel "1265," nonpowered, *13*		240 ____
38889	Nickel Plate Road GP9 Diesel "514," CC, *13*		480 ____
38890	Nickel Plate Road GP9 Diesel "452," CC, *13*		480 ____
38891	Nickel Plate Road GP9 Diesel "457," nonpowered, *13*		240 ____
38892	SP GP9 Diesel "3411," CC, *13*		480 ____
38893	SP GP9 Diesel "3415," CC, *13*		480 ____
38094	SP GP9 Diesel "3419," nonpowered, *13*		240 ____
38895	Wabash GP9 Diesel "484," CC, *13*		480 ____
38896	Wabash GP9 Diesel "488," CC, *13*		480 ____
38897	Wabash GP9 Diesel "491," nonpowered, *13*		240 ____
38918	Chessie System SD40-2 Diesel "7609," CC, *13*		530 ____
38919	Chessie System SD40-2 Diesel "7611," CC, *13*		530 ____
38920	Chessie System SD40-2 Diesel "7614," nonpowered, *13*		240 ____
38921	SP SD40T-2 Diesel Locomotive "8322," CC, *13*		530 ____
38922	SP SD40T-2 Diesel Locomotive "8326," CC, *13*		530 ____
38923	SP SD40T-2 Diesel, nonpowered, *13*		260 ____
38924	B&O SD40-2 Diesel "7602," CC, *13*		530 ____
38925	B&O SD40-2 Diesel "7607," CC, *13*		530 ____

			Exc	Mint
___	38926	B&O SD40-2 Diesel "7611," nonpowered, *13*		240
___	38933	Conrail SD40-2 Diesel "6424," CC, *13*		530
___	38934	Conrail SD40-2 Diesel "6437," CC, *13*		530
___	38935	Conrail SD40-2 Diesel "6468," nonpowered, *13*		240
___	38936	UP SD40-2 Diesel "2929," CC, *13*		530
___	38937	UP SD40-2 Diesel "2932," CC, *13*		530
___	38938	UP SD40-2 Diesel "2947," nonpowered, *13*		240
___	38939	NS SD40-2 Diesel "3355," CC, *13*		530
___	38940	NS SD40-2 Diesel "3365," CC, *13*		530
___	38941	NS SD40-2 Diesel "3379," nonpowered, *13*		240
___	38942	Central of Georgia NS Heritage ES44AC Diesel, CC, *12*		550
___	38943	Central of Georgia NS Heritage ES44AC Diesel, CC, *12*		550
___	38944	Central of Georgia NS Heritage ES44AC Diesel, nonpowered, *12*		280
___	38945	Conrail NS Heritage ES44AC Diesel, CC, *12*		550
___	38946	Conrail NS Heritage ES44AC Diesel, CC, *12*		550
___	38947	Conrail NS Heritage ES44AC Diesel, nonpowered, *12*		280
___	38948	Interstate NS Heritage ES44AC Diesel Locomotive "8105," CC, *12*		550
___	38949	Interstate NS Heritage ES44AC Diesel, CC, *12*		550
___	38950	Interstate NS Heritage ES44AC Diesel, non-powered, *12*		280
___	38951	LV NS Heritage ES44AC Diesel, CC, *12*		550
___	38952	LV NS Heritage ES44AC Diesel, CC, *12*		550
___	38953	LV NS Heritage ES44AC Diesel, nonpowered, *12*		280
___	38954	Nickel Plate Road NS Heritage ES44AC Diesel, CC, *12*		550
___	38955	Nickel Plate Road NS Heritage ES44AC Diesel, CC, *12*		550
___	38956	Nickel Plate Road NS Heritage ES44AC Diesel, nonpowered, *12*		280
___	38957	N&W NS Heritage ES44AC Diesel, CC, *12*		550
___	38958	N&W NS Heritage ES44AC Diesel, CC, *12*		550
___	38959	N&W NS Heritage ES44AC Diesel, nonpowered, *12*		280
___	38960	PRR NS Heritage ES44AC Diesel, CC, *12*		550
___	38961	PRR NS Heritage ES44AC Diesel, CC, *12*		550
___	38962	PRR NS Heritage ES44AC Diesel, nonpowered, *12*		280
___	38963	Southern NS Heritage ES44AC Diesel, CC, *12*		550
___	38964	Southern NS Heritage ES44AC Diesel, CC, *12*		550
___	38965	Southern NS Heritage ES44AC Diesel, nonpowered, *12*		280
___	38966	NS Heritage ES44AC Diesel, CC, *12*		550
___	38967	NS Heritage ES44AC Diesel, CC, *12*		550
___	38968	NS Heritage ES44AC Diesel, nonpowered, *12*		280
___	38969	North Pole Central GP35 Diesel "2525," CC, *13*		500
___	38970	North Pole Central GP35 Diesel "2512," CC, *13*		500
___	38971	North Pole Central GP35 Diesel "2513," nonpowered, *13*		260

		Exc	Mint
38972	Reading GP35 Diesel "3625," CC, *13*		500 ___
38973	Reading GP35 Diesel "3630," CC, *13*		500 ___
38974	Reading GP35 Diesel "3633," nonpowered, *13*		260 ___
38975	AT&SF GP35 Diesel "3312," CC, *13*		500 ___
38976	AT&SF GP35 Diesel "3318," CC, *13*		500 ___
38977	AT&SF GP35 Diesel "3329," nonpowered, *13*		260 ___
38978	Alaska GP35 Diesel "2501," CC, *13*		500 ___
38979	Alaska GP35 Diesel "2503," CC, *13*		500 ___
38980	Alaska GP35 Diesel "2502," nonpowered, *13*		260 ___
38981	B&O GP35 Diesel "2506," CC, *13-14*		500 ___
38982	B&O GP35 Diesel "2511," CC, *13-14*		500 ___
38983	B&O GP35 Diesel "2517," nonpowered, *13-14*		260 ___
38984	C&O GP35 Diesel "3515," CC, *13-14*		500 ___
38985	C&O GP35 Diesel "3521," CC, *13-14*		500 ___
38986	C&O GP35 Diesel "3526," nonpowered, *13-14*		260 ___
38987	MP GP35 Diesel "603," CC, *13*		500 ___
38988	MP GP35 Diesel "607," CC, *13*		500
38989	MP GP35 Diesel "611," nonpowered, *13*		260 ___
38990	GM&O GP35 Diesel "603," CC, *13-14*		500 ___
38991	GM&O GP35 Diesel "607," CC, *13-14*		500 ___
38992	GM&O GP35 Diesel "611," nonpowered, *13-14*		260 ___
38993	WM GP35 Diesel "3576," CC, *13*		500 ___
38994	WM GP35 Diesel "3578," CC, *13*		500 ___
38995	WM GP35 Diesel "3580," nonpowered, *13*		260 ___
38996	CSX GP35 Diesel "4355," CC, *13*		500 ___
38997	CSX GP35 Diesel "4363," CC, *13*		500 ___
38998	CSX GP35 Diesel "4390," nonpowered, *13*		260 ___
38999	NS GP35 Diesel "2916," CC, *13*		500 ___
39008	PRR Heavyweight Passenger Car 4-pack, *00*		225 ___
39009	PRR Indian Rock Heavyweight Combination Car, *00*		50 ___
39010	PRR Andrew Carnegie Heavyweight Passenger Coach, *00*		60 ___
39011	PRR Solomon P. Chase Heavyweight Passenger Coach, *00*		60 ___
39012	PRR Skyline View Heavyweight Observation Car, *00*		50 ___
39013	D&O Heavyweight Passenger Car 4-pack, *00*		400 ___
39016	B&O Heavyweight Passenger Car 4-pack, *00*		200 ___
39017	B&O Harper's Ferry Heavyweight Combination Car, *00*		50 ___
39018	B&O Youngstown Heavyweight Passenger Coach, *00*		50 ___
39019	B&O New Castle Heavyweight Passenger Coach, *00*		50 ___
39020	B&O Chicago Heavyweight Observation Car, *00*		50 ___
39028	LL Heavyweight Passenger Car 3-pack, *00*		195 ___
39029	LL Irvington Heavyweight Coach "2625," *00*		60 ___
39030	LL Madison Heavyweight Coach "2627," *00*		60 ___
39031	LL Manhattan Heavyweight Coach "2628," *00*		60 ___
39032	UP Madison Passenger Car 4-pack, *00*		275 ___
39038	SP Madison Baggage Car "6015," *01*		NRS ___
39039	SP Madison Coach Car "1978," *01*		NRS ___

			Exc	Mint
___	39040	SP Madison Coach "1975," *01*		NRS
___	39041	SP Madison Observation Car "2951," *01*		NRS
___	39042	N&W Heavyweight Passenger Car 4-pack, *00*		325
___	39047	B&O Heavyweight Passenger Car 2-pack, *01*		160
___	39050	PRR Heavyweight Passenger Car 2-pack, *01*		215
___	39053	Alaska Streamliner Car 2-pack, *01*		90
___	39056	NYC Streamliner Car 2-pack, *01*		75
___	39059	Santa Fe Streamliner Car 2-pack, *01*		100
___	39062	B&O Streamliner Car 2-pack, *01*		75
___	39065	PRR Streamliner Car 4-pack, *01*		165
___	39082	Blue Comet Heavyweight Passenger Car 2-pack, *02*		325
___	39085	"Freedom Train" Heavyweight Passenger Car 3-pack, *03*		260
___	39092	PRR Streamliner Car 2-pack, *01*		70
___	39099	Alton Limited Heavyweight Passenger Car 2-pack, *03*		230
___	39100	William Penn Congressional Coach, *00*		115
___	39101	Molly Pitcher Congressional Coach, *00*		100
___	39102	Betsy Ross Congressional Vista Dome Car, *00*		100
___	39103	Alexander Hamilton Congressional Observation Car, *00*		100
___	39104	Phoebe Snow Car, StationSounds, *99*		255
___	39105	Milwaukee Road Hiawatha Car, StationSounds, *99*		235
___	39106	CP Aluminum Passenger Car 2-pack, *00*		185
___	39107	CP Blair Manor Aluminum Passenger Coach "2553," *00*		115
___	39108	CP Craig Manor Aluminum Passenger Coach "2554," *00*		110
___	39109	"Spirit of the Century" Aluminum Passenger Car 4-pack, *99*		520
___	39110	"Spirit of the Century" Full Vista Dome Car, *99–00*		100
___	39111	"Spirit of the Century" Full Vista Dome Car, *99–00*		100
___	39112	"Spirit of the Century" Full Vista Dome Car, *99–00*		100
___	39113	"Spirit of the Century" Skytop Observation Car, *99–00*		100
___	39118	Texas Special Garland Aluminum Passenger Coach "1203," StationSounds, *99–00*		220
___	39119	Southern Aluminum Passenger Car 4-pack, *00*		350
___	39120	Southern Grand Junction Aluminum Passenger/Baggage Car, *00*		280
___	39121	Southern Charlottesville Aluminum Passenger Coach "812," *00*		90
___	39122	Southern Roanoke Aluminum Passenger Coach "814," *00*		250
___	39123	Southern Memphis Aluminum Observation Car "1152," *00*		90
___	39124	Amtrak Superliner Aluminum Passenger Car 4-pack, *02*		405
___	39129	Santa Fe Superliner Aluminum Passenger Car 4-pack, *02*		305
___	39141	RI Aluminum Passenger Car 4-pack, *01*		400
___	39146	UP Aluminum Passenger Car 4-pack, *01*		285

		Exc	Mint
39151	CP Aluminum Passenger Car 2-pack, *01*		315 ___
39154	PRR Congressional Aluminum Passenger Car 2-pack, *02*		195 ___
39155	PRR Congressional Baggage Car, *02*		105 ___
39156	PRR Robert Morris Congressional Coach, *02*		100 ___
39157	Southern Aluminum Passenger Car 2-pack, *01*		290 ___
39160	KCS Aluminum Passenger Car 2-pack, *01*	200	260 ___
39163	Erie-Lack. Aluminum Passenger Car 2-pack, *01*		230 ___
39166	Texas Special Aluminum Passenger Car 2-pack, *01*	300	430 ___
39169	ACL Aluminum Passenger Car 4-pack, *01*		360 ___
39179	NP Aluminum Passenger Car 2-pack, *02*		305 ___
39182	WP Aluminum Passenger Car 2-pack, *02*		280 ___
39185	Rio Grande Aluminum Passenger Car 2-pack, *02*		290 ___
39194	UP Aluminum Passenger Car 2-pack, *02*		220 ___
39197	CP Aluminum Passenger Coach, StationSounds, *02*		225 ___
39198	PRR Aluminum Passenger Coach, StationSounds, *02*		210 ___
39200	Hellgate Bridge Boxcar #2 "1900-2000," *00 u*		55 ___
39202	Lionel Centennial Boxcar "1900-2000," *00*		46 ___
39203	Postwar "6464" Series X, 3 cars, *01*		115 ___
39204	New Haven Boxcar "6464-725," *01*		44 ___
39205	Alaska Boxcar "6464-825," *01*		55 ___
39206	NYC Boxcar "6464-900," *01*		40 ___
39207	UP Boxcar "508500," red, *00*		50 ___
39208	UP Boxcar "903658," silver, *00*		42 ___
39209	UP Boxcar "500200," yellow, *00*		40 ___
39210	6530 Fire Fighting Car, *00*		37 ___
39211	Postwar "6464" Boxcar 3-pack #2, *00*		85 ___
39212	Postwar "6464" SP&S Boxcar, *00*		NRS ___
39213	Postwar "6464" Wabash Boxcar, *00*		NRS ___
39214	Postwar "6464" Kansas, Oklahoma & Gulf Boxcar, *00*		NRS ___
39216	PRR DD Boxcar "47211," *01*		46 ___
39220	B&LE Heavyweight Boxcar "82101," *01*		41 ___
39221	L&N Heavyweight Boxcar "109829," *01*		41 ___
39222	Conrail Heavyweight Boxcar "269198," *01*		44 ___
39223	Postwar "6464" Archive Boxcar Set, 3-pack, *02*		125 ___
39227	Postwar "6468" Automobile Boxcar 3-pack, *01*		95 ___
39236	WP Boxcar "6464-250," *01*		55 ___
39238	Elvis Boxcar, *03*		36 ___
39239	P&LE Boxcar "22300, *02*		35 ___
39240	Pennsylvania Boxcar "118747," *02*		32 ___
39241	PC Boxcar "252455," *02*		28 ___
39242	Postwar "6464" Boxcar 3-pack #1, Archive Collection, *03–04*		80 ___
39243	Soo Line Boxcar, Archive Collection		35 ___
39247	NYC DD Boxcar "6468," *02–03*		32 ___
39248	Lackawanna DD Boxcar with hobo, *03*		45 ___
39250	Campbell's Kids Centennial Boxcar, *03–04*		40 ___

Exc Mint

			Mint
____	39252	Lenny Dean 60th Anniversary Boxcar, 04	38
	39253	No. 6464 Boxcar 3-pack #2, Archive	
____		Collection, 04	100
____	39257	WP Boxcar "6464-100," boys set add-on, 03	50
____	39258	Elvis Presley "All Shook Up" Boxcar, 03–04	40
____	39259	Buick Centennial Boxcar, 03	35
____	39260	New Haven Boxcar, 04	40
	39262	Elvis Presley "Elvis Has Left the Building"	
____		Boxcar, 04	38
____	39263	M&StL Boxcar, Postwar Celebration Series, 05	35
	39267	No. 6464 Boxcar 3-pack #3, Archive	
____		Collection, 05	100
____	39271	State of Maine Boxcar, 04	35
	39273	No. 6464 Boxcar 3-pack #4, Archive	
____		Collection, 06	100
____	39281	Florida State University Boxcar, 07	45
____	39282	Purdue University Boxcar, 08	50
____	39283	University of Virginia Boxcar, 08	50
____	39284	Penn State University Boxcar, 06–07	45
	39285	U.S. Military Academy at West Point Boxcar,	
____		08	50
____	39286	University of Illinois Boxcar, 06–07	45
____	39287	University of Alabama Boxcar, 06–07	45
____	39289	University of Oklahoma Boxcar, 06–08	50
	39290	Postwar "6464" Boxcar 2-pack,	
____		rare variations, 08	100
____	39291	University of Michigan Boxcar, 06–07	45
____	39292	Monopoly Boxcar 3-pack, 08	135
____	39296	UPS Centennial Boxcar #3, 08–09	55
____	39297	Macy's Parade Boxcar, 07	55
____	39298	Monopoly Boxcar 3-pack #2, 08	135
____	39299	Lenny Dean Commemorative Boxcar, 08	50
____	39229	B&O DD Boxcar, 01	40
____	39302	University of Maryland Boxcar, 08	50
____	39303	Villanova University Boxcar, 08	50
____	39304	Auburn University Boxcar, 08	50
____	39308	CP Rail "6565" Boxcar "58700," 08–10	55
____	39309	Macy's Parade Boxcar, 08	50
____	39310	Monopoly Boxcar 3-pack #3, 09–10	165
____	39316	New Haven Automobile Boxcar, 09–10	60
____	39317	Wizard of Oz Boxcar #1, 09–10	60
____	39318	Wizard of Oz Boxcar #2, 09–10	60
____	39319	Boy Scouts "Scout Law" Add-on Boxcar, 10	60
____	39321	Lionel Art Boxcar 2-pack, 10	116
____	39325	Macy's Parade Boxcar, 09	45
____	39326	UPS Centennial Boxcar #4, 10–11	60
____	39328	Monopoly Boxcar 3-pack #4, 10–11	170
____	39332	Holiday Boxcar, 10	60
____	39334	Coca-Cola Christmas Boxcar, 10	68
____	39335	Thomas Kinkade Boxcar, 10, 12	60
	39336	Angela Trotta Thomas "My Turn Yet, Dad?"	
____		Boxcar, 10	60
____	39337	George Washington Boxcar, 11–12	60
____	39338	Abraham Lincoln Boxcar, 11–12	60

		Exc	Mint
39339	Theodore Roosevelt Boxcar, *11–12*		60 ____
39340	Thomas Jefferson Boxcar, *11–12*		60 ____
39342	Strasburg Boxcar, *11*		55 ____
39343	New Jersey Central Boxcar, *10*		45 ____
39344	Monopoly Boxcar 3-pack #5, *11–12*		165 ____
39345	Monopoly Tennessee Avenue Boxcar, *11*		55 ____
39346	Monopoly Atlantic Avenue Boxcar, *11*		55 ____
39347	Monopoly Illinois Avenue Boxcar, *11*		55 ____
39348	Lionel NASCAR Collectables Boxcar, *11–12*		60 ____
39350	Thomas Kinkade "All Aboard for Christmas" Boxcar, *12–13*		60 ____
39351	Peanuts Thanksgiving Boxcar, *12*		70 ____
39354	Monopoly North Carolina Avenue Boxcar, *12*		70 ____
39358	Boy Scouts "Prepared For Life" Boxcar, *12*		60 ____
39359	Thanksgiving Boxcar, *12*		60 ____
39360	Boy Scouts Cub Scout Boxcar, *12–13*		60 ____
39362	Thomas Kinkade "Emerald City" Boxcar, *12–14*		70 ____
39363	Peanuts Halloween Boxcar, *12*		65 ____
39364	Christmas Boxcar, *13*		60 ____
39376	Monopoly Boxcar 2-pack, States and Vermont Avenues, *13–14*		130 ____
39379	Monopoly Boxcar 2-pack, Mediterranean and St. James Avenues, *13–14*		130 ____
39383	Prewar "2719" Boxcar, *13*		65 ____
39385	U.S. Navy 1-D Tank Car, *13–14*		65 ____
39386	U.S. Marines 1-D Tank Car, *13–14*		65 ____
39387	U.S. Air Force 1-D Tank Car, *13–14*		65 ____
39388	U.S. National Guard 1-D Tank Car, *13–14*		65 ____
39389	U.S. Coast Guard 1-D Tank Car, *13–14*		65 ____
39391	U.S. Army Flatcar, *13–14*		65 ____
39392	U.S. Navy Flatcar, *13–14*		65 ____
39393	U.S. Marines Flatcar, *13–14*		65 ____
39394	U.S. Air Force Flatcar, *13–14*		65 ____
39395	U.S. National Guard Flatcar, *13–14*		65 ____
39396	U.S. Coast Guard Flatcar, *13–14*		65 ____
39398	Santa's Flyer Reefer, *13*		43 ____
39399	U.S. Army 1-D Tank Car, *13–14*		65 ____
39400	Republic Steel Slag Car 3-pack (std O), *04*		100 ____
39404	Republic Steel Hot Metal Car 3-pack (std O), *04*		130 ____
39411	Jones & Laughline Hot Metal Car 3-pack (std O), *05*		190 ____
39423	Postwar "3460" LL Flatcar with trailers, *05*		45 ____
39424	U.S. Steel 16-wheel Flatcar with girders, *05*		70 ____
39425	Hood's Flatcar with milk container, traditional, *05*		55 ____
39426	Nestle Nesquik Flatcar with milk container, traditional, *05*		55 ____
39428	Bethlehem Steel Slag Car #4 (std O), *05*		60 ____
39429	Bethlehem Steel Hot Metal Car #8 (std O), *05*		70 ____
39430	Youngstown Sheet & Tube Slag Car #7 (std O), *05*		60 ____
39431	Youngstown Sheet & Tube Hot Metal Car #11 (std O), *05*		70 ____

____	39435	Postwar "6477" Flatcar with pipes, *06*	50
____	39436	Postwar "6262" Wheel Car, *06*	50
____	39437	Supplee Flatcar with milk container, *06*	60
____	39439	6827 Flatcar with P&H power shovel, *04*	50
____	39440	6828 Flatcar with P&H truck crane, *04*	50
____	39443	U.S. Steel Slag Car 3-pack #2 (std O), *06*	170
____	39447	Postwar "6561" LL Cable Reel Car, Archive Collection, *06–07*	55
____	39450	Postwar "6414" Evans Auto Loader, Archive Collection, *06*	70
____	39452	White Bros. Flatcar with milk container, *07*	60
____	39457	Postwar "6175" Flatcar with rocket, *08*	55
____	39458	Postwar "6844" Flatcar with missiles, *08*	55
____	39463	Postwar "6430" Flatcar with trailers, *08*	55
____	39468	Allis-Chalmers Car "52369," *08–09*	60
____	39469	Christmas Egg Nog Barrel Car, *08*	50
____	39470	UP Well Car "147128," *08*	65
____	39471	Postwar "6264" Flatcar, *08*	60
____	39472	ATSF Culvert Gondola, *08*	60
____	39473	Play-Doh Vat Car, *08*	55
____	39475	UPS Flatcar with trailer, *08*	65
____	39476	Bethlehem Steel 16-wheel Flatcar, *08*	75
____	39477	Christmas Flatcar with reindeer trailers, *08*	60
____	39478	Postwar "6475" Pickles Vat Car, *08*	55
____	39479	Postwar "6404" Flatcar with brown automobile, *08*	50
____	39480	Western & Atlantic Cannon Flatcar, *09*	60
____	39482	CSX WM Track Maintenance Car "6812," *11*	65
____	39483	CSX P&LE Gondola "69812," *11*	65
____	39484	Cocoa Marsh Vat Car, *10–12*	60
____	39486	Deep Sea Challenger Submarine Car, *11*	60
____	39488	Reese's Vat Car, *10*	60
____	39490	Western & Atlantic Cannonball Flatcar, *10*	55
____	39497	Christmas Reindeer Stock Car, *10–11*	60
____	39498	CNJ Gondola with culvert pipes, *11*	55
____	39499	Alaska Oil Barrel Ramp Car, *11*	50
____	39502	Monongahela NS Heritage ES44AC Diesel, nonpowered, *13*	280
____	39530	PRR 1955 Pickup Truck, CC, *13*	180
____	39531	UP 1955 Pickup Truck, CC, *13*	180
____	39532	ATSF 1955 Pickup Truck, CC, *13–14*	180
____	39533	CP 1955 Pickup Truck, CC, *13–14*	180
____	39534	D&RGW 1955 Pickup Truck, CC, *13*	180
____	39535	GN 1955 Pickup Truck, CC, *13*	180
____	39536	MKT 1955 Pickup Truck, CC, *13–14*	180
____	39537	NYC 1955 Pickup Truck, CC, *13*	180
____	39538	Nickel Plate Road 1955 Pickup Truck, CC, *13*	180
____	39539	NP 1955 Pickup Truck, CC, *13–14*	180
____	39540	Southern 1955 Pickup Truck, CC, *13*	180
____	39541	SP 1955 Pickup Truck, CC, *13–14*	180
____	39542	Weyerhaeuser 1955 Pickup Truck, CC, *13–14*	180
____	39543	Texas Special F3 B Unit, *13–14*	230
____	39544	Texas Special F3 B Unit, CC, *13–14*	380
____	39547	PRR F3 B Unit, *13–14*	230

39548	PRR F3 B Unit, CC, *13–14*	380 ____
39554	NS GP35 Diesel "3918," CC, *13*	500 ____
39555	NS GP35 Diesel "2915," nonpowered, *13*	260 ____
39556	CP GP35 Diesel "5004," CC, *13–14*	500 ____
39557	CP GP35 Diesel "5007," CC, *13–14*	500 ____
39558	CP GP35 Diesel "5009," nonpowered, *13–14*	260 ____
39562	BN GP35 Diesel "2533," CC, *13–14*	500 ____
39563	BN GP35 Diesel "2509," CC, *13–14*	500 ____
39564	BN GP35 Diesel "2523," nonpowered, *13–14*	260 ____
39565	ATSF Dash-9 Diesel "612," CC, *13*	530 ____
39566	ATSF Dash-9 Diesel "623," CC, *13*	530 ____
39567	ATSF Dash-9 Diesel "631," nonpowered, *13*	260 ____
39568	BC Rail Dash-9 Diesel "4641," CC, *13*	530 ____
39569	BC Rail Dash-9 Diesel "4647," CC, *13*	530 ____
39570	BC Rail Dash-9 Diesel "4652," nonpowered, *13*	260 ____
39571	BNSF Dash-9 Diesel "4023," CC, *13*	530 ____
39572	BNSF Dash-9 Diesel "4037," CC, *13*	530 ____
39573	BNSF Dash-9 Diesel "4046," nonpowered, *13*	260 ____
39574	C&NW Dash-9 Diesel "8605," CC, *13*	530 ____
39575	C&NW Dash-9 Diesel "8610," CC, *13*	530 ____
39576	C&NW Dash-9 Diesel "8622," nonpowered, *13*	260 ____
39577	SP Dash-9 Diesel "8112," CC, *13*	530 ____
39578	SP Dash-9 Diesel "8123," CC, *13*	530 ____
39579	SP Dash-9 Diesel "8129," nonpowered, *13*	260 ____
39580	UP Dash-9 Diesel "9599," CC, *13*	530 ____
39581	UP Dash-9 Diesel "9714," CC, *13*	530 ____
39582	UP Dash-9 Diesel "9717," nonpowered, *13*	260 ____
39583	CSX Dash-9 Diesel "9036," CC, *13*	530 ____
39584	CSX Dash-9 Diesel "9048," CC, *13*	530 ____
39585	CSX Dash-9 Diesel "9051," nonpowered, *13*	260 ____
39586	NS Dash-9 Diesel "9310," CC, *13*	530 ____
39587	NS Dash-9 Diesel "9322," CC, *13*	530 ____
39588	NS Dash-9 Diesel "9334," nonpowered, *13*	260 ____
39589	CN Dash-9 Diesel "2534," CC, *13*	530 ____
39590	CN Dash-9 Diesel "2547," CC, *13*	530 ____
39591	CN Dash-9 Diesel "2570," nonpowered, *13*	260 ____
39592	CNJ NS Heritage SD70ACe Diesel "1071," CC, *13*	530 ____
39593	CNJ NS Heritage SD70ACe Diesel "1831," CC, *13*	530 ____
39594	CNJ NS Heritage SD70ACe Diesel "1834," nonpowered, *13*	260 ____
39595	DL&W NS Heritage SD70ACe Diesel "1074," CC, *13*	530 ____
39596	DL&W NS Heritage SD70ACe Diesel "1853," CC, *13*	530 ____
39597	DL&W NS Heritage SD70ACe Diesel "1856," nonpowered, *13*	260 ____
39598	Monongahela NS Heritage ES44AC Diesel "8025," CC, *12*	550 ____
39599	Monongahela NS Heritage ES44AC Diesel "1901," CC, *12*	550 ____
39600	PRR E8 AA Diesel Set, CC, *13*	930 ____
39603	B&O E9 AA Diesel Set, CC, *13*	930 ____
39606	FEC E9 AA Diesel Set, CC, *13*	930 ____

			Exc	Mint
____	39609	SP E9 AA Diesel Set, CC, *13*		930
____	39612	SP E9 AA Diesel Set, CC, *13*		930
____	39612	UP E9 AA Diesel Set, CC, *13*		930
____	39615	CB&Q E9 AA Diesel Set, CC, *13*		930
____	39618	MILW E9 AA Diesel Set, CC, *13*		930
____	39621	KCS E9 AA Diesel Set, CC, *13*		930
____	39624	Erie NS Heritage SD70ACe Diesel "1068," CC, *13*		530
____	39625	Erie NS Heritage SD70ACe Diesel "1832," CC, *13*		530
____	39626	Erie NS Heritage SD70ACe Diesel "1835," nonpowered, *13*		260
____	39627	Illinois Terminal NS Heritage SD70ACe Diesel "1072," CC, *13*		530
____	39628	Illinois Terminal NS Heritage SD70ACe Diesel "1896," CC, *13*		530
____	39629	Illinois Terminal NS Heritage SD70ACe Diesel "1899," nonpowered, *13*		260
____	39630	NYC NS Heritage SD70ACe Diesel "1066," CC, *13*		530
____	39631	NYC NS Heritage SD70ACe Diesel "1831," CC, *13*		530
____	39632	NYC NS Heritage SD70ACe Diesel "1834," nonpowered, *13*		260
____	39633	Reading NS Heritage SD70ACe Diesel "1067," CC, *13*		530
____	39634	Reading NS Heritage SD70ACe Diesel "1833," CC, *13*		530
____	39635	Reading NS Heritage SD70ACe Diesel "1836," nonpowered, *13*		260
____	39636	Savannah & Atlanta NS Heritage SD70ACe Diesel "1065," CC, *13*		530
____	39637	Savannah & Atlanta NS Heritage SD70ACe Diesel "1915," CC, *13*		530
____	39638	Savannah & Atlanta NS Heritage SD70ACe Diesel "1918," nonpowered, *13*		260
____	39639	Virginian NS Heritage SD70ACe Diesel "1069," CC, *13*		530
____	39640	Virginian NS Heritage SD70ACe Diesel "1907," CC, *13*		530
____	39641	Virginian NS Heritage SD70ACe Diesel "1910," nonpowered, *13*		260
____	39642	Wabash NS Heritage SD70ACe Diesel "1070," CC, *13*		530
____	39643	Wabash NS Heritage SD70ACe Diesel "1877," CC, *13*		530
____	39644	Wabash NS Heritage SD70ACe Diesel "1880," nonpowered, *13*		260
____	39645	PC NS Heritage SD70ACe Diesel "1073," CC, *13*		530
____	39646	PC NS Heritage SD70ACe Diesel "1968," CC, *13*		530
____	39647	PC NS Heritage SD70ACe Diesel "1971," nonpowered, *13*		260
____	51008	Burlington Pioneer Zephyr Diesel Passenger Set, RailSounds, *04*		875
____	51009	Prewar "269E" Steam Freight Set, TrainSounds, *06*		630

		Exc	Mint
51010	Prewar "246E" Steam Passenger Set, TrainSounds, *07–08*		630 ___
51012	Christmas Tinplate Freight Set, *08*		675 ___
51014	Prewar "291W" Red Comet Passenger Car Set, *08*		675 ___
51220	NYC Imperial Castle Passenger Coach, *93 u*		500 ___
51221	NYC Niagara County Passenger Coach, *93 u*		500 ___
51222	NYC Cascade Glory Passenger Coach, *93 u*		500 ___
51223	NYC City of Detroit Passenger Coach, *93 u*		500 ___
51224	NYC Imperial Falls Passenger Coach, *93 u*		500 ___
51225	NYC Westchester County Passenger Coach, *93 u*		500 ___
51226	NYC Cascade Grotto Passenger Coach, *93 u*		500 ___
51227	NYC City of Indianapolis Passenger Coach, *93 u*		500 ___
51228	NYC Manhattan Island Observation Car, *93 u*		500 ___
51229	NYC Diner "680," *93 u*		500 ___
51230	NYC Baggage Car "5017," *93 u*		500 ___
51231	NYC Century Club Passenger Coach, *93 u*		500 ___
51232	NYC Thousand Islands Observation Car, *93 u*		500 ___
51233	NYC Diner "684," *93 u*		500 ___
51234	NYC Baggage Car "5020," *93 u*		500 ___
51235	NYC Century Tavern Passenger Coach, *93 u*		500 ___
51236	NYC City of Toledo Passenger Coach, *93 u*		500 ___
51237	NYC Imperial Mansion Passenger Coach, *93 u*		500 ___
51238	NYC Imperial Palace Passenger Coach, *93 u*		500 ___
51239	NYC Cascade Spirit Passenger Coach, *93 u*		500 ___
51240	NYC Diner "681," *93 u*		500 ___
51241	NYC City of Chicago Passenger Coach, *93 u*		500 ___
51242	NYC Imperial Garden Passenger Coach, *93 u*		500 ___
51243	NYC Imperial Fountain Passenger Coach, *93 u*		500 ___
51244	NYC Cascade Valley Passenger Coach, *93 u*		500 ___
51245	NYC Diner "685," *93 u*		500 ___
51300	Shell Semi-Scale 1-D Tank Car "8124," *91*	50	135 ___
51301	Lackawanna Semi-Scale Reefer "7000," *92*	119	161 ___
51401	PRR Semi-Scale Boxcar "100800," *91*	84	128 ___
51402	C&O Semi-Scale Stock Car "95250," *92*	98	138 ___
51501	B&O Semi-Scale Hopper "532000," *91*	78	108 ___
51502	LL Steel Die-cast Ore Car "6486-3" (SSS), *96*		80 ___
51503	LL Steel Die-cast Ore Car "6486-1" (SSS), *96*		80 ___
51504	LL Steel Die-cast Ore Car "6486-2" (SSS), *96*		70 ___
51600	NYC Depressed Center Flatcar with transformer "6418," *96*		105 ___
51701	NYC Semi-Scale Caboose "19400," *91*	84	123 ___
51702	PRR N-8 Caboose "478039," *91–92*	300	385 ___
52054	Carail Boxcar, *94 u*		280 ___
52066	Trainmaster Tractor and Trailer, *94 u*		101 ___
52069	Carail Tractor and Trailer, *94 u*		64 ___
52070	Knoebel's Boxcar #1, *95 u*		64 ___
52075	United Auto Workers Boxcar, *95 u*		90 ___
52082	Steamtown Lackawanna Boxcar, *95 u*		90 ___
52132	Knoebel's Boxcar #2, *99 u*		81 ___
52133	Knoebel's Boxcar #3, *98 u*		93 ___
52134	Knoebel's Boxcar #4, *00 u*		93 ___

Exc Mint

		Exc	Mint
_____ 52136A	Christmas Special Tractor and Trailer, *97*		NRS
_____ 52136B	Frisco Special Tractor and Trailer, *98*		NRS
_____ 52137	Red Wing Shoes Boot Oil Tank Car, *98*		63
_____ 52141	Zep Manufacturing Boxcar, *96*		82
_____ 52158	Monopoly Mint Car "M-0539," *98*		340
52159	Monopoly Depressed Center Flatcar with transformer, *98*		
_____			95
_____ 52160	Monopoly Water Works Tank Car, *98*		105
_____ 52161	Monopoly SP-type Caboose "M-1006," *98*		55
_____ 52168	Carail Flatcar with Trailer "17455," *99 u*		95
52169	Zep Manufacturing Flatcar with trailer "62734," *99 u*		
_____			63
_____ 52174	REA Baggage Car "0083," *00 u*		400
_____ 52181	Monopoly Set #2, 4-pack, *99*		295
_____ 52182	Monopoly Railroads Boxcar "M0636," *99 u*		78
_____ 52183	Monopoly Jail Car "M-1131," *99*		75
52184	Monopoly Free Parking Flatcar with 2 autos, *99*		
_____			60
_____ 52185	Monopoly Chance Gondola "M-0893," *99*		50
_____ 52187	Madison Hardware Flatcar with 2 trailers, *99*		98
52188	Carail Aquarium with 2 autos, 25th Anniversary, *99*		
_____			95
_____ 52189	Monopoly 4-6-4 Hudson Locomotive, *99*		540
_____ 52207	Lionel Lines SD40 Diesel, traditional, *00*		600
_____ 52208	Lionel Lines Extended Vision Caboose, *00 u*		200
52209	World's Fair Sleeper/Roomette Car "0183," *01 u*		
_____			170
_____ 52218	Monopoly 4-4-2 Steam Freight Set, *00 u*		388
52219	Monopoly 4-6-4 Hudson Locomotive, bronze, *00 u*		
_____			530
_____ 52224A	SP Flatcar with Navajo tractor and trailer, *01*		25
52224B	SP Flatcar with Trailer Flatcar Service tractor and trailer, *01*		
_____			25
52225	Monopoly 4-6-4 Hudson Locomotive, pewter, *01 u*		
_____			495
_____ 52231	British Columbia 1-D Tank Car, *00 u*		65
_____ 52235	World's Fair Vista Dome Car "0283," *02 u*		NRS
52249	Knoebel's Amusement Park 75th Anniversary Boxcar, *01 u*		
_____			89
_____ 52253	San Pedro Boxcar, *02*		NRS
_____ 52262	Plasticville Boxcar, *01 u*		120
_____ 52263	World's Fair Combination Car "0383," *02*		NRS
_____ 52279	Dragoon & Northern Ore Car, *02*		25
_____ 52282	Western Pacific Feather Boxcar, red, *03*		365
_____ 52315/20	PRR FM Diesel and Caboose, *04 u*		440
_____ 52330	B&O Museum Fundraiser Boxcar, *03 u*		100
_____ 52371	NYC Flatcar with tanker trailer, *05 u*		150
62162	Postwar "262" Automatic Crossing Gate and Signal, *99–14*		
_____			60
_____ 62180	Railroad Signs, set of 14, *99–04, 08–14*		10
_____ 62181	Telephone Pole Set, *99–04, 08–14*		10
_____ 62283	Die-cast Illuminated Bumpers, *99–14*		27
_____ 62709	Rico Station Kit, *99–00*		46
_____ 62716	Short Extension Bridge, *99–03, 07–14*		15
_____ 62900	Lockon, *99–13*		3

Number	Description	Exc	Mint
62901	Ives Track Clips, 12 pieces (027), *99–10, 13–14*	5	___
62905	Lockon with wires, *99–10, 13–14*	7	___
62909	Smoke Fluid, *99–12*	7	___
62927	Lubrication/Maintenance Set, *99–14*	25	___
62985	The Lionel Train Book, *99–03*	12	___
65014	Half Curved Track (027), *99–14*	1	___
65019	Half-Straight Track (027), *99–14*	1	___
65020	90-degree Crossover (027), *99–14*	11	___
65021	27" Manual Switch, left hand (027), *99–14*	17	___
65022	27" Manual Switch, right hand (027), *99–14*	18	___
65023	45-degree Crossover (027), *99–14*	11	___
65024	35" Straight Track (027), *99–14*	5	___
65033	27" Diameter Curved Track (027), *99–14*	2	___
65038	9" Straight Track (027), *99–14*	2	___
65041	Insulator Pins, dozen (027), *99–04, 06, 13–14*	3	___
65042	Steel Pins, dozen (027), *99–04, 06–09, 13–14*	3	___
65049	42" Diameter Curved Track (027), *99–14*	3	___
65113	54" Diameter Curved Track (027), *99–14*	3	___
65121	27" Path Remote Switch, left hand (027), *99–14*	43	___
65122	27" Path Remote Switch, right hand (027), *99–14*	43	___
65149	Uncoupling Track (027), *99–14*	12	___
65165	72" Path Remote Switch, right hand (O), *99–14*	125	___
65166	72" Path Remote Switch, left hand (O), *99–14*	125	___
65167	42" Remote Switch, right hand (027), *99–14*	25	___
65168	42" Remote Switch, left hand (027), *99–14*	25	___
65500	10" Straight Track (O), *99–14*	2	___
65501	31" Diameter Curved Track (O), *99–14*	2	___
65504	Half Curved Track (O), *99–14*	2	___
65505	Half Straight Track (O), *99–14*	2	___
65514	Half Curved Track (027), *99–03*	3	___
65523	40" Straight Track (O), *99–14*	7	___
65530	Remote Control Track (O), *99–14*	38	___
65540	90-degree Crossover (O), *99–14*	16	___
65543	Insulator Pins, dozen (O), *99–14*	3	___
65545	45-degree Crossover (O), *99–14*	27	___
65551	Steel Pins, dozen (O), *99–14*	3	___
65554	54" Diameter Curved Track (O), *99–14*	4	___
65572	72" Diameter Curved Track (O), *99–14*	5	___
81000	BNSF Waffle-sided Boxcar "496464," *14*	45	___
81001	SP&S Flatcar with bulkheads, *14*	45	___
81002	UP 3-D Tank Car, *14*	45	___
81003	CP Bilevel Auto Carrier, *14*	45	___
81004	B&O Depressed-Center Flatcar with transformer, *14*	45	___
81005	Maine Central 2-bay Hopper "1005," *14*	45	___
81006	PRR Hi-Cube Boxcar "31010," *14*	45	___
81007	Seaboard Waffle-sided Boxcar "25335," *14*	45	___
81008	Central of Georgia Boxcar "5818," *14*	45	___
81009	Southern 2-D Tank Car "951005," *14*	45	___
81010	FEC Gondola "6121" with reels, *14*	45	___

		Exc	Mint
____ 81011	PFE Reefer "33280," *14*		45
____ 81012	T&P 1-D Tank Car, *14*		45
____ 81013	Frisco Boxcar "700117," *14*		45
____ 81014	D&RGW Ore Car "31101," *14*		45
____ 81015	B&M Reefer "1878," *14*		45
____ 81016	Coaling Station, *14*		110
____ 81017	Barrel Loading Building, *14*		43
____ 81019	Short Tunnel, *14*		45
____ 81021	B&M Paul Revere GP9 Diesel Freight Set, *14*		500
____ 81023	Jersey Central Yard Boss 0-4-0 Steam Freight Set, *14*		500
____ 81024	Christmas Train Set, *02–04*		150
____ 81025	Lackawanna Pocono Berkshire Steam Freight Set, *14*		480
____ 81027	Thomas the Tank Engine Set, *01–04*		120
____ 81028	Marquette GP38 Diesel Freight Set, *14*		430
____ 81029	C&NW Windy City GP38 Diesel Freight Set, *14*		400
____ 81030	UP Gold Coast Flyer Steam Freight Set, *14*		430
____ 81031	Dinosaur LionChief Diesel Freight Set, *14*		175
____ 81063	Classic Automatic Gateman, *14*		80
____ 81064	Construction Zone Signs #2, *14*		10
____ 81066	Milwaukee Road Double-sheathed Boxcar "8775" (std O), *14*		80
____ 81076	Pennsylvania Salt 8,000-gallon 1-D Tank Car "4724" (std O), *14*		73
____ 81077	Pere Marquette 8,000-gallon 1-D Tank Car "71710" (std O), *14*		73
____ 81078	NYC 8,000-gallon 1-D Tank Car "107898" (std O), *14*		73
____ 81079	NKP 8,000-gallon 1-D Tank Car "50277" (std O), *14*		73
____ 81080	BN 8,000-gallon 1-D Tank Car "977100" (std O), *14*		73
____ 81081	Alaska Steel-sided Reefer "10806" (std O), *14*		80
____ 81090	NS Hi-Cube Boxcar 2-Pack (std O), *14*		190
____ 81094	Conrail "Big Blue" High-Cube Boxcar Diesel Freight Set, CC, *14*		970
____ 81095	Conrail Hi-Cube Boxcar 2-Pack (std O), *14*		190
____ 81101	Polar Express LionChief 10th Anniversary Steam Passenger Set, *14*		400
____ 81134	BN SD70MAC Diesel "9424," CC, *14*		550
____ 81135	BN SD70MAC Diesel "9431," CC, *14*		550
____ 81137	BNSF SD70MAC Diesel "9858," CC, *14*		550
____ 81138	BNSF SD70MAC Diesel "9860," CC, *14*		550
____ 81141	Conrail SD70MAC Diesel "4138," CC, *14*		550
____ 81142	PFE Steel-sided Reefers 3-Pack (std O), *14*		300
____ 81144	CSX SD70MAC Diesel "781," CC, *14*		550
____ 81147	KCS SD7CMAC Diesel "3950," CC, *14*		550
____ 81148	KCS SD7CMAC Diesel "3953," CC, *14*		550
____ 81151	Alaska SD7CMAC Diesel "4002," CC, *14*		550
____ 81152	Alaska SD7CMAC Diesel "4005," CC, *14*		550
____ 81153	CSX SD70MAC Diesel "778," CC, *14*		550
____ 81154	UP ES44AC Diesel "7361," CC, *14*		550
____ 81155	UP ES44AC Diesel "7388," CC, *14*		550
____ 81160	CSX ES44AC Diesel "937," CC, *14*		550

		Exc	Mint
81161	CSX ES44AC Diesel "944," CC, *14*		550 ___
81169	Iowa Interstate ES44AC Diesel "504," CC, *14*		550 ___
81170	Iowa Interstate ES44AC Diesel "507," CC, *14*		550 ___
81171	Ferromex ES44AC Diesel "4617," CC, *14*		550 ___
81172	Ferromex ES44AC Diesel "4626," CC, *14*		550 ___
81176	CN ES44AC Diesel "2812," CC, *14*		550 ___
81177	CN ES44AC Diesel "2818," CC, *14*		550 ___
81179	2-8-2 Heavy Mikado Pilot Locomotive, CC, *14*		1300 ___
81182	L&N 2-8-2 Heavy Mikado Locomotive "1757," CC, *14*		1300 ___
81184	P&WV 2-8-2 Heavy Mikado Locomotive "1152," CC, *14*		1300 ___
81185	CNJ 2-8-2 Heavy Mikado Locomotive "845," CC, *14*		1300 ___
81186	Frisco 2-8-2 Heavy Mikado Locomotive "4126," CC, *14*		1300 ___
81187	C&IM 2-8-2 Heavy Mikado Locomotive "551," CC, *14*		1300 ___
81188	NYC 2-8-2 Heavy Mikado Locomotive "9506," CC, *14*		1300 ___
81192	GN 2-8-2 Heavy Mikado Locomotive "3148," CC, *14*		1300 ___
81195	PRR Boxcar, *14*		65 ___
81196	Timken Boxcar, *14*		65 ___
81197	Santa Fe Boxcar, *14*		65 ___
81198	GN Boxcar, *14*		65 ___
81199	PRR 1-D Tank Car, *14*		65 ___
81200	Timken 1-D Tank Car, *14*		65 ___
81201	GN 1-D Tank Car, *14*		65 ___
81202	Santa Fe 1-D Tank Car, *14*		65 ___
81203	PRR Flatcar, *14*		65 ___
81204	Santa Fe Flatcar, *14*		65 ___
81205	Timken Flatcar, *14*		65 ___
81206	GN Flatcar, *14*		65 ___
81207	CP H-24-66 Train Master Diesel "8900," CC, *14*		550 ___
81208	CP H-24-66 Train Master Diesel "8903," CC, *14*		550 ___
81209	CNJ H-24-66 Train Master Diesel "2401," CC, *14*		550 ___
81210	CNJ H-24-66 Train Master Diesel "2406," CC, *14*		550 ___
81211	Reading H-24-66 Train Master Diesel "801," CC, *14*		550 ___
81212	Reading H-24-66 Train Master Diesel "804," CC, *14*		550 ___
81213	SP H-24-66 Train Master Diesel "4803," CC, *14*		550 ___
81214	SP H-24-66 Train Master Diesel "4809," CC, *14*		550 ___
81215	Southern H-24-66 Train Master Diesel "6300," CC, *14*		550 ___
81216	Southern H-24-66 Train Master Diesel "6303," CC, *14*		550 ___
81217	N&W H-24-66 Train Master Diesel "151," CC, *14*		550 ___

		Exc	Mint
____	81218 N&W H-24-66 Train Master Diesel "164," CC, *14*		550
____	81219 Santa Fe E8 Diesel AA Set "84/85," CC, *14*		930
____	81222 PC E8 Diesel AA Set "4289/4325," CC, *14*		930
____	81225 RI E8 Diesel AA Set "647/648," CC, *14*		930
____	81228 C&O E8 Diesel AA Set "4027/4028," CC, *14*		930
____	81231 Erie E8 Diesel AA Set "822/823," CC, *14*		930
____	81234 MKT E8 Diesel AA Set "131/132," CC, *14*		930
____	81237 SAL E8 Diesel AA Set "3051/3055," CC, *14*		930
____	81240 Wabash E8 Diesel AA Set "1007/1011," CC, *14*		930
____	81243 Pilot M1a 4-8-2 Locomotive, CC, *14*		1500
____	81245 PRR M1a 4-8-2 Locomotive "6671," CC, *14*		1500
____	81246 PRR M1a 4-8-2 Locomotive "6764," CC, *14*		1500
____	81247 PRR M1a Coal Hauler Twin-hopper Steam Freight Set, CC, *14*		1800
____	81248 10" Girder Bridge Track, *14*		25
____	81250 FasTrack O-96 Curve, *14*		7
____	81251 FasTrack O-31 Manual Switch, right-hand, *14*		50
____	81252 FasTrack O-31 Manual Switch, left-hand, *14*		50
____	81253 FasTrack O-31 Remote Switch, right-hand, *14*		110
____	81254 FasTrack O-31 Remote Switch, left-hand, *14*		110
____	81256 Personalized Birthday Message Boxcar, *14*		80
____	81257 Amtrak Water Tower, *14*		35
____	81259 PRR Broadway Limited Steam Passenger Set, *14*		370
____	81263 CNJ LionChief Diesel Passenger Set, *14*		370
____	81264 Western Union Telegraph Steam Freight Set, *14*		370
____	81266 Amtrak LionChief FT Diesel Passenger Set, *14*		440
____	81279 Albert Hall LionChief European Steam Passenger Set, *14*		400
____	81286 Lionel Junction "Little Steam" Freight Set, *14*		175
____	81287 Lionel Junction UP Steam Freight Set, *14*		175
____	81288 Pet Shop Diesel Freight Set, *14*		175
____	81292 Valley Central 1-D Tank Car "45003," *14*		43
____	81294 LCS Sensor Track, *13–14*		95
____	81295 AT&SF LionChief 2-8-2 Locomotive "3158," *14*		430
____	81296 GN LionChief 2-8-2 Locomotive "3123," *14*		430
____	81297 PRR LionChief 2-8-2 Locomotive "9633," *14*		430
____	81299 Chessie System LionChief 2-8-2 Locomotive "2103," *14*		430
____	81301 NYC LionChief 4-6-4 Locomotive "5421," *14*		430
____	81302 C&O LionChief 4-6-4 Locomotive "308," *14*		430
____	81303 UP LionChief 4-6-4 Locomotive "674," *14*		430
____	81304 CN LionChief 4-6-4 Locomotive "5702," *14*		430
____	81307 B&O LionChief 4-6-2 Locomotive "5307," *14*		430
____	81308 CP LionChief 4-6-2 Locomotive "2469," *14*		430
____	81309 SP LionChief 4-6-2 Locomotive "3106," *14*		430
____	81311 Alaska LionChief 4-6-2 Locomotive "652," *14*		430
____	81325 LCS WiFi Module, *13–14*		180
____	81326 LCS Serial Converter #2, *14*		50
____	81331 Iron Arry Locomotive with LionChief Remote, *14*		140

Exc Mint

81332	Iron Bert Locomotive wLionChief Remote, *14*	140 ____
81419	Alien Ooze 1-D Tank Car, *14*	60 ____
81420	PRR Truss-rod Gondola with tarp, *14*	60 ____
81422	NS Water Tower, *14*	31 ____
81423	Sodor Coal and Scrap Cars 2-Pack, *14*	70 ____
81424	Sodor Crane Car and Work Caboose 2-Pack, *14*	70 ____
81430	Lionelville Shanty, *14*	22 ____
81432	PRR Girder Bridge, *14*	21 ____
81433	PRR Crossing Shanty, *14*	22 ____
81434	Pennsylvania Station Platform, *14*	23 ____
81435	N&W NS Heritage Quad Hopper with coal, *14*	55 ____
81436	Intermodal Container 4-Pack, *14*	43 ____
81437	York Peppermint Patty Vat Car, *14*	65 ____
81439	Halloween Pumpkinheads Handcar, *14*	85 ____
81440	Western Union Handcar, *14*	85 ____
81444	PRR MOW Tie-Jector Motorized Vehicle, CC, *14*	200 ____
81445	MOW Tie-Jector Motorized Vehicle, CC, *14*	200 ____
81446	Santa Fe Tie-Jector Motorized Vehicle, CC, *14*	200 ____
81447	NS Tie-Jector Motorized Vehicle, CC, *14*	200 ____
81448	Amtrak Tie-Jector Motorized Vehicle, CC, *14*	200 ____
81449	Zombie Motorized Trolley, *14*	100 ____
81451	St. Louis Motorized Trolley, *14*	100 ____
81452	Neil Young Texas Special F3 AA Diesels, CC, *13–14*	650 ____
81453	Neil Young PRR F3 AA Diesels, CC, *13–14*	650 ____
81462	PRR Broadway Limited Add-on Baggage Car, *14*	70 ____
81463	CNJ Water Tower, *14*	31 ____
81464	CNJ Montclair Add-on Passenger Car, *14*	60 ____
81465	SP Flatcar with piggyback trailers, *14*	70 ____
81466	BN Maxi-Stack Pair, *14*	125 ____
81469	GN Bilevel Stockcar "65385," *14*	60 ____
81475	DC Comics Batman M7 LionChief Subway Set, *14*	350 ____
81479	Batman Add-on M7 Subway Car 2-Pack, *14*	140 ____
81486	NYC Patrol Flatcar with helicopter, *14*	60 ____
81487	Ronald Reagan Presidential Boxcar, *14*	65 ____
81488	Andrew Jackson Presidential Boxcar, *14*	65 ____
81489	Warren G. Harding Presidential Boxcar, *14*	65 ____
81490	Dwight D. Eisenhower Presidential Boxcar, *14*	65 ____
81491	Jersey Central Coal Dump Car, *14*	55 ____
81492	Strasburg RR Searchlight Car, *14*	50 ____
81499	LCS Power Supply with DB9 cable, *13–14*	37 ____
81500	LCS Sensor Track 1' Cable, *13–14*	14 ____
81501	LCS Sensor Track 3' Cable, *13–14*	15 ____
81502	LCS Sensor Track 10' Cable, *13–14*	19 ____
81503	LCS Sensor Track 20' Cable, *13–14*	19 ____
81504	Ann Arbor FA-2 Diesel AA Set "53/53A," CC, *14*	750 ____
81507	B&O FA-2 Diesel AA Set "817/817A," CC, *14*	750 ____
81510	Erie FA-2 Diesel AA Set "736A/736D," CC, *14*	750 ____
81513	MKT FA-2 Diesel AA Set "331A/331C," CC, *14*	750 ____

			Exc	Mint
____	81516	NYC FA-2 Diesel AA Set "1075/1078," CC, 14		750
____	81519	PRR FA-2 Diesel AA Set "9608/9609," CC, 14		750
____	81522	Ann Arbor FB2 Diesel "53B," CC, 14		450
____	81523	B&O FB2 Diesel "817B," CC, 14		450
____	81524	Erie FB2 Diesel "736B," CC, 14		450
____	81525	MKT FB2 Diesel "331B," CC, 14		450
____	81526	NYC FB2 Diesel "3327," CC, 14		450
____	81527	PRR FB2 Diesel CC, 14		450
____	81528	Ann Arbor FB2 Diesel, nonpowered, 14		350
____	81529	B&O FB2 Diesel, nonpowered, 14		350
____	81530	Erie FB2 Diesel, nonpowered, 14		350
____	81531	MKT FB2 Diesel, nonpowered, 14		350
____	81532	NYC FB2 Diesel, nonpowered, 14		350
____	81533	PRR FB2 Diesel, nonpowered, 14		350
____	81568	4th of July Parade Car, 14		80
	81596	Weathered UP 4-12-2 Locomotive "9000," CC, 13		1400
	81597	Weathered B&O RF-16 Sharknose AA Diesels "855-857," CC, 13		830
	81600	Weathered PRR RF-16 Sharknose AA Diesels "2020A-2021A," CC, 13		830
____	81603	LionChief 72-Watt Power Supply, 14		55
____	81605	Santa Fe PS-1 Boxcar 5-Pack (std O), 14		380
____	81615	UP 1-D Tank Car, 14		45
____	81617	Pet Shop 1-D Tank Car, 14		45
____	81619	Reading PS-1 Boxcar "109448" (std O), 14		80
____	81620	Zombie Figure Pack, 14		23
____	81625	Amtrak Add-on Baggage Car, 14		85
____	81626	Barrel Shed, 14		35
____	81629	Lumber Shed Kit, 14		35
____	81635	Water Tower, 14		35
____	81639	LCS Accessory Switch Controller #2, 14		120
____	81640	LCS Block Power Controller #2, 14		120
	81644	Chessie System Baby Madison Passenger Car 3-Pack, 14		270
____	81649	SP Baby Madison Passenger Car 3-Pack, 14		270
____	81654	NYC Baby Madison Passenger Car 3-Pack, 14		270
____	81662	FasTrack O-31 Quarter Curved Track, 14		5
____	81680	Dinosaur 1-D Tank Car, 14		40
____	81686	PRR GL-a 2-bay Hopper 3-Pack (std O), 14		220
____	81687	LV GL-a 2-bay Hopper 2-Pack (std O), 14		146
____	81688	CB&Q GL-a 2-bay Hopper 3-Pack (std O), 14		220
____	81689	C&O GL-a 2-bay Hopper 3-Pack (std O), 14		220
____	81703	Santa Fe Hi-Cube Boxcar 2-Pack (std O), 14		190
	81704	Grand Trunk Hi-Cube Boxcar 2-Pack (std O), 14		190
	81705	Milwaukee Road Hi-Cube Boxcar 2-Pack (std O), 14		190
____	81706	Frisco Hi-Cube Boxcar 2-Pack (std O), 14		190
____	81707	NYC Hi-Cube Boxcar 2-Pack (std O), 14		190
____	81708	Santa Fe Hi-Cube Boxcar "36715" (std O), 14		95
	81710	Milwaukee Road Hi-Cube Boxcar "4980" (std O), 14		95
____	81711	Frisco Hi-Cube Boxcar "9125" (std O), 14		95

		Exc	Mint
81712	NYC Hi-Cube Boxcar "67282" (std O), *14*		95 ____
81725	UP Operating Merchandise Car, *14*		80 ____
81726	REA Operating Merchandise Car, *14*		80 ____
81729	Great Western Passenger Car Add-on 2-Pack, *14*		130 ____
81734	FasTrack Oval Track and Power Pack, *14*		200 ____
81735	FasTrack Figure-8 Track and Power Pack, *14*		250 ____
81736	Classic Lionel Catalogs Billboard Pack, *14*		13 ____
81737	Passenger Station, *14*		60 ____
81738	Lionel Auto Loader Cars 4-Pack, *14*		25 ____
81739	Santa Fe Baby Madison Passenger Car 3-Pack, *14*		270 ____
81744	CP Baby Madison Passenger Car 3-Pack, *14*		270 ____
81749	Pullman Baby Madison Passenger Car 3-Pack, *14*		270 ____
81759	NYC Coach/Diner 2-Pack, *14*		180 ____
81760	NYC Coach/Baggage Car 2-Pack, *14*		180 ____
81763	Pullman Baby Madison Passenger Car 3-Pack, *14*		180 ____
81768	Chessie System Coach/Diner 2-Pack, *14*		180 ____
81769	Chessie System Coach/Baggage Car 2-Pack, *14*		180 ____
81773	SP Coach/Diner 2-Pack, *14*		180 ____
81774	SP Coach/Baggage Car 2-Pack, *14*		180 ____
81778	Santa Fe Coach/Diner 2-Pack, *14*		180 ____
81779	Santa Fe Coach/Baggage Car 2-Pack, *14*		180 ____
81779	Pullman Coach/Baggage Car 2-Pack, *14*		180 ____
81783	CP Coach/Diner 2-Pack, *14*		180 ____
81784	CP Coach/Baggage Car 2-Pack, *14*		180 ____
81789	NH GL-a 2-bay Hopper 2-Pack (std O), *14*		146 ____
81793	Berwind GL-a 2-bay Hopper 3-Pack (std O), *14*		220 ____
81800	Southern 18' Aluminum Observation/Coach Car, 2-Pack (std O), *14*		320 ____
81801	Southern 18' Aluminum Combination/Vista Dome Car, 2-Pack (std O), *14*		320 ____
81806	PRR N5b Caboose "477814" (std O), *14*		95 ____
81807	Conrail N5b Caboose "22882" (std O), *14*		95 ____
81808	PC N5b Caboose "22802" (std O), *14*		95 ____
81809	LIRR N5b Caboose "2" (std O), *14*		95 ____
81810	Lionel Lines N5b Caboose "1402" (std O), *14*		95 ____
81812	RI 18' Aluminum Observation/Coach Car, 2-Pack (std O), *14*		320 ____
81813	RI 18' Aluminum Combination/Vista Dome Car, 2-Pack (std O), *14*		320 ____
81818	C&O 18' Aluminum Observation/Coach Car, 2-Pack (std O), *14*		320 ____
81819	C&O 18' Aluminum Combination/Vista Dome Car, 2-Pack (std O), *14*		320 ____
81824	P&WV GL-a 2-bay Hopper 2-Pack (std O), *14*		146 ____
81827	PC Round-roof Boxcar "100104" (std O), *14*		80 ____
81828	GN Round-roof Boxcar "5885" (std O), *14*		80 ____
81829	WP Round-roof Boxcar "10211" (std O), *14*		80 ____
81830	MKT 18' Aluminum Observation/Coach Car, 2-Pack (std O), *14*		320 ____

		Exc	Mint
81831	MKT 18' Aluminum Baggage/Diner Car, 2-Pack (std O), *14*		320
81836	Erie Double-sheathed Boxcar "71107" (std O), *14*		80
81837	Frisco Double-sheathed Boxcar "128528" (std O), *14*		80
81838	CNJ Double-sheathed Boxcar "14014" (std O), *14*		80
81839	Pacific Fright Express Steel-sided Reefer (std O), *14*		80
81840	UP Ca-4 Caboose with smoke "3880" (std O), *14*		90
81841	UP MOW Caboose "903224" (std O), *14*		90
81842	Wabash 18' Aluminum Dome-Observation/ Coach Car, 2-Pack (std O), *14*		320
81843	Wabash 18' Aluminum Combination/Vista Dome Car, 2-Pack (std O), *14*		320
81858	PRR GL-a 2-bay Hopper 3-Pack (std O), *14*		220
81862	FasTrack O-31 Curved Track 4-Pack, *14*		22
81866	RI 18' Aluminum Baggage/Diner Car, 2-Pack (std O), *14*		320
81869	C&O 18' Aluminum Baggage/Diner Car, 2-Pack (std O), *14*		320
81872	Wabash 18' Aluminum Baggage/Diner Car, 2-Pack (std O), *14*		320
81875	MKT 18' Aluminum Combination/Vista Dome Car, 2-Pack (std O), *14*		320
81878	Southern 18' Aluminum Baggage/Diner Car, 2-Pack (std O), *14*		320
81881	SP Crane Car, CC, *14*		500
81882	DT&I Crane Car, CC, *14*		500
81883	CSX Crane Car, CC, *14*		500
81884	Bethlehem Steel Crane Car, CC, *14*		500
81885	MOW Crane Car, CC, *14*		500
81886	SP Boom Car, RailSounds, CC, *14*		240
81887	DT&I Boom Car, RailSounds, CC, *14*		240
81888	CSX Boom Car, RailSounds, CC, *14*		240
81889	MOW Boom Car, RailSounds, CC, *14*		240
81890	Bethlehem Steel Boom Car, RailSounds, CC, *14*		240
81891	BNSF 52' Gondola "523300" with 3-piece covers (std O), *14*		80
81892	Bethlehem Steel 52' Gondola "303022" with 3-piece covers (std O), *14*		80
81893	GTW 52' Gondola "145391" with 3-piece covers (std O), *14*		80
81894	CSX 52' Gondola "709190" with 3-piece covers (std O), *14*		80
81895	North Pole Central 52' Gondola "128925" with 3-piece covers (std O), *14*		80
81896	NYC PS-5 Flatcar "506266" with piggyback trailers (std O), *14*		100
81897	Milwaukee Road PS-5 Flatcar "64660" with piggyback trailers (std O), *14*		100
81898	Lionel PS-5 Flatcar with piggyback trailers (std O), *14*		100
81899	CP PS-5 Flatcar "301000" with piggyback trailers (std O), *14*		100

		Exc	Mint
81900	UP PS-5 Flatcar "258255" with piggyback trailers (std O), *14*	100	___
81901	NYC Tractor and Piggyback Trailer, *14*	90	___
81902	Milwaukee Road Tractor and Piggyback Trailer, *14*	90	___
81903	Lionel Tractor and Piggyback Trailer, *14*	90	___
81904	CP Tractor and Piggyback Trailer, *14*	90	___
81905	UP Tractor and Piggyback Trailer, *14*	90	___
81908	PFE Steel-sided Reefers 3-Pack (std O), *14*	240	___
81912	New York Yankees Boxcar, *14*	70	___
81913	St. Louis Cardinals Boxcar, *14*	70	___
81914	Oakland Athletics Boxcar, *14*	70	___
81915	San Francisco Giants Boxcar, *14*	70	___
81916	Boston Red Sox Boxcar, *14*	70	___
81917	Los Angeles Dodgers Boxcar, *14*	70	___
81918	Cincinnati Reds Boxcar, *14*	70	___
81919	San Diego Padres Boxcar, *14*	70	___
81920	Detroit Tigers Boxcar, *14*	70	___
81921	Atlanta Braves Boxcar, *14*	70	___
81922	Baltimore Orioles Boxcar, *14*	70	___
81923	Minnesota Twins Boxcar, *14*	70	___
81924	Chicago White Sox Boxcar, *14*	70	___
81925	Chicago Cubs Boxcar, *14*	70	___
81926	Philadelphia Phillies Boxcar, *14*	70	___
81927	Cleveland Indians Boxcar, *14*	70	___
81928	New York Mets Boxcar, *14*	70	___
81929	Toronto Blue Jays Boxcar, *14*	70	___
81930	Miami Marlins Boxcar, *14*	70	___
81931	Angels Baseball Boxcar, *14*	70	___
81932	Pittsburgh Pirates Boxcar, *14*	70	___
81933	Texas Rangers Boxcar, *14*	70	___
81934	Milwaukee Brewers Boxcar, *14*	70	___
81935	Houston Astros Boxcar, *14*	70	___
81936	Colorado Rockies Boxcar, *14*	70	___
81937	Tampa Bay Rays Boxcar, *14*	70	___
81938	Seattle Mariners Boxcar, *14*	70	___
81939	Washington Nationals Boxcar, *14*	70	___
81940	Arizona Diamondbacks Boxcar, *14*	70	___
81941	Kansas City Royals Boxcar, *14*	70	___
81944	Rotary Beacon (yellow), *14*	85	___
81945	Polar Express Scale Coach, *14*	210	___
81946	FasTrack O-36 Remote Switch, right-hand, *14*	110	___
81947	FasTrack O-36 Remote Switch, left-hand, *14*	110	___
81948	FasTrack O-48 Remote Switch, right-hand, *14*	120	___
81949	FasTrack O-48 Remote Switch, left-hand, *14*	120	___
81950	FasTrack O-60 Remote Switch, right-hand, *14*	120	___
81951	FasTrack O-60 Remote Switch, left-hand, *14*	120	___
81952	FasTrack O-72 Remote Switch, right-hand, *14*	120	___
81953	FasTrack O-72 Remote Switch, left-hand, *14*	120	___
81954	FasTrack O-72 Remote Switch, wye, *14*	120	___
81968	Halloween Pacific Fright Express Caboose (std O), *14*	90	___

Exc | Mint

		Exc	Mint
__ 81969	PRR 18' Aluminum Parlor/Coach Car, 2-Pack (std O), *14*		320
__ 81972	B&O 18' Aluminum Baggage/Sleeper Car, 2-Pack (std O), *14*		320
__ 81975	SP 18' Aluminum Sleeper/Coach Car, 2-Pack (std O), *14*		320
__ 81978	UP 18' Aluminum Sleeper/Coach Car, 2-Pack (std O), *14*		320
__ 81981	KCS 18' Aluminum Sleeper/Coach Car, 2-Pack (std O), *14*		320
__ 99000	Keebler Elf Express Steam Freight Set, *99 u*		1020
__ 99001	Mickey's Holiday Express Freight Set, *99 u*		228
__ 99002	Looney Tunes Square Window Caboose, *99 u*		NRS
__ 99006	Keebler Bulkhead Flatcar, *99 u*		NRS
__ 99007	Smuckers Fudge 1-D Tank Car, *99 u*		80
__ 99008	Mickey's Merry Christmas Boxcar, *99 u*		NRS
__ 99009	Mickey's Holiday Express Square Window Caboose, *99 u*		NRS
__ 99013	Case Cutlery Tank Car "1889," *00 u*		NRS
__ 99014	Case Cutlery Gondola "1889," *00 u*		NRS
__ 99015	Case Cutlery Boxcar "1889," *00 u*		NRS
__ 99018	Case Cutlery Rolling Stock 3-pack, *00 u*		200
__ 79C95204C	Sears Santa Fe Diesel Freight Set, *71 u*	150	165
__ 79C9715C	Sears 4-unit Diesel Freight Set, *75 u*	50	65
__ 79C9717C	Sears 7-unit Steam Freight Set, *75 u*	150	165
__ 79N95223C	Sears 6-unit Diesel Freight Set, *74 u*	150	165
__ 79N9552C	Sears 6-unit Steam Freight Set, *72 u*	150	165
__ 79N9553C	Sears 6-unit Diesel Freight Set, *72 u*	150	165
__ 79N96178C	Sears 4-unit Steam Freight Set, *74 u*	50	65
__ 79N97082C	Sears Steam Freight Set, *70 u*		NRS
__ 79N97101C	Sears 5-unit Steam Freight Set, *72 u*	150	165
__ 79N98765C	Sears Logging Empire Set, *78 u*	100	115
__ T1428RRODTS	Tony Stewart NASCAR Steam Freight Set, *12–14*		300
__ T1828RRMMKB	Kyle Busch NASCAR Steam Freight Set, *12–14*		300
__ T2428RRDUJG	Jeff Gordon NASCAR Steam Freight Set, *12–14*		300
__ T4828RRLOJJ	Jimmy Johnson NASCAR Steam Freight Set, *12–14*		300
__ T4828RRLOJJ	Dale Earnhardt Jr. NASCAR Steam Freight Set, *12–14*		300
__ TX328RRGMDE	Dale Earnhardt NASCAR Steam Freight Set, *12–14*		300
__ UCS	Remote Control Track (O), *70*	4	7

Unnumbered Items

Item	Exc	Mint	
Amtrak Passenger Car Set, *89, 89 u*	640	770	___
B&A Hudson and Standard O Car Set, *86 u*	1500	1700	___
Baltimore & Ohio Set, *94, 96*		NRS	___
Black Cave Flyer Playmat, *82*		8	___
Blue Comet Set, *78–80, 87 u*	560	620	___
Burlington Texas Zephyr Set, *80, 80 u*	980	1150	___
C&NW Passenger Car Set, *93*	385	460	___
Cannonball Freight Playmat, *81–82*		8	___
Chesapeake & Ohio Set, *95–96*		NRS	___
Chessie System Special Set, *80, 86 u*	560	620	___
Chicago & Alton Limited Set, *81, 86 u*	560	620	___
Commando Assault Train Playmat, *83–84*		8	___
D&RGW California Zephyr Set, *92, 93*		900	___
Erie Set (FF 7), *93*	385	460	___
Erie-Lackawanna Passenger Car Set, *93, 94*	940	980	___
Favorite Food Freight Set, *81–82*	248	338	___
Frisco Set (FF 5), *91*	405	425	___
The General Set, *77–80*	240	285	___
GN Empire Builder Set, *92, 93*	620	730	___
Great Northern Set (FARR 3), *81, 81 u*	620	690	___
IC City of New Orleans Set, *85, 87, 93*	885	1045	___
Illinois Central Set, *91–92, 95*	255	285	___
Jersey Central Set, *86*	345	370	___
Joshua Lionel Cowen Set, *80, 80 u, 82*	540	580	___
L.A.S.E.R. Playmat, *81–82*		8	___
Lionel Lines Madison Car Set, *91, 93*	560	620	___
Lionel Lines Set, *82–84 u, 86, 86–87 u, 94–95*	530	620	___
Mickey Mouse Express Set, *77–78, 78 u*	1000	1693	___
Milwaukee Road Set (FF 2), *87, 90 u*	380	405	___
Mint Set, *79 u, 80–83, 84 u, 86 u, 87, 91 u, 93*	940	1073	___
Missouri Pacific Set, *95*		390	___
N&W Powhatan Arrow Passenger Car Set, *95*	370	445	___
N&W Powhatan Arrow Set, *81, 81 u, 82 u, 91 u*	1450	1700	___
New Haven Set, *94–95*		400	___
New York Central Set, *89, 91*	240	270	___
Nickel Plate Road Set (FF 6), *92*	385	460	___
Northern Pacific Set, *90–92*	190	250	___
NYC 20th Century Limited Set, *83, 83 u, 95*	980	1150	___
Pennsylvania Set, *79–80, 79–80 u, 81 u, 83 u*	1200	1350	___
Pennsylvania Set, *87–90, 95*	240	270	___

	Exc	Mint
___ Pennsylvania Set (FARR 5), *84–85, 89 u*	600	660
___ Pere Marquette Set, *93*	720	770
___ Rock Island & Peoria Set, *80–82*	240	315
___ Rocky Mountain Platform, *83–84*		8
___ Santa Fe Super Chief Set, *91, 91 u, 92 u, 93, 95*	1400	1700
___ Santa Fe Set (FARR 1), *79, 79 u*	460	580
___ Southern Crescent Limited Set, *77–78, 87 u*	540	650
___ Southern Pacific Daylight Diesel Set, *82–83, 82–83 u, 90 u*	2150	2300
___ Southern Set (FARR 4), *83, 83 u*	620	690
___ SP Daylight Steam Set, *90, 92, 93*	790	940
___ Spirit of '76 Set, *74–76*	570	690
___ Station Platform, *83–84*		8
___ Toys "R" Us Thunderball Freight Set, *75 u*		NRS
___ Union Pacific Set, *94*	430	500
___ Union Pacific Set (FARR 2), *80, 80 u*	540	580
___ UP Overland Route Set, *84, 92 u*	770	840
___ Wabash Set (FF 1), *86, 87*	755	905
___ Western Maryland Set (FF 4), *89*	345	405

Retail

11-1001	No. 400E Locomotive, black, brass trim (std)	900 ____
11-1002	No. 400E Locomotive, gray, nickel trim (std)	900 ____
11-1003	No. 400E Locomotive, gray, brass trim (std)	900 ____
11-1005	No. 390 Locomotive, green	600 ____
11-1006	No. 400E Locomotive, crackle black, brass trim	900 ____
11-1008	No. 400E Lionel Lines Locomotive	900 ____
11-1009	No. 400E Locomotive, blue, brass trim	900 ____
11-1010	No. 385E Locomotive (std)	700 ____
11-1012	No. 1835E Locomotive, black, nickel trim	700 ____
11-1013	AF No. 4694 Warrior Passenger Set	1400 ____
11-1014	AF No. 4694 Iron Monarch Passenger Set	1250 ____
11-1015	No. 392E Locomotive, black, brass trim	800 ____
11-1016	No. 392E Locomotive, gray, nickel trim	800 ____
11-1017	No. 400E Locomotive, blue, nickel trim (std)	900 ____
11-1018	No. 7 Lionel Locomotive (std)	900 ____
11-1019	No. 6 Pennsylvania Locomotive (std)	900 ____
11-1020	American Flyer No. 4696 Locomotive	1000 ____
11-1021	No. 400E Presidential Locomotive (std)	1000 ____
11-1022	No. 400E Red Comet Locomotive (std)	1000 ____
11-1023	No. 400E Locomotive, blue, brass trim (std)	900 ____
11-1024	No. 400E Locomotive, black, brass trim (std)	900 ____
11-1025	No. 400E Lionel Lines Locomotive (std)	900 ____
11-1026	No. 400E Locomotive, pink (std)	1000 ____
11-1027	No. 400E Locomotive, state green (std)	1000 ____
11-1028	No. 400E Locomotive, black, brass trim (std)	1000 ____
11-1029	No. 6 NYC Locomotive (std)	900 ____
11-1030	No. 6 General Locomotive (std)	900 ____
11-1031	No. 6 Texas Locomotive (std)	950 ____
11-2003	No. 8E Electric Locomotive, olive green (std)	500 ____
11-2004	No. 8E Electric Locomotive, dark olive green (std)	500 ____
11-2005	No. 8E Electric Locomotive, orange (std)	500 ____
11-2006	No. 8E Electric Locomotive, red/cream (std)	500 ____
11-2007	American Flyer Presidential Passenger Set (std)	1800 ____
11-2008	AF No. 4689 Presidential Locomotive, blue (std)	800 ____
11-2009	Big Brute Electric Engine, zinc chromate	1500 ____
11-2010	Big Brute Electric Engine, green	1500 ____
11-2015	Super 381 Electric Engine, state green (std)	1300 ____
11-2016	Super 381 MILW Electric Engine (std)	1300 ____
11-2017	No. 408E Electric Locomotive (std)	900 ____
11-2018	No. 408E Electric Locomotive, Mojave	900 ____
11-2019	No. 408E Electric Locomotive, pink	900 ____

____ **11-2020**	No. 9 Electric Locomotive, green	600
____ **11-2021**	No. 9 Electric Locomotive, orange	600
____ **11-2022**	No. 9 Electric Locomotive, gray, nickel trim	600
____ **11-2023**	No. 9 Electric Locomotive, dark green	600
____ **11-2024**	No. 8 Trolley (std)	530
____ **11-2025**	No. 9 Trolley (std)	650
____ **11-2026**	No. 8 Christmas Trolley (std)	570
____ **11-2027**	No. 381E Electric Locomotive, blue (std)	900
____ **11-2028**	No. 381E Electric Locomotive, brown (std)	900
____ **11-2029**	No. 381E Great Northern Electric Locomotive (std)	900
____ **11-2031**	No. 4689 President's Locomotive, red (std)	900
____ **11-2033**	Big Brute Electric Locomotive, brown (std)	1600
____ **11-2034**	Big Brute Electric Locomotive, orange (std)	1600
11-5001 ____	No. 384 Locomotive Passenger Set, black, brass trim	600
____ **11-5002**	No. 384 Locomotive Christmas Freight Set (std)	600
____ **11-5003**	No. 384 Locomotive LV Passenger Set (std)	600
____ **11-5004**	No. 384 Locomotive NYC Freight Set	600
____ **11-5006**	No. 384E Locomotive Girl's Passenger Set	600
____ **11-5007**	No. 386 Freight Set (std)	600
____ **11-5008**	No. 340E Coal Freight Set (std)	600
____ **11-5009**	No. 342E Baby State Passenger Set (std)	600
____ **11-5010**	No. 384E Blue Comet Passenger Set (std)	600
____ **11-5011**	No. 386 Christmas Freight Set (std)	600
____ **11-5012**	No. 342E Passenger Set (std)	600
____ **11-5013**	No. 318E Christmas Freight Set (std)	600
____ **11-5014**	No. 384E PRR Steam Passenger Set (std)	600
____ **11-5501**	No. 263E Steam Christmas Freight Set	600
____ **11-5502**	No. 263E Steam B&O Freight Set	600
____ **11-5505**	No. 249E Christmas Steam Passenger Set	500
____ **11-5506**	No. 299 Freight Set	450
____ **11-5507**	No. 269E Distant Control Freight Set	500
____ **11-5508**	Celebration Passenger Set	480
____ **11-5509**	No. 269E Christmas Distant Control Freight Set	500
____ **11-6001**	No. 263E Locomotive, black, brass trim	430
____ **11-6002**	No. 263E Locomotive, blue	430
____ **11-6003**	No. 277W Remote Control Work Train	680
____ **11-6004**	Blue Comet Distant Control Passenger Set	650
____ **11-6005**	No. 275W Distant Control Freight Set	600
____ **11-6006**	UP Streamliner Passenger Set, silver	800
____ **11-6007**	UP Streamliner Passenger Set, yellow	800
____ **11-6008**	No. 249E Steam Passenger Set, black, brass trim	600
____ **11-6009**	No. 249E Steam Passenger Set, blue	600
____ **11-6010**	No. 249E Steam Passenger Set, gray, nickel trim	600

11-6012	No. 260E Locomotive, black, brass trim	430 ____
11-6013	No. 255E Locomotive, gray, nickel trim	430 ____
11-6014	No. 255E Lionel Lines Locomotive	430 ____
11-6015	No. 279E Distant Control Passenger Set	750 ____
11-6016	No. 295E Distant Control Passenger Set	750 ____
11-6017	Hiawatha Distance Control Streamliner Set	900 ____
11-6018	Hiawatha Passenger Train Set	900 ____
11-6019	Hiawatha Distance Control Freight Set	900 ____
11-6020	UP City of Denver Passenger Set, green	590 ____
11-6021	UP City of Denver Passenger Set, yellow/brown	700 ____
11-6022	No. 262E Locomotive, black, brass trim	300 ____
11-6023	No. 262E Locomotive, black, nickel trim	300 ____
11-6024	No. 260E Locomotive, black, brass trim	450 ____
11-6025	No. 214 Armored Motor Car Set	400 ____
11-6028	No. 256 Electric Locomotive, orange	450 ____
11-6029	No. 214 Armored Motor Car Set	400 ____
11-6030	No. 295E Distant Control Passenger Set	750 ____
11-6031	No. 279E NYC Distance Control Passenger Set	700 ____
11-6033	No. 265E Commodore Vanderbilt Locomotive	430 ____
11-6036	No. 263E Baby Blue Comet Locomotive	460 ____
11-6037	Girls Freight Set	830 ____
11-6038	No. 284E Distant Control Freight Set	700 ____
11-6039	No. 616 Flying Yankee Passenger Set, black/chrome	590 ____
11-6040	No. 616 Flying Yankee Passenger Set, red/chrome	590 ____
11-6041	No. 616 Flying Yankee Passenger Set, green/chrome	590 ____
11-6046	No. 279E Distant Control Passenger Set	700 ____
11-6047	No. 264 Red Comet Locomotive	460 ____
11-6048	No. 263E Baby Blue Comet Locomotive, brass trim	500 ____
11-6050	No. 256 New Haven Electric Locomotive	500 ____
11-6051	No. 256 Great Northern Electric Locomotive	500 ____
11-6052	No. 263E Locomotive, black, nickel trim	500 ____
11-6053	No. 263E Chessie Locomotive	500 ____
11-6054	No. 263E Southern Locomotive	500 ____
11-6055	Boys Freight Set	900 ____
11-30004	No. 213 Cattle Car, cream/maroon (std)	130 ____
11-30005	No. 213 Cattle Car, terra-cotta/green (std)	130 ____
11-30006	No. 214 Boxcar, cream/orange (std)	130 ____
11-30007	No. 214 Boxcar, yellow/brown (std)	130 ____
11-30008	No. 214R Refrigerator Car, white/blue (std)	130 ____
11-30009	No. 215 Tank Car, silver, nickel trim (std)	130 ____
11-30010	No. 215 Tank Car, green, brass trim (std)	130 ____
11-30011	No. 215 Tank Car, white (std)	130 ____

____ **11-30012**	No. 216 Hopper Car, red (std)	130
____ **11-30013**	No. 217 Caboose, orange/maroon (std)	140
____ **11-30014**	No. 217 Caboose, red (std)	160
____ **11-30015**	No. 513 Cattle Car, green/orange, brass trim (std)	100
____ **11-30016**	No. 514 Boxcar, cream/orange (std)	100
11-30017 ____	No. 514R Refrigerator Car, ivory/peacock, brass trim (std)	100
____ **11-30018**	No. 515 Tank Car, terra-cotta, brass trim (std)	100
____ **11-30019**	No. 516 Hopper Car, red, brass trim (std)	120
____ **11-30020**	No. 517 Caboose, pea green/red (std)	120
____ **11-30021**	No. 212 Gondola, maroon (std)	110
____ **11-30022**	No. 212 Gondola, pea green (std)	110
11-30023 ____	No. 513 Cattle Car, cream/maroon, nickel trim (std)	100
11-30024 ____	No. 514R Refrigerator Car, white/blue, nickel trim (std)	100
____ **11-30025**	No. 515 Tank Car, silver, nickel trim (std)	100
____ **11-30026**	No. 516 Hopper Car, red, nickel trim (std)	100
____ **11-30027**	No. 517 Caboose, red, nickel trim (std)	120
____ **11-30028**	No. 520 Floodlight Car, green, nickel trim (std)	130
11-30029 ____	No. 520 Floodlight Car, terra-cotta, brass trim (std)	130
____ **11-30030**	No. 514R Christmas Refrigerator Car, (std)	100
____ **11-30031**	No. 514 Christmas Boxcar (std)	100
____ **11-30032**	No. 515 MTH/Lionel Tank Car (std)	100
____ **11-30033**	No. 211 Flatcar, black, brass trim, with wood (std)	120
____ **11-30034**	No. 211 Flatcar, black, nickel trim, with wood (std)	120
____ **11-30035**	No. 218 Dump Car, Mojave, nickel trim (std)	140
____ **11-30036**	No. 218 Dump Car, Mojave, brass trim (std)	140
____ **11-30037**	No. 219 Crane Car, white (std)	200
____ **11-30038**	No. 219 Crane Car, yellow, nickel trim (std)	200
____ **11-30039**	No. 219 Crane Car, yellow (std)	380
____ **11-30042**	No. 514 Boxcar, red/black (std)	100
____ **11-30043**	No. 512 Gondola, peacock, brass trim (std)	80
____ **11-30044**	No. 512 Gondola, green, nickel trim (std)	80
____ **11-30045**	No. 514 Boxcar, yellow/brown (std)	100
____ **11-30046**	No. 511 Flatcar, black, brass trim, with wood (std)	100
____ **11-30047**	No. 511 Flatcar, black, nickel trim, with wood (std)	100
____ **11-30048**	No. 216 Hopper Car, dark green (std)	130
____ **11-30050**	No. 219 Crane Car, white, brass trim (std)	380
____ **11-30051**	No. 514R NYC Refrigerator Car (std)	100
____ **11-30055**	No. 212 Gondola, gray (std)	110
____ **11-30056**	No. 213 Cattle Car, Mojave/maroon (std)	130
____ **11-30057**	No. 213 Cattle Car, terra-cotta/maroon (std)	130
____ **11-30058**	No. 214 Boxcar, terra-cotta/black, brass trim (std)	130

11-30059	No. 214R Refrigerator Car, white/peacock, brass trim (std)	130 ____
11-30060	No. 214R Refrigerator Car, ivory/peacock, brass trim (std)	130 ____
11-30061	No. 215 Tank Car, silver, brass trim (std)	130 ____
11-30062	No. 215 Tank Car, silver, nickel trim (std)	130 ____
11-30063	No. 217 Caboose, olive green (std)	140 ____
11-30064	No. 217 Lionel Lines Caboose (std)	140 ____
11-30065	No. 217 Caboose, pea green/red (std)	140 ____
11-30066	No. 217 Caboose, red/peacock (std)	160 ____
11-30067	No. 218 Dump Car, gray (std)	140 ____
11-30068	No. 218 Dump Car, pea green (std)	140 ____
11-30069	No. 218 Dump Car, peacock (std)	140 ____
11-30070	No. 219 Crane Car, peacock/dark green (std)	200 ____
11-30071	No. 219 Lionel Lines Crane Car (std)	380 ____
11-30072	No. 220 Floodlight Car, green, nickel trim (std)	140 ____
11-30073	No. 220 Floodlight Car, terra-cotta, brass trim (std)	140 ____
11-30074	No. 513 Cattle Car, orange/pea green (std)	100 ____
11-30075	No. 514 Christmas Boxcar (std)	100 ____
11-30076	No. 514R Refrigerator Car, ivory/blue (std)	100 ____
11-30077	No. 515 Tank Car, cream (std)	100 ____
11-30078	No. 515 Tank Car, ivory (std)	100 ____
11-30079	No. 515 Tank Car, orange (std)	100 ____
11-30080	No. 516 Christmas Hopper Car (std)	120 ____
11-30081	No. 516 Hopper Car, red (std)	120 ____
11-30082	No. 517 Caboose, red/black (std)	120 ____
11-30083	No. 520 Floodlight Car, green, nickel trim (std)	130 ____
11-30087	No. 516 Hopper Car, red, brass trim (std)	100
11-30088	AF 4018 Automobile Car, white/blue	150 ____
11-30089	AF 4020 Stock Car, blue	150 ____
11-30090	AF 4006 Hopper Car, red	150 ____
11-30091	AF 4017 Sand Car, green	150 ____
11-30092	AF 4010 Tank Car, cream/blue	150 ____
11-30093	AF 4022 Machine Car, orange	110 ____
11-30094	AF 4021 Caboose, red	160 ____
11-30095	AF 4018 Automobile Car, orange/maroon	130 ____
11-30096	AF 4022 Machine Car, blue	110 ____
11-30097	AF 4022 Machine Car, orange/green	110 ____
11-30098	AF 4010 Tank Car, blue	130
11-30099	AF 4017 Sand Car, maroon	130 ____
11-30100	AF 4006 Hopper Car, green	130 ____
11-30101	AF 4020 Stock Car, cream/maroon	130 ____
11-30102	AF 4021 Caboose, red/maroon	140 ____
11-30103	AF 4021 Caboose, cream/red	140 ____
11-30104	No. 215 Tank Car (std)	130 ____

____ **11-30105**	No. 214R Refrigerator Car (std)	130
____ **11-30107**	No. 214R Altoona 36 Lager Refrigerator Car (std)	130
____ **11-30108**	No. 214R Budweiser Refrigerator Car (std)	140
____ **11-30109**	No. 214R Burp-oh Beer Refrigerator Car (std)	130
____ **11-30110**	No. 214R Hood's Dairy Refrigerator Car (std)	130
____ **11-30111**	No. 214R Old Reading Refrigerator Car (std)	130
____ **11-30112**	No. 214R Palisades Park Refrigerator Car (std)	130
____ **11-30113**	No. 214 Circus Boxcar (std)	130
____ **11-30114**	No. 214 M&M's Christmas Boxcar (std)	140
____ **11-30115**	No. 215 Budweiser Tank Car (std)	140
____ **11-30116**	No. 215 Freedomland Tank Car (std)	130
____ **11-30117**	No. 215 Gulf Tank Car (std)	130
____ **11-30118**	No. 215 Tropicana Tank Car (std)	130
____ **11-30119**	No. 513 UP Cattle Car (std)	100
____ **11-30120**	No. 513 WM Cattle Car (std)	100
____ **11-30121**	No. 514 B&O Boxcar (std)	100
____ **11-30122**	No. 514 State of Maine Boxcar (std)	120
____ **11-30123**	No. 514R PFE Refrigerator Car (std)	100
____ **11-30124**	No. 514R Tropicana Refrigerator Car (std)	120
____ **11-30125**	No. 515 Anheuser Busch Tank Car (std)	110
____ **11-30126**	No. 515 Hooker Chemicals Tank Car (std)	100
____ **11-30127**	No. 516 Blue Coal Hopper Car (std)	100
____ **11-30128**	No. 516 Waddell Coal Hopper Car (std)	120
____ **11-30129**	No. 517 Pennsylvania Caboose (std)	120
____ **11-30130**	No. 517 Santa Fe Caboose (std)	140
____ **11-30131**	No. 215 Lionel Lines Tank Car (std)	130
____ **11-30134**	No. 515 Christmas Tank Car (std)	100
____ **11-30136**	No. 214 Christmas Boxcar (std)	150
____ **11-30137**	No. 214 UP Boxcar (std)	150
____ **11-30138**	No. 214R Horlacher's Brewing Refrigerator Car (std)	150
____ **11-30139**	No. 214R Coors Refrigerator Car (std)	140
____ **11-30140**	No. 215 Keystone Gasoline Tank Car (std)	150
____ **11-30141**	No. 215 Texaco Tank Car (std)	150
____ **11-30142**	No. 216 Peabody Hopper Car (std)	130
____ **11-30143**	No. 216 Pennsylvania Power & Light Hopper Car (std)	130
____ **11-30144**	No. 213 Cattle Car (std)	130
____ **11-30146**	No. 217 Jersey Central Caboose (std)	140
____ **11-30147**	No. 214 Jersey Central Boxcar (std)	130
____ **11-30148**	No. 214 U.S. Army Boxcar (std)	130
____ **11-30149**	No. 215 MTH/Lionel Tank Car	130
____ **11-30150**	No. 212 Lionel Lines Gondola (std)	130
____ **11-30151**	No. 212 Circus Gondola (std)	130
____ **11-30152**	No. 212 NYC Gondola (std)	130

LIONEL CORPORATION TINPLATE

Retail

11-30153	No. 214 MKT Boxcar (std)	150 ____
11-30154	No. 214 NYC Boxcar (std)	150 ____
11-30155	No. 215 C&O Tank Car (std)	150 ____
11-30156	No. 215 Shell Tank Car (std)	150 ____
11-30157	No. 216 Hopper Car, red, brass trim (std)	150 ____
11-30158	No. 216 LV Hopper Car (std)	150 ____
11-30159	No. 217 Pennsylvania Caboose (std)	160 ____
11-30160	No. 219 B&O Crane Car (std)	220 ____
11-30161	No. 219 Crane Car, ivory/red (std)	400 ____
11-30162	No. 219 Lionel Lines Crane Car (std)	220 ____
11-30163	No. 219 Crane Car, red/silver (std)	400 ____
11-30164	No. 514R Christmas Refrigerator Car (std)	120 ____
11-40001	Presidential Passenger Set, blue (std)	1200 ____
11-40002	No. 339 Pullman Car, green (std)	150 ____
11-40003	No. 332 Mail/Baggage Car, green (std)	150 ____
11-40004	No. 332 LV Ithaca Baggage Car	150 ____
11-40005	No. 339 LV Easton Passenger Coach	150 ____
11-40007	300 Series 3-Car Passenger Set, blue/silver (std)	400 ____
11-40009	3-Car State Passenger Set, green (std)	1200 ____
11-40010	Pennsylvania State Baggage Car, green (std)	400 ____
11-40011	Illinois State Coach Car, green (std)	400 ____
11-40012	Solarium State Car, green (std)	400 ____
11-40013	MILW 3-Car State Passenger Set (std)	1200 ____
11-40014	MILW State Baggage Car (std)	400 ____
11-40015	MILW State Passenger Coach (std)	400 ____
11-40016	MILW Solarium State Car (std)	400 ____
11-40017	3-Car Showroom Passenger Set, green (std)	1500 ____
11-40018	Showroom Passenger Coach, green (std)	500 ____
11-40019	3-Car Showroom Passenger Set, zinc chromate (std)	1500 ____
11-40020	Showroom Passenger Coach, zinc chromate (std)	500 ____
11-40021	3-Car Blue Comet Passenger Set (std)	1100 ____
11-40022	No. 432 Olbers Blue Comet Baggage Car (std)	380 ____
11-40023	No. 419 Tuttle Blue Comet Passenger Coach (std)	380 ____
11-40024	No. 4343 Diner Car	180 ____
11-40025	339 Series Passenger Car, pink	130 ____
11-40026	332 Series Baggage Car, pink	130 ____
11-40027	309 Series 3-Car State Passenger Set, brown (std)	1200
11-40028	Pennsylvania State Baggage Car, brown (std)	400 ____
11-40029	Illinois State Passenger Coach, brown (std)	400 ____
11-40030	Solarium State Car, brown (std)	400 ____
11-40031	State 3-Car Passenger Set, blue (std)	1200 ____
11-40032	Pennsylvania State Baggage Car, blue (std)	400 ____
11-40033	Illinois State Passenger Coach, blue (std)	400 ____

___	11-40034	Solarium State Car, blue (std)	400
___	11-40035	309 Series 3-Car Passenger Set, blue (std)	400
___	11-40036	309 Series 3-Car Passenger Set, green (std)	400
___	11-40037	309 Series 3-Car Passenger Set, red (std)	400
___	11-40038	No. 309 Passenger Coach (std)	140
___	11-40039	No. 310 Baggage Car (std)	140
___	11-40040	3-Car Blue Comet Passenger Set, nickel trim (std)	1100
___	11-40041	No. 432 Blue Comet Baggage Car, nickel trim (std)	380
___	11-40042	No. 423 Blue Comet Passenger Coach, nickel trim (std)	380
___	11-40043	3-Car Stephen Girard Set, brass trim	600
___	11-40044	No. 4427 Stephen Girard Baggage Car, brass trim	200
___	11-40045	No. 427 Stephen Girard Passenger Coach, brass trim	200
___	11-40046	3-Car Stephen Girard Set, nickel trim	600
___	11-40047	No. 4427 Stephen Girard Baggage Car, nickel trim	200
___	11-40048	No. 427 Stephen Girard Passenger Coach, nickel trim	200
___	11-40049	No. 418 3-Car Passenger Set, green, brass trim (std)	600
___	11-40050	No. 418 Diner, green, brass trim (std)	200
___	11-40051	No. 418 3-Car Passenger Set, orange, brass trim (std)	600
___	11-40052	No. 418 Diner, orange brass trim (std)	200
___	11-40053	No. 418 3-Car Passenger Set, Mojave, brass trim (std)	600
___	11-40054	No. 418 Diner, Mojave, brass trim (std)	200
___	11-40055	No. 418 3-Car Passenger Set, pink, brass trim (std)	600
___	11-40056	No. 418 Diner, pink, brass trim (std)	200
___	11-40057	Lionel 3-Car Pullman Passenger Set (std)	700
___	11-40058	Pennsylvania 3-Car Pullman Passenger Set (std)	700
___	11-40059	No. 332 Baggage Car (std)	140
___	11-40060	No. 339 Passenger Coach (std)	140
___	11-40061	Great Northern State 3-Car Passenger Set (std)	1200
___	11-40062	Great Northern State Baggage Car (std)	430
___	11-40063	Great Northern State Passenger Coach (std)	430
___	11-40064	Great Northern State Solarium Car (std)	430
___	11-40065	Presidential 3-Car Passenger Set (std)	1200
___	11-40066	Presidential Baggage Car (std)	430
___	11-40067	Presidential Passenger Coach (std)	430
___	11-40068	Red Comet 3-Car Passenger Set (std)	1140
___	11-40069	Red Comet Baggage Car (std)	400
___	11-40070	Red Comet Passenger Coach (std)	400

LIONEL CORPORATION TINPLATE

		Retail
11-40072	President's Passenger Set, red (std)	1300 ____
11-40073	No. 310 Baggage Car (std)	140 ____
11-40074	No. 309 Passenger Coach (std)	140 ____
11-40076	Green Comet 3-Car Passenger Set (std)	1140 ____
11-40077	NYC 3-Car Passenger Set, brown (std)	700 ____
11-40078	General 3-Car Pullman Passenger Set (std)	700 ____
11-40079	Green Comet Baggage Car (std)	400 ____
11-40080	Green Comet Passenger Coach (std)	400 ____
11-40081	Showroom 3-Car Passenger Set, brown (std)	1600 ____
11-40082	Showroom Passenger Coach, brown (std)	540 ____
11-40083	Showroom 3-Car Passenger Set, orange (std)	1600 ____
11-40084	Showroom Passenger Coach, orange (std)	540 ____
11-60033	No. 607 Christmas Coach Passenger	90 ____
11-70002	No. 2814 Boxcar, cream/orange	80 ____
11-70003	No. 2814R Refrigerator Car, white/brown	80 ____
11-70004	No. 2814R Christmas Refrigerator Car	80 ____
11-70005	No. 2814R Refrigerator Car, Ivory/peacock	80 ____
11-70006	No. 2815 Tank Car, silver	90 ____
11-70007	No. 2815 Tank Car, orange, nickel trim	80 ____
11-70008	No. 2817 Caboose, red/green	90 ____
11-70009	No. 2815 Christmas Tank Car	80 ____
11-70010	No. 2813 Cattle Car, cream/maroon	80 ____
11-70011	No. 2812 Gondola, apple green	80 ____
11-70012	No. 2811 Flatcar, silver	70 ____
11-70013	No. 2816 Hopper Car, red	90 ____
11-70014	No. 2816 Hopper Car, olive green	80 ____
11-70015	No. 2820 Floodlight Car, terra-cotta	90 ____
11-70016	No. 2815 Sunoco Tank Car	80 ____
11-70017	No. 2810 Crane Car, terra-cotta/maroon	180 ____
11-70018	No. 2811 Flatcar, maroon	70 ____
11-70019	No. 2814R MTH/Lionel Refrigerator Car	90 ____
11-70024	No. 2814 Christmas Boxcar	80 ____
11-70025	No. 2814 Boxcar, cream/orange	80 ____
11-70026	No. 2814 Boxcar, orange/brown	80 ____
11-70027	No. 2814 Boxcar, white brown	80 ____
11-70028	No. 2816 Christmas Hopper Car	80 ____
11-70029	No. 2817 Caboose, red/brown	90 ____
11-70030	No. 2812 Gondola, dark orange	70 ____
11-70031	No. 813 Cattle Car, brown	80 ____
11-70032	No. 2816 Hopper Car, black	80 ____
11-70033	No. 2820 Floodlight Car, light green	90 ____
11-70034	No. 2814R Refrigerator Car, white/brown	80 ____
11-70035	No. 2651 Flatcar, green	60 ____
11-70036	No. 2652 Gondola, red	60 ____

____ 11-70037	No. 2653 Hopper Car, black	60
____ 11-70038	No. 2654 Shell Tank Car, yellow	60
____ 11-70039	No. 2655 Boxcar, yellow/brown	60
____ 11-70040	No. 2656 Cattle Car, red/brown	60
____ 11-70041	No. 2657 Caboose, red/maroon	60
____ 11-70042	No. 659 Dump Car, green	60
____ 11-70043	No. 659 Dump Car, orange	60
____ 11-70045	No. 2814 Boxcar, yellow/brown	90
____ 11-70046	No. 2817 Caboose, red	100
____ 11-70047	No. 2814 Christmas Boxcar	80
____ 11-70048	No. 2815 Christmas Tank Car	90
____ 11-70049	No. 2814R Refrigerator Car, silver frame	90
____ 11-70050	No. 2814R Refrigerator Car, black frame	80
____ 11-70051	No. 2817 Caboose, red/maroon	90
____ 11-70052	No. 2654 Shell Tank Car, gray	60
____ 11-70053	No. 2654 Shell Tank Car, black	60
____ 11-70054	No. 2653 Hopper Car, green	60
____ 11-70055	No. 2653 Hopper Car, red	60
____ 11-70056	No. 2655 Boxcar, yellow/maroon	60
____ 11-70057	No. 2655 Boxcar, yellow/brown	60
____ 11-70058	No. 2656 Cattle Car, gray/red	60
____ 11-70059	No. 2656 Cattle Car, burnt orange	60
____ 11-70060	No. 659 Dump Car, blue	60
____ 11-70061	No. 900 Ammunition Car, gray	60
____ 11-70064	No. 2814R Hoods Dairy Refrigerator Car	80
____ 11-70065	No. 2814R Isaly's Refrigerator Car	80
____ 11-70066	No. 2814R Sheffield Farms Refrigerator Car	90
____ 11-70067	No. 2814R Palisades Park Refrigerator Car	80
____ 11-70068	No. 2654 UP Tank Car, yellow	60
____ 11-70069	No. 2654 M&M's Tank Car	70
____ 11-70070	No. 2654 Baker's Chocolate Tank Car	60
____ 11-70071	No. 2654 Budweiser Tank Car	70
____ 11-70072	No. 2655 Delaware & Hudson Boxcar	60
____ 11-70073	No. 2655 Railbox Boxcar	60
____ 11-70074	M&M's Christmas Boxcar	70
____ 11-70076	No. 2654 LL Tank Car, orange/blue	70
____ 11-70078	No. 900 Ammunition Car, green	60
____ 11-70079	No. 2820 LL Floodlight Car, black/orange	120
____ 11-70080	No. 2820 U.S. Army Air Corps Floodlight Car	120
____ 11-70081	No. 2810 Crane Car, yellow/red	180
____ 11-70082	No. 2810 Crane Car, white/red	180
____ 11-70083	No. 2660 Crane Car, cream/red	100
____ 11-70084	No. 2660 Crane Car, terra-cotta/maroon	100
____ 11-70085	No. 2660 Crane Car, yellow/red	100

LIONEL CORPORATION TINPLATE

Retail

11-70086	No. 2660 Crane Car, peacock/dark green	100
11-70087	No. 2813 LL Cattle Car, cream/tuscan	90
11-70088	No. 2813 LL Cattle Car, terra cotta/pea green	90
11-70089	No. 2810 B&O Crane Car	180
11-70091	No. 2815 LL Tank Car, cream, orange/blue	80
11-70092	No. 2810 Crane Car, blue	180
11-70095	No. 2820 LL Floodlight Car, black/peacock	120
11-70096	No. 2814 Southern Boxcar	90
11-70097	No. 2814 Chessie Boxcar	90
11-70098	No. 2814 Blue Comet Boxcar, nickel trim	90
11-70099	No. 2814 Blue Comet Boxcar, brass trim	90
11-80001	2600 Series 4-Car Blue Comet Passenger Set	430
11-80002	UP Articulated Baggage Car, silver	150
11-80003	UP Articulated Baggage Car, yellow	150
11-80004	UP Articulated Coach, silver	150
11-80005	UP Articulated Coach, yellow	150
11-80006	No. 2613 Series Pullman Coach, blue	110
11-80007	2600 Series 3-Car Passenger Set, red	300
11-80008	2600 Series 3-Car Passenger Set, green	300
11-80009	Milwaukee Road Articulated Baggage Car	150
11-80010	Milwaukee Road Articulated Coach	150
11-80011	Articulated Streamliner Baggage Car	150
11-80012	Articulated Streamliner Coach	150
11-80013	No. 2613 Series Pullman Coach, red	100
11-80014	No. 2613 Series Pullman Coach, green	100
11-80015	No. 605 Christmas Baggage Car	90
11-80016	710 Series 3-Car Passenger Set, blue	350
11-80017	No. 710 Series Baggage Car, blue	120
11-80018	No. 710 Series Passenger Coach, blue	120
11-80019	710 Series 3-Car Passenger Set, orange	350
11-80020	No. 710 Series Baggage Car, orange	120
11-80021	No. 710 Series Passenger Coach, orange	120
11-80022	710 Series 3-Car Passenger Set, red	350
11-80023	No. 710 Series Baggage Car, red	120
11-80024	No. 710 Series Passenger Coach, red	120
11-80025	No. 1695 3-Car Passenger Set, blue/silver	350
11-80026	No. 1685 Passenger Car, blue/silver	120
11-80027	1695 Series 3-Car Passenger Set, red/maroon	380
11-80028	No. 1695 Passenger Coach, red/maroon	130
11-80029	City of Denver Coach, yellow/green	110
11-80030	City of Denver Coach, green	110
11-80031	No. 605 Baggage Car	90
11-80032	No. 607 Passenger Coach	90
11-80034	No. 2613 NYC Pullman Car, LCCA 2012 Convention	100

____	**11-80036**	No. 605 Red Comet Baggage Car	90
____	**11-80039**	600 Series 3-Car Red Comet Passenger Set	270
____	**11-80040**	2600 Series 4-Car Blue Comet Passenger Set, brass trim	430
____	**11-80041**	No. 2613 Pullman Coach, brass trim	110
____	**11-80042**	Flying Yankee Chrome Coach	110
____	**11-80047**	710 Series 3-Car NH Passenger Set	400
____	**11-80048**	710 Series 3-Car GN Passenger Set	400
____	**11-80049**	2600 Series 4-Car Chessie Passenger Set	430
____	**11-80050**	2600 Series 4-Car Southern Passenger Set	430
____	**11-80051**	No. 2613 Chessie Pullman Coach	110
____	**11-80052**	No. 2613 Southern Pullman Coach	110
____	**11-80053**	No. 710 NH Baggage Car	140
____	**11-80054**	No. 710 NH Passenger Coach	140
____	**11-80055**	No. 710 GN Baggage Car	140
____	**11-80056**	No. 710 GN Passenger Coach	140
____	**11-90001**	No. 300 Hellgate Bridge, green/cream	500
____	**11-90002**	No. 300 Hellgate Bridge, silver/white	500
____	**11-90003**	No. 092 Signal Tower, cream/red	70
____	**11-90006**	No. 437 Switch Tower	280
____	**11-90007**	No. 155 Freight Shed	330
____	**11-90008**	No. 116 Passenger Station	400
____	**11-90009**	No. 438 Signal Tower	150
____	**11-90010**	No. 192 Villa Set	200
____	**11-90011**	No. 191 Villa	70
____	**11-90012**	No. 54 Street Lamp Set, green	45
____	**11-90013**	No. 54 Street Lamp Set, red	45
____	**11-90014**	No. 56 Gas Lamp Set, green	35
____	**11-90015**	No. 56 Gas Lamp Set, maroon	35
____	**11-90016**	No. 57 Corner Lamp Set, black	40
____	**11-90017**	No. 57 Corner Lamp Set, red	35
____	**11-90018**	No. 58 Lamp Set, single arc, cream	35
____	**11-90019**	No. 58 Lamp Set, single arc, dark green	35
____	**11-90020**	No. 59 Gooseneck Lamp Set, black	40
____	**11-90021**	No. 59 Gooseneck Lamp Set, maroon	40
____	**11-90022**	No. 1184 Bungalow (std)	200
____	**11-90023**	No. 1184 Bungalow (std)	200
____	**11-90024**	No. 1189 Villa (std)	300
____	**11-90025**	No. 1191 Villa (std)	300
____	**11-90026**	No.165 Magnetic Crane	300
____	**11-90027**	No. 441 Weighing Station (std)	380
____	**11-90028**	No. 69 Operating Warning Bell	50
____	**11-90029**	No. 78 Automatic Control Signal (std)	70
____	**11-90030**	No. 79 Flashing Railroad Signal	70
____	**11-90031**	No. 80 Operating Semaphore	70

LIONEL CORPORATION TINPLATE

		Retail
11-90032	No. 63 Lamp Post Set, aluminum	50 ____
11-90033	No. 87 Railroad Crossing Signal	50 ____
11-90034	No. 92 Floodlight Tower Set	160 ____
11-90035	No. 94 High Tension Tower Set	150 ____
11-90036	No. Automatic Block Signal (std)	70 ____
11-90037	No. 163 Freight Accessory Set, green cart	100 ____
11-90038	No. 163 Freight Accessory Set, orange cart	100 ____
11-90039	No. 208 Tools and Chest, dark gray	80 ____
11-90040	No. 208 Tools and Chest, silver	80 ____
11-90041	No. 550 Miniature Figures	100 ____
11-90042	No. 64 Lamp Post Set, light green	30 ____
11-90043	No. 85 Race Car Set	700 ____
11-90044	Straight Race Car Track Section	20 ____
11-90045	Inside Curve Race Car Track Section	20 ____
11-90046	Outside Curve Race Car Track Section	20 ____
11-90047	No. 55 Airplane & No. 49 Airport Set with mat	800 ____
11-90048	No. 49 Airport Mat	60 ____
11-90049	No. 90 Flagpole	50 ____
11-90050	No. 205 Merchandise Containers, 3 pieces (std)	130 ____
11-90052	No. 442 Diner	160 ____
11-90053	No. 43 Runabout Boat, red/white	450 ____
11-90054	No. 44 Speed Boat	450 ____
11-90055	No. 71 Telegraph Post Set, gray/red	80 ____
11-90056	Teardrop Lamp Set, pea green	20 ____
11-90057	No. 46 Crossing Gate	40 ____
11-90058	Small Oil Drum Set	20 ____
11-90060	No. 115 Passenger Station, beige/pea green	300 ____
11-90061	No. 115 Passenger Station, cream, orange/blue	300 ____
11-90062	No. 134 Lionel City Station with stop	330 ____
11-90063	No. 444 Roundhouse Section	500 ____
11-90064	No. 200 Turntable, red/black	200 ____
11-90065	No. 89 Flagpole, blue base (std)	50 ____
11-90066	No. 89 Flagpole, white base (std)	50 ____
11-90067	No. 89 American Flag Pole, white base (std)	50 ____
11-90068	Operating Industrial Crane	350 ____
11-90069	Operating Industrial Crane, TCA 2010 Convention	350 ____
11-90070	No. 552 Diner, orange/blue	200 ____
11-90071	No. 552 Diner, white/blue	200 ____
11-90072	No. 911 Country Estate, cream/red	140 ____
11-90073	No. 911 Country Estate, red/green	140 ____
11-90074	No. 912 Suburban Home, ivory/peacock	140 ____
11-90075	No. 912 Suburban Home, mustard/green	140 ____
11-90076	No. 913 Landscaped Bungalow, white/maroon	110 ____
11-90077	No. 913 Landscaped Bungalow, light green/peacock	110 ____

11-90078	AF No. 2050 Old Glory Flag Pole	100
____ **11-90079**	No. 43 Runabout Boat, orange/blue	400
11-90084	No. 57 Lamp Post Set, Lionel & American Flyer Aves.	
____		40
____ **11-90085**	No. 57 Lamp Post Set, orange, 21st St. & Fifth Ave.	40
____ **11-90086**	AF No. 2013 Corner Lamp Set, yellow	40
____ **11-90089**	No. 436 Power Station, cream	150
____ **11-90090**	No. 436 Power Station, terra-cotta	150
____ **11-90094**	No. 438 Signal Tower	160
____ **11-90095**	No. 116 Passenger Station	400
____ **11-90096**	No. 1184 Bungalow, gray/green	200
____ **11-90097**	No. 1184 Bungalow, white/maroon	200
____ **11-90098**	No. 1189 Villa (std)	300
____ **11-90099**	No. 1191 Villa (std)	300
____ **11-90100**	No. 442 Diner	160
____ **11-90101**	No. 54 Lamp Post Set, pea green	45
____ **11-90102**	No. 54 Lamp Post Set, state brown	45
____ **11-90103**	No. 58 Lamp Post Set, peacock	35
____ **11-90104**	No. 58 Lamp Post Set, orange	35
____ **11-90105**	No. 59 Lamp Post Set, dark green	40
____ **11-90106**	No. 59 Lamp Post Set, light green	40
____ **11-90107**	No. 92 Floodlight Tower Set	170
____ **11-90108**	No. 79 Flashing Signal	70
____ **11-90109**	No. 69 Warning Signal	50
____ **11-90110**	No. 94 High Tension Tower Set	170
____ **11-90111**	No. 57 Corner Lamp Set, orange, Lionel	40
____ **11-90112**	No. 57 Corner Lamp Set, blue, Lionel	40
____ **11-90113**	No. 57 Corner Lamp Set, blue/yellow	40
____ **11-90114**	No. 152 Operating Crossing Gate	40
____ **11-90115**	No. 153 Operating Block Signal	40
____ **11-90116**	No. 154 Highway Flashing Signal	40
____ **11-90117**	No. 437 Switch Signal Tower, cream/orange	300
____ **11-90118**	No. 437 Switch Signal Tower, terra-cotta/green	300
____ **11-90119**	AF No. 4230 Roadside Flashing Signal	100
____ **11-90120**	No. 200 Turntable, gray/green	200
____ **11-90121**	No. 200 Turntable, orange/blue	200
____ **11-90122**	No. 437 Switch Tower	280

Exc Mint

Artrain

		Exc	Mint	
9486	GTW "I Love Michigan" Boxcar, *87*		305	___
17885	1-D Tank Car, *90*	55	65	___
17891	GTW 20th Anniversary Boxcar, *91*	70	75	___
19425	CSX Flatcar with "Art in Celebration" trailer, *96*		80	___
52013	Norfolk Southern Flatcar with trailer, *92*	160	228	___
52024	Conrail Auto Carrier, *93*	80	90	___
52049	BN Gondola with coil covers, *94*	50	56	___
52097	Chessie System Reefer, *95*		34	___
52140	Union Pacific Bunk Car, *97*		37	___
52165	SP Caboose "6256," *98*		60	___
52197	Santa Fe GP38 Diesel, *99*		243	___
52227	"Artistry in Space" Boxcar, *00*		75	___
52255	30th Anniversary Flatcar with billboard, *01*		100	___
52283	Paint Vat Car, *02*		59	___
52331	Flatcar with "America's Railways" trailer, *03*		150	___
52349	Hometown Art Museum Hopper, purple, *04*		35	___
52350	"Native Views" 3-bay Hopper, *04*		65	___
52411	"35 Years" 1-D Tank Car, *06*		35	___

Carnegie Science Center

		Exc	Mint	
25085	Miniature Railroad & Village Boxcar, *09*		50	___
26750	Great Miniature Railroad & Village Boxcar, *99*		78	___
36202	Great Miniature Railroad 80th Anniversary Boxcar, *00*		110	___
36234	Great Miniature Railroad & Village Boxcar, *01*		50	___
52277	Carnegie Science Center 10th Anniversary Boxcar, *02*		60	___
52332	Miniature Railroad & Village Boxcar, *03*		58	___
52362	Miniature Railroad & Village 50th Anniversary Boxcar, *04*		50	___
52399	MRR&V Express Boxcar, *05*		50	___
52432	Miniature Railroad & Village Boxcar, *06*		50	___
52510	Miniature Railroad & Village Caboose, *08*		50	___

Chicagoland Railroad Club

		Exc	Mint	
52081	C&NW Boxcar "6464-555," *96*	40	68	___
52101	BN Maxi-Stack Flatcar "64287" with containers, *97*		82	___
52102	SF Extended Vision Caboose, red roof, *96*		75	___
52103	SF Extended Vision Caboose, black roof, *96*		75	___

			Exc	Mint
____	**52120**	Shedd Aquarium Car "3435-557," *98*		100
____	**52148**	REA/Santa Fe Operating Boxcar, *99*		70
____	**52170**	SP Operating Boxcar "52170-561," *99*		65
____	**52171**	UP Operating Boxcar "52171-561," *99*		65
____	**52178**	Burlington Operating Boxcar "52178-559," *00*		70
____	**52179**	ACL Operating Boxcar "52179-560," *00*		73
____	**52215**	C&NW 3-bay Cylindrical Hopper, *01*		60
____	**52216**	C&NW Cylindrical Hopper, *02*		60
____	**52223**	REA/Santa Fe Centennial Operating Boxcar, *00*		65
____	**52251**	PRR Express Car, green, *01*		67
____	**52259**	MP GP20 Diesel, traditional, *01*		250
____	**52292**	PRR Express Car, tuscan red, *02*		50
____	**52327**	City of Los Angeles Express Car, *04*		65
____	**52328**	City of New Haven Express Car, *04*		55
____	**52363**	City of New Orleans Express Car, *04*		55
____	**52364**	City of New York Express Car, *04*		65
____	**52388**	Great Northern Tool Car, *06*		48
____	**52389**	Great Northern Crew Car, *06*		48
____	**52390**	Great Northern Welding Caboose, *06*		78
____	**52391**	Great Northern Racing Crew Car, *06*		48
____	**52426**	City of San Francisco Express Car, *07*		55
____	**52427**	Rock Island Rocket Express Car, *07*		55
____	**52475**	Western Pacific UP Heritage Boxcar, *07*		60

Classic Toy Trains

____	**52126**	MILW Boxcar "21027" with CTT Logo, *97*		50

Dept. 56

____	**16270**	Heritage Village Boxcar "9796," *96*		56
____	**52096**	Snow Village Boxcar "9756," *95*		85
____	**52139**	Square Window Caboose "6256," *97*		72
____	**52157**	Holly Brothers 3-D Tank Car, *98*		85
____	**52175**	4-6-4 Hudson Locomotive, CC, *99*		350
____	**52199**	4-bay Hopper "6756," *00*		53
____	**52254**	"Happy Holidays" Gondola, *01*		35

Eastwood Automobilia

____	**16275**	Radio Flyer Boxcar "16275," *96*		50
____	**16757**	Johnny Lightning Auto Carrier "3435," *96*		90
____	**16985**	Flatcar with 2 Ford vans, *97*		49
____	**52044**	Vat Car, *95*		30
____	**52083**	PRR Flatcar "21697" with tanker, *95*		41
____	**52130**	Flatcar with Hot Wheels tanker, *97*		60

Gadsden-Pacific Division
Toy Train Operating Museum

		Exc	Mint
17872	Anaconda Ore Car, 88	60	72 ____
17878	Magma Ore Car, 89	45	55 ____
17881	Phelps Dodge Ore Car, 90	36	40 ____
17886	Cyprus Ore Car, 91	26	31 ____
19961	Inspiration Consolidated Copper Ore Car, 92	23	30 ____
52011	Tucson, Cornelia & Gila Bend Ore Car, 93	20	29 ____
52027	Pinto Valley Mine Ore Car, 94	20	29 ____
52071	Copper Basin Railway Ore Car, 95		30 ____
52089	SMARRCO Ore Car, 96		26 ____
52124	El Paso & Southwestern Ore Car, 97		40 ____
52164	SP Ore Car, 98		35 ____
52177	Arizona Southern Ore Car, 99		35 ____
52213	BHP Copper Ore Car, 00		29 ____
52248	Tombstone & Western Ore Car, 01		40 ____
52279	Dragoon & Northern Ore Car, 02		50 ____
52307	Twin Buttes Ore Car, 03		35 ____
52358	AJO & Southwestern Ore Car, 04		45 ____
52386	Ray & Gila Bend Ore Car, 05		45 ____
52541	Calabasas, Tuscon & Northwestern Ore Car, 06		45 ____
52473	Mascot & Western Ore Car, 07		90 ____
52524	Tucson, Globe & Northern Ore Car, 08		42 ____
52558	Port of Tucson Ore Car, 09		45 ____
52579	Rosemont Copper Ore Car, 10		40 ____
52588	ASARCO Ore Car, 11		40 ____
58513	Freeport-McMoRan Ore Car, 12		40 ____
58557	San Pedro & Southwestern Ore Car, 13		40 ____
58583	Arizona Eastern Ore Car, 14		42 ____

Houston Tinplate Operators Society

		Mint
8900	Sam Houston Mint Car, 00	120 ____
8901	Miracle Petroleum 1-D Tank Car, 01	100 ____
8902	USS Houston Submarine Car, 02	100 ____
8903	Railway Express Boxcar, 03	100 ____
8904	Lone Star Bay Window Caboose, 04	100 ____
8999	Lone Star Aquarium Car, mermaid or trout, 99	100 ____

Inland Empire Train Collectors Association

		Mint
1979	Boxcar, 79	15 ____
1980	SP-type Caboose, 80	14 ____
1981	Quad Hopper, 81	14 ____
1982	3-D Tank Car, 82	14 ____

CLUB CARS AND SPECIAL PRODUCTION

			Exc	Mint
____	1983	Reefer, *83*		14
____	1986	Bunk Car, *86*		14
____	7518	Carson City Mint Car, *84*	36	43

Lionel Central Operating Lines

____	1981	Boxcar, *81*		23
____	1986	Work Caboose, shell only, *86*		14
____	5724	Pennsylvania Bunk Car, *84*	30	39
____	6508	Canadian Pacific Crane Car, *83*		40
____	6907	NYC Wood-sided Caboose, *97*		50
____	9184	Erie Bay Window Caboose, *82*	17	21
____	9475	D&H "I Love NY" Boxcar, *85*		34
____	16342	CSX Gondola with coil covers, *92*		20
____	17221	NYC Boxcar, *95*		30

Lionel Collectors Association of Canada

____	5710	Canadian Pacific Reefer, *83*		215
____	5714	Michigan Central Reefer, *85*	120	150
____	6100	Ontario Northland Covered Quad Hopper, *82*		250
____	8103	Toronto, Hamilton & Buffalo Boxcar, *81*		150
____	8204	Algoma Central Boxcar, *82*		150
____	8507/08	Canadian National F3 Diesel AA, shells only, *85*		400
____	8912	Canada Southern Operating Hopper, *89*		95
____	9413	Napierville Junction Boxcar, *80*		10
____	9718	Canadian National Boxcar, *79*		20
____	17893	BAOC 1-D Tank Car "914," *91*		120
____	52004	Algoma Central Gondola "9215" with coil covers, *92*	70	90
____	52005	Canadian National F3 Diesel B Unit "9517," *93*		30
____	52006	Canadian Pacific Boxcar "930016" (std O), *93*		108
____	52115	Wabash Lake Railway 2-tier Auto Carrier "9519," *98*		100
____	52125	TH&B Gondola 2-pack, *99*		90
____	86009	Canadian National Bunk Car, *86*		115
____	87010	Canadian National Express Reefer, *87*		115
____	88011	Canadian National Caboose (std O), *88*		500
____	830005	Canadian National Boxcar, *83*		300
____	840006	Canadian Wheat Board Covered Quad Hopper, *84*		165
____	900013	Canadian National Flatcar with trailers, *90*		225

Lionel Collectors Club of America

LCCA National Convention Cars

		Exc	Mint	
6112	Commonwealth Edison Quad Hopper with coal, *83*	49	78	___
6323	Virginia Chemicals 1-D Tank Car, *86*	47	63	___
6567	Illinois Central Gulf Crane Car "100408," *85*	55	63	___
7403	LNAC Boxcar, *84*	21	24	___
9118	Corning Covered Quad Hopper, *74*	65	92	___
9155	Monsanto 1-D Tank Car, *75*	38	47	___
9159UP	UP Reefer, *10*		100	___
9212	Seaboard Coast Line Flatcar with trailers, *76*	22	31	___
9259	Southern Bay Window Caboose, *77*	31	41	___
9358	"Sands of Iowa" Covered Quad Hopper, *80*	24	33	___
9435	Central of Georgia Boxcar, *81*	25	29	___
9460	D&TS Automobile Boxcar, *82*	25	34	___
9701	Baltimore & Ohio Automobile Boxcar, *72*		170	___
9727	TA&G Boxcar, *73*	105	134	___
9728	Union Pacific Stock Car, *78*	23	26	___
9733	Airco Boxcar with tank car body, *79*	37	50	___
17870	East Camden & Highland Boxcar (std O), *87*	29	33	___
17873	Ashland Oil 3-D Tank Car, *88*	55	70	___
17876	Columbia, Newberry & Laurens Boxcar (std O), *89*	32	40	___
17880	D&RGW Wood-sided Caboose (std O), *90*	43	55	___
17887	Conrail Flatcar with Armstrong Tile trailer (std O), *91*	30	49	___
17888	Conrail Flatcar with Ford trailer (std O), *91*	42	80	___
17892	Conrail Flatcar with Armstrong and Ford Trailers (std O), *91*		140	___
17899	NASA Tank Car "190" (std O), *92*	45	51	___
27019	Imco PS-2 Covered Hopper, *09*		50	___
52023	D&TS 2-bay ACF Hopper "2601" (std O), *93*	35	40	___
52038	Southern Hopper "360794" with coal (std O), *94*	38	46	___
52074	Iowa Beef Packers Reefer "197095" (std O), *95*		32	___
52090	Pere Marquette DD Boxcar "71996" (std O), *96*		52	___
52110	CStPM&O Boxcar "71997" (std O), *97*	18	52	___
52151	Amtrak Express Baggage Boxcar "71998" (std O), *98*		64	___
52176	Fort Worth & Denver Boxcar "8277" (std O), *99*		55	___
52195	Double-stack Car with 2 containers, *00*		100	___
52244	Louisville & Nashville Horse Car "2001," *01*		50	___
52266	PRR "Coal Goes To War" Hopper "707025," *02*		86	___
52267	PRR "Coal Goes To War" Hopper "707026," *02*		92	___
52299	Las Vegas Mint Car, *03*		80	___
52343	MILW Milk Car, orange, *04*		160	___

CLUB CARS AND SPECIAL PRODUCTION

		Exc	Mint
____ 52344	MILW Milk Car, blue, 04		205
____ 52393	MKT Speeder, yellow, nonpowered, 05		20
____ 52394	Frisco Speeder, red, powered, 05		25
____ 52395	Frisco Flatcar, silver, 05		25
____ 52396	Frisco Flatcar with 2 speeders, 05		125
____ 52412	UP Auxiliary Power Car, 06		55
____ 52455	C&NW/UP Tank Car, 07		110
____ 52491	PS-2 Covered Hopper 2-pack, 08		140
____ 52507	NYC Water Tower, 08		83
____ 52514	ATSF Mint Car with Gold, 09		275
____ 52543	BNSF Mechanical Reefer, 09		140
____ 52559	UP Cylindrical Hopper, 10		100
____ 52562	D&RGW Uranium Transport Mint Car, 10		230
____ 58560	Southern Boxcar, 13		90
____ 72511	Alamo Mint Car, 11		150
____ 75511	Federal Reserve Mint Car, 11		200

LCCA Meet Specials

		Exc	Mint
____ 1130	Tender, 76		15
____ 6014-900	Frisco Boxcar (027), 75	17	30
____ 6483	Jersey Central SP-type Caboose, 82	24	28
____ 9016	Chessie System Hopper (027), 79	16	20
____ 9036	Mobilgas 1-D Tank Car (027), 78	20	22
____ 9142	Republic Steel Gondola, green or blue, with canisters, 77	15	23

Other LCCA Production

		Exc	Mint
____ 4001	RJ Corman Boxcar, 99		80
____ 4002	RJ Corman Boxcar, 99		40
____ 6464-2002	Maddox Retirement Boxcar, 02		100
____ 8068	Rock Island GP20 Diesel, 80	85	120
____ 9739	D&RGW Boxcar, 78	17	25
____ 9771	Norfolk & Western Boxcar, 77		32
____ 14154	Water Tower with LCCA plaque, 04		90
____ 17174	Great Northern 3-bay Hopper, 03		25
____ 17234	Port Huron & Detroit Boxcar, 00		45
____ 17377	American Railway Express Reefer "302," 06		48
____ 17412	Gondola, blue, 02		28
____ 17895	LCCA Tractor, 91	13	21
____ 17896	Lancaster Lines Tractor, 91	22	30
____ 18090	D&RGW 4-6-2 Locomotive and Tender, 90	230	303
____ 18483	C&O Ballast Tamper, 07		73
____ 18490	UP Ballast Tamper, yellow, 06		125
____ 19998	"Seasons Greetings" Boxcar, 03		40
____ 26023	Flatcar with bulldozer, 04		53
____ 26024	Flatcar with scraper, 04		63

CLUB CARS AND SPECIAL PRODUCTION

		Exc	Mint	
26049	Speedboat Willie Flatcar with boat, *05*		45	____
26132	UP 1-D Tank Car, *06*		27	____
26780	Operating Giraffe Car, green or pink, *05*		70	____
26791	UP Chase Gondola, red, *03*		32	____
26791	Rio Grande Chase Gondola, black, *06*		32	____
26795	Mrs. O'Leary's Dairy Farm Stock Car, *07*		100	____
26834	"La Cosa Nostra Railway" Operating Ice Car, *07*	25	75	____
29232	Lenny the Lion Hi-Cube, signed by Lenny Dean, *98*		63	____
52025	Madison Hardware Tractor and Trailer, *93*	13	18	____
52039	"Track 29" Bumper, *94*		23	____
52055	SOVEX Tractor and Trailer, *94*	15	22	____
52056	Southern Tractor and Trailer, *94*	17	23	____
52091	Lenox Tractor and Trailer, *95*		14	____
52092	Iowa Interstate Tractor and Trailer, *95*		20	____
52100	Grand Rapids Station Platform, *98*		23	____
52107	On-track Pickup, orange, *96*		50	____
52108	On-track Van, blue, *96*		35	____
52131	Beechcraft Airplane, blue, *97*		25	____
52138	Beechcraft Airplane, orange, *97*		25	____
52152	Ben Franklin and Liberty Bell Reefer, *98*		120	____
52153	6414 Auto Set, 4-pack, *98*		72	____
52206	SD40 Diesel and Extended Vision Caboose, *00*		650	____
52257	"Season's Greetings" Gondola, *01*		36	____
52273	Flatcar with submarine, *02*		219	____
52300	Halloween General Train, *04*		360	____
52348	Halloween General Sheriff and Outlaw Car, *04*		115	____
52405	Halloween General Add-on Cars, *06*		160	____
52406	Halloween General Cannon, *08*		135	____
52423	New Haven Alco Diesel Passenger Set, *09*		510	____
52468	Postwar "2434" Passenger Coach, *09*		75	____
52469	Postwar "2432" Passenger Coach, *09*		75	____
52581	Texas Special Milk Car, *10*		110	____
52582	Gondola with dinosaurs, *12*		45	____
58526	Texas Special Cow and Calf SW9 Switchers, *14*		375	____
58549	Texas Special Diamonds Mint Car, *14*		75	____

Lionel Operating Train Society

LOTS National Convention Cars

		Exc	Mint	
303	Stauffer Chemical 1-D Tank Car, *85*	85	210	____
3764	Kahn's Brine Tank Reefer, *81*	70	85	____
6111	L&N Covered Quad Hopper, *83*	37	42	____
6211	C&O Gondola with canisters, *86*	60	90	____
9414	Cotton Belt Boxcar, *80*	39	55	____

			Exc	Mint
___	16812	Grand Trunk 2-bay ACF Hopper (std O), 96		60
___	16813	Pennsylvania Power & Light Hopper with coal (std O), 97		78
___	17874	Milwaukee Road Log Dump Car "59629," 88	90	148
___	17875	Port Huron & Detroit Boxcar "1289," 89	40	48
___	17882	B&O DD Boxcar "298011" with ETD, 90	55	65
___	17890	CSX Auto Carrier "151161," 91	75	80
___	18890	Union Pacific RS3 Diesel "8805," 89	120	145
___	19960	Western Pacific Boxcar "1953" (std O), 92	47	66
___	38356	Dow Chemical 3-D Tank Car, 87	85	125
___	52014	BN TTUX Flatcar Set with N&W trailers, 93	165	205
___	52041	BN TTUX Flatcar Set with Conrail trailers, 94	60	85
___	52067	Burlington Operating Ice Car "50240," 95		60
___	52135	ATSF Reefer "22739," 98		55
___	52162	Gulf Mobile & Ohio DD Boxcar "24580," 99		65
___	52196	CP Maxi-Stack Flatcar "524115" with 2 containers, 00		95
___	52234	WM Well Car with transformer, 01		60
___	52261	Schlitz Beer Reefer "92132," 02		60
___	52281	PRR Operating Boxcar, 03		55
___	52342	Southern Stock Car, sound, 04		57
___	52346	D&H PS-2 Cement Hopper, 06		65
___	52347	SF SD80 MAC Diesel, TMCC, 04		350
___	52380/81	Virginian Coal Hopper, 05		50
___	52382	SF Extended View Caboose, 05		325
___	52425	SP&S Boxcar (std O), 07		90
___	52474	NYC Evans Auto Loader with 4 Studebakers, 08		82
___	52550	NC&StL Dixieland Boxcar, 09		73
___	52566	NH State of Maine Boxcar, 10		62
___	52580	Robin Hood Beer Double-sheathed Boxcar, 11		80
___	58553	UP Maxi-Stack Car with WP feather containers, 13		75
___	58575	H. J. Heinz Double-sheathed Boxcar, 14		70
___	80948	Michigan Central Boxcar, 82	145	230
___	121315	Pennsylvania Hi-Cube Boxcar, 84	125	343

LOTS Meet Specials

___	52413	Saratoga Brewery Reefer, 06		60
___	52456	Alpenrose Dairy Milk Car, 07		95
___	52506	Studebaker Automobile Parts Boxcar, 08		75
___	52552	Radioactive Waste Removal Car, 09		86

Other LOTS Production

___	1223	Seattle & North Coast Hi-Cube Boxcar, 86	150	200
___	52042	BN TTUX Flatcar "637500C" with CN trailer, 94	50	60
___	52048	Canadian National Tractor and Trailer "197993," 94	28	33

		Exc	Mint
52129	Lighted Billboard with Angela Trotta Thomas art, *97*		28 ____
52217	LOTS/LCCA 2000 Convention Billboard, *00*		10 ____
52260	National Aquarium in Baltimore Car, *01*		110 ____
52280	"More Precious than Gold" Mint Car, *02*		90 ____
52309	Patriotic Tank Car, *03*		68 ____
52359	Silver Anniversary Ore Car "1979," *04*		40 ____
52360	Silver Anniversary Ore Car "2004," *04*		40 ____
52419	Touring Layout Aquarium Car, *05*		90 ____
52523	Santa Fe Flatcar with trailer and tractor, *08*		88 ____
52553	Tennessee Aquarium Car, *09*	15	65 ____
52567	Santa Fe ACF 2-bay Hopper, *10*		58 ____
52590	Santa Fe Warbonnet Mint Car, *11*		75 ____
58535	Santa Fe ACF Transparent Boxcar, *12*		75 ____
58566	Virginia & Truckee Carson City Mint Car, *13*		70

Lionel Century Club

		Exc	Mint
14532	PRR Sharknose Diesel AA Set, LCC II, *00*		690 ____
18053	2-8-4 Berkshire Locomotive "726," *97*		705 ____
18057	6-8-6PRR S2 Steam Turbine Locomotive "671," *98*	320	568 ____
18058	4-6-4 Hudson Locomotive "773," *97*		734 ____
18068	Tender for PRR Steam Turbine Locomotive "773," *99*		210 ____
18135	NYC F3 Diesel AA Set, *99*		650 ____
18178	NYC F3 Diesel B Unit, *99*		230 ____
18314	PRR GG1 Electric "2332," *97*	490	560 ____
18340	FM Train Master Set, LCC II, *00*		900
24510	PRR Sharknose Diesel B Unit, LCC II, *00*		200 ____
28069	NYC 4-8-6 Niagara Locomotive "6024," CC, LCC II, *00*		920 ____
29173	Empire State Express Passenger Car 4-pack, LCC II, *02*		350 ____
29178	Empire State Express Passenger Car 2-pack, LCC II, *02*		175 ____
29181	Empire State Express Diner, LCC II, *02*		190 ____
29204	Boxcar "1900-2000," *96*		331 ____
29226	Berkshire Boxcar, *97*	115	145 ____
29227	GG1 Boxcar, *98*		55 ____
29228	PRR Turbine Boxcar "671," *99*		60 ____
29248	F3 Boxcar "2333," *99*		67 ____
31716	Niagara Milk Train Set, LCC II, *00*		300 ____
31726	PRR Sharknose Coal Train Set, LCC II, *00*		180 ____
31731	Train Master Freight Train Set, LCC II, *00*		180 ____
38000	NYC 4-6-4 Hudson Empire State Locomotive, LCC II, *02*		990 ____
38195	Santa Fe FT Diesel A Unit "170," *00*		NRS ____

		Exc	Mint
____ 39201	Hudson Boxcar "773," *00*		58
____ 39215	Niagara Boxcar, LCC II, *01*		48
____ 39217	Boxcar, LCC II, *00*		60
____ 39218	Gold Boxcar, LCC II, *00*		85
____ 39237	M-10000 Boxcar, LCC II, *00*		70
____ 39246	PRR Sharknose Boxcar, LCC II, *00*		55
____ 39265	Fairbanks-Morse Train Master Boxcar, LCC II, *00*		60
____ 39266	Empire State Boxcar, LCC II, *00*		40
____ 51007	UP M-10000 4-car Passenger Set, LCC II, *00*	600	970
____ 51249	UP Overland Route Sleeper Car, LCC II, *02*		120

Lionel Railroader Club

		Exc	Mint
____ 780	Boxcar, *82*	55	67
____ 781	Flatcar with trailers, *83*	40	50
____ 782	1-D Tank Car, *85*	40	43
____ 784	Covered Quad Hopper, *84*	50	60
____ 11183	Lincoln Funeral Train		800
____ 11319	PRR Tuscan K4 Locomotive, CC		900
____ 11320	PRR Tuscan K4 Locomotive		750
____ 12875	Tractor and Trailer, *94*	13	18
____ 12921	Illuminated Station Platform, *95*	19	22
____ 14274	Water Tower, *07*		20
____ 15034	50th Anniversary Mail Car, *10*		50
____ 15035	Holiday Boxcar, *10*		50
____ 16800	Ore Car, yellow, *86*	60	69
____ 16801	Bunk Car, blue, *88*	20	33
____ 16802	Tool Car, *89*	24	35
____ 16803	Searchlight Car, *90*	23	27
____ 16804	Bay Window Caboose, *91*	25	30
____ 16839	Covered Bridge, *11*		50
____ 18680	4-6-4 Hudson Locomotive, *00*		300
____ 18684	4-6-2 Pacific Locomotive, *99*		220
____ 18818	GP38-2 Diesel, *92*	100	117
____ 19399	Christmas Boxcar, *13*		60
____ 19437	Flatcar with trailer, *97*		55
____ 19473	Operating Log Dump Car "3351," *99*		38
____ 19685	Western Union Dining Car, *02*		47
____ 19695	Western Union 1-D Tank Car, *03*		22
____ 19774	Porthole Caboose, *99*		49
____ 19775	Stock Car, *99*		51
____ 19924	Boxcar, *93*	18	22
____ 19930	Quad Hopper with coal, *94*	14	20
____ 19935	1-D Tank Car, *95*	19	24
____ 19940	Vat Car, *96*		32
____ 19953	6464 Boxcar, *97*		35

CLUB CARS AND SPECIAL PRODUCTION

		Exc	Mint
19965	Aquarium Car "3435," 99		56 ____
19966	Gondola "9820" (std O), 98	18	32 ____
19978	Gold Membership Boxcar, 99		46 ____
19991	Gold Membership Boxcar, 00		65 ____
19992	Western Union Tool Car "3550," 00		50 ____
19993	Gold Membership Boxcar, 01		65 ____
19994	Western Union Passenger Car "1307," 01		60 ____
19995	25th Anniversary Boxcar (std O), 01		49 ____
24217	Animated Billboard, 08		30 ____
25631	Lincoln Train Passenger Car 2-pack		300 ____
25635	Red Passenger Car 3-pack, 12		420 ____
25635	Red Arrow Diner, 12		140 ____
26089	Western Union Gondola with handcar, 05		65 ____
26165	Western Union Reefer, 04		30 ____
26382	Flatcar with tractor and tanker, 08		60 ____
26413	Commemorative 4-bay Hopper, 08		68 ____
26636	"6830" 50th Anniversary Flatcar with submarine, 11		55 ____
26637	"6640" 50th Anniversary USMC Missile Launching Car, 11		65 ____
27940	"6469" Liquified Gas Tank Car, 13		50 ____
27943	"6416" Boat Loader, 13		50 ____
27944	"3413" Mercury Capsule Launch Car, 13		60 ____
27945	"6460-60" LV Covered Quad Hopper, 13		55 ____
28062	4-6-4 Hudson Locomotive, 00		1150 ____
28571	GP9 Diesel, CC, 07		250 ____
28665	Western Union 2-8-4 Berkshire Locomotive "665," 05		175 ____
29200	Lionel Boxcar "9700," 96		38 ____
29313	"3409" 50th Anniversary Helicopter Car, 11		70 ____
29657	"6413" 50th Anniversary Mercury Capsule Car, 12		55 ____
29658	"6465" 50th Anniversary Cities Service 2-D Car, 12		50 ____
29931	Holiday Boxcar, 05		25 ____
29939	30th Anniversary Boxcar, 06		50 ____
29941	Holiday Boxcar, 06		25 ____
29946	Holiday Boxcar, 07		37 ____
29947	Commemorative Boxcar, 07		30 ____
29957	Holiday Boxcar, 08		50 ____
29977	Holiday Boxcar, 11		60 ____
36521	Western Union Searchlight Caboose, 05		32 ____
36769	4th of July Lighted Boxcar, 03		70 ____
37968	Clock Tower with wreath, 11		43 ____
39249	Holiday Boxcar, 03		30 ____
39264	Holiday Boxcar, 04		50 ____
39352	"6445" 50th Anniversary Fort Knox Mint Car, 12		70 ____

CLUB CARS AND SPECIAL PRODUCTION

			Exc	Mint
___	39353	50th Anniversary Santa Fe Boxcar, 11		55
___	39496	"6475" 50th Anniversary Vat Car, 10		60
___	58632	1955 Maintenance of Way Truck, 13		165
___	81116	Polar Express Operating Billboard, 14		60
___	81117	Polar Express Flatcar with silver bell, 14		45

Lionel Railroad Club Milwaukee

			Mint
___	52116	MILW Flatcar "194797," black, with tractor and trailer, 97	76
___	52163	CMStP&P "Hiawatha" DD Automobile Boxcar, 98	60
___	52180	MILW Flatcar "194799," tuscan, with trailer, 99	75
___	52228	CMStP&P 1-D Water Tank Car "908309," 00	50
___	52229	MILW 1-D Diesel Fuel Tank Car "907797," 00	50
___	52230	1-D Tank Car 2-pack, 00	142
___	52246	CMStP&P "Olympian" Boxcar "194701," 01	67
___	52265	MILW/Zoological Society Aquarium Car "4701," orange, 02	55
___	52278	MILW/Zoological Society Aquarium Car "4702," blue, 03	95
___	52297	MILW Reefer "194703," yellow, 03	67
___	52298	MILW Flatcar "194704" with orange trailer, 04	115
___	52337	MILW/Zoological Society Motorized Aquarium Car, 04	90
___	52368	MILW Flatcar "472004," black, 05	65
___	52369	MILW Trailer Train Auto Carrier "194705," 05	85
___	52370	CMStP&P Milk Car "364," tan, 05	81
___	52387	CMStP&P Flatcar "194706," gray, 06	50
___	52400	MILW PS-2 2-bay Hopper "99607," orange, 06	85
___	52401	MILW PS-2 2-bay Hopper "98809," yellow, 06	65
___	52402	CMStP&P URTX Operating Ice Car "4706," 06	85
___	52428	CMStP&P 0-4-0 Switcher and Caboose Set, 60th Anniversary, 06	275
___	52429	CMStP&P 0-4-0 Switcher, 06	200
___	52430	CMStP&P Offset Cupola Caboose, 06	70
___	52458	MILW Stock Car "102721" (std O), 07	67
___	52466	CMStP&P Stock Car "105254" (std O), 07	67
___	52551	MILW "Big M" DD Boxcar "200947," yellow, 09	60
___	52572	MILW Reiman Aquarium Car, 11	75
___	52599	MILW 2-bay ACF Hopper, 12	60
___	58563	CMStP&P Round-Roof Boxcar, 13	70
___	58591	MILW Flatcar with auto frames, 14	60

Long Island Toy Train Locomotive Engineers

___	58520	Entenmann's Vat Car, 12	65
___	58556	Flatcar with U.S. Navy airplane, 13	70
___	58562	Entenmann's Quad Hopper, 14	74

Nassau Lionel Operating Engineers

		Exc	Mint	
8389	Long Island Boxcar, *89*	70	100	___
8390	Long Island Covered Quad Hopper, *90*	70	100	___
8391A	Long Island Bunk Car, *91*	70	90	___
8391B	Long Island Tool Car, *91*	70	90	___
8392	Long Island 1-D Tank Car, *92*	80	105	___
52007	Long Island RS3 Diesel "1552," *93*	120	250	___
52019	Long Island Boxcar, *93*	39	65	___
52020	Long Island Bay Window Caboose, *93*	65	95	___
52026	Long Island Flatcar "8394" with Grumman trailer, *94*	275	465	___
52061	Long Island Stern's Pickle Products Vat Car "8395," *95*		200	___
52072	Grumman Tractor, *94*		75	___
52076	Long Island Observation Car "8396," *96*		350	___
52112	Long Island Ronkonkoma Vista Dome Car "9783," *97*		300	___
52122	Meenan Oil 1-D Tank Car "8397" (std O), *97*		60	___
52123	Long Island Hicksville Diner Car "9883," *98*		300	___
52144	Long Island Flatcar with Grumman van, *99*		94	___
52145	Long Island Jamaica Passenger Coach, *99*		300	___
52145	Long Island Penn Station Passenger Coach, *99*		300	___
52166	Long Island Flatcar "8398" with Grumman trailer, *98*		77	___
52186	Grucci Fireworks Boxcar, *00*		72	___
52232	Central RR of Long Island Boxcar, *01*		60	___
52256	New York & Atlantic Boxcar "8302," *02*		58	___
52296	Long Island Flatcar with Republic tanker, *03*		78	___
52329	New York & Atlantic Caboose, *04*		80	___
52341	Long Island Flatcar with Pan Am trailer, *05*		85	___
52365	Long Island Flatcar with Lilco transformer, *04*		135	___
52420	Long Island 80th Anniversary Boxcar, *06*		45	___
52480	Long Island Flatcar with pipes, *08*		50	___
52409	Long Island Flatcar with P.C. Richard & Son trailer, *07*		67	___
52555	Martha Clara Vineyards Vat Car, *09*		58	___
52568	Flatcar with NY Islanders refrigerated trailer, *10*		62	___
52586	Flatcar with Cradle of Aviation Museum trailer, *11*		52	___
52592	Petland Discounts Aquarium Car, *11*		70	___
58500	Nassau County Firefighters Museum Tank Car, *12*		55	___
83131	Nathan's Famous Reefer, *13*		74	___
83132	Nathan's Famous Reefer, *13*		74	___

Railroad Museum of Long Island

			Exc	Mint
____	**52416**	RMLI 15th Anniversary LIRR Boxcar, *05*		170
____	**52433**	Atlantis Marine World Aquarium Car, *06*		145
____	**52453**	North Fork Bank Mint Car, *07*		90
____	**52497**	LIRR Flatcar with Entenmann's trailer and tractor, *08*		110
____	**52498**	Boeing Fairchild Container Car, *10*		75
____	**52548**	RMLI "Celebrating 175 Years of Railroading" Boxcar, *09*		90
____	**52557**	Entenmann's Operating Boxcar, *10*		90
____	**52570**	Riverhead Building Supply Boxcar, *11*		60
____	**52571**	Riverhead Visitor's Center Boxcar, *11*		60
____	**52577**	King Kullen Boxcar, *11*		60
____	**52595**	J. P. Holland Submarine Car, *12*		60
____	**58521**	Wonder Bread PS-2 Covered Hopper, *12*		60
____	**58551**	Flatcar with White Castle refrigerated trailer, *13*		60
____	**58554**	RCA Operating Radar Car, *13*		60

St. Louis Lionel Railroad Club

			Exc	Mint
____	**52099**	MP Flatcar with St. Louis trailer, *96*		65
____	**52104**	St. Louis tractor and trailer, *96*		20
____	**52117**	Wabash Flatcar with REA tractor and trailer, *97*		65
____	**52136A**	Christmas Tractor and Trailer, *97*		NRS
____	**52136B**	Frisco Tractor and Trailer, *98*		NRS
____	**52147**	Frisco Campbell TOFC Flatcar, *98*		75
____	**52150**	Frisco Campbell TOFC Flatcar, *98*		130
____	**52167**	ATSF Flatcar "831999" with Navajo trailer, *99*		75
____	**52190**	IC Flatcar with trailers, *00*		80
____	**52222**	Cotton Belt Flatcar with SP tractor and trailer, *01*		50
____	**52224A**	SP Flatcar with Navajo tractor and trailer, *01*		25
____	**52224B**	SP Flatcar with service tractor and trailer, *01*		25
____	**52258**	UP Flatcar with UP tractor and trailer, *02*		55
____	**52290**	UP Flatcar with tractor trailer, *03*		75
____	**52336**	U.S. Army Flatcar with tanker truck, *04*		125
____	**52371**	NYC Flatcar with Fire Company tanker truck, *05*		145
____	**52392**	PRR Flatcar with Hood's Milk tanker truck, *06*		100
____	**52440**	U.S.M.C. Flatcar with tractor and trailer, *07*		135
____	**52490**	Silver Special Flatcar with USA tractor and trailer, *08*		100
____	**52513**	Frisco Flatcar with U.S.A.F. trailer, *09*		120

Train Collectors Association

TCA National Convention Cars

		Exc	Mint	
511	St. Louis Baggage Car, *81*	36	41	___
2671-1968	TCA Tender, shell only, *68*	10	54	___
5734	REA Reefer, *85*	42	51	___
6315	Pittsburgh 1-D Tank Car, *72*	55	60	___
6436-1969	Open Quad Hopper, red, *69*	35	65	___
6464-1965	Pittsburgh Boxcar, blue, *65*	30	135	___
6464-1970	Chicago Boxcar, *70*	55	85	___
6464-1971	Disneyland Boxcar, *71*	210	240	___
6517-1966	Bay Window Caboose, *66*	41	168	___
6926	New Orleans Extended Vision Caboose, *86*	27	39	___
7205	Denver Combination Car, *82*	37	50	___
7206	Louisville Passenger Car, *83*	40	55	___
7212	Pittsburgh Passenger Car, *84*	41	50	___
7812	Houston Stock Car, *77*	12	25	___
8476	4-6-4 Locomotive "5484," *85*	255	310	___
9123	Dearborn 3-tier Auto Carrier, *73*	25	36	___
9319	"Silver Jubilee" Mint Car, *79*	105	130	___
9544	Chicago Observation Car, *80*		50	___
9611	Boston Hi-Cube Boxcar, *78*	21	26	___
9774	Orlando "Southern Belle" Boxcar, *75*	27	35	___
9779	Philadelphia Boxcar "9700-1976," *76*	26	34	___
9864	Seattle Reefer, *74*	37	52	___
11737	TCA 40th Anniversary F3 Diesel ABA Set, *93*	460	528	___
17879	Valley Forge Dining Car, *89*		60	___
17883	New Georgia Passenger Car, *90*	52	64	___
17898	Wabash Reefer "21596," *92*	41	44	___
19211	Vermont Railway Flatcars (2) with 4 trailers, *08*		160	___
52008	Bucyrus Erie Crane Car, *93*	44	49	___
52035	Yorkrail GP9 Diesel "1750," shell only, *94*	44	55	___
52036	TCA 40th Anniversary Bay Window Caboose, *94*	35	40	___
52037	Yorkrail GP9 Diesel "1754," *94*	125	150	___
52062	Skytop Observation Car, *95*	210	360	___
52085	Full Vista Dome Car, *96*		115	___
52106	City of Phoenix Diner, *97*		100	___
52142	Massachusetts Central Maxi-Stack Flatcar "5100-01," *98*		120	___
52143	City of Providence Passenger Car, *98*		140	___
52146	Ocean Spray Reefer, *98*		235	___
52155	City of San Francisco Baggage Car, *99*		140	___
52191	City of Grand Rapids Aluminum Passenger Car, *00*		135	___
52210	Rico Station, *00*		29	___
52220	City of Chattanooga Vista Dome Car, *01*		140	___

			Exc	Mint
____	**52221**	Norfolk Southern Boxcar, *01*		50
____	**52237**	Lionel Gondola, yellow, *01*		110
____	**52238**	Lionel Gondola, red, *01*		110
____	**52239**	Lionel Gondola, silver, *01*		110
____	**52240**	Lionel Gondola 3-pack, *01*		110
____	**52241**	Lionel Gondola, black, *02*		15
____	**52242**	Lionel Gondola, blue, *02*		35
____	**52250**	City of Chicago Combination Car, *02*		130
____	**52272**	Lionel Gondola, gold, *02*		80
____	**52276**	California Gold Mint Car, *03*		65
____	**52333**	Harmony Dairy Milk Car, *04*		90
____	**52338**	Lionel 50th Anniversary Mint Car, *04*		75
____	**52339**	50th Anniversary Convention Banquet Car with coin, *04*		360
____	**52340**	Train Order Building, *04*		90
____	**52373**	Montana Rail Link 2-car Set, *05*		90
____	**52374**	Montana Rail Link 2-bay Hopper, *05*		50
____	**52375**	Montana Rail Link Flatcar with pulp-wood logs, *05*		50
____	**52376**	GN Reefer, *05*		60
____	**52403**	T&P Stock Car (std O), *06*		75
____	**52414**	Flatcar with 3 snowmobiles, *07*		80
____	**52481**	Ben & Jerry's Reefer, *08*		95
____	**52500**	ATSF Grand Canyon Reefer, *09*		60
____	**52508**	Celebrate America Mint Car, *09*		95
____	**58544**	St. Louis Reefer, *13*		85
____	**58547**	Cotton Belt Blue Streak Merchandise Boxcar, *13*		75
____	**58571**	Bethlehem Steel PS-1 Boxcar, *14*		80
____	**58572**	Reading Philadelphia Mint Car, *14*		80

TCA Museum-Related and Other Cars

			Exc	Mint
____	**1018-1979**	Mortgage Burning Hi-Cube Boxcar, *79*	32	35
____	**5731**	L&N Reefer, *90*		95
____	**7780**	TCA Museum Boxcar, *80*		26
____	**7781**	Hafner Boxcar, *81*		26
____	**7782**	Carlisle & Finch Boxcar, *82*		26
____	**7783**	Ives Boxcar, *83*		26
____	**7784**	Voltamp Boxcar, *84*		23
____	**7785**	Hoge Boxcar, *85*		23
____	**9771**	Norfolk & Western Boxcar, *77*	24	31
____	**16811**	Rutland Boxcar "5477096," *96*		34
____	**52045**	Pennsylvania Dutch Milk Car "61052," *94*		90
____	**52051**	Baltimore & Ohio Sentinel Boxcar "6464095," *95*	36	42
____	**52052**	TCA 40th Anniversary Boxcar, *94*		90

CLUB CARS AND SPECIAL PRODUCTION

		Exc	Mint	
52063	NYC Pacemaker Boxcar "6464125," *95*		345	____
52064	Missouri Pacific Boxcar "6464150," *95*		370	____
52065	Pennsylvania Dutch Grain Operating Boxcar "9208," *96*		100	____
52118	Rio Grande Boxcar "5477097," *97*		53	____
52119	TCA Museum 20th Anniversary Boxcar, *97*		70	____
52128	Pennsylvania Dutch Pretzels Boxcar, *99*		80	____
52172	L&N "Share the Freedom" Boxcar "5477099," *99*		56	____
52198	Frisco Boxcar "5477000," *00*		43	____
52215	Museum Work Train Gondola with pipes, *03*		53	____
52226	Angela Trotta Thomas Boxcar "2000," *01*		100	____
52243	Museum Work Train 1-D Tank Car, *01*		50	____
52271	Museum Work Train Flatcar with wheel load, *02*		20	____
52289	National Toy Train Museum 25th Anniversary Bullion Car, *02*		75	____
52295	National Toy Train Museum Gondola with pipes, *03*		16	____
52310	Museum Work Train Boxcar, *04*		53	____
52311	50th Anniversary Golden Express Freight Set, *04*		450	____
52372	Museum Work Train Baggage Car, *05*		70	____
52408	N&W Caboose, *06*		55	____
52409	Museum Work Train Idler Caboose, *06*		68	____
52437	Museum Work Train Crane Car, *07*		78	____

TCA Bicentennial Special Set

		Exc	Mint	
1973	Bicentennial Observation Car, *76*	34	50	____
1974	Bicentennial Passenger Car, *76*	34	50	____
1975	Bicentennial Passenger Car, *76*	34	50	____
1976	Bicentennial U36B Diesel, *76*	115	165	____

Atlantic Division

		Exc	Mint	
1980	Atlantic Division Flatcar with trailers, *80*	28	34	____
6101	Burlington Northern Covered Quad Hopper, *82*	21	34	____
9186	Conrail N5c Caboose, *79*	22	30	____
9193	Budweiser Vat Car, *84*	80	110	____
9466	Wanamaker Boxcar, *83*	105	135	____
9788	Lehigh Valley Boxcar, *78*	19	24	____

Desert Division

		Exc	Mint	
52088	Desert Division 25th Anniversary On-track Step Van, *96*		120	____
52105	Superstition Mountain Operating Gondola "61997," *97*		80	____
52442	Verde Canyon Boxcar, *07*		55	____
52443	Grand Canyon Boxcar, *07*		55	____

Dixie Division

___	**27007/87**	Dixie Division 20th Anniversary PS-1 Boxcar, *06*	80
___	**52127**	Dixie Division 10th Anniversary Southern 3-bay Hopper, *98*	70

Eastern Division

___	**52059**	Clinchfield Quad Hopper "16413" with coal, *94*	85	110

Eastern Division: Washington, Baltimore & Annapolis Chapter

___	**9412**	Richmond, Fredericksburg & Potomac Boxcar, *79*	26
___	**9740**	Chessie System Boxcar, *76*	23
___	**9771**	Norfolk & Western Boxcar, *78*	30
___	**9783**	B&O Time-Saver Boxcar, *77*	30

Fort Pitt Division

___	**1984-30X**	Heinz Ketchup Boxcar, *84*	500

Great Lakes Division

___	**1983**	Churchill Downs Boxcar, *83*	200
___	**1983**	Churchill Downs Reefer, *83*	250
___	**9740**	Chessie System Boxcar, *76*	23

Great Lakes Division: Detroit-Toledo Chapter

___	**8957**	Burlington Northern GP20 Diesel, *80*		230
___	**8958**	Burlington Northern GP20 Diesel Dummy Unit, *80*		150
___	**9119**	Detroit & Mackinac Covered Quad Hopper, *77*	19	22
___	**9272**	New Haven Bay Window Caboose, *79*	19	22
___	**9401**	Great Northern Boxcar, *78*		23
___	**9730**	CP Rail Boxcar, *76*		27
___	**52000**	Detroit-Toledo Division Flatcar with trailer, *92*	70	85

Great Lakes Division: Three Rivers Chapter

___	**9113**	Norfolk & Western Quad Hopper, *76*	27	30

Great Lakes Division: Western Michigan Chapter

___	**9730**	CP Rail Boxcar, *74*	25

Lake & Pines Division

___	**52018**	3-M Boxcar, *93*	450

Lone Star Division

___	**7522**	New Orleans Mint Car with coin, *86*	420
___	**52093**	Lone Star Division Boxcar "6464696," *96*	32
___	**52585**	Texas Special Mint Car, *11*	62
___	**58512**	SP Daylight Mint Car, *12*	65
___	**58552**	Texas Special Mint Car with silver bars, *12*	65

Lone Star Division: North Texas Chapter

		Exc	Mint
9739	D&RGW Boxcar, *76*		20 ____

METCA

		Exc	Mint
10	Jersey Central F3 A Unit, shell only, *71*		25 ____
9272	New Haven Bay Window Caboose, *79*	21	25 ____
9754	New York Central Pacemaker Boxcar, *76*		31 ____
52485	New York Central Mint Car with copper load, *08*		120 ____
52486	Pennsylvania Mint Car, green, *09*		125 ____
52487	Pennsylvania Mint Car, tuscan, *09*		125 ____
52488	NYC Lightning Stripe Mint Car, *10*		60 ____
52574	Fort Knox 50th Anniversary Mint Car, *11*		100 ____
52583	B&O Capitol Dome Mint Car, *11*		100 ____
52596	LIRR Mint Car, *12*		100 ____
58523	Blue Comet Mint Car, *13*		69 ____
58534	Jersey Central Mint Car, *13*		69 ____
58569	Erie Lackawanna Mint Car, *14*		69 ____

Midwest Division

		Exc	Mint
4	C&NW F3 Diesel A Unit, shell only, *77*		80 ____
5	Midwest Division Covered Quad Hopper, *78*		43 ____
1287	C&NW Reefer, *84*		NRS ____
7600	Frisco "Spirit of '76" N5c Caboose "00003," *76*		38 ____
9872	PFE Reefer "00006," *79*		410 ____

Midwest Division: Museum Express

		Exc	Mint
9264	ICG Covered Quad Hopper, *78*	22	26 ____
9289	C&NW N5c Caboose, *80*	37	44 ____
9785	Conrail Boxcar, *77*		35 ____
9786	C&NW Boxcar, *79*		20 ____

NETCA

		Exc	Mint
1203	Boston & Maine NW2 Diesel, shell only, *72*		65 ____
5710	Canadian Pacific Reefer, *82*	38	45 ____
5716	Vermont Central Reefer, *83*	25	30 ____
6124	Delaware & Hudson Covered Quad Hopper, *84*	25	30 ____
8051	Hood's Milk Boxcar, *86*	44	75 ____
9181	Boston & Maine N5c Caboose, *77*	23	35 ____
9400	Conrail Boxcar, tuscan or blue, *78*	23	27 ____
9415	Providence & Worcester Boxcar, *79*	28	34 ____
9423	NYNH&H Boxcar, *80*	25	30 ____
9445	Vermont Northern Boxcar, *81*	29	39 ____
9753	Maine Central Boxcar, *75*	24	34 ____
9768	Boston & Maine Boxcar, *76*	32	39 ____
9785	Conrail Boxcar, *78*	22	26 ____

		Exc	Mint
___ 16911	B&M Flatcar with trailer, *95*		150
___ 22677	B&M Baked Beans Boxcar, *10*		45
___ 52001	B&M Quad Hopper with coal, *92*	50	75
___ 52016	B&M Gondola with coil covers, *93*	55	65
___ 52043	L.L. Bean Boxcar, *94*	110	210
___ 52080	B&M Flatcar "91095" with trailer, *95*		215
___ 52111	Ben & Jerry's Flatcar with trailer, *96*		313
___ 52212	Berkshire Brewing Reefer, *00*		155
___ 52236	Moxie Boxcar, *01*		160
___ 52270	Jenney Manufacturing Tank Car, *02*		150
___ 52306	NH Flatcar with New England Transportation trailer, *03*		150
___ 52352	Poland Spring Boxcar, *04*		131
___ 52379	CP Rail with W.B. Mason trailer, *05*		75
___ 52383	Fisk Tire Boxcar, *05*		108
___ 52397	D&H Flatcar with Vermont Railway trailer, *06*		90
___ 52418	Indian Motocycle Boxcar, *06*		190
___ 52434	New England Central Flatcar with Cabot's trailer, *07*		95
___ 52448	Oilzum Tanker 2-car Set, *08*		105
___ 52457	Cape Cod Potato Chip Boxcar, *07*		93
___ 52484A	Cabot's Reefer, *08*	100	250
___ 52484B	Bay State Beer Reefer, *09*		90
___ 52589	B&M Flatcar with Howard Johnson trailer, *11*		100
___ 58522	Grafton & Upton Flatcar with Spag's trailer, *12*		90

Ozark Division: Gateway Chapter

		Exc	Mint
___ 5700	Oppenheimer Reefer, *81*	55	110
___ 9068	Reading Bobber Caboose, *76*		20
___ 9601	Illinois Central Gulf Hi-Cube Boxcar, *77*		21
___ 9767	Railbox Boxcar, *78*		20
___ 52003	"Meet Me In St. Louis" Flatcar with trailer, *92*		520

Pacific Northwest Division

		Exc	Mint
___ 52077	Great Northern Hi-Cube Boxcar "9695," *95*		460

Rocky Mountain Division

		Exc	Mint
___ 1971-1976	Rocky Mountain Division Reefer, *76*		75

Sacramento Sierra Chapter

		Exc	Mint
___ 6401	Virginian Bay Window Caboose, *84*		35
___ 9301	U.S. Mail Operating Boxcar, *76*	26	38
___ 9414	Cotton Belt Boxcar, *80*		35
___ 9427	Bay Line Boxcar, *81*		30
___ 9444	Louisiana Midland Boxcar, *82*		35
___ 9452	Western Pacific Boxcar, *83*		35

CLUB CARS AND SPECIAL PRODUCTION

		Exc	Mint
9705	D&RGW Boxcar, 75		38 ____
9723	Western Pacific Boxcar, 73		29 ____
9726	Erie-Lackawanna Boxcar, 79		23 ____
9730	CP Rail Boxcar, 77		30 ____
9785	Conrail Boxcar, 78		22 ____

Southern Division

1976	FEC F3 Diesel ABA, shells only, 76		275 ____
1986	Southern Division Bunk Car, 86		30 ____
6111	L&N Covered Quad Hopper, 83	20	22 ____
9287	Southern N5c Caboose, 77	15	22 ____
9352	Trailer Train Flatcar with circus trailers, 80	29	55 ____
9403	Seaboard Coast Line Boxcar, 78		18 ____
9405	Chattahoochie Boxcar, 79		21 ____
9443	Florida East Coast Boxcar, 81		23 ____
9471	ACL Boxcar, 84		23 ____
9482	Norfolk & Southern Boxcar, 85		23 ____
16606	Southern Searchlight Car, 88	17	24 ____
19942	Southern Division 30th Anniversary Boxcar, 96		20 ____

Western Division

52275	Western Pacific Boxcar, 03		105 ____

Toy Train Operating Society

TTOS National Convention Cars

1984	Sacramento Northern Boxcar, 84	65	85 ____
1985	Snowbird Covered Quad Hopper, 85	42	55 ____
6017	SP-type Caboose, blue, 68	125	200 ____
6017	SP-type Caboose, brown, 69	200	300 ____
6057	SP-type Caboose, orange, 69	75	125 ____
6076	Santa Fe Hopper (O27), 70		85 ____
6167-1967	Hopper, olive drab with gold lettering, 67	25	85 ____
6257	SP-type Caboose, red, 69	125	200 ____
6476-1	LV Hopper, gray, 69	45	73 ____
6582	Portland Flatcar with wood, 86	44	55 ____
9326	Burlington Northern Bay Window Caboose, 82		25 ____
9347	Niagara Falls 3-D Tank Car, 79	38	46 ____
9355	Delaware & Hudson Bay Window Caboose, 82		50 ____
9361	C&NW Bay Window Caboose, 82	47	55 ____
9382	Florida East Coast Bay Window Caboose, 82		70 ____
9512	Summerdale Junction Passenger Car, 74	38	53 ____
9520	Phoenix Combination Car, 75	29	33 ____
9526	Snowbird Observation Car, 76	36	51 ____
9535	Columbus Baggage Car, 77	33	51 ____

CLUB CARS AND SPECIAL PRODUCTION

			Exc	Mint
___	9678	Hollywood Hi-Cube Boxcar, 78	25	32
___	9868	Oklahoma City Reefer, 80	36	44
___	9883	Phoenix Reefer, 83		50
___	17871	NYC Flatcar "81487" with Kodak and Xerox trailers, 87	185	217
___	17877	MKT 1-D Tank Car "3739469," 89	55	70
___	17884	Columbus & Dayton Terminal Boxcar (std O), 90	32	41
___	17889	SP Flatcar "15791" (std O) with trailer, 91	43	63
___	19963	Union Equity 3-bay ACF Hopper "86892" (std O), 92	30	38
___	52010	Weyerhaeuser DD Boxcar "838593" (std O), 93	20	40
___	52029	Ford 1-D Tank Car "12" (O27), 94	33	40
___	52030	Ford Gondola "4023," 94	23	29
___	52031	Ford Hopper "1458" (O27), 94	28	33
___	52057	Western Pacific Boxcar "64641995," 95	45	48
___	52087	New Mexico Central Boxcar "64641996," 96		55
___	52114	NYC Flatcar with Gleason and SASIB trailers, 97		58
___	52149	Conrail Flatcar with Blum coal shovel, 98		60
___	52192	SP Crane and Gondola Set, 00		75
___	52193	SP Gondola "6060," 00		50
___	52194	SP Crane Car "7111," 00		35
___	52231	British Columbia 1-D Tank Car, 01		25
___	52288	D&RGW Cookie Boxcar, 03		20
___	52293	D&RGW 1-D Tank Car, 03		40
___	52378	Las Vegas & Tonopah Boxcar, 05		70
___	52410	SP Flatcar with 2 trailers, 06		70
___	52441	Pennsylvania Operating Hopper, 07		60
___	52445	Pennsylvania Boxcar, 07		68
___	52545	Erie "6464" Boxcar, 09		50
___	58333	Sierra Railroad Sierra Beer Boxcar, 13		70

TTOS Division Cars

			Exc	Mint
___	52009	Sacramento Valley Division WP Boxcar, 93	34	44
___	52040	Wolverine Division GTW Flatcar with tractor and trailer, 94	42	51
___	52058	Central California Division Santa Fe Boxcar, 95	32	42
___	52086	Canadian Division Pacific Great Eastern Boxcar, 96		50
___	52113	Northeastern Division Genesee & Wyoming 3-bay Hopper, 97		34
___	52264	New Mexico Division Durango & Silverton Operating Hopper, 02		55

Other TTOS Production

		Exc	Mint	
1983	Phoenix 3-D Tank Car, *83*		100	___
17894	Southern Pacific Tractor, *91*	17	21	___
27148	BNSF "4427" PS2 Hopper, *06*		50	___
52021	Weyerhaeuser Tractor and Trailer, *93*	24	31	___
52022	Union Pacific Boxcar, *93*		400	___
52032	Ford 1-D Tank Car (O27) with Kughn inscription, *94*	70	95	___
52046	ACL Boxcar "16247," *94*		110	___
52053	Carail Boxcar, *94*	50	55	___
52068	Toy Train Parade Contadina Boxcar "16245," *94*		55	___
52078	Southern Pacific SD9 Diesel "5366," *96*		235	___
52079	Southern Pacific Bay Window Caboose, *96*	45	55	___
52084	Union Pacific I-Beam Flatcar "16380" with load, *95*		155	___
52384	Transparent Damage Control Boxcar, *03*		71	___
52451	Pennsylvania "X2454" Boxcar, *07*		175	___
52505	Forest Service/Smokey Bear Flatcar with airplane, *08*		45	___
52525	SP "X6454" Boxcar, *08*		45	___
52526	SP "X6454" Boxcar, *08*		90	___
52547	C&NW Reefer, *09*		84	___

TTOS Southwestern Division

		Exc	Mint	
19962	Southern Pacific 3-bay ACF Hopper "496035" (std O), *92*	50	65	___
52047	Cotton Belt Wood-sided Caboose (std O), smoke, *93–94*	60	68	___
52073	Pacific Fruit Express Reefer "459402" (std O), *95*		65	___
52098	National Bureau of Standards Boxcar (std O), *96*		47	___
52121	Mobilgas Tank Car "238" (std O), *97*		75	___
52154	Pacific Fruit Express Reefer "459403" (std O), *98*		53	___
52205	SP Overnight Merchandise Service Boxcar 5-pack, *00*		185	___
52287	Operating MX Missile Car, *02*		55	___
52385	Ward Kimball Boxcar, *05*		55	___
52431	Operating MX Missile Car, *06*		60	___
52476	Life Savers Tank Car, *07*		85	___
52515	Life Savers Wild Cherry Tank Car, *08*		77	___
52565	Life Savers Pep O Mint Tank Car, *09*		60	___
52569	Life Savers Butter Rum Tank Car, *10*		62	___
52591	Life Savers Wint O Green Tank Car, *11*		62	___
58548	Life Savers Bay Window Caboose, *13*		82	___

Virginia Train Collectors

			Exc	Mint
____	**7679**	Boxcar, *79*		17
____	**7681**	N5c Caboose, *81*		23
____	**7682**	Covered Quad Hopper, *82*		26
____	**7683**	Virginia Fruit Express Reefer, *83*		26
____	**7684**	Vitraco 3-D Tank Car, *84*		26
____	**7685**	Boxcar, *85*		27
____	**7686**	GP7 Diesel, *86*		100
____	**7692-1**	Baggage Car (027), *92*	35	45
____	**7692-2**	Combination Car (027), *92*	35	45
____	**7692-3**	Dining Car (027), *92*	35	45
____	**7692-4**	Passenger Car (027), *92*	35	45
____	**7692-5**	Vista Dome Car (027), *92*	35	45
____	**7692-6**	Passenger Car (027), *92*	35	45
____	**7692-7**	Observation Car (027), *92*	35	45
____	**7696**	20th Anniversary Station, *96*		65
____	**52060**	Tender "7694" with whistle, *94*		70

For more information on determining the condition of a box and a description of box types, see pages 8 and 9.

		Good (P-5)	Exc (P-7)
022	Switch Controller		8 ____
022	Remote Control Switches, pair (with both inserts)	7	27 ____
022	Remote Control Switches, pair (yellow, with both inserts)	10	38 ____
022A	Remote Control Switches, pair (with both inserts)	12	41 ____
025	Bumper	5	10 ____
026	Bumper	3	10 ____
30	Water Tower	18	65 ____
35	Boulevard Lamp		
38	Operating Water Tower	24	100 ____
40	Hookup Wire, 8 reels (dealer box)	33	145 ____
41	U.S. Army Switcher	10	50 ____
42	Picatinny Arsenal Switcher	25	67 ____
44	U.S. Army Mobile Launcher	30	98 ____
45	U.S. Marines Mobile Launcher	45	120 ____
45/45N	Automatic Gateman	7	27 ____
48	Super O Insulated Straight Track, 6 pieces (dealer box)	15	46 ____
49	Super O Insulated Curved Track, 6 pieces (dealer box)	15	55 ____
50	Section Gang Car (early classic)	5	57 ____
50	Section Gang Car (brown corrugated)	5	27 ____
50	Section Gang Car (orange picture)	20	45 ____
51	Navy Yard Switcher	23	79 ____
52	Fire Car	25	97 ____
53	Rio Grande Snowplow	30	86 ____
54	Ballast Tamper	15	46 ____
55	PRR Tie-Jector Car	15	50 ____
56	Lamp Post	2	10 ____
56	M&StL Mine Transport	30	119 ____
57	AEC Switcher	38	220 ____
58	Lamp Post	4	13 ____
58	Great Northern Rotary Snow Blower	51	175 ____
59	Minuteman Switcher	90	277 ____
60	Lionelville Rapid Transit Trolley (classic)	8	33 ____
60	Lionelville Rapid Transit Trolley (brown corrugated)	15	50 ____
64	Street Lamp	2	10 ____
65	Handcar	5	75 ____
68	Executive Inspection Car	10	134 ____
69	Maintenance Car	18	83 ____
70	Yard Light	2	10 ____
71	Lamp Post	2	5 ____

BOXES

		Good (P-5)	Exc (P-7)
75	Goose Neck Lamps	3	15
76	Boulevard Street Lamps	5	40
76	Boulevard Street Lamps (Hillside Checkerboard)	10	70
89	Flagpole	7	29
93	Water Tower	15	30
97	Coal Elevator	17	54
108	Trestle Set (ovestamped)	10	50
110	Graduated Trestle Set	1	11
111	Elevated Trestle Set	1	5
112	Remote Control Switches, pair (Super O)	10	25
112LH	Remote Control Super O Switch, left-hand	10	31
112RH	Remote Control Super O Switch, right-hand	10	31
114	Newsstand with horn	8	34
115	Passenger Station ("113-1, Star Corp." stamped on box)	25	140
118	Newsstand with whistle	10	42
123	Lamp Assortment	10	100
125	Whistle Shack	5	20
128	Animated Newsstand	17	40
132	Passenger Station	11	51
133	Passenger Station	10	35
138	Water Tower	5	30
140	Automatic Banjo Signal (classic)	3	18
142	Manual Switches, pair (Super O)	4	20
145	Automatic Gateman (brown corrugated)	5	22
145	Automatic Gateman (cellophane), *66*	12	62
148	Dwarf Trackside Signal	5	25
150	Telegraph Pole Set	4	20
151	Automatic Semaphore	4	14
151	Automatic Semaphore (narrower box, earlier postwar)	35	75
151	Automatic Semaphore (blister pack enclosure)	20	75
152	Automatic Crossing Gate	3	13
153	Automatic Block Control Signal	9	28
154	Automatic Highway Signal (cellophane)	5	25
154	Automatic Highway Signal (all other boxes)	3	12
155	Blinking Light Signal	5	35
156	Station Platform	19	60
157	Station Platform	9	39
160	Unloading Bin	22	119
161	Mail Pickup Set, with liner	10	45
163	Single Target Block Signal (white box)	20	65
164	Log Loader	30	69
175	Rocket Launcher	12	65
175-50	Dealer Display Box, 6 rockets	75	421
182	Magnetic Crane	19	78
192	Operating Control Tower	26	154
193	Industrial Water Tower	9	45
195	Floodlight Tower	5	25
195-75	Floodlight Extension, 8-bulb (classic)	4	54
195-75	Floodlight Extension, 8-bulb (white box)	5	59

BOXES

		Good (P-5)	Exc (P-7)
197	Rotating Radar Antenna	8	48 ___
197-15	Separate Sale Radar Head	30	115 ___
199	Microwave Relay Tower	5	30 ___
202	UP Alco Diesel A Unit	11	55 ___
204	Santa Fe Alco AA Set (master carton)	50	215 ___
204	Santa Fe Alco AA Set (P and T boxes)	19	93 ___
204T	Santa Fe Diesel Dummy A Unit		55 ___
208	Santa Fe Alco AA Set (master carton)	45	310 ___
208	Santa Fe Alco AA Set (P and T boxes)	22	99 ___
209	New Haven Alco AA Set (P and T boxes)	50	284 ___
209T	New Haven Diesel Dummy A Unit		160 ___
210	Texas Special Alco AA Set (P and T boxes)	9	50 ___
211	Texas Special Alco AA Set (P and T boxes)	28	248 ___
212	USMC Alco Diesel A Unit	43	110 ___
212T	USMC Diesel Dummy A Unit	171	459 ___
214	Plate Girder Bridge (classic)	2	14 ___
214	Plate Girder Bridge (Hillside orange picture)	9	34 ___
216	Burlington Alco Diesel A Unit	15	60 ___
217	B&M Alco AB Set (C and P boxes)	32	200 ___
217-16	Sleeve for 217 and 218 outer boxes		60 ___
218	Santa Fe Alco AA Set (master carton)	19	101 ___
218P	Santa Fe Alco Diesel A Unit	8	53 ___
218T	Santa Fe Diesel Dummy A Unit		40 ___
220	Santa Fe Alco AA Set (P and T boxes)	17	103 ___
221	2-6-4 Locomotive	12	60 ___
221T	Tender	5	20 ___
221W	Whistling Tender	7	35 ___
223P	Santa Fe Alco A Unit	15	60 ___
224	2-6-2 Locomotive	17	52 ___
224	U.S. Navy Alco AB Set (C and P boxes)	23	175 ___
225	C & O Alco Diesel A Unit	12	60 ___
226	B&M Alco Diesel AB Set (C and P boxes)	24	100 ___
226P	B&M Alco Diesel A Unit		60 ___
228P	CN Alco Diesel A Unit	20	65 ___
229C	M&StL Alco B Unit	8	35 ___
229P	M&StL Alco A Unit (brown corrugated)	8	50 ___
230P	C&O Alco A Unit	14	64 ___
231P	Rock Island Alco A Unit	8	51 ___
233	2-4-2 Scout Locomotive	10	45 ___
235	2-4-2 Scout Locomotive	20	78 ___
237	2-4-2 Scout Locomotive	10	39 ___
243	2-4-2 Scout Locomotive	10	33 ___
243W	Tender	5	20 ___
244T	Tender (overstamped 1625T box)	25	90 ___
245	2-4-2 Scout Locomotive	15	75 ___
246	2-4-2 Scout Locomotive		45 ___
247	2-4-2 Scout Locomotive	10	33 ___
247T	Tender	5	20 ___
248	2-4-2 Scout Locomotive	5	35 ___
250	2-4-2 Scout Locomotive	10	30 ___
250T	Tender	7	28 ___

BOXES

		Good (P-5)	Exc (P-7)
____ 252	Crossing Gate	3	10
____ 253	Block Control Signal	3	15
____ 256	Illuminated Freight Station	9	25
____ 257	Freight Station with diesel horn	10	30
____ 260	Bumper (Hagerstown checkerboard)	7	28
____ 260	Bumper (all other boxes)	4	10
____ 262	Highway Crossing Gate	4	
____ 264	Operating Forklift Platform	34	77
____ 282	Gantry Crane	20	65
____ 299	Code Transmitter Beacon Set	10	50
____ 308	Railroad Sign Set	2	15
____ 309	Yard Sign Set	2	10
____ 310	Billboard Set	1	10
____ 313	Bascule Bridge	40	140
____ 314	Scale Model Girder Bridge	3	15
____ 315	Trestle Bridge	35	140
____ 316	Trestle Bridge	5	15
____ 317	Trestle Bridge	8	33
____ 321	Trestle Bridge	5	15
____ 321-100	Trestle Bridge	5	20
____ 332	Arch-Under Trestle Bridge	3	23
____ 334	Operating Dispatching Board	10	45
____ 342	Culvert Loader	15	58
____ 345	Culvert Unoader	15	68
____ 350	Engine Transfer Table	8	56
____ 350-50	Transfer Table Extension	10	52
____ 352	Ice Depot	27	62
____ 353	Trackside Control Signal	3	15
____ 356	Operating Freight Station	8	28
____ 356-35	Baggage Trucks Set	20	100
____ 362	Barrel Loader	5	23
____ 362-78	Wooden Barrels		12
____ 364	Conveyor Lumber Loader	7	26
____ 365	Dispatching Station	15	53
____ 394	Rotary Beacon	5	30
____ 394-37	Rotating Beacon Cap		10
____ 395	Floodlight Tower	8	30
____ 397	Operating Coal Loader	7	22
____ 397	Operating Coal Loader (separate label on box)	10	30
____ 400	B&O Passenger Rail Diesel Car	25	60
____ 404	B&O Baggage-Mail Rail Diesel Car	30	110
____ 410	Billboard Blinker	2	10
____ 413	Countdown Control Panel	4	20
____ 415	Diesel Fueling Station	12	46
____ 419	Heliport Control Tower	19	125
____ 445	Switch Tower	6	21
____ 448	Missile Firing Range Set	15	80
____ 450	Operating Signal Bridge	2	10
____ 452	Overhead Gantry Signal	5	25
____ 455	Operating Oil Derrick	17	78
____ 456	Coal Ramp	10	42

BOXES

		Good (P-5)	Exc (P-7)
460	Piggyback Transportation Set	12	40 ____
460-150	Two Trailers	70	207 ____
461	Platform with truck and trailer	10	50 ____
462	Derrick Platform Set	60	200 ____
464	Lumber Mill	5	30 ____
465	Sound Dispatching Station	13	32 ____
470	Missile Launching Platform		15 ____
494	Rotary Beacon	5	25 ____
497	Coaling Station		58 ____
600	MKT NW2 Switcher	22	120 ____
601	Seaboard NW2 Switcher	25	91 ____
602	Seaboard NW2 Switcher	26	97 ____
610	Erie NW2 Switcher	15	113 ____
611	Jersey Central NW2 Switcher (overstamped 621 box)		140 ____
613	UP NW2 Switcher	22	129 ____
614	Alaska NW2 Switcher	27	128 ____
616	Santa Fe NW2 Switcher	25	95 ____
617	Santa Fe NW2 Switcher	30	130 ____
621	Jersey Central NW2 Switcher	23	80 ____
622	Santa Fe NW2 Switcher	33	120 ____
623	Santa Fe NW2 Switcher	18	64 ____
624	C&O NW2 Switcher	25	74 ____
626	B&O GE 44-ton Switcher	33	169 ____
628	Northern Pacific GE 44-ton Switcher	20	103 ____
629	Burlington GE 44-ton Switcher	28	181 ____
634	Santa Fe NW2 Switcher	33	152 ____
637	2-6-4 Locomotive	14	62 ____
637LTS	2-6-4 Locomotive and Tender (master carton)	40	180 ____
646	4-6-4 Locomotive	27	60 ____
665	4-6-4 Locomotive	17	57 ____
671	6-8-6 Steam Turbine Locomotive	27	76 ____
671R	6-8-6 Steam Turbine Locomotive		110 ____
671W	Whistle Tender	25	____
675	2-6-2 Locomotive, *47–49*	20	88 ____
681	6-8-6 Steam Turbine Locomotive	25	104 ____
682	6-8-6 Steam Turbine Locomotive	34	164 ____
685	4-6-4 Hudson Locomotive	22	74 ____
726	2-8-4 Berkshire Locomotive, *46*	87	198 ____
726	2-8-4 Berkshire Locomotive	50	105 ____
726RR	2-8-4 Berkshire Locomotive	26	77 ____
736	2-8-4 Berkshire Locomotive, *50*	53	123 ____
736	2-8-4 Berkshire Locomotive	25	66 ____
736LTS	2-8-4 Berkshire Locomotive and Tender (master carton)		178 ____
736W	Pennsylvania Tender	10	45 ____
746	N&W 4-8-4 Locomotive	63	170 ____
746LTS	N&W 4-8-4 Locomotive and Tender (master carton)	70	350 ____
746W	N&W Whistle Tender	30	110 ____
760	Curved Track	4	15 ____
773	4-6-4 Hudson Locomotive, *50*	53	287 ____

BOXES

			Good (P-5)	Exc (P-7)
____	**773**	4-6-4 Hudson Locomotive, *64–66*	58	179
	773LTS	4-6-4 Hudson Locomotive and Tender (master carton), *50*		
____			100	500
	773LTS	4-6-4 Hudson and Whistle Tender (master carton), *64–66*		
____			40	258
____	**773W**	NYC Tender	13	89
____	**810**	Milwaukee Road Freight Set	73	850
____	**920-2**	Tunnel Portals	7	15
____	**927**	Lubricating Kit	1	10
____	**928**	Maintenance and Lubricating Kit	5	20
____	**943**	Ammo Dump	2	10
____	**953**	Figure Set	10	50
____	**957**	Figure Set	10	55
____	**959**	Barn Set	7	52
____	**969**	Construction Set	5	45
____	**970**	Ticket Booth	7	35
____	**981**	Freight Yard Set	12	35
____	**984**	Railroad Set	10	75
____	**986**	Farm Set	18	110
____	**1001**	Diesel Freight Set		65
____	**1001**	2-4-2 Scout Locomotive	8	65
____	**1001T**	Tender	7	13
____	**1002**	Gondola	2	10
____	**X1004**	PRR Baby Ruth Boxcar	2	10
____	**1005**	Sunoco 1-D Tank Car	2	10
____	**1007**	Sunoco 1-D Tank Car	2	10
____	**1025**	Illuminated Bumper (O27)	3	10
____	**1032**	Transformer, 75 watts	2	10
____	**1033**	Transformer, 90 watts	5	16
____	**1034**	Transformer, 75 watts	2	10
____	**1043-500**	Transformer, 90 watts, ivory	15	75
____	**1044**	Transformer, 90 watts	2	10
____	**1045**	Operating Watchman	5	20
____	**1047**	Operating Switchman	23	105
____	**1060**	2-4-2 Locomotive (brown corrugated)	25	133
____	**1110**	2-4-2 Locomotive	5	20
____	**1112**	Scout Set	8	25
____	**1120**	2-4-2 Scout Locomotive	5	20
____	**1121**	O27 Remote Control Switches, pair	2	10
____	**1121LH**	O27 Remote Control Switch, left-hand	8	35
____	**1121RH**	O27 Remote Control Switch, right-hand	8	35
____	**1122**	O27 Remote Control Switches, pair	5	15
____	**1130**	2-4-2 Locomotive	6	25
____	**1130T**	Tender	3	13
____	**1130T-500**	Tender, pink, from Girls Set	18	180
____	**1232**	Transformer, 75 watts, made for export	4	20
____	**1407B**	Steam Switcher Work Set	40	360
____	**1417WS**	Steam Work Train Set		135
____	**1425B**	Steam Switcher Freight Set		190
____	**1432W**	O27 Steam Passenger Set		215
____	**1447WS**	Turbine Locomotive Set	30	150

BOXES

		Good (P-5)	Exc (P-7)
1453WS	O27 Steam Freight Set		90 ___
1457B	Santa Fe Freight Set (marked "1457"), *49*	100	200 ___
1457B	Santa Fe Freight Set , *50*		225 ___
1464W	Union Pacific Diesel Passenger Set		254 ___
1465	Steam Freight Set		63 ___
1467W	Union Pacific Freight Set	36	123 ___
1469WS	Steam Freight Set		50 ___
1471	Steam Freight Set		75 ___
1471WS	Steam Freight Set		55 ___
1479WS	Steam Freight Set	10	35 ___
1481WS	Steam Freight Set		80 ___
1483WS	Steam Freight Set	35	___
1485	Steam Freight Set		65 ___
1500	Steam Freight Set	20	___
1502WS	Steam Freight Set		600 ___
1503WS	Steam Freight Set	15	52 ___
1505WS	Steam Freight Set		90 ___
1507WS	Steam Freight Set		100 ___
1515WS	Steam Freight Set		100 ___
1517W	Texas Special Freight Set		105 ___
1519WS	Steam Freight Set		170 ___
1520W	Texas Special Passenger Set		675 ___
1521WS	Steam Work Train Set		380 ___
1525	Diesel Freight Set		80 ___
1529	Pennsylvania Diesel Freight Set		250 ___
1531W	Diesel Freight Set		90 ___
1533WS	Steam Freight Set	55	___
1534W	Burlington Diesel Passenger Set		421 ___
1537WS	Steam Freight Set	35	___
1538WS	Hudson Passenger Set	150	700 ___
1539W	Santa Fe Diesel Freight Set		250 ___
1542	Electric Freight Set	10	38 ___
1543	Lehigh Valley Freight Set		30 ___
1551W	Diesel Freight Set		55 ___
1557	Diesel Freight Set		88 ___
1559W	MILW Diesel Freight Set		90 ___
1569	UP Diesel Freight Set	35	___
1578S	Steam Passenger Set		500 ___
1581	Jersey Central Mixed Set		75 ___
1583WS	Steam Freight Set	25	70 ___
1587S	Girls Train Set	271	1151 ___
1590	Steam Freight Set	40	___
1591	USMC Military Set	83	724 ___
1599W	Texas Special Freight Set	47	129 ___
1600	Diesel Passenger Set		595 ___
1601W	Wabash GP7 Diesel Set	43	180 ___
1607WS	Steam Work Train Set	25	___
1608W	New Haven Passenger Set	80	676 ___
1615	B&M Diesel Freight Set		45 ___
1615	0-4-0 Locomotive	15	50 ___
1615LT	0-4-0 Locomotive and Tender (master carton)	25	98 ___

BOXES

			Good (P-5)	Exc (P-7)
____	1615T	Tender	7	58
____	1619W	Santa Fe Diesel Freight Set	40	125
____	1623W	NP Diesel Freight Set		165
____	1625	0-4-0 Locomotive	20	85
____	1625T	Tender	13	109
____	1625WS	Steam Freight Set	25	140
____	1633	U.S. Navy Diesel Freight Set		310
____	1648	Steam Freight Set		20
____	1650	Steam Military Set		100
____	1654	2-4-2 Locomotive	5	30
____	1655	2-4-2 Locomotive	10	50
____	1656	0-4-0 Locomotive	23	115
____	1656LTS	4-4-0 Locomotive and Tender (master carton)		225
____	1665	0-4-0 Locomotive	25	125
____	1666	2-6-2 Locomotive	10	50
____	1682T	Tender	10	
____	1800	General Gift Pack	13	110
____	1809	Western Gift Pack	8	60
____	1862	4-4-0 Civil War General Locomotive	30	100
____	1862T	Tender	15	60
____	1865	Western & Atlantic Coach	5	30
____	1866	Western & Atlantic Mail-Baggage Car	10	40
____	1872	4-4-0 Civil War General Locomotive	30	100
____	1872LTS	4-4-0 Locomotive and Tender (master carton)		400
____	1872T	Tender	5	38
____	1875	Western & Atlantic Coach	38	163
____	1875W	Western & Atlantic Coach, whistle	15	75
____	1876	Western & Atlantic Baggage Car	13	50
____	1877	Flatcar with fence and horses	5	48
____	2001	Track Make-up Kit (O27)		2000
____	2002	Track Make-up Kit (O27)		1800
____	2016	2-6-4 Locomotive	3	30
____	2018	2-6-4 Locomotive	6	33
____	2020	6-8-6 Steam Turbine Locomotive	22	72
____	2020W	Tender	11	38
____	2023	Union Pacific Alco AA Set (master carton)	38	89
____	2025	2-6-2 or 2-6-4 Locomotive	10	40
____	2026	2-6-2 or 2-6-4 Locomotive	10	40
____	2028	Pennsylvania GP7 Diesel	30	88
____	2029	2-6-4 Locomotive	12	53
____	2031	Rock Island Alco AA Set (master carton)	50	131
____	2032	Erie Alco AA Set (master carton)	24	83
____	2033	Uinion Pacific Alco AA Set (master carton)	25	80
____	2034	2-4-2 Scout Locomotive	6	66
____	2035	2-6-4 Locomotive	17	85
____	2036	2-6-4 Locomotive	9	58
____	2036LTS	2-6-4 Locomotive and Tender (master carton)		950
____	2037	2-6-4 Locomotive (brown corrugated)	6	29
____	2037-500	2-6-4 Locomotive, pink, from Girls Set	54	250
____	2046	4-6-4 Locomotive	23	60
____	2046T	Lionel Lines Tender, for export	25	88

BOXES

		Good (P-5)	Exc (P-7)
2046W	Lionel Lines Tender (early classic, with liner)	15	56 ____
2046W	Lionel Lines Tender (marked "2046")	13	128 ____
2046W-50	Pennsylvania Tender	7	43 ____
2055	4-6-4 Locomotive	10	67 ____
2055LTS	4-6-4 Locomotive and Tender (master carton)		255 ____
2056	4-6-4 Locomotive	15	50 ____
2065	4-6-4 Locomotive	13	65 ____
2113WS	Steam Freight Set	13	213 ____
2124W	GG1 Passenger Set	73	1570 ____
2126WS	Steam Turbine Passenger Set	60	968 ____
2139	GG1 Freight Set	60	1023 ____
2140WS	Steam Turbine Passenger Set	60	848 ____
2148WS	Hudson Passenger Set	132	2025 ____
2151W	F3 Freight Set		280 ____
2155WS	Berkshire Freight Set		75 ____
2159W	GG1 Freight Set	193	650 ____
2161W	Santa Fe Twin Diesel Freight Set	54	160 ____
2175W	Santa Fe Diesel Freight Set	35	118 ____
2177WS	Steam Freight Set		35 ____
2187WS	Steam Freight Set	30	____
2191W	Santa Fe Diesel Freight Set	35	150 ____
2193W	NYC Diesel Freight Set		90 ____
2201WS	Steam Freight Set	45	____
2203WS	Steam Freight Set		330 ____
2207W	Santa Fe Diesel Freight Set	38	145 ____
2209W	NYC Diesel Freight Set	40	____
2213WS	Steam Freight Set	35	____
2217WS	Steam Turbine Freight Set		200 ____
2217WS	Diesel Freight Set		425 ____
2222WS	Hudson Passenger Set	38	744 ____
2223W	Lackawanna FM Freight Set	315	588 ____
2227W	Santa Fe Diesel Freight Set		328 ____
2234W	Santa Fe Passenger Set	67	365 ____
2235W	Milwaukee Road Diesel Freight Set		175 ____
2239W	Illinois Central Freight Set	150	350 ____
2240	Wabash F3 AB Set (C and P boxes)		310 ____
2240	Wabash F3 AB Set (master carton)		850 ____
2240P	Wabash F3 A Unit	51	80 ____
2242	New Haven F3 AB Set (C and P boxes)	30	575 ____
2243	Santa Fe F3 AB Set (C and P boxes)	13	105 ____
2243	Santa Fe F3 AB Set (master carton)	30	130 ____
2243P	Santa Fe F3 A Unit	35	____
2244W	Wabash Passenger Set		1180 ____
2245	Texas Special F3 AB Set (C and P boxes)	25	275 ____
2245C	Texas Special F3 B Unit		135 ____
2254W	Pennsylvania GG1 Passenger Set, 55	38	1238 ____
2255W	Diesel Work Train Set	38	____
2257	SP-type Caboose	4	17 ____
2257WS	Steam Freight Set		85 ____
2259W	New Haven Electric Freight Set		195 ____
2263W	New Haven Freight Set		250 ____

BOXES		Good (P-5)	Exc (P-7)
____ **2265WS**	Steam Freight Set	27	140
____ **2267W**	Diesel Freight Set		250
____ **2269W**	B&O Diesel Freight Set	28	712
____ **2270W**	Jersey Central Passenger Set	83	985
____ **2271W**	Pennsylvania GG1 Freight Set	23	385
____ **2273W**	Milwaukee Road Diesel Freight Set	23	795
____ **2276W**	Budd Passenger Set	20	350
____ **2277WS**	Work Train Set		100
____ **2283W**	Steam Freight Set		125
____ **2289WS**	Berkshire Super O Freight Set	28	218
____ **2291W**	Rio Grande Diesel Freight Set	213	503
____ **2292WS**	Steam Passenger Set	83	915
____ **2293W**	Pennsylvania GG1 Freight Set	167	1035
____ **2295WS**	N&W Steam Freight Set	154	1038
____ **2296W**	Canadian Pacific Passenger Set	300	1548
____ **2297WS**	N&W Steam Freight Set	88	575
____ **2321**	Lackawanna FM Train Master Diesel	31	95
____ **2322**	Virginian FM Train Master Diesel		120
____ **2328**	Burlington GP7 Diesel	38	69
____ **2329**	Virginian Electric Locomotive	23	215
____ **2330**	Pennsylvania GG1 Electric Locomotive	48	293
____ **2331**	Virginian FM Train Master Diesel	25	116
____ **2332**	Pennsylvania GG1 Electric Locomotive	42	105
____ **2332-275**	Pennsylvania GG1 Electric Locomotive		270
____ **2333**	NYC F3 AA Set (P and T boxes)	35	205
____ **2333**	Santa Fe F3 AA Set (master carton)	40	170
____ **2337**	Wabash GP7 Diesel, 58	15	242
____ **2338**	MILW GP7 Diesel (classic)	13	72
____ **2338**	MILW GP7 Diesel (brown corrugated)	10	59
____ **2338**	MILW GP7 Diesel (brown corrugated marked "2338X")	33	120
____ **2339**	Wabash GP7 Diesel, *57*		135
____ **2340-10**	Pennsylvania GG1 Electric, tuscan	70	230
____ **2340-25**	Pennsylvania GG1 Electric, green, gold stripes		125
____ **2340-27**	Pennsylvania GG1 Electric, green, green stripes		160
____ **2341**	Jersey Central FM Train Master Diesel	113	938
____ **2343**	Santa Fe F3 AA Set (master carton)	53	123
____ **2343**	Santa Fe F3 AA Set (P and T boxes)	40	174
____ **2343C**	Santa Fe F3 B Unit	20	62
____ **2343P**	Santa Fe F3 A Unit	18	62
____ **2344**	NYC F3 AA Set (P and T boxes)	60	210
____ **2344C**	NYC F3 B Unit	20	75
____ **2344P**	NYC F3 A Unit	48	333
____ **2344T**	NYC F3 Dummy Unit	33	93
____ **2345**	Western Pacific F3 AA Set (brown corrugated)		170
____ **2346**	B&M GP9 Diesel		163
____ **2348**	M&StL GP9 Diesel	26	114
____ **2349**	Northern Pacific GP9 Diesel	57	167
____ **2349-12**	Sleeve for 2349 and 2359 outer boxes	15	138
____ **2350**	New Haven EP-5 Electric Locomotive	16	132
____ **2351**	Milwaukee Road EP-5 Electric Locomotive	13	173

BOXES

		Good (P-5)	Exc (P-7)
2352	Pennsylvania EP-5 Electric Locomotive	28	228 ____
2353	Santa Fe F3 AA Set (master carton)	82	250 ____
2353	Santa Fe F3 AA Set (P and T boxes)	40	125 ____
2354	NYC F3 AA Set (master carton)		175 ____
2354P	NYC F3 A Unit (brown corrugated)	80	170 ____
2355	Western Pacific F3 AA Set (P and T boxes)	55	375 ____
2356	Southern F3 AA Set (master carton)		400 ____
2356C	Southern F3 B Unit	33	316 ____
2356P	Southern F3 A Unit	28	125 ____
2356T	Southern F3 Dummy Unit	23	285 ____
2357	SP-type Caboose	4	13 ____
2358	Great Northern EP-5 Electric Locomotive	65	285 ____
2359	Boston & Maine GP9 Diesel		114 ____
2360-10	Pennsylvania GG1 Electric Locomotive, tuscan	33	234 ____
2360-25	Pennsylvania GG1 Electric Locomotive, green	24	195 ____
2363	Illinois Central F3 AB Set (C and P boxes)	130	376 ____
2363P	Illinois Central F3 A Unit		130 ____
2365	C&O GP7 Diesel	15	60 ____
2367C	Wabash F3 B Unit	18	226 ____
2367P	Wabash F3 A Unit	13	129 ____
2368	B&O F3 AB Set (master carton)	200	900 ____
2368C	B&O F3 B Unit	50	408 ____
2368P	B&O F3 A Unit	28	155 ____
2373	CP F3 AA Set (C and P boxes)	113	555 ____
2378	Milwaukee Road F3 AB Set (master carton)	178	888 ____
2378C	Milwaukee Road F3 B Unit	95	283 ____
2378P	Milwaukee Road F3 A Unit	90	246 ____
2379C	Rio Grande F3 B Unit	70	220 ____
2379P	Rio Grande F3 A Unit	93	204 ____
2383P	Santa Fe F3 Powered Unit	14	92 ____
2383T	Santa Fe F3 Dummy Unit	24	108 ____
2400	Maplewood Pullman Car	13	40 ____
2401	Hillside Observation Car	10	43 ____
2401	Hillside Observation Car	10	40 ____
2402	Chatham Pullman Car	10	40 ____
2403B	Tender with bell	17	75 ____
2404	Santa Fe Vista Dome Car	24	59 ____
2405	Santa Fe Pullman Car	21	61 ____
2406	Santa Fe Observation Car	18	50 ____
2408	Santa Fe Vista Dome Car	15	48 ____
2409	Santa Fe Pullman Car	13	48 ____
2410	Santa Fe Observation Car	13	45 ____
2411	Lionel Lines Flatcar	13	45 ____
2412	Santa Fe Vista Dome Car	10	40 ____
2414	Santa Fe Pullman Car	10	40 ____
2416	Santa Fe Observation Car	10	40 ____
2419	DL&W Work Caboose	9	53 ____
2420	DL&W Work Caboose with searchlight	17	80 ____
2421	Maplewood Pullman Car	10	36 ____
2422	Chatham Pullman Car	19	38 ____
2423	Hillside Observation Car	14	25 ____

BOXES

			Good (P-5)	Exc (P-7)
____	2426W	Hudson Tender (early classic)	40	245
____	2426W	Hudson Tender (middle classic)	51	225
____	2429	Livingston Pullman Car	10	53
____	2430	Pullman Car, blue	8	38
____	2431	Observation Car, blue	8	38
____	2432	Clifton Vista Dome Car	13	35
____	2434	Newark Pullman Car	10	35
____	2435	Elizabeth Pullman Car	10	55
____	2436	Mooseheart Observation Car	10	35
____	2440	Pullman Car, green	5	30
____	2441	Observation Car, green	5	30
____	2442	Pullman Car, brown	5	30
____	2442	Clifton Vista Dome Car	15	48
____	2443	Observation Car, brown	8	30
____	2444	Newark Pullman Car	15	52
____	2445	Elizabeth Pullman Car	25	118
____	2446	Summit Observation Car	15	52
____	2452	Pennsylvania Gondola	5	23
____	2452X	Pennsylvania Gondola	6	18
____	X2454	Pennsylvania Boxcar (marked "Box Car")	8	30
____	X2454	Pennsylvania Boxcar (marked "Merchandise Car")	17	49
____	2456	Lehigh Valley Hopper	10	34
____	2457	Pennsylvania N5-type Caboose	7	29
____	X2458	Pennsylvania Automobile Boxcar	5	30
____	2460	Bucyrus Erie Crane Car (box with toy logo)	10	65
____	2460	Bucyrus Erie Crane Car (box without toy logo)	15	64
____	2461	Transformer Car	15	60
____	2465	Sunoco 2-D Tank Car	5	15
____	2466T	Tender	5	15
____	2466W	Tender	13	37
____	2466WX	Tender	5	43
____	2472	PRR N5-type Caboose	2	12
____	2481	Plainfield Pullman Car	30	114
____	2482	Westfield Pullman Car	30	114
____	2483	Livingston Observation Car	30	114
____	2501W	M&StL Diesel Freight Set	18	220
____	2507W	New Haven Diesel Freight Set	28	541
____	2509WS	Super O Steam Freight Set	18	238
____	2511W	Pennsylvania Electric Work Set	70	323
____	2513W	Virginian Rectifier Set	18	413
____	2518W	Pennsylvania Electric Passenger Set	83	1023
____	2519W	Virginian Train Master Super O Freight Set	28	383
____	2521	President McKinley Observation Car	10	60
____	2522	President Harrison Vista Dome Car	22	75
____	2523	President Garfield Pullman Car	24	75
____	2523W	Santa Fe Super O Freight Set	18	290
____	2526W	Santa Fe Passenger Set	33	667
____	2527	Missile Launcher Set, yellow		100
____	2528	Super O General Set	38	
____	2530	REA Baggage Car	8	70

BOXES

		Good (P-5)	Exc (P-7)	
2530	REA Baggage Car (orange perforated)	155	475	____
2531	Silver Dawn Observation Car	18	59	____
2532	Silver Range Vista Dome Car	5	50	____
2533	Silver Cloud Pullman Car	24	92	____
2534	Silver Bluff Pullman Car	17	53	____
2537W	New Haven Freight Set	23	535	____
2541	Alexander Hamilton Observation Car	9	79	____
2541W	Santa Fe Super O Freight Set		650	____
2542	Betsy Ross Vista Dome Car	14	80	____
2543	William Penn Pullman Car	14	80	____
2543WS	Berkshire Freight Set	23	250	____
2544	Molly Pitcher Pullman Car	30	79	____
2544W	Santa Fe Passenger Set	73	1108	____
2550	B&O Baggage-Mail Rail Diesel Car	55	205	____
2551	Banff Park Observation Car	28	119	____
2551W	GN Electric Set	120	400	____
2552	Skyline 500 Vista Dome Car	33	127	____
2553	Blair Manor Pullman Car	64	198	____
2553WS	Berkshire Freight Set	99	273	____
2554	Craig Manor Pullman Car	78	196	____
2555	Sunoco 1-D Tank Car	8	40	____
2555	Sunoco 1-D Tank Car (overstamped 2755 box)	22	122	____
2559	B&O Passenger Rail Diesel Car	27	131	____
2560	Lionel Lines Crane Car	10	42	____
2561	Vista Valley Observation Car	30	125	____
2561	Vista Valley Observation Car (orange perforated)	125	190	____
2562	Regal Pass Observation Car	30	125	____
2562	Regal Pass Observation Car (orange perforated)	100	145	____
2563	Indian Falls Pullman Car	28	110	____
2572	Boston & Maine Military Set	18	155	____
2574	Santa Fe Military Set	85	418	____
2625	Irvington Pullman Car	10	148	____
2627	Madison Pullman Car	18	160	____
2628	Manhattan Pullman Car	13	128	____
2671T	Pennsylvania Tender, for export	22	85	____
2671W	Pennsylvania Tender	13	44	____
2671WX	Lionel Lines Tender	18	59	____
2755	Sunoco 1-D Tank Car	15	75	____
X2758	PRR Automobile Boxcar	5	30	____
2855	Sunoco 1-D Tank Car	25	129	____
3330	Flatcar with submarine kit	12	91	____
3330-100	Operating Submarine Kit, separate sale	60	250	____
3349	Turbo Missile Launch Car	2	10	____
3356	Operating Horse Car and Corral Set (classic)	13	45	____
3356	Operating Horse Car and Corral Set (orange picture)	19	80	____
3356-2	Horse Car	77	418	____
3356-100	Black Horses (classic)	4	17	____
3356-100	Black Horses (white box)	8	23	____
3356-150	Horse Car Corral	75	1000	____
3357	Hydraulic Maintenance Car	5	30	____

BOXES

			Good (P-5)	Exc (P-7)
___	3359	Lionel Lines Twin-bin Coal Dump Car	13	50
___	3360	Operating Burro Crane	15	65
___	3361	Operating Log Dump Car	5	30
___	3361X	Operating Log Dump Car	5	35
___	3362	Helium Tank Unloading Car	17	45
___	3364	Log Unloading Car	10	43
___	3366	Circus Car Corral Set	23	198
___	3366-100	White Horses	8	33
___	3370	W&A Outlaw Car	10	38
___	3376	Bronx Zoo Car	25	65
___	3376-160	Bronx Zoo Car	10	35
___	3410	Helicopter Car	20	100
___	3413	Mercury Capsule Car	10	57
___	3419	Helicopter Car	9	37
___	3424	Wabash Operating Boxcar	36	84
___	3424-75	Low Bridge Signal (marked "3424-75" or overstamped on 3424-100 box)	150	300
___	3424-100	Low Bridge Signal	5	20
___	3428	U.S. Mail Operating Boxcar	10	50
___	3434	Poultry Dispatch Car	15	65
___	3435	Traveling Aquarium Car	37	143
___	3444	Erie Operating Gondola	5	35
___	3451	Operating Log Dump Car	4	20
___	3454	PRR Operating Merchandise Car	24	125
___	3456	N&W Operating Hopper	10	35
___	3459	LL Operating Coal Dump Car (no toymaker's logo)	35	83
___	3459	LL Operating Coal Dump Car (toymaker's logo)	15	59
___	3461	LL Operating Log Car	4	20
___	3461X-25	Lionel Lines Operating Log Car, green	7	25
___	3462	Automatic Milk Car	15	53
___	X3464	NYC Operating Boxcar	5	20
___	3469X	LL Operating Coal Dump Car	5	20
___	3470	Target Launching Car	23	50
___	3472	Automatic Milk Car	12	33
___	3474	Western Pacific Operating Boxcar	4	35
___	3482	Automatic Milk Car	13	36
___	3484	Pennsylvania Operating Boxcar	9	30
___	3484-25	ATSF Operating Boxcar	7	33
___	3494-1	NYC Operating Boxcar	20	48
___	3494-150	Missouri Pacific Operating Boxcar	8	37
___	3494-275	State of Maine Operating Boxcar	10	70
___	3494-550	Monon Operating Boxcar	48	212
___	3494-625	Soo Operating Boxcar	52	199
___	3509	Satellite Launching Car	18	60
___	3512	Fireman and Ladder Car	20	52
___	3519	Satellite Launching Car	8	46
___	3520	Searchlight Car	7	25
___	3530	GM Generator Car	15	69
___	3530-50	Searchlight with pole and base, separate sale	25	63
___	3535	Security Car with searchlight	12	60
___	3540	Operating Radar Car	20	63

BOXES

		Good (P-5)	Exc (P-7)
3545	Operating TV Monitor Car	13	75 ___
3559	Operating Coal Dump Car	10	40 ___
3562-1	ATSF Operating Barrel Car	27	87 ___
3562-25	ATSF Operating Barrel Car, gray	25	54 ___
3562-50	ATSF Operating Barrel Car, yellow	18	60 ___
3562-75	ATSF Operating Barrel Car, orange	24	56 ___
3619	Helicopter Reconnaissance Car	8	59 ___
3620	Searchlight Car	7	27 ___
3650	Extension Searchlight Car	5	28 ___
3656	Armour Operating Cattle Car	15	45 ___
3656	Stockyard with cattle (set box with car box)	16	50 ___
3656-9	Cattle (marked "3656" on 4 sides, unnumbered tuck flaps)	8	19 ___
3656-9	Cattle (marked "3656" on 4 sides, "3656-44" on 1 tuck flap)	2	12 ___
3656-9	Cattle (marked "3656-34" on 4 sides, "3656-44" on 1 tuck flap)	2	10 ___
3656-9	Cattle (marked "3656" on 4 sides, "3656-44" on 1 tuck flap, OPS markings)	10	25 ___
3656-9	Cattle (unnumbered sides, marked "3656-44" on 1 tuck flap)	10	25 ___
3656-9	Cattle (unnumbered sides, marked "3656-34" on 1 tuck flap)	13	35 ___
3656-150	Corral Platform, separate sale	209	898 ___
3662	Automatic Milk Car (classic), *55*	10	40 ___
3662	Automatic Milk Car (orange picture), *64*	13	50 ___
3662	Automatic Milk Car (white box), *66*	15	55 ___
3665	Minuteman Operating Car	20	64 ___
3672	Bosco Operating Milk Car	33	127 ___
3830	Operating Submarine Car	5	33 ___
3854	Automatic Merchandise Car	88	375 ___
3927	Lionel Lines Track Cleaning Car	10	25 ___
4357	SP-type Caboose, electronic	28	93 ___
4452	PRR Gondola, electronic	15	84 ___
4454	Baby Ruth PRR Boxcar, electronic	18	65 ___
4457	PRR N5-type Caboose, tintype, electronic	23	111 ___
4671W	Tender	27	91 ___
5160	Viewing Stand	10	60 ___
5459	LL Coal Dump Car, electronic	15	92 ___
6001T	Tender	1	10 ___
6002	NYC Gondola	2	10 ___
X6004	Baby Ruth PRR Boxcar	2	10 ___
6007	Lionel Lines SP-type Caboose	2	15 ___
6012	Gondola	2	10 ___
6014	Boxcar	2	24 ___
6014-60	Frisco Boxcar, white	8	24 ___
6014-85	Bosco or Frisco Boxcar, orange (classic)	8	36 ___
6014-100	Airex Boxcar, red	5	25 ___
6014-150	Wix Boxcar	25	118 ___
6014-335	Frisco Boxcar	5	25 ___
6014-410	Frisco Boxcar	18	90 ___
6015	Sunoco 1-D Tank Car	4	16 ___

BOXES

		Good (P-5)	Exc (P-7)
6017	Lionel Lines SP-type Caboose	1	7
6017-50	U.S. Marine Corps SP-type Caboose (box marked "6017-60")	20	110
6017-85	Lionel Lines SP-type Caboose, gray	9	30
6017-100	B&M SP-type Caboose	18	64
6017-185	ATSF SP-type Caboose	3	15
6017-200	U.S. Navy SP-type Caboose	13	160
6017-235	ATSF SP-type Caboose	8	30
6019	Remote Control Track	2	3
6020W	Tender	5	45
6024	Nabisco Shredded Wheat Boxcar	5	25
6024-60	RCA Whirlpool Boxcar	15	54
6025	Gulf 1-D Tank Car (classic)	9	23
6025-60	Gulf 1-D Tank Car	3	10
6025-60	Gulf 1-D Tank Car (classic, overstamped 6024 box)	5	52
6025-85	Gulf 1-D Tank Car (classic)	5	52
6026W	Lionel Lines Tender	8	44
6027	Alaska SP-type Caboose	50	250
6029	Remote Control Uncoupling Track (classic)	2	7
6029	Remote Control Uncoupling Track (orange picture)	11	41
6032	Short Gondola	3	31
X6034	Baby Ruth PRR Boxcar	2	13
6035	Sunoco 1-D Tank Car	5	22
6037	Lionel Lines SP-type Caboose	2	10
6050	Lionel Savings Bank Boxcar	8	28
6050-110	Swift Boxcar	7	35
6057	Lionel Lines SP-type Caboose	4	20
6059	M&StL SP-type Caboose	15	25
6062	NYC Gondola	7	20
6066T	Tender	7	15
6110	2-4-2 Locomotive	4	20
6111-75	Flatcar with logs	12	51
6112-25	Canister Set	10	30
6112-85	Short Gondola (marked "Canister Car")	3	28
6112-135	Short Gondola (marked "Canister Car")	5	49
6119	DL&W Work Caboose, red	5	20
6119-25	DL&W Work Caboose, orange	7	25
6119-50	DL&W Work Caboose, brown	7	26
6119-75	DL&W Work Caboose	10	40
6119-100	DL&W Work Caboose (classic)	4	18
6119-100	DL&W Work Caboose (picture, perforated, or window)	6	36
6121	Flatcar with pipes	14	64
6121-60	Flatcar with pipes	14	77
6130	ATSF Work Caboose (cellophane)	10	35
6130	ATSF Work Caboose (Hagerstown checkerboard)	10	38
6130	ATSF Work Caboose (all other boxes)	5	33
6151	Flatcar with patrol truck	9	57
6162-60	Alaska Gondola	10	50

BOXES

		Good (P-5)	Exc (P-7)	
6162-110	NYC Gondola, blue (orange picture)	10	42	___
6162-110	NYC Gondola, red, separate sale (orange picture with label)	25	108	___
6175	Flatcar with rocket	10	34	___
6220	Santa Fe NW2 Switcher	25	125	___
6250	Seaboard NW2 Switcher	32	89	___
6257	SP-type Caboose	2	9	___
6257X	SP-type Caboose	10	41	___
6257-25	SP-type Caboose	2	10	___
6257-50	SP-type Caboose	2	10	___
6262	Flatcar with wheel load	5	28	___
6264	Flatcar with lumber, separate sale	33	125	___
6311	Flatcar with pipes	11	84	___
6315	Gulf 1-D Chemical Tank Car (classic)	20	43	___
6315	Gulf 1-D Chemical Tank Car (Hagerstown checkerboard)	30	53	___
6315-60	Gulf 1-D Chemical Tank Car (orange picture)	5	28	___
6342	NYC Gondola	22	210	___
6343	Barrel Ramp Car	5	38	___
6356	NYC Stock Car	4	31	___
6357	SP-type Caboose (classic)	2	13	___
6357	SP-type Caboose (orange perforated, overstamped)	12	111	___
6357-50	ATSF SP-type Caboose	88	338	___
6361	Timber Transport Car	8	35	___
6361	Timber Transport Car (Hagerstown checkerboard)	13	64	___
6362	Truck Car	6	46	___
6376	LL Circus Stock Car	7	32	___
6401	Flatcar, gray	25	107	___
6403B	Tender with bell	15	73	___
6405	Flatcar with piggyback van	5	32	___
6407	Flatcar with rocket	200	250	___
6411	Flatcar with logs	5	37	___
6413	Mercury Capsule Carrying Car	15	50	___
6414	Evans Auto Loader (classic)	20	57	___
6414	Evans Auto Loader (orange picture)	35	123	___
6414	Evans Auto Loader (orange picture, overstamped 6416 box)	23	183	___
6414	Evans Auto Loader (orange perforated), 59	12	77	___
6414	Evans Auto Loader (cellophane), 66	20	60	___
6414-25	Four Automobiles	180	713	___
6415	Sunoco 3-D Tank Car (classic)	5	23	___
6415	Sunoco 3-D Tank Car (orange picture)	24	42	___
6415	Sunoco 3-D Tank Car (cellophane)	31	49	___
6415	Sunoco 3-D Tank Car (Hillside checkerboard)	34	47	___
6415	Sunoco 3-D Tank Car (orange picture with label)	78	137	___
6416	Boat Transport Car	26	94	___
6417	PRR N5c Porthole Caboose	4	18	___
6417-1	PRR N5c Porthole Caboose, without "New York Zone"	7	29	___

BOXES

			Good (P-5)	Exc (P-7)
____	6417-25	Lionel Lines N5c Porthole Caboose	8	35
____	6417-50	Lehigh Valley N5c Porthole Caboose	26	89
____	6418	Machinery Car	18	72
____	6419	DL&W Work Caboose	7	40
____	6419-25	DL&W Work Caboose	5	20
____	6419-50	DL&W Work Caboose	9	40
____	6419-100	N&W Work Caboose	26	61
____	6420	DL&W Work Caboose with searchlight	12	49
____	6424	Twin Auto Flatcar		50
____	6424-60	Twin Auto Flatcar	10	52
____	6424-85	Twin Auto Flatcar	10	94
____	6424-110	Twin Auto Flatcar	10	99
____	6425	Gulf 3-D Tank Car	10	23
____	6427	Lionel Lines N5c Porthole Caboose	3	26
____	6427-60	Virginian N5c Porthole Caboose	40	138
____	6427-500	PRR N5c Porthole Caboose, sky blue, from Girls Set	33	109
____	6428	U.S. Mail Boxcar	10	50
____	6429	DL&W Work Caboose	43	169
____	6430	Flatcar with trailers	11	38
____	6431	Flatcar with vans and tractor (cellophane), *66*	42	160
____	6434	Poultry Dispatch Stock Car	7	49
____	6436-1	Lehigh Valley Open Quad Hopper, black	7	31
____	6436-25	Lehigh Valley Open Quad Hopper, maroon	7	27
____	6436-110	Lehigh Valley Open Quad Hopper, red	6	27
____	6436-500	Lehigh Valley Open Quad Hopper, lilac, from Girls Set	34	118
____	6436-1969	TCA Hopper (Hagerstown checkered)	5	55
____	6437	PRR N5c Porthole Caboose	3	15
____	6440	Flatcar with vans	13	38
____	6440	Green Pullman Car	10	40
____	6441	Green Observation Car	10	35
____	6442	Brown Pullman Car	10	48
____	6443	Brown Observation Car	10	39
____	6445	Fort Knox Gold Reserve Car	15	50
____	6446-25	N&W Covered Quad Hopper	11	36
____	6446-60	Lehigh Valley Covered Quad Hopper	118	363
____	6447	PRR N5c Porthole Caboose	52	223
____	6448	Exploding Target Range Boxcar	8	38
____	6452	Pennsylvania Gondola	3	31
____	X6454	Santa Fe, NYC, or Baby Ruth Boxcar	5	31
____	X6454	PRR Boxcar	10	29
____	X6454	PRR Boxcar (classic, overstamped 3464 box)	10	30
____	X6454	SP Boxcar	8	31
____	X6454	Erie Boxcar	9	37
____	6456	Lehigh Valley Short Hopper	2	12
____	6456-25	LV Short Hopper ("25" rubber-stamped on end flaps)	9	50
____	6456-75	Lehigh Valley Short Hopper	28	123
____	6457	SP-type Caboose	6	15
____	6460	Bucyrus Erie Crane Car	11	39
____	6460-25	Bucyrus Erie Crane Car, red cab	10	50

BOXES

		Good (P-5)	Exc (P-7)
6461	Transformer Car	7	30 ____
6462	NYC Gondola, black		30 ____
6462-25	NYC Gondola, green	10	24 ____
6462-75	NYC Gondola, red	3	18 ____
6462-125	NYC Gondola, red plastic	5	18 ____
6462-500	NYC Gondola, pink, from Girls Set	41	143 ____
6463	Rocket Fuel 2-D Tank Car	18	35 ____
6464-1	Western Pacific Boxcar	10	38 ____
6464-25	Great Northern Boxcar	12	42 ____
6464-50	M&StL Boxcar	7	32 ____
6464-50	M&StL Boxcar	3	25 ____
6464-50	M&StL Boxcar (overstamped with "S" and "Silver")	15	70 ____
6464-75	Rock Island Boxcar	7	58 ____
6464-100	Western Pacific Boxcar	33	75 ____
6464-125	NYC Pacemaker Boxcar	15	65 ____
6464-150	Missouri Pacific Boxcar	14	56 ____
6464-175	Rock Island Boxcar	8	58 ____
6464-200	Pennsylvania Boxcar	10	71 ____
6464-225	SP Boxcar	14	40 ____
6464-250	Western Pacific Boxcar (orange picture with label)	42	195 ____
6464-250	Western Pacific Blue Feather Boxcar (classic for 6464-100), *54*	100	450 ____
6464-250	Western Pacific Boxcar (cellophane)	23	88 ____
6464-275	State of Maine Boxcar	11	36 ____
6464-300	Rutland Boxcar, *55*	30	116 ____
6464-325	B&O Sentinel Boxcar	25	150 ____
6464-350	MKT Boxcar	23	110 ____
6464-375	Central of Georgia Boxcar	10	41 ____
6464-400	B&O Time-Saver Boxcar	5	36 ____
6464-425	New Haven Boxcar (classic)	9	32 ____
6464-425	New Haven Boxcar (Hagerstown)	10	44 ____
6464-450	Great Northern Boxcar	13	47 ____
6464-450	Great Northern Boxcar (cellophane)	15	74 ____
6464-475	B&M Boxcar	8	38 ____
6464-500	Timken Boxcar	9	54 ____
6484-510	NYC Pacemaker Boxcar	70	260 ____
6464-515	MKT Boxcar	53	260 ____
6464-525	M&StL Boxcar	5	46 ____
6464-650	D&RGW Boxcar (cellophane)	13	40 ____
6464-700	Santa Fe Boxcar	22	54 ____
6464-725	New Haven Boxcar (orange picture, "735" on box)	5	30 ____
6464-725	New Haven Boxcar (Hagerstown checkerboard)	22	67 ____
6464-825	Alaska Boxcar	56	197 ____
6464-900	NYC Boxcar	7	30 ____
6464-1970	TCA Boxcar	5	35 ____
6465	Gulf 2-D Tank Car, black (classic)	7	27 ____
6465-60	Gulf 2-D Tank Car, gray	5	28 ____

BOXES

		Good (P-5)	Exc (P-7)
6465-110	Cities Service 2-D Tank Car (orange perforated)	15	64
6465-160	Lionel Lines Tank Car (orange picture)	86	194
6465	Sunoco 2-D Tank Car (classic, overstamped 2465 box)	2	21
6465	Sunoco 2-D Tank Car (classic, overstamped 6555 box)	3	18
6465	Sunoco 2-D Tank Car (orange picture, 6464-900 label)	10	84
6465-60	Sunoco 2-D Tank Car (classic)	2	23
6465-85	Lionel Lines 2-D Tank Car (orange perforated)	33	75
6466W	Lionel Lines Tender (with liner)	8	28
6466WX	Lionel Lines Tender (with liner)	12	42
6467	Miscellaneous Car	15	35
6468	B&O Auto Boxcar, tuscan (marked "X")	35	95
6468	B&O Auto Boxcar, blue	5	23
6468-25	NH Auto Boxcar	5	40
6469	Liquified Gas Tank Car	15	60
6470	Explosives Boxcar	5	20
6472	Refrigerator Car	5	18
6473	Horse Transport Car	3	15
6475	Pickles Vat Car (orange picture)	9	80
6476	Lehigh Valley Short Hopper	6	13
6476-85	Lehigh Valley Short Hopper	16	68
6476-135	LV Short Hopper	9	29
6477	Miscellaneous Car with pipes	10	40
6482	Refrigerator Car	6	41
6500	Flatcar with Bonanza airplane	50	175
6501	Flatcar with jet boat	15	50
6511	Flatcar with pipes	7	25
6512	Cherry Picker Car	3	28
6517	Lionel Lines Bay Window Caboose	8	36
6517-60	Bay Window Caboose (TCA)	24	89
6517-75	Erie Bay Window Caboose	35	144
6518	Transformer Car	13	50
6519	Allis-Chalmers Flatcar (classic)	20	53
6519	Allis-Chalmers Flatcar (orange perforated)	21	92
6520	Searchlight Car	8	43
6530	Firefighting Instruction Car	10	43
6536	M&StL Open Quad Hopper	7	61
6544	Missile Firing Car	15	54
6555	Sunoco 1-D Tank Car	8	23
6556	MKT Stock Car	39	180
6557	SP-type Caboose	15	64
6560	Bucyrus Erie Crane Car (Hagerstown checkerboard)	14	55
6560	Bucyrus Erie Crane Car (all other boxes)	12	40
6560-25	Bucyrus Erie Crane Car, 8-wheel (with liner)	13	39
6561	Cable Car, 2 reels	5	27
6562-1	NYC Gondola, gray	8	23
6562-25	NYC Gondola, red	5	23
6562-50	NYC Gondola, black	8	30

BOXES

		Good (P-5)	Exc (P-7)
6572	REA Reefer (classic)	7	57 ___
6572	REA Reefer (orange picture)	5	25 ___
6636	Alaska Open Quad Hopper	10	50 ___
6646	Lionel Lines Stock Car	5	28 ___
6650	IRBM Rocket Launcher	9	38 ___
6654W	Whistle Tender	7	20 ___
6657	Rio Grande SP-type Caboose	25	131 ___
6660	Boom Car	8	63 ___
6670	Derrick Car	19	58 ___
6672	Santa Fe Refrigerator Car		25 ___
6736	Detroit & Mackinac Open Quad Hopper	17	64 ___
6800	Flatcar with airplane (classic)	20	74 ___
6800	Flatcar with airplane (orange perforated)	13	83 ___
6800-60	Airplane, separate sale	93	233 ___
6801	Flatcar with brown and white boat	5	36 ___
6801-50	Flatcar with yellow and white boat	10	43 ___
6801-60	Boat, separate sale	30	88 ___
6801-75	Flatcar with blue and white boat	11	36 ___
6802	Flatcar with girders (late classic)	10	33 ___
6802	Flatcar with girders (orange perforated)	35	65 ___
6803	Flatcar with USMC tank and sound truck	13	89 ___
6804	Flatcar with USMC trucks	13	88 ___
6805	Atomic Energy Disposal Flatcar	22	94 ___
6806	Flatcar with USMC trucks	13	115 ___
6807	Flatcar with boat	10	40 ___
6809	Flatcar with USMC trucks	10	93 ___
6810	Flatcar with trailer	7	35 ___
6812	Track Maintenance Car	8	43 ___
6814	Rescue Caboose	19	114 ___
6816	Flatcar with Allis-Chalmers bulldozer	31	143 ___
6816-100	Allis-Chalmers bulldozer	125	400 ___
6817	Flatcar with Allis-Chalmers motor scraper	36	166 ___
6818	Flatcar with transformer	5	30 ___
6819	Flatcar with helicopter	5	31 ___
6820	Aerial Missile Transport Car with helicopter	149	285 ___
6821	Flatcar with crates	5	20 ___
6822	Searchlight Car	5	23 ___
6823	Flatcar with IRBM missiles	10	38 ___
6825	Flatcar with arch trestle bridge	7	26 ___
6826	Flatcar with Christmas trees	16	50 ___
6827	Flatcar with Harnischfeger power shovel	14	118 ___
6828	Flatcar with Harnischfeger crane (cellophane, no crane kit box)	30	133 ___
6828	Flatcar with Harnischfeger crane (orange picture, no crane kit box)	13	53 ___
6828	Harnischfeger Crane Kit, used with flatcar	8	115 ___
6828-100	Harnischfeger Crane, separate sale	73	222 ___
6830	Flatcar with submarine	25	40 ___
6844	Missile Carrying Car	13	45 ___
9658	Steam Freight Set (Sears uncatalogued)		185 ___
11001	Steam Freight Set (advance catalog 1962)		10 ___

BOXES

		Good (P-5)	Exc (P-7)
____ 11242	Steam Freight Set	30	
____ 11268	Military Set		120
____ 11278	Steam Freight Set	25	
____ 11288	Steam Freight Set	50	
____ 11415	Steam Freight Set (advance catalog 1963)	9	55
____ 11420	Steam Freight Set		30
____ 11450	Steam Freight Set	25	
____ 11460	Steam Freight Set		30
____ 11560	Texas Special Set	15	25
____ 11580	Steam Freight Set (uncatalogued)		15
____ 11750	Steam Freight Set	20	
____ 12710	Steam Freight Set		55
____ 12730	Santa Fe Diesel Freight Set		185
____ 12760	Berkshire Freight Set		400
____ 12780	Santa Fe Passenger Set		550
____ 12800	B&M Diesel Freight Set		62
____ 12800X	B&M Diesel Freight Set		190
____ 12820	Virginian Train Master Freight Set	100	240
____ 13008	Super O Introductory Set		60
____ 13018	Santa Fe Space-age Military Set		1200
____ 13048	Super O Steam Freight Set	65	
____ 13058	Santa Fe Space-age Military Set		400
____ 13088	Santa Fe Passenger Set		1550
____ 13098	Steam Freight Set		300
____ 13118	Berkshire Freight Set		250
____ 13128	Santa Fe Space-age Military Set		650
____ 13150	Hudson Freight Set		900
____ 19151	Military Set (Allied Stores uncatalogued)		175
____ 19244	Steam Freight Set (Western Auto uncatalogued)	30	
____ 19394	CN Diesel Freight Set (uncatalogued)	33	125
____ 19561	UP Freight Set (Sears uncatalogued)		170
____ ECU-1	Electronic Control Unit	15	75
____ KW	Transformer, 190 watts	8	31
____ LW	Transformer, 125 watts	2	16
____ RCS	Remote Control Track	7	27
____ RW	Transformer, 110 watts	2	13
____ S	Transformer, 80 watts	3	15
____ TW	Transformer, 175 watts		25
____ UCS	Remote Control Track (O)	1	10
____ ZW	Transformer, 275 watts (orange, with inserts)	16	65
____ ZW	Transformer, 275 watts (yellow, with inserts)	20	105

Section 7
SETS

463W	Steam Freight Set, *45* (224, 2466W, 2458, 2452, 2555, 2457)	600 ___
1000W	027 Steam Freight Set, *55* (2016, 6026W, 6014, 6012, 6017)	250 ___
1001	027 Diesel Freight Set, *55* (610, 6012, 6014, 6017)	250 ___
1111	027 Scout Freight Set, *48* (1001, 1001T, 1002, 1005, 1007)	225 ___
1112	027 Scout Freight Set, *48* (1001 or 1101, 1001T, 1002, 1004, 1005, 1007)	250 ___
1113	027 Scout Freight Set, *50* (1120, 1001T, 1002, 1005, 1007)	114 ___
1115	027 Scout Freight Set, *49* (1110, 1001T, 1002, 1005, 1007)	188 ___
1117	027 Scout Freight Set, *49* (1110, 1001T, 1002, 1005, 1004, 1007)	150 ___
1119	027 Freight Scout Set, *51–52* (1110, 1001T, 1002, 1004, 1007)	158 ___
1400	027 Steam Passenger Set, *46* (221, 221T, two 2430, 2431)	600 ___
1400W	027 Steam Passenger Set, *46* (221, 221W, two 2430 2431)	720 ___
1401	027 Steam Freight Set, *46* (1654, 1654T, 2452X, 2465, 2472)	120 ___
1401W	027 Steam Freight Set, *46* (1654, 1654W, 2452X, 2465, 2472)	220 ___
1402	027 Steam Passenger Set, *46* (1666, 2466T, two 2440, 2441)	550 ___
1402W	027 Steam Passenger Set, *46* (1666, 2466W, two 2440, 2441)	550 ___
1403	027 Steam Freight Set, *46* (221, 221T, 2411, 2465, 2472)	400 ___
1403W	027 Steam Freight Set, *46* (221, 221W, 2411, 2465, 2472)	500 ___
1405	027 Steam Freight Set, *46* (1666, 2466T, 2452X, 2465, 2472)	145 ___
1405W	027 Steam Freight Set, *46* (1666, 2466W, 2452X, 2465, 2472)	250 ___
1407B	027 Steam Switcher Set, *46* (1665, 2403B, 2560, 2452X, 2419)	840 ___
1409	027 Steam Freight Set, *46* (1666, 2466T, 3559, 2465, 3454, 2472)	425 ___
1409W	027 Steam Freight Set, *46* (1666, 2466W, 3559, 2465, 3454, 2472)	418 ___
1411W	027 Steam Freight Set, *46* (1666, 2466WX, 2452X, 2465, 2454, 2472)	235 ___
1413WS	027 Steam Freight Set, *46* (2020, 2466WX, 2452X, 2465, 2454, 2472)	310 ___
1415WS	027 Steam Freight Set, *46* (2020, 2020W, 3459, 3454, 2465, 2472)	600 ___
1417WS	027 Steam Work Train Set, *46* (2020, 2020W, 2465, 3451, 2560, 2419)	700 ___

		Exc
1419WS	027 Steam Freight Set, *46* (2020, 2020W, 3459, 2452X, 2560, 2419, 97)	880
1421WS	027 Steam Freight Set, *46* (2020, 2020W, 3451, 2465, 3454, 2472, 164)	1100
1423W	027 Steam Freight Set, *48–49* (1655, 6654W, 6452, 6465, 6257)	290
1425B	027 Steam Switcher Freight Set, *48* (1656, 2403B, 6456, 6465, 6257X)	825
1425B	027 Steam Switcher Freight Set, *49* (1656, 6403B, 6456, 6465, 6257)	825
1426WS	027 Steam Passenger Set, *48–49* (2026, 6466WX, two 6440, 6441)	576
1427WS	027 Steam Freight Set, *48* (2026, 6466WX, 6454, 6465, 6257)	320
1429WS	027 Steam Freight Set, *48* (2026, 6466WX, 3451, 6454, 6465, 6257)	225
1430WS	027 Steam Passenger Set, *48–49* (2025, 6466WX, 2400, 2401, 2402)	800
1431	027 Steam Freight Set, *47* (1654, 1654T, 2452X, 2465, 2472)	150
1431W	027 Steam Freight Set, *47* (1654, 1654W, 2452X, 2465, 2472)	150
1432	027 Steam Passenger Set, *47* (221, 221T, two 2430, 2431)	850
1432W	027 Steam Passenger Set, *47* (221, 221W, two 2430 2431)	850
1433	027 Steam Freight Set, *47* (221, 221T, 2411, 2465, 2457)	375
1433W	027 Steam Freight Set, *47* (221, 221 W, 2411, 2465, 2457)	375
1434WS	027 Steam Passenger Set, *47* (2025, 2466WX, two 2440, 2441)	430
1435WS	027 Steam Freight Set, *47* (2025, 2466WX, 2452X, 2454, 2457)	222
1437WS	027 Steam Freight Set, *47* (2025, 2466WX, 2452X, 2465, 2454, 2472)	223
1439WS	027 Steam Freight Set, *47* (2025, 2466WX, 3559, 2465, 3454, 2457)	425
1441WS	027 Steam Work Train Set, *47* (2020, 2020W, 2560, 2461, 3451, 2419)	1223
1443WS	027 Steam Freight Set, *47* (2020, 2020W, 3459, 3462, 2465, 2457)	400
1445WS	027 Steam Freight Set, *48* (2025, 6466WX, 6454, 3559, 6465, 6357)	325
1447WS	027 Steam Work Train Set, *48* (2020, 6020W, 3451, 2461, 2460, 6419)	425
1447WS	027 Steam Work Train Set, *49* (2020, 6020W, 6461, 3461, 2460, 6419)	475
1449WS	027 Steam Freight Set, *48* (2020, 6020W, 3462, 3459, 6411, 6465, 6357)	430
1451WS	027 Steam Freight Set, *48* (2026, 6466WX, 6462, 3464, 6257)	265
1453WS	027 Steam Freight Set, *49* (2026, 6466WX, 3464, 6465, 3461, 6357)	325
1455WS	027 Steam Freight Set, *49* (2025, 6466WX, 6462, 6465, 3472, 6357)	375

SETS

Exc

1457B	027 Diesel Freight Set, *49–50* (6220, 3464, 6462, 6520, 6419)	600 ___
1459WS	027 Steam Freight Set, *49* (2020, 6020W, 6411, 3656, 6465, 3469, 6357)	1075 ___
1461S	027 Steam Freight Set, *50* (6110, 6001T, 6002, 6004, 6007)	175 ___
1463W	027 Freight Set, *50* (2036, 6466W, 6462, 6465, 6257)	200 ___
1463WS	027 Freight Set, *51* (2026, 6466W, 6462, 6465, 6257)	150 ___
1464W	027 UP Diesel Passenger Set, *50* (2023 AA, 2481, 2482, 2483)	1113 ___
1464W	027 UP Passenger Set, *51* (2023 AA, 2421, 2422, 2423)	1000 ___
1464W	027 UP Passenger Set, *52–53* (2033 AA, 2421, 2422, 2423)	635 ___
1465	027 Steam Freight Set, *52* (2034, 6066T, 6032, 6035, 6037)	180 ___
1467W	027 UP Diesel Freight Set, *50–51* (2023 AA, 6656, 6465, 6456, 6357)	500 ___
1467W	027 Erie Diesel Freight Set, *52–53* (2032 AA, 6656, 6456, 6465, 6357)	738 ___
1469WS	027 Steam Freight Set, *50–51* (2035, 6466W, 6462, 6465, 6456, 6257)	203 ___
1471WS	027 Steam Freight Set, *50–51* (2035, 6466W, 3469, 6465, 6454, 3461, 6357)	400 ___
1473WS	027 Steam Freight Set, *50* (2046, 2046W, 3464, 6465, 6520, 6357)	400 ___
1475WS	027 Steam Freight Set, *50* (2046, 2046W, 3656, 3461, 6472, 3469, 6419)	525 ___
1477S	027 Freight Set, *51–52* (2026, 6466T, 6012, 6014, 6017)	200 ___
1479WS	027 Freight Set, *52* (2056, 2046W, 6462, 6465, 6456, 6257)	353 ___
1481WS	027 Steam Freight Set, *51* (2035, 6466W, 3464, 3472, 6465, 6462, 6357)	415 ___
1483WS	027 Steam Freight Set, *52* (2056, 2046W, 3472, 6462, 6465, 3474, 6357)	693 ___
1484WS	027 Steam Passenger Set, *52* (2056, 2046W, 2421, 2422, 2423, 2429)	1268 ___
1485WS	027 Steam Freight Set, *52* (2025, 6466W, 6462, 6465, 6257)	135 ___
1500	027 Steam Freight Set, *53* (1130, 6066T, 6032, 6034, 6037)	150 ___
1500	027 Steam Freight Set, *54* (1130, 1130T, 6032, 6034, 6037)	125 ___
1501S	027 Steam Freight Set, *53* (2026, 6066T, 6032, 6035, 6037)	150 ___
1502WS	027 Steam Passenger Set, *53* (2055, 2046W, 2421, 2422, 2423)	750 ___
1503WS	027 Steam Freight Set, *53–54* (2055, 6026W, 6462, 6465, 6456, 6257)	353 ___
1505WS	027 Steam Freight Set, *53* (2046, 2046W, 6462, 6464-1, 6415, 6357)	450 ___
1507WS	027 Steam Freight Set, *53* (2046, 2046W, 6415, 6462, 3472, 6468, 6357)	450 ___

			Exc
1509WS	027 Steam Freight Set, *53*		
___	(2046, 2046W, 6456, 3520, 3469, 6460, 6419)		500
1511S	027 Steam Freight Set, *53*		
___	(2037, 6066T, 6032, 3474, 6035, 6037)		223
1513S	027 Steam Freight Set, *54–55*		
___	(2037, 6026T, 6012, 6014, 6015, 6017)		241
1515WS	027 Steam Freight Set, *54*		
___	(2065, 2046W, 6462, 6415, 6464-25, 6456-25, 6357)		383
1516WS	027 Passenger Set, *54*		
___	(2065, 2046W, 2434, 2432, 2436)		650
1517W	027 Diesel Freight Set, *54*		
___	(2245P/C AB, 6464-225, 6561, 6462-25, 6427)		1250
1519WS	027 Steam Freight Set, *54*		
___	(2065, 6026W, 6356, 6462-75, 3482, 3461-25, 6427)		550
1520W	027 Texas Special Passenger Set, *54*		
___	(2245P/C AB, 2432, 2435, 2436)		1700
1521WS	027 Steam Work Train Set, *54*		
___	(2065, 2046W, 3620, 6561, 6460, 3562, 6419)		700
1523	027 Diesel Work Train Set, *54*		
___	(6250, 6511, 6456-25, 6460-25, 6419-25)		700
1525	027 Diesel Freight Set, *55*		
___	(600, 6111, 6014, 6017)		100
1527	027 Steam Work Train Set, *55*		
___	(1615, 1615T, 6462-125, 6560, 6119)		500
1529	027 PRR Diesel Freight Set, *55*		
___	(2028, 6311, 6436, 6257)		650
1531W	027 Diesel Freight Set, *55*		
___	(2328, 6462-125, 6465, 6456 or 6456-25, 6257)		600
1533WS	027 Steam Freight Set, *55*		
___	(2055, 6026W, 3562-50, 6436, 6465, 6357)		450
1534W	027 Diesel Passenger Set, *55*		
___	(2328, 2432, 2434, 2436)		1000
1535W	027 Diesel Freight Set, *55*		
	(2243P/2243C AB, 6462-125, 6436, 6464-50 or		
___	6468X, 6257)		1650
1536W	027 Texas Special Passenger Set, *55*		
___	(2245P/C AB, two 2432, 2436)		1700
1537WS	027 Steam Freight Set, *55*		
___	(2065, 6026W, 3469, 6464-275, 3562-50, 6357)		500
1538WS	027 Steam Passenger Set, *55*		
___	(2065, 2046W, 2432, 2434, 2435, 2436)		900
1539W	027 Santa Fe Diesel Freight Set, *55*		
___	(2243P/C AB, 3620, 6446, 6561, 6560, 6419)		850
1541WS	027 Steam Freight Set, *55*		
___	(2065, 2046W, 3482, 6415, 3461-25, 3494-1, 6427)		600
1542	027 Electric Freight Set, *56*		
___	(520, 6014, 6012, 6017)		200
1543	027 Diesel Freight Set, *56*		
___	(627, 6121, 6112, 6017)		283
1545	027 Diesel Freight Set, *56*		
___	(628, 6424, 6014, 6025, 6257)		275
1547S	027 Steam Freight Set, *56*		
___	(2018, 6026T, 6121, 6112, 6014, 6257)		200
1549S	027 Diesel Work Train Set, *56*		
___	(1615, 1615T, 6262, 6560, 6119-25)		800

SETS		Exc
1551W	027 Diesel Freight Set, *56* (621, 6362, 6425, 6562-25, 6257)	400 ___
1552	027 Diesel Passenger Set, *56* (629, 2432, 2434, 2436)	1000 ___
1553W	027 MILW Diesel Freight Set, *56* (2338, 6430, 6462-125, 6464-425, 6346, 6257)	700 ___
1555WS	027 Steam Freight Set, *56* (2018, 6026W, 3361, 6464-400, 6462-125, 6257)	282 ___
1557W	027 Diesel Work Train Set, *56* (621, 6436, 6511, 3620, 6560, 6119-25)	500 ___
1559W	027 MILW Diesel Freight Set, *56* (2338, 6414, 3562-50, 6362, 3494-275, 6357)	800 ___
1561WS	027 Steam Freight Set, *56* (2065, 6026W, 3424, 6262, 6562-25, 6430, 6257)	500 ___
1562W	027 Diesel Passenger Set, *56* (2328, two 2442, 2444, 2446)	2000 ___
1563W	027 Wabash Diesel Freight Set, *56* (2240P/C AB, 6467, 3562-50, 6414, 3620, 6357)	1600 ___
1565WS	027 Steam Freight Set, *56* (2065, 6026W, 3662, 3650, 6414, 6346, 6357)	536 ___
1567W	027 Santa Fe Diesel Freight Set, *56* (2243P/C AB, 3356, 3424, 6430, 6672, 6357)	1200 ___
1569	027 UP Diesel Freight Set, *57* (202, 6014, 6111, 6112, 6017)	225 ___
1571	027 LV Diesel Freight Set, *57* (625, 6424, 6476, 6121, 6112, 6017)	400 ___
1573	027 Steam Freight Set, *57* (250, 250T, 6112, 6025, 6476, 6464-425, 6017)	190 ___
1575	027 MP Diesel Freight Set, *57* (205P/T AA, 6121, 6112, 6111, 6560-25, 6119-100)	320 ___
1577S	027 Steam Freight Set, *57* (2018, 1130T, 6014, 6121, 6464-475, 6111, 6112, 6017)	250 ___
1578S	027 Steam Passenger Set, *57* (2018, 1130T, 2432, 2434, 2436)	500 ___
1579S	027 Steam Freight Set, *57* (2037, 1130T, 6476, 6121, 6468-25, 6111, 6112, 6025, 6017)	225 ___
1581	027 Jersey Central Diesel Freight Set, *57* (611, 6464-650, 6424, 6024, 6025, 6476, 6560-25, 6119-100)	538 ___
1583WS	027 Steam Freight Set, *57* (2037, 6026W, 6482, 6112, 6646, 6121, 6476, 6017)	300 ___
1585W	027 Seaboard Diesel Freight Set, *57* (602, 6014, 6111, 6464-525, 6025, 6121, 6112, 6476, 6024, 6017)	447 ___
1586	027 Santa Fe Diesel Passenger Set, *57* (204P/T AA, two 2432, 2436)	668 ___
1587S	027 Steam Freight Set (Girls Set), *57–58* (2037-500, 1130T-500, 6462-500, 6464-515, 6436-500, 6464-510, 6427-500)	3160 ___
1589WS	027 Steam Freight Set, *57* (2037, 6026W, 6424, 6464-450, 6025, 6024, 6111, 6112, 6017)	500 ___
1590	027 Steam Freight Set, *58* (249, 250T, 6014, 6151, 6112, 6017)	300 ___

SETS

			Exc
1591	027 Military Set, *58*		
	(212, 6803, 6809, 6807, 6017-50)		803
1593	027 UP Diesel Work Set, *58*		
	(613, 6476, 6818, 6660, 6112, 6119-100)		650
1595	027 Military Set, *58*		
	(1625, 1625T, 6804, 6806, 6808, 6017-85)		1700
1597S	027 Steam Freight Set, *58*		
	(2018, 1130T, 6014, 6818, 6476, 6025, 6112, 6017)		375
1599	027 Texas Special Freight Set, *58*		
	(210P/T AA, 6801, 6014, 6424, 6112, 6465, 6017)		400
1600	027 Burlington Diesel Passenger Set, *58*		
	(216, 6572, 2432, 2436)		841
1601W	027 Wabash Diesel Freight Set, *58*		
	2337, 6800, 6464-425, 6801, 6810, 6017)		900
1603WS	027 Steam Freight Set, *58*		
	(2037, 6026W, 6424, 6014, 6818, 6112, 6017)		400
1605W	027 Santa Fe Diesel Freight Set, *58*		
	(208P/T AA, 6800, 6464-425, 6801, 6477, 6802, 6017)		900
1607WS	027 Steam Work Train Set, *58*		
	(2037, 6026W, 6465, 6818, 6464-425, 6660, 6112, 6119-100)		450
1608W	027 NH Diesel Passenger Set, *58*		
	(209P/T AA, two 2432, 2434, 2436)		1700
1609	027 Steam Freight Set, *59–60*		
	(246, 1130T, 6162-25, 6476, 6057)		92
1611	027 Alaska Diesel Freight Set, *59*		
	(614, 6825, 6162-60, 6465, 6027)		415
1612	027 General Set, *59–60*		
	(1862, 1862T, 1866, 1865)		313
1613S	027 B&O Steam Freight Set, *59*		
	(247, 247T, 6826, 6819, 6821, 6017)		300
1615	027 B&M Diesel Freight Set, *59*		
	(217P/C AB, 6800, 6464-475, 6812, 6825, 6017-100)		550
1617S	027 Steam Work Train Set, *59*		
	(2018, 1130T, 6816, 6536, 6812, 6670, 6119-100)		800
1619W	027 Santa Fe Diesel Freight Set, *59*		
	(218P/T AA, 6819, 6802, 6801, 6519, 6017-185)		450
1621WS	027 Steam Freight Set, *59*		
	(2037, 6026W, 6825, 6519, 6062, 6464-475, 6017)		325
1623W	027 NP Diesel Freight Set, *59*		
	(2349, 3512, 3435, 6424, 6062, 6017)		1600
1625WS	027 Steam Freight Set, *59*		
	(2037, 6026W, 6636, 3512, 6470, 6650, 6017)		400
1626W	027 Santa Fe Diesel Passenger Set, *59*		
	(208P/T AA, 3428, two 2412, 2416)		700
1627S	027 Steam Freight Set, *60*		
	(244, 244T, 6062, 6825, 6017)		150
1629	027 C&O Diesel Freight Set, *60*		
	(225, 6650, 6470, 6819, 6219)		295
1631WS	027 Steam Freight Set, *60*		
	(243, 243W, 6519, 6812, 6465, 6017)		250
1633	027 U.S. Navy Diesel Freight Set, *60*		
	(224P/C AB, 6544, 6830, 6820, 6017-200)		1300
1635WS	027 Steam Freight Set, *60*		
	(2037, 6026W or 243W, 6361, 6826, 6636, 6821, 6017)		460

SETS		Exc
1637W	O27 Santa Fe Diesel Freight Set, *60* (218P/T AA, 6475, 6175, 6464-475, 6801 or 6424-110, 6017-185)	550 ___
1639WS	O27 Steam Freight Set, *60* (2037, 6026W or 243W, 6816, 6817, 6812, 6530, 6560, 6119-100)	1250 ___
1640W	O27 Santa Fe Diesel Passenger Set, *60* (218P/T AA, 3428, two 2412, 2416, 1640-100)	750 ___
1641	O27 Steam Freight Set, *61* (246, 244T, 3362, 6162, 6057)	150 ___
1642	O27 Steam Freight Set, *61* (244, 1130T, 3376, 6405, 6119)	180 ___
1643	O27 C&O Diesel Freight Set, *61* (230, 3509, 6050, 6175, 6058)	385 ___
1644	O27 General Set, *61* (1862, 1862T, 3370, 1866, 1865)	367 ___
1645	O27 Diesel Freight Set, *61* (229, 3410, 6465-110, 6825, 6059)	250 ___
1646	O27 Steam Freight Set, *61* (233, 233W, 6162, 6343, 6476, 6017)	325 ___
1647	O27 U.S. Marines Military Set, *61* (45, 3665, 3519, 6830, 6448, 6814)	850 ___
1648	O27 Steam Freight Set, *61* (2037, 233W, 6062, 6465-110, 6519, 6476, 6017)	200 ___
1649	O27 Santa Fe Diesel Freight Set, *61* (218P/C AB, 6343, 6445, 6475, 6405, 6017)	500 ___
1650	O27 Steam Military Set, *61* (2037, 233W, 6544, 6470, 3330, 3419, 6017)	500 ___
1651	O27 Santa Fe Diesel Passenger Set, *61* (218P/T or 220T AA, two 2412, 2414, 2416)	675 ___
1800	General Gift Pack, *59–60* (1862, 1862T, 1865, 1866, 1877, storybook)	330 ___
1805	O27 Military Set (Land-Sea and Air Gift Pack), *60* (45, 3429, 3820, 6640, 6824)	2000 ___
1809	Western Gift Pack, *61* (244, 1130T, 3370, 3376, 1877, 6017)	300 ___
1810	Space Age Gift Pack, *61* (231, 3665, 3519, 3820, 6017)	500 ___
2100	Steam Passenger Set, *46* (224, 2466T, two 2442, 2443)	550 ___
2100W	Steam Passenger Set, *46* (224, 2466W, two 2442, 2443)	550 ___
2101	Steam Freight Set, *46* (224, 2466T, 2555, 2452, 2457)	350 ___
2101W	Steam Freight Set, *46* (224, 2466W, 2555, 2452, 2457)	350 ___
2103W	Steam Freight Set, *46* (224, 2466W, 2458, 3559, 2555, 2457)	338 ___
2105WS	Steam Freight Set, *46* (671, 2466W, 2555, 2454, 2457)	425 ___
2110WS	Steam Passenger Set, *46* (671, 2466W, three 2625)	1875 ___
2111WS	Steam Freight Set, *46* (671, 2466W, 3459, 2411, 2460, 2420)	795 ___
2113WS	Steam Freight Set, *46* (726, 2426W, 2855, 3854, 2857)	1900 ___

SETS

			Exc
2114WS	Steam Passenger Set, *46*		
____	(726, 2426W, three 2625)		2500
2115WS	Steam Work Train Set, *46*		
____	(726, 2426W, 2458, 3451, 2460, 2420)		1500
2120S	Steam Passenger Set, *47*		
____	(675, 2466T, two 2442, 2443)		500
2120WS	Steam Passenger Set, *47*		
____	(675, 2466WX, two 2442, 2443)		500
2121S	Steam Freight Set, *47*		
____	(675, 2466T, 2555, 2452, 2457)		400
2121WS	Steam Freight Set, *47*		
____	(675, 2466WX, 2555, 2452, 2457)		400
2123WS	Steam Freight Set, *47*		
____	(675, 2466WX, 2458, 3559, 2555, 2457)		450
2124W	PRR Electric Passenger Set, *47*		
	(2332 GG-1 green, 2625 Irvington, 2625 Madison,		
____	2625 Manhattan)		3200
2125WS	Steam Freight Set, *47*		
____	(671, 671W, 2411, 2454, 2452, 2457)		550
2126WS	Steam Passenger Set, *47*		
	(671, 671W, 2625 Irvington, 2625 Madison, 2625		
____	Manhattan)		1950
2127WS	Steam Work Train Set, *47*		
____	(671, 671W, 3459, 2461, 2460, 2420)		725
2129WS	Steam Freight Set, *47*		
____	(726, 2426W, 3854, 2411, 2855, 2457)		2000
2131WS	Steam Work Train Set, *47*		
____	(726, 2426W, 3462, 3451, 2460, 2420)		1200
2133W	Diesel Freight Set, *48*		
____	(2333P/T AA, 2458, 3459, 2555, 2357)		1350
2135WS	Steam Freight Set, *48*		
____	(675, 2466WX, 2456, 2411, 2357)		350
2135WS	Steam Freight Set, *49*		
____	(675, 6466WX, 6456, 6411, 6457)		350
2136WS	Steam Passenger Set, *48*		
____	(675, 2466WX, two 2442, 2443)		620
2136WS	Steam Passenger Set, *49*		
____	(675, 6466WX, two 6442, 6443)		638
2137WS	Steam Freight Set, *48*		
____	(675, 2466WX, 2458, 3459, 2456, 2357)		568
2139W	PRR Electric Freight Set, *49*		
____	(2332, 6456, 3464, 3461, 6457)		1400
2139W	PRR Electric Freight Set, *48*		
____	(2332, 2458, 3451, 2456, 2357)		1425
2140WS	Steam Passenger Set, *48–49*		
____	(671, 2671W, 2400, 2401, 2402)		1252
2141WS	Steam Freight Set, *48*		
____	(671, 2671W, 3451, 3462, 2456, 2357)		450
2143WS	Steam Work Train Set, *48*		
____	(671, 2671W, 3459, 2461, 2460, 2420)		700
2144W	PRR Electric Passenger Set, *48–49*		
____	(2332, 2625, 2627, 2628)		2300
2145WS	Steam Freight Set, *48*		
____	(726, 2426W, 3462, 2411, 2460, 2357)		815
2146WS	Steam Passenger Set, *48–49*		
____	(726, 2426W, 2625, 2627, 2628)		2000

SETS

Set	Description	Exc
2147WS	Steam Freight Set, *49* (675, 6466WX, 3472, 6465, 3469, 6457)	400 ___
2148WS	Hudson Passenger Set, *50* (773, 2426W, 2625, 2627, 2628)	5000 ___
2149B	Diesel Work Train Set, *49* (622, 6520, 3469, 2460, 6419)	690 ___
2150WS	Steam Passenger Set, *50* (681, 2671W, 2421, 2422, 2423)	1000 ___
2151W	Diesel Freight Set, *49* (2333P/T AA, 3464, 6555, 3469, 6520, 6457)	900 ___
2153WS	Steam Work Train Set, *49* (671, 2671W, 3469, 6520, 2460, 6419)	618 ___
2155WS	Steam Freight Set, *49* (726, 2426W, 6411, 3656, 2460, 6457)	795 ___
2159W	Electric Freight Set, *50* (2330, 3464, 6462, 3461, 6456, 6457)	3000 ___
2161W	Santa Fe Diesel Freight Set, *50* (2343P/T AA, 3469, 3464, 3461, 6520, 6457)	1500 ___
2163WS	Steam Freight Set, *50* (736, 2671WX, 6472, 6462, 6555, 6457)	550 ___
2163WS	Steam Freight Set, *51* (736, 2671WX, 6472, 6462, 6465, 6457)	500 ___
2165WS	Steam Freight Set, *50* (736, 2671WX, 3472, 6456, 3461, 6457)	600 ___
2167WS	Steam Freight Set, *50–51* (681, 2671W, 6462, 3464, 6457)	500 ___
2169WS	Hudson Freight Set, *50* (773, 2426W, 3656, 6456, 3469, 6411, 6457)	3000 ___
2171W	NYC Diesel Freight Set, *50* (2344P/T AA, 3469, 3464, 3461, 6520, 6457)	1400 ___
2173WS	Steam Freight Set, *50* (681, 2671W, 3472, 6555, 3469, 6457)	545 ___
2173WS	Steam Freight Set, *51* (681, 2671W, 3472, 6465, 3469, 6457)	550 ___
2175W	Santa Fe Diesel Freight Set, *50* (2343P/T AA, 6456, 3464, 6555, 6462, 6457)	1100 ___
2175W	Santa Fe Diesel Freight Set, *51* (2343 AA, 6456, 3464, 6465, 6462, 6457)	1100 ___
2177WS	Steam Freight Set, *52* (675, 2046W, 6462, 6465, 6457)	223 ___
2179WS	Steam Freight Set, *52* (671, 2046WX, 3464, 6465, 6462, 6457)	330 ___
2183WS	Steam Freight Set, *52* (726, 2046W, 3464, 6462, 6465, 6457)	575 ___
2185W	NYC Diesel Freight Set, *50* (2344P/T AA, 6456, 3464, 6555, 6462, 6457)	800 ___
2185W	NYC Diesel Freight Set, *51* (2344 AA, 6456, 3464, 6465, 6462, 6457)	800 ___
2187WS	Steam Freight Set, *52* (671, 2046WX, 6462, 3472, 3469, 6456, 6457)	649 ___
2189WS	Steam Freight Set, *52* (726, 2046W, 3520, 3656, 6462, 3461, 6457)	623 ___
2190W	Santa Fe Diesel Passenger Set, *52* (2343P/T AA, 2531, 2532, 2533, 2534)	2000 ___
2190W	Santa Fe Diesel Passenger Set, *53* (2353P/T AA, 2531, 2533, 2532, 2534)	1900 ___

SETS

			Exc
2191W	Santa Fe Diesel Freight Set, *52* (2343P/C/T ABA, 6462, 6656, 6456, 6457)		1350
2193W	NYC Diesel Freight Set, *52* (2344P/C/T ABA, 6462, 6656, 6456, 6457)		1040
2201WS	Steam Freight Set, *53* (685, 6026W, 6462, 6464-50, 6465, 6357)		544
2203WS	Steam Freight Set, *53* (681, 2046WX, 6415, 3520, 6464-25, 6417)		700
2205WS	Steam Freight Set, *53* (736, 2046W, 3484, 6415, 6468, 6456, 6417)		600
2207W	Santa Fe Diesel Freight Set, *53* (2353P/C/T ABA, 6462, 3484, 6415, 6417)		900
2209W	NYC Diesel Freight Set, *53* (2354P/C/T ABA, 6462, 3484, 6415, 6417)		1200
2211WS	Steam Freight Set, *53* (681, 2046WX, 3656, 6464-75, 3461, 6417)		700
2213WS	Steam Freight Set, *53* (736, 2046W, 3461, 3520, 3469, 6460, 6419)		560
2217WS	Steam Freight Set, *54* (682, 2046WX, 6464-175, 3562-25, 6356, 6417)		825
2219W	Diesel Freight Set, *54* (2321, 6456-25, 6464-50, 6462-25, 6415, 6417)		1400
2221WS	Steam Freight Set, *54* (646, 2046W, 6468, 3620, 3469, 6456-25, 6417-25)		600
2222WS	Steam Passenger Set, *54* (646, 2046W, 2530, 2531, 2532)		1800
2223W	Diesel Freight Set, *54* (2321, 6464-100, 3461-25, 3482, 6462-125, 6417-50)		1670
2225WS	Steam Work Train Set, *54* (736, 2046W, 3461-25, 3562 or 3562-25, 3620, 6460, 6419)		800
2227W	Santa Fe Diesel Freight Set, *54* (2353P/T AA, 3562-25, 6356, 6456-75, 6468, 6417-25)		1700
2229W	NYC Freight Set, *54* (2354P/T AA, 3562-25, 6356, 6456-75, 6468, 6417-25)		1300
2231W	Southern Diesel Freight Set, *54* (2356P/C/T ABA, 6511, 6561, 3482, 6415, 6417-25)		2200
2234W	Santa Fe Diesel Passenger Set, *54* (2353P/T AA, 2530, 2531, 2532, 2533)		1637
2235W	MILW Diesel Freight Set, *55* (2338, 6436-25, 6362, 6560, 6419)		575
2237WS	Steam Freight Set, *55* (665, 6026W, 3562-50, 6464-275, 6415, 6417)		400
2239W	Illinois Central Diesel Freight Set, *55* (2363P/C AB, 6672, 6464-125, 6414, 6517)		1700
2241WS	Steam Freight Set, *55* (646, 2046W, 3359, 6446, 3620, 6417)		550
2243W	Diesel Freight Set, *55* (2321, 3662, 6511, 6462-125, 6464-300, 6417)		1400
2244W	Wabash Diesel Passenger Set, *55* (2367P/C AB, 2530, 2531, 2533)		3500
2245WS	Steam Freight Set, *55* (682, 2046WX, 3562-25, 6436-25, 6561, 6560, 6419)		865

2247W Wabash Diesel Freight Set, *55*
(2367P/C AB, 6462-125, 3662, 6464-150, 3361, 6517)   2200 ___

2249WS Steam Freight Set, *55*
(736, 2046W, 6464-275, 6414, 3359, 3562-50, 6517)   700 ___

2251W Diesel Freight Set, *55*
(2331, 6464-275, 3562-50, 6414, 3359, 6517)   2000 ___

2253W PRR Electric Freight Set, *55*
(2340-25, 3361, 6464-300, 3620, 6414, 6417)   2700 ___

2254W PRR Electric Passenger Set, *55*
(2340, 2541, 2542, 2543, 2544)   5500 ___

2255W Diesel Work Train Set, *56*
(601, 3424, 6362, 6560, 6119-25)   725 ___

2257WS Steam Freight Set, *56*
(665, 2046W, 3361, 6346, 6467, 6462-125, 6427)   500 ___

2259W NH Electric Freight Set, *56*
(2350, 6464-425, 6430, 3650, 6511, 6427)   900 ___

2261WS Steam Freight Set, *56*
(646, 2046W, 3562-50, 6414, 6436-25, 6376, 6417)   570 ___

2263W NH Electric Freight Set, *56*
(2350, 3359, 6468-25, 6414, 3662, 6517)   1000 ___

2265WS Steam Freight Set, *56*
(736, 2046W, 3620, 3424, 6430, 6467, 6517)   675 ___

2267W Diesel Freight Set, *56*
(2331, 3562-50, 3359, 3361, 6560, 6419-50)   1700 ___

2269W B&O Diesel Freight Set, *56*
(2368P/C AB, 3356, 6518, 6315, 3361, 6517)   3200 ___

2270W Jersey Central Diesel Passenger Set, *56*
(2341, 2531, 2532, 2533)   5000 ___

2271W PRR Electric Freight Set, *56*
(2360-25, 3424, 3662, 6414, 6418, 6417)   2200 ___

2273W MILW Diesel Freight Set, *56*
(2378P/C AB, 342, 6342, 3562-50, 3662, 3359, 6517)   3500 ___

2274W PRR Electric Passenger Set, *56*
(2360, 2541, 2542, 2543, 2544)   4500 ___

2275W Wabash Diesel Freight Set, *57*
(2339, 3444, 6464-475, 6425, 6427)   790 ___

2276W Budd RDC Set, *57*
(404, two 2559)   2200 ___

2277WS Steam Work Train Set, *57*
(665, 2046W, 6446-25, 3650, 6560-25, 6119-75)   500 ___

2279W NH Electric Freight Set, *57*
(2350, 3424, 6464-425, 6424, 6477, 6427)   800 ___

2281W Santa Fe Diesel Freight Set, *57*
(2243P/C AB, 6464-150, 3361, 3562-75, 6560-25,
6119-75)   860 ___

2283WS Steam Freight Set, *57*
(646, 2046W, 3424, 3361, 6464-525, 6562-50, 6357)   675 ___

2285W Diesel Freight Set, *57*
(2331, 6418, 6414, 6425, 3662, 6517)   2000 ___

2287W MILW Electric Freight Set, *57*
(2351, 342, 6342, 6464-500, 3650, 6315, 6427)   2000 ___

2289WS Super O Steam Freight Set, *57*
(736, 2046W, 3359, 3494-275, 3361, 6430, 6427)   790 ___

2291W Super O Rio Grande Diesel Freight Set, *57*
(2379P/C AB, 3562-75, 3530, 3444, 6464-525, 6657)   2200 ___

SETS

			Exc
___	**2292WS**	Super O Steam Passenger Set, *57* (646, 2046W, 2530, 2531, 2532, 2533)	2000
___	**2293W**	Super O PRR Electric Freight Set, *57* (2360, 3662, 3650, 6414, 6518, 6417)	2900
___	**2295WS**	Super O Steam Freight Set, *57* (746, 746W, 342, 6342, 3530, 3361, 6560-25, 6419-100)	3000
___	**2296W**	Super O CP Diesel Passenger Set, *57* (2373P/T AA, 2551, 2552, 2553, 2554)	4667
___	**2297WS**	Super O Steam Freight Set, *57* (746, 746W, 264, 6264, 3356, 3662, 345, 6342, 6517)	2500
___	**2501W**	Super O Diesel Work Train Set, *58* (2348, 6464-525, 6802, 6560-25, 6119-100)	800
___	**2502W**	Super O Budd RDC Set, *58* (400, 2550, 2559)	2000
___	**2503WS**	Super O Steam Freight Set, *58* (665, 2046W, 3361, 6434, 6801, 6536, 6357)	550
___	**2505W**	Super O Electric Freight Set, *58* (2329, 6805, 6519, 6800, 6464-500, 6357)	1600
___	**2507W**	Super O Diesel Freight Set, *58* (2242P/C AB, 3444, 6464-425, 6424, 6468-25, 6357)	2000
___	**2509WS**	Super O Steam Freight Set, *58* (665, 2046W, 6414, 3650, 6464-475, 6805, 6357)	800
___	**2511W**	Super O Electric Work Set, *58* (2352, 3562-75, 3424, 3361, 6560-25, 6119-100)	1100
___	**2513W**	Super O Electric Freight Set, *58* (2329, 6556, 6425, 6414, 6434, 3359, 6427-60)	3000
___	**2515WS**	Super O Steam Freight Set, *58* (646, 2046W, 3662, 6424, 3444, 6800, 6427)	775
___	**2517W**	Super O Rio Grande Diesel Freight Set, *58* (2379P/C AB, 6519, 6805, 6434, 6800, 6657)	2550
___	**2518W**	Super O PRR Electric Passenger Set, *58* (2352, 2531, 2533, 2534)	1700
___	**2519W**	Super O Diesel Freight Set, *58* (2331, 6434, 3530, 6801, 6414, 6464-275, 6557)	1900
___	**2521WS**	Super O Steam Freight Set, *58* (746, 746W, 6805, 3361, 6430, 3356, 6424, 6557)	2000
___	**2523W**	Super O Santa Fe Diesel Freight Set, *58* (2383P/T AA, 264, 6264, 6434, 6800, 3662, 6517)	1300
___	**2525WS**	Super O Steam Work Train Set, *58* (746, 746W, 342, 345, 6519, 6518, 6560-25, 6419-100)	2300
___	**2526W**	Super O Santa Fe Diesel Passenger Set, *58* (2383P/T AA, 2530, 2531, two 2532)	1750
___	**2527**	Super O Missile Launcher Set, *59–60* (44, 3419, 6844, 6823, 6814, 943)	550
___	**2528WS**	Super O General Set, *59–61* (1872, 1872T, 1877, 1876, 1875W)	493
___	**2529W**	Super Electric Work Train Set, *59* (2329, 3512, 6819, 6812, 6560, 6119-25 or 6119-100)	1300
___	**2531WS**	Super O Steam Freight Set, *59* (637, 2046W, 3435, 6817, 6636, 6825, 6119-100)	1300
___	**2533W**	Super O GN Electric Freight Set, *59* (2358, 6650, 6414, 3444, 6470, 6357)	1800

SETS

		Exc
2535WS	Super O Steam Freight Set, *59* (665, 2046W, 3434, 6823, 3672, 6812, 6357)	900 ___
2537W	Super O NH Diesel Freight Set, *59* (2242P/C AB, 3435, 3650, 6464-275, 6819, 6427)	2500 ___
2539WS	Super O Steam Freight Set, *59* (665, 2046W, 3361, 6464-825, 3512, 6812, 6357, 464)	1017 ___
2541W	Super O Santa Fe Diesel Freight Set, *59* (2383P/T AA, 3356, 3512, 6519, 6816, 6427)	2400 ___
2543WS	Super O Steam Freight Set, *59* (736, 2046W, 264, 6264, 3435, 6823, 6434, 6812, 6557)	1588 ___
2544W	Super O Santa Fe Diesel Passenger Set, *59–60* (2383P/T AA, 2530, 2561, 2562, 2563)	2500 ___
2545WS	Super O Military Set, *59* (746, 746W, 175, 6175, 6470, 3419, 6650, 3540, 6517)	3000 ___
2547WS	Super O Steam Freight Set, *60* (637, 2046W, 3330, 6475, 6361, 6357)	600 ___
2549W	Super O Military Set, *60* (2349, 3540, 6470, 6819, 6650, 3535)	1158 ___
2551W	Super O GN Electric Freight Set, *60* (2358, 6828, 3512, 6827, 6736, 6812, 6427)	2300 ___
2553WS	Super O Steam Freight Set, *60* (736, 2046W, 3830, 3435, 3419, 3672, 6357)	1200 ___
2555W	Super O Santa Fe Freight Set with matching HO Set, *60* (2383P/T AA, 3434, 3366, 6414, 6464-900, 6357-50)	10000 ___
2570	Super O Santa Fe Work Train Set, *61* (616, 6822, 6828, 6812, 6736, 6130)	798 ___
2571	Super O Steam Freight Set, *61* (637, 736W, 3419, 6445, 6361, 6119-100)	550 ___
2572	Super O B&M Diesel Freight Set, *61* (2359, 6544, 3830, 6448, 3519, 3535)	800 ___
2573	Super O Steam Freight Sct, *61* (736, 736W, 3545, 6416, 6475, 6440, 6357)	1400 ___
2574	Super O Santa Fe Diesel Freight Set, *61* (2383P/T AA, 3665, 3419, 3830, 448, 6448, 6437)	1500 ___
2575	Super O PRR Electric Freight Set, *61* (2360, 6530, 6828, 6464-900, 6827, 6736, 6560, 6437)	2500 ___
2576	Super O Santa Fe Diesel Passenger Set, *61* (2383P/T AA, 2561, two 2562, 2563)	4000 ___
4109WS	Electronic Control Set, *46* (671R, 4424W, 4452, 4454, 5459, 4457)	745 ___
4110WS	Electronic Control Set, *48–49* (671R, 4671W, 4452, 5459, 4357, 151, 97)	2500 ___
11011	027 Diesel Freight Set, *62* (222, 3510, 6076, 6120)	75 ___
11201	027 Steam Freight Set, *62* (242, 1060T, 6042-75, 6502, 6047)	125 ___
11212	027 Santa Fe Diesel Freight Set, *62* (633, 3349, 6825, 6057)	375 ___
11222	027 Steam Freight Set, *62* (236, 1050T, 3357, 6343, 6119-100)	130 ___
11232	027 NH Diesel Freight Set, *62* (232, 3410, 6062, 6413, 6057-50)	500 ___

	SETS		Exc
	11242	027 Steam Freight Set, *62* (233, 233W, 6465-100, 6476, 6162, 6017)	120
	11252	027 Texas Special Space Set, *62* 211P/T AA, 3509, 6448, 3349, 6463, 6057)	500
	11268	027 C&O Diesel Freight Set, *62* (2365, 3619, 3470, 3349, 6501, 6017)	1000
	11278	027 Steam Freight Set, *62* (2037, 233W, 6473, 6162, 6050-110, 6825, 6017)	250
	11288	027 Space Set, *62* (229P/C AB, 3413, 6512, 6413, 6463, 6059)	1215
	11298	027 Steam Freight Set, *62* (2037, 233W, 6544, 3419, 6448, 3330, 6017)	500
	11308	027 Santa Fe Diesel Passenger Set, *62* (218P/T AA, two 2412, 2414, 2416)	600
	11311	027 Steam Freight Set, *63* (1062, 1061T, 6409-25, 6076-100, 6167-25)	100
	11321	027 Rio Grande Diesel Freight Set, *63* (221, 3309, 6076-75, 6042-75, 6167-50)	300
	11331	027 Steam Freight Set, *63* (242, 1060T, 6473, 6476-25, 6142, 6059-50)	100
	11341	027 Santa Fe Diesel Freight Set, *63* (634, 3410, 6407, 6014-325, 6463, 6059-50)	950
	11351	027 Steam Freight Set, *63* (237, 1060T, 6050-100, 6465-150, 6408, 6162, 6119-110)	250
	11361	027 Texas Special Space Set, *63* (211P/T AA, 3665-100, 3413-150, 6470, 6413, 6257-100)	750
	11375	027 Steam Freight Set, *63* (238, 234W, 6822-50, 6465-150, 6414-150, 6476-75, 6162, 6257-100)	700
	11385	027 Santa Fe Space Set, *63* (223P/218C AB, 3619-100, 3470-100, 3349-100, 3830-75, 6407, 6257-100 or 6017-235)	2000
	11395	027 Steam Freight Set, *63* (2037, 233W or 234W, 6464-725, 6469-50, 6536, 6440-50, 6560-50, 6119-100)	600
	11405	027 Santa Fe Diesel Passenger Set, *63* (218P/T AA, two 2412, 2414, 2416)	750
	11420	027 Steam Freight Set, *64* (1061, 1061T, 6042-250, 6167-25)	100
	11430	027 Steam Freight, *64* (1062, 1061T, 6176, 6142, 6167-125)	80
	11440	027 Rio Grande Diesel Freight Set, *64* (221, 3309, 6176-50, 6142-125, 6167-100)	200
	11450	027 Steam Freight Set, *64* (242, 1060T, 6473, 6142-75, 6176-50, 6059-50)	138
	11460	027 Steam Freight Set, *64* (238, 234W, 6014-335, 6465-150, 6142-100, 6176-75, 6119-100)	120
	11470	027 Steam Freight Set, *64* (237, 1060T, 6014-335, 6465-150, 6142-100, 6176-75, 6119-100)	150
	11480	027 Diesel Freight Set, *64* (213P/T AA, 6473, 6176-50, 6142-150, 6014-335, 6257-100 or 6059)	625

	SETS	Exc

11490 O27 Diesel Passenger Set, *64–65*
(212P/T AA, 2404, 2405, 2406) — 360 ___

11500 O27 Steam Freight Set, *64*
(2029, 234W, 6465-150, 6402-50, 6176-75,
6014-335, 6257-100 or 6059) — 275 ___

11500 O27 Steam Freight Set, *65*
(2029, 234W, 6465-150, 6402-50, 6076, 6014-335,
6257-100 or 6059) — 275 ___

11500 O27 Steam Freight Set, *66*
(2029, 234W, 6465-150, 6402-50, 6176-75,
6014-335, 6059) — 275 ___

11510 O27 Steam Freight Set, *64*
(2029, 1060T, 6465-150, 6402-50, 6176-75,
6014-335, 6257-100 or 6059) — 300 ___

11520 O27 Steam Freight Set, *65–66*
(242, 1062T, 6176, 3362/64, 6142, 6059) — 113 ___

11530 O27 Santa Fe Diesel Freight, *65–66*
(634, 6014, 6142, 6402, 6130) — 148 ___

11540 O27 Steam Freight Set, *65–66*
(239, 242T, 6473, 6465, 6176, 6119-100) — 210 ___

11550 O27 Steam Freight Set, *65–66*
(239, 234W, 6473, 6465, 6176, 6119) — 154 ___

11560 O27 Texas Special Freight Set, *65–66*
(211P/T AA, 6473, 6076, 6142, 6465, 6059) — 285 ___

11590 O27 Santa Fe Diesel Passenger Set, *66*
(212P/T AA, 2408, 2409, 2410) — 925 ___

11600 O27 Steam Freight Set, *68*
(2029, 234W, 6014, 6476, 6315, 6560, 6130) — 700 ___

11710 O27 Steam Freight Set, *69*
(1061, 1061T or 1062T, 6402, 6142, 6059) — 170 ___

11720 Diesel Freight Set, *69*
(2024, 6142, 6402, 6176, 6057) — 250 ___

11730 O27 UP Diesel Freight Set, *69*
(645, 6402, 6014-85, 6176, 6142, 6167-85) — 350 ___

11740 O27 RI Diesel Freight Set, *69*
(2041P/T AA, 6315, 6142, 6014-410, 6476, 6057) — 300 ___

11750 O27 Steam Freight Set, *69*
(2029, 234T, 6014-85, 6476, 6473, 6315, 6130) — 400 ___

11760 O27 Steam Freight Set, *69*
(2029, 234W, 6014-410, 6315, 6476, 3376, 6119) — 355 ___

12502 Prairie-Rider Gift Pack, *62*
(1862, 1862T, 3376, 1877 or 6473, 1866, 1865) — 600 ___

12512 Enforcer Gift Pack, *62*
(45, 3413, 3619, 3470, 3349, 6017) — 1100 ___

12700 Steam Freight Set, *64*
(736, 736W, 6464-725, 6162-100, 6414-75,
6476-125, 6437, no transformer) — 1000 ___

12710 Steam Freight Set, *64–66*
(736, 736W, 6464-725, 6162-100, 6414-75,
6476-125, 6437, LW transformer) — 1000 ___

12720 Santa Fe Diesel Freight Set, *64*
(2383P/T AA, 6464-725, 6162-100, 6414-75,
6476-125, 6437, no transformer) — 1500 ___

12730 Santa Fe Diesel Freight Set, *64–66*
(2383P/T AA, 6464-725, 6162-100, 6414-75,
6476-125, 6437, LW transformer) — 1138 ___

			Exc
SETS			
12740	Santa Fe Diesel Freight Set, *64*		
	(2383P/T AA, 3662, 6361, 6436-110, 6315-60,		
___	6464-525, 6822, 6437)		1500
12760	Steam Freight Set, *64*		
	(736, 736W, 3662, 6361, 6436-110, 6315-60,		
___	6464-525, 6822, 6437)		1100
12780	Santa Fe Diesel Passenger, *64–66*		
___	(2383P/T AA, 2521, 2522, two 2523)		2700
12800	B&M Diesel Freight Set, *65–66*		
___	(2346, 6428, 6436, 6464-475, 6415, 6017-100)		575
12820	Diesel Freight Set, *65*		
	(2322, 3662, 6822, 6361, 6464-725, 6436, 6315,		
___	6437)		1650
12840	Steam Freight Set, *66*		
___	(665, 736W, 6464-375, 6464-450, 6431, 6415, 6437)		925
12850	Diesel Freight Set, *66*		
	(2322, 3662, 6822, 6361, 6464-725, 6436, 6315,		
___	6437)		1700
13008	Super O Steam Freight Set, *62*		
___	(637, 736W, 3349, 6448, 6501, 6119-100)		500
13018	Super O Santa Fe Diesel Freight Set, *62*		
___	(616, 6500, 6650, 3519, 6448, 6017-235)		1200
13028	Super O Space Set, *62*		
___	(2359, 3665, 3349, 3820, 3470, 6017-100)		1000
13036	Super O General Set, *62*		
___	(1872, 1872T, 6445, 3370, 1876, 1875W)		980
13048	Super O Steam Freight Set, *62*		
___	(736, 736W, 6822, 6414, 3362, 6440, 6437)		720
13058	Super O Space Set, *62*		
___	(2383P/T AA, 3619, 3413, 6512, 470, 6470, 6437)		1600
13068	Super O PRR Electric Freight Set, *62*		
	(2360, 6464-725, 6828, 6416, 6827, 6530, 6475,		
___	6437)		3200
13078	Super O PRR Electric Passenger Set, *62*		
___	(2360, 2521, two 2522, 2523)		3500
13088	Super O Santa Fe Diesel Passenger Set, *62*		
___	(2383P/T AA, 2521, two 2522, 2523)		2500
13098	Super O Steam Freight Set, *63*		
___	(637, 736W, 6469, 6464-900, 6414, 6446, 6447)		2000
13108	Super O Santa Fe Space Set, *63*		
___	(617, 3665, 3419, 6448, 3830, 3470, 6119-100)		1000
13118	Super O Steam Freight Set, *63*		
	(736, 736W, 6446-60, 6827, 3362, 6315-60, 6560,		
___	6429)		1500
13128	Super O Santa Fe Space Set, *63*		
___	(2383P/T AA, 3619, 3413, 6512, 448, 6448, 64337)		1750
13138	Super O PRR Electric Freight Set, *63*		
	(2360, 6464-725, 6828, 6416, 6827, 6315-60,		
___	6436-110, 6437)		3800
13148	Super O Santa Fe Diesel Passenger Set, *63*		
___	(2383P/T AA, 2521, 2522, two 2523)		2500
13150	Super O Hudson Steam Freight Set, *64*		
	(773, 736W or 773W, 3434, 6361, 3662, 6415, 3356,		
___	6436-110, 6437)		2500

ABBREVIATIONS

Descriptions

AAR	Association of American Railroads (truck type)
AEC	Atomic Energy Commission
AF	American Flyer
CC	Command Control
DD	Double-door
EMD	Electro-Motive Division
ETD	End-of-train device
FARR	Famous American Railroad Series
FF	Fallen Flag Series
FM	Fairbanks-Morse
GE	General Electric
LL	Lionel Lines
MOW	Maintenance-of-way
MU	Multiple unit (commuter cars)
O	Lionel gauge (1¼" between outside rails)
OO	Lionel gauge (¾" between outside rails)
PFE	Pacific Fruit Express
REA	Railway Express Agency
SSS	Service Station Special
std	Standard gauge (2⅛" between outside rails)
std O	Standard O (scale length and dimension)
TMCC	TrainMaster Command Control
USMC	United States Marine Corps
1-D	One dome
2-D	Two dome
3-D	Three dome

ABBREVIATIONS

Railroad names

ACL	Atlantic Coast Line
ATSF	Atchison, Topeka & Santa Fe
B&A	Boston & Albany
BAR	Bangor & Aroostook
B&LE	Bessemer & Lake Erie
B&M	Boston & Maine
BN	Burlington Northern
BNSF	Burlington Northern Santa Fe
B&O	Baltimore & Ohio
C&IM	Chicago & Illinois Midland
C&EI	Chicago & Eastern Illinois
CB&Q	Chicago, Burlington & Quincy
CMStP&P	Chicago, Milwaukee, St. Paul & Pacific
CN	Canadian National
CNJ	Central of New Jersey
C&IM	Chicago & Illinois Midland
C&NW	Chicago & North Western
C&O	Chesapeake & Ohio
CP	Canadian Pacific
D&H	Delaware & Hudson
DL&W	Delaware, Lackawanna & Western
DM&IR	Duluth, Missabe & Iron Range
D&RGW	Denver & Rio Grande Western
D&TS	Detroit & Toledo Shore Line
DT&I	Detroit, Toledo & Ironton
EJ&E	Elgin, Joliet & Eastern
Erie-Lack.	Erie-Lackawanna
FEC	Florida East Coast
GM&O	Gulf, Mobile & Ohio
GN	Great Northern
GTW	Grand Trunk Western
IC	Illinois Central
ICG	Illinois Central Gulf
KCS	Kansas City Southern
L&N	Louisville & Nashville
LIRR	Long Island Railroad
LNAC	Louisville, New Albany & Corydon

Railroad names

LV	Lehigh Valley
MD&W	Minnesota, Dakota & Western
MKT	Missouri-Kansas-Texas
MN&S	Minneapolis, Northfield & Southern
MP	Missouri Pacific
MPA	Maryland & Pennsylvania
MILW	Milwaukee Road
M&StL	Minneapolis & St. Louis
NC&StL	Nashville, Chattanooga & St. Louis
NdeM	Nacionales de Mexico Railway
NH	New Haven
NKP	Nickel Plate Road
NP	Northern Pacific
NS	Norfolk Southern
N&W	Norfolk & Western
NYC	New York Central
NYNH&H	New York, New Haven & Hartford
NYO&W	New York, Ontario & Western
PC	Penn Central
P&E	Peoria & Eastern
P&LE	Pittsburgh & Lake Erie
PRR	Pennsylvania Railroad
RF&P	Richmond, Fredericksburg & Potomac
RI	Rock Island
SMARRCO	San Manuel Arizona Railroad Company
SP	Southern Pacific
SP&S	Spokane, Portland & Seattle
TA&G	Tennessee, Alabama & Georgia
TH&B	Toronto, Hamilton & Buffalo
T&P	Texas & Pacific
TP&W	Toledo, Peoria & Western
UP	Union Pacific
V&TRR	Virginia & Truckee Railroad
W&ARR	Western & Atlantic Railroad
WM	Western Maryland
WP	Western Pacific

Build Your Toy Train Library

Track Plans for Lionel FasTrack

This one-stop resource for Lionel FasTrack includes 25 mostly small and mid-sized plans collected from the pages of *Classic Toy Trains* magazine as well as new plans. Each plan includes a description, an illustration of the layout, and a list of FasTrack components. You'll also find essential track planning tips and learn how to adapt existing track plans to FasTrack.

10-8804 • $14.99

Greenberg's *Repair and Operating Manual for Lionel Trains, 1945–1969, 7th Edition*

Get 1,000+ repair and maintenance tips for Lionel locomotives, operating cars, accessories, transformers, light bulbs, and switches. Provides technical advice as well as handy techniques submitted by toy train collectors and operators.

10-8160 • $24.95

American Flyer Pocket Price Guide 1946-2015

Discover the value of your American Flyer toy trains. This essential pocket guide provides accurate current market values for American Flyer S gauge trains and accessories manufactured by A.C. Gilbert and Lionel. It is the only price guide with current and updated listings for American Flyer and other S scale trains.

10-8615 • $15.99

**Buy now from hobby shops!
To find a store near you, visit
www.HobbyRetailer.com
www.KalmbachStore.com
or call 1-800-533-6644**

Monday – Friday, 8:30 a.m. – 4:30 p.m. CT.
Outside the United States and Canada call 262-796-8776, ext. 661.

KALMBACH BOOKS

P23077

2XTT